HAVEN'T
I SEEN YOU
SOME-
WHERE
BEFORE?

SCRIPT & EDITING BY
JAMES L. LIMBACHER

A 1979 PRODUCTION BY
THE PIERIAN PRESS

HAVEN'T I SEEN YOU SOME-WHERE BEFORE?

REMAKES, SEQUELS AND SERIES IN MOTION PICTURES AND TELEVISION, 1896–1978

ISBN 0-87650-107-2
LC 79-84272

THE PIERIAN PRESS
5000 Washtenaw Ave.
Ann Arbor, MI 48104

CONTENTS

INTRODUCTION

Those interested in the visual media, whether they are teachers, librarians, film, radio and television personnel, film buffs, or researchers, are constantly searching for the sources of films seen in theaters and on television. Many times a story seems so familiar, but the producer has managed to disguise it so beautifully that there seems to be no way of discovering what it was adapted from and how many times it has been produced. The need to know this information usually leads the searcher to the local school or public library. This publication is designed to provide the needed information on thousands of titles which have been presented in the media *more than once*.

By gathering like contents together, this book gives film programmers a chance to choose the best version of a film for a given purpose. It also aids researchers in offering "tips" to find further information on related film materials. Every attempt has been made to bring like titles together, but there is bound to be much controversy over this book's contents. The accent has been put on the *basic* source. For instance, ROSE OF WASHINGTON SQUARE, FUNNY GIRL and FUNNY LADY are all films based on the life of entertainer Fanny Brice. The idea is to bring all films and television programs about Fanny Brice under one heading, not to go into secondary sources, which are available in a number of other books. ROSE OF WASHINGTON SQUARE is based on a story by John Larkin and Jerry Horwin and a screenplay by Nunnally Johnson. FUNNY GIRL is a musical comedy by Jule Styne and Bob Merrill with a book by Isobel Lennart, and FUNNY LADY is an original film musical by John Kander and Fred Ebb based on a story by Arnold Schulman and a screenplay by Schulman and Jay Presson Allen. This book will tell you only that these three films are based on the life of Fanny Brice. All the other material mentioned is easily found in any review or film yearbook.

Considering that this reference book is much larger than it was ever intended to be, only the basic information can be given, but further details are always available if needed from the books listed in the bibliography.

This is the only book which brings all this material together and users are encouraged to suggest additional titles for inclusion in the next edition and to challenge and correct existing material. Only then can this publication be the definitive source.

SCOPE AND ARRANGEMENT

This publication is limited to material which has been produced more than once. Each entry lists the title of the work, the releasing company or country of origin and the year of release of the first production, the source of the first production (book, play, comic strip, legend, screenplay, biography, etc.) and any other comments and related information, plus all known subsequent productions of the same material with the name of the releasing company and the year of release.

Dates vary from one information source to another on many of the titles and in every case in this edition, the earliest date found was used. Titles which were first made under another title are cross-indexed, as are those titles which were changed for television showing or theatrical re-release.

Modified letters (such as á, ñ, ö, and ø) are treated as regular letters (a, n and o), all accent marks having been omitted for the sake of simplicity in setting type for this edition.

SAMPLE ENTRY

The following example will make the purpose of this book clear:

SECRET HOUR, THE (PAR, 1928, based on the play, "They Knew What They Wanted," by Sidney Howard; also the basis for the 1957 musical drama, "The Most Happy Fella," by Frank Loesser)
LADY TO LOVE, A (MGM, 1930)
SEHSUCHT JEDER FRAU, DIE (GER, 1930)
THEY KNEW WHAT THEY WANTED (RKO, 1940)

THEY KNEW WHAT THEY WANTED   see SECRET HOUR, THE

For anyone wishing to know how many times Sidney Howard's play, "They Knew What They Wanted," has been produced, one would first check the title, which would refer him to "The Secret Hour" and three other subsequent productions, plus information on a musical stage version which has not yet been filmed.

SEQUELS AND SERIES

Appendices covering film sequels and film series appear at the end of this compendium.

THE SECOND TIME AROUND

Film-makers and television networks frequently go on "remake kicks" -- the dusting off of stories and plots on which the producing agency has exclusive rights and making of new versions. Every decade or so, producers reason, there is a new audience attending the movies and watching television and oldtimers don't seem to mind seeing the same plot again if it is done well -- and perhaps differently.

Not that a remake is done exactly as in its previous version. Usually great pains are taken to alter and vary the plot as well as the characters and sometimes setting and even period. A sturdy story such as Fox's WORKING GIRLS served as a story about three young girls going to the big city to seek fame, fortune and romance in 1931, then the plot surfaced again as a Loretta Young vehicle in 1938 titled THREE BLIND MICE and again in 1941 as MOON OVER MIAMI, with Betty Grable, Technicolor and a full complement of songs. In 1946, the plot appeared again as a musical, THREE LITTLE GIRLS IN BLUE, with Vera-Ellen and the period switched to the Gay Nineties. Most reviewers also feel that the same plot showed up again in Fox's second CinemaScope film, HOW TO MARRY A MILLIONAIRE with the addition of another play called LOCO. A good standard story can expect to have a long life in movies and many are now being resurrected for television.

Dashiell Hammett's famed story, THE MALTESE FALCON, was first a straight mystery story at Warner Brothers in 1931, then re-written as a comedy for Bette Davis in 1936 under the title of SATAN MET A LADY, then finally received its definitive classic status in John Huston's 1941 version with Humphrey Bogart and Mary Astor under its original title. After a long hiatus, it surfaced again in 1975 as a George Segal vehicle called BLACK BIRD and the end is probably not yet in sight. THE MALTESE FALCON was one of the exceptions to the rule that "the remake is never as good as the original," as the remakes of CIMARRON, STAGECOACH and MUTINY ON THE BOUNTY have proved.

There are also the "uncredited" remakes, many of which have been included in this listing for the sake of tipping off researchers to possible relationships between plots. Noted film scholars have often discovered plot similarities in diverse and seemingly unrelated material and there is no reason not to have them listed even though uncredited. One film scholar goes so far as to insist that RED RIVER is a disguised remake of MUTINY ON THE BOUNTY, that STAGECOACH harkens back to BOULE DE SUIF, and that Universal's CATTLE DRIVE seems to be lifted from MGM's CAPTAINS COURAGEOUS, so who is to say he isn't right?

Nearly all the great literary works have been put on film and later on television, although many of them were altered and watered down to fit the moral standards of the period. Since most taboos of the past are now acceptable, and as audiences mature, most great works will eventually end up on film or television.

Great books have been filmed with regularity, including Victor Hugo's LES MISERABLES, which has a dozen or more film versions to its credit (including two very cleverly-disguised versions), and THE THREE MUSKETEERS seems to have the longest list of remakes of them all. At least a dozen versions of CARMEN, DR. JEKYLL AND MR. HYDE, THE HOUND OF THE BASKERVILLES, RESURRECTION and other works have appeared and there is no reason to think that more are not on the way.

The opportunity of directors and writers to create an interesting remake sometimes causes changes merely for the sake of changes, negating the good things they have brought to a particular version. Few directors get a second chance with the same material (James Whale is one of the exceptions when he directed A KISS BEFORE THE MIRROR in 1933 and its remake, WIVES UNDER SUSPICION, a scant five years later, with the original the much better of the two), even though one might think that a second chance might lead to improvement. One need only compare Orson Welles' stylish version of MACBETH with Akira Kurosawa's Japanese version (THRONE OF BLOOD) of Ken Hughes' modern-dress gangster version (JOE MACBETH) to see how many variations can be done on the same theme. A comparison of THE DIARY OF A CHAMBERMAID (1946 American version and 1964 French version) shows how far films have come in telling a story in an adult manner.

The validity of remakes has often been debated by critics, industry personnel and audiences themselves, but as long as there are films and television, there will be remakes. Many are made with the best of intentions and they may sound wonderful in the conference room and look good in script form, but often as not, a story which broke box office records in 1935 may prove completely out of touch with the times in 1955 or 1975, even though rewriting and updating are meticulously done.

There is security in a good story, even though it has been done many times before, and it will show up again and again for economic and aesthetic reasons. Who ever thought that a satirical version of the Frankenstein legend (YOUNG FRANKENSTEIN) would break box-office records in 1975? Many mature movie fans remember the days when Warner Brothers used to remake virtually all its standard stories about every seven years or so without any complaints from viewers (most of them are listed in this book) and similar things are still being done today. Now it is television which is coming up with remakes of many old movies as well as some of its own earlier TV material!

HAVEN'T I SEEN YOU SOMEWHERE BE-FORE? is bound to be a controversial and perhaps even frustrating reference book, but it needn't be. No one is insisting that it is the be--all and end--all on the subject. The author hopes that readers and users will think of other remakes and add interesting sidelights to the titles already listed and, heaven forbid, even send in proof that an entry might be wrong. And wouldn't we be happy to have people in France, India, Russia and Sweden ferret out the original source and titles for entries from their countries which are incomplete and had to be marked "source unlisted"! My thanks to my friends Wolfram and Volker Hannemann for their help in providing sources for many of the German entries and to the staff of the Audio--Visual Division of the Dearborn Department of Libraries for their usual encourage-ment and cooperation.

To all researchers, librarians and just plain film and television buffs who will use this book, happy hunting!

James L. Limbacher

BIBLIOGRAPHY

The following reference works have been used to gather the material for this edition. There are many other secondary sources (periodicals, articles, conversations, suggestions from film scholars, buffs and librarians, and personal observations) too numerous to mention. Many of these publications will list the detailed information which might be needed for further research on any entry.

Alicoate, Charles. *Film Daily Yearbook* (Film Daily, through 1970)

American Film Institute Catalog. *Feature Films 1921--1930* (2 vols) and *1961--1970* (2 vols). (Bowker, 1971 and 1976)

Armes, Roy. *French Cinema* (2 volumes) (Barnes, 1966)

Boussinot, Roger. *L'Encyclopedie du Cinema* (Bordas, 1967)

Broadcast Information Bureau. *TV Feature Film Source Book* (Broadcast Information Bureau, annually)

Bucher, Felix. *Germany* (Barnes, 1970)

Cawkwell, Tom and John M. Smith. *The World Encyclopedia of the Film* (World, 1972)

Cowie, Peter. *International Film Guide* (Barnes, annually)

Cowie, Peter. *Sweden* (2 volumes). Barnes, 1970)

Dimmitt, Richard B. *A Title Guide to the Talkies, 1927–1963* (2 volumes) (Scarecrow, 1965)

Druxman, Michael B. *Make It Again, Sam* (Barnes, 1975)

Druxman, Michael B. *One Good Film Deserves Another* (Barnes, 1977)

Gifford, Denis. *British Cinema* (Barnes, 1968)

Gifford, Denis. *The British Film Catalogue, 1895–1970* (McGraw--Hill, 1973)

Halliwell, Leslie. *The Filmgoer's Companion* (4th edition). (Hill and Wang, 1974)

Hibbin, Nina. *Eastern Europe* (Barnes, 1969)

Lauritzen, Einar, and Gunnar Lundquist. *American Film--Index 1908--1915* (Akademibokhendlen, 1976)

Lee, Walt. *A Reference Guide to Fantastic Films* (3 volumes) (Chelsea--Lee, 1972)

Library of Congress. *Catalog of Copyright Entries. Motion Pictures 1896--1912, 1912--1939, 1940--1949, 1950--1959, 1960--1969* (5 vols.)

Limbacher, James L. *Feature Films on 8mm, 16mm and Videotape* (Bowker, biennially)

Low, Rachel. *The History of the British Film* (4 vols). (1948--49--50--71) reprints.

Manvell, Roger. *The International Encyclopaedia of Film* (Crown, 1972)

Martin, Marcel. *France* (Barnes, 1971)

Michael, Paul. *The American Movies Reference Book: The Sound Era* (Prentice Hall, 1969)

NICEM. *Index to 16mm Educational Films* (3 volumes) (National Information Center for Educational Media, University of Southern California, 1975)

New York Times Film Reviews, 1913--1968, 1969–1970, 1971--1972, 1973--1974 (7 vols. 3 supp. vols.) (Arno)

Parmentier, Ernest. *Filmfacts* (University of Southern California Cinema Department, annually)

Pickard, Roy. *A Companion to the Movies from 1903 to the Present Day* (Hippocrene, 1974)

Quigley, Martin J. *International Motion Picture Almanac* (Quigley, annually)

Sadoul, George. *Dictionary of Films* (University of California, 1972)

Spigelgass, Leonard. *Who Wrote the Movie and What Else Did He Write?* (The Academy of Motion Picture Arts and Sciences, and The Writers Guild of America, West, 1970)

Willis, John. *Screen World* (Crown, annually)

ABBREVIATIONS

AA   – Allied Artists
ABC – American Broadcasting Co.
AE   – Associated Exhibitors
AFI – American Film Institute
AFR – African nations
AFT – American Film Theater
AI   – American International
ALC – Alco
ALL – Allied
AMB – Ambassador/Conn
AP   – Associated Producers
API – API Productions
APO – Apollo
ARA – Arabia
ARC – American Releasing Corp.
ARG – Argentina
ARR – Arrow
ART – Artcraft
AST – Astor
AUS – Austria
AUT – Australia
AYW – Aywon

BFA – BFA Multimedia
BIO – Biograph
BIS – Bison
BJU – Bob Jones University
BOS – Bosworth
BRA – Brazil
BRI – Great Britain
BRO – Broadway Star
BRY – Bryanston
BTZ – Burroughs/Tarzan
BU   – Boston University
BUL – Bulgaria

CAL – University of California
CAN – Canada
CBS – Columbia Broadcasting System
CC   – Cinema Center
CEN – Centron
CFD – Classroom Film Dist.
CHA – Chadwick
CHI – Childhood
CHL – Chile
CHN – China
CHU – Churchill
CIN – Cinerama
CKY – Clara Kimball Young
CMC – Center for Mass Communications
COL – Columbia
COM – Comicolor
CON – Continental/Walter Reade

CPC – Colored Players Co.
CRO – Crown
CUB – Cuba
CZE – Czechoslovakia

DCA – Distributor's Corp. of America
DEN – Denmark
DER – DeRochemont
DIS – Walt Disney
DYN – Dynamic

EAS – Eastin
EBE – Encyclopaedia Britannica
ED   – Edison
EDU – Educational
EGY – Egypt
EL   – Eagle–Lion
ELE – Electronovision
EMB – Embassy/Avco–Embassy
EMP – Empire
EPI – Blumenthal–EPI
EQU – Equity
ESS – Essanay

FA   – Fine Arts
FBO – Film Booking Offices
FC   – Film Classics
FD   – First Division
FFH – Films for the Humanities
FIN – Finland
FLE – Flemish
FN   – First National
FNC – Films Incorporated
FOX – Fox/20th Century–Fox
FRA – France/French language version
FRO – Frohman

GAM – Gamma III
GER – Germany/German language version
GHA – Ghana
GN   – Grand National
GO   – Go Pictures
GOL – Goldwyn
GRE – Greece
GRI – D. W. Griffith

HAN – Handel
HK   – Hong Kong
HOD – Hodginson
HOF – Hoffberg
HOL – Holland/Netherlands
HUN – Hungary
HWD – Hollywood

IFB	– International Film Bureau	PAT	– Pathe
IN	– India	PBS	– Public Broadcasting System
INC	– Thomas H. Ince	PDC	– Producer's Distributing Corp.
IND	– independent American release	PEE	– Peerless–Brady–World
IR	– Image Resources	PER	– Peru
ISR	– Israel	PEW	– Peppercorn–Wormser
ITA	– Italy/Italian language version	PHI	– Phillippine Islands

JAM – Jamaica
JAP – Japan

KAL – Kalem
KE – Klaw and Erlanger
KEY – Keystone
KIN – King Features
KLE – Kleine
KOR – Korea

LCA – Learning Corp. of America
LES – Lesser
LIB – Liberty
LIO – Lionex
LIP – Lippert
LOP – Lopert
LUB – Lubin

MAC – Macmillan
MAJ – Majestic
MAS – Mascot
MAY – Mayfair
MEX – Mexico
MGM – Metro/Metro–Goldwyn/Metro–Goldwyn–
Mayer
MHF – McGraw–Hill
MOG – Mongolia
MOL – Monopol
MON – Monogram
MOT – March of Time
MUT – Mutual

NAT – National
NAV – National Audio–Visual Center
NBC – National Broadcasting Co.
NET – National Educational Television
NGP – National General
NIG – Nigeria
NOR – Norway
NTA – National Telefilm Associates
NWP – New World Pictures
NY – New York
NYF – New Yorker Films

OCE – Ocean
OFF – Official
OZ – Oz

PAL – Pallas
PAR – Famous Players–Lasky/Paramount

PIC – Pictura
PIO – Pioneer
PLC – Plunkett & Carroll
PLY – Plymouth
POL – Poland
POR – Portugal
POW – Powers
PP – Peter Pan
PPL – Popular Players
PRC – Producers Releasing Corp.
PRE – Preferred
PRI – Principal
PS – Popular Science
PUR – Puritan
PYR – Pyramid

RAD – Radim/Film Images
RAN – Rankin–Bass
RAY – Rayart
RC – Robertson–Cole
REA – Realart
REL – Reliable
REP – Republic
REX – Rex Beach
RIN – Ring
RKO – Radio/RKO–Radio
RUM – Rumania
RUS – Russia/Soviet Union

SA – South America
SAC – Sacred
SAS – Stage & Screen
SAU – Robert M. Saudek
SAV – Savoy
SEL – Selig
SEZ – Selznick
SG – Screen Guild
SOL – Solax
SPA – Spain/Spanish language version
STE – Sterling
STG – Steger
SUN – Sunset
SUR – Surinam
SWE – Sweden
SWI – Switzerland

TER – Terrytoons
TEX – Texture
TFC – Teaching Film Custodians
THA – Thanhouser
TIF – Tiffany

TIM -- Time–Life
TRI -- Triangle
TUN -- Tunisia
TUR -- Turkey
TV   -- television production

UA   -- United Artists
UMC -- Universal–Marion
UN   -- Universal/Universal–International
UPA -- United Productions of America
URU -- Uruguay
USC -- Univ. of Southern California

VEN -- Venezuela
VIC -- Victory
VIT -- Vitagraph

WAR -- Andy Warhol
WB   -- Warner Brothers
WHO -- Wholesome
WOO -- Woolner Brothers
WOR -- World
WW   -- World–Wide/Sono–Art
WWS -- Weston Woods Studios

YUG -- Yugoslavia

A.K.A. CASSIUS CLAY see FLOAT LIKE A BUTTERFLY, STING LIKE A BEE

ABBE CONSTANTIN, L' (FRA, 1925, based on a story by Ludovic Halevy)
  ABBE CONSTANTIN L' (FRA, 1933)

ABBOTT & COSTELLO MEET DR. JEKYLL AND MR. HYDE see DR JEKYLL AND MR. HYDE

ABBOTT & COSTELLO MEET FRANKENSTEIN (UN, 1948, based on a story by Robert Lees, Frederic I. Rinaldo and John Grant; remake uncredited)
  FRANKENSTEIN, THE VAMPIRE & CO. (MEX, 1961)

ABBOTT & COSTELLO MEET FRANKENSTEIN see FRANKENSTEIN

ABBOTT & COSTELLO MEET THE INVISIBLE MAN see INVISIBLE MAN, THE

ABBOTT & COSTELLO SHOW, THE (series) (CBS–TV, 1952, based on the characters of Abbott & Costello)
  ABBOTT & COSTELLO SHOW, THE (series) (HB, 1966)

ABDICATION see QUEEN CHRISTINA

ABDUL THE DAMNED (BRI, 1935, based on a book by Robert Neumann and made in two language versions)
  SULTAN ROUGE, LE (FRA, 1935)

ABE LINCOLN AND HIS STEPMOTHER see ABRAHAM LINCOLN

ABE LINCOLN IN ILLINOIS (RKO, 1940, based on the play by Robert E. Sherwood)
  ABE LINCOLN IN ILLINOIS (CBS–TV, 1951)
  ABE LINCOLN IN ILLINOIS (NBC–TV, 1954)
  ABE LINCOLN IN ILLINOIS (NBC–TV, 1964)

ABIE'S IRISH ROSE (PAR, 1929, based on the play by Anne Nichols)
  ABIE'S IRISH ROSE (UA, 1946)

ABISMOS DE PASION see WUTHERING HEIGHTS

ABOMINABLE SNOWMAN, THE (short) (IND, 1954, based on the legend)
  SNOW CREATURE (UA, 1954)
  CREATURE, THE (BRI–TV, 1955)
  MAN BEAST (ITA, 1957)
  ABOMINABLE SNOWMAN, THE (FOX, 1957)

ABOUT FACE see BROTHER RAT

ABSCHIED (GER, 1930, based on the book by Johannes R. Becher)
  ABSCHIED (GER, 1967)

ABRAHAM LINCOLN (FN, 1924, based on various screen-plays taken from the life of U.S. President Abraham Lincoln)
  ABRAHAM LINCOLN (short) (IND, n.d.)
  ABRAHAM LINCOLN (UA, 1930)
  ABRAHAM LINCOLN – STATESMAN (short) (IND, 1933)
  ABRAHAM LINCOLN, THE PIONEER (short) (IND, 1933)
  LINCOLN IN THE WHITE HOUSE (short) (WB, 1939)
  LINCOLN SPEAKS AT GETTYSBURG (short) (RAD, 1950)
  ABRAHAM LINCOLN (short) (EBE, 1951)
  ABRAHAM LINCOLN: A BACKGROUND STUDY (short) (COR, 1951)
  YOUNG LAWYER IN NEW SALEM, THE (short) (SAU, 1952)
  ABRAHAM LINCOLN (short) (CBS–TV, 1952)
  FACE OF LINCOLN, THE (short) (USC, 1954)
  EMANCIPATION PROCLAMATION, THE (short) (CBS–TV, 1955)
  ONE NATION INDIVISIBLE (short) (SAU, 1956)
  NEW SALEM (short) (MHF, 1956)
  LINCOLN AT GETTYSBURG (short) (PAT, n.d.)
  GROWING UP (short) (SAU, 1956)
  FRONTIER FAMILY (short) (SAU, 1956)
  DAY LINCOLN WAS SHOT, THE (NBC–TV, 1956)
  LINCOLN: NOR LONG REMEMBER (short) (IND, n.d.)
  END AND THE BEGINNING (short) (MHF, n.d.)
  ABE LINCOLN AND HIS STEPMOTHER (short) (IND–TV, 1958)
  ABRAHAM LINCOLN: THE WAR YEARS (short) (IND, 1959)
  ABRAHAM LINCOLN: YOUTH (short) (IND, 1959)
  ABRAHAM LINCOLN – THE ILLINOIS YEARS (short) (IND, 1959)
  MEET MR. LINCOLN (short) (NBC–TV, 1960)
  ABRAHAM LINCOLN (SAU, 1960)
  HOW CHANCE MADE LINCOLN PRESIDENT (IDE, n.d.)
  LINCOLN MURDER CASE, THE (ABC–TV, 1961)
  BOYHOOD OF ABRAHAM LINCOLN, THE (short) (COR, 1962)
  NEW SALEM STORY: LINCOLN LEGEND, THE (short) (TFC, 1963)
  GREAT DEBATE: LINCOLN VS. DOUGLAS, THE (short) (EBE, 1965)
  PALMETTO CONSPIRACY, THE: LINCOLN – PRESI-DENT–ELECT (short) (TFC, 1965)
  MOONLIGHT WITNESS: ABE LINCOLN, LAWYER (short) (TFC, 1965)
  ABRAHAM LINCOLN: A STUDY IN GREATNESS (IND, n.d.)
  LINCOLN'S LAST DAY (short) (TV, 1968)
  ABRAHAM LINCOLN AND THE EMANCIPATION PROC-LAMATION (short) (IND, 1970)
  THEY'VE KILLED PRESIDENT LINCOLN! (NBC–TV, 1971)
  LINCOLN: TRIAL BY FIRE (ABC–TV, 1974)
  LINCOLN CONSPIRACY, THE (SUN, 1976)

ABSINTHE see MADAME X

ABYSMAL BRUTE, THE (UN, 1923, based on the story by Jack London)
  CONFLICT (UN, 1936)

ACCENT ON YOUTH (PAR, 1935, based on the play by Samson Raphaelson)
  MR. MUSIC (PAR, 1950)
  BUT NOT FOR ME (PAR, 1960)

ACE OF SCOTLAND YARD see BLAKE OF SCOTLAND YARD

ACES HIGH see JOURNEY'S END

ACROSS THE PACIFIC (VIT, 1914, based on the book by Charles E. Blaney)

ACROSS THE PACIFIC (WB, 1926)

ACROSS TO SINGAPORE see ALL THE BROTHERS
    WERE VALIANT

ACT OF MURDER, AN (LIVE TODAY FOR TOMORROW)
    (UN, 1948, based on the book, "The Mills of God," by
    Ernst Lothar)
    ACT OF MURDER, AN (NBC–TV, 1955)

ACTION OF THE TIGER (MGM, 1957, based on the book
    by James Willard)
    ACTION OF THE TIGER (NBC–TV, 1964)

ACTRESS, THE (MGM, 1953, based on the play, "Years
    Ago," by Ruth Gordon)
    YEARS AGO (CBS–TV, 1960)

ACTRESS, THE see TRELAWNY OF THE "WELLS"

ADALENS POESI (SWE, 1928, based on a series of poems)
    ADALENS POESI (SWE, 1948)

ADAM AND EVE (VIT, 1912, based on the Bible story)
    ADAM AND EVE (GER, 1923)
    ADAM AND EVE (GER, 1928)
    ADAM AND EVE (ITA, 1950)
    ADAM AND EVE (IND, 1954)
    ADAM AND EVE (MEX, 1956)
    ADAM AND EVE (IND, 1957)
    ADAM AND EVE (CZE, 1962)
    BIBLE, THE (sequence) (FOX, 1966)
    BIBLE, LA (FRA, 1977)

ADAM HAD FOUR SONS (COL, 1941, based on the book,
    "Legacy," by Charles Donner)
    ADAM HAD FOUR SONS (NBC–TV, 1957)

ADAM'S RIB (MGM, 1949, based on a screenplay by Ruth
    Gordon and Garson Kanin)
    ADAM'S RIB (series) (ABC–TV, 1973)

ADDAMS FAMILY, THE (series) (ABC–TV, 1964, based on
    characters created by Charles Addams)
    ADDAMS FAMILY, THE (series) (NBC–TV, 1973)
    HALLOWE'EN WITH THE NEW ADDAMS FAMILY
    (NBC–TV, 1977)

ADDIO, FRATELLO CRUDELE see MY SISTER, MY
    LOVE

ADDIO GROVINEZZA! (ITA, 1911, source unknown)
    ADDIO GROVINEZZA! (ITA, 1913)
    ADDIO GROVINEZZA! (ITA, 1918)
    ADDIO GROVINEZZA! (ITA, 1940)

ADMIRABLE CRICHTON, THE see BACK TO NATURE

ADMIRAL BYRD see EXPEDITION TO ANTARCTICA

ADOLESCENCE (ARG, 1941, source unknown)
    MY FIRST GIRL FRIEND (ARG, 1966)

ADOLF HITLER: THE RISE TO POWER see HITLER
    GANG, THE

ADORABLE (FOX, 1933, based on a story by Billy Wilder
    and Paul Frank)
    IHRE HOHEIT BEFIEHLT (GER, 1933)

PRINCESS A VOUS ORDRES (FRA, 1933)

ADORABLE JULIA see JULIA, DU BIST ZAUBERHAFT

ADRIENNE LECOUVREUR (FRA, 1913, based on the play
    by Eugene Scribe and Ernst Legouve; also the basis for
    an opera by Cilea in 1902)
    DREAM OF LOVE (MGM, 1928)
    ADRIENNE LECOUVREUR (FRA, 1938)

ADULT VERSION OF DR. JEKYLL AND MR. HYDE see
    DR. JEKYLL AND MR. HYDE

ADULTRESS, THE see THERESE RAQUIN

ADVENTURE IN IRAQ see GREEN GODDESS, THE

ADVENTURE IN MANHATTAN see THREE HOURS

ADVENTURE ISLAND see EBB TIDE

ADVENTURE TO THE CENTER OF THE EARTH see
    VOYAGE AU CENTRE DE LA TERRE

ADVENTURER, THE (short) (MUT, 1917, based on a
    screenplay by Charlie Chaplin and elaborated on in the
    remake)
    SECOND HUNDRED YEARS, THE (short) (MGM, 1927)

ADVENTURES AT RUGBY see TOM BROWN'S SCHOOL
    DAYS

ADVENTURES IN DIPLOMACY (FRA, 1914, based on the
    book by Jacques Futrelle)
    ELUSIVE ISABEL (UN, 1916)

ADVENTURES OF A YOUNG MAN see WORLD OF NICK
    ADAMS, THE

ADVENTURES OF BARON MUNCHAUSEN, THE see
    BARON DE CRAC

ADVENTURES OF BLACK BEAUTY, THE see BLACK
    BEAUTY

ADVENTURES OF CUCURUCHITO AND PINOCCHIO
    see PINOCCHIO

ADVENTURES OF DR. DOLITTLE (short) (GER, 1928,
    based on the stories by Hugh Lofting)
    DR. DOLITTLE IN THE LION'S DEN (short) (GER, 1928)
    DR. DOLITTLE'S TRIP TO AFRICA (short) (GER, 1928)
    DR. DOLITTLE (FOX, 1967)
    GOOD DOCTOR AIBOLIT, THE (RUS, 1967)
    ADVENTURES OF DR. DOLITTLE (series) (NBC–TV,
    1970)

ADVENTURES OF DON JUAN see DON JUAN

ADVENTURES OF DON QUIXOTE see DON QUIXOTE

ADVENTURES OF FRANK AND JESSE JAMES see
    JAMES BOYS, THE

ADVENTURES OF GERARD, THE see BRIGADIER
    GERARD

ADVENTURES OF GOOD SOLDIER SCHWEIK, THE see
    DOBRY VOJAK SVEJK

ADVENTURES OF HUCKLEBERRY FINN see HUCKLE–
BERRY FINN

ADVENTURES OF JUDGE ROY BEAN (series) (TV,
1955, based on an actual character from western
America)
LIFE AND TIMES OF JUDGE ROY BEAN (NGP, 1973)

ADVENTURES OF KIT CARSON, THE see KIT CARSON

ADVENTURES OF LONG JOHN SILVER, THE see LONG
JOHN SILVER

ADVENTURES OF MARCO POLO, THE (UA, 1938, based
on the writings of Marco Polo)
MARCO POLO'S TRAVELS (short) (EBE, 1955)
FABULOUS ADVENTURES OF MARCO POLO (FRA/
EGY/ITA/YUG, 1965)
MARCO THE MAGNIFICENT (MGM, 1966)
MARCO POLO (AI, 1962)
TRAVELS OF MARCO POLO, THE (TV, 1972)
MARCO (CIN, 1973)
MARCO POLO JR. (AUT, 1973)
MARCO POLO (CHN, 1976)

ADVENTURES OF MARK TWAIN, THE (WB, 1944, based
on the life and works of the noted American humorist
and writer)
MARK TWAIN (short) (IND, 1946)
MARK TWAIN: BACKGROUND FOR HIS WORKS
(short) (COR, 1957)
MARK TWAIN'S MISSISSIPPI (MGM, 1960)
MARK TWAIN'S AMERICA (NBC–TV, 1960)
MARK TWAIN GIVES AN INTERVIEW (short) (COR,
1961)
MARK TWAIN (short) (WOL, 1963)
MARK TWAIN TONIGHT! (TV, 1967)
MARK TWAIN'S TOM SAWYER AND HUCKLEBERRY
FINN (BRI/FRA–TV, 1967)

ADVENTURES OF MARTIN EDEN, THE see MARTIN
EDEN

ADVENTURES OF MR. PICKWICK, THE see PICKWICK
PAPERS, THE

ADVENTURES OF OZZIE AND HARRIET, THE (series)
(TV, 1952, based on a radio series)
HERE COME THE NELSONS (UN, 1952)
OZZIE'S GIRLS (series) (TV, 1973)

ADVENTURES OF PENROD AND SAM, THE see
PENROD

ADVENTURES OF PICASSO, THE see PICASSO: LE
PEINTRE ET SON MODELE

ADVENTURES OF PINOCCHIO see PINOCCHIO

ADVENTURES OF PRINCE ACHMED, THE see ALADDIN

ADVENTURES OF ROBIN HOOD see ROBIN HOOD AND
HIS MERRY MEN

ADVENTURES OF ROBINSON CRUSOE, THE see
ROBINSON CRUSOE

ADVENTURES OF SADIE see BACK TO NATURE

ADVENTURES OF SCARAMOUCHE, THE see SCARA–
MOUCHE

ADVENTURES OF SINBAD see SINBAD THE SAILOR

ADVENTURES OF SINBAD THE NAVIGATOR, THE see
SINBAD THE SAILOR

ADVENTURES OF SIR LANCELOT see SWORD OF
LANCELOT

ADVENTURES OF THE 3 MUSKETEERS, THE see
THREE MUSKETEERS, THE

ADVENTURES OF TIL L'ESPIEGLE see TIL EULENS--
PIEGEL

ADVENTURES OF TOM SAWYER, THE see TOM SAWYER

ADVENTURES OF WILLIAM TELL see GUILLAUME
TELL ET LE CLOWN

ADVENTURESS, THE see DESERT BRIDE and KEYHOLE,
THE

ADVENTUROUS LIFE OF CATHERINE I OF RUSSIA
(GER, 1929, based on the life of the Russian empress)
CZARINA'S SECRET, THE (short) (MGM, 1928)
CATHERINE THE GREAT (UA, 1934)
SCARLET EMPRESS, THE (PAR, 1934)
CATHERINE DE RUSSIE (FRA/ITA, 1962)
GREAT CATHERINE (BRI, 1969)

ADVICE TO THE LOVELORN (UA, 1933, based on the
book by Nathaniel West)
MISS LONELYHEARTS (UA, 1958)

AFFAIR see PASSION FIRE

AFFAIR DE LA RUE DE LOURCINE, L' (FRA, 1923,
based on the play by Eugene Labiche, Albert Monnier
and Eduard Martin)
AFFAIR DE LA RUE DE LOURCINE, L' (FRA, 1930)

AFFAIR DREYFUS, L' (FRA, 1899, based on a historical
incident)
DREYFUS (GER, 1931)
DREYFUS CASE, THE (BRI, 1931)
J'ACCUSE! (FRA, 1938)
DREYFUS CASE, THE (GER, 1940)
DREYFUS CASE, THE (short) (CBS–TV, 1953)
I ACCUSE! (MGM, 1958)
DREYFUS AFFAIR, THE (ITA--TV, 1968)

AFFAIR DU COURIER DE LYON, L' see COURIER DE
LYON, LE

AFFAIR IN MONTE CARLO see VIERUNDZWANZIG
STUNDEN AUS DEM LEBEN EINER FRAU

AFFAIR OF YOUNG NOSZTY WITH MARI TOTH (HUN,
1928, based on the book by Kalman Mikszath)
IHR LEIBHUSAR (AUS/GER/HUN, 1937)
AFFAIR OF YOUNG NOSZTY WITH MARI TOTH
(HUN, 1960)

AFFAIR TO REMEMBER, AN see LOVE AFFAIR

AFFAIRE CLEMENCEAU, L' see CLEMENCEAU CASE,

AFFAIRS OF DOBIE GILLIS, THE   (MGM, 1953, based on stories by Max Schulman)
  MANY LOVES OF DOBIE GILLIS, THE   (series)   (CBS–TV, 1959)
  WHATEVER HAPPENED TO DOBIE GILLIS?   (CBS–TV, 1977)

AFFAIRS OF JIMMY VALENTINE, THE   see   RETURN OF JIMMY VALENTINE, THE

AFFAIRS OF LADY HAMILTON, THE   see   ROMANCE OF LADY HAMILTON, THE

AFFAIRS OF MESSALINA   see   MESSALINA

AFRAID TO LOVE   see   MARRIAGE OF KITTY

AFRICA AND SCHWEITZER   see   DR. SCHWEITZER

AFRICA – TEXAS STYLE   (PAR, 1967, based on a screen–play by Andy White)
  COWBOY IN AFRICA   (series)   (ABC–TV, 1967)

AFRICAN MANHUNT   see   DARK RAPTURE

AFRICAN QUEEN, THE   (UA, 1951, based on the book by C.S. Forester)
  AFRICAN QUEEN, THE   (series)   (CBS–TV, 1977)

AFTER DEATH   see   KLARA MILITCH

AFTER FIVE   (PAR, 1915, based on the play by William C. DeMille and Cecil B. DeMille)
  NIGHT CLUB, THE   (PAR, 1925)

AFTER HIS OWN HEART   (GOL, 1919, based on the story by Ben Ames Williams)
  TOO BUSY TO WORK   (FOX, 1932)

AFTER MANY YEARS   (BIO, 1908, based on the poem, "Enoch Arden," by Alfred, Lord Tennyson)
  ENOCH ARDEN   (BIO, 1911)
  ENOCH ARDEN   (BRI, 1914)
  ENOCH ARDEN   (MUT, 1915)
  FATAL MARRIAGE, THE   (RC, 1922)

AFTER SIX DAYS   see   CAIN AND ABEL

AFTER THE WELSH RABBIT   see   DREAM OF A RARE–BIT FIEND

AGAINST ALL FLAGS   (UN, 1953, based on the book by Aeneas MacKenzie)
  KING'S PIRATE, THE   (UN, 1967)

AGE OF DISCRETION   see   UNKNOWN BLONDE

AGE OF ELIZABETH, THE   (short)   (EBE, n.d., based on the life and times of Queen Elizabeth I)
  ENGLAND OF ELIZABETH, THE   (short)   (IFB, 1960)

AGE OF INNOCENCE, THE   (WB, 1924, based on the book by Edith Wharton and a subsequent play by Margaret Ayer Barnes)
  AGE OF INNOCENCE, THE   (RKO, 1934)

AGE OF KENNEDY, THE   see   MAKING OF THE

AGE OF KINGS   (BRI–TV, 1960, based on various sequences from Shakespeare plays)
  WARS OF THE ROSES, THE   (BRI–TV, 1964)

AGE OF KINGS   see also   HENRY V, RICHARD II and RICHARD III

AGONIE DES AIGLES, L'   (FRA, 1921, based on a story by Georges D'Esparbes)
  AGONIE DES AIGLES, L'   (FRA, 1933)
  AGONIE DES AIGLES, L'   (FRA, 1951)

AGONIES OF AGNES, THE   see   PERILS OF PAULINE, THE

AGONY COLUMN, THE   see   BLIND ADVENTURE, THE

AH, WILDERNESS   (MGM, 1935, based on the play by Eugene O'Neill and subsequently the basis for the musical comedy, "Take Me Along" in 1959)
  SUMMER HOLIDAY   (MGM, 1948)
  AH, WILDERNESS   (ABC–TV, 1951)
  AH, WILDERNESS   (CBS–TV, 1955)
  AH, WILDERNESS   (NBC–TV, 1959)

AHASUERUS   see   WANDERING JEW, THE

AHNFRAU, DIE   see   BILD DER AHNFRAU, DAS

AIDA   (ED, 1911, based on the opera by Verdi, later the basis for a musical stage version with a Civil War setting, "My Darlin' Aida," in 1953)
  AIDA   (ITA, 1954)

AIGLON, L'   (FRA, 1913, based on the play by Edmond Rostand)
  AIGLON, L'   (FRA, 1931)

AJKA ALLADIN   see   ALADDIN

ALADDIN   (BRI, 1898, based on tales from the Arabian Nights)
  ALADIN   (FRA, 1900)
  ALADIN   (FRA, 1906)
  ALADDIN AND THE WONDERFUL LAMP   (FOX, 1917)
  ALADDIN   (IND, 1923)
  ONE ARABIAN NIGHT   (BRI, 1923)
  ALADDIN AND THE WONDERFUL LAMP   (IN, 1926)
  ADVENTURES OF PRICE ACHMED   (GER, 1926)
  ALADDIN AND THE WONDERFUL LAMP   (IN, 1930)
  ALADDIN AND THE WONDERFUL LAMP   (IN, 1933)
  ALADDIN AND THE WONDERFUL LAMP   (short)   (COM, 1934)
  AJKA ALLADIN   (IN, 1935)
  ALADDIN   (HOL, 1936)
  ALLADIN KA BETA   (IN, 1939)
  ALADDIN AND HIS WONDERFUL LAMP   (short)   (PAR, 1939)
  ADVENTURES OF PRINCE ACHMED   (GER, 1942)
  1001 NIGHTS   (COL, 1945)
  ALADDIN   (PHI, 1947)
  THIEF OF DAMASCUS   (COL, 1951)
  ALADDIN AND HIS WONDERFUL LAMP   (IN, 1951)
  ALADDIN AND HIS LAMP   (MON, 1952)
  ALADDIN   (BRI, 1952)
  ALLADIN KA BETA   (IN, 1955)
  ALADDIN AND THE MAGIC LAMP   (HUN, 1955)

ALADDIN AND THE WONDERFUL LAMP (IN, 1957)
ALADDIN (CBS--TV, 1958)
ALADIN (FRA/ITA, 1961)
WONDERS OF ALADDIN (MGM, 1961)
SINBAD, ALI BABA AND ALADDIN (IN, 1963)
I AM ALADDIN (IN, 1965)
ALADDIN (CBS--TV, 1967)
ALADDIN AND HIS MAGIC LAMP (RUS, 1967)
ALADDIN AND HIS WONDERFUL LAMP (FRA, 1969)
ALADDIN (AUT--TV, 1969)

ALADDIN AND THE MAGIC LAMP see ALADDIN

ALADDIN AND THE WONDERFUL LAMP see ALADDIN

ALADIN see ALADDIN

ALAMO, THE see REMEMBER THE ALAMO

ALAS SOBRE EL CHACO see STORM OVER THE ANDES

ALASKA SEAS see SPAWN OF THE NORTH

ALBERT SCHWEITZER see DR. SCHWEITZER

ALCADE DE ZALAMEA, L' (SPA, 1914, based on a book
    by Pedro Calderon de la Barca)
  RICHTER VON ZALAMEA, DER (GER, 1920)
  RICHTER VON ZALAMEA, DER (GER, 1956)

ALEKO see GYPSIES, THE

ALEXANDER HAMILTON see CHRONICLES OF
    AMERICA: ALEXANDER HAMILTON

ALEXANDER THE GREAT (SWE, 1917, based on the life
    of the noted ruler)
  TRIUMPH OF ALEXANDER THE GREAT, THE (short)
    (MHF, 1955)
  ALEXANDER THE GREAT (UA, 1956)
  ALEXANDER THE GREAT AND THE HELLENISTIC
    AGE (short) (COR, 1964)

ALEXANDRA (GER, 1914, source unknown)
  ALEXANDRA (GER, 1922)

ALFREDO, ALFREDO see FILUMENA MARTURANO

ALF'S BUTTON (BRI, 1921, based on the play by W.A.
    Darlington)
  ALF'S BUTTON (BRI, 1930)
  ALF'S BUTTON AFLOAT (BRI, 1938)

ALF'S BUTTON AFLOAT see ALF'S BUTTON

ALGIERS see PEPE LE MOKO

ALI BABA (FRA, 1902, based on a legend and an operetta
    by Oscar Asche)
  ALI BABA AND THE FORTY THIEVES (FRA, 1907)
  ALI BABA (ITA, 1911)
  ALI BABA AND THE FORTY THIEVES (FOX, 1918)
  CHU CHIN CHOW (BRI, 1923)
  CHU CHIN CHOW (MGM, 1925)
  ALI BABA AND THE FORTY THIEVES (IN, 1926)
  CHU CHIN CHOW (BRI, 1934)
  ALI BABA (IN, 1934)
  ALI BABA (IN, 1937)
  ALI BABA (IN, 1939)

ALI BABA AND THE FORTY THIEVES (EGY, 1941)
  ALI BABA AND THE FORTY THIEVES (UN, 1944)
  SON OF ALI BABA (UN, 1951)
  THIEF OF DAMASCUS (COL, 1951)
  ALI BABA AND THE FORTY THIEVES (FRA, 1954)
  CAVE OF ALI BABA (ARG, 1954)
  ALI BABA AND THE FORTY THIEVES (NBC--TV, 1958)
  SINBAD, ALI BABA AND ALADDIN (IN, 1963)
  SWORD OF ALI BABA (UN, 1965)
  ALI BABA AND THE 40 THIEVES (short) (TV, 1967)
  ALI BABA AND THE FORTY THIEVES OF BAGDAD
    (IRAN, 1967)
  ALI BABA AND THE 40 THIEVES (JAP, 1971)

ALI BABA AND THE FORTY THIEVES see ALI BABA

ALI BABA AND THE FORTY THIEVES OF BAGDAD see
    ALI BABA

ALIAS JIMMY VALENTINE (WOR, 1915, based on the play
    by Paul Armstrong. Armstrong worked on the screenplay
    for the 1936 version using another story. Also a popular
    radio series)
  ALIAS JIMMY VALENTINE (MGM, 1920)
  ALIAS JIMMY VALENTINE (MGM, 1929)
  RETURN OF JIMMY VALENTINE (MGM, 1929)

ALIAS SMITH AND JONES (ABC--TV, 1971, based on a
    teleplay)
  ALIAS SMITH AND JONES (series) (ABC--TV, 1972)

ALIAS THE DEACON (UN, 1927, based on the play by John
    B. Hymer and Leroy Clemens)
  HALF A SINNER (UN, 1934)
  ALIAS THE DEACON (UN, 1940)

ALIAS THE DOCTOR (WB, 1932, based on a play by Emric
    Foeldes)
  CAS DU DOCTEUR BRENNER, LA (FRA, 1932)

ALIBI (FRA, 1938, based on the story by Marcel Achard)
  ALIBI (REP, 1943)

ALICE see ALICE DOESN'T LIVE HERE ANYMORE

ALICE ADAMS (AE, 1923, based on the book by Booth
    Tarkington)
  ALICE ADAMS (RKO, 1935)

ALICE DOESN'T LIVE HERE ANYMORE (WB, 1974, based
    on a screenplay by Robert Getchell)
  JERRY (pilot) (WB--TV, 1974)
  ALICE (series) (CBS--TV, 1976)

ALICE IN WONDERLAND (BRI, 1903, based on the books
    by Lewis Carroll)
  ALICE IN WONDERLAND (FRA, 1909)
  ALICE'S ADVENTURES IN WONDERLAND (ED, 1910)
  ALICE IN WONDERLAND (IND, 1915)
  ALICE IN WONDERLAND (IND, 1920)
  ALICE IN WONDERLAND (PAT, 1927)
  ALICE THROUGH THE LOOKING GLASS (PAT, 1928)
  ALICE IN WONDERLAND (IND, 1931)
  ALICE IN WONDERLAND (PAT, 1933)
  ALICE IN WONDERLAND (FRA, 1948)
  ALICE IN WONDERLAND (CBS--TV, 1950)
  ALICE IN WONDERLAND (DIS, 1951)
  ALICE IN WONDERLAND (BRI, 1951)
  ALICE IN WONDERLAND (ABC--TV, 1954)

ALICE IN WONDERLAND (NBC--TV, 1955)
ALICE IN WONDERLAND (NBC--TV, 1959)
ALICE IN WONDERLAND (ABC--TV, 1966)
ALICE IN WONDERLAND (NBC--TV, 1966)
ALICE IN WONDERLAND IN PARIS (CHI, 1966)
ALICE THROUGH THE LOOKING GLASS (NBC--TV, 1967)
ALICE IN WONDERLAND (RAN, 1972)
ALICE'S ADVENTURES IN WONDERLAND (BRI, 1972)
ALICE IN WONDERLAND (HB, 1976)
ALICE THROUGH THE LOOKING GLASS (BRI--TV, 1976)
ALICIA EN LA ESPANA DE LAS MARAVILLAS (SPA, 1978)

ALICE IN WONDERLAND IN PARIS see ANATOLE, FROWING PRINCE, THE, and MANY MOONS

ALICE THROUGH THE LOOKING GLASS see ALICE IN WONDERLAND

ALICE'S ADVENTURES IN WONDERLAND see ALICE IN WONDERLAND

ALICIA EN LA ESPANA DE LAS MARAVILLAS see ALICE IN WONDERLAND

ALL ABOUT EVE (FOX, 1950, based on the short story and radio play by Mary Orr)
APPLAUSE (CBS--TV, 1973)

ALL FOR A WOMAN (GER, 1921, based on the play by Georg Buchner)
DANTON (GER, 1931)

ALL IN THE FAMILY (series) (CBS--TV, 1971, based on the British television series, "Til Death Us Do Part")
MAUDE (series) (CBS--TV, 1972)
GOOD TIMES (series) (CBS--TV, 1973)

ALL IN THE FAMILY see also TILL DEATH US DO PART

ALL MY SONS (UN, 1948, based on the play by Arthur Miller)
ALL MY SONS (FRA--TV, 1969)

ALL NIGHT LONG see OTHELLO

ALL THAT MONEY CAN BUY see DEVIL AND DANIEL WEBSTER, THE

ALL THE BROTHERS WERE VALIANT (MGM, 1923, based on the story by Ben Ames Williams)
ACROSS TO SINGAPORE (MGM, 1928)
ALL THE BROTHERS WERE VALIANT (MGM, 1953)

ALL THE KING'S MEN (COL, 1949, based on the book by Robert Penn Warren)
ALL THE KING'S MEN (NBC--TV, 1958)

ALL THE KING'S MEN see SECOND WIFE

ALL THE WAY HOME (PAR, 1963, based on the book "A Death in the Family," by James Agee and the play by Tad Mosel)
ALL THE WAY HOME (NBC--TV, 1971)

ALL THE WORLD'S WOMEN see DON JUAN

ALLADIN KA BETA see ALADDIN

ALLE TAGE IST KEIN SONNTAG (GER, 1935, source unknown)
ALLE TAGE IST KEIN SONNTAG (GER, 1959)

ALLES UM EINE FRAU see KAMERADEN

ALLUMETTE SUEDOISE, L' (RUS, 1915, based on the book by Anton Chekhov)
ALLUMETTE SUEDOISE (RUS, 1922)
ALLUMETTE SUEDOISE (RUS, 1954)

ALMENRAUSCH UND EDELWEISS (GER, 1927, based on the play by Dr. H. Schmidt and H. Nevert)
ALMENRAUSCH UND EDELWEISS (GER, 1957)

ALMOST A HONEYMOON (BRI, 1930, based on the play by Walter Ellis)
ALMOST A HONEYMOON (BRI, 1938)

ALMOST HUMAN (PAT, 1927, based on the story, "The Bar Sinister," by Richard Harding Davis)
IT'S A DOG'S LIFE (MGM, 1955)

ALOHA see ALOHA OE

ALOHA OE (BRI, 1915, based on the screenplay by J.G. Hawks and Thomas H. Ince)
ALOHA (TIF, 1931)

ALOISE see MAGIC MIRROR OF ALOYSE

ALOMA OF THE SOUTH SEAS (PAR, 1926, based on the play by John B. Hymer and Leroy Clemens)
ALOMA OF THE SOUTH SEAS (PAR, 1941)

ALONG CAME JONES (RKO, 1945, based on the book by Alan LeMay)
ALONG CAME JONES (NBC--TV, 1955)

ALRAUNE (GER, 1918, based on the book by Hanns Heinz Ewers)
ALRAUNE (HUN, 1918)
ALRAUNE AND THE GOLEM (GER, 1919)
UNHOLY LOVE (GER, 1928)
DAUGHTER OF EVIL (GER, 1930)
UNNATURAL (MANDRAKE) (GER, 1952)

ALRAUNE AND THE GOLEM see ALRAUNE

ALT PAA ET BRAET see C'EST PAS PARCE QU' ON A REIN A DIRE QU'IL FAUT FERMER SA GUEULE

ALTE GAUNER, DER see VIEUX TRICHEUR, LE

ALTE LIED, DAS (GER, 1930, based on the book "Stine Irrungen, Wirrungen," by Theodor Fontane)
ALTE LIED, DAS (GER, 1945)

ALWAYS A BRIDE see BRIDES ARE LIKE THAT

ALWAYS GOODBYE see GALLANT LADY

ALWAYS IN MY HEART see DAUGHTERS COURAGEOUS

AMANTS DE VERONE, LES see ROMEO AND JULIET

AMANTS TERRIBLES, LES see PRIVATE LIVES

AMATEUR GENTLEMAN (BRI, 1920, based on the book
    by Jeffrey Farnol)
    AMATEUR GENTLEMAN (IND, 1926)
    AMATEUR GENTLEMAN (BRI, 1936)

AMAZING DR. CLITTERHOUSE, THE (A SLIGHT CASE
    OF MURDER) (WB, 1938, based on the play by Barre
    Lyndon)
    STOP, YOU'RE KILLING ME (WB, 1952)

AMAZING MRS. HOLLIDAY, THE (UN, 1943, based on the
    story by Sonya Levien)
    AMAZING MRS. HOLLIDAY, THE (NBC--TV, 1955)

AMAZING QUEST OF MR. ERNEST BLISS, THE (BRI,
    1920, based on the book by E. Phillips Oppenheim)
    AMAZING QUEST, THE (BRI, 1924)
    ROMANCE AND RICHES (BRI, 1936)
    STAIRWAY TO HEAVEN (BRI, 1946)
    STAIRWAY TO HEAVEN (NBC--TV, 1951)

AMBROSE'S FIRST FALSEHOOD (short) (KEY, 1914,
    based on a Mack Sennet plot which was elaborated upon
    in subsequent versions by Stan Laurel)
    WE FAW DOWN (short) (MGM, 1928)
    BE BIG (short) (MGM, 1931)
    CAROTTIERS, LES (short) FRA, 1931)
    CALAVERAS, LOS (short) (SPA, 1931)
    BE BIG (short) (GER, 1931)
    SONS OF THE DESERT (MGM, 1934)

AMELIA EARHART see FLIGHT FOR FREEDOM

AMERICAN ASSASSINS, THE see NOVEMBER 22 AND
    THE WARREN REPORT

AMERICAN IN ORBIT, AN (short) (UNI, 1962, based on
    the career of astronaut John Glenn Jr.)
    VOYAGE OF FRIENDSHIP 7 (short) NAV, 1962)
    FLIGHT OF THE FRIENDSHIP 7 (short) (IND, 1962)
    FRIENDSHIP 7 (NAV, 1962)
    JOHN GLENN STORY, THE (short) (NAV, 1963)
    JOHN GLENN JR. (short) (WOL, 1963)
    FLIGHT OF THE SPIRIT OF ST. LOUIS AND THE
      FRIENDSHIP 7 (short) (MHF, 1967)

AMERICAN ROAD, THE (short) (IND, 1953, based on the
    life of industrialist Henry Ford)
    HENRY FORD (short) (MHF, 1962)
    TIN LIZZIE TYCOON, THE (MGM, 1963)
    HENRY FORD (short) (PAT, 1964)
    HENRY FORD'S MIRROR OF AMERICA (short)
      (IND, 1965)
    HENRY FORD'S AMERICA (CAN--TV, 1976)
    HENRY FORD'S ROAD TO HAPPINESS (PBS--TV, 1978)

AMERICAN SUICIDE CLUB, THE see SUICIDE CLUB,
    THE

AMERICAN TRADITION, THE (sequence) (NET--TV,
    1966, based on the life and work of composer Charles
    Ives)
    GOOD DISSONANCE LIKE A MAN, A (IND, 1977)

AMERICAN TRAGEDY, AN (PAR, 1931, based on the book
    by Theodore Dreiser)
    PLACE IN THE SUN, A (PAR, 1951)
    PLACE IN THE SUN, A (CBS--TV, 1954)
    AMERICAN TRAGEDY, AN (ITA--TV, 1962)

AMI FRITZ, L' (FRA, 1919, based on material by
    Erckmann--Chatrian)
    AMI FRITZ, L' (FRA, 1933)

AMLETO see HAMLET

AMMENKONIG, DER see TAL DES LEBENS, DAS

AMOK see LOI ET LE DEVOIR, LA

AMOR AUDAZ see SLIGHTLY SCARLET

AMORE DE AMORE E ANTIGONE (ITA, 1911, based on the
    play by Sophocles)
    ANTIGONE (CBS--TV, 1954)
    ANITGONE (ITA--TV, 1956)
    ANTIGONE (NBC--TV, 1956)
    ANTIGONE (GRE, 1961)
    ANTIGONE (CAN--TV, 1963)
    ANTIGONE (CZE--TV, 1964)
    YEAR OF THE CANNIBALS, THE (ITA, 1969)
    ANTIGONE (PBS--TV, 1972)

AMOROUS ADVENTURES OF DON QUIXOTE AND SAN--
    CHO PANZA see DON QUIXOTE

AMOUR CHANTE, L' (FRA, 1930, based on a screenplay by
    J. Bousquet and H. Falk)
    PROFESSOR DE MI MUJER, EL (SPA, 1930)
    KOMM' ZU MIR ZUM RENDEZ--VOUS (GER, 1930)

AMOUR ESPAGNOL see CARMEN

AMOUR GUIDE, L' see WAY TO LOVE, THE

AMOUR MAITRE DES CHOSES, L' see FLAME OF LOVE,
    THE

AMOUREAUX, LES see EPERVIER, L'

AMOURS DE ROCAMBOLE, LES see ROCAMBOLE

AMPHITRYON see JUPITER SMITTEN

AN DER SCHONEN BLAUEN DONAU (GER, 1926, based
    on the play by Franz Hiesel)
    AN DER SCHONEN BLAUEN DONAU (GER, 1955)
    AN DER SCHONEN BLAUEN DONAU (GER, 1965)

ANASTASIA see ANASTASIA, DIE FALSCHE ZAREN--
    TOCHTER

ANASTASIA, DIE FALSCHE ZARENTOCHTER (GER,
    1927, based on historical events and the play by Marcelle
    Maurette, adapted by Guy Bolton)
    ANASTASIA (FOX, 1956)
    IS ANNA ANDERSON ANASTASIA? (GER, 1956)
    ANASTASIA (NBC--TV, 1967)

ANATOLE (MH, 1950, based on the story by Eve Titus)
    ALICE IN WONDERLAND IN PARIS (CHI, 1966)

ANATOMIST, THE see BODY SNATCHER, THE

ANCIENT MARINER, THE (FOX, 1925, based on the poem
    by Samuel Taylor Coleridge)
    RIME OF THE ANCIENT MARINER, THE (short)
      CAL, 1953)
    ANCIENT MARINER, THE (CBS--TV, 1957)

RIME OF THE ANCIENT MARINER, THE (short)
(IND, 1967)
RIME OF THE ANCIENT MARINER, THE (BRI–TV,
1974)

AND NOW MIGUEL (IND, 1954, based on the book by
Joseph Krumgold)
AND NOW MIGUEL (UN, 1966)

AND THEN THERE WERE NONE (FOX, 1945, based on the
book and play, "Ten Little Indians," by Agatha Christie)
TEN LITTLE INDIANS (NBC–TV, 1959)
TEN LITTLE INDIANS (BRI, 1965)
TEN LITTLE INDIANS (EMB, 1975)

ANDALUSIAN NIGHTS see CARMEN

ANDERE, DER (GER, 1912, based on the book by Paul
Lindau)
ANDERE, DER (GER, 1915)
ANDERE, DER (GER, 1924)
ANDERE, DER (MAN WITHIN, THE) (GER, 1930)
ANDERE, DER (GER, 1929)

ANDERE ICH, DAS (GER, 1918, based on the book by
Heinrich Spoerl)
ANDERE ICH, DAS (GER, 1941)

ANDERE SEITE, DIE see JOURNEY'S END

ANDERSSONSKANS KALLE (SWE, 1922, based on a
screenplay)
ANDERSSONSKANS KALLE (SWE, 1934)
ANDERSSONSKANS KALLE (SWE, 1950)

ANDREAS HOFER (GER, 1909, source unknown)
ANDREAS HOFER (GER, 1929)

ANDREI RUBLEV (RUS, 1964, source unknown)
PASSION OF ANDREW, THE (RUS, 1966)

ANDREW JACKSON see OLD HICKORY

ANDREW JOHNSON see TENNESSEE JOHNSON

ANDROCLES AND THE LION (FRA, 1912, based on the
play by George Bernard Shaw)
ANDROCLES AND THE LION (RKO, 1951)
ANDROCLES AND THE LION (NBC–TV, 1967)

ANDY GRIFFITH SHOW, THE (series) (CBS–TV, 1960,
based on a teleplay)
GOMER PYLE USMC (series) (CBS–TV, 1964)
MAYBERRY RFD (series) (CBS–TV, 1968)

ANGE NU, L' see FRAULEIN ELSE)

ANGEL AND SINNER see WOMAN DISPUTED, A

ANGEL FROM TEXAS, AN see BUTTER AND EGG MAN,
THE

ANGEL OF MERCY (short) (MGM, 1939, based on the
work of Clara Barton, Founder of the Red Cross)
FLAG OF HUMANITY, THE (short) (IND, n.d.)
HEROISM OF CLARA BARTON, THE (short) (CBS–TV,
1956)

ANGEL STREET see GASLIGHT

ANGEL WITH THE TRUMPET, THE see ENGEL MIT DER
POSAUNE, DER

ANGORA LOVE (short) (MGM, 1929, based on a screenplay
by Stan Laurel and elaborated upon in subsequent films)
LAUGHING GRAVY (short) (MGM, 1931)
CHIMP, THE (MGM, 1932)

ANGST see ANGST, DIE SCHWACHE STUNDE EINER
FRAU

ANGST, DIE SCHWACHE STUNDE EINER FRAU (GER,
1928, based on the book, "Angst," by Stefan Sweig)
VERTIGE D'UN SOIR (FRA, 1936)
ANGST (GER, 1954)

ANIMAL KINGDOM, THE (RKO, 1932, based on the play
by Philip Barry)
ONE MORE TOMORROW (WB, 1946)
ANIMAL KINGDOM, THE (NBC–TV, 1952)
ANIMAL KINGDOM, THE (NBC–TV, 1957)

ANIMALS AND BRIGANDS see FOUR MUSICIANS OF
BREMEN

ANJUMAN see ROMEO AND JULIET

ANNA AND THE KING OF SIAM (FOX, 1946, based on the
book by Margaret Landon)
KING AND I, THE (FOX, 1956)
ANNA AND THE KING (series) (CBS–TV, 1972)

ANNA BOLEYN see DECEPTION and HENRY VIII

ANNA CHRISTIE (FN, 1923, based on the play by Eugene
O'Neill, later presented as a stage musical comedy, "New
Girl in Town," in 1958)
HARBOR IN THE FOG (JAP, 1923)
ANNA CHRISTIE (GER, 1930)
ANNA CHRISTIE (MGM, 1930)
ANNA CHRISTIE (ABC–TV, 1952)

ANNA KARENINA (GER, 1910, based on the book by Leo
Tolstoy)
ANNA KARENINA (FRA, 1911)
ANNA KARENINA (RUS, 1911)
ANNA KARENINA (RUS, 1914)
ANNA KARENINA (FOX, 1915)
ANNA KARENINA (ITA, 1917)
ANNA KARENINA (GER, 1919)
ANNA KARENINA (HUN, 1920)
LOVE (MGM, 1927)
ANNA KARENINA (FRA, 1934)
ANNA KARENINA (MGM, 1935)
ANNA KARENINA (BRI, 1948)
ANNA KARENINA (IN, 1952)
ANNA KARENINA (RUS, 1953)
ANNA KARENINA (ARG, 1956)
ANNA KARENINA (ARA, 1961)
ANNA KARENINA (NET–TV, 1964)
ANNA KARENINA (RUS, 1967)
ANNA KARENINA (RUS, 1971)
ANNA KARENINA (RUS, 1975)
ANNA KARENINA (series) (BRI–TV, 1977)

ANNA LUCASTA (COL, 1949, based on the play by Philip
Yordan)
ANNA LUCASTA (UA, 1958)

ANNABELLE LEE   see   AVENGING CONSCIENCE, THE

ANNE OF GREEN GABLES   (REA, 1919, based on the
     books of L.M. Montgomery. Later the basis of a 1968
     musical comedy)
     ANNE OF GREEN GABLES   (RKO, 1934)
     ANNE OF WINDY POPLARS   (RKO, 1940)

ANNE OF THE THOUSAND DAYS   see   DECEPTION

ANNE OF WINDY POPLARS   see   ANNE OF GREEN
     GABLES

ANNIE GET YOUR GUN   see   ANNIE OAKLEY

ANNIE LAURIE   (BRI, 1916, based on the story by Alma
     Taylor)
     ROMANCE OF ANNIE LAURIE   (BRI, 1920)
     ANNIE LAURIE   (MGM, 1927)

ANNIE OAKLEY   (RKO, 1935, based on a historical
     character and a musical comedy by Irvin Berlin)
     ANNIE GET YOUR GUN   (MGM, 1950)
     ANNIE OAKLEY   (series)   (ABC–TV, 1953)
     ANNIE GET YOUR GUN   (NBC--TV, 1957)
     ANNIE GET YOUR GUN   (NBC--TV, 1967)

ANOTHER FINE MESS   see   DUCK SOUP

ANOTHER MAN'S SHOES   see   PHANTOM BUCCANEER,
     THE

ANOTHER PART OF THE FOREST   (UN, 1948, based on
     the play by Lillian Hellman)
     ANOTHER PART OF THE FOREST   (NET–TV, 1972)

ANOTHER PASSOVER OF REMBRANDT VAN RIJN
     (TV, 1953, based on the teleplay by Morton Wishengrad)
     ANOTHER PASSOVER OF REMBRANDT VAN RIJN
     (TV, 1968)

ANSEL ADAMS, PHOTOGRAPHER   (short)   (IFB, 1958,
     based on the works of the noted photographer)
     POINT OF VIEW   (short)   (NET--TV, 1960)
     TECHNIQUE   (short)   (NET--TV, 1962)

ANTARCTICA   see   EXPEDITION TO ANTARCTICA

ANTHONY AND CLEOPATRA   (VIT, 1908, based on the
     play by William Shakespeare)
     ANTONY AND CLEOPATRA   (ITA, 1913)
     ANTONY AND CLEOPATRA   (ITA, 1918)
     ANTONY AND CLEOPATRA   (short)   (BRI, 1951)
     ANTONY AND CLEOPATRA   (BRI–TV, 1962)
     ANTONY AND CLEOPATRA   (ITA–TV, 1965)
     ANTONY AND CLEOPATRA   (ITA, 1971)
     ANTONY AND CLEOPATRA   (ITA, 1971)
     ANTONY AND CLEOPATRA   (BRI, 1972)
     ANTONY AND CLEOPATRA   (ABC–TV, 1973)

ANTHONY AND CLEOPATRA   see also   CLEOPATRA

ANTIGONE   see   AMORE DE AMORE E ANTIGONE, GLI

ANTINEA   see   ATLANTIDE, L'

ANTOMES, LES   (ITA, 1954, based on material by Eduardo
     de Filippo)
     ANTOMES, LES   (ITA, 1967)

ANTONIO GAUDI   (short)   (IND, 1964, based on the life of
     the noted architect)
     ANTONIO GAUDI: AN UNFINISHED VISION   (SPA,
     1974)

ANY MAN'S WIFE   see   MICHAEL O'HALLERAN

ANYTHING GOES   (PAR, 1936, based on the musical comedy
     by Howard Lindsay, Russell Crouse and Cole Porter)
     (TV Title: TOPS IS THE LIMIT)
     ANYTHING GOES   (CBS–TV, 1950)
     ANYTHING GOES   (NBC–TV, 1954)
     ANYTHING GOES   (PAR, 1956)

APACHE TRAIL   (MGM, 1942, based on the story, "Stage
     Station," by Ernest Haycox; the 1952 film used much
     stock footage from the 1942 film)
     APACHE WAR SMOKE   (MGM, 1952)

APACHE UPRISING   see   BROKEN ARROW

APACHE WAR SMOKE   see   APACHE TRAIL

A--PLUMBING WE WILL GO   (short)   (COL, 1940, based on
     a screenplay by Elwood Ullman)
     SCHEMING SCHEMERS   (short)   (COL, 1956)

APOCALYPSE NOW   see   MISSIONS

APOKAL   see   EERIE TALES

APPLAUSE   see   ALL ABOUT EVE

APPLE OF HIS EYE, THE   (CBS--TV, 1952, based on the play
     by Kenyon Nicholson and Charles Robinson)
     APPLE OF HIS EYE, THE   (CBS–TV, 1959)

APPLESAUCE   see   BRIDES ARE LIKE THAT

APRES L'AMOUR   (FRA, 1924, based on the book by Pierre
     Wolff and Henri Duvernois)
     APRES L'AMOUR   (FRA, 1931)
     APRES L'AMOUR   (FRA, 1947)

APRIL LOVE   see   HOME IN INDIANA

ARAB, THE   (PAR, 1915, based on the play by Edgar Selwyn)
     ARAB, THE   (MGM, 1924)
     ONE STOLEN NIGHT   (WB, 1929)
     BARBARIAN, THE   (MGM, 1933)

ARABIAN NIGHTS   (GER, 1920, based on tales from the
     Arabian Nights)
     ARABIAN NIGHTS   (UA, 1924)
     TALES OF 1001 ARABIAN NIGHTS   (FRA/RUS, 1926)
     ARABIAN NIGHTS   (IN, 1926)
     MILLE DE DEUTIEME NUIT, LA   (FRA, 1933)
     BLACK ROSE   (IN, 1935)
     ARABIAN NIGHTS   (UN, 1943)
     THOUSAND AND ONE NIGHTS, A   (COL, 1945)
     SONG OF SHEHERAZADE   (UN, 1947)
     DESERT HAWK   (UN, 1950)
     GOLDEN BLADE, THE   (UN, 1953)
     HUSN KA CHOR   (IN, 1953)
     SABU AND THE MAGIC RING   (AA, 1957)
     ARABIAN NIGHTS   (NBC–TV, 1960)
     CHEHERAZADE   (FRA/ITA/SPA, 1962)
     THOUSAND AND ONE NIGHTS, A   (JAP, 1969)
     ARABIAN NIGHTS   (RAN, 1972)

ARABIAN NIGHTS   see also   KISMET

ARCHER   see   UNDERGROUND MAN

ARCHIE   see   ARCHIE'S FUN HOUSE

ARCHIE'S FUN HOUSE   (series)   (CBS–TV, 1968, based on
   the comic strip, "Archie Andrews," by Bob Montana)
   SABRINA, THE TEEN–AGE WITCH   (series)   (CBS--TV,
      1970)
   ARCHIE'S TV FUNNIES   (series)   (CBS–TV, 1971)
   ARCHIE   (ABC–TV, 1976)
   ARCHIE SITUATION COMEDY MUSICAL VARIETY
      SHOW, THE   (ABC–TV, 1978)

ARCHIE'S TV FUNNIES   see   ARCHIE'S FUN HOUSE

ARCHY AND MEHITABEL   (NET–TV, 1960, based on the
   book by Don Marquis)
   SHINBONE ALLEY   (AA, 1970)

ARCTIC FURY   see   TUNDRA

ARENES SANGLANTES   (SPA, 1912, based on the book by
   Vincente Blasco Ibanez)
   BLOOD AND SAND   (PAR, 1922)
   BLOOD AND SAND   (FOX, 1941)

AREN'T WE ALL?   see   KISS IN THE DARK, A

ARGENT, L'   (FRA, 1929, based on the book by Emile
   Zola)
   ARGENT, L'   (FRA, 1936)

ARGYLE CASE, THE   (IND, 1917, based on the play by
   Harriet Ford and Harold J. O'Higgins)
   ARGYLE CASE, THE   (WB, 1929)

ARIANE   (GER, 1931, based on the book by Claude Anet)
   ARIANE   (FRA, 1931)
   ARIANE   (BRI, 1931)
   ARIANE   (UA, 1934)
   LOVE IN THE AFTERNOON   (AA, 1957)   (Reissue title:
      FASCINATION)

ARISTOTLE   see   OUR INHERITANCE FROM HISTORIC
   GREECE

ARIZONA   (HE COMES UP SMILING)   (PAR, 1918, based
   on the play by Augustus Thomas)
   WOMEN ARE LIKE THAT   (COL, 1931)

ARIZONA MAHONEY   see   STAIRS OF SAND

ARIZONIAN, THE   (RKO, 1935, based on a story by Dudley
   Nichols)
   MARSHAL OF MESA CITY   (RKO, 1940)

ARLESIENNE, L'   (FRA, 1909, based on a book by Alphonse
   Daudet. Also the basis for the opera by Francesco Cilea)
   ARLESIENNE, L'   (FRA, 1922)
   ARLESIENNE, L'   (FRA, 1930)
   ARLESIENNE, L'   (FRA, 1941)

ARME, KLEINE EVA   (GER, 1921, based on the book by
   Paul Langenscheidt)
   ARME, KLEINE EVA   (GER, 1931)

ARMS AND THE MAN   see   CHOCOLATE SOLDIER, THE

AROUND THE CORNER   see   ROSIE O'GRADY

AROUND THE WORLD IN 18 MINUTES   see   'ROUND THE
   WORLD IN 80 DAYS

AROUND THE WORLD IN 80 DAYS   see   'ROUND THE
   WORLD IN 80 DAYS

AROUND THE WORLD IN 80 MINUTES   see   'ROUND THE
   WORLD IN 80 DAYS

AROUND THE WORLD IN 79 DAYS   see   'ROUND THE
   WORLD IN 80 DAYS

ARRASTAO, LES AMANTS DE LA MER   see   ETERNAL
   RETURN, THE

ARRIVISTE, L'   (FRA, 1914, based on a book by Felicien
   Champsaur)
   ARRIVISTE, L'   (FRA, 1924)

ARROWSMITH   (UA, 1931, based on the book by Sinclair
   Lewis)
   ARROWSMITH   (NBC–TV, 1950)
   ARROWSMITH   (NBC–TV, 1954)
   ARROWSMITH   (CBS–TV, 1960)

ARSENE LUPIN   (BRI, 1916, based on the play by Maurice
   le Blanc and Francois de Crosset)
   ARSENE LUPIN   (VIT, 1917)
   ARSENE LUPIN   (MGM, 1932)

ARSENIC AND OLD LACE   (WB, 1944, based on the play by
   Joseph Kesselring)
   ARSENIC AND OLD LACE   (CBS–TV, 1955)
   ARSENIC AND OLD LACE   (NBC–TV, 1962)
   ARSENIC AND OLD LACE   (ABC--TV, 1968)

ART CARNEY MEETS PETER AND THE WOLF   see
   PETER AND THE WOLF

ARTISTEN   (GER, 1927, source unknown)
   ARTISTEN   (GER, 1935)

ARZT AUS LEIDENSCHAFT   (GER, 1936, source unknown)
   ARZT AUS LEIDENSCHAFT   (GER, 1959)

AS NO MAN HAS LOVED   see   DEATH OF NATHAN
   HALE, THE

AS YOU DESIRE ME   (MGM, 1932, based on the play,
   "Comme tu me Veux," by Luigi Pirandello)
   COMME TU ME VEUX   (URU, 1944)

AS YOU LIKE IT   (KAL, 1908, based on the play by
   William Shakespeare)
   AS YOU LIKE IT   (VIT, 1912)
   AS YOU LIKE IT   (BRI, 1913)
   LOVE IN A WOOD   (BRI, 1916)
   AS YOU LIKE IT   (UA, 1936)

AS YOUNG AS YOU FEEL   (FOX, 1951, based on a story by
   Paddy Chayevsky)
   GREAT AMERICAN HOAX, THE   (CBS--TV, 1957)

ASCHENBROEDEL   see   CINDERELLA AND THE FAIRY
   GODMOTHER

ASHENPUTTE   see   CINDERELLA AND THE FAIRY

GODMOTHER

ASCHERMITTWOCH see KABALE UND LIEBE

ASI ES LA VIDA see WHAT A MAN

ASPERN PAPERS, THE see LOST MOMENT, THE

ASPHALT (GER, 1928, based on a story and screenplay by
    Rolf E. Valloo)
  ASPHALT (GER, 1951)

ASPHALT JUNGLE, THE (MGM, 1950, based on the book
    by W.R. Burnett)
  BADLANDERS, THE (MGM, 1958)
  ASPHALT JUNGLE, THE (series) (ABC--TV, 1961)
  CAIRO (MGM, 1963)
  COOL BREEZE (MGM, 1972)

ASSASSINATION OF JULIUS CAESAR see JULIUS
    CAESAR

ASSOMMOIR, L' (FRA, 1909, based on the book by Emile
    Zola)
  DRINK (BRI, 1917)
  ASSOMMOIR, L' (FRA, 1921)
  ASSOMMOIR, L' (FRA, 1933)
  GERVAISE (FRA, 1956)

AT SWORD'S POINT see THREE MUSKETEERS, THE

AT THE STROKE OF TWELVE see MIDNIGHT ALIBI

AT THE VILLA ROSE (BRI, 1920, based on the book by
    A.E.W. Mason)
  AT THE VILLA ROSE (BRI, 1930)
  MYSTERY AT THE VILLA ROSE (FRA, 1930)
  AT THE VILLA ROSE (HOUSE OF MYSTERY) (BRI,
    1939)

ATATURK, FOUNDER OF MODERN TURKEY (short)
    (BRI--TV, n.d., based on the life of the noted leader)
  ATATURK, FATHER OF MODERN TURKEY (short)
    (CBS--TV, 1960)
  INCREDIBLE TURK, THE (short) (IND, n.d.)
  ATATURK (short) (IND, 1971)

ATHLETE INCOMPLET, L' see POOR NUT, THE

ATLANTIC (GER, 1929, based on a historical incident and
    various screenplays and teleplays)
  ATLANTIC (BRI, 1929)
  ATLANTIC (FRA, 1929)
  S.O.S. EISBERG (GER, 1933)
  TITANIC (GER, 1943)
  TITANIC! (FOX, 1953)
  NIGHT TO REMEMBER, A (NBC--TV, 1956)
  NIGHT TO REMEMBER, A (BRI, 1958)

ATLANTIDE, L' (FRA, 1920, based on the book by Pierre
    Benoit and the legend of the lost continent of Atlantis)
  MISSING HUSBANDS (MGM, 1922)
  ATLANTIDE, L' (FRA, 1932)
  ATLANTIDE, L' (BRI, 1932)
  ATLANTIDE, L' (GER, 1932)
  LOST ATLANTIS (IND, 1939)
  SIREN OF ATLANTIS (UA, 1948)
  DESERT LEGION (UN, 1953)
  ATLANTIDE, L' (FRA, 1960)

LOST CONTINENT, THE (MGM, 1961)
  ANTINEA (ITA, 1961) (also called LOST KINGDOM,
    THE, JOURNEY UNDER THE DESERT and QUEEN
    OF ATLANTIS)
  END OF ATLANTIS (FRA/ITA, 1961)
  CONQUEROR OF ATLANTIS (EGY/ITA, 1965)
  WARLORDS OF ATLANTIS (BRI, 1978)

ATTEMPT TO ASSASSINATE THEODORE ROOSEVELT,
    THE see TEDDY, THE ROUGH RIDER

ATTILA (ITA, 1917, based on historical events and the
    character of Atilla the Hun)
  SIGN OF THE PAGAN (UN, 1954)
  ATTILA, THE HUN (ITA, 1958)

ATTILA, THE HUN see ATTILA

AU COEUR DE LA VIE see OCCURRENCE AT OWL
    CREEK BRIDGE, AN

AU PAYS DES TENEBRES (FRA, 1912, based on the book,
    "Germinal," by Emile Zola)
  GERMINAL (FRA, 1913)
  GERMINAL (FRA/HUN/ITA, 1963)

AU TEMPS DES PREMIERS CRETIENS see QUO VADIS?

AUBERGE ROUGE, L' (FRA, 1912, based on a story by
    Honore de Balzac)
  AUBERGE ROUGE, L' (FRA, 1923)
  AUBERGE ROUGE, L' (FRA, 1951)

AUCTION BLOCK, THE (MGM, 1917, based on the book by
    Rex Beach)
  AUCTION BLOCK, THE (MGM, 1926)

AUF DU REEPERBAHN NACHTS UM HALB EINS (GER,
    1929, source unknown)
  AUF DU REEPERBAHN NACHTS UM HALB EINS
    (GER, 1954)

AUF WIEDERSEHN, FRANZISKA (GER, 1936, source
    unknown)
  AUF WIEDERSEHN, FRANZISKA (GER, 1941)

AUFERSTEHUNG see RESURRECTION

AUGUST VERMEYLEN (short) (HOL, 1963, based on the
    life and work of August Vermeylen)
  IN DE VOETSPOREN VAN AUGUST VERMEYLEN
    (HOL, 1972)

AUGUSTE DER STARKE (GER, 1922, source unknown)
  AUGUSTE DER STARKE (GER, 1936)

AULD LANGE SYNE see LIFE OF ROBERT BURNS,
    THE

AUNTIE MAME (WB, 1958, based on the book by Patrick
    Dennis and a play by Jerome Lawrence and Robert E. Lee)
  MAME (WB, 1974)

AUS DEM LEBEN EINES TAUGENICHTS see TAUGEN--
    ICHTS, DER

AUS DEM TAGEBUCH EINEN FRAUENAERZTIN (GER,
    1932, source unknown)
  AUS DEM TAGEBUCH EINEN FRAUENAERZTIN

(GER, 1939)

AVALANCHE (JAP, 1937, source unknown)
　AVALANCHE (JAP, 1952)

AVE MARIA (GER, 1936, based on the book by Daniel–
　　Rops)
　AVE MARIA (GER, 1953)

AVEC ANDRE GIDE see VIE COMMENCE DEMAIN, LA

AVENGERS, THE (series) (BRI–TV, 1966, based on a
　　teleplay)
　NEW AVENGERS, THE (BRI–TV, 1976)

AVENGING CONSCIENCE, THE (GRI, 1914, based on the
　　story, "The Tell–Tale Heart," by Edgar Allan Poe)
　TELL–TALE HEART, THE (short) (IND, 1927)
　TELL–TALE HEART, THE (short) (IND, 1928)
　BUCKET OF BLOOD (BRI, 1934)
　TELL–TALE HEART (short) (MGM, 1941)
　TELL–TALE HEART, THE (short) (POL, 1947)
　HISTOIRES EXTRAORDINAIRES (FRA, 1949)
　HEARTBEAT (short) (IND--TV, 1950)
　TELL–TALE HEART, THE (short) (BRI, 1953)
　TELL–TALE HEART, THE (TV, 1953)
　TELL–TALE HEART, THE (short) (COL, 1953)
　CALYPSO (MANFISH) (BRI, 1956)
　TELL–TALE HEART, THE (IND, 1958)
　BUCKET OF BLOOD (AI, 1959)
　MASTER OF HORROR (ARG, 1960)
　TELL–TALE HEART, THE (BRI, 1960)
　TELL–TALE HEART, THE (BRI, 1963)
　TELL–TALE HEART, THE (IND, 1966)
　TELL–TALE HEART, THE (GER, 1967)
　VERRATERISCHE HERZ, DAS (short) (GER, 1968)
　TELL–TALE HEART, THE (AFI, 1971)
　CASK OF AMONTILLADO, THE (NBC–TV, 1971)

ANNABELLE LEE (SA, 1972)
LEGEND OF HORROR (IND, 1972)
TELL–TALE HEART, THE (short) (POL–TV, 1972)

AVENTURES DES PIEDS–NICKELES, LES (FRA, 1918,
　　based on a story by Louis Forton)
　AVENTURES DES PIEDS–NICHELES, LES (FRA, 1947)

AVENTURIER, L' (FRA, 1924, based on a book by Alfred
　　Capus)
　AVENTURIER, L' (FRA, 1934)

AVENTURIERS, LES (FRA, 1966, based on a story by Jose
　　Giovanni)
　LOI DU SURVIVANT, LA (FRA, 1967)

AVIATEUR, L' see AVIATOR, THE

AVIATOR, THE (WB, 1929, based on the play by James
　　Montgomery)
　GOING WILD (WB, 1930)
　AVIATEUR, L' (FRA, 1931)

AWAKENING, THE (POL, 1934)
　AWAKENING, THE (CZE, 1959)

AWAKENING OF GALATEA, THE see GALATEA

AWAY FROM IT see NIGHT

AWFUL TRUTH, THE (PDC, 1925, based on the play by
　　Arthur Richman)
　AWFUL TRUTH, THE (PAT, 1929)
　AWFUL TRUTH, THE (COL, 1937)
　AWFUL TRUTH, THE (NBC–TV, 1950)
　LET'S DO IT AGAIN (COL, 1953)

AZ ORDOG see DEVIL, THE

BABBITT (WB, 1924, based on the book by Sinclair Lewis)
  BABBITT (WB, 1934)

BABE RUTH STORY, THE (AA, 1949, based on the life of
    the noted athlete)
  BABE RUTH – THAT EVER–LOVIN' BABE (MGM–TV,
  1962)

BABES IN THE WOODS see HANSEL AND GRETEL

BABES IN TOYLAND (TV TITLE: MARCH OF THE
    WOODEN SOLDIERS) (MGM, 1934, based on the
    operetta by Victor Herbert)
  BABES IN TOYLAND (NBC–TV, 1950)
  BABES IN TOYLAND (NBC–TV, 1954)
  BABES IN TOYLAND (NBC–TV, 1955)
  BABES IN TOYLAND (NBC–TV, 1960)
  BABES IN TOYLAND (DIS, 1961)

BABY MINE (MBM, 1917, based on the play by Margaret
    Mayo)
  BABY MINE (MGM, 1928)

BABY TAKE A BOW see SQUARE CROOKS

BACHELOR FATHER (MGM, 1931, based on a play by
    Edward Childs Carpenter)
  PERE CELIBATAIRE, LE (FRA, 1931)

BACHELOR MOTHER see KLEINE MUTTER

BACHELOR PARTY (NBC–TV, 1954, based on a teleplay by
    Paddy Chayevsky)
  BACHELOR PARTY (UA, 1957)

BACHELOR'S FOLLY (WW, 1931, based on the play, "The
    Calendar," by Edgar Wallace)
  CALENDAR, THE (BRI, 1948)

BACHPAN see TOM SAWYER

BACK BAY ROMANCE see LATE GEORGE APLEY, THE

BACK FROM ETERNITY see FIVE CAME BACK

BACK PAY (IND, 1922, based on a story by Fannie Hurst)
  BACK PAY (FB, 1930)

BACK STREET (UN, 1932, based on the book by Fannie
    Hurst)
  BACK STREET (UN, 1941)
  BACK STREET (UN, 1961)

BACK TO GOD'S COUNTRY (FN, 1919, based on a story by
    James Oliver Curwood)
  BACK TO GOD'S COUNTRY (UN, 1927)
  BACK TO GOD'S COUNTRY (UN, 1953)

BACK TO NATURE (VIT, 1912, based on "Admirable
    Crichton," by J.M. Barrie. Also the basis for the
    British musical comedy, "Our Man Crichton," 1964)
  SHIPWRECKED (KAL, 1913)
  MAN OF HER CHOICE, A (POW, 1914)
  MASTER AND MAN (BRI, 1915)
  ADMIRABLE CRICHTON, THE (BRI, 1918)
  MALE AND FEMALE (PAR, 1919)
  MASTER AND MAN (BRI, 1929)
  WE'RE NOT DRESSING (PAR, 1934)
  BACK TO NATURE (CHN, 1936)

ADVENTURES OF SADIE (OUR GIRL FRIDAY) (BRI,
    1953)
  PARADISE LAGOON (BRI, 1957)
  ADMIRABLE CRICHTON, THE (NBC–TV, 1968)

BACKTRACK see LAREDO

BAD AUF DER TENNE (GER, 1943)
  BAD AUF DER TENNE (GER, 1956)

BAD DAY AT BLACK ROCK (MGM, 1954, based on the
    story, "Bad Time at Hondo," by Howard Breslin)
  PLATINUM HIGH SCHOOL (MGM,1961)

BAD FLOWER, THE see NOSFERATU

BAD GIRL (FOX, 1931, based on the book by Vina Delmar)
  MARIDA Y MUJER (SPA, 1932)
  MANHATTAN HEARBEAT (FOX, 1940)

BAD LORD BYRON see PRINCE OF LOVERS, THE

BAD MAN, THE (FN, 1923, based on the play by Porter Emerson
    Browne)
  LOPEZ LE BANDIT (FRA, 1930)
  BAD MAN, THE (FN, 1930)
  HOMBRE MALO, EL (SPA, 1930)
  WEST OF SHANGHAI (WB, 1937)
  BAD MAN, THE (MGM, 1941)

BAD MEN OF THUNDER GAP (PRC, 1942, based on a screenplay by
    Elmer Clifton)
  THUNDERGAP OUTLAWS (EL, 1947)

BAD SISTER see FLIRT, THE

BAD SLEEP WELL, THE see HAMLET

BAD TIME AT HONDO see BAD DAY AT BLACK ROCK

BADDEST DADDY IN THE WHOLE WORLD, THE see
    FLOAT LIKE A BUTTERLY, STING LIKE A BEE

BADGE OF POLICEMAN O'ROON, THE (FRA, 1913, based
    on a story by O. Henry)
  DR. RHYTHM (PAR, 1938)

BADGER'S GREEN (BRI, 1934, based on the play by R.C.
    Sherriff)
  BADGER'S GREEN (BRI, 1948)

BADLANDERS, THE see ASPHALT JUNGLE, THE

BADLANDS OF DAKOTA see WILD BILL HICKOCK

BADMAN'S COUNTRY see THREE OUTLAWS

BADSHAH DAMPATI see ESMERELDA

BAGDAD THIRUDAN see THIEF OF BAGDAD, THE

BAGNOSTRAFLING, DER see VAUTRIN

BAILOUT AT 43,000 (CBS–TV, 1955, based on the teleplay
    by Paul Monash)
  BAILOUT AT 43,000 (UA, 1957)

BALAKLAVA see CHARGE OF THE LIGHT BRIGADE,
    THE

BALAOO (FRA, 1913, based on a story by Gaston Leroux)
  WIZARD, THE (FOX, 1927)
  DR. RENAULT'S SECRET (FOX, 1942)

BALL OF FIRE (UA, 1941, based on a screenplay by Billy
    Wilder and Thomas Monroe)
  SONG IS BORN, A (UA, 1947)

BALLERINA, THE (FRA, 1938, based on the book, "Le
    Morte du Cygne," by Paul Morand)
  UNFINISHED DANCE, THE (MGM, 1947)

BALLET BY DEGAS (SHORT) (MAC, 1951, based on the
    works of the noted painter)
  DEGAS, MASTER OF MOTION (SHORT) (USC, 1957)
  DEGAS (SHORT) MAC, n.d.)
  DEGAS (SHORT) (UNI, 1967)
  DEGAS DANCERS (short) (TIM, 1970)
  DEGAS (IND, 1973)

BALLET GIRL, THE (WOR,1916) based on the book by
    Sir Compton Mackenzie)
  CARNIVAL (BRI, 1921)
  DANCE PRETTY LADY (BRI, 1931)
  CARNIVAL (COL, 1935)
  CARNIVAL (BRI, 1946)

BALLET OF ROMEO AND JULIET, THE see ROMEO AND
    JULIET

BALZAC (SHORT) (RAD, 1950, based on the life and works
    of author Honore de Balzac)
  BALZAC A PARIS (Short) (MHF, 1964)

BANDIT OF SHERWOOD FOREST see ROBIN HOOD AND
    HIS MERRY MEN

BANDITS OF CORSICA see CORSICAN BROTHERS, THE

BANDITS OF FRA DIAVOLO see FRA DIAVOLO

BANDWAGON, THE see DANCING IN THE DARK

BANG THE DRUM SLOWLY (TV, 1956, based on the book
    by Mark Harris)
  BANG THE DRUM SLOWLY (PAR, 1973)

BAR SINISTER, THE see ALMOST HUMAN

BARABBAS (FRA, 1919, based on a story in the Bible)
  WHICH WILL YOU HAVE? (BRI, 1949)
  BARABBAS (SWE, 1952)
  WINE OF MORNING (IND, 1955)
  GIVE US BARABBAS (NBC–TV, 1961)
  BARRABBAS (COL, 1962)
  GIVE US BARABBAS (NBC–TV, 1968)

BARBARA FRIETCHIE (VIT, 1908, based on the poem by
    John Greenleaf Whittier. Also the basis for the musical
    comedy, "My Maryland," in 1927)
  BARBARA FRIETCHIE (MGM, 1915)
  BARBARA BRIETCHIE (PDC, 1924)

BARBARIAN, THE see ARAB, THE

BARBARIAN AND THE LADY, THE see TARAS BULBA

BARBE–BLEUE (short) (FRA, 1901, based on the story by
    Charles Perrault)

BARBE––BLEUE (short) (FRA, c1910)
BARBE––BLEUE (short) (FRA, 1936)
BARBE–BLEUE (FRA, 1951)

BARBE–BLEUE see also BLUEBEARD

BARBER OF SEVILLE, THE (FRA, 1904, based on the play
    by Beaumarchais and the opera by Giacomo Rossini)
  BARBER OF SEVILLE, THE (SWE, 1908)
  BARBER OF SEVILLE, THE (ITA, 1913)
  FIGARO (FRA, 1929)
  BARBER OF SEVILLE, THE (GER/SPA, 1937)
  BARBER OF SEVILLE, THE (ITA, 1946)
  BARBER OF SEVILLE, THE (FRA, 1947)
  BARBER OF SEVILLE, THE (ITA, 1955)
  BARBER OF SEVILLE, THE (CBS–TV, 1965)
  BARBER OF SEVILLE, THE (FRA/GER, 1973)

BARBERO DE NAPOLEON see NAPOLEON'S BARBER

BAREFOOT BOY (COL, 1924, based on the poem by John
    Greenleaf Whittier)
  BAREFOOT BOY (MON, 1938)

BAREFOOT IN THE PARK (PAR, 1967, based on the play by
    Neil Simon)
  BAREFOOT IN THE PARK (series) (ABC–TV, 1970)

BARETTA see TOMA

BARKER, THE (FN, 1928, based on the play by John Kenyon
    Nicholson)
  HOOP–LA (FOX, 1933)
  BILLY ROSE'S DIAMOND HORSESHOE (FOX, 1945)
  BARKER, THE (CBS–TV, 1950)
  BARKER, THE (TV, 1952)

BARNABY RUDGE see DOLLY VARDEN

BARNET (SWE, 1912)
  BARNET (SWE, 1940)

BARNEY MILLER see LIFE AND TIMES OF BARNEY
    MILLER, THE

BARON DE CRAC (FRA, 1909)
  HALLUCINATIONS OF BARON MUNCHAUSEN (FRA
    1911)
  ADVENTURES OF BARON MUNCHAUSEN, THE (ITA,
    1914)
  ADVENTURES OF BARON MUNCHAUSEN (BRI, 1915)
  MUNCHAUSEN (short) (GER, 1920)
  NOTHING BUT THE TRUTH (short) (IND, 1927)
  ADVENTURES OF BARON MUNCHAUSEN (GER, 1928)
  ADVENTURES OF BARON MUNCHAUSEN (RUS, 1929)
  BARON PRASIL (CZE, 1940)
  MUNCHAUSEN (GER, 1943)
  ADVENTURES OF BARON MUNCHAUSEN (short) (CAN
    1947)
  MUNCHAUSEN (ITA, 1947)
  MUNCHAUSEN IN AFRICA (GER, 1958)
  FABULOUS BARON MUNCHAUSEN, THE (CZE, 1959)
  BARON PRASIL (CZE, 1961)

BARON FANTOME, LE (SWE, 1927, based on a story by
    Serge de Poligny)
  BARON FANTOME, LE (FRA, 1944)

BARON OF ARIZONA, THE (LIP, 1950, based on a historical

incident)
BARON OF ARIZONA, THE (short) (TV, 1956)

BARON PRASIL   see   BARON DE CRAC

BARON TSIGANE, LE   see   ZIGEUNER BARON, DER

BARON'S AFRICAN WAR, THE   see   SECRET SERVICE IN
DARKEST AFRICA

BARRETTS OF WIMPOLE STREET, THE (TV TITLE:
FORBIDDEN ALLIANCE) (MGM, 1934, based on the
play by Rudolf Besier)
BARRETTS OF WIMPOLE STREET, THE (CBS–TV, 1950)
BARRETTS OF WIMPOLE STREET, THE (CBS–TV,
1955)
BARRETTS OF WIMPOLE STREET, THE (NBC–TV,
1956)
BARRETTS OF WIMPOLE STREET, THE (MGM, 1957)

BARRICADE   see   SEA WOLVES, THE

BARRIER, THE (REX, 1917, based on the book by Rex Beach)
BARRIER, THE (MGM, 1926)
BARRIER, THE (PAR, 1937)

BARTERED BRIDE, THE (CZE, 1933, based on the operetta
by Bederich Smetana)
BARTERED BRIDE, THE (CZE, 1933)

BARTLEBY (short) (IND, 1970, based on the story by Her--
man Melville)
BARTLEBY (BRI, 1971)
BARTLEBY THE SCRIVENER (PBS–TV, 1978)

BARTLEBY THE SCRIVENER   see   BARTLEBY

BARTON MYSTERY, THE (BRI, 1920, based on the play
by Walter Hackett)
BARTON MYSTERY, THE (BRI, 1932)

BAS--FONDS, LES   see   LOWER DEPTHS, THE

BASS FIDDLE, THE (short) (MHF, c1960, based on a short
story by Anton Chekhov)
ROMANCE WITH A DOUBLE BASS (CAN, 1978)

BAT, THE   see   CIRCULAR STAIRCASE, THE

BAT MASTERSON (series) (NBC–TV, 1958, based on the
legendary lawman in the old West)
HEROES AND VILLAINS (sequence) (NET--TV, 1965)

BAT WHISPERS, THE   see   CIRCULAR STAIRCASE, THE

BATAILLE, LA (FRA, 1923, based on the book by Claude
Farrere)
BATTLE, THE (PAR, 1924)
BATAILLE, LA (FRA, 1933)
THUNDER IN THE EAST (UA, 1935)

BATALION (CZE, 1927, source unknown)
BATALION (CZE, 1937)

BATMEN OF AFRICA   see   DARKEST AFRICA

BATTEMENT AU COEUR   see   BATTICUORE

BATTICUORE (ITA, c1938, based on the screenplay by Hans)

Wilhelm, Max Kolpe and Michel Duran)
BATTEMENT AU COEUR (FRA, 1939)
HEARTBEAT (RKO, 1946)

BATTLE, THE   see   BATAILLE, LA and DANGER LINE

BATTLE BEYOND THE SUN   see   NEBO ZOWET

BATTLE CIRCUS (MGM, 1952, based on the experiences of
the wartime mobile Army surgical hospital units. The
former is based on material by Allen Rivkin and Laura Kerr
and the latter on a book by Richard Hooker)
M*A*S*H (FOX, 1970)
M*A*S*H (series) (CBS--TV, 1972)

BATTLE OF STALINGRAD (RUS, 1949, based on historical
incidents)
BATTLE OF STALINGRAD (RUS, 1970)

BATTLE OF THE SEXES (BIO, 1913, based on the book by
Daniel Carson Goodman)
BATTLE OF THE SEXES (UA, 1928)

BATTLE OF THE SEXES (MUT, 1914, based on the book by
Adela Rogers St. John)
SINGLE STANDARD, THE (MGM, 1929)

BATTLING BELLHOP, THE   see   KID GALAHAD

BAWDY ADVENTURES OF TOM JONES, THE   see   TOM
JONES

BE BIG   see   AMBROSE'S FIRST FALSEHOOD

BE MINE TONIGHT   see   TELL ME TONIGHT

BEACH HOLIDAY   see   BEACH PARTY

BEACH PARTY (AI, 1963, based on a screenplay by Lou
Rusoff)
BEACH HOLIDAY (GER, 1971)

BEACHCOMBER, THE (BRITISH TITLE: VESSEL OF
WRATH) (BRI, 1938, based on the book, "Vessel of
Wrath," by M. Somerset Maugham)
BEACHCOMBER, THE (UA, 1955)

BEACON HILL   see   UPSTAIRS AND DOWNSTAIRS

BEANSTALK JACK   see   JACK AND THE BEANSTALK

BEANY AND CECIL   see   TIME FOR BEANY, A

BEAST, THE   see   BEAUTY AND THE BEAST

BEATRIX (ITA, 1919, based on a story by Honore de Balzac)
BEATRIX (ITA, 1920)

BEAU BRUMMEL (VIT, 1912, based on the play by Clyde
Fitch)
BEAU BRUMMEL (WB, 1924)
BEAU BRUMMEL (MGM, 1954)

BEAU GESTE (PAR, 1926, based on the books by Sir Percival
Christopher Wren)
BEAU SABREUR (PAR, 1928)
BEAU IDEAL (RKP, 1931)
BEAU GESTE (PAR, 1939)
BEAU GESTE (UN, 1966)

LAST REMAKE OF BEAU GESTE, THE (UN, 1977)

BEAU HUNKS (MGM, 1931, based on a screenplay by H.M.
    Walker)
    DEUX LEGIONAIRES, LES (FRA, 1931)
    FLYING DEUCES (RKO, 1939)

BEAU IDEAL see BEAU GESTE

BEAU SABREUR see BEAU GESTE

BEAUTIFUL DREAMER see SWANEE RIVER

BEAUTY AND THE BARGE (BRI, 1914, based on the play
    by W.W. Jacobs)
    BEAUTY AND THE BARGE (BRI, 1937)

BEAUTY AND THE BEAST (FRA, 1899, based on the legend)
    BEAUTY AND THE BEAST (BRI, 1905
    BEAUTY AND THE BEAST (FRA, 1908)
    BEAUTY AND THE BEAST (UN, 1913)
    BEAUTY AND THE BEAST (IND, 1916)
    BEAUTY AND THE BEAST (ITA, 1921)
    BEAUTY AND THE BEAST (short) (WB, 1936)
    BEAUTY AND THE BEAST (FRA, 1948)
    BEAUTY AND THE BEAST (NBC–TV, 1958)
    BEAUTY AND THE BEAST (UA, 1962)
    BEAUTY AND THE BEAST (ABC–TV, 1968)
    BEAUTY AND THE BEAST (PBS–TV, 1973)
    BEAUTY AND THE BEAST (NBC–TV, 1976)
    BEAST, THE (FRA, 1976)

BEAUTY AND THE BOSS (WB, 1932, based on the play,
    "Church Mouse," by Ladislaus Fodor)
    CHURCH MOUSE, THE (BRI, 1934)

BEAUTY OF LIFE, THE (POL, 1921, based on the book by
    Stefan Zeromski)
    BEAUTY OF LIFE, THE (POL, 1930)

BECKET see MARTYRDOM OF THOMAS A BECKET

BECKY SHARP see VANITY FAIR

BEDAZZLED see FAUST

BEDLAM IN PARADISE see HEAVENLY DAZE

BEETHOVEN see BEETHOVEN UND DAS VOLK

BEETHOVEN CONCERTO see BEETHOVEN UND DAS
    VOLK

BEETHOVEN – DAYS IN A LIFE see BEETHOVEN UND
    DAS VOLK

BEETHOVEN: ORDEAL AND TRIUMPH see BEETHOVEN
    UND DAS VOLK

BEETHOVEN UND DAS VOLK (GER, 1912, based on the
    life and works of the noted composer Ludwig van Bee--
    thoven)
    BEETHOVEN (AUS, 1927)
    LIFE OF BEETHOVEN, THE (GER, 1929)
    BEETHOVEN (short) (GER, 1931)
    BEETHOVEN (FRA, 1937)
    BEETHOVEN CONCERTO (RUS, 1937)
    EROICA (AUS, 1949)
    BEETHOVEN AND HIS MUSIC (short) (COR, 1954)

TORMENT OF BEETHOVEN, THE (short) (CBS--TV, 1955)
BEETHOVEN: ORDEAL AND TRIUMPH (ABC–TV, 1967)
BEETHOVEN – DAYS IN A LIFE (GER, 1976)

BEFORE THE REVOLUTION see CHARTERHOUSE OF
    PARMA, THE

BEGEGNUNG MIT WERTHER see WERTHER

BEGGAR STUDENT, THE (GER, 1922, based on the opera,
    "Bettel--Student, Der," by Carl Millocher and R. Gene, and
    the book by Victorien Sardou)
    BEGGAR STUDENT, THE (GER, 1927)
    BEGGAR STUDENT, THE (BRI, 1931)
    BEGGAR STUDENT, THE (GER, 1931)
    BEGGAR STUDENT, THE (GER, 1936)
    BEGGAR STUDENT, THE (GER, 1956)
    MAZURKA DER LIEBE (GER, 1957)

BEGGAR'S OPERA, THE see THREE--PENNY OPERA, THE

BEHIND THE HIGH WALL see BIG GUY

BEHIND THE IRON MASK see MAN IN THE IRON MASK,
    THE

BEHIND THE MAKE–UP (PAR, 1930, based on a story by
    Mildred Cram)
    MAQUILLAGE (FRA, 1931)

BEHOLD MY WIFE (PAR, 1920, based on the book "Trans--
    lation of a Savage, The," by Sir Gilbert Parker)
    BEHOLD MY WIFE (PAR, 1934)

BEHOLD THE MAN see PASSION PLAY, THE

BEHOLD THE WOMEN see IN THE BALANCE

BEI DER BLONDEN KATHREIN (GER, 1934, source unknown)
    BEI DER BLONDEN KATHREIN (GER, 1959)

BEL–AMI (GER, 1939, based on a book by Guy de Maupas--
    sant)
    PRIVATE AFFAIRS OF BEL–AMI (UA, 1947)
    BEL–AMI (AUS/FRA, 1955)
    BEL–AMI (SWE, 1976)

BELL, BOOK AND CANDLE (COL, 1958, based on the play
    by John van Druten)
    BELL, BOOK AND CANDLE (short) (NBC--TV, 1976)

BELL FOR ADANO, A (FOX, 1945, based on the book by
    John Hershey)
    BELL FOR ADANO, A (NBC–TV, 1945)
    BELL FOR ADANO, A (CBS–TV, 1956)
    BELL FOR ADANO, A (NBC–TV, 1967)

BELLA (RUS, 1913, based on the books, "Heroes of Our
    Time, The," by Mikhail Liermontov)
    TAMAGNE (RUS, 1916)
    HEROES OF OUR TIME, THE (RUS, 1927)
    PRINCESS MARY, THE (RUS, 1955)
    BELLA/MAXIME MAXIMYTCH/TAMAGNE (RUS, 1967)

BELLA DONNA (PAR, 1915, based on a novel by Robert S.
    Hichens)
    BELLA DONNA (PAR, 1918)
    BELLA DONNA (PAR, 1923)
    BELLA DONNA (BRI, 1935)

TEMPTATION   (UN, 1946)

BELLE AU BOIS DORMANT, LA (short)   (FRA, 1902)
   BELLE AU BOIS DORMANT, LA (short)   (FRA, 1935)

BELLE ETOILE, LA   see   O. HENRY'S FULL HOUSE

BELLE GARCE, UNE   (FRA, 1931, based on a novel by
   Charles–Henry Hirsch)
   BELLE GARCE, UNE   (FRA, 1947)

BELLE LOLA, UNE DAME AUX CAMELIAS, LA   see
   DAME AUX CAMELIAS, LA

BELLE MEUNIERE, LA   see   MEUNIERE DEBAUCHEE,
   LA

BELLE OF NEW YORK   (SEZ, 1919, based on the play by
   Hugh Morton and Gustave Kerker)
   BELLE OF NEW YORK   (MGM, 1952)

BELLE RUSSE, LA   (IND, 1914, based on the play by David
   Belasco)
   BELLE RUSSE, LA   (FOX, 1919)

BELLE STAR   (FOX, 1941, based on the life and legend of
   the famed lady bandit)
   MONTANA BELLE   (RKO, 1952)

BELLS, THE   (REL, 1913, based on the book, "Le Juif
   Polonois," by Erckmann–Chatrian and the play by Leopold
   Lewis)
   BELLS, THE   (BRI, 1914)
   BELLS, THE   (FRA, 1918)
   BELLS, THE   (PAT, 1918)
   POLISH, JEW, THE   (AUS/BEL, 1925)
   BELLS, THE   (CHA, 1926)
   JUIF POLONAIS, LE   (AUS, 1931)
   BURGOMEISTER, THE   (AUS, 1935)
   POLISH JEW, THE   (FRA, 1937)

BELLS, THE   (ED, 1913, based on the poem by Edgar Allan
   Poe)
   BELLS, THE   (IND, 1926)

BELLS OF ST. MARYS, THE   (RKO, 1945, based on a story
   by Leo McCarey)
   BELLS OF ST. MARYS, THE   (CBS–TV, 1959)

BELOVED ELEKTRA   see   ELEKTRA

BELOVED INFIDEL   (FOX, 1959, based on incidents in the
   life of the noted author)
   F. SCOTT FITZGERALD   (ABC–TV, 1972)
   F. SCOTT FITZGERALD AND THE LAST OF THE
   BELLES   (ZBC–TV, 1974)
   SCREENTEST   (ABC–TV, 1974)
   F. SCOTT FITZGERALD IN HOLLYWOOD   (ABC–TV,
   1976)

BELOVED ROGUE, THE   see   IF I WERE KING

BELOVED VAGABOND   (FRA, 1916, based on the book by
   William J. Locke)
   BELOVED VAGABOND   (BRI, 1923)
   BELOVED VAGABOND   (FBO, 1924)
   BELOVED VAGABOND   (BRI, 1936)
   BELOVED VAGAOND   (FRA, 1936)

BELOW ZERO (short)   (MGM, 1930, based on a story by
   Leo McCarey)
   TIEMBA Y TITUBEA (short)   (SPA, 1930)
   BELOW ZERO (short)   (GER, 1930)

BEN–GURION   see   DAVID BEN–GURION

BEN–HUR   (KAL, 1907, based on the book by Gen. Lew Wal-
   lace)
   BEN–HUR   (MGM, 1926)
   BEN–HUR   (MGM, 1959)

BENEATH THE 12–MILE REEF   (FOX, 1953, based on the
   same basic story with stock footage from the former used
   in the remake)
   SECRETS OF THE PURPLE REEF   (FOX, 1960)

BENEDICT ARNOLD   see   BETRAYAL: BENEDICT ARNOLD

BENGAL TIGER   see   TIGER SHARK

BENITO CERENO   (NET–TV, 1965, based on the play by
   Robert Lowell taken from "The Old Glory")
   BENITO CERENO   (FRA, 1969)

BENITO MUSSOLINI (short)   (CBS–TV, 1955, based on the
   life of the Italian dictator)
   MUSSOLINI (short)   (CBS–TV, 1959)
   FASCIST REVOLUTION, THE (short)   (NET–TV, 1959)
   RISE AND FALL OF BENITO MUSSOLINI   (WOL, 1963)
   DEATH OF A DICTATOR   (TV, 1964)
   BLOOD ON THE BALCONY   (IND, 1964)

BENJAMIN FRANKLIN   see   OUR BILL OF RIGHTS

BENSON MURDER CASE, THE   (PAR, 1930, based on the book
   by S.S. van Dyne)
   CORPUS DELECTI, THE   (ARG' 1930)
   CUERPO DELITO, EL   (SPA, 1930)

BERG, THE   see   ATLANTIC

BERGE IN FLAMMEN   see   GUILLAUME TELL ET LE
   CLOWN

BERKELEY SQUARE   (FOX, 1933, based on the play by
   John L. Balderston)
   I'LL NEVER FORGET YOU (BRITISH TITLE: HOUSE
   ON THE SQUARE, THE)   (FOX, 1951)
   BERKELEY SQUARE   (CBS–TV, 1951)
   BERKELEY SQUARE   (NBC–TV, 1959)

BERLIN STORIES   see   I AM A CAMERA

BERNADETTE   see   SONG OF BERNADETTE, THE

BERNADETTE OF LOURDES   see   SONG OF BERNADETTE,
   THE

BERTH MARKS (short)   (MGM, 1929, based on a story by
   Leo McCarey and elaborated upon in the feature remakes)
   HOUSE OF ERRORS   (PRC, 1942)
   BIG NOISE, THE   (FOX, 1944)

BERTRAND RUSSELL (short)   NBC–TV, 1951, based on the
   life of philosopher Bertrand Russell)
   BERTRAND RUSSELL (short)   (NBC–TV, 1958)
   BERTRAND RUSSELL DISCUSSES THE ROLE OF THE
   INDIVIDUAL (short)   (COR, 1961)

BERTRAND RUSSELL DISCUSSES POWER (short)
(COR, 1961)
BERTRAND RUSSELL DISCUSSES HAPPINESS (short)
(COR, 1961)
BERTRAND RUSSELL DISCUSSES PHILOSPHY (short)
(COR, 1961)
LIFE AND TIMES OF BERTRAND RUSSELL, THE
(BRI–TV, 1967)

BERYL CORONET, THE (short) (BRI, 1912, based on the
story by Sir Arthur Conan Doyle)
BERYL CORONET, THE (short) (BRI, 1921)

BESESSENE, DER see FRAULEIN VON SCUDERI, DAS

BESPOKE OVERCOAT, THE see OVERCOAT, THE

BEST MAN WINS see JUMPING FROG

BEST OF EVERYTHING, THE (FOX, 1959, based on the
book by Rona Jaffe)
BEST OF EVERYTHING, THE (series) (ABC–TV, 1970)

BEST PEOPLE, THE (PAR, 1925, based on the play by David
Grey and Avery Hopwood)
FAST AND LOOSE (PAR, 1930)

BEST YEARS OF OUR LIVES, THE (RKO, 1946, based on
the book by McKinlay Kantor)
RETURNING HOME (ABC–TV, 1975)

BESTIE IM MENSCHEN, DIE (GER, 1920, based on the
book "La Bete Humaine," by Emile Zola)
BETE HUMAINE, LA (FRA, 1938)
HUMAN DESIRE (COL, 1954)

BETE HUMAINE, LA see BESTIE IM MENSCHEN, DIE

BETRAYAL: BENEDICT ARNOLD (short) (TFC, 1953,
based on the life of the American statesman)
BENEDICT ARNOLD'S PLOT AGAINST WEST POINT
(short) (CBS–TV, 1956)

BETRAYER, THE see VANINA VANINI

BETROTHED, THE (ITA, 1913)
PROMESSI SPOSI, I (ITA, 1938)

BETTELSTUDENT, DER see BEGGAR STUDENT, THE

BETTER 'OLE, THE (BRI, 1919, based on the play by Bruce
Bairnsfeather and Arthur Eliot)
BRITISH TITLES: CARRY ON and ROMANCE OF OLD
BILL, THE
BETTER 'OLE, THE (WB, 1926)

BETWEEN TWO WOMEN (TV TITLE: SURROUNDED BY
WOMEN) (MGM, 1937, based on a story by Erich von
Stroheim)
BETWEEN TWO WOMEN (MGM, 1944)

BETWEEN TWO WORLDS see OUTWARD BOUND

BETWEEN US GIRLS see FRUCHTSHEN

BEVERLY OF GRAUSTARK (KE, 1914, based on a story
by George Barr McCutcheon)
BEVERLY OF GRAUSTARK (BIO, 1916)
BEVERLY OF GRAUSTARK (MGM, 1926)

BEWARE MY LOVELY see MAN, THE

BEWARE! THE BLOB! see BLOB, THE

BEWITCHED (ABC–TV, 1964, based on a teleplay)
TABITHA (ABC–TV, 1976)
TABITHA (series) (ABC–TV, 1977)

BEYOND LOVE AND EVIL (FRA, 1969, source unknown)
EUGENIE – THE STORY OF HER JOURNEY INTO
PERVERSION (GER, 1969)

BEZHIN MEADOW (RUS, 1935, based on the book, "A
Sportsman's Sketches," by Ivan Turgenev)
BEZHIN MEADOW (short) (RUS, 1966)
BIRJUK (LONE WOLF) (RUS, 1977)

BIALIK – POET OF A PEOPLE see BIALIK – POET OF
TRANSITION

BIALIK – POET OF TRANSITION (ABC–TV, 1962, based
on the life and works of the noted poet)
BIALIK – POET OF A PEOPLE (CBS–TV, 1963)

BIBERPELZ, DER (GER, 1928, based on the play by Gerhart
Hauptmann)
BIBERPELZ, DER (GER, 1937)
BIBERPELZ, DER GER, 1949)

BIBLE, THE see ADAM AND EVE, CAIN AND ABEL, and
NOAH'S ARK

BICHON (FRA, 1935, based on a book by Jean de Letraz)
BICHON (FRA, 1947)

BIG BAD WOLF, THE see THREE LITTLE PIGS, THE

BIG BOW MYSTERY, THE see PERFECT CRIME, THE

BIG BROTHER (PAR, 1923, based on a book by Rex Beach)
YOUNG DONOVAN'S KID (RKO, 1931)

BIG CAGE, THE (UN, 1933, stock footage from the first film
was used extensively in the other two later films)
CAPTIVE WILD WOMAN (UN, 1943)
JUNGLE WOMAN (UN, 1944)

BIG DEAL AT LAREDO (NBC–TV, 1962, based on a teleplay
by Sidney Carroll)
BIG HAND FOR THE LITTLE LADY, A (WB, 1966)

BIG FIGHT, THE (WW, 1930, based on the play by David
Belasco and Sam H. Harris)
FUERZA DEL QUERER, LA (SPA, 1930)

BIG GUY (UN, 1939, based on the story, "No Power on Earth,"
by Wallace Sullivan and Richard K. Polimer)
BEHIND THE HIGH WALL (UN, 1956)

BIG HAND FOR THE LITTLE LADY, A see BIG DEAL AT
LAREDO

BIG–HEARTED HERBERT (WB, 1934, based on a story by
Sophie Kerr)
FATHER IS A PRINCE (WB, 1940)

BIG HOUSE, THE (MGM, 1930, based on a story by Frances
Marion)
MENSCHEN HINTER GETTERN (GER, 1930)

PRESIDIO, EL (SPA, 1930)
BIG HOUSE, THE (FRA, 1930)

BIG NOISE, THE (FN, 1928, based on a story by Ben Hecht)
BIG NOISE, THE (WB, 1936)

BIG NOISE, THE see BERTH MARKS

BIG OPERATOR, THE see JOE SMITH, AMERICAN

BIG POND, THE (PAR, 1930, based on the play by George
Middleton and A.E. Thomas)
GRAND MER, LE (FRA, 1930)

BIG RIPOFF, THE (NBC–TV, 1975, based on a teleplay)
MCCOY (series) (NBC–TV, 1975)

BIG SHOW, THE see HOUSE OF STRANGERS

BIG SLEEP, THE (WB, 1946, based on the book by Raymond
Chandler)
BIG SLEEP, THE (NBC–TV, 1950)
BIG SLEEP, THE (UA, 1978)

BIG STAMPEDE, THE see LAND BEYOND THE LAW

BIG TRAIL, THE (FOX, 1930, based on a story by Hal J.
Evarts)
HORIZONTES NUEVOS, LE (SPA, 1931)
GROSSE FAHRT, DIE (GER, 1931)
PISTE DES GEANTS, LA (FRA, 1931)

BIG TREES, THE see VALLEY OF THE GIANTS

BIGAMIE see LIVING CORPSE, THE

BILD DER AHNFRAU, DAS (GER, 1917, based on the novel,
"Die Ahnfrau," by Franz Grillparzer)
AHNFRAU, DIE (AUS, 1920)

BILDNIS DES DORIAN GRAY see PICTURE OF DORIAN
GRAY, THE

BILL BUMPER'S BARGAIN see FAUST

BILL OF DIVORCEMENT, A (BRI, 1922, based on the play
by Clemence Dane)
BILL OF DIVORCEMENT, A (TV TITLE: NEVER TO
LOVE (RKO, 1932)
BILL OF DIVORCEMENT, A (CZE, 1933)
BILL OF DIVORCEMENT, A (RKO, 1940)

BILLY BUDD (CBS–TV, 1952, based on the book, "Billy
Budd, Foretopman," by Herman Melville. Also the basis
for an opera by Sir Benjamin Britten in 1951 and the
musical drama, "Billy," in 1969)
BILLY BUDD (ABC–TV, 1955)
BILLY BUDD (CBS–TV, 1959)
BILLY BUDD (AA, 1962)

BILLY JACK GOES TO WASHINGTON see MR. SMITH
GOES TO WASHINGTON

BILLY MITCHELL COURT MARTIAL, THE see COURT
MARTIAL OF BILLY MITCHELL, THE

BILLY ROSE'S DIAMOND HORSESHOE see BARKER,
THE

BILLY THE KID (VIT, 1911, based on the incidents in the
life of the bandit. Also the basis for a musical, "Wanted,"
in 1972)
BILLY THE KID (MGM, 1930)
BILLY THE KID (MGM, 1941)
DEATH OF BILLY THE KID, THE (NBC–TV, 1955)
PARSON AND THE OUTLAW, THE (COL, 1957)
LEFT–HANDED GUN, THE (WB, 1958)
TALL MAN, THE (series) (NBC–TV, 1960)
MAN WHO KILLED BILLY THE KID, THE (SPA, 1968)
FEW BULLETS MORE, A (ITA, 1969)

BIOGRAPHY see BIOGRAPHY OF A BACHELOR GIRL

BIOGRAPHY OF A BACHELOR GIRL (MGM, 1935, based on
the play, "Biography," by S.N. Behrman)
BIOGRAPHY (CBS–TV, 1950)

BIRD OF PARADISE (RKO, 1932, based on the play by
Richard Walton Tully)
BIRD OF PARADISE (FOX, 1951)

BIRDS AND THE BEES, THE see LADY EVE, THE

BIRJUK see BEZHIN MEADOW

BIRTH OF MODERN BOXING, THE see GENTLEMAN JIM

BIRTH OF OUR SAVIOR, THE see PASSION PLAY, THE

BISCUIT EATER, THE (PAR, 1940, based on the story by
James Street)
BISCUIT EATER, THE (DIS, 1972)

BISHOP'S CANDLESTICKS, THE see CHEMINEAU, LE

BITTER SWEET (BRI, 1933, based on the operetta by Noel
Coward)
BITTER SWEET (MGM, 1940)

BLACK ARROW, THE (ED, 1912, based on the book by
Robert Louis Stevenson)
BLACK ARROW, THE (serial) (COL, 1944)
BLACK ARROW, THE (NBC–TV, 1960)
BLACK ARROW, THE (HB, 1971)
BLACK ARROW, THE (AUT, 1972)

BLACK BART (UN, 1948, based on a story by Luci Ward
and Jack Natteford)
RIDE TO HANGMAN'S TREE, THE (UN, 1967)

BLACK BEAUTY (BRI, 1907, based on a screenplay by Lewis
Fitzhamon)
BLACK BEAUTY (BRI, 1910)

BLACK BEAUTY (BRI, 1906, based on the book by Anna
Sewall)
BLACK BEAUTY (BRI, 1910)
YOUR OBEDIENT SERVANT (ED, 1917)
BLACK BEAUTY (VIT, 1921)
BLACK BEAUTY (MON, 1933)
BLACK BEAUTY (FOX, 1946)
COURAGE OF BLACK BEAUTY (FOX, 1957)
BLACK BEAUTY (BRI, 1971)
ADVENTURES OF BLACK BEAUTY (series) (BRI–TV,
1972)
BLACK BEAUTY (NBC–TV, 1978)

BLACK CAT see EERIE TALES

BLACK DRAGON OF MANANAR see G--MEN VS. THE
    BLACK DRAGON

BLACK EAGLE, THE see DOUBROVSKY

BLACK-EYED SUSAN (BRI, 1908, based on the play by
    Douglas Jerrold)
  BLACK--EYED SUSAN (BRI, 1913)

BLACK EYES (BRI, 1937, based on the book, "Yeux Noire,
    Les," by V. Tourjansky)
  BLACK EYES (BRI, 1939)

BLACK FOX, THE see ROMAN DE RENARD, LE

BLACK MAGIC see CAGLIOSTRO

BLACK 107, THE (IND, 1913, based on a true--to--life inci--
    dent involving the persecution of Russian Jews in Kiev)
  TERRORS OF RUSSIA, THE (ITA/USA, 1913)

BLACK ORCHIDS (UN, 1916, based on a story by Rex
    Ingram)
  TRIFLING WOMEN (MGM, 1922)

BLACK ORPHEUS see LEGEND OF ORPHEUS

BLACK PATH OF FEAR, THE see CHASE, THE

BLACK PIRATE, THE (UA, 1926, based on a story by Elton
    Thomas; remake written by Milton Kibbee)
  CRIMSON PIRATE, THE (WB, 1952)

BLACK ROSE, THE see ARABIAN NIGHTS

BLACK ROSES see SVARTA ROSAR

BLACK SHIELD OF FALWORTH, THE see MEN OF IRON

BLACK SUNDAY (n.d., 1960, source unknown)
  VII (RUS, 1967)

BLACK TULIP (BRI, 1921, based on the book by Alexandre
    Dumas)
  BLACK TULIP (BRI, 1937)
  BLACK TULIP (series) (BRI-TV, 1971)

BLACK WATCH (FOX, 1929, based on a story by Talbot
    Mundy)
  KING OF THE KHYBER RIFLES (FOX, 1953)

BLACK WIDOW, THE (serial) (REP, 1947, based on a screen-
    play by various authors. The remake is an edited version
    of the serial)
  SOMBRA, THE SPIDER WOMAN (REP, 1966)

BLACKBEARD (SEL, 1912, based on the legend)
  BLACKBEARD THE PIRATE (RKO, 1952)

BLACKBEARD THE PIRATE see BLACKBEARD

BLACULA see DRACULA

BLAISE PASCAL see UNIVERSE OF NUMBERS

BLAKE OF SCOTLAND YARD (serial) (UN, 1927,
    based on a screenplay by Robert F. Hill)
  ACE OF SCOTLAND YARD (serial) (UN, 1929)
  BLAKE OF SCOTLAND YARD (IND, 1937)

BLANCHEVILLE MONSTER see FALL OF THE HOUSE
    OF USHER and PRELUDE

BLAUE MAUS, DIE (GER, 1912, source unknown)
  BLAUE MAUS, DIE (GER, 1928)

BLAZE O'GLORY (WW, 1930, based on a story by Thomas
    Boyd)
  SOMBRAS DE GLORIA (SPA, 1930)

BLAZING THE OVERLAND TRAIL see OVERLAND WITH
    KIT CARSON

BLEAK HOUSE see JO, the CROSSING SWEEPER

BLIND ADVENTURE, THE (VIT, 1917, based on the book,
    "Agony Column," by Earl Derr Biggers)
  SECOND FLOOR MYSTERY (WB, 1930)
  PASSAGE FROM HONG KONG (WB, 1941)

BLIND ALLEY (COL, 1939, based on the play by James
    Warwick)
  DARK PAST, THE (COL, 1949)

BLIND PREJUDICE see ESTHER AND MORDECAI

BLINKY (UN, 1923, based on a story by Gene Markey)
  RANGE COURAGE (UN, 1927)

BLITHE SPIRIT (BRI, 1944, based on the play by Noel
    Coward. Later the basis for the musical comedy, "High
    Spirits," in 1964)
  BLITHE SPIRIT (CBS-TV, 1956)
  BLITHE SPIRIT (NBC-TV, 1966)

BLOB, THE (PAR, 1958, based on the idea by Irvine H.
    Millgate)
  BEWARE! THE BLOB! (IND, 1972)

BLOCKHEADS see SOLDIER MAN

BLONDE SAINT see ISLE OF LIFE, THE

BLONDE TROUBLE see JUNE MOON

BLONDER TRAUM, EIN (GER, 1932, based on a screenplay
    by Billy Wilder and Walter Reisch)
  REVE BLONDE, UNE (FRA, 1932)
  HAPPILY EVER AFTER (BRI, 1932)

BLOOD AND ROSES see STRANGE CASE OF DAVID
    GRAY, THE

BLOOD AND SAND see ARENES SANGLANTES

BLOOD BROTHER see BROKEN ARROW

BLOOD DEMON see PIT AND THE PENDULUM, THE

BLOOD FOR BLOOD see HAMLET

BLOOD FOR DRACULA see NOSFERATU

BLOOD FOR LOVE see HAMLET

BLOOD ON THE BALCONY see BENITO MUSSOLINI

BLOODTHIRSTY BUTCHERS see SWEENEY TODD

BLOODY BRIDE, THE   see   STRANGE CASE OF DAVID
   GRAY, THE

BLOTTO   see   THEIR PURPLE MOMENT

BLUE ANGEL, THE   (GER, 1929, based on the book, "Prof.
   Unrath," by Heinrich Mann)
   BLUE ANGEL, THE   (PAR, 1930)
   BLUE ANGEL, THE   (FOX, 1959)

BLUE BIRD, THE   (BRI, 1910, based on the play by Maurice
   Maeterlinck)
   BLUE BIRD, THE   (RUS, 1911)
   BLUE BIRD, THE   (PAR, 1918)
   BLUE BIRD, THE   (FOX, 1940)
   BLUE BIRD, THE   (FOX/RUS, 1976)

BLUE HOTEL, THE   (CBS–TV, 1957, based on the story by
   Stephen Crane)
   BLUE HOTEL, THE   (TV, n.d.)
   BLUE HOTEL, THE   (LCA, 1977)

BLUE KNIGHT, THE   (NBC–TV, 1974, based on the book by
   Joseph Wambaugh)
   BLUE KNIGHT, THE (series)   (CBS–TV, 1975)

BLUE LAGOON, THE   (BRI, 1923, based on the book by
   H. DeVere Stacpoole)
   BLUE LAGOON, THE   (BRI, 1949)

BLUE MOUNTAINS   (JAP, 1949, source unknown)
   BLUE MOUNTAINS   (JAP, 1957)

BLUE SKIES   (FOX, 1929, based on the story, "The Matron's
   Report," by Frederick Hazlitt Brennan)
   LITTLE MISS NOBODY   (FOX, 1936)

BLUE VEIL, THE   see   VOILE BLEU, LE

BLUEBEARD   (FRA, 1898, based on the life of the noted
   lady–killer)
   BLUEBEARD   (FRA, 1907)
   BLUEBEARD   (ED, 1909)
   BLUEBEARD   (FRA, 1910)
   BLUEBEARD   (FRA, 1936)
   BLUEBEARD   (PRC, 1944)
   BLUEBEARD   (CIN, 1972)

BLUEBEARD   see   MONSIEUR VERDOUX

BLUEBEARD'S EIGHTH WIFE   (PAR, 1923, based on the
   book by Alfred Savoir)
   BLUEBEARD'S EIGHTH WIFE   (PAR, 1938)

BLUES ACCORDING TO LIGHTNIN' HOPKINS, THE
   (short)   (IND, 1970, based on the life of the noted blues
   singer)
   SAM "LIGHTNIN' " HOPKINS   (short)   (IND, 1971)

BLUFFEUR, LE   see   HIGH PRESSURE

BLUMENFRAU VON LINDENAU, DIE   (AUS/GER, 1931,
   based on the play by Bruno Frank)
   STORM IN A TEACUP   (BRI, 1937)
   STORM IN A TEACUP   (NBC--TV, 1950)
   STURM IM WASSERGLAS   (GER, 1960)

BOCCACCIO   see   DECAMERON, THE

BLUEBEARD'S TEN HONEYMOONS   see   MONSIEUR
   VERDOUX

BLUME VON HAWAII   see   FLOWER OF HAWAII, THE

BOAT FROM SHANGHAI   see   SHADOWS

BOB & CAROL & TED & ALICE   (COL, 1969, based on a
   screenplay by Paul Mazursky and Larry Tucker)
   BOB & CAROL & TED & ALICE   (series)   (ABC–TV, 1973)

BOB, SON OF BATTLE   see   TO THE VICTOR

BOBBY DEERFIELD   see   IN THE ANTEROOM OF DEATH

BODY AND SOUL   (UA, 1947, based on a screenplay by Abra–
   ham Polonsky)
   BODY AND SOUL   (CBS--TV, 1959)

BODY SNATCHER, THE   (RKO, 1945, based on a story by
   Robert Louis Stevenson and the lives of Burke and Hare)
   MANIA   (BRI, 1960)
   ANATOMIST, THE   (BRI, 1961)
   BURKE AND HARE – BODY SNATCHERS   (BRI, 1971)

BOHEME, LA   see   VIE DE BOHEME, LA

BOHEMIAN GIRL, THE   (BRI, 1922, based on a operetta by
   Michael William Balfe)
   BOHEMIAN GIRL, THE   (SEZ, 1923)
   BOHEMIAN GIRL, THE   (short)   (BRI, 1927)
   BOHEMIAN GIRL, THE   (MGM, 1936)
   SWING OPERA, A   (short)   (WB, 1939)

BOLD ADVENTURE   see   TIL EULENSPIEGEL

BOLD CABALLERO, THE   see   MARK OF ZORRO, THE

BON PETIT DIABLE, UN   see   GOOD LITTLE DEVIL, THE

BONAVENTURE   see   THUNDER ON THE HILL

BONDMAN, THE   (FOX, 1916, based on the book by Sir Hall
   Caine)
   BONDMAN, THE   (WW, 1929)

BONHEUR DES DAMES, AN   see   ZUM PARADIES DER
   DAMEN

BONNE CHANCE   (FRA, 1935, based on a story by Sacha Guitry)
   LUCKY PARTNERS   (RKO, 1940)

BONNIE AND CLYDE   see   BONNIE PARKER STORY, THE

BONNIE PARKER STORY, THE   (AI, 1958, based on histor–
   ical incidents)
   BONNIE AND CLYDE   (WB, 1967)

BONNIE PRINCE CHARLE   (BRI, 1923, based on historical
   incidents and characters)
   BONNIE PRINCE CHARLIE   (BRI, 1948)

BONS PETITES DIABLES, LES   see   BRATS

BOOBS IN ARMS   see   SLIPPING WIVES

BOOK OF RUTH, THE   (COL, 1931, based on the Bible story)
   RUTH   (short)   (BRI, 1948)
   STORY OF RUTH, THE   (short)   (IND, n.d.)

STORY OF RUTH, THE   (NBC–TV, 1954)
STORY OF RUTH, THE   (short) (CBS–TV, 1957)
STORY OF RUTH, THE   (FOX, 1960)

BOOKER T. WASHINGTON (short) (EBE, 1951, based on
    the life of the noted educator)
    BOOKER T. WASHINGTON (short) (BFA, 1967)

BORDER LAW (COL, 1931, the first two films are based
    on a story by Stuart Anthony and the others have a simi–
    lar story content)
    WHITLIN' DAN (TIF, 1932)
    FIGHTING RANGER, THE (COL, 1933)
    TRAITOR, THE (PUR, 1936)
    LAW OF THE TEXAN (COL, 1937)
    RIDERS OF THE ROCKIES (GN, 1937)

BORDER LEGION (MGM, 1919, based on the book by Zane
    Grey)
    BORDER LEGION (PAR, 1924)
    BORN TO THE WEST (PAR, 1926)
    BORDER LEGION (PAR, 1930)
    LAST ROUNDUP, THE (PAR, 1934)
    BORN TO THE WEST HELL TOWN (PAR, 1937)
    BORDER LEGION (REP, 1940)

BORDER TERROR, THE see CABALLERO'S WAY

BORDERTOWN (WB, 1935, written by different authors but
    plots are similar)
    THEY DRIVE BY NIGHT (WB, 1941)
    BLOWING WILD (WB, 1953)

BORIS GODOUNOV (RUS, 1907, based on the story by
    Alexander Pushkin and the opera by Modest Mussorgsky)
    BORIS GUDOUNOV (RUS, 1955)

BORN FOR GLORY see BROWN ON "RESOLUTION"

BORN FREE (COL, 1966, based on the book by Joy
    Adamson)
    BORN FREE (series) (NBC–TV, 1974)

BORN TO THE WEST see BORDER LEGION

BORN YESTERDAY (COL, 1950, based on the play by
    Garson Kanin)
    BORN YESTERDAY (NBC–TV, 1956)

BOSSU, LE (FRA, 1913, based on a novel by Paul Feval (pere)
    BOSSU, LE (FRA, 1925)
    BOSSU, LE (FRA, 1934)
    BOSSU, LE (FRA, 1944)
    SERMENT DE LAGARDERE, LE (ARG, 1955)

BOSUN'S MATE (BRI, 1914, based on a story by W.W.
    Jacobs)
    BOSUN'S MATE (BRI, 1953)

BOTTLE IMP, THE see IMP OF THE BOTTLE, THE

BOUDOIR DIPLOMAT (UN, 1930, based on the play by
    Rudolph Lothar and Fritz Gottwald)
    BOUDOIR DIPLOMAT (GER, 1930)
    DON JUAN DIPLOMATICO (SPA, 1930)
    BOUDOIR DIPLOMATIQUE (FRA, 1931)

BOUDOIR DIPLOMATIQUE see BOUDOIR
    DIPLOMAT,

THE

BOUGHT AND PAID FOR (IND, 1916, based on the play by
    George Broadhurst)
    BOUGHT AND PAID FOR (PAR, 1922)

BOULE DE SUIF see STAGECOACH and WOMAN
    DISPUTED, A

BOUNTY COURT MARTIAL see MUTINY ON THE
    BOUNTY

BOURRASQUE DE NEIGE, LA (RUS, 1918, based on the
    story by Alexander Pushkin)
    BOURRASQUE DE NEIGE, LA (RUS, 1964)
    UND DER REGEN VERWISCHT JEDE SPUR (GER, 1973)

BOY CRIED MURDER, THE see WINDOW, THE

BOY FROM NEW ORLEANS: A TRIBUTE TO LOUIS
    ARMSTRONG see SATCHMO THE GREAT

BOY OF FLANDERS, A see DOG OF FLANDERS, A

BOYHOOD OF GEORGE WASHINGTON, THE see MOUNT
    VERNON IN VIRGINIA

BOYHOOD OF GEORGE WASHINGTON CARVER, THE see
    STORY OF DR. CARVER, THE

BOYHOOD OF THOMAS EDISON, THE see YOUNG TOM
    EDISON

BOYS FROM SYRACUSE, THE see COMEDY OF ERRORS

BOYS OF PAUL STREET, THE (HUN, 1917, based on the
    play by Ferenc Molnar)
    BOYS OF PAUL STREET, THE (HUN, 1924)
    PAUL STREET BOYS, THE (HUN, 1929)
    NO GREATER GLORY (COL, 1934)
    BOYS OF PAUL STREET (POL, 1969)
    PAUL STREET BOYS, THE (HUN, 1969)

BRADY BUNCH, THE (series) (ABC–TV, 1969, based on a
    teleplay)
    BRADY KIDS (series) (ABC–TV, 1972)

BRAIN, THE see LADY AND THE MONSTER, THE

BRANDED SOUL, THE see IRON STAIR, THE

BRANNINGAR (SWE, 1912, source unknown)
    BRANNINGAR (SWE, 1935)

BRAQUE (short) (FRA, n.d., based on the life and work of
    the noted artist)
    GEORGES BRAQUE (short) (RAD, n.d.)

BRASHER DOUBLOON, THE see TIME TO KILL

BRASS BOTTLE, THE (BRI, 1914, based on the book by
    F. Anstey)
    BRASS BOTTLE, THE (FN, 1923)
    BRASS BOTTLE, THE (UN, 1964)

BRASS BOWL, THE (ED, 1914, based on the book by Louis J.
    Vance)
    BRASS BOWL, THE (FOX, 1931)

BRAT, THE (MGM, 1919, based on the play by Maude
    Fulton)
  BRAT, THE (FOX, 1931)
  GIRL FROM AVENUE A, THE (FOX, 1940)

BRATS (short) (MGM, 1930, based on a story by Leo
    McCarey)
  GLUCKLICHE KINDHEIT (short) (GER, 1930)
  BONS PETITES DIABLES, LES (short) (FRA, 1930)
  BRATS (short) (SPA, 1930)

BRAVE ENGINEER, THE (short) (DIS, 1950, based on the
    legend)
  CASEY JONES (series) (TV, 1957)

BRAVE LITTLE TAILOR (short) (DIS, 1938, based on the
    story, "Seven in One Blow," by the Brothers Grimm)
  GALLANT LITTLE TAILOR (BRI, 1954)
  BRAVE LITTLE TAILOR (GER, 1969)

BRAVE SOLDIER SCHWEIK see GOOD SOLDIER
    SCHWEIK

BREAK THE NEWS see MORT EN FUITE, LE

BREAKERS see BRANNINGAR

BREAKING POINT, THE see TO HAVE AND HAVE NOT

BREATH OF SCANDAL, A see HIS GLORIOUS NIGHT

BREMENTOWN MUSICIANS see FOUR MUSICIANS OF
    BREMEN

BRENNENDE ACKER, DER (GER, 1913, based on a screen-
    play by Thea von Harbou)
  BRENNENDE ACKER, DER (GER, 1922)

BRENNENDES GEHEIMNIS (GER, 1923, based on the book
    by Stefan Zweig)
  BRENNENDES GEHEIMNIS (GER, 1933)

BREWSTER'S MILLIONS (PAR, 1914, based on the book by
    George Barr McCutcheon and the play by Winchell Smith)
  BREWSTER'S MILLIONS (PAR, 1921)
  MISS BREWSTER'S MILLIONS (PAR, 1926)
  BREWSTER'S MILLIONS (BRI, 1935)
  BREWSTER'S MILLIONS (UA, 1945)
  3 ON A SPREE (BRI, 1961)

BRIDE BY MISTAKE see RICHEST GIRL IN THE WORLD,
    THE

BRIDE FOR A SINGLE NIGHT see TESS OF THE STORM
    COUNTRY

BRIDE OF FRANKENSTEIN see FRANKENSTEIN

BRIDE OF LAMMERMOOR see LUCIA DI LAMMERMOOR

BRIDE OF THE REGIMENT see LADY IN ERMINE, THE

BRIDE OF VENGEANCE see LUCRETIA BORGIA

BRIDES ARE LIKE THAT (WB, 1936, based on the play,
    "Applesauce," by Barry Connors)
  ALWAYS A BRIDE (WB, 1940

BRIDES OF DRACULA see NOSFERATU

BRIDGE, THE see OCCURENCE AT OWL CREEK BRIDGE,
    AN

BRIDGE OF SAN LUIS REY (MGM, 1929, based on the
    book by Thornton Wilder)
  BRIDGE OF SAN LUIS REY, THE (UA, 1944)
  BRIDGE OF SAN LUIS REY, THE (CBS–TV, 1958)

BRIEF EINER UNBEKANNTEN see NARKOSE

BRIEF ENCOUNTER (BRI, 1946, based on the play by Noel
    Coward)
  BRIEF ENCOUNTER (NBC–TV, 1961)
  BRIEF ENCOUNTER (ABC–TV, 1973)

BRIGADIER GERARD (BRI, 1915, based on the book, "Ex-
    ploits of Brigadier Gerard, The" by Sir Arthur Conan
    Doyle)
  FIGHTING EAGLE, THE (PAT, 1927)
  ADVENTURES OF GERARD (UA, 1970)

BRIGADOON (MGM, 1954, based on the musical by Alan
    Jay Lerner and Frederick Loewe)
  BRIGADOON (ABC–TV, 1966)

BRIGAND BROTHERS, THE (RUS, 1912, based on the story
    by Alexander Pushkin)
  BRIGAND BROTHERS, THE (RUS, 1972)

BRIGHAM YOUNG, FRONTIERSMAN (FOX, 1940, based
    on the life of the Mormon leader)
  BRIGHAM YOUNG, COLONIZER (short) (IND, n.d.)
  DRIVEN WESTWARD (short) (TFC, 1948)

BRIGHT LIGHTS (TIF, 1929, based on a story by Richard
    Connell)
  BRIGHT LIGHTS (WB, 1935)

BRITAIN CROWNS A QUEEN see KING IS DEAD, LONG
    LIVE THE QUEEN, THE

BRITANNICUS (FRA, 1908, based on the book by Jean
    Racine)
  BRITANNICUS (FRA, 1912)

BRITISH INTELLIGENCE see THREE FACES EAST

BROADWAY (UN, 1929, based on the play by Philip Dunning
    and George Abbott)
  BROADWAY (UN, 1942)
  BROADWAY (CBS–TV, 1955)

BROADWAY BILL (COL, 1934, based on a story by Mark
    Hellinger)
  RIDING HIGH (PAR, 1950)

BROADWAY MELODY (MGM, 1929, based on a story by
    Edmund Goulding)
  TWO GIRLS ON BROADWAY (MGM, 1940

BROADWAY MUSKETEERS see THREE ON A MATCH

BRODERNA OSTERMANS HUSKORS (SWE, 1925, source
    unknown)
  BRODERNA OSTERMANS HUSKORS (SWE, 1932)

BROKEN ARROW (FOX, 1950, based on the book, "Blood
    Brother," by Elliott Arnold)
  BLOOD AROTHER (BCS–TV, 1956)

BROKEN ARROW (series) (ABC--TV, 1956)

BROKEN BLOSSOMS (GRI, 1919, based on the book, "The Chink and the Child," by Thomas Burke)
BROKEN BLOSSOMS (BRI, 1936)

BROKEN DISHES see TOO YOUNG TO MARRY

BROKEN LANCE see HOUSE OF STRANGERS

BROKEN LULLABY see PAX DOMINE

BROKEN MELODY (BRI, 1928, based on the play by Herbert Keith and James Leader)
BROKEN MELODY (BRI, 1934)

BROKEN WING, THE (IND, 1923, based on the play by Paul Dickey and Charles Goddard)
BROKEN WING, THE (PAR, 1932)

BRONTE SISTERS, THE see DEVOTION

BROOCH, THE see DAMNED DON'T CRY, THE

BROOKLYN ORCHID see COME CLEAN

BROTHER RAT (WB, 1938, based on the play by John Monks Jr. and Fred Finklehoffe)
BROTHER RAT (NBC--TV, 1939)
ABOUT FACE (WB, 1952)

BROTHER SUN, SISTER MOON see ST. FRANCIS OF ASSISI

BROTHERS (BRI, 1914, based on the book by L.A.G. Strong)
BROTHERS (BRI, 1941)

BROTHERS KARAMAZOV, THE (RUS, 1915, based on the book by Feyodor Dostoyevsky)
KARAMAZOV (GER, 1920)
KARAMAZOV (GER, 1931)
BROTHERS KARAMAZOV, THE (ITA, 1947)
BROTHERS KARAMAZOV, THE (MGM, 1958)
BROTHERS KARAMAZOV, THE (RUS, 1968)

BROWN BOMBER, THE see SPIRIT OF YOUTH

BROWN OF HARVARD (SEL, 1917, based on the book and play by Rida Johnson Young and Gilbert P. Coleman)
BROWN OF HARVARD (MGM, 1926)

BROWN ON "RESOLUTION" (FOREVER ENGLAND) (British Title: BORN FOR GLORY) (BRI, 1935, based on the book by C.S. Forrester)
SAILOR OF THE KING (FOX, 1953)

BROWN SUGAR (BRI, 1922, based on the play by Lady Arthur Lever)
BROWN SUGAR (BRI, 1931)

BROWNING VERSION, THE (BRI, 1951, based on the play by Terrence Rattigan)
BROWNING VERSION, THE (NBC--TV, 1955)
BROWNING VERSION, THE (CBS--TV, 1959)

BRUCE LEE AND I (CHN, 1975, based on the life of the Oriental film actor)

BRUCE LEE – THE TRUE STORY (CHN, 1976)

BRUCE LEE – THE TRUE STORY see BRUCE LEE AND I

BRUTUS see JULIUS CAESAR

BUCCANEER, THE (PAR, 1938, based on the book, "LaFitte the Pirate," by Lyle Saxon)
BUCCANEER, THE (ABC--TV, 1951)
BUCCANEER, THE (PAR, 1958)

BUCHSE DER PANDORA, DIE see LULU

BUCK ROGERS (serial) (UN, 1939, based on the comic strip by Phil Nowland and Lt. Richard Calkins: "Planet Out-laws" is a condensation of the serial)
PLANET OUTLAWS (UN, 1939)
BUCK ROGERS IN THE 25TH CENTURY (series) (ABC--TV, 1950)

BUCKAROO KID, THE (UN, 1926, based on the book, "O Promise Me," by Peter B. Kyne)
FLAMING GUNS (UN, 1933)

BUCKET OF BLOOD see AVENGING CONSCIENCE, THE

BUDDAH see GOTAMA, THE BUDDAH

BUDDENBROOKS, DIE (GER, 1923, based on the book by Thomas Mann)
BUDDENBROOKS I AND II (GER, 1959)

BUDDHA see BUDDHISM

BUDDHISM (NET--TV, 1960, based on the life and philosophy of the noted religious leader)
BUDDHA, THE (short) (RAD, n.d.)
BUDDHISM (short) (CAN, 1962)
BUDDHIST WORLD, THE (short) (COR, 1963)
BUDDAH (LOP, 1963)

BUDDHIST WORLD, THE see BUDDHISM

BUFFALO BILL (BRI, 1911, based on historical characters and incidents)
BUFFALO BILL ON THE U.P. TRAIL (SUN, 1926)
BUFFALO BILL (FOX, 1944)
BUFFALO BILL RIDES AGAIN (SG, 1947)
BUFFALO BILLY IN TOMAHAWK TERRITORY (UA, 1952)
BUFFALO BILL (ITA, 1963)
DON'T TOUCH WHITE WOMEN! (FRA, 1974)

BUFFALO BILL IN TOMAHAWK TERRITORY see BUFFA-LO BILL

BUFFALO BILL ON THE U.P. TRAIL see BUFFALO BILL

BUFFALO BILL RIDES AGAIN see BUFFALO BILL

BUGLES IN THE AFTERNOON see CUSTER'S LAST STAND

BULLDOG DRUMMOND (HOD, 1922, based on the book by Sapper (Herman Cyril McNeile)
BULLDOG DRUMMOND (BRI, 1923)
BULLDOG DRUMMOND (UA, 1929)

BULLDOG DRUMMOND AT BAY (BRI, 1937, based on the

book by Sapper (Herman Cyril McNeile)
BULLDOG DRUMMOND AT BAY (COL, 1947)

BULLDOG DRUMMOND IN AFRICA (PAR, 1938, based on
  the book, "The Challenge," by Sapper (Herman April McNeile)
CHALLENGE, THE (FOX, 1948)

BULLDOG DRUMMOND STRIKES BACK (UA, 1934,
  based on the book by Sapper (Herman Cyril McNeile)
BULLDOG DRUMMOND STRIKES BACK (COL, 1947)

BULLDOG DRUMMOND'S PERIL see BULLDOG DRUM--
  MOND'S THIRD ROUND

BULLDOG DRUMMOND'S SECRET POLICE see TEMPLE
  TOWER

BULLDOG DRUMMOND'S THIRD ROUND (BRI, 1925,
  based on the book, "The Third Round," by Sapper (Her--
  man Cyril McNeile)
BULLDOG DRUMMOND'S PERIL (PAR, 1938)

BULLET FOR PRETTY BOY, A see PRETTY BOY FLOYD

BULLETS FOR O'HARA see PUBLIC ENEMY'S WIFE

BULLFIGHTERS, THE see DO DETECTIVES THINK?

BUNDLE OF JOY see BACHELOR MOTHER

BUNKER BEAN see HIS MAJESTY, BUNKER BEAN

BURDEN AND GLORY OF JOHN F. KENNEDY, THE see
  MAKING OF THE PRESIDENT – 1960, THE

BUREAU OF MISSING PERSONS (WB, 1933, based on a
  story with remake uncredited)
MISSING WITNESSES (WB, 1937)

BURGLAR, THE (WOR, 1917, based on the play by Augustus
  Thomas)
FAMILY SECRET, THE (UN, 1924)

BURGLAR, THE (COL, 1957, based on the book by David
  Goodis)
BURGLARS, THE (COL, 1972)

BURGLARS, THE see BURGLAR, THE

BURGOMEISTER, THE see BELLS, THE

BURGOS SOLAR DEL CID see CID, EL

BURIDAN see TOUR DE NESLE, LA

BURIDAN, LE HEROS DE LA TOUR DE NESLE see TOUR

DE NESLE, LA

BURIED ALIVE see GREAT ADVENTURE, THE

BURKE AND HARE – BODY SNATCHERS see BODY
  SNATCHERS, THE

BURLESQUE ON CARMEN see CARMEN

BURN, WITCH, BURN see WEIRD WOMAN

BURNING BRIGHT (PBS--TV, 1959, based on the play by
  John Steinbeck)
BURNING BRIGHT (PBS--TV, 1966)

BURNING DAYLIGHT (BOS, 1914, based on the book by Jack
  London)
BURNING DAYLIGHT (MGM, 1920)
BURNING DAYLIGHT (FN, 1928)

BURNING THE WIND see MAN IN THE SADDLE

BURNING TRAIL, THE see SUNDOWN SLIM

BURNT WINGS (UN, 1920, based on the play, "The Primrose
  Path," by Bayard Veiller)
PRIMROSE PATH, THE (RKO, 1940)

BUS STOP (TV TITLE: WRONG KIND OF WOMAN, THE
  (FOX, 1956, based on the play by William Inge)
CHERIE (ABC--TV, 1959)
BUS STOP (series) (ABC--TV, 1961)

BUSTER SE MARIE see SPITE MARRIAGE

BUT NOT FOR ME see ACCENT ON YOUTH

BUT THE FLESH IS WEAK (MGM, 1932, based on the play,
  "Truth Game," by Ivor Novello)
FREE AND EASY (MGM, 1941)

BUTCH CASSIDY AND THE SUNDANCE KID see THREE
  OUTLAWS

BUTTER AND EGG MAN, THE (FN, 1928, based on the play
  by George S. Kaufman)
TENDERFOOT, THE (WB, 1932)
HELLO, SWEETHEART (BRI, 1935)
DANCE, CHARLIE, DANCE (WB, 1937)
ANGEL FROM TEXAS, AN (WB, 1940)
THREE SAILORS AND A GIRL (WB, 1953)

BUTTON WAR, THE see GENERALS WITHOUT BUTTONS

BY THE LIGHT OF THE SILVERY MOON see PENROD

BYRD AT THE POLES see EXPEDITION TO ANTARCTICA

CABALLERO DE FRAC, UN see EVENING CLOTHES

CABELLERO DELA NOCHE, EL see DICK TURPIN

CABALLERO'S WAY (FRA, 1914, based on a story by O.
   Henry)
   BORDER TERROR, THE (UN, 1919)
   IN OLD ARIZONA (FOX, 1929)
   RETURN OF THE CISCO KID (FOX, 1939)

CABARET see I AM A CAMERA and SENSATION
   HUNTERS

CABINET OF CALIGARI, THE see CABINET OF DR.
   CALIGARI

CABINET OF DR. CALIGARI, THE (GER, 1919, based on
   the story by Karl Mayer and Hans Janowitz)
   CABINET OF CALIGARI, THE (FOX, 1962)
   VENGEANCE OF DR. CALIGARI, THE (GER, 1970)

CABIRIA (ITA, 1914, source unknown)
   CABIRIA (ITA, 1921)

CAESAR AND CLEOPATRA (UA, 1946, based on the play
   by George Bernard Shaw)
   CAESAR AND CLEOPATRA (NBC–TV, 1956)
   CAESAR AND CLEOPATRA (CBS–TV, 1959)

CAFE HOSTESS see HERMAN

CAGED (WB, 1950, based on a screenplay by Virginia Kellogg
   and Bernard C. Schoenfeld)
   HOUSE OF WOMEN (WB, 1962)

CAGLIOSTRO (FRA, 1909, based on the book, "Memoirs of
   a Physician," by Alexandre Dumas)
   LEGEND OF CAGLIOSTRO (GER, 1920)
   COUNT CAGLIOSTRO (GER, 1920)
   CAGLIOSTRO (FRA, 1928)
   CAGLIOSTRO (ITA, 1928)
   CAGLIOSTRO (GER, 1930)
   BLACK MAGIC (UA, 1949)
   CAGLIOSTRO (ITA, 1975)

CAIN AND ABEL (FRA, 1910, based on a Bible story)
   CAIN AND ABEL (VIT, 1911)
   BIBLE, THE (short) (SAC, 1921)
   AFTER SIX DAYS (ART, 1922)
   OLD TESTAMENT, THE (ITA, 1963)
   THE BIBLE (sequence) (FOX, 1966)
   BIBLE, LA (FRA, 1977)

CAIN AND MABEL see GREAT WHITE WAY, THE

CAINE MUTINY, THE (COL, 1954, based on the book by
   Herman Wouk)
   CAINE MUTINY COURT MARTIAL, THE (CBS–TV,
   1955)

CAINE MUTINY COURT MARTIAL see CAINE MUTINY,
   THE

CAIRO see ASPHALT JUNGLE, THE

CAIUS JULIUS CAESAR see JULIUS CAESAR

CAKAJI NA GODOTA see CEKAJI NA GODOTA

CALAIS–DOUVRES see NIE WIEDER LIEBE

CALAMITY JANE (WB, 1953, based on a screenplay by James
   O'Hanlon with songs by Sammy Fain and Paul Francis
   Webster; Calamity Jane's real name was Martha Jane Canary)
   CALAMITY JANE (CBS–TV, 1963)

CALAMITY JANE see CAUGHT and WILD BILL HICKOCK

CALAMITY JANE AND SAM BASS see CAUGHT

CALAMITY NAMED JANE, A see CAUGHT

CALAVERAS, LOS see AMBROSE'S FIRST FALSEHOOD

CALENDAR, THE (BRI, 1931, based on the play by Edgar
   Wallace)
   CALENDAR, THE (BRI, 1948)

CALENDAR, THE see BACHELOR'S FOLLY

CALL NORTHSIDE 777 see RAILROADED

CALL OF THE FLESH (MGM, 1930, based on the story by
   Dorothy Farnum)
   SEVILLA DE MIS AMORES (SPA, 1930)
   CHANTEUR DE SEVILLE, LE (FRA, 1935)

CALL OF THE NORTH, THE (PAR, 1914, based on the book,
   "Conjurer's House," by Stewart Edward White)
   CALL OF THE NORTH, THE (PAR, 1921)

CALL OF THE WILD, THE (BIO, 1908, based on the book by
   Jack London)
   CALL OF THE WILD, THE (PAT, 1923)
   CALL OF THE WILD, THE (UA, 1935)
   CALL OF THE WILD, THE (GER, 1971)
   CALL OF THE WILD, THE (NBC–TV, 1977)

CALL TO DANGER (CBS–TV, 1965, based on a teleplay)
   MISSION: IMPOSSIBLE (series) (CBS–TV, 1966)

CALLED BACK (AUT, 1911, based on the book by Hugh
   Conway)
   CALLED BACK (BRI, 1914)
   CALLED BACK (BRI, 1933)

CALLING NORTHSIDE 777 see RAILROADED

CALLING PHILO VANCE see KENNEL MURDER CASE,
   THE

CALYPSO see AVENGING CONSCIENCE, THE and THE
   GOLDEN BEETLE

CALZONIN INSPECTOR see REVIZOR

CAMELIA, PASSION SAUVAGE see DAME AUX CAME–
   LIAS, LA

CAMELOT see SWORD IN THE STONE, THE

CAMEO KIRBY (PAR, 1914, based on the play by Booth
   Tarkington and Harry Leon Wilson)
   CAMEO KIRBY (FOX, 1923)
   CAMEO KIRBY (FOX, 1929)

CAMERAMAN, THE (MGM, 1928, based on a screenplay by
   Clyde Bruckman and Lew Lipton. Remake uncredited)

WATCH THE BIRDIE   (MGM, 1950)

CAMILLE   see   DAME AUX CAMELIAS, LA

CAMILLE 2000   see   DAME AUX CAMELIAS, LA

CAMINO DEL INFIERNO   see   MAN WHO CAME BACK,
    THE

CAMP VOLANT   (FRA, 1930, source unknown)
    MARCO THE CLOWN   (GER, 1930)

CANADIAN MOUNTIES VS. ATOMIC INVADERS   (serial)
    (REP, 1953, based on an original screenplay. Remake is
    a condensation of the serial)
    MISSILE BASE AT TANIAK   (REP, 1966)

CANAVAN, THE MAN WHO HAD HIS WAY   see   DANGER
    SIGNAL

CANCAO DO BERCO   see   SARAH AND SON

CANDIDATE FOR PRESIDENT   see   THIEF, THE

CANDIDE   (FRA, n.d., based on the book by Voltaire)
    CANDIDE   (FRA, 1960)

CANDY   (short)   (BU, 1966, based on the book by Terry
    Southern and Mason Hoffenberg)
    CANDY   (CIN, 1968)

CANNON   (CBS–TV, 1971, based on an original teleplay)
    CANNON   (series)   (CBS–TV, 1971)

CANNONBALL, THE   (short)   (COL, 1931, based on a screen-
    play by Del Lord, et. al.)
    FIREMAN SAVE MY CHOO CHOO   (short)   (COL, 1940)

CANTERVILLE GHOST, THE   (BRI, 1940, based on the
    story by Oscar Wilde)
    CANTERVILLE GHOST, THE   (MGM, 1943)
    CANTERVILLE GHOST, THE   (NBC–TV, 1950)
    CANTERVILLE GHOST, THE   (short)   (IND, 1950)
    CANTERVILLE GHOST, THE   (CBS–TV, 1953)
    CANTERVILLE GHOST, THE   (ABC–TV, 1966)
    WORLD OF HORROR   (sequence)   (POL, 1968)
    CANTERVILLE GHOST, THE   (CAN–TV, 1972)

CAP PERDU   see   CAPE FORLORN

CAPE FORLORN   (n.d., 1930, source unknown)
    MENSCHEN IM KAFIG LE CAP PERDU   (GER, 1930)
    CAP PERDU   (FRA, 1930)

CAPETOWN AFFAIR   see   PICKUP ON SOUTH STREET

CAPITAINE FRACASSE, LE   (ITA, 1918, based on a book by
    Theophile Gautier)
    CAPITAINE FRACASSE, LE   (FRA, 1928)
    CAPITAINE FRACASSE, LE   (FRA, 1942)
    CAPITAINE FRACASSE, LE   (FRA/ITA, 1961)

CAPITAN, LE   (FRA, 1945, based on the book by Michel
    Zevaco)
    CAPITAN, LE   (FRA/ITA, 1960)

CAPPOTTO, IL   see   OVERCOAT, THE

CAPTAIN APPLEJACK   see   STRANGERS OF THE NIGHT

CAPTAIN BLOOD   (VIT, 1924, based on the book by Rafael
    Sabatini)
    CAPTAIN BLOOD   (WB, 1935)
    FORTUNES OF CAPTAIN BLOOD   (COL, 1950)
    CAPTAIN PIRATE   (COL, 1952)
    CAPTAIN WITHOUT A COUNTRY   (WB–TV, 1956)
    SON OF CAPTAIN BLOOD   (ITA/SPA, 1961)

CAPTAIN CAUTION   see   TWO LOST WORLDS

CAPTAIN FROM CASTILLE, THE   (FOX, 1947, based on
    the book by Samuel Shellabarger)
    SPANISH CONQUEST IN THE NEW WORLD   (short)
    (TFC, 1947)
    BALBOA OF DARIEN   (short)   (CFD, 1952)

CAPTAIN FROM KOPENIK, THE   (GER, 1907, based on the
    play by Karl Zuckmayer)
    CAPTAIN FROM KOPENIK, THE   (GER, 1926)
    CAPTAIN FROM KOPENIK, THE   (GER, 1931)
    PASSPORT TO HEAVEN   (TV TITLE: I WAS A CRIMI-
    NAL)   (FC, 1945)
    CAPTAIN FROM KOPENIK, THE   (GER, 1956)

CAPTAIN FURY   see   TWO LOST WORLDS

CAPTAIN HORATIO HORNBLOWER   (WB, 1951, based on
    the book by C.S. Forester)
    HORNBLOWER   (BRI–TV, 1963)

CAPTAIN JANUARY   (PRI, 1924, based on the story by
    Laura E. Richards)
    CAPTAIN JANUARY   (FOX, 1936)

CAPTAIN JOHN SMITH, EXPLORER   (short)   (IND, 1948,
    based on the life of the American pioneer)
    CAPTAIN JOHN SMITH POCAHONTAS   (UA, 1953)
    CAPTAIN JOHN SMITH – FOUNDER OF VIRGINIA
    (short)   (EBE, 1955)

CAPTAIN KIDD   (UA, 1945, based on a historical figure)
    CAPTAIN KIDD AND THE SLAVE GIRL   (UA, 1954)
    TRIAL OF CAPTAIN KIDD   (ABC–TV, 1957)

CAPTAIN KIDD AND THE SLAVE GIRL   see   CAPTAIN
    KIDD

CAPTAIN MARVEL   see   SHAZAM!

CAPTAIN MEPHISTO AND THE TRANSFORMATION
    MACHINE   see   MANHUNT OF MYSTERY ISLAND

CAPTAIN NEMO AND THE UNDERWATER CITY   see
    20,000 LEAGUES UNDER THE SEA

CAPTAIN PIRATE   see   CAPTAIN BLOOD

CAPTAIN WITHOUT A COUNTRY   see   CAPTAIN BLOOD

CAPTAINS COURAGEOUS   (MGM, 1937, based on the book
    by Rudyard Kipling)
    CAPTAINS COURAGEOUS   (ABC–TV, 1977)

CAPTAIN'S DAUGHTER, THE   (RUS, n.d., source unknown)
    CAPTAIN'S DAUGHTER, THE   (RUS, 1959)

CAPITAINE FRACASSE, LE   (FRA, 1927, based on the book
    by Theophile Gautier)
    CAPITAINE FRACASSE, LE   (FRA, 1942)
    CAPITAINE FRACASSE, LE   (FRA, 1961)

CAPTIVE CITY (UA, 1952, based on a story by Alvin M.
    Joseph Jr.)
  CAPTIVE CITY (NBC–TV, 1954)

CAPTIVE CUBA: YEARS UNDER CASTRO see FIDEL
    CASTRO STORY, THE

CAPTIVE WILD WOMAN see BIG CAGE, THE

CARAVAN (FOX, 1934, based on a story by Melchior
    Lengyel)
  CARAVANE (FRA, 1934)

CARAVANE see CARAVAN

CARD, THE (BRI, 1922, based on the book by Arnold
    Bennett)
  PROMOTER, THE (BRI, 1952)

CARDBOARD LOVER, THE (MGM, 1928, based on the play,
    "Dans sa candeur naive" by Jacques Deval)
  HER CARDBOARD LOVER (BRI, 1929)
  PASSIONATE PLUMBER, THE (MGM, 1931)
  PLOMBIER AMOUREUX, LE (FRA, 1932)
  HER CARDBOARD LOVER (MGM, 1942)

CARDINAL MINDSZENTY see GUILTY OF TREASON

CARDINAL RICHELIEU see RICHELIEU

CARDINAL WOLSEY see HENRY VIII

CARDINAL'S EDICT, THE see RICHELIEU

CARIBBEAN MYSTERY see MURDER IN TRINIDAD

CARL AND ANNA see OLD HEIDELBERG

CARL SANDBURG (short) (NBC–TV, 1958, based on the
    life and works of the noted poet)
  VISIT WITH CARL SANDBURG, A (short) (IND, n.d.)
  CARL SANDBURG AT GETTYSBURG (CBS–TV, 1961)
  CARL SANDBURG DISCUSSES HIS WORK (short)
    (COR, 1961)
  CARL SANDBURG DISCUSSES LINCOLN (short)
    (COR, 1961)

CARMEN (SEL, 1908, based on the story by Prosper Merimee;
    also the basis for the Bizet opera in 1875)
  CARMEN (ITA, 1909)
  CARMEN (SPA, 1910)
  CARMEN (FRA, 1910)
  CARMEN (IND, 1912)
  CARMEN (THA, 1913)
  CARMEN (ITA, 1913)
  CARMEN (MOL, 1913)
  AMOUR ESPAGNOL (DEN/GER, 1913)
  CARMEN (SPA, 1914)
  CARMEN (PAR, 1915)
  CARMEN (FOX, 1915)
  CARMEN (ITA, 1916)
  BURLESQUE ON CARMEN (ESS, 1916)
  GYPSY BLOOD (GER, 1918)
  CARMEN (short) (BRI, 1922)
  CARMEN (FRA, 1926)
  LOVES OF CARMEN, THE (FOX, 1927)
  CARMEN (SPA, 1928)
  CARMEN (BRI, 1929)
  GIPSY BLOOD (BRI, 1931)

  IDOL OF SEVILLE, THE (short) (EDU, 1932)
  CARMEN (GER, 1933)
  ANDALUSIAN NIGHTS (GER/SPA, 1938)
  CARMEN (SPA, 1940)
  CARMEN (FRA/ITA, 1942)
  CARMEN (ARG, 1943)
  LOVES OF CARMEN, THE (COL, 1948)
  CARMEN DE LA TRIANA (SPA, 1949)
  CARMEN (NBC–TV, 1953)
  CARMEN (ITA/SPA, 1953)
  CARMEN JONES (FOX, 1954)
  CARMEN DE RONDA, LA (SPA, 1959)
  CARMEN (CBS–TV, 1961)
  CARMEN DE TRASTVERE (FRA/ITA, 1962)
  CARMEN (CZE, 1966)
  CARMEN BABY (IND, 1967)
  HOMME, L'ORGUEIL ET LA VENGEANCE, L' (GER/ITA,
    1968)
  CARMEN (AUS, 1970)

CARMEN, BABY see CARMEN

CARMEN DE RONDA, LA see CARMEN

CARMEN DE TRASTVERE see CARMEN

CARMEN JONES see CARMEN

CARMILLA see STRANGE CASE OF DAVID GRAY, THE

CARNET DU BAL, UN (FRA, 1937, based on a screenplay by
    Julien Duvivier and Ladislas Bus–Fekete)
  LYDIA (UA, 1941)

CARNET DU CABARET see TEN CENTS A DANCE

CARNIVAL see BALLET GIRL, THE

CAROLINE CHERIE (FRA, 1950, based on the book by
    Cecil Saint–Laurent)
  CAROLINE CHERIE (FRA/GER/ITA, 1967)

CAROTTIERS, LES see AMBROSE'S FIRST FALSEHOOD

CAROUSEL see TRIP TO PARADISE, A

CARPETBAGGERS, THE (PAR, 1964, based on the book by
    Harold Robbins)
  NEVADA SMITH (PAR, 1966)
  NEVADA SMITH (NBC–TV, 1975)

CARREFOUR (FRA, 1932, based on a story by Hans Kafka)
  DEAD MAN'S SHOES (BRI, 1939)
  CROSSORADS (MGM, 1942)

CARRIERE D'UNE CHANTEUSE DES RUES, LA (RUS,
    1915, based on the story, "La Victoire inutile," by Anton
    Chekhov)
  FIN DE LA MAISON LOUNTICH, LA (RUS, 1924)

CARRY ON see BETTER 'OLE, THE

CARRY ON, NURSE (BRI, 1960, based on the play, "Ring for
    Catty," by Patrick Cargill and Jack Beale)
  TWICE AROUND THE DAFFODILS (BRI, 1962)

CARTA, LA see LETTER, THE

CARTOUCHE (RKO, 1957, screenplay based on the life of the legendary 18th century highwayman)
CARTOUCHE (FRA, 1964)

CARAVAGGIO (short) (IND, n.d., based on the life of the noted paint.)
CARAVAGGIO AND THE BAROQUE (short) (MHF, 1961)

CARYL OF THE MOUNTAINS (SEL, 1914, based on the story by James Oliver Curwood)
PERILS OF THE WILD (AMB, 1935)

CAS DU DOCTEUR BRENNER, LA see ALIAS THE DOCTOR

CASABLANCA (WB, 1942, based on the play by Murray Burnett and Joan Alison)
WHO HOLDS TOMORROW (NBC–TV, 1955)
CASABLANCA (series) (ABC–TV, 1955)
CHEAP DETECTIVE, THE (COL, 1978)

CASANOVA (HUN, 1918, based on the memoirs of the legendary lover)
CASANOVA'S ERSTE UND LETZTE LIEBE (AUS, 1920)
CASANOVA (ITA, 1927)
LOVES OF CASANOVA (FRA, 1933)
ADVENTURES DE CASANOVA, LES (FRA, 1940)
CASANOVA (FRA/ITA, 1955)
SINS OF CASANOVA (FOX, 1957)
CASANOVA '70 (ITA, 1965)
DERNIERES ROSES DE CASANOVA, LES (CZE, 1966)
CASANOVA, YOUTH AND ADOLESCENCE (ITA, 1969)
CASANOVA (BRI–TV, 1971)
NEW EROTIC ADVENTURES OF CASANOVA, THE (IND, 1978)
CASANOVA AND COMPANY (IND, 1978)

CASANOVA AND COMPANY see CASANOVA

CASANOVA BROWN see LITTLE ACCIDENT

CASANOVA'70 see CASANOVA

CASANOVA, YOUTH AND ADOLESCENCE see CASA–NOVA

CASBAH see PEPE LE MOKO

CASCARRABIAS see GRUMPY

CASE AGAINST PAUL RYKER, THE (NBC–TV, 1963, based on a teleplay by Seeleg Lester)
SERGEANT RYKER (UN, 1968)

CASE FOR A YOUNG HANGMAN, A see GULLIVER'S TRAVELS

CASE FOR DR. MUDD, THE see PRISONER OF SHARK ISLAND, THE

CASE OF BECKY, THE (PAR, 1915, based on the play by Edward Locke)
CASE OF BECKY, THE (REA, 1921)

CASE OF CHARLES PEACE, THE see LIFE OF CHARLES PEACE, THE

CASE OF THE BLACK PARROT, THE see IN THE NEXT ROOM

CASE OF THE FRIGHTENED LADY, THE see FRIGHT–ENED LADY

CASEY AT THE BAT (short) (VIT, 1913, based on the poem by Ernest L. Thayer)
CASEY AT THE BAT (short) (IND, 1920)
CASEY AT THE BAT (PAR,1927)
CASEY BATS AGAIN (short) (DIS, 1953)

CASEY JONES see BRAVE ENGINEER, THE

CASH ON DEMAND (TV, n.d., based on a teleplay by Jacques Gillies)
CASH ON DEMAND (COL, 1962)

CASK OF AMONTILLADO, THE see AVENGING CON–SCIENCE, THE and SEALED ROOM, THE

CASSURE, LA (RUS, 1929, based on the book by Boris Lavreniov)
CASSURE, LA (RUS, 1952)
CASSURE, LA (RUS, 1971)

CASTA DIVA see DIVINE SPARK, THE

CASTE (ED, 1913, based on the play by T.W. Robinson)
CASTE (BRI, 1915)

CASTLE IN THE DESERT see CHINESE PARROT, THE

CASTLE ON THE HUDSON see 20,000 YEARS IN SING SING

CAT AND THE CANARY, THE (UN, 1927, based on the play by John Willard)
GATO, EL (SPA, 1930
CAT CREEPS, THE (UN, 1930)
VOLUNTAD DEL MUERTO, LA (SPA, 1930)
CAT AND THE CANARY, THE (PAR, 1939)
CAT AND THE CANARY, THE (NBC–TV, 1960)
CAT AND THE CANARY, THE (BRI, 1978)

CAT CREEPS see CAT AND THE CANARY

CAT ON A HOT TIN ROOF (MGM, 1958, based on the play by Tennessee Williams)
CAT ON A HOT TIN ROOF (NBC--TV, 1976)

CAT WOMEN OF THE MOON (AST, 1953, source unknown)
MISSILE TO THE MOON (AST, 1959)

CATCH MY SOUL see OTHELLO

CATCH–22 (short) (ABC--TV, n.d., based on the book by Joseph Heller)
CATCH–22 (PAR, 1970)

CATERED AFFAIR, THE (NBC–TV, 1955, based on the teleplay by Paddy Chayefsky)
CATERED AFFAIR, THE (MGM, 1956)

CATERPILLAR see ONCE UPON A TIME

CATHERINE DE RUSSIE see ADVENTUROUS LIFE OF
    CATHERINE I OF RUSSIA

CATHERINE THE GREAT see ADVENTUROUS LIFE OF
    CATHERINE I OF RUSSIA and FORBIDDEN PARA-
    DISE

CATHY COME HOME (BRI–TV, 1966, based on a teleplay
    by Neil Dunn)
    POOR COW (BRI, 1967)

CAUGHT (PAR, 1931, based on the life of the western pioneer)
    CALAMITY JANE AND SAM BASS (UN, 1949)
    CALAMITY JANE (WB, 1953)
    CALAMITY NAMED JANE, A (short) (TV, 1954)
    HEROES AND VILLAINS (sequence) (NET–TV, 1965)

CAUGHT IN THE FOG (WB, 1928, based on the book, "Five
    Fragments," by George Dyer)
    FOG OVER FRISCO (WB, 1934)
    SPY SHIP (WB, 1942)

CAVALCADE (FOX, 1933, based on the play by Noel Coward)
    CAVALCADE (CBS–TV, 1955)

CAVALLERIA RUSTICANNA (ARG, 1909, based on the
    story by Giovanni Verga and the opera by Pietro Mascagni)
    CAVALLERIA RUSTICANNA (FRA, 1909)
    CAVALLERIA RUSTICANNA (ITA, 1916)
    CAVALLERIA RUSTICANNA (ITA, 1917)
    CAVALLERIA RUSTICANNA (ITA, 1925)
    VENDETTA (IND, 1932)
    CAVALLERIA RUSTICANNA (ITA, 1939)
    CAVALLERIA RUSTICANNA (FATAL DESIRE) (ITA,
    1953)

CAVE, THE see PLATO'S CAVE

CAVE OF ALI BABA see ALI BABA

CE COCHON DE MORIN (FRA, 1925, based on a book by
    Guy de Maupassant)
    CE COCHON DE MORIN (FRA, 1933)
    TERREUR DES DAMES, LA (FRA, 1956)

CE N'EST PAS UNE CHOSE SERIEUSE (ITA, 1920, based
    on the play by Luigi Pirandello)
    CE N'EST PAS UNE CHOSE SERIEUSE (ITA, 1936)

CE QUE L'ON NE DIT PAS (POL, 1924, based on the book by
    Gabriela Zapolska)
    CE QUE L'ON NE DIT PAS (POL, 1939)

CEILING ZERO (WB, 1936, based on the play by Frank Wead)
    INTERNATIONAL SQUADRON (WB, 1941)

CEKAJI NA GODOTA (CZE, 1966, based on the play by
    Samuel Beckett)
    WAITING FOR GODOT (NET–TV, 1961)
    WAITING FOR GODOT (NET–TV, 1968)

CELEBRATED JUMPING FROG OF CALAVERAS COUNTY,
    THE see JUMPING FROG

CELL 2455 – DEATH ROW (COL, 1955, based on the life and
    death of Caryl Chessman)
    KILL ME IF YOU CAN (NBC–TV, 1977)

CELLE QUI N'ETAIT PLUS see DIABOLIQUE

CELUI–LA (POL, 1921, based on the book by Gabriela
    Zapolska)
    WARSCHAUER ZITADELLE, DIE (GER, 1930)
    WARSCHAUER ZITADELLA, DIE (GER, 1937)

CENDRILLON see CINDERELLA AND THE FAIRY
    GODMOTHER

CENERENTOLA, LA see CINDERELLA AND THE FAIRY
    GODMOTHER

CERTAIN WOMEN (JAP, 1942, source unknown)
    CERTAIN WOMEN (JAP, 1954)

CESAR see FANNY

CESAR BIROTTEAU (FRA, 1911, based on a story by Honore
    de Balzac)
    CESAR BIROTTEAU (ITA, 1921)

CESAR BORGIA (DEN, 1908, based on a novel by Victor
    Hugo)
    LUCRECE BORGIA (FRA, 1909)
    LUCRECE BORGIA (ITA, 1910)
    LUCRECE BORGIA (ITA, 1910)
    FESTIN DES BORGIA, LE (ITA, 1910)
    ETERNAL SIN, THE (SEZ, 1917)
    BORGIA, LES (ITA, 1919)
    LUKREZIA BORGIA (GER, 1922)
    LUCRECE BORGIA (FRA, 1935)
    LUCRECIA BORGIA (ITA, 1940)
    LUCRECE BORGIA (ARG, 1947)
    NUITS DE LUCRECE BORGIA, LES (FRA/ITA, 1959)
    LUCRECE BORGIA, L'AMANTE DU DEMON (AUS/ITA,
    1968)

C'EST PAS PARCE QU'ON A REIN A DIRE QU'IL FAUT
    FERMER SA GUEULE (FRA, 1976, based on a screen-
    play by Jean Halain and Jacques Bresnard)
    GOING FOR BROKE (ALT PAA ET BRAET) (DEN, 1977)

C'ETAIT UN MUSICIEN see ES WAR EIN MUSIKUS

CHAGALL see GLIMPSE OF THE INNER LIFE OF MARC
    CHAGALL, A

CHAGALL – AN ARTIST'S PRAYER see GLIMPSE OF THE
    INNER LIFE OF MARC CHAGALL, A

CHAGRINLIEDER, DAS see PEAU D'ANE

CHAIKA see SEA GULL, THE

CHAIN LIGHTNING (WB, 1950, based on a story by J.
    Raymond Prior)
    SHOCK WAVE (ABC–TV, 1955)

CHALLENGE, THE (BRI, 1938, based on a screenplay by
    Emeric Pressberger, Patrick Kirwan and Milton Rosmer)
    CHALLENGE, THE (GER, 1938)

CHALLENGE, THE see BULLDOG DRUMMOND IN AFRICA

CHALLENGE FOR ROBIN HOOD see ROBIN HOOD AND
    HIS MERRY MEN

CHALLENGE TO LASSIE (MGM, 1949, based on the book,

"Greyfriar's Bobby," by Eleanor Atkinson
GREYFRIAR'S BOBBY (DIS, 1961)

CHAMBER OF HORRORS (BRI, 1940, based on the book, "Door with the Seven Locks, The," by Edgar Wallace)
DOOR WITH THE SEVEN LOCKS, THE (GER, 1962)
DOOR WITH THE SEVEN LOCKS, THE (BRI, 1965)

CHAMBER OF HORRORS see MYSTERY OF THE WAX MUSEUM

CHAMP, THE (MGM, 1931, based on a story by Frances Marion)
CLOWN, THE (MGM, 1953)
CHAMP, THE (MGM, 1978)

CHAMPAGNE WALTZ (PAR, 1935, based on a story by Billy Wilder and H.S. Kraft)
EMPEROR WALTZ, THE (PAR, 1948)

CHAMPION (UA, 1949, based on a story by Ring Lardner)
CHAMPION (CBS--TV, 1955)

CHANGELING see WOMAN GOD CHANGED, THE

CHANGING OF SILAS MARNER, THE see FAIR EX-CHANGE, A

CHANSON D'UNE NUIT, LES see TELL ME TONIGHT

CHANT DE L'AMOUR TRIOMPHANT, LE see SONG OF LOVE TRIUMPHANT, THE

CHANT DE LA FLEUR ROUGE, LA see DANS LES REMOUS

CHANTEUR DESEVILLE LE see CALL OF THE FLESH

CHAPEAU see ITALIAN STRAW HAT, THE

CHAPEAU DE PAILLE D'ITALIE (FRA, 1911, based on the play by Eugene Labiche, Marc--Michel and Jacques Feydeau; also the basis for two musicals, "Horse Eats Hat" and "Chapeau")
CHAPEAU DE PAILLE D'ITALIE (FRA, 1927)
FLORENTINE HUT, DER (GER, 1939)
CHAPEAU DE PAILLE D'ITALIE (FRA, 1940)
STRAW HAT, THE (CZE, 1971)

CHAPTER IN HER LIFE, A see JEWELL

CHARGE OF THE LIGHT BRIGADE, THE (BIO, 1903, based on the poem by Alfred, Lord Tennyson)
CHARGE OF THE LIGHT BRIGADE, THE (ED, 1912)
CHARGE OF THE LIGHT BRIGADE, THE (BRI, 1914)
JAWS OF HELL (BRI, 1928)
CHARGE OF THE LIGHT BRIGADE, THE (WB, 1936)
CHARGE OF THE LIGHT BRIGADE, THE (BRI, 1968)

CHARIOTS OF THE GODS see IN SEARCH OF ANCIENT ASTRONAUTS

CHARLATAN, THE (BRI, 1916, based on the play by Ernest Pascal and George Praskins)
CHARLATAN, THE (UN, 1929)

CHARLEMAGNE AND HIS EMPIRE (short) (COR, 1961, based on the life of the noted conqueror)
CHARLEMAGNE: UNIFIER OF EUROPE (short)

(EBE, 1964)
CHARLEMAGNE: HOLY BARBARIAN (short) (LCA, 1968)

CHARLES DE GAULLE see TRIALS OF CHARLES DE GAULLE, THE

CHARLES DICKENS: BACKGROUND FOR HIS WORKS see DICKENS WALKED HERE

CHARLES DICKENS CHRISTMAS, A see PICKWICK PAPERS, THE

CHARLES DICKENS SHOW, THE see CHRISTMAS CAROL, A, LITTLE EMILY, and OLD CURIOSITY SHOP, THE

CHARLES PEACE, KING OF CRIMINALS see LIFE OF CHARLES PEACE, THE

CHARLEY'S AUNT PDC, 1925, based on the play by Brandon Thomas)
CHARLEYS' AUNT (SWE, 1926)
CHARLEY'S AUNT (COL, 1930
CHARLEY'S TANTE (GER, 1934)
MARRAINE DE CHARLEY, LA (FRA, 1935)
CHARLEY'S (BIG HEARTED) AUNT (BRI, 1939)
CHARLEY'S AUNT (FOX, 1940)
WHERE'S CHARLEY? (WB, 1951)
CHARLEY'S TANTE (GER, 1956)
CHARLEY'S AUNT (CBS--TV, 1957)
MARRAINE DE CHARLEY, LA (FRA, 1959)
CHARLEY'S TANTE (AUS, 1963)
CHARLEY'S AUNT (BRI--TV, 1967)
CHARLEY'S AUNT IN A MINI--SKIRT (SPA, 1967)

CHARLEY'S AUNT IN A MINI--SKIRT see CHARLEY'S AUNT

CHARLEY'S TANTE see CHARLEY'S AUNT

CHARLIE CHAN CARRIES ON (FOX, 1931, based on the book by Earl Derr Diggers)
ERAN TRECE (SPA, 1931)
CHARLIE CHAN'S MURDER CRUISE (FOX, 1940)

CHARLIE CHAN'S COURAGE see CHINESE PARROT, THE

CHARLIE CHAN'S GREATEST CASE see HOUSE WITH-OUT A KEY, THE

CHARLIE CHAN'S MURDER CRUISE see CHARLIE CHAN CARRIES ON

CHARLIE'S ANGELS (ABC--TV, 1976, based on a teleplay)
CHARLIE'S ANGELS (series) (ABC--TV, 1976)

CHARLY see TWO WORLDS OF CHARLY GORDON, THE

CHARM OF LA BOHEME, THE see VIE DE BOHEME, LA

CHARM SCHOOL (PAR, 1921, based on a story by Alice Duer Miller)
SOMEONE TO LOVE (PAR, 1928)
COLLEGIATE (PAR, 1936)

CHARMING SINNERS (PAR, 1929, based play, "The Constant Wife, W. by W. Somerset Maugham)

FINDEN SIE, DASS CONSTANZE SICH RICHTIG VER–
HALT? (GER, 1962)

CHARTERHOUSE OF PARMA, THE (FRA, source unknown)
BEFORE THE REVOLUTION (ITA, 1967)
CHARTERHOUSE OF PARMA, THE (FRA, 1969)

CHASE, THE (UA, 1946, based on the book, "The Black
Path of Fear," by Cornell Woolrich)
CHASE, THE (NBC–TV, 1954)

CHASE, THE see NUISANCE, THE

CHASER, THE see NUISANCE, THE

CHASING YESTERDAY see CRIME DE SYLVESTRE
BONNARD, LA

CHASSEUR DE CHEZ MAXIM'S, LE (FRA, 1927, based on
the play by Yves Mirande and Gustave Quinson)
CHASSUUR DE CHEZ MAXIM'S, LE (FRA, 1939)
CHASSEUR DE CHEZ MAXIM'S LE, (FRA, 1953)

CHAT BOTTE, LE (FRA, 1903, based on the story by Charles
Perrault)
CHAT BOTTE, LE (FRA, 1908)

CHATEAU HISTORIQUE (FRA, 1923, based on material by
Alexandre Bisson and Julien Berr de Turique)
FEMMES SONT FOLIES, LES (FRA, 1950)

CHATELAINE DU LIBAN, LA (FRA, 1926, based on a book
by Pierre Benoit)
CHATELAINE DU LIBAN, LA (FRA, 1933)
CHATELAINE DU LIBAN, LA (FRA, 1956)

CHATTERBOX, THE see SMOOTH AS SATIN

CHEAP DETECTIVE, THE see CASABLANCA and
MALTESE FALCON, THE

CHEAT, THE (PAR, 1915, based on a story by Hector Turn–
bull)
CHEAT, THE (PAR, 1923)
CHEAT, THE (PAR, 1931)
FORFAITURE (FRA, 1937)

CHEATING CHEATERS (SEL, 1919, based on a play by Max
Marcin)
CHEATING CHEATERS (UN, 1927)
CHEATING CHEATERS (UN, 1934)

CHECKERS (FOX, 1919, based on a story by Henry Blossom)
CHECKERS (FOX, 1938)

CHEHERAZADE see ARABIAN NIGHTS

CHEMIN DU PARADIS, LE see DREI VON DER TANK--
STELLE, DIE

CHEMINEAU, LE (FRA, 1906, based on the book, "Les
Miserables," by Victor Hugo)
PRICE OF A SOUL (ED, 1909)
GALLERY SLAVE, THE (VIT, 1910)
MISERABLES, LES (FRA, 1911)
MISERABLES, LES (BRI, 1912)
MISERABLES, LES (FOX, 1917)
MISERABLES, LES (short) (BRI, 1922)
MISERABLES, LES (UN, 1925)

MISERABLES, LES (FRA, 1925)
MISERABLES, LES (UN, 1927)
BISHOP'S CANDLESTICKS, THE (PAR, 1929)
JEAN VALJEAN (JAP, 1929)
MISERABLES, LES (FRA, 1933)
MISERABLES, LES (UA, 1935)
GAVROCHE (RUS, 1937)
MISERABLES, LES (MEX, 1943)
MISERABLES, LES (ITA, 1946)
MISERABLES, LES (JAP, 1950)
MISERABLES, LES (FRA, 1952)
MISERABLES, LES (FOX, 1952)
BISHOP'S CANDLESTICKS, THE (CBS–TV, 1953)
MISERABLES, LES (IN, 1955)
MISERABLES, LES (FRA/ITA, 1957)
MISERABLE ONES, THE (TUR, 1967)

CHEMINEAU, LE (FRA, 1917, based on the book by Jean
Richepin)
CHEMINEAU, LE (FRA, 1927)
CHEMINEAU, LE (FFA, 1935)

CHERI see COME OUT OF THE KITCHEN

CHERI–BIBI (FRA, 1913, based on the book by Gaston
Leroux)
CHERI--BIBI (FRA, 1914)
NOUVELLE AURORE, LA (FRA, 1919)
PHANTOM OF PARIS, THE (MGM, 1931)
CHERI--BIBI (SPA, 1931)
FANTOME DE PAIRS, LE (FRA, 1931)
CHERI–BIBI (FRA, 1937)
CHERI–BIBI (FRA/ITA, 1955)

CHERIE see BUS STOP

CHESS PLAYER, THE (FRA, 1927, source unknown)
CHESS PLAYER, THE (FRA, 1937)

CHEVALIER DE MAISON--ROUGE, LE (FRA, 1912, based
on the novel by Alexandre Dumas (pere)
PRINCE AU MASQUE ROUGE, LE (ITA, 1953)

CHEVALIER DE PARDAILLAN, LE (FRA/ITA, 1962, based
on the book, "Pardaillan," by Michel Zevaco)
HARDI, PARDAILLAN (FRA/ITA, 1964)

CHEVRE AUX PIEDS D'OR, LA (FRA, 1926, based on a
novel by Charles--Henry Hirsch)
DANSEUSE ROUGE, LA (FRA, 1937)

CHEYENNE (WB, 1947, based on a screenplay by Alan LeMay
and Thames Williamson)
CHEYENNE (series) (ABC–TV, 1955)

CHICAGO (PAT, 1927, based on the play by Maurine Watkins)
ROXIE HART (FOX, 1942)

CHICAGO DEADLINE (PAR, 1949, based on a screenplay by
Tiffany Thayer)
FAME IS THE NAME OF THE GAME (UN, 1966)

CHICAGO PICASSO, THE see PICASSO: LE PEINTRE ET
SON MODELE

CHICK (BRI, 1928, based on the book by Edgar Wallace)
CHICK (BRI, 1936)

CHICKEN EVERY SUNDAY (FOX, 1949, based on the book

by Rosemary Taylor and the play by Julius and Philip Epstein)
HEFFERNAN FAMILY, THE (CBS–TV, 1956)

CHICKEN WAGON FAMILY see DIXIE MERCHANT

CHICKENS COME HOME see LOVE 'EM AND WEEP

CHIEN JAUNE, LE (FRA, 1932, based on the book by Georges Simenon)
CHIEN JAUNE, LE (FRA–TV, 1968)

CHIENNE, LA (FRA, 1931, based on the book by Georges de la Fouchardiere)
SCARLET STREET (UN, 1945)

CHILD IS BORN, A see LIFE BEGINS

CHILD IS WAITING, A (CBS–TV, 1957, based on the tele–play by Abby Mann)
CHILD IS WAITING, A (UA, 1963)

CHILD OF DIVORCE see WEDNESDAY'S CHILD

CHILD OF FATE see MYSTERIES OF PARIS

CHILDREN HAND IN HAND (JAP, 1947, source unknown)
CHILDREN HAND IN HAND (JAP, 1962)

CHILDREN OF CAPTAIN GRANT, THE see IN SEARCH OF THE CASTAWAYS

CHILDREN OF THE SUN see MARCH AU SOLEIL, LE

CHILDREN'S HOUR, THE see THESE THREE

CHIMES AT MIDNIGHT see MERRY WIVES OF WINDSOR, THE

CHIMP, THE see ANGORA LOVE

CHINA: THE SOCIAL REVOLUTION see RED CHINA

CHINESE BUNGALOW, THE (BRI, 1926, based on the play by Mathieson Lang and Marian Osmond)
CHINESE BUNGALOW, THE (BRI, 1931)
CHINESE DEN (BRI, 1941)

CHINESE DEN see CHINESE BUNGALOW, THE

CHINESE NIGHTINGALE, THE see EMPEROR'S NIGHT–INGALE, THE

CHINESE PARROT, THE (UN, 1927, based on the book by Earl Derr Biggers)
CHARLIE CHAN'S COURAGE (FOX, 1934)
CASTLE IN THE DESERT (FOX, 1942)

CHINESE PRINCESS WHITE SNOW see SNOW WHITE

CHINESE PUZZLE (BRI, 1919, based on the play by Leon M. Lion and Frances Barclay)
CHINESE PUZZLE (BRI, 1932)

CHINESE RING, THE see MR. WONG IN CHINATOWN

CHING, CHING, CHINAMAN see SHADOWS

CHIP OF THE FLYING U (SEL, 1914, based on the book by B.M. Bower)

CHIP OF THE FLYING U (UN, 1926)
CHIP OF THE FLYING U (UN, 1939)

CHIRURGIE (RUS, 1909, based on the book by Anton Chekhov)
CHIRURGIE (RUS, 1939)

CHOCOLATE SOLDIER, THE (IND, 1914, based on the play, "Arms and the Man," by George Bernard Shaw. Also the basis for Oscar Straus' operetta, "The Chocolate Soldier," in 1908)
ARMS AND THE MAN (BRI, 1932)
ARMS AND THE MAN (GER, 1938)
ARMS AND THE MAN (CBS–TV, 1953)
CHOCOLATE SOLDIER, THE (NBC–TV, 1955)
ARMS AND THE MAN (NBC–TV, 1957)
HEROES (HELDEN) (GER, 1958)

CHOCOLATE SOLDIER, THE see also GUARDSMAN, THE

CHOEKI JAHACHINEN (JAP, n.d., source unlisted)
CHOEKI JAHACHINEN – KARI SHUTSUGOKU (JAP, 1967)

CHOPIN see LIFE OF CHOPIN, THE

CHOPINIANA see SYLPHIDES, LES

CHORAL VON LEUTEHEN, DER (GER, 1933, based on the book by Walter von Molo)
FRIDERICUS (GER, 1936)

CHORUS LADY, THE (PAR, 1915, based on the play by James Forbes)
CHORUS LADY, THE (PDC, 1924)

CHRIST see LIFE OF CHRIST, THE

CHRISTIAN, THE (VIT, 1914, based on the book by Hall Caine)
CHRISTIAN, THE (BRI, 1915)
CHRISTIAN, THE (MGM, 1922)

CHRISTINE see LIEBELEI

CHRISTMAS AT THE NOEDEBO VICARAGE (DEN, 1934, source unknown)
NOEDEBO VICARAGE (DEN, 1974)

CHRISTMAS CAROL, A (BRI, 1901, based on the book by Charles Dickens. Also the basis for a Canadian musical, "Mr. Scrooge," in 1963)
CHRISTMAS CAROL, A (ED, 1910)
DREAM OF OLD SCROOGE (ITA, 1910)
SCROOGE (IND, 1912)
SCROOGE (BRI, 1913)
CHRISTMAS CAROL, A (BRI, 1914)
RIGHT TO BE HAPPY, THE (UN, 1916)
SCROOGE (short) (BRI, 1922)
SCROOGE (BRI, 1923)
SCROOGE (short) (BRI, 1928)
SCROOGE (BRI, 1935)
CHRISTMAS CAROL, A (MGM, 1938)
CHRISTMAS CAROL, A (BRI, 1951)
CHRISTMAS CAROL, A (ABC–TV, 1953)
CHRISTMAS CAROL, A (CBS–TV, 1954)
STINGIEST MAN IN TOWN, THE (NBC–TV, 1956)
CHRISTMAS CAROL, A (short) (BRI, 1960)
MR. MAGOO'S CHRISTMAS CAROL (NBC–TV, 1962)
SCROOGE (BRI, 1970)

CHRISTMAS CAROL, A (AUT–TV, 1970)
CHRISTMAS CAROL, A (ABC–TV, 1971)
CHARLES DICKENS SHOW, THE (BRI, 1973)
PASSION OF CAROL, THE (IND, 1975)
HONEYMOONER'S CHRISTMAS SPECIAL, THE (ABC–
    TV, 1977)
ENERGY CAROL, AN (short) (CAN–1977)

CHRISTMAS IN CONNECTICUT (WB, 1945, based on a story
    by Aileen Hamilton)
CHRISTMAS IN CONNECTICUT (NBC–TV, 1956)

CHRISTMAS IN JULY (PAR, 1940, based on a screenplay
    by Preston Sturges)
CHRISTMAS IN JULY (NBC–TV, 1954)

CHRISTMAS NIGHT (RUS, 1913, based on a story by Nikolai
    Gogol)
CHRISTMAS NIGHT (RUS, 1928)
CHRISTMAS NIGHT (RUS, 1952)
CHRISTMAS NIGHT (RUS, 1961)

CHRISTOPHER BEAN see PRENEZ GARDE A LA PEIN–
    TURE

CHRISTOPHER COLUMBUS see COMING OF COLUMBUS

CHRISTUS see PASSION PLAY, THE

CHRONICLE OF ANNA MAGDELENA BACH see JOHANN
    SEBASTIAN BACH

CHRONICLES OF AMERICA: ALEXANDER HAMILTON
    (short) (IND, 1923, based on the life of statesman
    Alexander Hamilton)
ALEXANDER HAMILTON (WB, 1931)
ALEXANDER HAMILTON (short) (EBE, 1951)
HAMILTON–BURR DUEL (short) (CBS–TV, 1956)
LAUNCHING THE NEW GOVERNMENT 1789–1800
    (short) (COR, 1958)

CHRONICLES OF AMERICA: COLUMBUS see COMING
    OF COLUMBUS, THE

CHRONICLES OF AMERICA: DANIEL BOONE (short)
    (IND, 1923, based on the life of American trailblazer)
DANIEL BOONE THRU THE WILDERNESS (SUN, 1926)
DANIEL BOONE (RKO, 1936)
DANIEL BOONE (short) (EBE, 1950)
YOUNG DANIEL BOONE (MON, 1950)
DANIEL BOONE, TRAILBLAZER (REP, 1956)
DANIEL BOONE (series) (NBC–TV, 1964)
DANIEL BOONE IN AMERICA'S STORY (short) (COR,
    1968)
YOUNG DAN'L BOONE (CBS–TV, 1977)

CHRONICLES OF AMERICA: WOLFE AND MONTCALM
    (short) (IND, 1923, based on the lives and exploits of
    explorers Wolf and Montcalm)
WOLFE AND MONTCALM (short) (CAN, 1958)

CHU CHIN CHOW see ALI BABA AND THE FORTY
    THIEVES

CHUANG–TSE TESTS HIS WIFE (CHN, 1913, based on the
    opera, "Cosi Fan Tutte," by Wolfgang Amadeus Mozart)
THEY ALL DO IT (DEN, 1956)

CHUMP AT OXFORD, A see FROM SOUP TO NUTS

CHURCH MOUSE, THE see BEAUTY AND THE BOSS

CHURCHILL – CHAMPION OF FREEDOM see CHURCH–
    ILL – MAN OF THE CENTURY

CHURCHILL – MAN OF THE CENTURY (short) (BRI,
    1955, based on the life of the British prime minister)
CHURCHILL – MAN OF THE CENTURY (CBS–TV,
    1957)
VALIANT YEARS, THE (series) ((TV, 1961)
CHURCHILL OBITUARY (BRI–TV, 1965)
CHURCHILL – CHAMPION OF FREEDOM (short) (BRI,
    1965)
FIRST CHURCHILLS, THE (series) (BRI–TV, 1971)
OTHER WORLD OF WINSTON CHURCHILL, THE (BRI–
    TV, 1967)
CHURCHILL THE MAN (TV, 1972)
YOUNG WINSTON (BRI, 1972)
GATHERING STORM, THE (NBC–TV, 1974)

CHURCHILL OBITUARY see CHURCHILL – MAN OF THE
    CENTURY

CHURCHILL THE MAN see CHURCHILL – MAN OF THE
    CENTURY

CHUTE DE TROIE, LA (ITA, 1910, based on the book, "The
    Iliad," by Homer)
HELENA, DER UNTERGANG TROJAS (GER, 1924)
PRIVATE LIFE OF HELEN OF TROY (FN, 1927)
HELEN OF TROY (SWE, 1951)
FACE THAT LAUNCHED A THOUSAND SHIPS, THE
    (ITA, 1954)
HELEN OF TROY (WB, 1956)

CIAO, GULLIVER see GULLIVER'S TRAVELS

CID, LE (ITA, 1910, based on a book by Guillen de Castro
    and Pierre Corneille)
CID, EL (AA, 1961)
BURGOS SOLAR DEL CID (short) (SPA, n.d.)

CIGALE, LA (RUS, 1915, based on the book by Anton Chekhov)
CIGALE, LA (RUS, 1955)

CIGALE ET LA FOURMI, LA (FRA, 1897, based on a fable
    by Jean de la Fontaine)
CIGALE ET LA FOURMI, LA (FRA, 1909)
JUGENDRAUSCH (GER,1927)
CIGALE ET LA FOURMI, LA (FRA, 1954)

CIMARRON (RKO, 1931, based on the book by Edna Ferber)
CIMARRON (MGM, 1961)

CINDER ELFRED see CINDERELLA AND THE FAIRY
    GODMOTHER

CINDERELLA see CINDERELLA AND THE FAIRY GOD–
    MOTHER

CINDERELLA AND THE FAIRY GODMOTHER (BRI,
    1898, based on the story by Charles Perrault, the opera
    by G. Rossini and the ballet by Serge Prokofiev. Also the
    basis for the British musical, "I Gotta Shoe"
CENDRILLON (FRA, 1899)
CINDERELLA (BRI, 1900)
CENDRILLON (FRA, 1905)
CINDERELLA (BRI, 1907)
CENDRILLON (FRA, 1907)

CENERENTOLA, LA (ITA, 1909)
CINDERELLA (THA, 1911)
CINDERELLA (SEL, 1912)
MAGIC SLIPPERS, THE (FRA, 1912)
CINDERELLA (BRI, 1912)
CINDERELLA'S SLIPPER (VIT, 1913)
MAGIC SLIPPERS, THE (ITA, 1913)
CINDERELLA (BRI, 1913)
MAGIC SLIPPERS, THE (PAR, 1914)
CINDER ELFRED (BRI, 1914)
ASCHENBROEDEL (GER, 1914)
CRIPPLED HAND, THE (UN, 1916)
CINDERELLA AND THE MAGIC SLIPPERS (WHO, 1917)
CINDERELLA (PAR, 1918)
ASCHENPUTTE (GER, 1922)
VERLORENE SCHUH, DER (GER, 1923)
CINDERELLA'S FELLER (short) (WB, 1940)
CINDERELLA (CBS–TV, 1942)
CINDERELLA ON STRINGS (AUT, 1947)
MAGIC SLIPPERS, THE (RUS, 1947)
CINDERELLA (CBS–TV, 1947)
MAGIC SLIPPERS, THE (ITA, 1948)
CINDERELLA (DIS, 1949)
CINDERELLA (HOL, 1953)
CINDERELLA (short) (BRI, 1954)
GLASS SLIPPER, THE (MGM, 1955)
CINDERELLA (IND, 1956)
CINDERELLA (CBS–TV, 1957)
CINDERELLA (short) (IND, 1958)
CINDERFELLA (PAR, 1960)
GLASS SLIPPER, THE (RUS, 1960)
GLASS SLIPPER, THE (GER, 1963)
GLASS SLIPPER, THE (ITA, 1963)
CINDERELLA (CBS–TV, 1965)
GLASS SLIPPER, THE (GER, 1966)
CINDERELLA (CHI, 1966)
CINDERELLA (short) (CAN, 1967)
HEY, CINDERELLA (CBS–TV, 1969)
SOULIERS DE CENTRILLON, LES (RUM, 1969)
CINDERELLA (RAN, 1972)
CINDERELLA (IND–TV, 1972)
SLIPPER AND THE ROSE, THE (BRI, 1975)
3 NUTS FOR CINDERELLA (CZE, 1975)
CINDERELLA (IND, 1977)
CINDERELLA 2000 (IND, 1977)
CINDY (ABC–TV, 1978)

CINDERELLA ON STRINGS see CINDERELLA AND THE
FAIRY GODMOTHER

CINDERELLA 2000 see CINDERELLA AND THE FAIRY
GODMOTHER

CINDERELLA'S FELLER see CINDERELLA AND THE
FAIRY GODMOTHER

CINDERELLA'S SLIPPER see CINDERELLA AND THE
FAIRY GODMOTHER

CINDERFELLA see CINDERELLA AND THE FAIRY
GODMOTHER

CINDY see CINDERELLA AND THE FAIRY GODMOTHER

CINQ GENTLEMEN MAUDITS, LES (FRA, 1931, source
unknown)
FUNF VERFLUCHTEN GENTLEMEN (GER, 1931)

CINQ SOUS DE LAVAREDE, LES (FRA, 1913, based on a
story by Paul d'Ivoi and Henri Chabrillat)
CINQ SOUS DE LAVAREDE, LES (FRA, 1927)
CINQ SOUS DE LAVAREDE, LES (FRA, 1938)

CIRCLE, THE (MGM, 1925, based on the play by W. Somerset
Maugham)
STRICTLY UNCONVENTIONAL (MGM, 1930)

CIRCLE OF LOVE see RONDE, LA

CIRCULAR STAIRCASE, THE (SEL, 1915, based on the book
by Mary Roberts Rinehart)
BAT, THE (UA, 1926)
BAT WHISPERS, THE (UA, 1931)
CIRCULAR STAIRCASE, THE (CBS–TV, 1956)
BAT, THE (AA, 1959)
BAT, THE (NBC–TV, 1960)

CIRCUS DAYS (FN, 1923, based on the book, "Toby Tyler,"
by James Otis)
TOBY TYLER (DIS, 1959)

CIRCUS OF FEAR see PSYCHO–CIRCUS

CIRCUS TRAGEDY (SWE, 1943, based on an actual incident)
ELVIRA MADIGAN (SWE, 1968)

CISCO KID, THE see BORDER TERROR, THE

CISSY see KING STEPS OUT, THE

CITADEL, THE (MGM, 1938, based on the book by A.J.
Cronin)
CITADEL, THE (NBC–TV, 1950)

CITIES AND YEARS (RUS, n.d., source unknown)
CITIES AND YEARS (GER/RUS, 1974)

CITY AFTER MIDNIGHT see THAT WOMAN OPPOSITE

CITY LIMITS (MON, 1934, based on the book by Jack Wood--
ford)
FATHER STEPS OUT (MON, 1941)

CITY OF BEAUTIFUL NONSENSE, THE (BRI, 1919, based
on the book by Ernest Temple Thurston)
WORLD OF WONDERFUL REALITY, THE (BRI, 1924)
CITY OF BEAUTIFUL NONSENSE, THE (BRI, 1935)

CITY OF SILENT MEN (PAR, 1921, based on the book, "The
Quarry," by John A. Moroso)
SHADOW OF THE LAW (PAR, 1930)

CITY STREETS see LADIES OF THE MOB

CIVIL WAR: POSTWAR PERIOD see TENNESSEE JOHN–
SON

CLAIRVOYANT, THE (BRI, 1935, based on the book by
Ernst Lothar)
PREDICTION, THE (NBC–TV, 1960)

CLARA SCHUMANN STORY, THE see SONG OF LOVE

CLARENCE (PAR, 1922, based on the play by Booth Tarking–
ton)
CLARENCE (PAR, 1931)
CLARENCE (PAR, 1937)

CLARENCE, THE CROSS–EYED LION (ABC–TV, 1965, based on a screenplay by Art Arthur and Marshall Thomp–son)
DAKTARI (series) (CBS–TV, 1966)

CLASH BY NIGHT (RKO, 1952, based on the play by Clifford Odets)
CLASH BY NIGHT (CBS–TV, 1957)

CLAUDIA (FOX, 1943, based on the play by Rose Franken)
CLAUDIA (series) (NBC–TV, 1952)

CLAW, THE (SEL, 1918, based on the book by Cynthia Stockley)
CLAW, THE (UN, 1927)

CLAW MONSTER, THE see PANTHER GIRL OF THE KONGO

CLEMENCEAU CASE, THE (IND, 1915, based on the book, "L'Affaire Clemenceau" by Aledandre Dumas (fils)
FALL DOBRONOWSKA, DER (GER, 1917)
AFFAIRE CLEMENCEAU, L' (ITA, 1918)

CLEOPATRA (FRA, 1910, based on historical incidents and characters and the book by Plutarch)
CLEOPATRA (IND, 1912)
CLEOPATRA (FOX, 1917)
CLEOPATRA, QUEEN OF THE NILE (GER, 1911)
CLEOPATRA (PAR, 1934)
INTIMATE LIFE OF MARK ANTHONY AND CLEOPATRA, THE (MEX, 1946)
SERPENT OF THE NILE (COL, 1953)
LEGIONS OF THE NILE (ITA, 1959)
QUEEN FOR CAESAR, A (FRA, 1962)
CLEOPATRA (FOX, 1963)

CLEOPATRA, QUEEN OF THE NILE see CLEOPATRA

CLERK AND THE COAT, THE see OVERCOAT, THE

CLIMAX, THE (UN, 1930, based on the play by Edward Locke)
CLIMAX, THE (UN, 1944)

CLIMBERS, THE (LUB, 1915, based on the play by Clyde Fitch)
CLIMBERS, THE (VIT, 1919)
CLIMBERS, THE (WB, 1927)

CLOAK, THE see OVERCOAT, THE

CLOCHEMERLE see SCANDALS OF CLOCHEMERLE, THE

CLOCKWORK ORANGE, A see VINYL

CLOWN, THE (SWE, n.d., source unknown)
CLOWN, THE (SWE, 1926)

CLOWN, THE see CHAMP, THE

CLUB DE FEMMES (FRA, 1936, based on a book by Jacques Deval)
CLUB DE FEMMES (FRA/ITA, 1956)

CLUE OF THE NEW PIN, THE (BRI, 1929, based on the book by Edgar Wallace)
CLUE OF THE NEW PIN, THE (BRI, 1961)

COAST OF THE SKELETONS see SANDERS OF THE RIVER

COCU MAGNIFIQUE, LE (BEL, 1946, based on a book by Fernand Crommelnyck)
COCU MAGNIFIQUE, LE (FRA/ITA, 1964)

CODE OF THE MOUNTED see WHEELS OF FATE, THE

CODE OF THE WEST (PAR, 1925, based on the book by Zane Grey)
HOME ON THE RANGE (PAR, 1934)
CODE OF THE WEST (RKO, 1947)

CODE 645 see G–MEN NEVER FORGET

CODIGO PENAL, EL see CRIMINAL CODE, THE

COEUR DE LA CASBAH, AU see PHAEDRA

COIFFEUR POUR DAMES (FRA, 1931, source unlisted)
COIFFEUR POUR DAMES (FRA, 1952)

COLE YOUNGER, GUNFIGHTER see DESPERADO, THE

COLLEEN BAWN, THE (AUT, 1911, based on the play by Dion Boucicault)
LILY OF KILLARNEY (short) (BRI, 1922)
COLLEEN BAWN, THE (BRI, 1924)
LILY OF KILLARNEY (BRI, 1929)
LILY OF KILLARNEY (BRI, 1934)

COLLEGE SCANDAL, (PAR, 1935, based on a story by Beulah Marie Dix and Bertram Millhauser)
SWEATER GIRL (PAR, 1942)

COLLEGE WIDOW (LUB, 1915, based on the play by George Ade. Also the basis for the musical comedy, "Leave it to Jane," by Jerome Kern in 1917)
COLLEGE WIDOW (WB, 1927)
FAIR CO–ED (MGM, 1927)
FRESHMAN LOVE (WB, 1936)

COLLEGIATE see SOMEONE TO LOVE

COLLIER DE LA REINE (FRA, 1912, based on the book by Alexandre Dumas (pere)
COLLIER DE LA REINE (FRA, 1929)
COLLIER DE LA REINE (FRA, 1946)

COLLUSION see UNKNOWN BLONDE

COLOMBA (FRA, 1920, based on the book by Prosper Merimee)
COLOMBA (FRA, 1947)
VENDETTA (RKO, 1950)
COLOMBA (FRA, 1953)
COLOMBA (FRA–TV, 1968)

COLONEL CHABERT (FRA, 1910, based on the book by Honore de Balzac)
COLONEL CHABERT (GER, 1918)
COLONEL CHABERT (ITA, 1920)
COLONEL CHABERT (FRA, 1924)
COLONEL CHABERT (GER, 1932)
COLONEL CHABERT (FRA, 1943)

COLOR ME DEAD see D.O.A.

COLORADO (UN, 1915, based on the play by Augustus Thomas)
  COLORADO (UN, 1921)

COLORADO TERRITORY see HIGH SIERRA

COLT .45 (WB, 1950, based on a screenplay by Thomas Blackburn)
  COLT .45 (series) (ABC–TV, 1958)

COMBAT, THE (VIT, 1919, based on a story by Edward J. Montagne and Ralph Ince)
  COMBAT, THE (UN, 1926)

COME BACK, LITTLE SHEBA (PAR, 1952, based on the play by William Inge)
  COME BACK, LITTLE SHEBA (NBC–TV, 1977)

COME CLEAN (short) (MGM, 1931, based on a screenplay by H.M. Walker and elaborated upon in the remake)
  BROOKLYN ORCHID (UA, 1942)

COME ON, DANGER (RKO, 1932, based on a story by Bennett Cohen)
  RENEGADE RANGER (RKO, 1939)
  OKLAHOMA RAIDERS (UN, 1944)

COME OUT OF THE KITCHEN (PAR, 1919, based on a story by Alice Duer Miller; also the basis of the musical comedy, "The Magnolia Lady," in 1924)
  HONEY (PAR, 1930)
  SALGA DE LA COCINA (SPA, 1930)
  JEDE FRAU HAT ETWAS (GER, 1930)
  CHERI (FRA, 1931)
  COME OUT OF THE PANTRY (BRI, 1935)
  SPRING IN PARK LANE (BRI, 1948)

COME OUT OF THE PANTRY see COME OUT OF THE KITCHEN

COMEDY OF ERRORS, A (VIT, 1908, based on the play by William Shakespeare)
  BOYS FROM SYRACUSE, THE (UN, 1940)
  COMEDY OF ERRORS (NBC–TV, 1949)
  COMEDY OF ERRORS (GER, 1964)

COMING OF CHRIST, THE see PASSION PLAY, THE

COMIN' THRO' THE RYE (BRI, 1916, based on the book by Helen Mathers)
  COMIN' THRO' THE RYE (BRI, 1924)

COMIN' THRO' THE RYE see LIFE OF ROBERT BRUNS, THE

COMING OF COLUMBUS, THE (SEL, 1912, based on the life of the noted explorer)
  CHRISTOPHER COLUMBUS (GER, 1922)
  CHRONICLES OF AMERICA: COLUMBUS (short) (IND, 1923)
  CRISTOFORO COLOMBO (ITA, 1937)
  STORY OF CHRISTOPHER COLUMBUS, THE (short) (EBE, 1948)
  CHRISTOPHER COLUMBUS (BRI, 1949)
  CHRISTOPHER COLUMBUS (short) (EBE, 1954)
  STORY OF CHRISTOPHER COLUMBUS, THE (short) (UNI, n.d.)
  CHRISTOPHER COLUMBUS (short) (CHU, 1962)
  CHRISTOPHER COLUMBUS (short) (MAC, 1964)

COMME TU ME VEUX see AS YOU DESIRE ME

COMMISSIONER MANAGES THE TOWN WELL, THE (ARG, 1936, based on the play by Claudio Martinez Payva)
  COMMISSIONER MANAGES THE TOWN WELL, THE (ARG, 1967)

COMMON CLAY (PAT, 1919, based on the play by Cleves Kinkead)
  COMMON CLAY (FOX, 1930)
  DEL MISMO BARRO (SPA, 1930)
  PRIVATE NUMBER (FOX, 1936)

COMMON LAW IND, 1916, based on the book by Robert W. Chambers)
  COMMON LAW (SEZ, 1923)

CONCERT, THE (GOL, 1921, based on the book and play by Hermann Bahr)
  FASHIONS IN LOVE (PAR, 1929)
  KONZERT, DAS (GER, 1931)
  DELPHINE (FRA, 1931)
  KONZERT, DAS (GER, 1944)
  NICHTS ALS ARGER MIT DER LIEBE (AUS, 1956)

CONDE DE MONTE CRISTO, EL see COUNT OF MONTE CRISTO

CONDEMNED MEN see WHITE ZOMBIE

CONEY ISLAND (FOX, 1943, based on a screenplay by George Seaton)
  WABASH AVENUE (FOX, 1950)

CONFESSION see MAZURKA and WIFE TRAP, THE

CONFLICT see ABYSMAL BRUTE, THE

CONGO LANDING see RED DUST

CONGO MAISIE see RED DUST

CONGRES S'AMUSE, LE see CONGRESS DANCES

CONGRESS DANCES (UA, 1932, based on a story by Norbert Falk)
  CONGRES S'AMUSE, LE (FRA, 1932)
  KONGRESS TANZT, DER (GER, 1932)
  CONGRESS DANCES (REP, 1957)

CONJURE WIFE see WEIRD WOMAN

CONN THE SHAUGRAUN see MURPHY'S WAKE

CONNECTICUT RABBIT IN KING ARTHUR'S COURT, A see CONNECTICUT YANKEE IN KING ARTHUR'S COURT, A.

CONNECTICUT YANKEE, A see CONNECTICUT YANKEE IN KING ARTHUR'S COURT, A

CONNECTICUT YANKEE IN KING ARTHUR'S COURT, A (FOX, 1921, based on the book by Mark Twain. Also the basis of a musical comedy, "A Connecticut Yankee," in 1927.
  CONNECTICUT YANKEE, A (FOX, 1931)
  CONNECTICUT YANKEE, A (PAR, 1949)
  CONNECTICUT YANKEE IN KING ARTHUR'S COURT, A (ABC–TV, 1954)

CONNECTICUT YANKEE, A (NBC–TV, 1955)
CONNECTICUT YANKEE IN KING ARTHUR'S COURT,
A (AUT–TV, 1970)
CONNECTICUT RABBIT IN KING ARTHUR'S COURT,
A (short) (CBS–TV, 1978)
CONNECTICUT YANKEE IN KING ARTHUR'S COURT,
A (PBS–TV, 1978)

CONOCESA TU MUJER? see DON'T BET ON WOMEN

CONQUERING HORDE, THE see NORTH OF '36

CONQUERING POWER, THE see EUGENIE GRANDET

CONQUEROR, THE (FOX, 1917, based on the biography
of the American leader)
MAN OF CONQUEST (REP, 1939)
TESTING OF SAM HOUSTON (CBS–TV, 1963)
SAM HOUSTON (CBS–TV, 1963)
SAM HOUSTON (NBC–TV, 1964)
HONORABLE SAM HOUSTON, THE (ABC–TV, 1975)

CONQUEROR, THE see GENGHIS KHAN

CONQUEROR OF ATLANTIS see ATLANTIDE, L'

CONQUEST see MARIA WALEWSKA and NAPOLEON

CONQUEST OF CANAAN, THE (FRO, 1916, based on the
book by Booth Tarkington)
CONQUEST OF CANAAN, THE (PAR, 1921)

CONQUISTADOR see ROMANCE OF THE RIO GRANDE

CONSTANT NYMPH, THE (BRI, 1928, based on the book
and play by Margaret Kennedy and Basil Dean. Also the
basis of the 1933 musical comedy, "Nymph Errant)
CONSTANT NYMPH, THE (BRI, 1934)
CONSTANT NYMPH, THE (WB, 1943)

CONSTANT WIFE, THE see CHARMING SINNERS

CONTE UGOLINO, IL see DANTE'S INFERNO

CONTRE–ENQUETE see THOSE WHO DANCE

CONVERSATION WITH ROBERT FROST, A see ROBERT
FROST

CONVERSATION WITH WALTER GROPIUS, A see
WALTER GROPIUS

CONVERSION OF FERDYS PISTORA, THE (CZE, 1931,
based on the book by Frantisek Langer)
SAINTE PECHERESSE, LA (CZE, 1970)

CONVERSATION WITH ELEANOR ROOSEVELT, A see
ELEANOR ROOSEVELT – THE FIRST LADY OF THE
WORLD

CONVICT 99 (BRI, 1909, based on the book by Marie
Connor and Robert Leighton)
CONVICT 99 (BRI, 1919)

CONVICTED see CRIMINAL CODE, THE

COOGAN'S BLUFF (UN, 1968, based on a story by Herman
Miller)
McCLOUD: WHO KILLED MISS USA? (UN, 1970)

McCLOUD (series) (NBC–TV, 1971)

COOL BREEZE see ASPHALT JUNGLE, THE

COOL MIKADO, THE see FAN–FAN

COP AND THE ANTHEM, THE see O. HENRY'S FULL
HOUSE and BELLE ETOILE, LA

COP–OUT see INCONNUS DANS LA MAISON, LES

COPPELIA OU LA POUPEE ANIMEE (FRA, 1900, based on
the children's story and the ballet by Leo Delibes)
POUPEE VIVANTE, LA (FRA, 1908)
PUPPE, DIE (GER, 1919)
POUPEE DE CIRE (SWE, 1962)
COPPELIA (BRI–TV, 1964)
DR. COPPELIUS (CHI, 1966)
COPPELIA (AUS, 1967)
MYSTERIOUS HOUSE OF DR. COPPELIUS, THE (GER,
1976)

COQUETTE (UA, 1929, based on the play by George Abbott
and Preston Bridgers)
COQUETTE (ABC–TV, 1955)

CORBEAU, LE (FRA, 1948, based on a screenplay, "The
Scarlet Pen," by Louis Chavanie)
THIRTEENTH LETTER, THE (FOX, 1951)

CORDONNIERS DE PROVINCE, LES see SHOEMAKERS OF
PROVINCE, THE

CORIOLANUS (CBS–TV, 1951, based on the play by William
Shakespeare)
CORIOLANUS (BRI–Tv, 1962)
CORIOLANUS (NET–TV, 1965)
THUNDER OF BATTLE (ITA, n.d.)

CORN IS GREEN, THE (WB, 1945, based on the play by
Emlyn Williams)
CORN IS GREEN, THE (NBC–TV, 1956)

CORNER BAR, THE (series) (ABC–TV, 1972, based on a
teleplay)
CORNER BAR, THE (series) (ABC–TV, 1973)

CORNER IN WHEAT, A (BIO, 1909, based on the story, "The
Pit," by Frank Norris)
PIT, THE (IND, 1917)

CORNERED (WB, 1924, based on a play by Dodson Mitchell
and Zelda Sears)
ROAD TO PARADISE, (WB, 1930

CORONATION OF QUEEN ELIZABETH OF ENGLAND see
KING IS DEAD, LONG LIVE THE QUEEN, THE

CORPUS DELECTI, THE see BENSON MURDER CASE, THE

CORSICAN BROTHERS, THE (BRI, 1897, based on the book
by Alexandre Dumas)
CORSICAN BROTHERS, THE (BRI, 1902)
CORSICAN BROTHERS, THE (BRI, 1908)
CORSICAN BROTHERS, THE ED, 1912)
CORSICAN BROTHERS, THE (UN, 1915)
CORSICAN BROTHERS, THE (FRA, 1917)
CORSICAN BROTHERS, THE (UN, 1919)
FRERES CORSES, LES (FRA, 1938)

CORSICAN BROTHERS, THE (UA, 1941)
BANDITS OF CORSICA (UA, 1953)
CORSICAN BROTHERS, THE (ARG, 1954)
CORSICAN BROTHERS, THE (FRA/ITA, 1960)
START THE REVOLUTION WITHOUT ME (WB, 1970)

COSI FAN TUTTE see CHUANG--TSE TESTS HIS WIFE

COSSACKS, THE (RUS, 1928, based on the book by Leo
   Tolstoy)
COSSACKS, THE (MGM, 1928)
COSSACKS, THE (RUS, 1957)

COTTAGE ON DARTMOOR (BRI, 1929, based on the book
   by Herbert Price)
WIRTHAUS VON DARTMOOR, DAS (GER, 1964)

COUNSELLOR--AT--LAW (UN, 1933, based on the play by
   Elmer Rice)
COUNSELLOR--AT--LAW (ABC--TV, 1951)

COUNSEL'S OPINION (BRI, 1933, based on the play by
   Gilbert Wakefield)
DIVORCE OF LADY X, THE (BRI, 1938)

COUNT CAGLIOSTRO see CAGLIOSTRO

COUNT DRACULA see NOSFERATU

COUNT OF MONTE CRISTO, THE (SEL, 1908, based on the
   book by Alexandre Dumas)
COUNT OF MONTE CRISTO, THE (ITA, 1908)
COUNT OF MONTE CRISTO, THE (IND, 1910)
COUNT OF MONTE CRISTO, THE (POW, 1911)
COUNT OF MONTE CRISTO, THE (ITA, 1911)
COUNT OF MONTE CRISTO, THE (SEL, 1912)
COUNT OF MONTE CRISTO, THE (PAR, 1913)
COUNT OF MONTE CRISTO, THE (ITA, 1915)
MONTE CRISTO (FRA, 1917)
COUNT OF MONTE CRISTO, THE (GER, 1919)
MONTE CRISTO (FOX, 1922)
MONTE CRISTO (FRA/GER, 1928)
GRAFIN VON MONTE CRISTO, DER (GER, 1932)
COUNT OF MONTE CRISTO, THE (UA, 1934)
CONDE DE MONTE CRISTO, EL (MEX, 1941)
SON OF MONTE CRISTO (UA, 1941)
COUNT OF MONTE CRISTO, THE (FRA, 1942)
COUNT OF MONTE CRISTO, THE (FRA/ITA, 1943)
RETURN OF MONTE CRISTO, THE (COL, 1946)
WIFE OF MONTE CRISTO, THE (PRC, 1946)
SECRET OF MONTE CRISTO (FRA, 1948)
COUNT OF MONTE CRISTO, THE (FRA, 1953)
TESTAMENT OF MONTE CRISTO, THE (ARG/MEX,
   1953)
COUNT OF MONTE CRISTO, THE (FRA/ITA, 1954)
COUNT OF MONTE CRISTO, THE (series) (TV, 1955)
COUNT OF MONTE CRISTO, THE (CBS--TV, 1958)
SECRET OF MONTE CRISTO, THE (BRI, 1960)
COUNT OF MONTE CRISTO, THE (FRA/ITA, 1961)
COREEN (IN, 1967)
UNDER THE SIGN OF MONTE CRISTO (FRA/ITA, 1968)
COUNT OF MONTE CRISTO, THE (BRI, 1971)
COUNT OF MONTE CRISTO, THE (HB, 1973)
COUNT OF MONTE CRISTO, THE (series) (TV, 1974)
COUNT OF MONTE CRISTO, THE (NBC--TV, 1975)

COUNTERFEIT KILLER, THE see FACELESS MAN, THE

COUNTERFEIT TRAIL, THE (UN, 1919, based on a story by

Dorothy Rochfort)
COUNTERFEIT TRAIL, THE (UN, 1924)

COUNTERSPY see DAVID HARDING, COUNTERSPY

COUNTESS MARITZA (GER, 1925, based on the operetta by
   Emmerich Kalman)
COUNTESS MARITZA (GER, 1932)
COUNTESS MARITZA (GER, 1958)

COUNTESS OF MONTE CRISTO, THE (GER, 1932, based
   on a story by Walter Fleisher)
COUNTESS OF MONTE CRISTO, THE (UN, 1934)

COUNTRY BEYOND, THE (FOX, 1926, based on the book by
   James Oliver Curwood)
COUNTRY BEYOND, THE (FOX, 1936)

COUNTRY COUSIN, THE see COUNTRY MOUSE, THE

COUNTRY GIRL, THE (PAR, 1954, based on the play by
   Clifford Odets)
COUNTRY GIRL, THE (NBC--TV, 1974)

COUNTRY MOUSE, THE (short) (GER, 1921, based on the
   children's story)
TOWN RAT AND THE COUNTRY RAT (FRA, 1926)
COUNTRY MOUSE, THE (short) (WB, 1935)
COUNTRY COUSIN (DIS, 1936)
COUNTRY MOUSE AND CITY MOUSE (short) (COR,
   1962)

COUNTRY MOUSE AND THE CITY MOUSE, THE see
   COUNTRY MOUSE, THE

COUP DE FEU, LE see DETTE OUBLIEE, LA

COUP DE VENT (FRA/ITA, 1935, based on a book by Gio-
   vacchino Forzano)
WINDSTOSS, EIN (GER, 1942)

COUPABLE, LE (FRA, 1918, based on a book by Francois
   Coppee)
COUPABLE, LE (FRA, 1936)

COUPABLES INNOCENTS, LES (RUS, 1916, based on the
   play by Alexandre Ostrovksy)
COUPABLES INNOVENTS, LES (RUS, 1945)

COUPS DE FEU see DETTE OUBLIEE, LA

COURAGE (WB, 1930, based on the play by Tom Barry)
MY BILL (WB, 1938)

COURAGE OF BLACK BEAUTY see BLACK BEAUTY

COURIER DE LYON, LE (FRA, 1911, based on the book by
   Maxime Valoris and Marc Mario)
AFFAIRE DU COURIER DE LYON, L' (FRA, 1923)
COURIER DE LYON, LE (FRA, 1938)

COURIER OF THE KING see RED AND THE BLACK, THE

COURSE DU FLAMBEAU, LA (FRA, 1917, baeed on a novel
   by Paul Hevvieu)
COURSE DU FLAMBEAU, LA (FRA, 1925)

COURT MARTIAL OF BILLY MITCHELL, THE (WB, 1955,
   based on historical events and characters)

BILLY MITCHELL COURT MARTIAL, THE (CBS–TV, 1956)

COURT–MARTIAL OF GEORGE ARMSTRONG CUSTER, THE see CUSTER'S LAST STAND

COURTSHIP OF EDDIE'S FATHER, THE (MGM, 1963, based on the book by Mark Toby)
COURTSHIP OF EDDIE'S FATHER, THE (series) (ABC–TV, 1969)

COURTSHIP OF MILES TANDISH, THE see WOOING OF MILES STANDISH, THE

COUSIN BETTE (FRA, n.d., based on the book by Honore de Balzac)
COUSIN BETTE (series) (BRI–TV, 1971)

COUSIN KATE (VIT, 1920, based on the play by Hubert Henry Davies)
STRICTLY MODERN (WB, 1930)

COWBOY AND THE LADY, THE (MGM, 1915, based on the play by Clyde Fitch)
COWBOY AND THE LADY, THE (PAR, 1922)

COWBOY FROM BROOKLYN (WB, 1938, based on the play, "Howdy Stranger," by Robert Sloane and Louis Pelletier Jr.)
TWO GUYS FROM TEXAS (WB, 1948)

COWBOY IN AFRICA see AFRICA – TEXAS STYLE

COWBOY IN MANHATTAN see YOU'RE A SWEETHEART

COWBOY QUARTERBACK see FAST COMPANY

COWBOYS, THE (WB, 1972, based on the book by William Dale Jennings)
COWBOYS, THE (series) (ABC–TV, 1974)

CRACK–UP (RKO, 1946, based on the story, "Madman's Holiday," by Fredric Brown)
CRACK–UP (CBS–TV, 1956)

CRADLE SNATCHERS, THE (FOX, 1927, based on the play by Russell Medcraft and Norma Mitchell)
WHY LEAVE HOME (FOX, 1929)
LET'S FACE IT (PAR, 1943)

CRADLE SONG (PAR, 1933, based on the play by G.M. Martinez Sierra)
CRADLE SONG (NBC–TV, 1956)
CRADLE SONG (NBC–TV, 1960)

CRAIG'S WIFE (PAT, 1928, based on the play by George Kelly)
CRAIG'S WIFE (COL, 1934)
HARRIET CRAIG (COL, 1950)
CRAIG'S WIFE (TV, 1952)
CRAIG'S WIFE (NBC–TV, 1954)

CRAINQUEBILLE (FRA, 1922, based on a story by Anatole France)
CRAINQUEBILLE (FRA, 1934)
MORT AUX VACHES (FRA, 1953)

CRASH, THE (WB, 1929, based on a story by Frank L. Packard)
PAGES FROM LIFE (WB, 1932)

CRASHING HOLLYWOOD see LIGHTS OUT

CRAZY LIKE A FOX (short) (PAT, 1926, source unlisted)
WRONG MISS WRIGHT, THE (short) (COL, 1927)

CREATION CAN'T BE BOUGHT see MARTIN EDEN

CREATURE, THE see ABOMINABLE SNOWMAN, THE

CREATURE OF DESTRUCTION see SHE CREATURE, THE

CREEPING SHADOWS (BRI, 1931, based on a play by Will Scott)
LIMPING MAN, THE (BRI, 1936)
LIMPING MAN, THE (BRI, 1953)

CRICKET ON THE HEARTH, THE (BIO, 1909, based on the story by Charles Dickens)
CRICKET ON THE HEARTH, THE (BIO, 1914)
CRICKET ON THE HEARTH, THE (RUS, 1915)
GRILLON DU FOYER, LE (FRA, 1921)
CRICKET ON THE HEARTH, THE (SEZ, 1923)
GRILLON DU FOYER, LE (FRA, 1933)
CRICKET ON THE HEARTH, THE (short) (IND, 1949)
CRICKET ON THE HEARTH, THE (NBC--TV, 1967)
CRICKET ON THE HEARTH, THE (UPA, 1968)

CRIME AND CRIME see RAUSCH

CRIME AND PUNISHMENT (RUS, 1910, based on the book by Feydor Dostoyevsky)
CRIME AND PUNISHMENT (RUS, 1913)
CRIME AND PUNISHMENT (PAR,1917)
CRIME AND PUNISHMENT (RUS, 1922)
RASKOLNIKOV (GER, 1923)
CRIME AND PUNISHMENT (RUS, 1926)
CRIME AND PUNISHMENT (IND, 1929)
CRIME AND PUNISHMENT (FRA, 1935)
CRIME AND PUNISHMENT (COL, 1935)
CRIME AND PUNISHMENT (SWE, 1945)
FEAR (MON, 1946)
CRIME AND PUNISHMENT (IND, 1948)
MOST DANGEROUS SIN, A (FRA, 1956)
PICKPOCKET (FRA, 1959)
CRIME AND PUNISHMENT USA (AA, 1959)
MURDERER, THE (CAN–TV, 1966)
CRIME AND PUNISHMENT (RUS, 1969)
SONYA AND THE MADMAN (EGY, 1977)

CRIME AND PUNISHMENT USA see CRIME AND PUNISH–MENT

CRIME DE LORD ARTHUR SAVILE, LE see LORD ARTHUR SAVILE'S CRIME

CRIME DE SYLVESTRE BONNARD, LE (FRA, 1929, based on a book by Anatole France)
CHASING YESTERDAY (RKO, 1935)

CRIME DOCTOR see PERFECT CRIME, THE

CRIME DU BOUIF, LA (FRA, 1921, based on a story by Georges de la Fouchardiere)
CRIME DU BOUIF, LA (FRA, 1933)
CRIME DU BOUIF, LA (FRA, 1951)

CRIME IN THE STREETS (ABC–TV, 1954, based on the teleplay by Reginald Rose)
CRIME IN THE STREETS (AA, 1956)

CRIME OF DR. CRESPI, THE see PRELUDE

CRIME OF DR. HALLET, THE UN, 1938, based on a story
by Lester Cole and Carl Dreher)
STRANGE CONQUEST (UN, 1946)

CRIME OF GIOVANNI EPISCOPO, THE see GIOVANNI
EPISCOPO

CRIME OF P. GARINE, THE see HYPERBOLOIDE DE L
L'INGENIEUR GARINE, L'

CRIME SCHOOL see MAYOR OF HELL

CRIMES AT THE DARK HOUSE see WOMAN IN WHITE,
THE

CRIMINAL AT LARGE see FRIGHTENED LADY

CRIMINAL CODE, THE (COL, 1931, based on the play by
Martin Flavin)
CODIGO PENAL, EL (MEX, 1931)
CRIMINEL (FRA, 1932)
PENITENTIARY (COL, 1938)
CONVICTED (COL, 1950)

CRIMINAL LAWYER see STATE'S ATTORNEY

CRIMINEL see CRIMINAL CODE, THE

CRIMSON CIRCLE, THE (BRI, 1922, based on the book by
Edgar Wallace)
ROTE KREIS, DER (BRI/GER, 1928)
CRIMSON CIRCLE, THE (BRI, 1936)
ROTE KREIS, DER (GER, 1959)

CRIMSON GHOST, THE (serial) (REP, 1946, based on a
screenplay by various authors. Remake is a condensation
of the serial)
CYCLOTRODE X (REP, 1966)

CRIMSON PIRATE, THE see BLACK PIRATE, THE

CRIPPLED HAND, THE see CINDERELLA AND THE
FAIRY GODMOTHER

CRISTOFORO COLOMBO see COMING OF COLUMBUS

CROIX DU BOIS (FRA, 1932, based on the book by Roland
Dorgeles)
ROAD TO GLORY, THE (FOX, 1926)
ROAD TO GLORY, THE (FOX, 1936)

CROMWELL (BRI, 1911, based on historical incidents
and characters)
CROMWELL (COL, 1970)

CROOK'S HONOR (GER, 1932, source unknown)
CROOK'S HONOR (GER, 1966)

CROONER, THE (WB, 1932, based on a story by Rian James)
MR. DODD TAKES THE AIR (WB, 1937)

CROSS MY HEART see TRUE CONFESSION

CROSS OF LORAINE, THE (MGM, 1943, based on the
character of Heydrich in Nazi Germany)
HANGMEN ALSO DIE (UA, 1943)

CROSSED SWORDS see PRINCE AND THE PAUPER, THE

CROSSROADS see CARREFOUR

CROWD ROARS, THE (WB, 1932, based on a story by Howard
Hawks)
FOULE HURLE, LA (FRA, 1932)
INDIANAPOLIS SPEEDWAY (WB, 1939)

CROWD ROARS, THE (MGM, 1937, based on a story by
George Bruce)
KILLER MCCOY (MGM, 1947)

CROWDED IDOL, THE see SPIRIT OF ST. LOUIS, THE

CRUCIBLE, THE (U.S. TITLE: WITCHES OF SALEM)
(FRA, 1958, based on the play by Arthur Miller)
CRUCIBLE, THE (CBS–TV, 1967)

CRUCIFIXION OF JESUS see PASSION PLAY, THE

CRUCIFIXION OF PHILIP STRONG, THE see MARTYR–
DOM OF PHILIP STRONG, THE

CRUISER EMDEN, THE see EMDEN, THE

CRY THE BELOVED COUNTRY (U.S. Title: AFRICAN
FURY) (BRI, 1952, based on the book by Alan Paton)
LOST IN THE STARS (AFT, 1973)

CUBA: CHANGE UNDER CASTRO see FIDEL CASTRO
STORY, THE

CUCURUCHITO AND PINOCCHIO see PINOCCHIO

CUERPO DELITO, EL see BENSON MURDER CASE, THE

CUP OF LIFE, THE (INC, 1915, based on a story by Carey
Wilson)
CUP OF LIFE, THE (PAR, 1920)

CUREE, LA (ITA, 1916, based on the book by Emile Zola)
CUREE, LA (FRA/ITA, 1966)

CURFEW MUST NOT RING TONIGHT (BRI, 1912, based
on the poem by Rose Thorpe)
CURFEW MUST NOT RING TONIGHT (BRI, 1923)

CURIOUS CASE OF UNCLE TOM'S CABIN, THE see
UNCLE TOMS' CABIN

CURLEY TOP see DADDY LONG LEGS

CURSE OF FRANKENSTEIN see FRANKENSTIEN

CURSE OF THE CRYING WOMEN, THE see LLORONA,
LA

CURSE OF THE KARNSTEINS see STRANGE CASE OF
DAVID GRAY, THE

CURSE OF THE WRAYDONS (BRI, 1946, based on the play,
"Springheeled Jack, the Terror of London," author
unknown)
GHOST FOR SALE, A (BRI, 1952)

CUSTER AT THE WASHITA see CUSTER'S LAST STAND

CUSTER OF THE WEST see CUSTER'S LAST STAND

CUSTER: THE AMERICAN SURGE WESTWARD see
    CUSTER'S LAST STAND

CUSTER'S LAST FIGHT see CUSTER'S LAST STAND

CUSTER'S LAST RAID see CUSTER'S LAST STAND

CUSTER'S LAST STAND (SEL, 1909, based on historical
    incidents and characters)
  CUSTER'S LAST RAID (INC, 1912)
  CUSTER'S LAST FIGHT (IND, 1925)
  FLAMING FRONTIER (UN, 1926)
  THEY DIED WITH THEIR BOOTS ON (WB, 1941)
  BUGLES IN THE AFTERNOON (WB, 1952)
  CUSTER: THE AMERICAN SURGE WESTWARD (short)
    (ABC–TV, 1966)
  LEGEND OF CUSTER (series) (ABC–TV, 1967)
  CUSTER OF THE WEST (CIN, 1968)
  CUSTER AT THE WASHITA (short) (IND–TV, 1968)
  DON'T TOUCH WHITE WOMEN! (FRA, 1974)
  RED SUNDAY (short) (PYR, 175)
  COURT–MARTIAL OF GEORGE ARMSTRONG CUSTER,
    THE (ABC--TV, 1977)

CYCLOTRODE X see CRIMSON GHOST, THE

CYNARA (UA, 1932, based on the play by H.M. Harwood
    and Robert Gore–Browne)
  CYNARA (ABC–TV, 1955)

CYRANO AND D'ARTAGNAN see CYRANO DE BERGER-
    AC and THREE MUSKETEERS, THE

CYRANO DE BERGERAC (FRA, 1900, based on the play,
    "Cyrano de Bergerac," by Edmond Rostand; also the
    basis for two musicals, "The White Plume," in 1938 and
    "Cyrano" in 1973)
  CYRANO (ITA, 1909)
  CYRANO DE BERGERAC'S ADVENTURES (FRA, 1909)
  CYRANO ET D'ASSOUCY (FRA, 1909)
  CYRANO DE BERGERAC (ITA, 1923)
  CYRANO DE BERGERAC (FRA, 295)
  CYRANO DE BERGERAC (FRA, 1945)
  CYRANO DE BERGERAC (NBC–TV, 1949)
  CYRANO DE BERGERAC (UA, 1950)
  CYRANO DE BERGERAC (NBC–TV, 1955)
  CYRANO AND D'ARTAGNAN (FRA/ITA/SPA, 1962)
  CYRANO DE BERGERAC (NBC–TV, 1962)
  MAGOO IN THE KING'S SERVICE (UPA, 1964)
  CYRANO DE BERGERAC (PBS–TV, 1973)
  CYRANO (ABC–TV, 1973)

CYRANO DE BERGERAC'S ADVENTURES see CYRANO
    DE BERGERAC

CZAR IVAN THE TERRIBLE see IVAN THE TERRIBLE

CZARDAS PRINCESS, THE see CZARDASFURSTIN, DIE

CZARDASFURSTIN, DIE (GER, 1926, based on the operetta
    by Emmerich Kalman, Bela Jenbach and Leo Stein)
  CZARDASFURSTIN, DIE (FRA/GER, 1934)
  CAARDASFURSTIN, DIE (GER, 1951)
  CZARDASFURSTIN, DIE (GER/HUN, 1971)

CZARINA see FORBIDDEN PARADISE

CZARINA'S SECRET, THE see ADVENTUROUS LIFE OF
    CATHERINE I OF RUSSIA

CZECH YEAR see CHRISTMAS CAROL, A

D-DAY (CBS-TV, 1955, based on historical events in the
    1940's)
    D-DAY: THE SIXTH OF JUNE (FOX, 1956)
    D-DAY (series) (TV, 1958)
    D-DAY (WOL-TV, 1962)
    D-DAY PLUS 20 YEARS (CBS-TV, 1964)

D.O.A. (UA, 1949, based on a screenplay by Russell Rouse
    and Clarence Greene)
    COLOR ME DEAD (AUT, 1969)

DADDY LONG LEGS (FN, 1919, based on a story by Jean
    Webster. Also the basis for the British musical comedy,
    "Love from Judy,")
    DADDY LONG LEGS (FOX, 1931)
    CURLY TOP (FOX, 1935)
    VADERTJE LANGBEEN (HOL, 1938)
    DADDY LONG LEGS (FOX, 1955)

DADDY'S GONE A HUNTING (MGM, 1925, based on the
    play by Zoe Atkins)
    WOMEN LOVE ONCE (PAR, 1931)

DAFFODIL MYSTERY, THE (GER, 1961, based on the book
    by Edgar Wallace)
    DEVIL'S DAFFODIL, THE (BRI, 1962)

DAG HAMMARSKJOLD see PORTRAIT OF DAG HAM-
    MARSKJOLD, A

DAKTARI see CLARENCE, THE CROSS-EYED LION

DALTON GANG, THE see WHEN THE DALTONS RODE

DALTON GIRLS, THE see WHEN THE DALTONS RODE

DALTONS MUST DIE, THE see WHEN THE DALTONS
    RODE

DALTONS RIDE AGAIN, THE see WHEN THE DALTONS
    RODE

DAMA ATREVIDA, LA see LADY WHO DARED, THE

DAMAGED GOODS (IND, 1914, based on the play by Eugene
    Brieux)
    DAMAGED GOODS (BRI, 1915)
    DAMAGED GOODS (BRI, 1919)
    DAMAGED GOODS (IND, 1937)

DAME AUX CAMELIAS, LA (DEN, 1907, based on the book
    by Alexandre Dumas. Also the basis for Verdi's opera,
    "La Traviata," in 1853)
    LADY OF THE CAMELLIAS (ITA, 1909)
    CAMILLE (IND, 1912)
    DAME AUX CAMELLIAS, LA (FRA, 1912)
    CAMILLE (FOX, 1917)
    CAMILLE (IND, 1917)
    PRIMAVER AM DIE KAMELIENDAME (GER, 1917)
    CAMILLE (MGM, 1921)
    LADY OF THE CAMELIAS (short) (BRI, 1922)
    LOVER OF CAMILLE, THE (WB, 1924)
    DAME AUX CAMELIAS, LA (SWE, 1925)
    CAMILLE (FN, 1927)
    TRAVIATA, LA (short) (BRI, 1927)
    WILD GRASS (CHN, 1930)
    RED PEACOCK, THE GER, n.d.)
    DAME AUX CAMELIAS, LA (FRA, 1934)
    DAME AUX CAMELIAS, LA (EGY, 1941)

DAMA DE LAS CAMELIAS, LA (MEX, 1944)
    LOST ONE, THE (COL, 1948)
    CAMILLE (NBC-TV, 1948)
    TRAVIATA, LA SIGNORASENZA COMELIE, LA
        (ITA, 1953)
    CAMILLE (FRA, 1952)
    CAMELIA', PASSION SAUVAGE (MEX, 1952)
    MUJER DE LAS CAMELLIAS, LA (ARG, 1953)
    CAMILLE (CBS-TV, 1953)
    FILLE D'AMOUR, TRAVIATA '53 (FRA/ITA, 1953)
    CAMILLE (NBC-TV, 1954)
    BELLE LOLA, UN DAME AUX CAMELIAS, LA (FRA/
        ITA/SPA, 1962)
    TRAVIATA, LA (FRA/ITA, 1967)
    CAMILLE 2000 (IND, 1969)
    GIRL AT LUNA PARK, THE (GRE, 1968)

DAME DE CHEZ MAXIM, LA (FRA, 1912, based on the
    play by Georges Feydeau)
    DAME DE CHEZ MAXIM, LA (ITA, 1923)
    GIRL FROM MAXIM'S, THE (BRI, 1933)
    DAME DE CHEZ MAXIM, LA (FRA, 1933)
    DAME DE CHEZ MAXIM, LA (FRA, 1950)

DAME DE MONSOREAU, LA (ITA, 1909, based on the
    book by Alexandre Dumas [pere])
    DAME DE MONSOREAU, LA (FRA, 1913)
    DAME DE MONSOREAU, LA (FRA, 1922)

DAME DE PIQUE see PIQUE DAME

DAME IN SCHWARZ, DIE see WOMEN IN BLACK

DAMES AUX CHAPEAUX VERTS, CES (WOMEN IN GRE-
    EN HATS) (FRA, 1929, based on the book by Germaine
    Acremant)
    DAMES AUX CHAPEAUX VERTS, CES (FRA, 1937)
    DAMES AUX CHAPEAUX VERTS, CES (FRA, 1948)

DAMIEN see GREAT HEART, THE

DAMN YANKEES (WB, 1958, based on the book, "The
    Year the Yankees Lost the Pennant, " by Douglas Wallop)
    DAMN YANKEES (NBC-TV, 1967)

DAMNATION OF FAUST, THE see FAUST

DAMNED DON'T CRY, THE (WB, 1950, based on the
    story, "The Brooch," by William Faulkner
    BROOCH, THE (CBS-TV, 1953)

DAMOISELLE PAYSANNE, UNE (RUS, 1912, based on
    the story by Alexander Pushkin)
    DAMOISELLE PAYSANNE, UNE (RUS, 1917)

DAMON AND PYTHIAS (UN, 1914, based on the legend)
    DAMON AND PYTHIAS (ITA, 1962)

DAMON DES MEERS, see SEA BEAST, THE

DANCE, CHARLIE, DANCE see BUTTER AND EGG
    MAN, THE

DANCE OF DEATH (DEN, 1908, based on the play by
    August Strindberg)
    DANCE OF DEATH (DEN/GER, 1912)
    DANCE OF DEATH (NOR, 1916)
    DANCE OF DEATH (GER, 1920)
    DANCE OF DEATH (GER, 1925)

DANCE OF DEATH (FRA/ITA, 1946)
PAARUNGER (Couplings) (GER, 1967)
DANCE OF DEATH (BRI, 1968)

DANCE OF LIFE, THE (PAR, 1929, based on the play, "Bur-
lesque," by George Manker Watters and Arthur Hopkins)
SWING HIGH SWING LOW (PAR, 1937)
BURLESQUE (NBC–TV, 1940)
WHEN MY BABY SMILES AT ME (FOX, 1948)
BURLESQUE (CBS–TV, 1951)
BURLESQUE (IND,-TV, 1952)
BURLESQUE (ABC–TV, 1954)
BURLESQUE (CBS–TV, 1955)

DANCE PRETTY LADY see BALLET BIRL, THE

DANCERS, THE (FOX, 1925, baded on the play by Gerald
Du Maurier and Viola Tree)
DANCERS, THE (FOX, 1930)

DANCER'S WORLD, A (short) (CAN, 1959, based on the
works of choreographer Martha Graham)
MARTHA GRAHAM DANCE COMPANY, THE (IND, 1977)

DANCING GIRLS OF IZO (JAP, 1933, source unknown)
DANCING GIRLS OF IZO (JAP, 1954)
DANCING GIRLS OF IZO (JAP, 1960)
DANCING GIRLS OF IZO (JAP, 1963)

DANCING IN THE DARK (FOX, 1949, based on the mus-
ical, "The Bandwagon," by George S. Kauffman, Howard
Dietz and Arthur Schwartz)
BANDWAGON, THE (MGM, 1953)

DANGER LINE (FBO, 1924, based on the book, "The Battle,"
by Claude Farrere)
BATTLE, THE (FRA, 1934)

DANGER ON THE RIVER see MISSISSIPPI GAMBLER

DANGER SIGNAL (KLE, 1915, based on the story, "Canavan,
the Man Who Had His Way," by Rupert Hughes)
IT HAD TO HAPPEN (FOX, 1936)

DANGEROUS (WB, 1935, based on a screenplay by Laird
Doyle)
SINGAPORE WOMAN (WB, 1941)

DANGEROUS CHRISTMAS OF RED RIDING HOOD, THE
see PETIT CHAPERON ROUGE, LE

DANGEROUS FEMALE see MALTESE FALCON, THE

DANGEROUS PARADISE see VICTORY

DANGERS OF THE CANADIAN MOUNTED (serial) (REP,
1948, based on a screenplay by various authors. Remake
is a condensation of the serial)
RCMP AND THE TREASURE OF GENGIS KHAN (REP,
1966)

DANIEL see DANIEL IN THE LION'S DEN

DANIEL BOONE see CHRONICLES OF AMERICA; DAN-
IEL BOONE

DANIEL IN THE LION'S DEN (FRO, 1905, based on a
story in the Bible)
DANIEL (VIT, 1913)

DANIEL WEBSTER (short) (EBE, 1951, based on the
life of the American statesman)
WEBSTER'S SACRIFICE TO SAVE THE UNION (short)
(CBS–TV, 1955)
DANIEL WEBSTER (short) (SAU, 1965)
LAST WILL OF DANIEL WEBSTER, THE (short)
(TFC, 1967)

DANNY BOY (BRI, 1934, based on a screenplay by Oswald Mitchell and H. Barr–Carson)
DANNY BOY (BRI, 1941)

DANS LES REMOUS (SWE, 1919, based on the book,
"Chant de la fleur rouge, Le, " by Johannes Linnankow-
sky)
CHANT DE LA FLEUR ROUGE, LE (SWE, 1934)
CHANT DE LA FLEUR ROUGE, LE (SWE, 1956)

DANS SA CANDEUR NAIVE see CARDBOARD LOVER,
THE

DANS UNE ILE PERDUE see VICTORY

DANSE MACABRE see DANZA MACABRE, LA

DANSEUSE ROUGE, LA see CHEVRE AUX PIEDS
D'OR, LA

DANTE'S INFERNO (ITA, 1909, based on the book, "The
Inferno," by Dante)
INFERNO (ITA, 1910)
DANTE'S INFERNO (IND, 1911)
DANTE'S INFERNO (FOX, 1924)
MACISTE IN HELL (ITA, 1931)
HELLEVISION (IND, 1939)
CONTE UGOLINO, IL (ITA, 1949)
DANTE'S INFERNO (CBS–TV, 1952)
WITCHES' CURSE, THE (ITA, 1960)

DANTON see ALL FOR A WOMAN

DANZA MACABRE, LA (ITA, 1963, based on the story,
"Danse Macabre," by Edgar Allan Poe)
THROW ME TO THE VAMPIRE (MEX, 1964)
IN THE GRIP OF THE SPIDER (FRA/GER/ITA, 1971)

DAPHNE (ITA, 1936 source unknown)
DAPHNE (FRA–TV, 1964)

DARBY AND JOAN see IRON STAIR, THE

DARK CORNER, THE (FOX, 1946, based on a story by
Leo Rosten)
DARK CORNER, THE (CBS–TV, 1957)

DARK EYES (FRA, 1934, source unknown)
PETERSBRUGER NACHTE (GER, 1924)
PETERSBURG NIGHTS (RUS, 1934)
SCHWARZE AUGEN (GER, 1951)
PETERSBURGER NACHTE (GER, 1958)

DARK EYES OF LONDON, THE (HUMAN MONSTER)
(BRI, 1940, based on the book by Edgar Wallace)
DEAD EYES OF LONDON, THE (GER, 1961)

DARK HAZARD (WB, 1934, based on the book by W.R.
Burnett)
WINE, WOMEN AND HORSES (WB, 1937)
DARK PAGE, THE see SCANDAL SHEET

DARK PAST, THE see BLIND ALLEY

DARK RAPTURE (UN, 1938, based on documentary foot-
     age)
   AFRICAN MANHUNT (REP, 1955)

DARK SWAN, THE (WB, 1924, based on a story by Ernest
     Pascal)
   WEDDING RINGS (FN, 1930)

DARK VICTORY (WB, 1939, based on the play by George
     Emerson Brewer Jr. and Bertram Bloch)
   DARK VICTORY (NBC–TV, 1951)
   DARK VICTORY (ABC–TV, 1954)
   DARK VICTORY (CBS–TV, 1955)
   DARK VICTORY (NBC–TV, 1957)
   STOLEN HOURS (UA, 1963)
   DARK VICTORY (NBC–TV, 1976)

DARKEST AFRICA (serial) (REP, 1936, based on a screen-
     play by various authors. The remake is a condensation
     of the serial)
   BATMEN OF AFRICA (REP, 1966)

DARLING OF PARIS, THE see ESMERELDA

D'ARTAGNAN see THREE MUSTETEERS, THE

D'ARTAGNAN AGAINST THE THREE MUSKETEERS see
   THREE MUSKETEERS, THE

D'ARTAGNAN THE BRAVE see THREE MUSKETEERS
   THE

DARWIN AND EVOLUTION (short) (MHF, 1961, based on
     theories of the noted scientist Charles Darwin)
   DARWIN'S FINCHES (short) (BFA, 1961)
   DARWIN AND THE THEORY OF NATURAL SELECTION
   (short) (COR, 1967)

DATE WITH JUDY, A (MGM, 1948, suggested by the radio
     series)
   DATE WITH JUDY, A (series) (ABC–TV, 1951)

DAUGHTER OF DESTINY see WARRIOR'S HUSBAND
   THE

DAUGHTER OF EVIL see ALRAUNE

DAUGHTER OF THE CAPTAIN, THE (RUS, 1914, based
     on the story   by Alexander Pushkin)
   DAUGHTER OF THE CAPTAIN, THE (RUS, 1928)
   DAUGHTER OF THE CAPTAIN, THE (ITA, 1947)
   TEMPEST, THE (FRA/ITA/RUS, 1958)

DAUGHTER OF THE DONS see MAN IN THE SADDLE

DAUGHTER OF THE REGIMENT see KING'S DAUGH-
   TER, THE

DAUGHTERS COURAGEOUS (WB, 1939, based on a play by
     Dorothy Bennett and Irving White)
   ALWAYS IN MY HEART (WB, 1942)

DAUGHTERS OF DARKNESS see BLOOD AND ROSES

DAUGHTERS OF DESTINY see JOAN OF ARC

DAUGHTERS OF MADAME SANS–GENE, THE see

MADAME SANS–GENE

DAVE BRUBECK see JAZZ OF DAVE BRUBECK, THE

DAVID AND BATHSHEBA (FOX, 1951, based on the Bible
     story)
   DAVID AND BATHSHEBA (CBS–TV, 1960)

DAVID AND CATRIONA see KIDNAPPED

DAVID AND GOLIATH (KAL, 1908, based on the Bible
     story)
   DAVID AND GOLIATH (FRA, 1909)
   DAVID AND GOLIATH (ITA, 1959)

DAVID AND MR. MACAWBER see LITTLE EMILY

DAVID BALFOUR see KIDNAPPED

DAVID BEN–GURION (short) (NBC–TV, 1958, based
     on the life of the Israeli leader)
   BEN–GURION (short) (WOL, 1963)

DAVID COPPERFIELD see LITTLE EMILY

DAVID GARRICK (BRI, 1912, based on the play by T.W.
     Robinson)
   DAVID GARRICK (BRI, 1913)
   DAVID GARRICK (BRI, 1914)
   DAVID GARRICK (PAL, 1916)
   DAVID GARRICK (short) (BRI, 1922)
   DAVID GARRICK (BRI, 1928)
   GREAT GARRICK, THE (WB, 1937)

DAVID GOLDER (FRA, 1930, based on the book by Irene
     Nemirovski)
   MY DAUGHTER JOY (OPERATION X) (BRI, 1949)

DAVID HARDING, COUNTERSPY (COL, 1950, based on
     the radio series)
   COUNTERSPY (series) (TV, 1958)
DAVID HARUM (MUT, 1915, based on the book by Ed-
     ward Noyes Wescatt. Also the basis for a daytime radio
     serial in the 1930's and 1940's
   DAVID HARUM (FOX, 1934)

DAVID LIVINGSTONE see LIVINGSTONE

DAVY CROCKETT, INDIAN SCOUT see KIT CARSON

DAWN see NURSE CAVELL

DAWN ON THE GREAT DIVEDE see WHEELS OF FATE

DAWN PATROL (WB, 1930, based on the story, "Flight
     Commander," by John Monk Saunders)
   DAWN PATROL (WB, 1938)
   (TV Titles: FLIGHT COMMANDER and
               LAST FLIGHT)

DAWN TRAIL, THE (COL, 1930, based on a story by For-
     rest Sheldon; remake uncredited
   TEXAS STAMPEDE (COL, 1939)

DAY DREAMS see HAMLET

DAY MANOLETE WAS KILLED, THE see MANOLETE

DAY OF TRIUMPH see PASSION PLAY, THE

DAY THE EARTH STOOD STILL, THE (FOX, 1951, based
    on story by Harry Bates; remake uncredited)
    IMMEDIATE DISASTER (BRI, 1954)

DAY THE WORLD ENDED (AI, 1956, source unknown)
    IN THE YEAR 2889 (AI, 1966)

DAY WELL SPENT, A (AUS, 1916, based on the play "Einen
    jux willer sich Machen" by Johann Nestroy)
    DAY WELL SPENT, A (GER, 1928)
    EINMALEINS DER LIEBE (GER, 1935)
    EINMAL KEINE SORGERN HABEN (AUS/GER, 1953)
    DAY WELL SPENT, A (GER, 1957)

DAYBOOKS OF EDWARD WESTON, THE see PHOTO-
    GRAPHER

DAYBREAK see JOUR SE LEVE, LE

DAYDREAMER, THE see QUEEN OF THE SEA

DE BOTE EN BOTE see DUCK SOUP

DE FRENTE MARCHEN see DOUGHBOYS

DEAD END KIDS ON DRESS PARADE see SHIPMATES
    FOREVER

DEAD EYES OF LONDON, THE see DARK EYES OF
    LONDON

DEADMAN'S SHOES see CARREFOUR

DEAD RINGER see OTHER, THE

DEAL A BLOW (CBS–TV, n.d., based on the teleplay by
    Robert Dozier)
    YOUNG STRANGER, THE (RKO, 1957)

DEATH AND THE MAIDEN see FAHRMANN MARIA

DEATH DRUMS ALONG THE RIVER see SANDERS OF
    THE RIVER

DEATH IN THE FAMILY, A see ALL THE WAY HOME

DEATH OF A DICTATOR see BENITO MUSSOLINI

DEATH OF A SALESMAN (COL, 1951, based on the play
    by Arthur Miller. Also the basis of a Scandinavian opera
    in 1961)
    DEATH OF A SALESMAN (BRI–TV, 1957)
    YOU CAN'T CROSS THE BRIDGE (RUS, 1961)
    DEATH OF A SALESMAN (CBS–TV, 1966)

DEATH OF BILLY THE KID, THE see BILLY THE KID

DEATH OF MANOLETE see MANOLETE

DEATH OF NATHAN HALE, THE (ED, 1911,based on a
    story by Edward Hale and the play, "Nathan Hale," by
    Clyde Fitch
    NATHAN HALE (short) (KIN, 1913)
    HEART OF A HERO, THE (WOR, 1916)
    MAN WITHOUT A COUNTRY, THE (UN, 1917)
    MAN WITHOUT A COUNTRY, THE (AS NO MAN HAS
    LOVED) (FOX, 1925)
    MAN WITHOUT A COUNTRY, THE (short) (WB, 1938)
    MAN WITHOUT A COUNTRY, THE (NBC–TV, 1950)

STORY OF NATHAN HALE, THE (CBS–TV, 1963)
MAN WITHOUT A COUNTRY, THE (ABC–TV, 1973)

DEATH OF NELSON (BRI, 1896, based on a song by Braham)
    DEATH OF NELSON (BRI, 1905)

DEATH OF PRESIDENT KENNEDY, THE see MAKING
    OF THE PRESIDENT–1960, THE

DEATH OF SITTING BULL see SITTING BULL

DEATH OF STALIN, THE see STALIN ERA, THE

DEATH OF STONEWALL JACKSON, THE see UNDER
    SOUTHERN STARS

DEATH TAKES A HOLIDAY (PAR, 1934, based on the play
    by Alberto Casella)
    DEATH TAKES A HOLIDAY (ABC–TV, 1954)
    DEATH TAKES A HOLIDAY (ABC–TV, 1971)

DEBOUT LES MORTS! (FRA, 1917, based on the book,
    "The Four Horsemen of the Apocalypse," by Vicente Blasco Iba
    FOUR HORSEMEN OF THE APOCALYPSE, THE (MGM,
    1921)
    FOUR HORSEMEN OF THE APOCALYPSE, THE (MGM,
    1961)

DEBT OF HONOR (BRI, 1922, based on a story by H.C.
    "Sapper" McNeile)
    DEBT OF HONOR (BRI, 1936)

DECAMERON, THE (ITA, 1912, based on stories by Gio-
    vani Boccacio)
    LIEBELIST UND LUST (GER, 1922)
    DECAMERON NIGHTS (BRI, 1924)
    DECAMERON NIGHTS (GER, 1924)
    DECAMERON NIGHTS (GER, 1928)
    BOCCACIO (GER, 1936)
    DECAMERON NIGHTS (RKO, 1952)
    BOCCACIO '70 (FRA,/ITA, 1962)
    DECAMERON, THE (ITA, 1971)
    UNCENSORED DECAMERON (GER, 1972)

DECAMERON NIGHTS see DECAMERON, THE

DECEMBER BRIDE (series) (CBS–TV, 1954, based on a
    teleplay)
    PETE AND GLADYS (series) (CBS–TV, 1960)

DECEMBER 7, 1941: PEARL HARBOR (CBS–TV, 1955,
    based on historical incidents)
    DECEMBER 7 (UA–TV, 1963)

DECEPTION (ANNE BOLEYN) (BRI, 1921, based on a histori–
    cal incident)
    ANNE OF THE THOUSAND DAYS (UN, 1969)

DECEPTION see JEALOUSY

DECLARATION OF INDEPENDENCE, THE (short) (WB,
    1938, based on the life of President John Adams)
    OUR CONSTITUTION (short) (IND, n.d.)
    VICE–PRESIDENT'S STORY, THE (short) (IND, n.d.)
    LAUNCHING THE NEW GOVERNMENT (short) (COR,
    1958)
    JOHN YANKEE: JOHN ADAMS AND THE BOSTON
    MASSACRE (short) (IND, n.d.)
    JOHN ADAMS (SAU, 1964)

1776 (COL, 1973)

DECLASSE (FN, 1925, based on the play by Zoe Atkins)
HER PRIVATE LIFE (FN, 1929)

DECLINE AND FALL OF JOSEF STALIN, THE see
STALIN ERA, THE

DEDALE, LE (FRA, 1917, based on the novel by Paul
Hervieu)
DEDALE, LE (FRA, 1926)

DEEP PURPLE, THE (WOR, 1915, based on the play by
Paul Armstrong and William Mizner)
DEEP PURPLE, THE (IND, 1920)

DEEP WATER see FROGMEN, THE

DEERSLAYER, THE (VIT, 1913, based on the book by
James Fenimore Cooper)
DEERSLAYER, THE (SEZ, 1923)
DEERSLAYER, THE (REP, 1943)
DEERSLAYER, THE (FOX, 1943)
DEERSLAYER, THE (series) (FRA–TV, 1968)

DEGAS see BALLET BY DEGAS

DEHEIMNISSE VON LONDON, DIE see OLIVER TWIST

DEL MISMO BARRO see COMMON CLAY

DELIVERANCE (IND, 1919, based on the life of Helen
Keller)
HELEN KELLER IN HER OWN STORY (DER, 1956)
MIRACLE WORKER, THE (CBS–TV, 1957)
HELEN KELLER: THE WORLD I SEE (MGM–TV, 1961)
MIRACLE WORKER, THE (UA, 1962)

DELPHINE see FASHIONS IN LOVE

DELUSIONS OF GRANDEUR see RUY BLAS

DEMI–VIERGES, LES (ITA, 1916, based on the book by
Marcel Prevost)
DEMI–VIERGES, LES (FRA, 1924)
DEMI–VIERGES, LES (FRA, 1936)

DEMOCRACY IN EDUCATION: JOHN DEWEY (short)
(IND–TV, n.d., based on the life of the noted educator)
HUMANISM: JOHN DEWEY (short) (IND, n.d.)

DEMON BARBER OF FLEET STREET see SWEENEY
TODD

DEN FORGYLLDA LERGOKEN (SWE, 1924, source
unknown)
FIA JANSSON FRAN SODER (SWE, 1944)

DENTA PER DENTA see MEADURE FOR MEASURE

DENTE PER DENTE see MEASURE FOR MEASURE

DEPUTY, THE see TIN STAR, THE

DERBY (GER, 1926, based on the book by Ernst Klein)
DERBY (GER, 1949)

DERNIER REFUGE see LOCATAIRE, LA

DERNIER TOURNANT, LE (FRA, 1939, based on the book,
"The Postman Always Rings Twice,"by James M. Cain)
OSSESSIONE (ITA, 1942)
POSTMAN ALWAYS RINGS TWICE, THE (MGM, 1946)

DERNIER TSAR, LE see RASPUTIN, THE BLACK MONK

DERNIERS JOURS DE POMPEII, LES see ULTIMO GIORNO
DE POMPEII, L'

DESARROI see ODETTE

DESDEMONA see OTHELLO

DESERT BRIDE, THE (COL, 1939, based on the story,
"The Adventuress," by Ewart Adamson and Elmer Harris)
KEYHOLE, THE (WB, 1933)
ROMANCE ON THE HIGH SEAS (WB, 1948)

DESERT CRUCIBLE, THE see RAINBOW TRAIL

DESERT FOX, THE see DESERT VICTORY

DESERT GOLD (PAR, 1919, based on the book by Zane Grey)
DESERT GOLD (PAR, 1936)

DESERT HAWK see ARABIAN NIGHTS

DESERT LEGION see ATLANTIDE, L'

DESERT SONG, THE (WB, 1929, based on the operetta by
Frank Mandell, Oscar Hammerstein II and Otto Harbach)
RED SHADOW, THE (short) (WB, 1932)
DESERT SONG, THE (WB, 1943)
DESERT SONG, THE (WB, 1953)
DESERT SONG, THE (NBC–TV, 1955)

DESERT VICTORY (NAV, 1943, based on the life of the
German field marshal)
DESERT FOX, THE (FOX, 1951)
ROMMEL (short) (CBS–TV, 1960)
ERWIN ROMMEL (short) (WOL, 1963)
ERWIN ROMMEL (short) (WOL, 1965)

DESIGNING WOMAN see WOMAN OF THE YEAR

DESIRE see PEAU DE CHAGRIN, LA and SCHONEN
TAGE IN ARANJUWZ, DIE

DESIRE ME see HEIMKEHR

DESIRE UNDER THE ELMS see WOMAN AT THE FAIR

DESPERADO, THE (AA, 1954, based on a book by Clifton
Adams)
COLE YOUNGER, GUNFIGHTER (AA, 1958)

DESPERATE HOURS, THE (PAR, 1955, based on the play
by Joseph Hayes)
DESPERATE HOURS, THE (ABC–TV, 1967)

DESPERATION see DRIVEN

DESTRY see DESTRY RIDES AGAIN

DESTRY RIDES AGAIN (UN, 1932, based on the book by
Max Brand)
DESTRY RIDES AGAIN (UN, 1939)
FRENCHIE (UN, 1951)

DESTRY (UN, 1954)
DESTRY (series) (ABC–TV, 1964)

DETECTIVE, THE see FATHER BROWN, DETECTIVE

DETECTIVE STORY (PAR, 1951, based on the play by
    Sidney Kinglsey)
DETECTIVE STORY (GER–TV, 1963)

DETTE OUBLIEE, LA (RUS, 1911, based on the story,
    "Le Coup de Feu," by Alexander Pushkin)
COUPS DE FEU (FRA, 1939)
COUP DE FEU, LE (ITA, 1941)
COUP DE FEU, LE (POL–TV, 1965)
COUP DE FEU, LE (RUS, 1967)

DEUX FONT LA PAIRE, LES see MORTE EN FUITE, LE

DEUX GAMINES, LES (FRA, 1920, based on a book by
    Arthur Bernede)
DEUX GAMINES, LES (FRA, 1936)
DEUX GAMINES, LES (FRA, 1951)

DEUX GOSSES, LES (FRA, 1912, based on a book by
    Pierre Decourcelle)
DEUX GOSSES, LES (FRA, 1924)
DEUX GOSSES, LES (FRA, 1936)
DEUX GOSSES, LES (ITA, 1951)

DEUX LEGIONAIRES, LES see BEAU HUNKS

DEUX ORPHELINES, LES see   TWO ORPHANS

DEUX TIMIDES, LES (FRA, 1927, based on the play by
    Eugene Labiche and Marc–Michel)
DEUX TIMIDES, LES (FRA, 1941)

DEVDAS (IN, 1935, source unknown)
DEVDAS (IN, 1956)

DEVIL AND DANIEL WEBSTER, THE (ALL THAT MONEY
    CAN BUY) (RKO, 1941, based on the story by Stephen
    Vincent Benet)
DEVIL AND DANIEL WEBSTER, THE (NBC–TV, 1960)
DEVIL AND DANIEL WEBSTER, THE (CBS–TV, 1962)

DEVIL AND THE MAN FROM SMALAND, THE see HIN
OCH SMALANNIGEN

DEVIL BAT, THE (PRC, 1941, based on a story by George
    Bricker)
FLYING SERPENT, THE (PRC, 1946)

DEVIL IS A WOMAN, THE see WOMAN AND THE PUPPET,
THE

DEVILS, THE see JOAN OF THE ANGELS

DEVIL'S ASSISTANT, THE (FRA, 1913, based on a story
    by G. Vertriebe)
DEVIL'S ASSISTANT, THE (MUT, 1917)

DEVIL'S BROTHER, THE see FRA DIAVOLO

DEVIL'S DAFFODIL, THE see DAFFODIL MYSTERY, THE

DEVIL'S DAUGHTER, THE see GIOCONDA, LA and
PHAEDRA

DEVIL'S DISCIPLE, THE (NBC–TV, 1955, based on the
    play by George Bernard Shaw)
DEVIL'S DESCIPLE, THE (UA, 1959)

DEVIL'S HOLIDAY (PAR, 1930, based on a screenplay by
    Edmund Goulding)
SONTAG DES LEBENS (GER, 1930)
FIESTA DEL DIABLO, LA (SPA, 1930)
VACANCES DU DIABLE, LES (FRA, 1931)

DEVIL'S MATE, THE (MON, 1933, based on a screenplay by
    Leonard Fields and David Silverstein)
I KILLED THAT MAN (MON, 1941)

DEVILS OF LOUDON, THE see JOAN OF THE ANGELS

DEVIL'S PLAYGROUND, THE see LADY WHO DARED,
THE and SUBMARINE

DEVOTION (WB, 1946, based on the life and work of the
    Bronte Sisters)
BRONTE SISTERS, THE (short) (IFB, 1970)

DHANWAN see ESMERELDA

DHRUVA (IN, 1934, based on a myth)
DHRUVA (IN, 1936)
DHRUVA (IN, 1937)

DIABLOTINS ROUGES, LES (RUS, 1923, based on a book
    by Pavel Bliakhine)
VENGEURS INSAISISSABLES, LES (RUS, 1967)

DIABOLIQUE (FRA, 1956, based on a book, "Celle qui
    n'etait plus," by Pierre Boileau and Thomas Marcejac)
REFLECTIONS ON MURDER (ABC–TV, 1974)

DIAL M FOR MURDER (BRI–TV, 1952, based on the play
    by Frederick Knott)
DIAL M FOR MURDER (WB, 1954)
DIAL M FOR MURDER (NBC–TV, 1956)
DIAL M FOR MURDER (ABC–TV, 1967)

DIAL 999 (BRI, 1938, based on the book, "The Way Out,"
    by Bruce Graeme)
DIAL 999 (THE WAY OUT) (BRI, 1955)

DIAMOND NECKLACE, THE (BRI, 1921, based on the story,
    "La Parure," by Guy de Maupassant)
PEARL NECKLACE, THE (CHN, 1925)

DIARY OF A CHAMBERMAID (UA, 1946, based on the
    book by Octave Mirbeau)
DIARY OF A CHAMBERMAID (FRA, 1964)

DIARY OF A LOST GIRL see TAGEBUCH EINER VER–
LORENEN, DAS

DIARY OF A MADMAN (UA, 1963, based on the story,
    "Le Norla," by Guy de Maupassant)
DIARY OF A MADMAN (short) (CAN, 1965)
NORLA, LE (short) (FRA, 1967)
DIARY OF A MADMAN (CBS–TV, 1967)
SOFI (IND, 1968)

DIARY OF ANNE FRANK, THE (FOX, 1959, based on the
    book by Anne Frank)
WHO KILLED ANNE FRANK? (short) (CBS–TV, 1964)
DIARY OF ANNE FRANK, THE (ABC–TV, 1967)

DICHTUNG UND WAHRHEIT (GER, 1917, based on the life of Johann Wolfgang von Goethe and an operetta by Franz Lehar)
SOHN DER GOTTER, DER JUNGE GOETHE, DER (GER, 1918)
GOETHE – EIN DOKUMENT DEUTSCHER KULTUR (GER, 1919)
FRIEDERIKE VON SESENHEIM, DIE JUGENDGELIEBTE, GOETHES FRUHLINGSTRAUM (GER, 1930)
FRIEDERIKE (GER, 1932)
GOETHE LEBT . . . ! (GER, 1932)
GOETHE – DER WERDEGANG (GER, 1932)

DICK TURPIN'S LAST RIDE TO YORK (BRI, 1906, based on the legend)
DICK TURPIN (BRI, 1912)
ADVENTURES OF DICK TURPIN (BRI, 1912)
DICK TURPIN'S RIDE TO YORK (BRI, 1913)
DICK TURPIN'S RIDE TO YORK (BRI, 1922)
DICK TURPIN (FOX, 1925)
DICK TURPIN (BRI, 1929)
CABALLERO DE LA NOCHE, EL (SPA, 1932)

LADY AND THE BANDIT, THE (COL, 1951)
DICK TURPIN – HIGHWAYMAN (BRI, 1956)
LEGEND OF YOUNG DICK TURPIN (DIS, 1965)

DICKENS CHRONICLE, A see DICKENS WALKED HERE

DICKENS WALKED HERE (short) (IND, n.d. based on the life and works of author Charles Dickens)
CHARLES DICKENS: BACKGROUND FOR HIS WORKS (short) (COR, 1949)
WORKS OF CHARLES DICKENS, THE (short) (HOF, n.d.)
DICKENS CHRONICLE, A (MHF, 1963)

DICTATOR, THE (PAR, n.d., based on the play by Richard Harding Davis)
DICTATOR, THE (PAR, 1922)

DICTATOR, THE (LOVES OF A DICTATOR) (BRI, 1935, based on a screenplay by Benn W. Levy)
KING IN SHADOW (GER, 1957)

DID I BETRAY? see SCHWARZE ROSEN

DID YOU HEAR THE ONE ABOUT THE TRAVELING SALESLADY? see FIRST TRAVELING SALESLADY, THE

DILLINGER, (MON, 1945, based on historical incidents and characters)
LAST DAYS OF JOHN DILLINGER, THE (CBS–TV, 1971)
DILLINGER (AI, 1973)

DINDON, LE (FRA, 1913, based on a play by George Feydeau)
DINDON, LE (FRA/ITA, 1923)
DINDON, LE FRA, 1951)

DINKY DOODLE IN UNCLE TOM'S CABIN see UNCLE TOM'S CABIN

DINNER AT EIGHT (MGM, 1933, based on the play by Edna Ferber and George S. Kauffman)
DINNER AT EIGHT (CBS–TV, 1955)

DINO (CBS–TV, 1956, based on the teleplay by Reginald Rose)

DINO (AA, 1957)

DIOS DEL MAR, EL see SEA GOD, THE

DIPLOMACY (PAR, 1916, based on the book by Victorien Sardou)
DIPLOMACY (PAR, 1926)

DIRNENTRAGODIE (GER, 1931, based on a book by Wilhelm Braun)
ZWISCHEN NACHT UND MORGEN (GER, 1931)
ZWISCHEN NACHT UND MORGEN (GER, 1944)

DIRTY GERTIE FORM HARLEM, USA see SADIE THOMPSON

DIRTY LITTLE BILLY see BILLY THE KID

DIRTYMOUTH (IND, 1971, based on incidents in the life of comedian Lenny Bruce)
LENNY BRUCE ON TV (short) (NYF, 1972)
LENNY (UA, 1974)

DISCOVERY OF RADIUM, THE see MADAME CURIE

DISHONORABLE DISCHARGE see TO HAVE AND HAVE NOT

DISRAELI (BRI, 1916, based on a play by Louis N. Parker and incidents in the life of the British prime minister)
DISRAELI (UA, 1921)
DISRAELI (WB, 1929)
PRIME MINISTER, THE (BRI, 1941)
INVINCIBLE MR. DISRAELI, THE (NBC–TV, 1963)

DISTANT JOURNEY see GHETTO TEREZIN

DIVE BOMBER see SUBMARINE D–1

DIVIDED HEART, THE (BRI, 1954, based on a screenplay by Jack Whittingham and Richard Hughes)
DIVIDED HEART, THE (NBC–TV, 1952)

DIVINE COMEDY, THE see PURGATORY

DIVINE LADY, THE see ROMANCE OF LADY HAMILTON, THE

DIVINE SPARK, THE (BRI, 1935, based on a story by Walter Reisch)
CASTA DIVA (ITA, 1935)
CASTA DIVA (FRA/ITA, 1954)

DIVORCE OF LADY X, THE see COUNSEL'S OPINION

DIVORCONS (BIO, 1915, based on the play by Victorien Sardou and Emile de Nejac)
LET'S GET A DIVORCE (PAR, 1918)
KISS ME AGAIN (WB, 1925)
DON'T TELL THE WIFE (WB, 1927)
THAT UNCERTAIN FEELING (UA, 1941)

DIXIE MERCHANT (FOX, 1924, based on the book, "Chicken Wagon Family," by Berry Benefield)
CHICKEN WAGON FAMILY (FOX, 1939)

DO DETECTIVES THINK? (short) (PAT, 1927, based on a screenplay by Hal Roach and elaborated upon in the remakes)

GOING BYE BYE (short) (MGM, 1934)
BULLFIGHTERS, THE (FOX, 1945)

DO NOT FOLD, SPINDLE OR MUTILATE (ABC–TV,
    1971, based on a teleplay)
SNOOP SISTERS, THE (series) (NBC–TV, 1972)

DOBIE GILLIS see AFFAIRS OF DOBIE GILLIS, THE

DOBUTSU TAKARAJIMA see PIRATE'S TREASURE

DOCE HOMBRES SIN PIEDAD see 12 ANGRY MEN

DOCK BRIEF (CBS–TV, 1958, based on the play by John
    Mortimer)
DOCK BRIEF (BRI–TV, 1959)
TRIAL AND ERROR (BRI, 1962)

DOCKS OF NEW ORLEANS see MR. WONG, DETECTIVE

DR. BLACK AND MR. HYDE see DR. JEKYLL AND MR.
    HYDE

DR. COPPELIUS see COPPELIA, THE ANIMATED DOLL

DR. CRIPPEN see DR. CRIPPEN AN BORD

DR. CRIPPEN AN BORD (GER, 1942 , based on incidents
    in the life of the notorious criminal)
DR. CRIPPEN LEBT (GER, 1958)
DR. CRIPPEN (BRI, 1964)

DR. CRIPPEN LEBT see DR. CRIPPEN AN BORD

DR. DOLITTLE see ADVENTURES OF DR. DOLITTLE

DR. FAUSTUS see FAUST

DR. GEORGE WASHINGTON CARVER see STORY OF
    DR. CARVER, THE

DOCTOR GLAS (SWE, 1942, based on the play by Hjalmar
    Soderberg)
DOCTOR GLAS (DEN, 1967)

DR. HEIDEGGER'S EXPERIMENT (NBC–TV, 1950, based
    on a story by Nathaniel Hawthorne)
DR. HEIDEGGER'S EXPERIMENT (short) (IND, 1954)
TWICE TOLD TALES (UA, 1963)

DR. JEKYLL see DR. JEKYLL AND MR. HYDE

DR. JEKYLL AND MISS HYDE see DR. JEKYLL AND MR.
    HYDE

DR. JEKYLL AND MR. HYDE (SEL, 1908, based on the
    book by Robert Louis Stevenson. Also the basis for a
    musical play, "After You, Mr. Hyde," in 1968)
DR. JEKYLL AND MR. HYDE (DEN, 1910)
DUALITY OF MAN, THE (BRI, 1910)
DR. JEKYLL AND MR. HYDE (NOR, 1910)
DR. JEKYLL AND MR. HYDE (THA, 1911)
DR. JEKYLL AND MR. HYDE (ED, 1913)
DR JEKYLL AND MR. HYDE (UN, 1913)
DR. JEKYLL AND MR. HYDE (BRI, 1914)
EIN SELTSAMER FALL (GER, 1914)
HORRIBLE HYDE (LUB, 1915)
DR. JEKYLL AND MR. HYDE (PAR, 1920)
DR. JEKYLL AND MR. HYDE (ARR, 1920)

DR. JEKYLL AND MR. HYDE (ARR, 1920)
DR. JEKYLL AND ME. HYSE (PIO, 1920)
JANUSKOPF (GER, 1920)
DR. PYCKLE AND MR. PRIDE (short) (FBO, 1925)
DR. JEKYLL AND MR. HYDE (PAR, 1932)
DR. JEKYLL AND MR. HYDE (MGM, 1941)
DR. JEKYLL AND MR. MOUSE (short) (MGM, 1947)
HOMBRE Y LA BESTIA (ARG, 1950)
DR. JEKYLL (ITA, 1951)
DR. JEKYLL AND MR. HYDE (CBS– TV, 1951)
ABBOTT & COSTELLO MEET DR. JEKYLL AND MR.
    HYDE (UN, 1953)
SHADA KALO (IN, 1953)
DR. JEKYLL AND MR. HYDE (CBS–TV, 1955)
DR. JEKYLL AND MR. HYDE (NBC–TV, 1957)
DR. JEKYLL'S HYDE (short) (WB, 1958)
TESTAMENT DU DOCTEUR CORDELIER, LA (FRA–
    TV, 1959)
UGLY DUCKLING, THE (BRI, 1959)
MY FRIEND JEKYLL (ITA, 1960)
HOUSE OF FRIGHT (JEKYLL'S INFERNO) (BRI, 1961)
TESTAMENT DU DOCTEUR CORDELIER, LA (FRA,
    1961)
NUTTY PROFESSOR, THE (PAR, 1963)
PACT WITH THE DEVIL (MEX, 1968)
STRANGE CASE OF DR. JEKYLL AND MR. HYDE (ABC–
    TV, 1968)
I, MONSTER (BRI, 1970)
DR. JEKYLL AND SISTER HYDE (BRI, 1971)
MAN WITH TWO HEADS, THE (BRI, 1971)
ADULT VERSION OF JEKYLL AND HYDE (IND, 1972)
DR. JEKYLL AND MR. HYDE (NBC–TV, 1973)
DR. BLACK AND MR. HYDE (IND, 1976)

DR. JEKYLL AND MR. MOUSE see DR. JEKYLL AND MR.
    HYDE

DR. JEKYLL AND SISTER HYDE see DR. JEKYLL AND
    MR. HYDE

DR. JEKYLL'S HYDE see DR. JEKYLL AND MR. HYDE

DR. KNOCK see KNOCK

DR. ORLOW (GER, 1927, source unknown)
DR. ORLOW (GER, 1932)

DR. PRAETORIUS (GER, 1933, based on the play by Kurt
    Goetz)
FRAUENARZT DR. PRAETORIUS (GER, 1950)
PEOPLE WILL TALK (FOX, 1951)
DR. PRAETORIUS (GER, 1965)

DR. PYCKLE AND MR. PRIDE see DR. JEKYLL AND MR.
    HYDE

DR. RENAULT'S SECRET see BALAOO

DR. RHYTHM see BADGE OF POLICEMAN O'ROON, THE

DR. SATAN'S ROBOT see MYSTERIOUS DR. SATAN

DR. SCHWEITZER (FRA, 1952, based on the life of the
    noted scientist and musician)
AFRICA AND SCHWEITZER (short) (IND, n.d.)
ALBERT SCHWEITZER (IND, 1957)
ALBERT SCHWEITZER – THE THREE AVENUES OF A
    MIND (USC, 1962)

LEGACY OF ALBERT SCHWEITZER, THE (WB–TV, 1968)

DR. SIMON LOCKE (series) (CAN–TV, 1971, based on a screenplay)
POLICE SURGEON (series) (CAN–TV, 1972)

DR. SYN (BRI, 1937, based on the book by Russell Thorndyke)
NIGHT CREATURES (BRI, 1962)
DR. SYN – ALIAS THE SCARECROW (DIS, 1964)

DR. SYN – ALIAS THE SCARECROW see DR. SYN

DOCTORS AND NURSES see NURSES, THE

DOCTOR'S HOSPITAL see ONE OF OUR OWN

DOCTOR'S SECRET, THE (PAR, 1929, based on the play, "Half an Hour," by James M. Barrie)
DOCTOR'S SECRET, THE (POL, 1930)
SECRETO DEL DOCTOR, EL (SPA, 1930)
DOCTOR'S SECRET, THE (SWE, 1930)
SECRET DU DOCTEUR, LA (FRA, 1930)

DODSWORTH (UA, 1936, based on the book by Sinclair Lewis)
DODSWORTH (CBS–TV, 1950)
DODSWORTH (NBC–TV, 1956)

DOG OF FLANDERS, A (THA, 1914, based on a story by Ouida)
BOY OF FLANDERS, A (MGM, 1924)
DOG OF FLANDERS, A (RKO, 1935)
DOG OF FLANDERS, A (FOX, 1959)
DOG OF FLANDERS, A (series) (GER–TV, 1976)

DOG'S LIFE, A see ZIVOT JE PES

DOLLARS AND CENTS see DOLLARS AND THE WOMAN

DOLLARS AND THE WOMAN (LUB, 1916, based on a story by Albert Payson Terhune)
DOLLARS AND THE WOMAN (VIT, 1920)

DOLL'S HOUSE, A (THA, 1911, based on the play by Hendrick Ibsen)
DOLL'S HOUSE, A (IND, 1915)
DOLL'S HOUSE, A (UN, 1917)
HER SACRIFICE (RUS, 1917)
DOLL'S HOUSE, A (PAR, 1918)
DOLL'S HOUSE, A (UA, 1922)
NORA (GER, 1923)
CASA DE MUNECAS (ARG, 1943)
NORA (GER, 1944)
DOLL'S HOUSE, A (NBC–TV, 1959)
DOLL'S HOUSE, A (CBS–TV, 1955)
DOLL'S HOUSE, A (PAR, 1973)
DOLL'S HOUSE, A (BRI, 1973)

DOLLY VARDEN (BRI, 1906, based on the book, "Barnaby Rudge," by Charles Dickens)
BARNABY RUDGE (ED, 1913)
BARNABY RUDGE (BRI, 1915)

DOMBEY AND SON (BRI, 1917, based on the book by Charles Dickens)
DOMBEY AND SON (IND, 1919)

DON CARLOS (ITA, 1909, based on the book by Fredrich von Schiller)
DON CARLOS (FRA, 1909)
DON CARLOS (GER, 1910)
DON CARLOS (ITA, 1917)
CARLOS UND ELISABETH (GER, 1924)
DON CARLOS (AUS, 1960)

DON CESAR DE BAZAN (KAL, 1915, based on the story by Adolphy d'Ennery and Philippe Dumanoir, adapted from "Ruy Blas" by Victor Hugo)
ROSITA (UA, 1923)
SPANISH DANCER, THE (PAR, 1923)

DON GIOVANNI see DON JUAN

DON JUAN (FRA, 1905, based on a poem by Lord Byron. Also the basis of Mozart's opera in 1787)
DON GIOVANNI (ITA, 1907)
END OF DON JUAN, THE (FRA, 1911)
DON JUAN AND FAUST (FRA, 1922)
DON JUAN AND THE THREE WOMEN (GER, 1922)
DON JUAN (GER, 1922)
DON JUAN (short) (BRI, 1922)
DON JUAN (SPA, 1924)
DON JUAN (WB, 1926)
DON JUAN AND THE GIRL'S SCHOOL (GER, 1928)
ADVENTURES OF DON JUAN (WB, 1948)
DON JUAN (SPA, 1950)
DON GIOVANNI (BRI, 1954)
DON JUAN (GER, 1956)
PANTALOONS (FRA, 1956)
DON GIOVANNI (DCA, 1957)
DON JUAN (short) (POL, 1963)
ALL THE WORLDS WOMEN (BRA, 1967)
DON GIOVANNI (ITA, 1970)
DON JUAN, OR IF DON JUAN WERE A WOMAN (FRA, 1973)

DON JUAN (FRA, 1907, based on the play by Moliere)
DON JUAN GER, 1922)
DON JUAN (FRA/SPA, 1955)

DON JUAN AND FAUST see DON JUAN AND FAUST

DON JUAN AND THE GIRL'S SCHOOL see DON JUAN

DON JUAN AND THE 3 WOMEN see DON JUAN

DON JUAN DIPLOMATICO see BOUDOIR DIPLOMAT

DON JUAN IN HELL (NET–TV, 1960, based on the play , "Man and Superman," by George Bernard Shaw)
DON JUAN IN HELL (NET–TV, 1965)

DON JUAN, OR IF DON JUAN WERE A WOMAN see DON JUAN

DON JUAN TENORIO (SPA, 1908, based on the book by Jose Zorrilla y Moral)
DON JUAN TENORIO (SPA, 1922)

DON PAISIBLE, LE (RUS, 1930, based on a book by Mikhail Cholokhov)
  DON PAISIBLE, LE (RUS, 1958)

DON QUICHOTTE see DON QUIXOTE

DON QUIXOTE (FRA, 1903, based on the book by Miguel Cervantes)
  DON QUIXOTE (FRA, 1908)
  DON QUIXOTE (SPA, 1908)
  DON QUIXOTE (short) (FRA, 1909)
  DON QUIXOTE (FRA, 1913)
  DON QUIXOTE (TRI, 1915)
  DON QUIXOTE (ITA, 1915)
  PASSIONATE FRIENDS, THE (BRI, 1923)
  DON QUIXOTE (GER/SPA, 1926)
  DON QUIXOTE (DEN, 1926)
  DON QUIXOTE (BRI, 1933)
  DON QUIXOTE (GER, 1933)
  DON QUIXOTE (FRA, 1933)
  DON QUIXOTE (short) (IND, 1934)
  DON QUIXOTE (BRI, 1935)
  DON QUIXOTE DE LA MANCHA (SPA, 1947)
  DON QUIXOTE (MEX, 1955)
  DON QUIXOTE (ITA, 1956)
  DON QUIXOTE (RUS, 1957)
  I, DON QUIXOTE (CBS–TV, 1959)
  DON QUIXOTE (YUG, 1961)
  DULCINEA (SPA, 1962)
  DON QUIXOTE (VS. THE SYSTEM) (short) (RAD, 1962)
  GIRL FROM LA MANCHA, THE (ITA, 1963)
  MR. MAGOO'S STORY BOOK (UPA, 1964)
  DON QUICHOTTE (series) (FRA,–TV, 1965)
  DON QUIXOTE (short) (FRA/GER/SPA, 1967)
  DULCINEA DEL TOBOSO (FRA/GER/SPA 1967)
  MAINLY ON THE PLAINS (NBC–TV, 1967)
  DON QUIXOTE AND SANCHO PANZA (ITA, 1968)
  MAN OF LA MANCHA (UA, 1972)
  DON QUIXOTE (AUT, 1973)
  ADVENTURES OF DON QUIXOTE (BRI–TV, 1973)
  AMOUROUS ADVENTURES OF DON QUIXOTE AND SANCHO PANZA (IND, 1976)

DON QUIXOTE AND SANCHO PANZA see DON QUIXOTE

DON QUIJOTE DE LA MANCHA see DON QUIXOTE

DONA MENTIRAS see LADY LIES, THE

DONA PERFECTA (MEX, 1949, based on the book by Benito Perez)
  DONA PERFECTA (SPA, 1977)

DONKEY SKIN see PEAU D'ANE

DONKOSAKENLIED, DAS (GER, 1929, source unknown)
  DONKOSAKENLIED, DAS (GER, 1956)

DONOGOO–TONKA (GER, 1936, based on the book by Jules Romains)
  DONOGOO–TONKA (FRA, 1936)

DONOVAN'S BRAIN see LADY AND THE MONSTER, THE

DON'T BET ON WOMEN (FOX, 1931, based on the story, "All Women are Bad," by William Anthony McGuire)
  CONOCESA TU MUJER? (SPA, 1931)
DON'T MARRY (FOX, 1928, based on a story by Philip Klein and Sidney Lanfield
  DOS MAS UNO (SPA, 1934)

DON'T TELL THE WIFE see DIVORCONS

DON'T TOUCH WHITE WOMEN! see BUFFALO BILL and CUSTER'S LAST STAND

DOOMED BATALLION (UN, 1932, based on a story by Luis Trenker)
  SKI PATROL (UN, 1940)

DOOR WITH THE SEVEN LOCKS, THE see CHAMBER OF HORRORS

DOPPELBRAUTIGAM, DIE see ZIVOT JE PES

DOPPELTE LOTTCHEN, DAS (GER, 1950, based on a book by Erich Kastner)
  TWICE UPON A TIME (BRI, 1953)
  PARENT TRAP, THE (DIS, 1961)

DORA (BRI, 1910, based on a poem by Alfred Lord Tennyson)
  DORA (BRI, 1912)

DORA THE SPY (ITA, 1917, based on the book, "Dora," by Victorien Sardou)
  DORA THE SPY (ITA/SPA, 1943)

DORF·IN DER HEIMAT, DAS see POLE POPPENSPALER

DORIAN GRAY see PICTURE OF DORIAN GREY, THE

DOROTHY AND THE SCARECROW OF OZ (SEL, 1910, based on the books by Frank Baum)
  LAND OF OZ (SEL, 1910)
  PATCHWORK GIRL OF OZ, THE (PAR, 1914)
  HIS MAJESTY, THE SCARECROW OF OZ (OZ, 1914)
  MAGIC CLOAK OF OZ, THE (OZ, 1914)
  RAGGED GIRL OF OZ, THE (OZ, 1919)
  WIZARD OF OZ, THE (IND, 1925)
  WIZARD OF OZ, THE (short) (IND, 1933)
  WIZARD OF OZ, THE (MGM, 1939)
  LAND OF OZ, THE (NBC–TV, 1960)
  TALES OF THE WIZZARD OF OZ (series) (TV, 1961)
  RETURN TO OZ (UA–TV, 1963)
  FANTASY . . . 3 (SPA, 1967)
  WONDERFUL LAND OF OZ, THE (CHI, 1969)
  JOURNEY BACK TO OZ (IND, 1977)
  WIZARD OF OZ, THE (IND, 1977)
  OZ (AUT, 1976)
  20TH CENTURY OZ (IND, 1977)
  WIZ, THE (UN, 1978)

DOS MAS UNO see DON'T MARRY

DOTHBOY'S HALL see NICHOLAS NICKLEBY

DOUBLE–DECKERS, THE see MAGNIFICENT 6½, THE

DOUBLE DOOR (PAR, 1936, based on the play by Elizabeth McFadden)
  DOUBLE DOOR (NBC–TV, 1947)

DOUBLE–DYED DECEIVER, THE (MGM, 1920, based on a story by O. Henry)
  TEXAN, THE (PAR, 1930)
  LLANO KID, THE (PAR, 1939)

DOUBLE EVENT   (BRI, 1921, based on a play by Sidney
    Blow and Douglas Hoare)
    DOUBLE EVENT   (BRI, 1934)

DOUBLE IDENTITY   see   RIVER'S END

DOUBLE INDEMNITY   (PAR, 1944, based on the book by
    James M. Cain)
    DOUBLE INDEMNITY   (NBC--TV, 1954)
    DOUBLE INDEMNITY   (ABC--TV, 1973)

DOUBLE LIFE, A   (UN, 1948, based on a screenplay by
    Ruth Gordon and Garson Kanin)
    DOUBLE LIFE, A   (NBC–TV, 1973)

DOUBLE LIFE, A   see also   OTHELLO

DOUBLE SUICIDE   (JAP, 1969, source unknown)
    SHADOW RIVER   (GER, 1975)

DOUBROVSKY   (RUS, 1911, based on the book by Alexan--
    der Pushkin)
    DOUBROVSKY   (RUS, 1913)
    EAGLE, THE   (UA, 1925)
    DOUBROVSKY   (RUS, 1936)
    BLACK EAGLE, THE   (ITA, 1946)
    VENGEANCE OF THE BLACK EAGLE, THE   (ITA, 1951)
    DOUBROVSKY   (ITA/YUG, 1959)
    SONS OF THE BLACK EAGLE, THE   (ITA, 1968)

DOUBTING THOMAS   (FOX, 1935, based on the play, "The
    Torch Bearers," by George Kelly)
    TOO BUSY TO WORK   (FOX, 1939)

DOUCE, LA   (RUS, 1960, based on a book by Feyodor
    Dostoyevsky)
    FEMME DOUCE, UNE   (FRA, 1969)

DOUGHBOYS   (MGM, 1930, based on a story by Al Boasberg
    and Sidney Lazarus)
    DE FRENTE MARCHEN   (SPA, 1930)

DOUGHNUTS   (WW, 1964, based on the Homer Price stories
    by Robert McCloskey)
    HOMER AND THE WACKY DOUGHNUT MACHINE
    (ABC--TV, 1978)

DOVE, THE   (UA, 1928, based on the play by Willard Mack)
    GIRL OF THE RIO, THE   (RKO, 1932)
    GIRL AND THE GAMBLER, THE   (RKO, 1939)

DOVER--CALAIS   see   NIE WIEDER LIEBE

DOVER ROAD, THE   see   LITTLE ADVENTURESS, THE

DOWN TO EARTH   see   HERE COMES MR. JORDAN

DOWNY GIRL   see   DUNUNGEN

DRACULA   see   NOSFERATU

DRACULA HAS RISEN FROM THE GRAVE   see
    NOSFERATU

DRACULA TODAY   see   NOSFERATU

DRACULA VS. FRANKENSTEIN   see   NOSFERATU

DRACULA'S DAUGHTER   see   NOSFERATU

DRAGON'S BLOOD   see   SIEGFRIED

DRAKE OF ENGLAND   see   DRAKE'S LOVE STORY

DRAKE'S LOVE STORY   (BRI, 1913, based on the life of the
    noted seaman)
    DRAKE OF ENGLAND   (BRI, 1935)
    SIR FRANCIS DRAKE'S LIFE AND VOYAGES   (short)
    (COR, 1956)
    SIR FRANCIS DRAKE   (short)   (EBE, 1957)
    SIR FRANCIS DRAKE   (series)   (BRI--TV, 1962)

DRAMA OF KRISHNA   (IN, 1935, based on a legend)
    DRAMA OF KRISHNA   (IN, 1945)

DRAMA VON MAYERLING   see   MAYERLING

DRAME A LA CHASSE, UN   (RUS, 1913, based on the book
    by Anton Chekhov)
    DRAME A LA CHASSE, UN   (RUS, 1918)
    SUMMER STORM   (UA, 1944)

DREAM GIRL   (PAR, 1948, based on the play by Elmer Rice.
    Also the basis of a musical comedy, "Skyscraper," in 1965)
    DREAM GIRL   (NBC--TV, 1955)

DREAM NO MORE   (ISR, 1948, based on a screenplay by
    Joseph Krumgold)
    DREAM NO MORE   (ISR, n.d.)

DREAM OF A RAREBIT FIEND   (ED, 1906, based on a
    screenplay, author unknown)
    AFTER THE WELSH RABBIT   (ED, 1913)
    DREAM OF A RAREBIT FIEND   (IND, 1921)

DREAM OF BUTTERFLY, THE   see   MADAME BUTTERFLY

DREAM OF LOVE   (short)   (MGM, 1939, based on the life and
    music of composer Franz Liszt)
    LISZT AND HIS MUSIC   (short)   (COR, 1957)
    SONG WITHOUT END   (COL, 1960)
    MAESTRO FRANZ LISZT AT WEIMAR   (short)   (TFC,
    1961)
    VIRTUOSO FRANZ LISZT AS COMPOSER   (short)
    (TFC, 1961)
    LISZTOMANIA   (BRI, 1975)

DREAM OF LOVE   see   ADRIENNE LECOUVREUR

DREAM OF OLD SCROOGE   see   CHRISTMAS CAROL, A

DREAM THAT WOULDN'T DOWN, THE   see   FATHER OF
    THE SPACE AGE, THE

DREAM WOMAN   see   WOMAN IN WHITE, THE

DREAMING LIPS   see   MELO

DREAMS OF YOUTH   (JAP, 1923, source unknown)
    DREAMS OF YOUTH   (JAP, 1928)

DREI FRAUEN VON URBAN HELL, DIE   (GER, 1928,
    based on the book, "Hell in Frauensee," by Vicki Baum)
    LAC--AIX--DAMES   (FRA, 1934)

DREI VON DER TANKSTELLE, DIE   (GER, 1930, based on
    the book by Paul Frank and Franz Schulz)
    CHEMIN DU PARADIS, LE   (FRA, 1930)
    DREI VON DER TANKSTELLE, DIE   (GER, 1955)

DREIGROSCHENOPER, DIE   see   THREE--PENNY OPERA,

THE

DREIMADERLHAUS, DAS (GER, 1918, based on a story
    by Rudolf Hans Bartsch)
    DREI MADERL UM SCHUBERT (GER, 1936)
    DREIMADERLHAUS, DAS (AUS, 1958)

DRESSED TO KILL (FOX, 1928, based on a story by William
    M. Conselman)
    TALL, DARK AND HANDSOME (FOX, 1941)
    LOVE THAT BRUTE (FOX, 1950)

DREYFUS CASE, THE see AFFAIR DREYFUS, L'

DRIFTING (UN, 1923, based on a play by John Colton)
    SHANGHAI LADY (UN, 1929)

DRINK see ASSOMMOIR, L'

DRIVEN (IND, 1916, based on the book, "The Evolution of
    Katherine," by E. Temple Thurston)
    DESPERATION (UN, 1917)

DRIVEN WESTWARD see BRIGHAM YOUNG,
    FRONTIERSMAN

DRUMS OF JEOPARDY, THE (IND, 1924, based on the book
    by Harold McGrath)
    DRUMS OF JEOPARDY, THE (TIF, 1931)

DRUNKARD, THE see OLD--FASHIONED, THE

DU SANG L'AUBE see MARE NOSTRUM

DUALITY OF MEN see DR. JEKYLL AND MR. HYDE

DUBARRY (IND, 1915, based on a play by David Belasco)
    MADAME DUBARRY (FOX, 1918)
    PASSION (GER, 1918)
    MADAME DUBARRY (MGM, 1919)
    DUBARRY, VON HEUTE EINE (GER, 1926)
    MADAME DUBARRY (MGM, 1928)
    DUBARRY -- WOMAN OF PASSION (UA, 1930)
    MADAME DUBARRY (WB, 1934)
    I GIVE MY HEART (BRI, 1936)
    DUBARRY, DIE (GER, 1951)
    MADAME DUBARRY (ITA, 1953)
    MADAME DUBARRY (FRA, 1954)

DUBARRY, VON HEUTE EINE see DUBARRY

DUBARRY -- WOMAN OF PASSION see DUBARRY

DUBROVSKY see EAGLE, THE

DUCHESSE DE DANTZIG, LA see MADAME SANS--GENE

DUCHESSE DE LANGEAIS, LA (FRA, 1910, based on a
    story by Honore de Balzac)
    ETERNAL FLAME, THE (FN, 1922)
    LIEBE (GER, 1927)
    DUCHESSE DE LANGEAIS, LA (FRA, 1942)

DUCK SOUP (short) (PAT, 1927, based on a screenplay by
    Hal Roach and elaborated upon in the remake)
    ANOTHER FINE MESS (short) (MGM, 1930)
    DE BOTE EN BOTE (short) (MGM, 1930)

DUDE RANGER, THE (FOX, 1934, based on a story by Zane
    Grey)
    ROLL ALONG COWBOY (FOX, 1937)

DUE ORFANELLE, LE see TWO ORPHANS

DUEL, THE (RUS, 1961, based on the book by Anton
    Chekhov)
    HOMME NI BON NI MAUVAIS, UN (RUS, 1973)

DUEL AT ICHIJOLI TEMPLE (JAP, 1941, source unknown)
    DUEL AT ICHIJOLI TEMPLE (JAP, 1955)
    DUEL AT ICHIJOLI TEMPLE (JAP, 1964)

DUEL AT THE O.K. CORRAL see GUNFIGHT AT THE
    O.K. CORRAL

DUFFY OF SAN QUENTIN (WB, 1954, based on a book by
    Clinton T. Duffy and Dean Jennings)
    STEEL CAGE, THE (UA, 1954)

DUFFY'S TAVERN (PAR, 1945, based on a radio series by
    various authors)
    DUFFY'S TAVERN (series) (NBC--TV, 1954)

DULCINEA see DON QUIXOTE

DULCINEA DEL TOBOSO see DON QUIXOTE

DULCY (FN, 1923, based on the play by George S. Kauffman
    and Marc Connelly)
    NOT SO DUMB (MGM, 1930)
    DULCY (NBC--TV, 1939)
    DULCY (MGM, 1940)

DUMB LUCK see RANSOM OF RED CHIEF, THE

DUMMKOPF, DER see IDIOT, THE

DUMMY, THE (PAR, 1917, based on the play by Harvey
    O'Higgins and Harriet Ford)
    DUMMY, THE (PAR, 1929)

DUNJA see POSTMASTER, THE

DUNUNGEN (SWE, 1919, based on the play by Selma
    Lagerlof)
    DUNUNGEN (SWE, 1941)

DURAND OF THE BADLANDS (FOX, 1917, based on the
    story by Maibelle Heikes Justice)
    DURAND OF THE BADLANDS (FOX, 1925)

DUST BE MY DESTINY (WB, 1939, based on the book by
    Jerome Odlum)
    I WAS FRAMED (WB, 1942)

DUVET, LE (SWE, 1919, based on the book by Selma
    Lagerlof)
    DUVET, LE (SWE, 1941)

DWENADZET STULOW see IT'S IN THE BAG

DYBBUK, THE (POL, 1937, based on a legend and the play
    by S. Anski)
    DYBBUK, THE (GER, 1938)
    DYBBUK, THE (CBS--TV, 1949)
    DYBBUK, THE (NET--TV, 1960)
    DYBBUK, THE (GER/ISR, 1967)

EAGLE, THE (UA, 1925, based on the book, "Dubrovsky,"
    by Alexander Pushkin)
  DUBROVSKY (RUS, 1936)
  VIGILANTES ARE COMING (REP, 1936)
  VINDICATORE (ITA, 1959)

EAGLE IN A CAGE see NAPOLEON

EARLY LIFE OF DAVID COPPERFIELD, THE see LITTLE
    EMILY

EARLY LIGHT OF DAWN, THE see SONG OF A NA-
    TION

EARLY TO BED see ICH BEI TAG UND DU BEI NACHT

EARTH SPIRIT see LULU

EARTHBOUND (GOL, 1920, based on a story by Basil King)
  EARTHBOUND (FOX, 1940)

EASIEST PROFESSION, THE see SCANDALS OF
    CLOCHEMERLE, THE

EASIEST WAY, THE (CKY, 1917, based on the play by
    Eugene Walter)
  EASIEST WAY, THE (MGM, 1931)
  QUANT ON EST BELLE (FRA, 1931)

EAST IS WEST (FN, 1922, based on the play by Samuel
    Shipman and John B. Hymer)
  EAST IS WEST (UN, 1930)
  ORIENTE Y OCCIDENTE (SPA, 1930)

EAST LYNNE (BRI, 1902, based on a story by Mrs. Henry
    Wood)
  EAST LYNNE (VIT, 1908)
  EAST LYNNE (BRI, 1910)
  EAST LYNNE (BRI, 1913) (2 versions)
  EAST LYNNE (BIO, 1915)
  EAST LYNNE (FOX, 1916)
  EAST LYNNE (HOD, 1921)
  EAST LYNNE (IND, 1921)
  EAST LYNNE (AUT, 1922)
  EAST LYNNE (short) (BRI, 1922)
  EAST LYNNE (FOX, 1926)
  EX--FLAME (IND, 1930)
  EAST LYNNE (FOX, 1931)

EAST SIDE, WEST SIDE (FOX, 1927, based on the book by
    Felix Riesenberg)
  SKYLINE (FOX, 1931)

EASY COME, EASY GO (PAR, 1928, based on a play by
    Owen Davis)
  ONLY SAPS WORK (PAR, 1930)

EASY TO WED see LIBELED LADY

EAUX PRINTANIERES, LES see FRUHLINGSFLUTEN

EBB TIDE (SEL, 1915, based on the story by Robert Louis
    Stevenson and Lloyd Osbourne)
  EBB TIDE (PAR, 1922)
  EBB TIDE (BRI, 1932)
  EBB TIDE (PAR, 1937)
  ADVENTURE ISLAND (PAR, 1947)
  REFLUX OU L'ENFER AU PARADIS, LE (FRA, 1962)

EBBERODS BANK (SWE, 1926, source unknown)
  EBBERODS BANK (SWE, 1935)
  EBBERODS BANK (SWE, 1947)

ECHEC AU ROI see ROYAL BED, THE

ECOLE DES COCOTTES, L' (FRA, 1934, based on the play
    by Paul Armont and Marcel Gerbidou)
  ECOLE DES COCOTTES, L' (FRA, 1938)

ECSTASY (CZE, 1933, based on a screenplay by Jacques A.
    Koerpel)
  ECSTASY 70 (GER/ITA, 1969)

ECSTASY 70 see ECSTASY

EDDIE (NBC--TV, 1958, based on a teleplay, "Sammy," by
    Ken Hughes)
  SMALL WORLD OF SAMMY LEE (BRI--TV, n.d.)
  SMALL WORLD OF SAMMY LEE, THE (BRI, 1963)

EDELWEISSKONIG, DER (GER, 1938, based on the book
    by Ludwig Ganghofer)
  EDELWEISSKONIG, DER (GER, 1957)

EDGAR ALLAN POE (BIO, 1909, based on the poem, "The
    Raven," by Edgar Allan Poe)
  RAVEN, THE (FRA, 1912)
  RAVEN, THE (IND, 1912)
  RAVEN, THE (ESS, 1915)
  RAVEN, THE (UN, 1935)
  RAVEN, THE (short) (PAR, 1942)
  RAVEN, THE (IND, 1948)
  RAVEN, THE (IND, 1954)
  RAVEN, THE (AI, 1962)

EDGAR ALLAN POE: BACKGROUND FOR HIS WORKS
    (short) (COR, 1958, based on the life and works of the
    noted American author)
  POE: A VISIT WITH THE AUTHOR (short) (IND, n.d.)
  EDGAR ALLAN POE (short) (USC, 1962)
  EDGAR ALLAN POE (short) (PAR, 1971)

EDGE OF THE CITY see MAN IS TEN FEET TALL, A

EDIPO RE see OEDIPUS REX

EDISON THE MAN see YOUNG TOM EDISON

EDITH CAVELL see NURSE CAVELL

EDUCATION DE PRINCE (FRA, 1926, based on a book by
    Maurice Donnay)
  EDUCATION DE PRINCE (FRA, 1938)

EDUCATION SENTIMENTALE, UNE (FRA, 1961, based on
    the book by Harold Brodkey)
  FIRST LOVE (PAR, 1977)

EDVARD MUNCH (short) (RAD, 1968, based on the life
    and work of the impressionist painter)
  EDVARD MUNCH (NOR/SWE, 1976)

EDWARD, MY SON (MGM, 1949, based on the play by
    Robert Morley and Noel Langley)
  EDWARD, MY SON (CBS-TV, 1955)

EDWARD STEICHEN see FAMILY OF MAN, THE

EERIE TALES (GER, 1919, based on the story, "The Black Cat," by Edgar Allan Poe)
SCHWARZE KATZE, DIE (GER, 1932)
LIVING DEAD, THE (GER, 1934)
BLACK CAT, THE (UN, 1934)
BLACK CAT, THE (UN, 1941)
BLACK CAT, THE (short) (IND, 1957)
TALES OF TERROR (AI, 1962)
BLACK CAT, THE (IND, 1965)
BLACK CAT (BRI, 1966)
APOKAL (GER, 1971)
TUO VIZIO E UNA STANZA CHIUSA E SOLO IO NE NO LA CHIARE, IL (ITA, 1972)
SABBATH OF THE BLACK CAT, THE (AUT, 1973)

EFFECT OF GAMMA RAYS ON MAN--IN--THE--MOON MARIGOLDS (TV, 1966, based on the play by Paul Zindel)
EFFECT OF GAMMA RAYS ON MAN--IN--THE--MOON MARIGOLDS (FOX, 1972)

EFFI BRIEST see SCHRITT VOM WEGE, DER

EGG AND I, THE (UN, 1947, based on the book by Betty McDonald)
EGG AND I, THE (series) (CBS--TV, 1951)

EGGHEADS ROBOT (BRI, 1971, source unknown)
TROUBLESOME DOUBLE, THE (BRI, 1971)

EHESKANDAL IM HAUSE FROMONT JUN. UND RISLER SEN. see FROMONT JEUNE ET RISLER AINE

EHESTREIK (GER, 1930, based on the book by Julius Pohl)
EHESTREIK (GER, 1935)
EHESTREIK (GER, 1953)

EID DES STEPHAN HULLER, DER (GER, 1912, based on a story by Felix Hollaender)
VARIETY (GER, 1925)
VARIETIES (FRA/GER, 1935)

EIGHT GIRLS IN A BOAT see 8 MAEDELS IN BOOT

EIGHT IRON MEN (COL, 1952, based on the play, "A Sound of Hunting," by Harry Brown)
SOUND OF HUNTING, A (NBC--TV, 1951)
EIGHT IRON MEN (NBC--TV, 1955)
SOUND OF HUNTING, A (CBS--TV, 1962)

EIN BREIRA (short) (IND, n.d., source unlisted)
EIN BREIRA (short) (BRI, c1967)

EIN LIED GEHT UM DIE WELT (GER, 1933, based on the book by Ernst Neubach and Heinz Goldberg)
EIN LIED GEHT UM DIE WELT (GER, 1958)

EIN SELTSAMER FALL see DR. JEKYLL AND MR. HYDE

EIN TOLLER TAG see FIGARO'S WEDDING

EINE FRAU, DIE WEISS WAS SIE WILL (CZE/GER, 1934, based on the operetta by Louis Verneuil, Alfred Gruenwald and Oscar Straus)
EINE FRAU, DIE WEISS WAS SIE WILL (GER, 1958)

EINE SIEBZEHNJAHRIGE see GEFAHRLICHE LIEBE

EINGEBILDETE DRANKE, DU (GER, 1920, source unknown)

EINGEBILDETE DRANKE, DU (GER, 1952)

EINMAL EINE GROSSE DAME SEIN (GER, 1934, source unknown)
EINMAL EINE GROSSE DAME SEIN (GER, 1957)

EINMAL KEINE SORGEN HABEN see DAY WELL SPENT, A

EINMALEINS DER LIEVE see DAY WELL SPENT, A

EKEL, DAS (GER, 1931, based on the book by Hans Reismann and Toni Impekoven)
EKEL, DAS (GER, 1939)

EL DORADO see RIO BRAVO

EL GRECO TREASURES see GRECO, EL

ELEANOR ROOSEVELT – THE FIRST LADY OF THE WORLD (MGM--TV, 1962, based on the life of the first lady of President Franklin Delano Roosevelt)
ELEANOR ROOSEVELT STORY, THE (IND, 1965)
ELEANOR ROOSEVELT STORY (short) (STE, 1965)
FIRST LADY OF THE WORLD: ELEANOR ROOSEVELT, THE (short) (PAR, 1974)
CONVERSATION WITH ELEANOR ROOSEVELT, A (short) (IND, n.d.)

ELEKTRA (VIT, 1910, based on the play by Euripides)
ELECTRA (LOP, 1963)
BELOVED ELEKTRA (HUN, 1975)

ELEPHANT BOY (BRI, 1937, based on the book, "Tomai of the Elephants," by Rudyard Kipling)
ELEPHANT BOY (series) (AUT--TV, 1973)

11TH COMMANDMENT, THE see JEDENACTE PRIKAZANI

ELF SCHILL SCHEN OFFIZIERE, DIE (GER, 1926, source unknown)
ELF SCHILL SCHEN OFFIZIERE, DIE (GER, 1932)

ELI WHITNEY (short) (EBE, 1951, based on the life and works of the noted inventor)
ELI WHITNEY (short) (MAC, n.d.)
ELI WHITNEY INVENTS THE COTTON GIN (short) (CBS--TV, 1956)

ELIXIRS OF THE DEVIL, THE see HOFFMANN'S ERZAHLUNGEN

ELIZABETH R see QUEEN ELIZABETH

ELIZABETH THE QUEEN see QUEEN ELIZABETH

ELMER THE GREAT see FAST COMPANY

ELUSIVE ISABEL see ADVENTURES IN DIPLOMACY

ELUSIVE PIMPERNEL, THE see SCARLET PIMPERNEL, THE

ELVIRA MADIGAN see CIRCUS TRAGEDY

ELVIS ON TOUR see ELVIS -- THAT'S THE WAY IT IS

ELVIS -- THAT'S THE WAY IT IS (MGM, 1971, documen--taries on the noted popular singer)

ELVIS ON TOUR   (MGM, 1973)

EMANCIPATION PROCLAMATION, THE   see   ABRAHAM
    LINCOLN

EMDEN, THE   (GER, 1926, source unknown)
    CRUISER EMDEN, THE   (GER, 1932)

EMERGENCY   (series)   (NBC--TV, 1971, based on a teleplay)
    EMERGENCY PLUS FOUR   (series)   (NBC–TV, 1973)

EMERGENCY WEDDING   see   YOU BELONG TO ME

EMIL AND THE DETECTIVE   see   EMIL UND DIE
    DETEKTIVE

EMIL UND DIE DETEKTIVE   (GER, 1923, based on the
    book by Erich Kastner)
    EMIL UND DIE DETEKTIVE   (GER, 1931)
    EMIL THE DETECTIVE   (BRI, 1931)
    EMIL AND THE DETECTIVE   (BRI, 1934)
    FIVE LITTLE MORAL ONES   (CHN, 1937)
    EMIL UND DIE DETEKTIVE   (GER, 1954)
    EMIL AND THE DETECTIVES   (DIS, 1964)

EMILE VERHAEREN   (short)   (BEL, 1954, based on the
    life of Emile Verhaeren)
    EMILE VERHAEREN   (HOL--TV, 1967)
    EMILE VERHAEREN   (FRA--TV, 1973)

EMILIA GALOTTI   (GER, 1913, based on the book by
    Gotthold Ephriam Lessing)
    EMILIA GALOTTI   (GER, 1918)
    EMILIA GALOTTI   (GER, 1957)

EMILIANO ZAPATA   see   VIVA ZAPATA

EMMA   (MGM, 1932, based on a story by Frances Marion)
    EMMA   (NBC--TV, 1954)

EMMA HAMILTON   see   ROMANCE OF LADY HAMILTON,
    THE

EMPEROR AND THE GOLEM, THE   see   GOLEM, THE

EMPEROR HIROHITO   see   HIROHITO

EMPEROR JONES, THE   (BRI, 1933, based on the play by
    Eugene O'Neill)
    EMPEROR JONES, THE   (NBC--TV, 1955)

EMPEROR OF PORTUGAL, THE   see   TOWER OF LIES

EMPEROR WALTZ, THE   see   CHAMPAGNE WALTZ

EMPEROR'S CANDLESTICKS, THE   see   LEUCHTER DES
    KAISERS, DIE

EMPEROR'S NEW CLOTHES, THE   (short)   (UPA, 1952,
    based on the story by Hans Christian Andersen)
    EMPEROR'S NEW CLOTHES, THE   (NBC--TV, 1958)
    EMPEROR'S NEW CLOTHES, THE   (short)   (MAC, 1958)
    EMPEROR'S NEW CLOTHES, THE   (RAN, 1972)

EMPEROR'S NEW CLOTHES, THE   see also   HANS
    CHRISTIAN ANDERSEN

EMPEROR'S NIGHTINGALE, THE   (CZE, 1951, based on
    the story by Hans Christian Andersen)

CHINESE NIGHTINGALE, THE   (GER/HOL, 1964)

EMPEROR'S SNUFFBOX   THE   see   CITY AFTER MIDNIGHT

EMPIRE   (series)   (NBC-TV, 1962, based on a teleplay)
    REDIGO   (series)   (NBC-TV, 1963)

EMPRESS WU   (CHN, 1939, source unknown)
    EMPRESS WU   (CHN, 1963)

EMPRESS YANG KWEI FEI   (MAGNIFICENT CONCUBINE)
    (JAP, 1955)
    YANG KWEI FEI   (HK, 1962)

EN CADA PUERTO UN AMOR   see   WAY FOR A SAILOR

ENAMORADA   (MEX, 1949, based on a screenplay by Inigo
    de Martino Noreiga and Emilio Fernandez)
    TORCH, THE   (EL, 1950)

ENCHANTED COTTAGE, THE   (FN, 1924, based on the
    book by Sir Arthur Wing Pinero)
    ENCHANTED COTTAGE, THE   (RKO, 1945)
    ENCHANGED COTTAGE, THE   (NBC--TV, 1955)

ENCHANTED ISLAND   see   OMOO--OMOO, THE SHARK
    GOD

ENCHANTED NUTCRACKER, THE   see   NUTCRACKER,
    THE

END AND THE BEGINNING   see   ABRAHAM LINCOLN

END OF A GUN   see   GUNFIGHTER, THE

END OF ATLANTIS   see   ATLANTIDE, L'

END OF DON JUAN, THE   see   DON JUAN

END OF THE DALTON GANG, THE   see   WHEN THE
    DALTONS RODE

END OF THE GAME   see   JUDGE AND HIS HANGMAN,
    THE

ENDE VOM LIED, DAS   (GER, 1914, based on a story by
    Joseph Conrad)
    ENDE VOM LIED, DAS   (GER, 1919)

ENEMY AGENT   see   RADIO PATROL

ENEMY OF THE PEOPLE, AN   (TV, 1966, based on the play
    by Hendrick Ibsen)
    ENEMY OF THE PEOPLE, AN   (WB, 1977)

ENFANT DE L'AMOUR, L'   (FRA, 1930, based on a book
    by Henry Bataille)
    ENFANT DE L'AMOUR, L'   (FRA, 1944)

ENFANT DE VOLUPTE, L'   (RUS, 1915, based on a book
    by Gabriele D'Annunzio)
    ENFANT DE VOLUPTE, L'   (ITA, 1917)

ENFANT DU CARNAVAL, L'   (FRA, 1921, source unknown)
    ENFANT DU CARNAVAL, L'   (FRA, 1934)

ENFANT PRODIQUE, L'   see   PARABLE OF THE PRODIGAL
    SON, THE

ENFANTS DE LA SCENE, LES see TOSCA, LA

ENFORCER, THE (WB, 1951, based on the life of gangster
    Lepke Buchalter)
    LEPKE (CBS--TV, 1959)
    MURDER INC. (FOX, 1960)
    LEPKE (WB, 1975)

ENGEL MIT DER POSAUNE, DER (AUS, 1948, based on the
    book by Ernst Lothar)
    ANGEL WITH THE TRUMPET, THE (BRI, 1950)

ENGLAND OF ELIZABETH, THE see AGE OF ELIZABETH,
    THE

ENGLISHMAN'S HOME, AN (BRI, 1914, based on the play
    by Guy de Maurier)
    ENGLISHMAN'S HOME, AN (MADMEN OF EUROPE)
    (BRI, 1939)

ENIGMA, THE (FRA, 1919, based on a novel by Paul Hervieu)
    MAIN QUI A TUE, LA (BEL/FRA, 1924)

ENIGMA OF CHARLES DE GAULLE see TRIALS OF
    CHARLES DE GAULLE, THE

ENIGMATIQUE MR. PARKES, L' see SLIGHTLY SCARLET

ENMEI--IN NO SEMUSHI see ESMERELDA, LA

ENOCH ARDEN see AFTER MANY YEARS

ENSIGN PULVER see MR. ROBERTS

ENTEBBE COUNTDOWN see VICTORY AT ENTEBBE

ENTER MADAME (MGM, 1922, based on the play by Gilda
    Varesi Archibald and Dorothea Donn--Byrne)
    ENTER MADAME (PAR, 1934)

ENTERTAINER, THE (BRI, 1960, based on the play by John
    Osborne)
    ENTERTAINER, THE (NBC--TV, 1976)

ENTFUEHRUNG INS GLUECK (GER, 1951, based on a
    story by Karl Hartl)
    WONDER KID, THE (BRI, 1951)

EPERVIER, L' (FRA, 1924, based on a story by Pierre
    Decourcelle and Paul Rouget)
    EPERVIER, L' (FRA, 1933)

EPIC THAT NEVER WAS, THE (BRI, 1967, based on the
    book by Robert Graves)
    I, CLAUDIUS (series) (BRI--TV, 1976)

EQUIPAGE, L' (LAST FLIGHT, THE) (FRA, 1927, based
    on the book, by Joseph Kessel.
    FLIGHT INTO DARKNESS (FRA, 1935)
    WOMAN I LOVE, THE (RKO, 1937)

ERAN TRECE see CHARLIE CHAN CARRIES ON

ERASMUS (short) (BEL, 1963, based on the life of Erasmus)
    ERASMUS, CIVIS TOTIUS MUNDI (short) (FLE--TV,
    1969)

ERBFORSTER, DER (GER, 1915, based on the book by
    Otto Ludwig)

ERBFORSTER, DER (GER, 1944)

ERDGEIST see LULU

ERIC HOFFER, THE PASSIONATE STATE OF MIND
    (CBS--TV, n.d., based on the life and times of philosopher
    Eric Hoffer)
    ROLE OF THE WEAK, THE (short) (NET--TV, 1965)
    ERIC HOFFER: THE CROWDED LIFE (IND--TV, 1977)

ERIE WAR, THE see OVERTHROW OF THE TWEED RING,
    THE

ERLKONIG, DER see ROI DES AULNES, LE

ERLKONIGS TOCHTER see ROI DES AULNES, LE

EROICA see BEETHOVEN UND DAS VOLK

EROTIKON, VERS LE BONHEUR (SWE, 1920, based on the
    story, "Le Renard Bleu,"by Ferenc Herczeg)
    BLAUFUCHS, DER (GER, 1938)

ERWIN ROMMEL see DESERT VICTORY

ES WAR EIN MUSIKUS (GER, 1933, based on a song by
    Frederick Schwarz)
    C'ETAIL UN MUSICIEN (FRA, 1933)

ESCADRON BLANC, L' (ITA, 1936, based on the book by
    Joseph Peyre)
    ESCADRON BLANC, L' (FRA, 1948)

ESCALVAS DE LA MODA see ON YOUR BACK

ESCAPADE see MASKERADE

ESCAPE (RKO, 1930, based on the play by John Galsworthy)
    ESCAPE (FOX, 1948)

ESCAPE EPISODE (IND, 1944, source unknown)
    ESCAPE EPISODE (IND, 1946)

ESCAPE FROM CRIME see PICTURE SNATCHER

ESCAPE IN THE DESERT see PETRIFIED FOREST, THE

ESCAPE ME NEVER (BRI, 1935, based on the play by Margaret
    Kennedy)
    ESCAPE ME NEVER (WB, 1947)

ESCAPE ROUTE CAPE TOWN see PICK--UP ON SOUTH
    STREET

ESCUELA DE VAGABUNDOS see MY MAN GODFREY

ESMERELDA, LA (FRA, 1905, based on the book, "Notre
    Dame de Paris," by Victor Hugo; also the basis for the
    1978 musical, "Quasimodo")
    ESMERELDA (BRI, 1906)
    NOTRE DAME DE PARIS (FRA, 1911)
    NOTRE DAME DE PARIS (ITA, 1911)
    NOTRE DAME (FRA, 1913)
    DARLING OF PARIS, THE (FOX, 1916)
    ESMERELDA (short) (BRI, 1922)
    HUNCHBACK OF NOTRE DAME, THE (UN, 1923)
    ENMEI--IN NO SEMUSHI (JAP, 1925)
    DHANWAN (IN, 1937)
    HUNCHBACK OF NOTRE DAME, THE (RKO, 1939)

BADSHAH DAMPATI (IN, 1953)
HUNCHBACK OF NOTRE DAME, THE (NBC--TV, 1954)
HUNCHBACK OF NOTRE DAME, THE (AA, 1956)
HUNCHBACK OF NOTRE DAME, THE (BRI–TV, 1977)

ESPOIRS (FRA, 1940, based on the novel, "Romeo und
Julia auf dem Dorfe," by Gottfried Keller)
ROMEO UND JULIA AUF DEM DORFE (SWI, 1941)
ROMEO UND JULIA AUF DEM DORFE (GER, 1944)

ESPOUSE DU RADELIER, L' (FIN, 1923, source unknown)
ESPOUSE DU RADELIER, L' (FIN, 1933)

ESTHER see ESTHER AND MORDECAI

ESTHER AND MORDECAI (KLE, 1910, based on a Bible
story)
MARRIAGE OF ESTHER, THE (KLE, 1910)
ESTHER (IND, 1914)
ESTHER (BRI, 1916)
BLIND PREJUDICE (IND, 1921)
ESTHER AND THE KING (FOX, 1960)
ESTHER (short) (CBS--TV, 1961)

ESTHER AND THE KING see ESTHER AND MORDECAI

ESTRELLADOS see FREE AND EASY

ETAIT UNE FOIS, IL (FRA, 1933, based on a book
"L'Epervier," by Francis de Croisset)
VISAGE DE FEMME, UN (SWE, 1938)
WOMAN'S FACE, A (MGM, 1941)

ETERNAL FLAME, THE see DUCHESSE DE LANGEAIS,
LA

ETERNAL LOVE (UA, 1929, based on a story by Jakob
Christoph Heer)
KONIG DER BERNINA, DER (AUS/SWI, 1957)

ETERNAL MARI, L' see GATTE, DER

ETERNAL MELODIES see LITTLE NIGHT MUSIC, A

ETERNAL RETURN, THE (FRA, 1943, based on the legend)
ARRASTAO, LES AMANTS DE LA MER (FRA, 1967)
TRISTAN AND ISOLDE (FRA, 1973)

ETERNAL SAPHO, THE see SAPHO

ETERNAL SIN, THE see LUCRETIA BORGIA

ETERNAL WALTZ (GER, 1936, based on an operetta)
ETERNAL WALTZ (FRA, 1936)

ETOILES D'EGER, LES (HUN, 1923, based on a book by
Geza Gardonyi)
ETOILES D'EGER, LES (HUN, 1968)

EUGEN ONEGIN (RUS, 1911, based on the poem by Alex--
ander Pushkin and the opera by Peter Illytch Tchaikovsky)
EUGEN ONEGIN (RUS, 1959)

EUGENE ARAM (BRI, 1914, based on the book by Edward
Bulwer Lytton)
EUGENE ARAM (ED, 1915)
EUGENE ARAM (BRI, 1919)
EUGENE ARAM (BRI, 1924)

EUGENIE GRANDET (FRA, 1910, based on the story by
Honore de Balzac)
EUGENIE GRANDET (ITA, 1913)
CONQUERING POWER, THE (MGM, 1921)
EUGENIE GRANDET (ITA, 1946)
EUGENIE GRANDET (SPA, 1953)

EUGENIE – THE STORY OF HER JOURNEY INTO PER–
VERSION see BEYOND LOVE AND EVIL

EUREKA STOCKADE (AUT, 1907, based on events in
Australia during the 1850 gold rush)
LOYAL REBEL, THE (AUT, 1915)
EUREKA STOCKADE (AUT, 1919)
EUREKA STOCKADE (BRI, 1949)

EVA PERON see PERON AND EVITA

EVANGELINE (IND, 1909, based on the poem by Henry
Wadsworth Longfellow)
EVANGELINE (BOS, 1912)
EVANGELINE (CAN, 1913)
EVANGELINE (FOX, 1919)
EVANGELINE (FOX, 1929)

EVE KNEW HER APPLES see IT HAPPENED ONE NIGHT

EVEL KNIEVEL (IND, 1971, based on the life of stunt man
Evel Knievel)
VIVA KNIEVEL! (WB, 1977)

EVELYN PRENTICE (MGM, 1934, based on the book by
W. E. Woodward)
STRONGER THAN DESIRE (MGM, 1939)

EVEN IN THE WEST THERE WAS GOD ONCE UPON A
TIME see TREASURE ISLAND

EVENING CLOTHES (PAR, 1927, based on the play, "The
Man in Dress Clothes," by Andre Picard and Yves Mirande)
HOMME EN HABIT, UN (FRA, 1931)
CABALLERO DE FRAC, UN (SPA, 1931)

EVENING WITH THE ROYAL BALLET, AN see SLEEPING
BEAUTY and SYLPHIDES, LES

EVER SINCE EVE see HEIR TO THE HORRAH, THE

EVER THE BEGINNING see MY GIRL TISA

EVERY GIRL SHOULD BE MARRIED see BACHELOR
MOTHER

EVERYBODY DOES IT see WIFE, HUSBAND AND
FRIEND

EVERYBODY'S OLD MAN see WORKING MEN, THE

EVERYMAN (BRI, 1913, based on the play, author unknown)
EVERYMAN (IND, 1914)
OLD PLAY OF EVERYMAN (DEN, 1915)
SUMMONING OF EVERYMAN (n.d., 1956)
SALZBURG EVERYMAN, THE (AUS, 1961)

EVERYTHING THAT LIVES (JAP, 1934, source unknown)
EVERYTHING THAT LIVES (JAP, 1955)

EVIL FOREST, THE see PARSIFAL

EVIL OF FRANKENSTEIN see FRANKENSTEIN

EVOLUTION OF KATHERINE, THE see DRIVEN

EWIGER WALZER see WALTZES FROM VIENNA

EX–BAD BOY see WHOLE TOWN'S TALKING, THE

EXECUTIVE SUITE (MGM, 1954, based on the book by
     Cameron Hawley)
   EXECUTIVE SUITE (series) (CBS--TV, 1976)

EX–FLAME see EAST LYNNE

EX--LADY see ILLICIT

EXPEDITION TO ANTARCTICA (short) (TFC, 1948,
     based on the exploits of the noted explorer)
   ANTARCTICA (short) (IND, n.d.)
   NORTH POLE EXPLORATION (short) (IND, n.d.)
   BYRD AT THE POLES (short) (PAT, 1953)
   RICHARD E. BYRD (short) (WOL, 1961)
   ADMIRAL BYRD (short) (CBS–TV, 1960)
   TRIO (sequence) (MGM–TV, 1963)

ADMIRAL BYRD (WOL, 1965)

EXPERT, THE see WELCOME HOME

EXPOSE ME LOVELY see FALCON TAKES OVER, THE

EXQUISITE SINNER, THE (MGM, 1926, based on the book,
     "Escape," by Alden Brooks)
   HEAVEN ON EARTH (IND, 1960)

EYE FOR EYE (MGM, 1918, based on a story by Henry
     Kistemaeckers)
   OCCIDENT, L' (FRA, 1928)
   OCCIDENT, L' (FRA, 1938)

EYES OF YOUTH (EQU, 1919, based on the play by Charles
     Guernon and Max Marcin)
   LOVE OF SUNYA, THE (UA, 1927)

EYES WITHOUT A FACE (HORROR CHAMBER OF DR.
     FAUSTUS) (FRA, 1959, based on a screenplay by
     Georges Franju and other authors)
   SHADOWMAN (FRA–TV, 1975)

FDR – THE PRICE OF PEACE see FIGHTING PRESI–
DENT, THE

FDR -- THE VOICE OF CHANGE see FIGHTING PRESI--
DENT, THE

F.P.I. ANTWORTET NICHT (GER, 1933, based on the book
  by Curt Siodmak)
  F.P.I. ANTWORTET NICHT (FRA, 1933)
  F.P.I. ANTWORTET NICHT (BRI, 1933)

F. SCOTT FITZGERALD AND "THE LAST OF THE
  BELLES" see BELOVED INFIDEL

FABIOLA see MYSTERY OF THE CATACOMBS

FABLE OF MAY (CZE, 1921, source unknown)
  FABLE OF MAY (CZE, 1940)

FABLE OF THE FISHERMAN AND THE FISH (RUS,
  1913, based on the folk tale)
  FISH AND THE FISHERMAN (RUS, 1952)
  FISHERMAN AND HIS WIFE, THE (short) (WW, 1970)
  FISHERMAN AND HIS WIFE, THE (short) (IND, 1977)

FABLES FROM HANS CHRISTIAN ANDERSEN see
  HANS CHRISTIAN ANDERSEN, LITTLE MATCH
  GIRL, THE and RED SHOES, THE

FABULOUS BARON MUNCHAUSEN, THE see BARON
  DE CRAC

FABULOUS SYCAMORES, THE see YOU CAN'T TAKE
  IT WITH YOU

FACE AT THE WINDOW, THE (AUS, 1919, based on the
  book by F. Brooke Warren)
  FACE AT THE WINDOW, THE (BRI, 1920)
  FACE AT THE WINDOW, THE (BRI, 1932)
  FACE AT THE WINDOW, THE (BRI, 1939)

FACE OF LINCOLN, THE see ABRAHAM LINCOLN

FACE OF THE FROG, THE see MARK OF THE FROG,
  THE

FACE THAT LAUNCHED A THOUSAND SHIPS, THE see
  CHUTE DE TROIE, LA

FACE TO FACE see HENRY MOORE

FACE TO FACE: WALT WHITMAN 100 YEARS HENCE
  see WALT WHITMAN: BACKGROUND FOR HIS
  WORKS

FACELESS MAN, THE (NBC--TV, 1966, based on a teleplay)
  COUNTERFEIT KILLER, THE (UN, 1968)

FAGIN see OLIVER TWIST

FAHRMANN MARIA (GER, 1935, based on a legend)
  STRANGLER OF THE SWAMP (PRC, 1945)

FAHRT INS ABENTEUER (GER, 1926, source unknown)
  FAHRT INS ABENTEUER (GER, 1943)

FAHRT INS GLUCK, DIE (GER, 1926, based on a story by
  Thea von Harbou)
  FAHRT INS GLUCK, DIE (GER, 1945)

FAILURE see ONE MAN'S JOURNEY

FAIR COED see COLLEGE WIDOW

FAIR EXCHANGE, A (BIO, 1909, based on the book,
  "Silas Marner," by George Eliot)
  CHANGING OF SILAS MARNER, THE (VIT, 1911)
  SILAS MARNER (ED, 1913)
  SILAS MARNER (THA, 1916)
  SILAS MARNER (AE, 1921)

FAISEUR, LE (FRA, 1936, based on the story, "Mercadet,"
  by Honore de Balzac)
  LOVABLE CHEAT, THE (FC, 1949)

FAITH HEALER, THE (REL, 1912, based on the play by
  William Vaughn Moody)
  FAITH HEALER, THE (PAR, 1921)

FAITH, HOPE AND HOGAN (short) (IND, n.d., based on
  the life of golfer Ben Hogan)
  FOLLOW THE SUN (FOX, 1951)

FAITHFUL HEART (BRI, 1922, based on the play by
  Monckton Hoffe)
  FAITHFUL HEART (BRI, 1932)

FALCON TAKES OVER, THE (RKO, 1942, based on the
  book, "Farewell My Lovely," by Raymond Chandler)
  MURDER MY SWEET (RKO, 1944)
  FAREWELL MY LOVELY (EMB, 1975)
  EXPOSE ME LOVELY (IND, 1976)

FALL DERUGA, DER (GER, 1938, based on a book by
  Ricarda Huch)
  . . . UND NICHTS ALS DIE WAHRHEIT (GER, 1958)

FALL DOBRONOWSKA, DER see CLEMENCEAU CASE,
  THE

FALL OF BABYLON, THE (KLE, 1910, based on a Bible
  story)
  FALL OF BABYLON (sequence from INTOLERANCE)
  (GRI, 1916)

FALL OF BERLIN, THE (POL, 1945, based on historical
  events)
  FALL OF BERLIN, THE (RUS, 1949)

FALL OF THE HOUSE OF USHER, THE (FRA, 1927,
  based on the story by Edgar Allan Poe)
  FALL OF THE HOUSE OF USHER, THE (short) (IND,
  1928)
  FALL OF THE HOUSE OF USHER, THE (short) (BRI,
  1941)
  FALL OF THE HOUSE OF USHER, THE (IND, 1942)
  FALL OF THE HOUSE OF USHER, THE (BRI, 1948)
  FALL OF THE HOUSE OF USHER, THE (BRI, 1950)
  FALL OF THE HOUSE OF USHER, THE (BRI, 1952)
  FALL OF THE HOUSE OF USHER, THE (short) (IND,
  1955)
  FALL OF THE HOUSE OF USHER, THE (NBC–TV,
  1956)
  HOUSE OF USHER, THE (AI, 1960)
  BLANCHEVILLE MONSTER (ITA/SPA, 1963)

FALL OF THE ROMANOFFS see RASPUTIN, THE
  BLACK MONK

FALL OF TROY see CHUTE DE TROIE, LA

FALLEN IDOL, THE (BRI, 1948, based on the story, "The
    Basement Room," by Graham Greene)
    FALLEN IDOL, THE (CBS--TV, 1959)

FALSCHER VON LONDON, DER see FORGER, THE

FALSE WITNESS see RAILROADED

FALSTAFF see MERRY WIVES OF WINDSOR, THE

FALSTAFF, THE TAVERN KNIGHT see MERRY WIVES
    OF WINDSOR, THE

FAME IS THE NAME OF THE GAME see CHICAGO
    DEADLINE

FAMILIE SCHIMEK (GER, 1925, source unknown)
    FAMILIE SCHIMEK (GER, 1935)
    FAMILIE SCHIMEK (GER, 1956)

FAMILY (CHN, 1941, source unknown)
    FAMILY (CHN, 1957)

FAMILY (mini--series) (ABC--TV, 1977, based on a tele--
    play)
    FAMILY (series) (ABC--TV, 1977)

FAMILY HOLVAK, THE see GREATEST GIFT, THE

FAMILY OF MAN, THE (short) (NAV, 1955, based on the
    life and work of the noted photographer)
    EDWARD STEICHEN (NET--TV, 1962)
    THIS IS EDWARD STEICHEN (short) (CAR, 1966)

FAMILY SECRET, THE see BURGLAR, THE and SECRET
    OF POLICHINELLE, THE

FAMILY UPSTAIRS, THE (FOX, 1926, based on the play by
    Harry Delf)
    HARMONY AT HOME (FOX, 1929)
    STOP, LOOK AND LOVE (FOX, 1939)

FAN, THE see LADY WINDERMERE'S FAN

FAN--FAN (FOX, 1918, based on the opera by Gilbert and
    Sullivan. Stage versions include "The Hot Mikado,"
    "The Swing Mikado," and "The Black Mikado")
    MIKADO, THE (BRI, 1939)
    MIKADO, THE (CBS--TV, 1959)
    MIKADO, THE (NBC--TV, 1960)
    COOL MIKADO, THE (BRI, 1963)
    MIKADO, THE (CAN--TV, 1963)
    MIKADO, THE (BRI, 1967)
    GENTLEMEN OF TITIPU (TV, 1973)

FANCY PANTS see RUGGLES OF RED GAP

FANFARE D'AMOUR see FIRST A GIRL

FANFARE OF LOVE see FIRST A GIRL

FANFAREN DER LIEBE see FIRST A GIRL

FANNY (FRA, 1932, based on a trilogy by Marcel Pagnol)
    FANNY (ITA, 1933)
    SCHWARZE WALFISCH, DER (GER, 1934)
    PORT OF SEVEN SEAS (MGM, 1938)

FANNY (WB, 1961)

FANNY HAWTHORN see HINDLE WAKES

FANNY HILL (HOL, 1966, based on the book by John
    Cleland)
    FANNY HILL (SWE, 1969)
    YOUNG EROTIC FANNY HILL, THE (IND, 1970)

FANRIK STALS SAGNER (SWE, 1909, based on a poem,
    author unknown)
    FANRIK STALS SAGNER (SWE, 1925)

FANTASIA see WIZARD'S APPRENTICE, THE

FANTASTIC VOYAGE (FOX, 1966, based on a story by
    Otto Klement and Jay Lewis Bixby)
    FANTASTIC VOYAGE (series) (ABC--TV, 1968)

FANTASY ISLAND see RETURN TO FANTASY ISLAND

FANTASY . . . 3 see DOROTHY AND THE SCARECROW
    OF OZ and QUEEN OF THE SEA

FANTOMAS (FRA, 1913, based on stories by Pierre
    Souvestre and Marcel Allain)
    FANTOMAS UNDER THE SHADOW OF THE
        GUILLOTINE (FRA, 1913)
    FANTOMAS, THE CROOKED DETECTIVE (FRA, 1914)
    FANTOMAS, THE FALSE MAGISTRATE (FRA, 1914)
    FANTOMAS (serial) (FOX, 1920)
    FANTOMAS (FRA, 1931)
    FANTOMAS (IND, 1934)
    MR. FANTOMAS (BEL, 1937)
    FANTOMAS (FRA, 1947)
    FANTOMAS AGAINST FANTOMAS (FRA, 1948)
    FANTOMAS (FRA/ITA, 1964)
    FANTOMAS STRIKES BACK (FRA, 1965)
    FANTOMAS VS. SCOTLAND YARD (FRA/ITA, 1967)

FANTOMAS AGAINST FANTOMAS see FANTOMAS

FANTOMAS STRIKES BACK see FANTOMAS

FANTOMAS, THE CROOK DETECTIVE see FANTOMAS

FANTOMAS, THE FALSE MAGISTRATE see FANTOMAS

FANTOMAS UNDER THE SHADOW OF THE GUILLOTINE
    see FANTOMAS

FANTOMAS VS. SCOTLAND see FANTOMAS

FANTOME DE PARIS, LE see CHERI--BIBI

FAR FROM THE MADDING CROWD (IND, 1911, based on
    the book by Thomas Hardy)
    FAR FROM THE MADDING CROWD (BRI, 1915)
    FAR FROM THE MADDING CROWD (MUT, 1916)
    FAR FROM THE MADDING CROWD (MGM, 1967)

FAREWELL MY LOVELY see FALCON TAKES OVER,
    THE

FAREWELL TO ARMS, A (PAR, 1932, based on the book by
    Ernest Hemingway)
    FORCE OF ARMS (WB, 1951)
    FAREWELL TO ARMS, A (CBS--TV, 1955)

FAREWELL TO ST. PETERSBURG see WALTZES FROM VIENNA

FARMER TAKES A WIFE, THE (FOX, 1935, based on the play by Max Gordon and the book, "Rome Haul," by Walter D. Edmonds)
  FARMER TAKES A WIFE, THE (NBC–TV, 1940)
  FARMER TAKES A WIFE, THE (FOX, 1953)

FARMER'S DAUGHTER, THE (RKO, 1947, based on a play, "Juurakon Hulda," by Juhani Tervapaa)
  FARMER'S DAUGHTER, THE (series) (ABC–TV, 1962)

FARMER'S WIFE (BRI, 1928, based on the play by Eden Philpotts)
  FARMER'S WIFE (BRI, 1941)

FASCHING (GER, 1921, based on the play by Ferenc Molnar)
  FASCHING (GER, 1939)

FASCINATION see ARIANE

FASCIST REVOLUTION, THE see BENITO MUSSOLINI

FASHIONS IN LOVE see CONCERT, THE

FAST AND LOOSE see BEST PEOPLE, THE

FAST COMPANY (PAR, 1929, based on the play, "Elmer the Great," by Ring Lardner and George M. Cohan)
  ELMER THE GREAT (WB, 1933)
  COWBOY QUARTERBACK (WB, 1939)

FAST WORK (short) (MGM, 1930, based on a screenplay by Leo McCarey and elaborated upon in the remake)
  MANY SAPPY RETURNS (short) (COL, 1939)

FASTEST GUN ALIVE, THE see LAST NOTCH, THE

FATAL DESIRE see CAVALLERIA RUSTICANNA

FATAL MARRIAGE, THE see AFTER MANY YEARS

FATHER, THE (SWE, 1912, based on the play by August Strindberg)
  FATHER, THE (SWE, 1969)

FATHER BROWN see FATHER BROWN, DETECTIVE

FATHER BROWN, DETECTIVE (PAR, 1935,
  DETECTIVE, THE (COL, 1954)
  FATHER BROWN (series) (BRI–TV, 1974)

FATHER IS A PRINCE see BIG HEARTED HERBERT

FATHER OF THE BRIDE (MGM, 1950, based on the book by Edward Streeter)
  FATHER'S LITTLE DIVIDEND (MGM, 1951)
  FATHER OF THE BRIDE (series) (CBS–TV, 1961)

FATHER OF THE SPACE AGE, THE (short) (NAV, 1961, based on the life and work of scientist Dr. Robert Goddard)
  DREAM THAT WOULDN'T DOWN, THE (short) (NAV, 1965)

FATHER SERGIUS (RUS, 1917, based on a story by Leo Tolstoy)

FATHER SERGIUS (FRA, 1946)

FATHER STEPS OUT see CITY LIMITS

FATHER VOJTECK (CZE, 1929, source unknown)
  FATHER VOJTECK (CZE, 1937)

FATHERS AND CHILDREN (RUS, 1915, based on the book by Ivan Turgenev)
  FATHERS AND CHILDREN (RUS, 1959)

FATHER'S SON (FN, 1930, based on the book, "Old Fathers and Young Sons," by Booth Tarkington)
  FATHER'S SON (WB, 1941)

FAUBOURG MONTMARTRE (FRA, 1924, based on a book by Henri Duvernois)
  FAUBOURG MONTMARTRE (FRA, 1932)

FAUST (FRA, 1896, based on a legend, the book by Goethe and operas by Charles Gounod in 1859 and Berlioz in 1946)
  FAUST ET MARGUERITE (FRA, 1897)
  FAUST AND MEPHISTOPHELES (BRI, 1898)
  FAUST AND MARGUERITE (ED, 1900)
  DAMNATION OF FAUST, THE (FRA, 1903)
  FAUST AND MARGUERITE (FRA, 1904)
  FAUST (FRA, 1906)
  FAUST (FRA, 1907)
  FAUST (BRI, 1907)
  FAUST (SEL, 1908)
  FAUST (BOS, 1908)
  FAUST (ED, 1909)
  FAUST (FRA, 1909)
  FAUST (BRI, 1910)
  FAUST (ITA, 1910)
  FAUST (GER, 1910)
  TOUT PETIT FAUST, LE (FRA, 1910)
  FAUST (BRI, 1911)
  FAUST (FRA, 1911)
  BILL BUMPER'S BARGAIN (ESS, 1911)
  FAUST (CZE, 1912)
  FAUST AND THE LILY (BIO, 1913)
  FAUST (DEN, 1914)
  FAUST (ITA, 1916)
  FAUST (GER, 1921)
  FOUNTAIN OF YOUTH (IND, 1921)
  FAUST (short) (BRI, 1922)
  DON JUAN AND FAUST (FRA, 1922)
  FAUST (short) (BRI, 1923)
  FAUST (GER, 1926)
  FAUST (MGM, 1926)
  FAUST (short) (BRI, 1927)
  FAUST (WB, 1929)
  WALPURGIS NIGHT (short) (EDU, 1932)
  FAUST (short) (BRI, 1936)
  PAN TWARDOWSKI (POL, 1937)
  LEGEND OF FAUST (ITA, 1948)
  FAUST AND THE DEVIL (FRA/ITA, 1950)
  MARGUERITE OF THE NIGHT (FRA/ITA, 1955)
  STUDIO OF DR. FAUST (SWE, 1956)
  JOHANES DOKTOR FAUST (short) (CZE, 1958)
  OUT OF REACH OF THE DEVIL (CZE, 1959)
  FAUST (GER, 1960)
  FAUST (IND, 1964)
  FAUST (RUM, 1967)
  BEDAZZLED (FOX, 1967)
  DR. FAUSTUS (BRI, 1968)
  STRANGE CASE OF DR. FAUSTUS, THE (SPA, 1971)

FAUST (short) (PNX, 1973)

FAUST AND MARGUERITE see FAUST

FAUST AND MEPHISTOPHELES see FAUST

FAUST AND THE DEVIL see FAUST

FAUST AND THE LILY see FAUST

FAUTEUIL 47, LE (FRA/GER, 1926, based on the book by
    Louis Verneuil)
    FAUTEUIL 47, LE (FRA, 1937)

FAWLTY TOWERS (series) (BRI--TV, 1976, based on a
    British teleplay)
    SNAVELY (short) (ABC--TV, 1978)

FAZIL (FOX, 1928, based on the play, "L' Insoumise,"
    by Pierre Frondaie)
    LEY DEL HAREN, LA (SPA, 1931)

FEAR see CRIME AND PUNISHMENT

FEAR IN THE NIGHT (PAR, 1947, based on the story,
    "Nightmare," by William Irish)
    NIGHTMARE (UA, 1956)

FEAR STRIKES OUT (CBS--TV, 1955, based on the
    biography of Jimmy Piersall and a story by Piersall and Al
    Hirschberg)
    FEAR STRIKES OUT (PAR, 1957)

FEATHERED SERPENT, THE see SQUEAKER, THE

FEATHERTOP see LORD FEATHERTOP

FEDERAL AGENTS VS. UNDERWORLD, INC. (serial)
    (REP, 1948, based on a screenplay by various authors.
    The remake is a condensation of the serial)
    GOLDEN HANDS OF KURIGAI (REP, 1966)

FEDORA (FRA/ITA, 1913, based on the play by Victorien
    Sardou; also the basis for the opera by Umberto Giordano
    in 1898)
    PRINCESS ROMANOFF (FOX, 1915)
    FEDORA (ITA, 1916)
    WHITE NIGHTS (FEDORA) (HUN, 1916)
    FEDORA (PAR, 1918)
    FEDORA (GER, 1925)
    WOMAN FROM MOSCOW, THE (PAR, 1928)
    FEDORA (FRA, 1934)
    FEDORA (ITA, 1938)

FEDRA WEST see DEVIL'S DAUGHTER, THE

FELDHERRNHUGEL, DER (AUS, 1921, based on the play
    by Alexander Roda Roda and Carl Rossler)
    FELDHERRNHUGEL, DER (GER, 1926)
    FELDHERRNHUGEL, DER (GER, 1932)
    FELDHERRNHUGEL, DER (AUS, 1953)

FEMALE HAMLET see HAMLET

FEMME DE CLAUDE, LA (FRA, 1916, based on the book
    by Alexandre Dumas [fils])
    FEMME DE CLAUDE, LA (ITA, 1917)

FEMME DE LA MORT, LA see SUICIDE CLUB, THE

FEMME DE TRENTE ANS, LA (FRA/ITA, 1919, based on a
    story by Honore de Balzac)
    IF WOMEN ONLY KNEW (RC, 1921)

FEMME DOUCE, UNE see DOUCE, LA

FEMME ET LE PANTIN, LA see WOMAN AND THE
    PUPPET, THE

FEMME NUE, LA (ITA, 1914, based on a book by Henry
    Bataille)
    FEMME NUE, LA (ITA, 1918)
    FEMME NUE, LA (FRA, 1926)
    FEMME NUE, LA (FRA, 1932)
    FEMME NUE, LA (FRA, 1949)

FEMMES COLLANTES, LES (FRA, 1920, based on a book
    by Leon Gandillot)
    FEMMES COLLANTES, LES (FRA, 1938)

FEMMES SONT FOLIES, LES see CHATEAU HISTORIQUE

FERIEN VOM ICH (GER, 1934, based on the book by Paul
    Keller)
    FERIEN VOM ICH (GER, 1952)
    FERIEN VOM ICH (GER, 1963)

FERRAGUS (FRA, 1909, based on a book by Honore de
    Balzac)
    FERRAGUS (FRA, 1923)

FEU MATHIAS PASCAL (FRA, 1925, based on the play by
    Luigi Pirandello)
    LATE MATTHEW PASCAL, THE (RUS, 1925)
    LIVING DEAD, THE (FRA, 1927)
    HOMME DE NULLE PART, L' (FRA/ITA, 1936)
    LATE MATTHEW PASCAL, THE (ITA, 1937)

FEUERSCHIFF, DAS (GER, 1922, based on a story by
    Siegfried Lenz)
    FEUERSCHIFF, DAS (GER, 1963)

FEUERZANGENBOWLE, DIE see SUCH A BOOR

FEW BULLETS MORE, A see BILLY THE KID

FIA JANSSON FRAN SODER see DEN FORGYLLDA
    LERGOKEN

FIACRE NO. 13, LE (ITA, 1916, based on a book by Xavier
    de Montepin)
    FIACRE NO. 13, LE (FRA, 1947)

FIANCEE OF THE TSAR, THE (RUS, 1911, based on the
    story by Liev Miei and the opera by Nickolai Rimsky--
    Korsakov)
    FIANCEE OF THE TZAR, THE (RUS, 1965)

FIANCES, LES (ITA, 1911, based on the book by Alessandro
    Manzoni)
    FIANCES, LES (ITA, 1913) (2 versions)
    FIANCES, LES (ITA, 1916)
    FIANCES, LES (ITA, 1919)
    FIANCES, LES (ITA, 1923)
    FIANCES, LES (ITA, 1941)
    FIANCES, LES (ITA/SPA, 1963)

FIDDLER ON THE ROOF see TEVYA

FIDEL see FIDEL CASTRO STORY, THE

FIDEL CASTRO STORY, THE (IND, n.d., based on the life
    of Cuban dictator Fidel Castro)
    INSIDE CUBA TODAY (short) (IND, 1963)
    FIDEL CASTRO (short) (WOL, 1963)
    CUBA: CHANGE UNDER CASTRO (IND, n.d.)
    CUBA UNDER CASTRO (IND, n.d.)
    CAPTIVE CUBA: YEARS UNDER CASTRO (IND, n.d.)
    CUBA: BAY OF PIGS (NBC--TV, 1965)
    FIDEL (NYF, 1969)

FIDELE BAUER, DER (GER, 1927, based on the operetta
    by Leo Fall)
    FIDELE BAUER, DER (GER, 1951)

FIEND WHO WALKED THE WEST, THE see KISS OF
    DEATH

FIESCO (GER, 1913, based on the book, "Die Verschworung
    des fiesco zu Genua," by Friedrich von Schiller)
    VERSCHWORUNG ZU GENUA (GER, 1920)

FIESTA DEL DIABLO, LA see DEVIL'S HOLIDAY

FIFI see MADEMOISELLE MODISTE

FIFTY FATHOMS DEEP (COL, 1931, based on a story by
    Dorothy Howell)
    MON AMI TIM (FRA, 1932)

FIFTY MILLION FRENCHMEN (WB, 1931, based on the
    musical by Herbert Fields, E. Ray Goetz and Cole
    Porter)
    PAREE, PAREE (short) (WB, 1934)

FIGARO see BARBER OF SEVILLE, THE and FIGARO'S
    WEDDING

FIGARO'S WEDDING (ITA, 1913, based on the play by
    Beaumarchais and the opera by Wolfgang Amadeus
    Mozart)
    MARRIAGE OF FIGARO, THE (GER, 1920)
    FIGARO (FRA, 1929)
    EIN TOLLER TAG (GER, 1945)
    MARRIAGE OF FIGARO, THE (GER, 1949)
    MARRIAGE OF FIGARO, THE (FRA, 1959)
    MARRIAGE OF FIGARO, THE (FRA, 1963)

FIGHTING CARAVANS (PAR, 1931, based on a book by
    Zane Grey)
    WAGON WHEELS (PAR, 1934)

FIGHTING COWARD, THE (PAR, 1924, based on the book,
    "Magnolia," by Booth Tarkington)
    RIVER OF ROMANCE (PAR, 1927)
    MISSISSIPPI (PAR, 1935)

FIGHTING DEVIL DOGS, THE (serial) (REP, 1938, based
    on a screenplay by various authors. Remake is a conden-
    sation of the serial)
    TORPEDO OF DOOM, THE (REP, 1966)

FIGHTING EAGLE, THE see BRIGADIER GERARD

FIGHTING MUSKETEERS, THE see THREE
    MUSKETEERS, THE

FIGHTING PRESIDENT, THE (short) (UN, 1933, based on

the life of President Franklin Delano Roosevelt)
    ROOSEVELT STORY, THE (UA, 1947)
    F.D.R. (short) (OFF, n.d.)
    SUNRISE AT CAMPOBELLO (WB, 1960)
    F.D.R. -- THE VOICE OF CHANGE (MGM--TV, 1961)
    FDR -- THE PRICE OF PEACE (MGM--TV, 1961)
    FRANKLIN DELANO ROOSEVELT (MHF, 1963)
    F.D.R. -- THIRD TERM TO PEARL HARBOR (IND, n.d.)
    F.D.R. (series) (ABC--TV, 1965)
    HUNDRED DAYS, THE (short) (ABC--TV, 1966)
    HUNDRED DAYS, THE (short) (BRI--TV, 1971)
    FRANKLIN D. ROOSEVELT (series) (PAR, 1974)
    FRANKLIN D. ROOSEVELT'S HYDE PARK (short)
    (PAR, 1975)

FIGHTING RANGER, THE see BORDER LAW

FIL A LA PATTE, UN (FRA, 1919, based on a play by
    Georges Feydeau)
    FIL A LA PATTE, UN (FRA, 1924)
    FIL A LA PATTE, UN (FRA, 1934)
    FIL A LA PATTE, UN (FRA, 1954)

FILE 113 (BIO, 1915, based on a book by Emile Gaboriau)
    THOU SHALT NOT STEAL (FOX, 1917)
    FILE 113 (HOL, 1932)

FILE OF THE GOLDEN GOOSE, THE see T-MEN

FILLE D'AMOUR, TRAVIATA '53 see DAME AUX
    CAMELIAS, LA

FILLE DE IORIO, LA (ITA, 1911, based on a book by
    Gabriele D'Annunzio)
    FILLE DE IORIO, LA (ITA, 1916)

FILLE DE LA TOURBIERE, LA (SWE, 1917, based on the
    book by Selma Lagerlof)
    MAEDCHEN VOM MOORHOF, DAS (GER, 1935)
    FILLE DE LA TOURBIERE, LA (FIN, 1939)
    MAEDCHEN VOM MOORHOF, DES (SWE, 1947)
    MAEDCHEN VOM MOORHOF, LA (GER, 1958)

FILLE ET LE GARCON, LA see ZWEI HERZEN UND EIN
    SCHLAG

FILS DE L'AUTRE, LE see WOMAN BETWEEN, THE

FILUMENA MARTURANO (ITA, 1951, based on material
    by Eduardo de Filippo; the 1973 film is an uncredited
    remake)
    MARRIAGE ITALIAN STYLE (FRA/ITA, 1964)
    ALFREDO, ALFREDO (ITA, 1973)

FIN DE LA MAISON LOUNTICH, LA see CARRIERE
    D'UNE CHANTEUSE DES RUES, LA

FINANZEN DES GROSSHERZOGS, DIE (GER, 1923,
    based on a novel by Frank Heller)
    FINANZEN DES GROSSHERZOGS, DIE (GER, 1934)

FINDEN SIE, DASS CONSTANZE SICH RICHTIG
    VERHALT? see CHARMING SINNERS

FINISHING TOUCH, THE see ONE WEEK

FIREMAN, SAVE MY CHOO CHOO see CANNONBALL,
    THE

FIRES OF FATE (BRI, 1923, based on the book, "Tragedy of the Korosko," by Sir Arthur Conan Doyle.
   FIRES OF FATE (BRI, 1932)

FIRE–TONGUE BOWL, THE see SUCH A BOOR

FIRMA HEIRATET (GER, 1913, source unknown)
   FIRMA HEIRATET (GER, 1931)

FIRST A GIRL (ONCE A WOMAN) (BRI, 1935, based on the play, "Viktor und Viktoria," by Reinhold Schunzel)
   FANFARE D'AMOUR (FRA, 1935)
   FANFAREN DER LIEBE (GER, 1948)
   SOME LIKE IT HOT (UA, 1959)

FIRST AND THE LAST, THE see STRANGER, THE

FIRST CHURCHILLS, THE see CHURCHILL – MAN OF THE CENTURY

FIRST IMPRESSIONS see PRIDE AND PREJUDICE

FIRST LOVE (RUS, 1915, based on the book by Ivan Turgenev)
   FIRST LOVE (SPA, 1941)
   FIRST LOVE (RUS, 1969)
   FIRST LOVE (GER, 1970)
   FIRST LOVE (POL--TV, 1971)

FIRST LOVE see EDUCATION SENTIMENTALE, UNE

FIRST MEN IN THE MOON, THE (BRI, 1911, based on the book by H. G. Wells)
   FIRST MEN IN THE MOON, THE (BRI, 1919)
   FIRST MEN IN THE MOON, THE (COL, 1964)

FIRST OFFENCE see MAUVAISE GRAINE

FIRST TRAVELING SALESLADY, THE (RKO, 1956, based on a story by Stephen Longstreet)
   DID YOU HEAR THE ONE ABOUT THE TRAVELING SALESLADY? (UN, 1968)

FIRST YEAR, THE (FOX, 1926, based on the play by Frank Craven)
   FIRST YEAR, THE (FOX, 1932)

FISH see LIFE AND TIMES OF BARNEY MILLER, THE

FISH AND THE FISHERMAN see FABLE OF THE FISHER--MAN AND THE FISH

FISHERMAN AND HIS WIFE, THE see FABLE OF THE FISHERMAN AND THE FISH

FISTFUL OF DOLLARS, A see YOJIMBO

FIVE CAME BACK (RKO, 1939, based on a story by Richard Connell)
   BACK FROM ETERNITY (RKO, 1956)

FIVE FINGERS (FOX, 1952, based on the book by L. C. Moyzisch)
   OPERATION CICERO (CBS--TV, 1956)
   FIVE FINGERS (series) (NBC--TV, 1959)

FIVE FRAGMENTS, THE see CAUGHT IN THE FOG

FIVE LITTLE MORAL ONES see EMIL UND DIE DETEKTIVE

FIVE SINISTER STORIES see SUICIDE CLUB, THE

5--STAR FINAL (WB, 1931, based on a story by Byron Morgan)
   TWO AGAINST THE WORLD (ONE FATAL HOUR) (WB, 1936)

FIVE WEEKS IN A BALLOON (FOX, 1962, based on the book by Jules Verne)
   FANTASTIC BALLOON TRIP, THE (MEX, 1976)

FIXER--UPPERS, THE see SLIPPING WIVES

FLACHSMANN ALS ERZIEHER (GER, 1921, based on a book by Otto Ernst)
   FLACHSMANN ALS ERZIEHER (GER, 1930)

FLAG LIEUTENANT, THE (BRI, 1919, based on the play by W. P. Drury and Leo Tovar)
   FLAG LIEUTENANT, THE (BRI, 1926)
   FURTHER ADVENTURES OF THE FLAG LIEUTENANT, THE (BRI, 1927)
   FLAG LIEUTENANT, THE (BRI, 1932)

FLAG OF HUMANITY, THE see ANGEL OF MERCY

FLAGERMUSEN see FLEDERMAUS, DIE

FLAGPOLE JITTERS see HOCUS POCUS

FLAMBEE, LA (FRA, 1917, based on a story by Henry Kistemaeckers)
   FLAMBEE, LA (FRA, 1934)

FLAME, THE see MONTMARTRE

FLAME AND THE FLESH see NAPLES AU BAISER DE FEU

FLAME OF LOVE, THE (BRI, 1930, based on a story by Monckton Hoffe and Ludwig Wolff)
   AMOUR MAITRE DES CHOSES, L' (FRA, 1930)
   HAITANG (GER, 1930)

FLAME OF NEW ORLEANS, THE (UN, 1941, based on a screenplay by Norman Krasna)
   SCARLET ANGEL (UN, 1953)

FLAME OVER INDIA see WAGONMASTER

FLAMING FORTIES see TENNESSEE'S PARDNER

FLAMING FRONTIER see CUSTER'S LAST STAND

FLAMING FRONTIERS see HEROES OF THE WEST

FLAMING GUNS see BUCKAROO KID, THE

FLAMING ROAD (WB, 1949, based on the play by Robert and Sally Wilder)
   FLAMINGO ROAD (NBC--TV, 1956)

FLAMME, LA (FRA, 1925, based on the book by Charles Mere)
   FLAMME, LA (FRA, 1936)

FLAW, THE (BRI, 1933, based on a story by Brandon Fleming)

FLAW, THE (BRI, 1955)

FLEDERMAUS, DIE (GER, 1923, based on the operetta by
    Johann Strauss Jr.)
  FLEDERMAUS, DIE (GER, 1931)
  WALTZ TIME (BRI, 1933)
  FLEDERMAUS, DIE (GER, 1937)
  FLEDERMAUS, DIE (GER, 1945)
  WALTZ TIME (BRI, 1945)
  FLEDERMAUS (ABC--TV, 1952)
  FLEDERMAUS, DIE (GER, 1955)
  ROSALINDA (NBC--TV, 1956)
  OH, ROSALINDA! (BRI, 1961)
  FLEDERMAUS, DIE (AUS/GER, 1962)
  FLAGERMUSEN (DEN, 1968)

FLEET'S IN, THE (PAR, 1928, based on a play by Kenyon
    Nicholson and Charles Robinson)
  LADY BE CAREFUL (PAR, 1936)
  FLEET'S IN, THE (PAR, 1942)
  SAILOR BEWARE (PAR, 1951)

FLESH AND FANTASY see LORD ARTHUR SAVILLE'S
  CRIME

FLESH AND THE FIENDS see BODY SNATCHER, THE

FLESH AND WOMAN see GRAND JEU, LE

FLESH FOR FRANKENSTEIN see FRANKENSTEIN

FLESH FOR THE ORCHID see NO ORCHIDS FOR MISS
  BLANDISH

FLEURS TARDIVES, LES (RUS, 1917, based on the book
    by Anton Chekhov)
  FLEURS TARDIVES, LES (RUS, 1970)

FLEUVE FIDELE, LE see YEAR 1863

FLICKEN I FRACK (SWE, 1926, source unknown)
  FLICKEN I FRACK (SWE, 1956)

FLIGHT COMMANDER see DAWN PATROL

FLIGHT FOR FREEDOM (RKO, 1943, based on the life of
    aviator Amelia Earhart)
  MYSTERY OF AMELIA EARHART, THE (short) (CBS--
    TV, 1971)
  AMELIA EARHART (NBC--TV, 1976)

FLIGHT INTO DANGER (NBC--TV, 1956, based on a story
    by Arthur Hailey)
  ZERO HOUR (PAR, 1958)
  TERROR IN THE SKY (CBS--TV, 1971)

FLIGHT INTO DARKNESS see EQUIPAGE, L'

FLIGHT OF THE FRIENDSHIP 7 see AMERICAN IN
  ORBIT, AN

FLIGHT OF THE SPIRIT OF ST. LOUIS AND THE FRIEND--
  SHIP 7 see AMERICAN IN ORBIT, AN

FLINTSTONES, THE (series) (HB, 1960, based on a teleplay)
  PEBBLES AND BAM BAM (series) (CBS--TV, 1971)

FLIRT, THE (UN, 1916, based on the book by Booth Tarking--
  ton)

FLIRT, THE (UN, 1922)
  BAD SISTER (UN, 1931)
  BAD SISTER (UN, 1948)

FLOAT LIKE A BUTTERFLY, STING LIKE A BEE (GRO,
    1969, based on the life of the champion prize--fighter)
  A.K.A. CASSIUS CLAY (UA, 1970)
  BADDEST DADDY IN THE WHOLE WORLD, THE (NYF,
    1973)
  MUHAMMAD ALI -- SKILL, BRAINS AND GUTS (IND,
    1975)
  GREATEST, THE (IND, 1977)
  I AM THE GREATEST: THE ADVENTURES OF
    MUHAMMAD ALI (series) (NBC--TV, 1977)

FLOATING WEEDS see STORY OF FLOATING WEEDS,
  THE

FLORADORA GIRL, THE see PAINTED DAUGHTERS

FLORENCE NIGHTINGALE (BRI, 1915, based on the
    biography of the noted nurse)
  WHITE ANGEL (BRI, 1936)
  LADY WITH THE LAMP (BRI, 1951)
  HOLY TERROR, THE (NBC--TV, 1965)

FLORENTINE HUT, DER see CHAPEAU DE PAILLE
  D'ITALIE

FLORETTE & PATAPON (ITA, 1913, based on the book by
    Pierre Veber and Maurice Hennequin)
  FLORETTE & PATAPON (GER, 1927)

FLOTTANS KAVALJERER see SPOKBARONEN

FLOWER OF HAWAII, THE (GER, 1933, based on the
    operetta by Paul Abraham)
  FLOWER OF HAWAII, THE (GER, 1953)

FLOWERS FOR ALGERNON see TWO WORLDS OF
  CHARLY GORDON, THE

FLOWING GOLD (FN, 1924, based on the book by Rex
    Beach)
  FLOWING GOLD (WB, 1940)

FLUTE MAGIQUE, LA see MAGIC FLUTE, THE

FLY AWAY HOME see DAUGHTERS COURAGEOUS

FLYING BANDIT, THE see THIEF OF BAGDAD, THE

FLYING DEUCES see BEAU HUNKS

FLYING DUTCHMAN, THE (FBO, 1923, based on a legend.
    Also the basis for the opera by Richard Wagner in 1843)
  PANDORA AND THE FLYING DUTCHMAN (MGM, 1951)
  FLYING DUTCHMAN, THE (GER, 1965)

FLYING FIFTY--FIVE, (BRI, 1923, based on the book by
    Edgar Wallace)
  FLYING FIFTY--FIVE (BRI, 1939)

FLYING SERPENT, THE see DEVIL BAT, THE

FLYING SQUAD (BRI, 1929, based on the book by Edgar
    Wallace)
  FLYING SQUAD (BRI, 1932)
  FLYING SQUAD (BRI, 1940)

FOG OVER FRISCO   see   CAUGHT IN THE FOG

FOHN   (GER, 1920, based on a story by Arnold Franck and
   Lad Vayda)
   WHITE HELL OF PITZ PALU, THE   (GER, 1929)
   WHITE ICE   (GER, 1945)
   FOHN (WHITE HELL)   (GER, 1950)

FOLIES BERGERE   (FRA, 1935, based on a play by Rudolph
   Lothar and Hans Adler)
   FOLIES BERGERE   (UA, 1935)
   THAT NIGHT IN RIO   (FOX, 1941)
   ON THE RIVIERA   (FOX, 1951)

FOLKET I SIMLANGSDALEN   (SWE, 1924, source unknown)
   FOLKET I SIMLANGSDALEN   (SWE, 1947)

FOLLOW THE FLEET   see   SHORE LEAVE

FOLLOW THE SUN   see   FAITH, HOPE AND HOGAN

FONTAINE DE BAKHTCHISSARAI, LA   (RUS, 1909, based
   on the story by Alexander Pushkin)
   FONTAINE DE BAKHTCHISSARAI, LA   (RUS, 1954)

FOOL, THE   (BRI, 1913, based on the poem by Rudyard
   Kipling)
   FOOL THERE WAS, A   (FOX, 1914)
   FOOL THERE WAS, A   (FOX, 1922)

FOOL KILLER, THE   (NBC–TV, 1956, based on the book by
   Helen Eustis)
   FOOL KILLER, THE   (IND, 1965)

FOOL OF THE FAMILY   see   ESCAPE ME NEVER

FOOL THERE WAS, A   see   FOOL, THE

FOOLISH VIRGIN, THE   (IND, 1917, based on the book by
   Thomas Dixon)
   FOOLISH VIRGIN, THE   (COL, 1924)

FOOL'S PARADISE   (PAR, 1921, based on the story, "Laurels
   and the Lady," by Leonard Merrick)
   MAGNIFICENT LIE, THE   (PAR, 1931)

FOOL'S REVENGE, A   (BIO, 1909, based on the opera,
   "Rigoletto," by Giuseppe Verdi)
   RIGOLETTO   (GER, 1918)
   RIGOLETTO   (short)   (BRI, 1922)
   RIGOLETTO   (short)   (BRI, 1926)
   RIGOLETTO   (short)   (BRI, 1927)
   RIGOLETTO   (ITA, 1947)
   RIGOLETTO   (CON, 1950)
   RIGOLETTO   (ITA, 1954)
   RIGOLETTO   (ITA, 1959)
   RIGOLETTO   (NBC–TV, 1959)

FOOTLIGHTS   (PAR, 1921, based on a story by Rita Weiman)
   SPOTLIGHT, THE   (PAR, 1927)

FOOTLIGHTS OF FATE   (VIT, 1916, based on the book,
   "Joan Thursday," by Louis Joseph Vance)
   GREATER THAN MARRIAGE   (VIT, 1924)

FOR LOVE OR MONEY   (UN, 1939, based on a story by
   various authors)
   NOOSE HANGS HIGH, THE   (EL, 1948)

FOR THE LOVE OF ADA   (series)   (BRI–TV, n.d., based on
   a teleplay)
   TOUCH OF GRACE, A   (series)   (ABC–TV, 1973)

FOR WHOM THE BELL TOOLS   (PAR, 1943, based on the
   book by Ernest Hemingway)
   FOR WHOM THE BELL TOLLS   (CBS–TV, 1959)

FORBIDDEN ALLIANCE   see   BARRETTS OF WIMPOLE
   STREET, THE

FORBIDDEN FRUIT   see   GOLDEN CHANCE, THE

FORBIDDEN LOVE   see   QUEEN WAS IN THE PARLOR,
   THE

FORBIDDEN MUSIC (LAND WITHOUT MUSIC)   (BRI, 1938,
   based on an operetta by Fritz Koselka and Armin Robinson)
   MUSICA PROIBITA   (ITA, 1942)

FORBIDDEN PARADISE   (PAR, 1921, based on the play,
   "The Czarina," by Lajos Biro and Melchior Lengyel)
   CATHERINE THE GREAT   (BRI, 1934)
   ROYAL SCANDAL, A   (FOX, 1945)

FORBIDDEN PLANET   see   TEMPEST, THE

FORBIDDEN VALLEY   (UN, 1938, based on the book,
   "Mountains Are My Kingdom," by Stuart Hardy)
   SIERRA   (UN, 1950)

FORCE OF EVIL   see   FAREWELL TO ARMS

FOREIGN INTRIGUE   (series)   (CROSS–CURRENT, DATE–
   LINE EUROPE, and OVERSEAS ADVENTURE)   (TV,
   1951, based on a teleplay)
   FOREIGN INTRIGUE   (UA, 1956)

FOREVER   see   PETER IBBETSON

FOREVER ENGLAND   see   BROWN ON "RESOLUTION"

FOREVER FEMALE   (PAR, 1953, based on a book by J. M.
   Barrie)
   FOREVER FEMALE   (NBC–TV, 1955)

FORFAITURE   see   CHEAT, THE

FORGER, THE   (BRI, 1928, based on the book by Edgar
   Wallace)
   FALSCHER VON LONDON, DER   (GER, 1961)

FORGET–ME–NOT   (GER, 1935, based on a screenplay by
   Hugh Gray and Arthur Wimperis)
   FORGET–ME–NOT (FOREVER YOURS)   (BRI, 1936)

FORGOTTEN COMMANDMENTS   see   LIFE OF MOSES,
   THE

FORGOTTEN FACES   see   HELIOTROPE

FORGOTTEN WOMEN   (MON, 1931, based on a screenplay
   by W. Scott Darling)
   FORGOTTEN WOMEN   (MON, 1949)

FORLORN RIVER   (PAR, 1926, based on a book by Zane
   Grey)
   FORLORN RIVER   (PAR, 1937)

FORSTERCHRISTL, DIE (GER, 1925, based on the operetta
    by Bernhard Buchbinder and Georg Jarno)
    FORSTERCHRISTL, DIE (GER, 1931)
    FORSTERCHRISTL, DIE (GER, 1952)
    FORSTERCHRISTL, DIE (GER, 1962)

FORSYTE SAGA, THE see THAT FORSYTE WOMAN

FORT APACHE, THE BRONX see SATURDAY NIGHT
    AT FORT APACHE

FORTUNE HUNTER, THE (VIT, 1920, based on a story by
    Winchell Smith)
    FORTUNE HUNTER, THE (WB, 1927)

FORTUNES OF CAPTAIN BLOOD see CAPTAIN BLOOD·

41ST, THE (RUS, 1926, source unknown)
    41ST, THE (RUS, 1956)

45 MINUTES FROM BROADWAY (FN, 1920, based on a
    musical by George M. Cohan)
    45 MINUTES FROM BROADWAY (NBC--TV, 1959)

44--CALIBRE MYSTERY, THE (UN, 1917, based on a story
    by T. Shelly Sutton)
    44--CALIBRE MYSTERY, THE (UN, 1922)

40 LITTLE MOTHERS see MIOCHE, LE

40 POUNDS OF TROUBLE see LITTLE MISS MARKER

FORTY WINKS see LORD CHUMLEY

FORVANDLINGEN see METAMORPHOSIS

FOSTERS, THE see GOOD TIMES

FOULE HURLE, LA see CROWD ROARS, THE

FOUNTAIN OF YOUTH see FAUST

FOUR DAUGHTERS (WB, 1938, based on a book by Fannie
    Hurst)
    YOUNG AT HEART (WB, 1954)

FOUR DEVILS, THE (DEN, 1911, based on the story by
    Herman Bang)
    FOUR DEVILS, THE (DEN, 1920)
    FOUR DEVILS, THE (FOX, 1928)

FOUR FEATHERS (BRI, 1915, based on the book by A. E.
    W. Mason)
    FOUR FEATHERS (BRI, 1918)
    FOUR FEATHERS (BRI, 1921)
    FOUR FEATHERS (PAR, 1929)
    FOUR FEATHERS (BRI, 1939)
    STORM OVER THE NILE (BRI, 1956)
    FOUR FEATHERS (NBC--TV, 1978)

FOUR HORSEMEN OF THE APOCALYPSE, THE see
    DEBOUT LES MORTS!

FOUR JACKS AND A JILL see STREET GIRL

FOUR JUST MEN (BRI, 1921, based on the book by Edgar
    Wallace)
    SECRET FOUR, THE (BRI, 1939)
    FOUR JUST MEN (series) (BRI,-TV, 1957)

FOUR MEN AND A PRAYER (FOX, 1938, based on the
    book by David Garth)
    FURY AT FURNACE CREEK (FOX, 1948)

FOUR MUSICIANS OF BREMEN (short) (DIS, 1922, based
    on the fairy tale)
    ANIMALS AND BREIGANDS (CZE, 1946)
    BREMENTOWN MUSICIANS (short) (GER, 1954)
    TOWN MUSICIANS, THE (short) (IND, 1954)
    TRAVELING MUSICIANS, THE (short) (IND, 1967)
    BREMENTOWN MUSICIANS (short) (RUS, 1969)
    MUPPET MUSICIANS OF BREMEN (TV, 1972)
    IN THE TRACKS OF THE BREMEN MUSICIANS (short)
        (RUS, 1975)

FOUR MUSKETEERS, THE see THREE MUSKETEERS,
    THE

FOUR NIGHTS OF A DREAMER see WHITE NIGHTS

FOUR SONS (FOX, 1928, based on a story by I. A. R. Wylie)
    FOUR SONS (FOX, 1940)

FOUR STEPS IN THE CLOUDS (ITA, 1943, based on a
    screenplay by Cesare Zavattini and Piero Tellini)
    VIRTUOUS BIGAMIST, THE (FRA/ITA, 1957)

FOUR WALLS (MGM, 1928, based on the play by Dana
    Burnet and George Abbott)
    STRAIGHT IS THE WAY (MGM, 1934)

FOURPOSTER, THE (COL, 1952, based on the play by Jan
    de Hartog. Also the basis for the musical comedy, "I Do!
    I Do!")
    FOURPOSTER, THE (NBC--TV, 1955)
    REISENRAD, DAS (GER, 1961)
    FOURPOSTER, THE (CBS--TV, 1962)

14 HOURS (FOX, 1951, based on a story by Joel Sayre)
    MAN ON THE LEDGE (CBS--TV, 1955)

FOURTEENTH MAN, THE (PAR, 1920, based on the play,
    "Man from Blankley's, The," by F. Anstey)
    MAN FROM BLANKLEY'S, THE (WB, 1930)
    GUEST OF HONOR (BRI, 1934)

FOURTH IN SALVADOR, THE (BIO, 1917, based on the
    story, "Roads of Destiny," by O. Henry)
    ROADS OF DESTINY (MGM, 1921)

FRA DIAVOLO (GER, 1906, based on the opera by Daniel
    Auber and the book by Eugene Scribe)
    FRA DIAVOLO (SOL, 1912)
    FRA DIAVOLO (short) (BRI, 1922)
    FRA DIAVOLO (GER, 1926)
    FRA DIAVOLO (ITA, 1931)
    FRA DIAVOLO (FRA, 1931)
    FRA DIAVOLO (GER, 1931)
    DEVIL'S BROTHER, THE (MGM, 1933)
    FRA DIAVOLO (ITA, 1938)
    FRA DIAVOLO (ITA, 1941)
    FRA DIAVOLO (ITA, 1960)
    LAST CHARGE, THE (ITA, 1964)
    LEGEND OF FRA DIAVOLO (short) (ITA, 1964)
    BANDITS OF FRA DIAVOLO (ITA, 1968)

FRANCESCA DA RIMINI, OR THE TWO BROTHERS (VIT,
    1907, based on a story from "The Inferno" by Dante
    Alighieri)

FRANCESCA DA RIMINI (VIT, 1910)

FRANCIS JOINS THE WACS (UN, 1954, based on a story
    by Herbert Baker)
    SERGEANT WAS A LADY, THE (UN, 1961)

FRANCIS MARION, THE SWAMP FOX see GENERAL
    MARION, THE SWAMP FOX

FRANCIS OF ASSISI see ST. FRANCIS OF ASSISI

FRANKENSTEIN (ED, 1910, based on the book by Mary
    Shelley)
    LIFE WITHOUT SOUL (OCE, 1915)
    FRANKENSTEIN (UN, 1931)
    BRIDE OF FRANKENSTEIN (UN, 1935)
    SON OF FRANKENSTEIN (UN, 1939)
    FRANKENSTEIN MEETS THE WOLF MAN (UN, 1943)
    GHOST OF FRANKENSTEIN (UN, 1942)
    HOUSE OF FRANKENSTEIN (UN, 1945)
    ABBOTT & COSTELLO MEET FRANKENSTEIN (UN,
    1948)
    FRANKENSTEIN (ABC--TV, 1952)
    CURSE OF FRANKENSTEIN (BRI, 1957)
    FRANKENSTEIN 1970 (AA, 1958)
    FRANKENSTEIN'S DAUGHTER (AST, 1958)
    REVENGE OF FRANKENSTEIN (BRI, 1958)
    EVIL OF FRANKENSTEIN, THE (BRI, 1964)
    MR. MAGOO – MAN OF MYSTERY (UPA, 1964)
    FRANKENSTEIN CREATED WOMAN (BRI, 1966)
    FRANKENSTEIN JR. (series) (CBS–TV, 1966)
    FRANKENSTEIN MUST BE DESTROYED (BRI, 1969)
    HORROR OF FRANKENSTEIN (BRI, 1970)
    MOSAIC – FRANKENSTEIN 1980 (ITA, 1972)
    LADY FRANKENSTEIN (IND, 1972)
    FRANKENSTEIN (ABC--TV, 1973)
    FRANKENSTEIN: THE TRUE STORY (NBC--TV, 1973)
    FLESH FOR FRANKENSTEIN (FRA/ITA, 1973)
    VICTOR FRANKENSTEIN (IRE/SWE, 1977)

FRANKENSTEIN CREATED WOMAN see FRANKENSTEIN

FRANKENSTEIN MEETS THE WOLF MAN see
    FRANKENSTEIN

FRANKENSTEIN MUST BE DESTROYED see FRANKEN--
    STEIN

FRANKENSTEIN 1970 see FRANKENSTEIN

FRANKENSTEIN: THE TRUE STORY see FRANKEN–
    STEIN

FRANKENSTEIN, THE VAMPIRE & CO., see ABBOTT &
    COSTELLO MEET FRANKENSTEIN

FRANKENSTEIN'S DAUGHTER see FRANKENSTEIN

FRANKIE AND JOHNNY see HER MAN

FRATE FRANCESCO (ITA, n.d., source unknown)
    FRATE FRANCESCO (ITA, 1928)

FRAU CHENEY'S ENDE see LAST OF MRS. CHENEY,
    THE

FRAU WIE DU, EINE (GER, 1933, source unknown)
    FRAU WIE DU, EINE (GER, 1939)

FRAUENARZT DR. PRAETORIUS (GER, 1950, based on
    a story, "Dr. Med. Hiob Praetorius," by Curt Goetz)
    PEOPLE WILL TALK (FOX, 1951)
    DR. PRAETORIUS (GER, 1964)

FRAUENPARADIES (GER, 1922, source unknown)
    FRAUENPARADIES (GER, 1939)

FRAULEIN ELSE (GER, 1929, based on the book by Arthur
    Schnitzler)
    ANGE NU, L' (ARG, 1946)

FRAULEIN JULIE see MISS JULIE

FRAULEIN VON BARNHELM, DAS see MINNA VON
    BARNHELM

FRAULEIN VON SCUDERI, DAS (ITA, 1911, based on a
    novel by Ernst Theodor Amadeus Hoffmann)
    BESESSENE, DER (GER, 1919)
    JUWELEN (AUS, 1930)
    TODLICHEN TRAUME, DIE (GER, 1950)
    SCHATZE DES TEUFELS, DIE (SWE, 1955)

FREAKS (MGM, 1932, based on the story, "Spurs," by
    Tod Robbins)
    SHE FREAK (IND, 1967)

FRECKLES (VIT, 1912, based on the book by Gene Stratton
    Porter)
    FRECKLES (PAR, 1917)
    FRECKLES (RKO, 1928)
    FRECKLES (RKO, 1935)
    FRECKLES COMES HOME (MON, 1942)
    FRECKLES (FOX, 1961)

FRECKLES COMES HOME see FRECKLES

FREDERIC CHOPIN see LIFE OF CHOPIN

FREDERICK DOUGLAS see HOUSE ON CEDAR HILL,
    THE

FREE AND EASY (MGM, 1930, based on a story by Richard
    Schayer)
    ESTRELLADOS (SPA, 1930)
    PICK A STAR (MGM, 1937)

FREE AND EASY see BUT THE FLESH IS WEAK

FREE SOUL, A (MGM, 1931, based on the book by Adela
    Rogers St. Johns)
    GIRL WHO HAD EVERYTHING, THE (MGM, 1953)

FRENCH LEAVE (BRI, 1930, based on the play by Reginald
    Berkeley)
    FRENCH LEAVE (BRI, 1937)

FRENCHIE see DESTRY RIDES AGAIN

FRENTE MARCHEN, DE see DOUGHBOYS

FRERES BRIGANDS, LES see BRIGAND BROTHERS,
    THE

FRERES CORSES, LES see CORICAN BROTHERS, THE

FRESHMAN LOVE see COLLEGE WIDOW

FREUD see SECRET OF SIGMUND FREUD, THE

FREUT EUCH DES LEBENS (GER, 1920, source unknown)
   FREUT EUCH DES LEBENS (GER, 1934)

FRIDERICUS see CHORAL VON LEUTHEN, DER

FRIEDERIKE see DICHTUNG UND WAHRHEIT

FRIEDERIKE VON SESENHEIM, DIE JUGENDGELIEBTE,
   GOETHES FRUHLINGSTRAUM see DICHTUNG
   UND WAHRHEIT

FRIEDRICH SCHILLER (GER, 1923, source unknown)
   FRIEDRICH SCHILLER (GER, 1940)

FRIENDLY ENEMIES (PDC, 1925, based on the play by
   Samuel Shipman and Aaron Hoffman)
   FRIENDLY ENEMIES (UA, 1942)

FRIENDLY PERSUASION (AA, 1956, based on the book
   by Jessamyn West)
   FRIENDLY PERSUASION (ABC--TV, 1975)

FRIENDSHIP (FOX, 1929, based on a screenplay by Eugene
   Walter)
   NOMBRE DE LA AMISTAD, EN (SPA, 1930)

FRIENDSHIP 7 see AMERICAN IN ORBIT, AN

FRIGHTENED LADY (BRI, 1932, based on the book, "The
   Case of the Frightened Lady," by Edgar Wallace)
   CRIMINAL AT LARGE (BRI, 1933)
   CASE OF THE FRIGHTENED LADY, THE (BRI, 1940)
   INDIAN SCARF (GER, 1963)
   INDIAN SCARF, THE (BRI, 1965)

FROG, THE see MARK OF THE FROG, THE

FROG PRINCESS, THE (short) (RUS, 1928, based on a
   fairy tale)
   FROG PRINCESS, THE (short) (COR, 1957)

FROG WENT A'COURTIN' (WW, 1961, based on the folk
   tune)
   MR. FROG WENT A'COURTIN' (CAN, 1977)

FROGMEN, THE (FOX, 1951, based on a book by Oscar
   Millard)
   DEEP WATER (CBS--TV, 1957)

FROHLICHE WEINBERG, DER (GER, 1927, based on the
   play by Carl Zuckmayer)
   FROHLICHE WEINBERG, DER (GER, 1952)

FROM PRECINCT TO PRESIDENT (CBS--TV, 1958, based
   on the life of President Harry S. Truman)
   TRUMAN YEARS, THE (short) (TFC, 1961)
   HARRY TRUMAN, THE EARLY YEARS (short) (WOL,
   1962)
   H.S.T.: DAYS OF DECISION (MGM--TV, 1963)
   HARRY TRUMAN, THE PRESIDENCY (short) (WOL,
   1964)

FROM SOUP TO NUTS (short) (MGM, 1928, based on a
   screenplay by Leo McCarey)
   CHUMP AT OXFORD, A (UA, 1940)

FROM THE EARTH TO THE MOON see TRIP TO THE
MOON, A

FROM THE MANGER TO THE CROSS see PASSION PLAY,
THE

FROMONT JEUNE ET RISLER AINE (GER, 1914, based
   on a book by Alphonse Daudet)
   FROMONT JEUNE ET RISLER AINE (FRA, 1921)
   EHESKANDAL IM HAUSE FROMONT JUN. UND RISLER
   SEN. (GER, 1927)
   FROMONT JEUNE ET RISLER AINE (FRA, 1941)

FRONT PAGE, THE (UA, 1931, based on the play by Ben
   Hecht and Charles MacArthur)
   HIS GIRL FRIDAY (COL, 1940)
   THRILL OF BRAZIL, THE (COL, 1946)
   FRONT PAGE, THE (CBS--TV, 1949)
   FRONT PAGE, THE (TV, 1953)
   FRONT PAGE, THE (CBS--TV, 1970)
   FRONT PAGE, THE (UN, 1974)

FRONTIER FAMILY see ABRAHAM LINCOLN

FRONTIER MARSHAL (FOX, 1934, based on the book by
   Stuart N. Lake and western legend)
   FRONTIER MARSHAL (FOX, 1938)
   MY DARLING CLEMENTINE (FOX, 1946)
   POWDER RIVER (FOX, 1953)
   LIFE AND LEGEND OF WYATT EARP (series) (ABC--
   TV, 1955)
   HEROES AND VILLAINS (sequence) (NET--TV, 1965)

FRONTIER UPRISING see KIT CARSON

FROU--FROU (ITA, 1918, based on the play by Henri Meilhac
   and Ludovic Halevy)
   FROU--FROU (FRA, 1923)
   TOY WIFE, THE (MGM, 1938)

FROWNING PRINCE, THE (short) (FRA, 1962, based on
   a fairy tale)
   ALICE IN WONDERLAND IN PARIS (CHI, 1966)

FRUCHTCHEN (AUS, 1934, based on the play, "The Green
   Fruit," by Jacques Thery and Regis Gignoux)
   BETWEEN US GIRLS (UN, 1942)

FRUHLINGS ERWACHEN (AUS, 1923, based on the book
   by F. Wedekind)
   FRUHLINGS ERWACHEN (GER, 1929)

FRUHLINGSFLUTEN (GER, 1924, based on the book by
   Ivan Turgenev)
   EAUX PRINTANIERES, LES (CZE, 1967)

FRUTA AMARGA, LA see MIN AND BILL

FUERZA DEL DESEO, LA see OF HUMAN BONDAGE

FUERZA DEL QUERER, LA see BIG FIGHT, THE

FUERZA Y NOBLEZA (SPA, 1919, based on the life of
   Prizefighter Jack Johnson)
   GREAT WHITE HOPE, THE (FOX, 1970)
   JACK JOHNSON (CON, 1970)

FUGA A DUE VOCI (ITA, n.d., based on a screenplay by
   Carlo Bragaglia)
   ONE NIGHT WITH YOU (BRI' 1948)

FUGITIVE, THE   (RKO, 1947, based on the book, "Laby--
    rinthine Ways, The," by Graham Greene)
  POWER AND THE GLORY, THE   (NET-TV, 1959)
  POWER AND THE GLORY, THE   (ABC-TV, 1961)

FUHRMANN HENSCHEL   (GER, 1918, based on the play
    by Gerhart Hauptmann)
  FUHRMANN HENSCHEL   (GER, 1922)
  FUHRMANN HENSCHEL   (GER, 1956)

FUN AND FANCY FREE   see   JACK AND THE BEANSTALK

FUNF VERFLUCHTEN GENTLEMEN   see   CINQ GENTLE-
    MEN MAUDITS, LES

FUNNY GIRL   see   ROSE OF WASHINGTON SQUARE

FUNNY LADY   see   ROSE OF WASHINGTON SQUARE

FURIES, THE   see   KING LEAR

FURST FAMILY OF WASHINGTON, THE   (ABC-TV, 1973,
    based on a teleplay)
  THAT'S MY MAMA   (series)   (ABC-TV, 1974)

FURST VON PAPPENHEIM, DER   (GER, 1927, based on the
    operetta by Arnold and Bach)
  FURST VON PAPPENHEIM, DER   (GER, 1952)

FURTHER ADVENTURES OF THE FLAG LIEUTENANT,
    THE   see   FLAG LIEUTENANT, THE

FURUSATO   (JAP, 1922, source unknown)
  FURUSATO   (JAP, 1930)

FURY AT FURNACE CREEK   see   FOUR MEN AND A
    PRAYER

G--MEN NEVER FORGET (serial) (REP, 1947, based on a
screenplay by various authors; the remake is a condensed
version of the serial)
CODE 645 (REP, 1966)

G--MEN VS. THE BLACK DRAGON (serial) (REP, 1942,
based on a screenplay by various authors; remake is a
condensed version of the serial)
BLACK DRAGON OF MAZANAR (REP, 1966)

GABLES MYSTERY, THE (BRI, 1931, based on the play by
Jack Celestin and Jack di Leon)
MAN AT SIX, THE (BRI, 1938)

GABRIEL GRUB, THE SURLY SEXTON see PICKWICK
PAPERS, THE

GABY see WATERLOO BRIDGE

GADFLY, THE (RUS, 1928, based on the story by Ethel
Voynich)
GADFLY, THE (RUS, 1955)

GAIS LURONS, LES see GLUECKSKINDER

GAITES DE L'ESCADRON, LES (FRA, 1912, based on a
book by Georges Courteline)
GAITES DE L'ESCADRON, LES (FRA, 1932)
GAITES DE L'ESCADRON, LES (FRA/ITA, 1955)

GALAS DE LA PARAMOUNT see PARAMOUNT ON
PARADE

GALATHEA (FRA, 1910, based on a legend)
AWAKENING OF GALATHEA (POW, 1911)
GALATHEA (GER, 1935)

GALEERENSTRAFLING, DER see VAUTRIN

GALILEO see STAR GAZERS

GALLANT LADY (UA, 1934, based on a story by Gilbert
Emery and Franc Rhodes)
ALWAYS GOODBYE (FOX, 1938)

GALLANT LITTLE TAILOR see BRAVE LITTLE TAILOR

GALLEY SLAVE, THE see CHEMINEAU, LE

GAMBLER, THE (GER, n.d., based on the book, "The
Possessed," by Fyodor Dostoyevsky)
GAMBLER, THE (FRA, n.d.)
GREAT SINNER, THE (MGM, 1949)
GAMBLER, THE (CZE/RUS, 1973)
GAMBLER, THE (PAR, 1974)

GAMBLERS, THE (VIT, 1919, based on the play by Charles
Klein)
GAMBLERS, THE (WB, 1929)

GAMBLING HOUSE see MR. LUCKY

GAMBLING ON THE HIGH SEAS see SPECIAL AGENT

GAME OF DEATH, THE see MOST DANGEROUS GAME,
THE

GAME OF LIFE AND DEATH, THE see HAMLET

GANDHI see MAHATMA GANDHI

GANESH AVATAR (IN, 1922, based on a legend)
GANESH AVATAR (IN, 1925)

GANOVENEHRE (GER, 1933, based on the book by Charles
Rudolph)
GANOVENEHRE (GER, 1966)

GANZER KERL, EIN (GER, 1935, based on the book by
Wolfgang Marken)
GANZER KERL, EIN (GER, 1939)

GARCON ENSORCELE, LE (RUS, 1956, based on the book
"Merveilleux Voyage de Nils Holgersson," by Selma
Lagerlof)
MARVELOUS VOYAGE OF NILS HOLGERSSON, THE
(SWE, 1962)

GARCONNE, LA (FRA, 1923, based on the book by Victor
Margueritte)
GARCONNE, LA (FRA, 1935)
GARCONNE, LA (FRA, 1956)

GARDE DU CORPS, LE (HUN, 1918, based on the play by
Ferenc Molnar)
GARDEOFFIZIER, DER (AUS, 1925)
GUARDSMAN, THE (MGM, 1931)
CHOCOLATE SOLDIER, THE (MGM, 1941)

GARDEN IN THE SEA, A see LOST MOMENT, THE

GARDEN OF ALLAH, THE (SEL, 1916, based on the book
by Robert Hitchens)
GARDEN OF ALLAH, THE (MGM, 1927)
GARDEN OF ALLAH, THE (UA, 1936)

GARRISON'S FINISH (SEL, 1914, based on the book by
W. B. F. Ferguson)
GARRISON'S FINISH (IND, 1923)

GASLIGHT (ANGEL STREET and MURDER IN THORNTON
SQUARE) (BRI, 1940, based on the play, "Angel Street,"
by Patrick Hamilton)
GASLIGHT (MGM, 1943)
ANGEL STREET (NBC--TV, 1948)
ANGEL STREET (TV, 1952)
ANGEL STREET (NBC--TV, 1958)

GASPARONE (GER, 1937, based on the book by F. Zell
and Richard Genee)
GASPERONE (GER, 1956)

GASSCHEN ZUM PARADIES, DAS see ULICKA V RAJI

GATHERING STORM, THE see CHURCHILL -- MAN OF
THE CENTURY

GATTE, DER (GER, 1922, based on a book, "L'Eternal
Mari," by Feyodor Dostoyevsky)
HOMME AU CHAPEAU ROND, L' (FRA, 1946)

GAUGHIN IN TAHITI -- SEARCH FOR PARADISE see
PAUL GAUGHIN

GAUNT STRANGER, THE see RINGER, THE

GAVROCHE see CHEMINEAU, LE

GAY BANDITTI, THE see YOUNG IN HEART, THE

GAY CABALLERO, THE (FOX, 1932, based on the book
   by Tom Gill)
GAY CABALLERO, THE (FOX, 1940)

GAY DECEIVER, THE (MGM, 1926, based on the play,
   "Toto," by Leo Ditrichstein)
SU ULTIMA NOCHE (SPA, 1931)

GAY LORD QUEX, THE (BRI, 1917, based on the play by
   Arthur Wing Pinero)
GAY LORD QUEX, THE (GOL, 1919)

GAY MASQUERADE (JAP, 1928, source unknown)
GAY MASQUERADE (JAP, 1958)

GAY MUSKETEER, THE see THREE MUSKETEERS, THE

GAY SISTERS, THE (WB, 1942, based on the book by
   Stephen Longstreet)
GAY SISTERS, THE (NBC–TV, 1956)

GAY SWORDSMAN, THE see THREE MUSKETEERS, THE

GAZEBO, THE (MGM, 1959, based on the play by Alec
   Coppel)
JO (FRA, 1971)

GEFAHRDETE MADCHEN (GER, 1927, source unknown)
GEFAHRDETE MADCHEN (GER, 1958)

GEFAHRLICHE ALTER, DAS (GER, 1911, based on the
   book by Karin Michaelis)
GEFAHRLICHE ALTER, DES (GER, 1927)

GEFAHRLICHE LIEBE (GER, 1929, based on the book,
   "Die Siebzehnjahrigen," by Max Dreyer)
EINE SIEBZEHNJAHRIGE (GER, 1934)

GEFAHRLICHES SPIEL (GER, 1919, source unknown)
GEFAHRLICHES SPIEL (GER, 1937)

GEHEIME KURIER, DER see RED AND THE BLACK,
   THE

GEHEIMNIS DER ROTEN KATZE, DAS (GER, 1931, source
   unknown)
GEHEIMNIS DER ROTEN KATZE, DAS (GER, 1949)

GEIER–WALLY, DIE (GER, 1921, based on the book by
   Wilhelmine von Hillern)
GEIER–WALLY, DIE (GER, 1940)
GEIER–WALLY, DIE (GER, 1956)

GEISTERSEHER, DER (GER, 1915, based on the book by
   Friedrich von Schiller)
GEISTERSEHER, DER (GER, 1927)

GELD AUF DER STRASSE (GER, 1922, source unknown)
GELD AUF DER STRASSE (GER, 1930)

GELIEBTE, DIE (GER, 1926, based on the play by Alexander
   Brody)
GELIEBTE, DIE (GER, 1939)

GEMINI MAN, THE see INVISIBLE MAN, THE

GENERAL, THE (UA, 1927, based on Andrew's Raid during

the Civil War)
GREAT LOCOMOTIVE CHASE, THE (DIS, 1956)

GENERAL, THE see GENERAL DOUGLAS Mac ARTHUR

GENERAL DOUGLAS Mac ARTHUR – I SHALL RETURN
   (short) (IND, n.d., based on the life of the noted American
   general)
Mac ARTHUR STORY, THE (short) (RKO, 1951)
Mac ARTHUR (short) (WB, n.d.)
Mac ARTHUR LIBERATES MANILLA (short) (UNI,
   n.d.)
Mac ARTHUR -- AMERICA'S FIRST SOLDIER (short)
   (IND, n.d.)
GENERAL, THE (MGM--TV, 1962)
Mac ARTHUR STORY, THE (short) (NAV, 1964)
OLD SOLDIER – A BIOGRAPHY OF DOUGLAS
   Mac ARTHUR, THE (short) (IND, 1964)
Mac ARTHUR VS. TRUMAN (short) (FNC, 1964)
OLD SOLDIER: DUTY, HONOR, COUNTRY (short)
   (IND, 1964)
GENERAL, THE (short) (EBE, 1966)
GENERAL, THE (WOL, 1967)
Mac ARTHUR (UNI, 1977)

GENERAL GEORGE C. MARSHALL (short) (CBS–TV,
   1955, based on the life and work of the noted U.S. general)
GENERAL MARSHALL (short) (CBS–TV, 1961)
MARSHALL (short) (IND, n.d.)

GENERAL JOHN REGAN (BRI, 1921, based on the play by
   George A. Birmingham)
GENERAL JOHN REGAN (BRI, 1933)

GENERAL MARION, THE SWAMP FOX (IND, 1911, based on
   the life of the guerilla chief in the American Revolution)
FRANCIS MARION, THE SWAMP FOX (KAL, 1914)

GENERAL PERSHING (short) (IND, n.d., based on the life
   of the World War I Navy commander)
PERSHING STORY, THE (short) (NAV, 1959)
JOHN J. PERSHING (short) (NAV, 1960)
PERSHING (short) (NAV, 1963)
GENERAL PERSHING -- THE IRON COMMANDER
   (short) (IND, 1964)
PERSHING VS. LUDENDORFF (short) (FNC, 1964)
GENERAL PERSHING (short) (WOL, 1965)

GENERAL TOPTYGUINE, LE (RUS, 1910, based on the
   book by Nikolai Niekrassov)
GENERAL TOPTYGUINE, LE (RUS, 1929)

GENERALS WITHOUT BUTTONS (FRA, 1936, based on
   the book by Louis Perguad)
WAR OF THE BUTTONS (THE BUTTON WAR) (FRA, 1962
GENGHIS KHAN (PHI, 1953, based on a historical character)
CONQUERER, THE (RKO, 1956)
KING OF THE MONGOLS (JAP, 1964)
GENGHIS KHAN (COL, 1965)

GENIUS, THE see SITTING PRETTY

GENS DE HEMSO see HEMSOBORNA

GENTLE JULIA (FOX, 1924, based on the book by Booth
   Tarkington)
GENTLE JULIA (FOX, 1936)

GENTLEMAN AFTER DARK, A see HELIOTROPE

GENTLEMAN JIM (WB, 1942, based on the life of boxer
James Corbett)
BIRTH OF MODERN BOXING, THE (short) (CBS–TV,
1955)

GENTLEMAN OF LEISURE, A (PAR, 1915, based on the
play by John Stapleton and P. G. Wodehouse)
GENTLEMAN OF LEISURE, A (PAR, 1923)

GENTLEMEN OF TITIPU see FAN–FAN

GENTLEMEN PREFER BLONDES (PAR, 1928, based on
the book by Anita Loos)
GENTLEMEN PREFER BLONDES (FOX, 1953)

GEORGE FRIEDRICH HANDEL see GREAT MR. HANDEL,
THE

GEORGE M! see YANKEE DOODLE DANDY

GEORGE SAND see SONG TO REMEMBER, A

GEORGE WASHINGTON see MOUNT VERNON IN
VIRGINIA

GEORGE WASHINGTON CARVER see STORY OF DR.
CARVER, THE

GEORGES BRAQUE see BRAQUE

GERMINAL see AU PAYS DES TENEBRES

GERN HAB' ICH DIE FRAU'N GEHUSST see PAGANINI

GERONIMO (PAR, 1939, based on historical incidents and
the character of Geronimo)
WALK THE PROUD LAND (UN, 1956)
GERONIMO'S REVENGE (ABC–TV, 1960)
GERONIMO (UA, 1962)

GERONIMO see also LIVES OF A BENGAL LANCER and
PLAINSMAN, THE

GERVAISE see ASSOMMOIR, L'

GESCHICHTE VOM KLEINEN MUCK, DER (GER, 1922,
based on a story by Wilhelm Hauff)
GESCHICHTE VOM KLEINEN MUCK, DER (GER, 1953)

GESCHIEDENE FRAU, DIE (GER, 1926, based on the
operetta by Victor Leon and Leo Fall)
GESCHIEDENE FRAU, DIE (GER, 1953)
GESCHMINKTE JUGEND (GER, 1929, source unknown)
GESCHMINKTE JUGEND (GER, 1960)

GESPENSTER, KONNEN DIE TOTEN LEBEN? see GHOSTS

GESTERN UND HEUTE see MAEDCHEN IN UNIFORM

GET CARTER (MGM, 1971, based on the book, "Jack's
Return Home," by Ted Lewis)
HIT MAN (MGM, 1972)

GET–RICH–QUICK WALLINGFORD (AUT, 1916, based
on the play by George M. Cohan)
GET–RICH–QUICK WALLINGFORD (PAR, 1921)

GETAWAY, THE see PUBLIC HERO NO. 1

GETTING GERTIE'S GARTER (PDC, 1927, based on the
play by Avery Hopwood and Wilson Collison)
NIGHT OF THE GARTER, A (BRI, 1933)
GETTING GERTIE'S GARTER (UA, 1945)

GHETTO TEREZIN (DISTANT JOURNEY) (CZE, 1950,
based on people and incidents in the Terezin concentration
camp during World War II)
TEREZIN REQUIEM, THE (CBS–TV, 1964)
TEREZIN (short) (IND, 1969)

GHOST AND MRS. MUIR, THE (FOX, 1947, based on the
book by R. A. Dick)
STRANGER IN THE NIGHT (CBS–TV, 1956)
GHOST AND MRS. MUIR, THE (series) (NBC–TV, 1968)
GHOST AND MRS. MUIR, THE (series) (ABC–TV, 1968)

GHOST BREAKER, THE (PAR, 1914, based on the play by
Paul Dickey and Charles W. Goddard)
GHOST BREAKER, THE (PAR, 1922)
GHOST BREAKERS, THE (PAR, 1940)
SCARED STIFF (PAR, 1953)

GHOST BREAKERS, THE see GHOST BREAKER, THE

GHOST FOR SALE, A see CURSE OF THE WRAYDONS

GHOST OF FRANKENSTEIN see FRANKENSTEIN

GHOST TRAIN, THE (BRI, 1927, based on the play by
Arnold Ridley)
GHOST TRAIN, THE (BRI, 1931)
GHOST TRAIN, THE (BRI, 1941)
GHOST TRAIN, THE (JAP, 1949)
SPOEGELSESTOGET (DEN, 1976)

GHOSTS (RUS, 1914, based on the play, "Ghosts," by
Hendrik Ibsen)
GHOSTS (IND, 1915)
GESPENSTER, KONNEN DIE TOTEN LEBEN? (GER,
1922)

GHOST'S STORY, THE see EARTHBOUND

GHOUL, THE (BRI, 1933, based on the book by Frank King)
NO PLACE LIKE HOMICIDE (WHAT A CARVE UP) (BRI,
1961)

GIANTS OF THESSALY, THE (ITA, 1961, based on a legend)
JASON AND THE ARGONAUTS (COL, 1963)

GIBBSVILLE see TURNING POINT OF JIM MALLOY,
THE

GILBRATER (FRA, 1939, source unknown)
GIBRALTER (BRI, 1961)

GIFT FOR HEIDI, A see HEIDI

GIFT OF LOVE, THE see SENTIMENTAL JOURNEY

GIFT OF LOVE, THE see SACRIFICE, THE

GIFT OF THE MAGI, THE see SACRIFICE, THE

GIFTAS (SWE, 1926, source unknown)
GIFTAS (SWE, 1955)

GIGI (FRA, 1950, based on a story by Colette)

GIGI   (MGM, 1958)

GIGOLETTE   (FRA, 1921, based on a book by Pierre
    Decourcelle)
    GIGOLETTE   (FRA, 1937)
GILDED LILY, THE   (PAR, 1921, based on a story by Mel-
    ville Baker and Jack Kirkland)
    GILDED LILY, THE   (PAR, 1935)

GILLIGAN'S ISLAND   (series)   (CBS–TV, 1964, based on
    a teleplay)
    NEW ADVENTURES OF GILLIGAN   (series)   (ABC–TV,
    1974)

GINGERBREAD COTTAGE   see   HANSEL AND GRETEL

GINGERBREAD HOUSE, THE   see   HANSEL AND GRETEL

GIOCONDA, LA   (ITA, 1911, based on the book by Gabriel
    d'Annunzio and the opera by Amilcare Ponchielli)
    DEVIL'S DAUGHTER, THE   (FOX, 1915)
    GIOCONDA, LA   (ITA, 1916)

GIOCONDA SMILE, THE   see   WOMAN'S VENGEANCE, A

GIOVANNI EPISCOPO   (ITA, 1916, based on a book by
    Gabriele D'Annunzio)
    CRIME OF GIOVANNI EPISCOPO, THE   (ITA, 1947)

GIPSY BLOOD   see   CARMEN

GIRL AND HER TRUST, A   see   LONEDALE OPERATOR,
    THE

GIRL AND THE GAMBLER, THE   see   DOVE, THE

GIRL AT LUNA PARK, THE   see   DAME AUX CAMELIAS,
    LA

GIRL CRAZY   (RKO, 1932, based on the musical by George
    and Ira Gershwin)
    GIRL CRAZY   (MGM, 1943)
    WHERE THE BOYS MEET THE GIRLS   (MGM, 1966)

GIRL FROM AVENUE A, THE   see   BRAT, THE

GIRL FROM HAVANA, THE   see   LEATHERNECKS HAVE
    LANDED, THE

GIRL FROM LENINGRAD, THE (WINGS OF VICTORY)
    (RUS, 1941, based on a screenplay by Serge Mikhailov
    and Mikhail Rosenberg)
    THREE RUSSIAN GIRLS   (UA, 1944)

GIRL FROM MAXIM'S, THE   see   DAME DE CHEZ MAXIM,
    LA

GIRL FROM MONTE CARLO   see   NIGHT WATCH, THE

GIRL OF LA MANCHA   see   DON QUIXOTE

GIRL FROM TENTH AVENUE, THE   see   OUTCAST, THE

GIRL FROM THE MARSH CROFT, THE   see   TOSEN
    FRAN STORMYTORPET

GIRL IN A DRESS COAT   see   FLICKAN I FRANCK

GIRL IN EVERY PORT, A   (FOX, 1926, based on a screenplay
    by Howard Hawks)
    GOLDIE   (FOX, 1931)

GIRL MOST LIKELY, THE   see   TOM, DICK AND HARRY

GIRL OF THE GOLDEN WEST, THE   (PAR, 1914, based
    on the play by David Belasco. Also the basis for the
    Giacomo Puccini opera, "La Fanciulla del West," in 1910)
    GIRL OF THE GOLDEN WEST, THE   (FN, 1923)
    GIRL OF THE GOLDEN WEST, THE   (FN, 1930)
    GIRL OF THE GOLDEN WEST, THE   (MGM, 1938)

GIRL OF THE LIMBERLOST   (FBO, 1924, based on the book
    by Gene Stratton Porter)
    GIRL OF THE LIMBERLOST   (MON, 1934)
    ROMANCE OF THE LIMBERLOST   (MON, 1938)
    GIRL OF THE LIMBERLOST   (COL, 1945)

GIRL OF THE RIO   see   DOVE, THE

GIRL ON THE GREEN MOUNTAIN, THE   see   PEER GYNT

GIRL ON THE SUBWAY   see   PRETTY BABY

GIRL WHO CAME BACK, THE   (PAR, 1918, based on the
    play, "Leah Kleschna," by C. M. S. McLellan)
    MORAL SINNER, THE   (PAR, 1924)

GIRL WHO DANCED INTO LIFE, THE   see   RED SHOES,
    THE

GIRL WHO HAD EVERYTHING, THE   see   FREE SOUL, A

GIRL WHO LIKED PURPLE FLOWERS, THE   (HUN, 1935,
    source unknown)
    GIRL WHO LIKED PURPLE FLOWERS, THE   (HUN, 1974)

GIRL WHO RAN WILD, THE   see   M'LISS

GIRLS ABOUT TOWN   (PAR, 1931, based on the play, "The
    Greeks Had a Word for It," by Zoe Atkins)
    GREEKS HAD A WORD FOR THEM, THE   (THREE
    BROADWAY GIRLS)   (UA, 1932)
    HOW TO MARRY A MILLIONAIRE   (FOX, 1953)

GIRLS AT SEA   see   MIDDLE WATCH

GIRL'S DORMITORY   (FOX, 1936, based on a play by
    Ladislaus Fodor)
    VERY YOUNG LADY, A   (FOX, 1941)

GIRLS IN UNIFORM   see   MAEDCHEN IN UNIFORM

GIT ALONG LITTLE DOGIES   (REP, 1937, based on a
    screenplay by Dorrell and Stuart McGowan)
    STARDUST ON THE SAGE   (REP, 1942)

GITANILLA, LA   (SPA, 1914, based on a story by Cervantes)
    GITANILLA, LA   (SPA, 1923)
    GITANILLA, LA   (SPA, 1940)

GIUSEPPE VERDI   (ITA, 1938, based on the life of the noted
    composer)
    VERDI   (series)   (ITA--TV, 1974)

GIVE US BARABBAS   see   BARABBAS

GLAD EYE, THE   (BRI, 1920, based on the play, "The Zebra,"
    by Jose Levy, Paul Armont and Nicholas Nancey)

GLAD EYE, THE (BRI, 1927)

GLANZ UND ELEND DER KURTISANEN see MOREL, DER MEISTER DER KETTE

GLAS WASSER, EIN (GER, 1923, based on the book, "Le Verre d'Eau," by Eugene Scribe)
GLAS WASSER, DAS (GER, 1960)

GLASS KEY, THE (PAR, 1935, based on the book by Dashiell Hammett)
GLASS KEY, THE (PAR, 1942)

GLASS MENAGERIE, THE (WB, 1950, based on the play by Tennessee Williams)
GLASS MENAGERIE, THE (CBS-TV, 1966)
GLASS MENAGERIE, THE (ABC-TV, 1973)

GLASS OF WATER, A see GLAS WASSER, EIN

GLASS SLIPPER, THE see CINDERELLA AND THE FAIRY GODMOTHER

GLASS WEB, THE (UN, 1953, based on a screenplay by Robert Blees and Leonard Lee)
GLASS WEB, THE (NBC-TV, 1956)

GLIMPSE OF THE INNER LIFE OF MARC CHAGALL, A (short) (ABC-TV, 1962, based on the life and work of the noted painter)
CHAGALL (short) (FRA, 1963)
CHAGALL – AN ARTIST'S PRAYER (short) (CBS-TV, 1963)
HOMAGE TO CHAGALL – THE COLORS OF LOVE (CAN-TV, 1977)

GLOCKE I, DIE (GER, 1917, based on the book, "Das Lied von der glocke," by Freidrich von Schiller)
GLOCKE II, DIE (GER, 1921)

GLORIOUS BETSY (WB, 1928, based on the play by Rita Johnson Young)
HEARTS DIVIDED (WB, 1936)

GLORY OF CLEMENTINA, THE (ED, 1915, based on a story by William J. Locke)
GLORY OF CLEMENTINA, THE (RC, 1922)

GLORY OF GOYA, THE see GOYA – THE DISASTERS OF WAR

GLU, LA (FRA, 1913, based on the book by Jean Richepin)
GLU, LA (FRA, 1927)
GLU, LA (FRA, 1937)

GLUCKLICHE KINDHEIT see BRATS

GLUECKSKINDER (GER, 1936, source unknown)
GAIS LURONS, LES (FRA, 1936)

GO AND GET IT (IND, 1920, based on a story by Marion Fairfax. Remake uncredited)
MONSTER AND THE GIRL, THE (PAR, 1941)

GO-BETWEEN, THE (CBS-TV, 1962, based on the book by L.P. Hartley)
GO-BETWEEN, THE (BRI, 1971)

GODCHILD, THE see THREE GODFATHERS

GO--GETTER, THE (PAR, 1923, based on a story by Peter B. Kyne)
GO--GETTER, THE (WB, 1937)

GOD'S CLAY (BRI, 1919, based on the book by Claude and Alice Askew)
GOD'S CLAY (BRI, 1928)

GOD'S COUNTRY see GOD'S COUNTRY AND THE WOMAN

GOD'S COUNTRY AND THE WOMAN (VIT, 1916, based on the book by James Oliver Curwood)
GOD'S COUNTRY AND THE WOMAN (VIT, 1920)
GOD'S COUNTRY AND THE WOMAN (WB, 1936)
GOD'S COUNTRY (SG, 1946)

GODSPELL see PASSION PLAY, THE

GOETHE -- DER WERDEGANG see DICHTUNG UND WAHRHEIT

GOETHE – EIN DOKUMENT DEUTSCHER KULTUR see DICHTUNG UND WAHRHEIT

GOETHE LEBT . . . ! see DICHTUNG UND WAHRHEIT

GOING BYE BYE see DO DETECTIVES THINK?

GOING FOR BROKE see C'EST PAS PARCE QU' ON A REIN A DIRE QU'IL FAUT FERMER SA GUEULE

GOING MY WAY (PAR, 1944, based on a story by Leo McCarey)
GOING MY WAY (series) (ABC-TV, 1962)

GOING PLACES see HOTTENTOT, THE

GOING WILD see AVIATOR, THE

GOLD (GER, 1934, based on a screenplay by Rolf E. Vanloo; the 1953 film used much stock footage from the 1934 German production)
OR, L' (FRA, 1934)
MAGNETIC MONSTER, THE (UA, 1953)

GOLD AND SILVER WORLD see TOPAZE

GOLD BUG, THE see SCARABEE D'OR, LE

GOLD DIGGERS, THE (WB, 1923, based on the play by Avery Hopwood)
GOLD DIGGERS OF BROADWAY (WB, 1929)
GOLD DIGGERS OF 1933 (WB, 1933)
PAINTING THE CLOUDS WITH SUNSHINE (WB, 1951)
GOLD DIGGERS, THE (TV, 1952)

GOLD DIGGERS OF BROADWAY see GOLD DIGGERS, THE

GOLD DIGGERS OF 1933 see GOLD DIGGERS, THE

GOLD HUNTERS see TRAIL OF THE YUKON

GOLDBERGS, THE (series) (CBS-TV, 1949, based on the radio series by Gertrude Berg)
MOLLY (PAR, 1950)
GOLDBERGS, THE (series) (TV, 1954)

GOLDEN BEETLE, THE (ITA, 1911, based on the story,
  "The Gold Bug," by Edgar Allen Poe)
  CALYPSO (BRI, 1956)

GOLDEN BLADE, THE see ARABIAN NIGHTS

GOLDEN CHANCE, THE (PAR, 1915, based on a screen--
  play by Jeannie McPherson)
  FORBIDDEN FRUIT (PAR, 1921)

GOLDEN DREAM (MGM, 1922, based on the book by Zane
  Grey)
  ROCKY MOUNTAIN MYSTERY (PAR, 1935)

GOLDEN GIRL (FOX, 1951, based on the life of the
  entertainer)
  LOTTA CRABTREE (short) (TV, 1954)

GOLDEN HANDS OF KURIGAI see FEDERAL AGENTS
  VS. UNDERWORLD, INC.

GOLDEN PRINCESS, THE see TENNESSEE'S PARDNER

GOLDEN SALAMANDER, THE (BRI, 1950, based on the
  book by Victor Canning)
  GOLDEN SALAMANDER, THE (FRA, 1968)

GOLDEN TOUCH, THE see KING MIDAS

GOLDENE KALB, DAS (GER, 1917, based on a screenplay
  by Franz Herczeg)
  GOLDENE KALB, DAS (GER, 1924)

GOLDIE see GIRL IN EVERY PORT, A

GOLDILOCKS see TEDDY BEARS, THE

GOLDILOCKS AND THE THREE BEARS see TEDDY
  BEARS, THE

GOLEM, DER (GER, 1914, based on a legend)
  GOLEM (DEN, 1916)
  GOLEM AND THE DANCER (GER, 1917)
  GOLEM, DER (GER, 1920)
  GOLEM'S LAST ADVENTURE (AUS, 1921)
  GOLEM, LA (FRA, 1936)
  GOLEM, LE (FRA, 1966)
  IT! (BRI, 1966)
  GOULVE, LA (FRA, 1971)

GOLEM AND THE DANCER, THE see GOLEM, THE

GOLGOTHA (FRA, 1937, based on a Bible story)
  GOLGOTHA (RUM, 1966)

GOMER PYLE USMC see ANDY GRIFFITH SHOW, THE

GONZAGUE (FRA, 1922, based on the book by Pierre
  Veber)
  GONZAGUE OU L'ACCORDEUR (short) (FRA, 1933)

GONZAGUE OU L'ACCORDEUR see GONZAGUE

GOOD AND NAUGHTY (PAR, 1926, based on the play,
  "Naughty Cinderella," by Rene Peter and Henri Falk)
  THIS IS THE NIGHT (PAR, 1932)

GOOD BAD GIRL (COL, 1931, based on a story by Winifred

Van Duzer)
  PASADO ACUSA, EL (SPA, 1931)

GOOD COMPANIONS, THE (BRI, 1933, based on the book
  by J.B. Priestley; also the basis for the Johnny Mercer
  musical comedy)
  GOOD COMPANIONS, THE (BRI, 1957)

GOOD DISSONANCE LIKE A MAN, A see AMERICAN
  TRADITION, THE

GOOD DOCTOR DIBOLIT, THE see ADVENTURES OF
  DR. DOLITTLE

GOOD FAIRY, THE (UN, 1935, based on the play by Ferenc
  Molnar. Also the basis for the musical comedy, "Make a
  Wish," in 1951)
  I'LL BE YOURS (UN, 1947)
  GOOD FAIRY, THE (NBC--TV, 1956)

GOOD LITTLE DEVIL, THE (PAR, 1914, based on a story,
  "Un Bon Petit Diable," by Comtesse de Segur)
  BON PETIT DIABLE, UN (FRA, 1923)

GOOD NEWS (MGM, 1930, based on the musical comedy by
  Brown, DeSylva and Henderson)
  GOOD NEWS (MGM, 1947) (TV title: HIP HIP HAPPY)

GOOD OLD SOAK, THE see OLD SOAK, THE

GOOD SOLDIER SCHWEIK, THE (CZE, 1925, based on the
  book by Jaroslav Hasek)
  SCHWEIK AT THE FRONT (CZE, 1926)
  SCHWEIK IN RUSSIAN CAPTIVITY (CZE, 1927)
  SCHWEIK IN CIVILIAN LIFE (CZE, 1927)
  DOBRY VOJAK SVEJK (CZE, 1931)
  GOOD SOLDIER SCHWEIK, THE (GER, 1931)
  SCHWEIK'S NEW ADVENTURE (BRI, 1942)
  GOOD SOLDIER SCHWEIK, THE (RUS, 1943)
  BRAVE SOLDIER SCHWEIK (short) (CZE, 1954)
  GOOD SOLDIER SCHWEIK, THE (CZE, 1956)
  GOOD SOLDIER SCHWEIK, THE (GER, 1959)
  SCHWEJKS FLEGELJAHRE (GER, 1963)
  ADVENTURES OF GOOD SOLDIER SCHWEIK, THE
  (series) (GER--TV, 1976)

GOOD, THE BAD AND THE UGLY, THE (ITA, 1966, the
  second is a parody of the first)
  HANDSOME, THE UGLY AND THE STUPID, THE (ITA,
  1967)

GOOD TIMES (series) (CBS--TV, 1974, based on a teleplay)
  FOSTERS, THE (series) (BRI--TV, 1975)

GOOD TIMES see also ALL IN THE FAMILY

GOODBYE AGAIN (WB, 1933, based on the play by George
  Haight and Alan Scott)
  HONEYMOON FOR THREE (WB, 1941)

GOODBYE BROADWAY see SHANNONS OF BROADWAY,
  THE

GOODBYE, GULLIVER see GULLIVER'S TRAVELS

GOODBYE, MR. CHIPS (MGM, 1939, based on the book by
  James Hilton)
  GOODBYE, MR. CHIPS (MGM, 1969)

GOOSE HANGS HIGH, THE (PAR, 1929, based on a play
    by Lewis Beach)
  THIS RECKLESS AGE (PAR, 1932)

GOOSE WOMAN, THE (UN, 1925, based on a story by Rex
    Beach)
  PAST OF MARY HOLMES, THE (RKO, 1933)

GOPAL KRISHNA (IN, 1928, based on a myth)
  GOPAL KRISHNA (IN, 1938)

GORILLA, THE (FN, 1927, based on a play by Ralph Spence)
  GORILLA, THE (FN, 1931)
  GORILLA, THE (FOX, 1939)

GOSPEL ACCORDING TO ST. MATTHEW, THE see
    PASSION PLAY, THE

GOSPEL ROAD, THE see PASSION PLAY, THE

GOTAMA THE BUDDAH (IN, 1956, based on the life of the
    religious leader)
  BUDDAH (LOP, 1963)

GOTZ VON BERLICHINGEN (ITA, 1910, based on the book
    by Goethe)
  GOTZ VON BERLICHINGEN (GER, 1922)
  GOTZ VON BERLICHINGEN (GER, 1925)
  GOTZ VON BERLICHINGEN (AUS, 1955)

GOVERNOR'S LADY, THE (PAR, 1915, based on the play
    by Alice Bradley)
  GOVERNOR'S LADY, THE (FOX, 1923)

GOYA see GOYA – THE DISASTERS OF WAR

GOYA -- THE DISASTERS OF WAR (short) (RAD, 1952,
    based on the life and works of painter Francisco Goya)
  GLORY OF GOYA, THE (short) (PIC, 1953)
  GOYA (short) (SPA, n.d.)
  GOYA (short) (IND, 1955)
  GOYA (short) (MHF, 1957)
  GOYA (UNI, 1973)
  GOYA (short) (IND, 1973)

GOYO–KIN (JAP, 1966, based on a screenplay)
  MASTER GUNFIGHTER, THE (IND, 1975)

GRADY see STEPTOE AND SON

GRAFIN MARIZA see COUNTESS MARITZA

GRAFIN VON MONTE CRISTO, DER see COUNT OF
    MONTE CRISTO, THE

GRAND BLUFF, LE (FRA, 1933, source unknown)
  GRAND BLUFF, LE (FRA, 1957)

GRAND DUCHESS AND THE WAITER, THE see LOST –
    A WIFE

GRAND DUKE'S FINANCES, THE (GER, 1923, based on the
    book by Franz Heller)
  GRAND DUKE'S FINANCES, THE (GER, 1934)

GRAND HOTEL (MGM, 1932, based on the book, "Menschen
    im Hotel," by Vicki Baum)
  WEEKEND AT THE WALDORF (MGM, 1945)
  MENSCHEN IM HOTEL (FRA/GER, 1959)

GRAND JEU, LE (FRA, 1934, based on the book by Rene
    Masson)
  GRAND JEU, LE (FRA/ITA, 1954)

GRAND MER, LE see BIG POND, THE

GRANDE BRETECHE, LA (FRA, 1909, based on the story
    by Honore de Balzac)
  SEUL AMOUR, UN (FRA, 1943)
  TRUE AND THE FALSE, THE (SWE/USA, 1955)
  GRANDE BRETECHE, LA (short) (BRI--TV, 1974)

GRANDMOTHER, THE (CZE, 1921, based on the book by
    Bozena Nemcova)
  GRANDMOTHER, THE (CZE, 1931)
  GRANDMOTHER, THE (CZE, 1940)
  GRANDMOTHER, THE (CZE–TV, 1971)

GRANDS, LES (FRA, 1916, based on the book by Pierre
    Veber and Serge Basset)
  GRANDS, LES (FRA, 1924)
  GRANDS, LES (FRA, 1936)

GRANT AND LEE AT APPOMATTOX see SUNSET AT
    APPOMATTOX

GRAPES OF WRATH, THE (FOX, 1940, based on the book
    by John Steinbeck)
  GRAPES OF WRATH, THE (NBC--TV, 1974)

GRASS HARP, THE (NBC--TV, 1952, based on the play by
    Truman Capote)
  GRASS HARP, THE (PBS--TV, 1960)

GRASSHOPPER AND THE ANT (FRA, 1897, based on a
    fairy tale)
  GRASSHOPPER AND THE ANT (RUS, 1912)
  GRASSHOPPER AND THE ANT (FRA, 1954)
  GRASSHOPPER AND THE ANT (BRI, 1954)

GRAUSTARK (ESS, 1915, based on the story by George
    Barr McCutcheon)
  GRAUSTARK (FN, 1925)

GRAY GHOST, THE (serial) (UN, 1917, based on the book,
    "Loot," by Arthur Somers Roche)
  LOOT (UN, 1919)

GRAZIELLA (FRA, 1912, based on a book by Alphonse
    de Lamartine)
  GRAZIELLA (FRA, 1926)

GREAT ADVENTURE, THE (BRI, 1915, based on the book,
    "Buried Alive," by Arnold Bennett and the play, "The
    Great Adventure," also by Bennett. Also the basis for
    the musical comedy, "Darling of the Day," in 1968)
  BURIED ALIVE (RUS, 1916)
  GREAT ADVENTURE, THE (FN, 1921)
  HIS DOUBLE LIFE (PAR, 1933)
  HOLY MATRIMONY (FOX, 1943)

GREAT ADVENTURES OF WILD BILL HICKOCK see
    WILD BILL HICKOCK

GREAT AMERICAN BEAUTY CONTEST, THE see PRIX
    DE BEAUTE

GREAT AMERICAN HOAX, THE see AS YOUNG AS YOU
    FEEL

GREAT BODHISATTVA PASS, THE (JAP, 1935, source unknown)
GREAT BODHISATTVA PASS, THE (JAP, 1957)
GREAT BODHISATTVA PASS II, THE (JAP, 1958)
GREAT BODHISATTVA PASS III, THE (JAP, 1959)

GREAT CATHERINE see ADVENTUROUS LIFE OF CATHERINE I OF RUSSIA

GREAT COMMANDMENT, THE see PASSION PLAY, THE

GREAT DEBATE: LINCOLN VS. DOUGLAS, THE see ABRAHAM LINCOLN

GREAT DESIGN, THE see STALIN ERA, THE

GREAT DIVIDE, THE (LUB, 1915, based on the play by William Vaughan Moody)
GREAT DIVIDE, THE (MGM, 1925)
GREAT DIVIDE, THE (FN, 1929)
WOMAN HUNGRY (FN, 1931)

GREAT EXPECTATIONS (PAR, 1917, based on a book by Charles Dickens)
GREAT EXPECTATIONS (DEN, 1921)
GREAT EXPECTATIONS (UN, 1934)
GREAT EXPECTATIONS (BRI, 1947)
GREAT EXPECTATIONS (NBC–TV, 1953)
GREAT EXPECTATIONS (BRI, 1974)

GREAT GARRICK, THE see DAVID GARRICK

GREAT GATSBY, THE (PAR, 1926, based on the book by F. Scott Fitzgerald)
GREAT GATSBY, THE (PAR, 1949)
GREAT GATSBY, THE (NBC–TV, 1955)
GREAT GATSBY, THE (CBS–TV, 1958)
GREAT GATSBY, THE (PAR, 1974)

GREAT GAY ROAD, THE (BRI, 1920, based on a book by Tom Gallon)
GREAT GAY ROAD, THE (BRI, 1931)

GREAT HEART, THE (short) (MGM, 1938, based on the life and work of Father Damien at the Molokai Leper Colony)
DAMIEN (PBS–TV, 1978)

GREAT HOUDINI, THE see HOUDINI

GREAT IMPERSONATION, THE (PAR, 1921, based on the book by E. Phillips Oppenheim)
GREAT IMPERSONATION, THE (UN, 1935)
GREAT IMPERSONATION, THE (UN, 1942)
GREAT IMPERSONATION, THE (CBS–TV, 1955)
GREAT IMPERSONATION, THE (TV, 1960)

GREAT LIE, THE (WB, 1941, based on the book by Polan Banks)
GREAT LIE, THE (NBC–TV, 1957)

GREAT LOCOMOTIVE CHASE, THE see GENERAL, THE

GREAT McGINTY, THE (PAR, 1940, based on a screenplay by Preston Sturges)
GREAT McGINTY, THE (NBC–TV, 1955)

GREAT MAGOO, THE see SHOOT THE WORKS

GREAT MISSOURI RAID, THE (PAR, 1950, based on a story by Frank Gruber)
WARPATH (PAR, 1951)

GREAT MISSOURI RAID, THE see also JAMES BOYS, THE

GREAT MR. HANDEL, THE (BRI, 1943, based on the life and works of the noted composer)
GEORGE FRIEDRICH HANDEL (short) (IND, n.d.)
HANDEL AND HIS MUSIC (short) (COR, 1957)

GREAT NORTHFIELD MINNESOTA RAID, THE see JAMES BOYS, THE

GREAT O'MALLEY, THE see MAKING OF O'MALLEY, THE

GREAT PIE MYSTERY, THE (short) (COL, 1931, based on a screenplay by John A. Waldron)
SPOOK LOUDER (short) (COL, 1943)

GREAT SINNER, THE see GAMBLER, THE

GREAT WALTZ, THE see WALTZES FROM VIENNA

GREAT WHITE HOPE, THE see FUERZA Y NOBELZA

GREAT WHITE SILENCE, THE see SCOTT ANTARCTIC EXPEDITION

GREAT WHITE WAY, THE (MGM, 1924, based on the story, "Cain and Mabel," by H.C. Witwer)
CAIN AND MABEL (WB, 1936)

GREAT ZIEGFELD, THE (MGM, 1936, based on the life of the noted showman)
ZIEGFELD: A MAN AND HIS WOMAN (NBC–TV, 1978)

GREATER THAN A CROWN see LADY FROM LONG--ACRE, THE

GREATER THAN MARRIAGE see FOOTLIGHTS OF FATE

GREATEST, THE see FLOAT LIKE A BUTTERFLY, STING LIKE A BEE

GREATEST GIFT, THE (NBC--TV, 1975, based on a teleplay)
FAMILY HOLVAK, THE (series) (NBC–TV, 1975)

GREATEST SHOW ON EARTH, THE (PAR, 1952, based on a story and screenplay by various authors)
GREATEST SHOW ON EARTH, THE (series) (ABC–TV, 1963)

GREATEST STORY EVER TOLD, THE see PASSION PLAY, THE

GRECO, EL (short) (PIC, n.d., based on the life and works of the noted painter)
GRECO, EL (short) (IND, n.d.)
GRECO, EL (short) (IND, 1970)
EL GRECO TREASURES (short) (MAC, n.d.)

GREED see LIFE'S WHIRLPOOL

GREEKS HAD A WORD FOR THEM, THE see GIRLS ABOUT TOWN

GREEN ARCHER, THE (serial) (PAT, 1925, based on
    stories by Edgar Wallace)
  GREEN ARCHER, THE (serial) (COL, 1940)
  GREEN ARCHER, THE (GER, 1961)

GREEN CARNATION, THE see OSCAR WILDE

GREEN FRUIT, THE see FRUCHTCHEN

GREEN GODDESS, THE (MGM, 1923, based on the play by
    William Archer)
  GREEN GODDESS, THE (WB, 1929)
  ADVENTURES IN IRAQ (WB, 1943)

GREEN HAT, THE see WOMAN OF AFFAIRS, A

GREEN PASTURES, THE (WB, 1936, based on the play by
    Marc Connelly)
  GREEN PASTURES, THE (TV, 1951)
  GREEN PASTURES, THE (NBC–TV, 1957)
  GREEN PASTURES, THE (NBC–TV, 1959)

GREENE MURDER CASE, THE (PAR, 1929, based on the
    book by S.S. Van Dine)
  NIGHT OF MYSTERY (PAR, 1937)

GREIFER, DER (GER, 1930, source unknown)
  GREIFER, DER (GER, 1958)

GRETEL AND LIESEL see KOHLHEISEL'S DAUGHTERS

GREYFRIAR'S BOBBY see CHALLENGE TO LASSIE

GRIBOUILLE see HEART OF PARIS

GRIGORI RASPUTIN AND THE GREAT RUSSIAN
    REVOLUTION see RASPUTIN, THE BLACK MONK

GRILLON DU FOYER, LE see CRICKET ON THE
    HEARTH

GRIMM'S FAIRY TALES see HANSEL AND GRETEL

GRINSENDE GESICHT, DAS see HOMME QUI RIT, L'

GRIP OF IRON, THE (BRI, 1913, based on the book, "The
    Stranglers of Paris," by Belot and the play by Arthur
    Shirley)
  GRIP OF IRON, THE (BRI, 1920)

GRISSOM GANG, THE see NO ORCHIDS FOR MISS
    BLANDISH

GROSSE CHANCE, DIE (GER, 1934, source unknown)
  GROSSE CHANCE, DIE (GER, 1957)

GROSSE FAHRT, DIE see BIG TRAIL, THE

GROSSE FREIHEIT see PALOMA, LA

GROSSE LIEBE, DIE (GER, 1932, source unknown)
  GROSSE LIEBE, DIE (GER, 1942)

GROSSE LIEBESSPIEL, DAS see RIEGEN, DER

GROSSE PREIS, DER (GER, 1922, source unknown)
  GROSSE PREIS, DER (GER, 1944)

GROSSE UNBEKANNTE, DIE (GER, 1924, source unknown
  GROSSE UNBEKANNTE, DIE (GER, 1927)

GROSSE UND DIE KLEINE WELT, DIE (GER, 1927,
    based on the book by Hugo M. Kritz)
  GROSSE UND DIE KLEINE WELT, DIE (GER, 1936)

GROSSTADTNACHT (GER, 1933, based on the book, "Der
    Zobelpelz," by Wilhelm Lichtenberg)
  GROSSTADTNACHT (GER, 1950)

GROWING UP see ABRAHAM LINCOLN

GRUMPY (PAR, 1923, based on the play by Horace Hodges
    and Thomas Wigney Percyval)
  GRUMPY (PAR, 1930)
  CASCARRABIAS (SPA, 1930)

GRUN IST DIE HEIDE (GER, 1932, based on the book by
    Harmann Lons)
  GRUN IST DIE HEIDE (GER, 1951)

G'SCHICHTEN AUS DEM WIENERWALD (GER, 1928,
    based on the play by Odeon Horvath)
  G'SCHICHTEN AUS DEM WIENERWALD (GER, 1934)

GUARDSMAN, THE (GER, 1927, based on the play by
    Ferenc Molnar)
  GUARDSMAN, THE (MGM, 1931)
  CHOCOLATE SOLDIER, THE (MGM, 1941)
  GUARDSMAN, THE (CBS--TV, 1955)

GUERASSIM AND MOUMOU (RUS, 1919, based on the book,
    "Moumou," by Ivan Turgenev)
  MOUMOU (RUS, 1959)

GUERNICA -- PABLO PICASSO see PICASSO: LE
    PEINTRE ET SON MODELE

GUERRE DES VALSES, LA see WALTZKREIG

GUESS WHO'S COMING TO DINNER (COL, 1967, based on
    a screenplay by William Rose)
  GUESS WHO'S COMING TO DINNER (ABC–TV, 1975)

GUEST, THE see WHERE LOVE IS, GOD IS

GUEST IN THE HOUSE (UA, 1944, based on the play by
    Hagar Wilde and Dale Eunson)
  GUEST IN THE HOUSE (TV, 1953)
  GUEST IN THE HOUSE (CBS–TV, 1955)

GUEST OF HONOR see FOURTEENTH MAN, THE

GUEUX AU PARADIS, LES (FRA, 1945, based on the book
    by Gaston Martens)
  SCHELME IM PARADIES, DIE (GER–TV, 1965)

GILLAUME TELL ET LE CLOWN (FRA, 1898, based on the
    story by Friedrich Schiller, the opera by Giocchino
    Rossini; also the basis for the German musical, "Tell," in
    1977)
  WILLIAM TELL (BRI, 1900)
  GUILLAUME TELL (FRA, 1903)
  WILLIAM TELL (DEN, 1908)
  WILHELM TELL (GER, 1913)
  WILLIAM TELL (PAR, 1914)
  WILHELM TELL (GER, 1915)
  WILHELM TELL (GER, 1923)
  WILLIAM TELL (IND, 1924)
  WILHELM TELL (GER, 1925)
  WILHELM TELL (GER, 1934)

WILLIAM TELL (short) (UN, 1934)
WILLIAM TELL (IND, 1939)
JASPER TELL (short) (PAR, 1945)
WILLIAM TELL (ITA, 1948)
WILHELM TELL (AUS, 1956)
ADVENTURES OF WILLIAM TELL (series) (TV, 1957)
BERGE IN FLAMMEN (SWI, 1960)
MR. MAGOO'S FAVORITE HEROES (UPA, 1964)

GUILTY AS HELL (PAR, 1932, based on a play, "Riddle
     Me This," by Daniel N. Rubin)
  NIGHT CLUB SCANDAL (PAR, 1937)

GUILTY OF TREASON (EL, 1949, based on historical
     incidents and characters)
  CARDINAL MINDSZENTY (CBS–TV, 1954)

GUL SANOVAR (IN, 1928, based on a fairy tale)
  GUL SANOVAR (IN, 1934)

GULBAKAVALI (IN, 1947, based on a myth)
  GULBAKAVALI (IN, 1955)

GULLIVER IN LILLIPUT see GULLIVER'S TRAVELS

GULLIVER IN THE LAND OF GIANTS see GULLIVER'S
     TRAVELS

GULLIVER'S TRAVELS (FRA, 1902, based on the book by
     Jonathan Swift)
  GULLIVER'S TRAVELS (LUB, 1903)
  VOYAGE OF GULLIVER TO LILLIPUT AND THE
     HOUSE OF GIANTS (FRA, 1903)
  GULLIVER IN THE LAND OF GIANTS (SPA, 1905)
  GULLIVER IN LILLIPUT (FRA, 1923)
  GULLIVER'S TRAVELS (IND, 1933)
  GULLIVER'S TRAVELS (short) (DIS, 1934)
  NEW GULLIVER, THE (RUS, 1935)
  GULLIVER'S TRAVELS (PAR, 1939)
  LAST VOYAGE OF GULLIVER (POL, 1960)
  THREE WORLDS OF GULLIVER, THE (COL, 1960)
  GULLIVER'S TRAVELS BEYOND THE MOON (JAP,
     1965)
  INCREDIBLE WORLD OF MARK O'GULLIVER, THE
     (short) (IND, c1967)
  ADVENTURES OF GULLIVER, THE (series) (ABC–TV,
     1969)
  CASE FOR A YOUNG HANGMAN, A (CZE, 1970)
  CIAO, GULLIVER (ITA, 1970)
  GULLIVER'S TRAVELS (BEL/BRI, 1977)
  GULLIVER'S TRAVELS (SUN, 1978)

GULLIVER'S TRAVELS BEYOND THE MOON see
     GULLIVER'S TRAVELS

GUN LAW (FBO, 1929, based on a story by Oliver Drake)
  GUN LAW (RKO, 1938)

GUN RUNNERS, THE see TO HAVE AND HAVE NOT

GUNFIGHT AT ABILENE see SHOWDOWN AT ABILENE

GUNFIGHT AT COMANCHE CREEK see LAST OF THE
     BADMEN

GUNFIGHT AT THE O.K. CORRAL (CBS–TV, 1953, based
     on historical incidents and characters)
  DUEL AT THE O.K. CORRAL (NBC–TV, 1954)
  GUNFIGHT AT THE O.K. CORRAL (PAR, 1957)
  SHOWDOWN AT THE O.K. CORRAL (CBS–TV, 1972)

GUNFIGHT AT THE O.K. CORRAL (PAR, 1957, based on
     a book, "The Killer," by George Scullin)
  HOUR OF THE GUN (UA, 1967)

GUNFIGHTER, THE (FOX, 1950, based on a story by
     William Bowers and Andre de Toth)
  END OF A GUN (CBS–TV, 1957)

GUNGA DIN (RKO, 1939, based on the poem by Rudyard
     Kipling)
  SERGEANTS 3 (UA, 1962)
  MR. MAGOO'S FAVORITE HEROES (UPA, 1964)
  LAST BLAST, THE (IND, 1964)

GUNN see PETER GUNN

GUY FAWKES (BRI, 1907, based on historical incidents and
     characters)
  GUY FAWKES (BRI, 1923)

GUYS AND DOLLS see VERY HONORABLE GUY, A

GYPSIES, THE (RUS, 1910, based on the story by Alexander
     Pushkin and the opera by Serge Rachmaninoff)
  GYPSY, THE (ITA, 1913)
  ALEKO (RUS, 1954)

GYPSY, THE see GYPSIES, THE

GYPSY BARON, THE see ZIGEUNERBARON, DER

GYPSY BLOOD see CARMEN

GYPSY COLT see LASSIE COME HOME

GYPSY MELODY see JUANITA

H.M.S. PINAFORE (NBC–TV, 1959, based on operetta by
    Gilbert and Sullivan)
  H.M.S. PINAFORE (NBC–TV, 1960)
  H.M.S. PINAFORE (CBS–TV, 1973)

H.S.T.: DAYS OF DECISION see FROM PRECINCT TO
    PRESIDENT

HADJI MURAD see WHITE DEVIL

HAITANG see FLAME OF LOVE, THE

HAKUCHI see IDIOT, THE

HALF A SINNER see ALIAS THE DEACON

HALF A SIXPENCE see KIPPS

HALF AN ANGEL see HALF ANGEL

HALF AN HOUR see DOCTOR'S SECRET

HALF ANGEL (FOX, 1936, based on a story by F. Tennyson
    Jesse)
  HALF AN ANGEL (FOX, 1951)

HALF HOLIDAY see SATURDAY AFTERNOON

HALF WAY TO HEAVEN (PAR, 1929, based on the book,
    "Here Comes the Bandwagon," by H.L. Gates)
  SOMBRAS DEL CIRCO (SPA, 1929)
  MI–CHEMIN DU CIEL, A (FRA, 1930)

HALF WIT'S HOLIDAY (short) (COL, 1947, based on a
    screenplay by Zion Meyers)
  PIES AND GUYS (short) (COL, 1958)

HALLOWE'EN WITH THE NEW ADDAMS FAMILY see
    ADDAMS FAMILY, THE

HALLUCINATION see LORD ARTHUR SAVILLE'S
    CRIME

HALLUCINATIONS OF BARON MUNCHAUSEN see BARON
    DE CRAC

HALSINGAR (SWE, 1923, source unknown)
  HALSINGAR (SWE, 1933)

HALTA LENA OCH VINDOGDE PER (SWE, 1924, source
    unknown)
  HALTA LENA OCH VINDOGDE PER (SWE, 1933)
  LATA LENA OCH GLAOGDA PER (SWE, 1947)

HAMELIN see PIED PIPER OF HAMELIN, THE

HAMILE see HAMLET

HAMILTON–BURR DUEL see CHRONICLES OF AMER–
    ICA: ALEXANDER HAMILTON

HAMLET (FRA, 1900, based on the play by William Shake–
    speare)
  HAMLET (BRI, 1904)
  HAMLET (BRI, 1905)
  AMLETO (ITA, 1907)
  HAMLET, PRINCE OF DENMARK (FRA, 1907)
  AMLETO (ITA, 1908)
  HAMLET (FRA, 1909)

  AMLETO (ITA, 1910)
  HAMLET (DEN, 1910)
  HAMLET (BRI, 1910)
  HAMLET (FRA, 1910)
  HAMLET (NOR, 1911)
  HAMLET (FRA, 1911)
  HAMLET (BRI, 1912)
  HAMLET (BRI, 1913)
  AMLETO (ITA, 1914)
  HAMLET (IND, 1915)
  HAMLET (BRI, 1916)
  AMLETO (ITA, 1917)
  HAMLET (GER, 1919)
  HAMLET (BRI, 1920)
  HAMLET (GER, 1922)
  DAY DREAMS (short) (FN, 1923)
  BLOOD FOR BLOOD (IN, 1927)
  KHUN–E–NAHAK (IN, 1928)
  BLOOD FOR LOVE (IN, 1935)
  STRANGE ILLUSION (PRC, 1945)
  HAMLET (BRI, 1948)
  I, HAMLET (ITA, 1952)
  HAMLET (NBC–TV, 1953)
  KHUN––E–NAHAK (IN, 1953)
  PRINCE OF PLAYERS (sequence) (FOX, 1955)
  REST IS SILENCE, THE (GER, 1959)
  HAMLET (CBS–TV, 1959)
  BAD SLEEP WELL, THE (JAP, 1960)
  HAMLET (GER, 1960)
  OPHELIA (FRA, 1962)
  HAMLET (RUS, 1964)
  HAMLET (ELE, 1964)
  HAMLET IN EISINORE (BRI–TV, 1964)
  HAMILE (GHA, 1965)
  HAMLET (series) (BRI–TV, c1965)
  HE WANTED TO BECOME KING (GRE, 1967)
  THAT DIRTY STORY OF THE WEST (ITA, 1968)
  HAMLET (BRI, 1969)
  HAMLET (NBC–TV, 1970)
  GAME OF LIFE AND DEATH, THE (BRA, 1972)
  JOHNNY HAMLET (ITA, 1972)
  ONE HAMLET LESS (ITA, 1973)
  HAMLET (BRI–TV, 1973)
  VILLAGE PERFORMANCE OF HAMLET, A (YUG, 1973)
  GAY HAMLET, A (BRI, 1976)
  HAMLET (BRI, 1976)
  FEMALE HAMLET (TUR, 1977)
  HAMLET (BRI, 1978)

HAMLET IN ELSINORE see HAMLET

HAMLET, PRINCE OF DENMARK see HAMLET

HAMPELMANN, DER (GER, 1930, source unlisted)
  HAMPELMANN, DER (GER, 1938)

HANDEL AND HIS MUSIC see GREAT MR. HANDEL, THE

HANDS OF A STRANGLER see HANDS OF ORLAC, THE

HANDS OF ORLAC, THE (GER, 1924, based on the book by
    Maurice Renard)
  HANDS OF ORLAC, THE (IND, 1928)
  MAD LOVE (MGM, 1935)
  HANDS OF A STRANGLER (BRI/FRA, 1960)

HANDS OF THE RIPPER see LODGER, THE

HANDSOME, THE UGLY, AND THE STUPID, THE see

GOOD, THE BAD AND THE UGLY, THE

HANDY ANDY (FOX, 1934, based on the play, "Merry
    Andrew," by Lewis Beach)
  YOUNG AS YOU FEEL (FOX, 1940)

HANGED MAN, THE see RIDE THE PINK HORSE

HANGMEN ALSO DIE see CROSS OF LORAINE, THE

HANNELES HIMMELFAHRT (GER, 1922, based on a
    novel by Gerhart Hauptmann)
  HANNELES HIMMELFAHRT (GER, 1934)

HANNON CAMBIATO FACCIA see NOSFERATU

HANS BRINKER see HANS BRINKER OR THE SILVER
    SKATES

HANS BRINKER OR THE SILVER SKATES (NBC–TV, 1958,
    based on the book by Mary Mapes Dodge)
  HANS BRINKER OR THE SILVER SKATES (GER,
    1962)
  HANS BRINKER (NBC–TV, 1969)
  HANS BRINKER (TV, 1973)

HANS CHRISTIAN ANDERSEN (RKO, 1962, based on the
    life and works of Hans Christian Andersen)
  HANS CHRISTIAN ANDERSEN (BRI, 1950)
  HANS CHRISTIAN ANDERSEN (HOF, 1952)
  HANS CHRISTIAN ANDERSEN (series) (TV, 1955)
  THUMBELINA (RUS, 1964)
  FABLES FROM HANS CHRISTIAN ANDERSEN (JAP,
    1968)
  WORLD OF HANS CHRISTIAN ANDERSEN, THE (UA,
    1971)

HANS CHRISTIAN ANDERSEN see also EMPEROR'S NEW
    CLOTHES, THE, EMPEROR'S NIGHTINGALE, THE,
    and UGLY DUCKLING, THE

HANS IM GLUCK (GER, 1936, based on the book by Henrik
    Pontoppidan)
  HANS IM GLUCK (GER, 1949)

HANSEL AND GRETEL (ED, 1909, based on the fairy tale
    by the Brothers Grimm)
  BABES IN THE WOODS (FRA, 1913)
  BABES IN THE WOODS (FOX, 1917)
  HANSEL AND GRETEL (UN, 1923)
  STORY OF HANSEL AND GRETEL (GER, c1923)
  HANSEL AND GRETEL (AUS, 1924)
  BABES IN THE WOODS (short) (FBO, 1925)
  BABES IN THE WOODS (short) (DIS, 1933)
  HANSEL AND GRETEL (TV, 1943)
  GINGERBREAD COTTAGE (short) (CZE, 1951)
  STORY OF HANSEL AND GRETEL (short) (BFA, 1951)
  HANSEL AND GRETEL (short) (FOX, 1952)
  HANSEL AND GRETEL (CHI, 1954)
  HANSEL AND GRETEL (RKO, 1954)
  HANSEL AND GRETEL (short) (GER, 1955)
  GRIMM'S FAIRY TALES (GER, 1955)
  HANSEL AND GRETEL (NBC–TV, 1958)
  HANSEL AND GRETEL GET LOST IN THE WOODS
    (GER, 1970)
  HANSEL AND GRETEL (NET–TV, 1971)
  WHO SLEW AUNTIE ROO? (BRI, 1971)

HANSEL AND GRETEL GET LOST IN THE WOODS see
    HANSEL AND GRETEL

HANUMAN JANUMAN (IN, 1925, based on a myth)
  HANUMAN JANUMAN (IN, 1953)

HAPPILY EVER AFTER see BLONDER TRAUM, EIN

HAPPY DAYS (FOX, 1930, based on a screenplay by Sidney
    Lanfield and Edwin Burke)
  IN TIMES LIKE THESE (CBS–TV, 1956)

HAPPY DAYS see LOVE AND THE HAPPY DAYS

HAPPY ENDING (BRI, 1925, based on the play by Ian Hay)
  HAPPY ENDING (BRI, 1931)

HAPPY EVER AFTER (BRI, 1932, source unlisted)
  HAPPY EVER AFTER (GER, 1932)

HAPPY--GO--LUCKY seee TILLY OF BLOOMSBURY

HAPPY HOOKER, THE see LIFE AND TIMES OF XAVIERA
    HOLLANDER, THE

HAPPY IS THE BRIDE see QUIET WEDDING

HARA KIRI see MADAME BUTTERFLY

HARBOR IN THE FOG see ANNA CHRISTIE

HARBOUR LIGHTS (BRI, 1914, based on the play by George
    Sims and Henry Pruitt)
  HARBOUR LIGHTS (BRI, 1923)

HARD HOMBRE (ALL, 1932, based on a screenplay by E.
    Morton Hough)
  TRAILIN' TROUBLE (GN, 1937)

HARD LUCK DAME see MALTESE FALCON, THE

HARDI, PARDAILLAN see CHEVALIER DE PARDAILLAN,
    LE

HAREM DREAM see KISMET

HARISCHANDRA (IN, 1912, source unknown)
  HARISCHANDRA (IN, 1935)
  HARISCHANDRA (IN, 1951)
  HARISCHANDRA (IN, 1959)

HARLOW (ELE, 1965, based on the life of actress Jean
    Harlow)
  HARLOW (PAR, 1965)

HARMONY AT HOME see FAMILY UPSTAIRS, THE

HAROLD TEEN (FN, 1928, based on the comic strip by Carl
    Ed)
  HAROLD TEEN (WB, 1934)

HARRIET CRAIG see CRAIG'S WIFE

HARRY TRUMAN see FROM PRECINCT TO PRESIDENT

HARVETSTER, THE (FBO, 1927, based on the book by Gene
    Stratton Potter)
  HARVESTER, THE (REP, 1936)

HARVEY (UN, 1950, based on the play by Mary Chase)
  HARVEY (CBS–TV, 1958)
  HARVEY (CBS–TV, 1960)
  HARVEY (NBC–TV, 1972)

HAS ANYBODY SEEN MY GAL? (UN, 1952, based on a
  story by Eleanor H. Porter)
  HAS ANYBODY SEEN MY GAL? (NBC–TV, 1956)

HASTY HEART, THE (WB, 1949, based on the play by John
  Patrick)
  HASTY HEART, THE (CBS–TV, 1958)

HAT, COAT AND GLOVE (RKO, 1934, based on a story by
  William Speyer)
  NIGHT OF ADVENTURE, A (RKO, 1944)

HATFIELDS AND THE McCOYS, THE see ROSEANNA
  McCOY

HATFUL OF RAIN, A (FOX, 1957, based on the play by
  Michael V. Gazzo)
  HATFUL OF RAIN, A (ABC–TV, 1968)

HATS OFF see HIS MUSICAL CAREER

HAUNTED GOLD see PHANTOM CITY

HAUNTED SHIP, THE see JACK LONDON'S TALES OF
  THE FISH PATROL

HAUNTING SHADOWS see HOUSE OF A THOUSAND
  CANDLES, THE

HAUNTS OF THE VERY RICH see OUTWARD BOUND

HAUPTMANN VON KOPENIK, DER see CAPTAIN FROM
  KOPENIK, THE

HAUS DER LUGE see WILD DUCK, THE

HAUS IN MONTEVIDEO, DAS see HOUSE IN MONTEVI-
  DEO, THE

HAVSGAMAR see PA LIVETS ODEVAGAR

HAWK OF THE WILDERNESS (serial) (REP, 1938, based
  on the book by William L. Chester; the remake is an abridge-
  ment of the original serial)
  LOST ISLAND OF KIOGA (REP, 1966)

HAWKEYE see LAST OF THE MOHICANS, THE

HAY QUE CASAR AL PRINCIPE see PAID TO LOVE

HE COMES TO SMILING see ARIZONA

HE COULDN'T TAKE IT (MON, 1934, based on a story by
  Dore Schary)
  HERE COMES KELLY (MON, 1943)

HE HIRED THE BOSS see TEN DOLLAR RAISE

HE IS RISEN see PASSION PLAY, THE

HE WANTED TO BECOME KING see HAMLET

HE WHO GETS SLAPPED (RUS, 1916, based on the play
  by Leonid Andreyev)

HE WHO GETS SLAPPED (MGM, 1924)
HE WHO GETS SLAPPED (PBS–TV, 1961)

HEAD OF A TYRANT see JUDITH OF HOLOFERNES

HEAD OF JANUS, THE see DR. JEKYLL AND MR. HYDE

HEAD OF PANCHO VILLA, THE see LIFE OF VILLA

HEADLESS HORSEMAN, THE see LEGEND OF SLEEPY
  HOLLOW, THE

HEALTHY, WEALTHY AND DUMB (short) (COL, 1938,
  based on a screenplay by Searle Kramer)
  MISSED FORTUNE, A (short) (COL, 1951)

HEART IS A FORGOTTEN HOTEL, THE (TV, 1955, based
  on the teleplay by Arnold Schulman; also the basis for
  the musical comedy, "Golden Rainbow")
  HOLE IN THE HEAD (UA, 1959)

HEART OF A CHILD (BRI, 1915, based on the book by Frank
  Danby)
  HEART OF A CHILD (MGM, 1920)
  HEART OF A CHILD (BRI, 1958)

HEART OF A HERO see DEATH OF NATHAN HALE, THE

HEART OF DARKNESS see MISSIONS

HEART OF MARYLAND (VIT, 1921, based on a play by David
  Belasco)
  HEART OF MARYLAND (MGM, 1927)

HEART OF PARIS (FRA, 1939, based on a screenplay by
  Marcel Archard)
  LADY IN QUESTION, THE (COL, 1940)

HEART O' THE HILLS (ED, 1916, based on the story by
  John Fox Jr.)
  HEART O' THE HILLS (FN, 1919)
  HILLBILLY, THE (ALL, 1924)

HEART OF THE THIEF, THE see PATHS TO PARADISE

HEART OF THE WILD, THE (IND, 1918, based on the book,
  "Pierre of the Plains," by Edgar Selwyn)
  OVER THE BORDER (PAR, 1922)
  THREE ROGUES (FOX, 1931)
  PIERRE OF THE PLAINS (MGM, 1942)
  OVER THE BORDER (MON, 1950)

HEART SONG see ICH UND DIE KAISERIN

HEARTBEAT see AVENGING CONSCIENCE, THE and
  BATTICUORE

HEARTS AFIRE (WOR, 1915, based on the book, "Hearts in
  Exile," by John Oxellam)
  HEARTS IN EXILE (WB, 1929)

HEARTS AND MASKS (SEL, 1914, based on the book by
  Harold McGrath)
  HEARTS AND MASKS (FBO, 1920)

HEARTS DIVIDED see GLORIOUS BETSY

HEARTS IN EXILE see HEARTS AFIRE

HEARTS OF THE WEST   (MGM, 1975, based on a screenplay
    by Rob Thompson)
  RIDING HIGH   (pilot)   (NBC--TV, 1977)

HEAT LIGHTNING   (WB, 1934, based on the play by Leon
    Abrams and George Abbott)
  HIGHWAY WEST   (WB, 1941)

HEAVEN ON EARTH   see   EXQUISITE SINNER, THE

HEAVENLY DAZE   (short)   (COL, 1949, based on a screen-
    play)
  BEDLAM IN PARADISE   (short)   (COL, 1955)

HEDDA   see   HEDDA GABLER

HEDDA GABLER   (IND, 1917, based on the play by Henrick
    Ibsen)
  HEDDA GABLER   (ITA, 1919)
  HEDDA GABLER   (ITA, 1923)
  HEDDA GABLER   (GER, 1924)
  HEDDA GABLER   (NBC--TV, 1950)
  HEDDA GABLER   (ABC--TV, 1954)
  HEDDA GABLER   (CAN--TV, 1955)
  HEDDA GABLER   (GER--TV, 1960)
  HEDDA GABLER   (CBS--TV, 1963)
  HEDDA   (BRI, 1975)

HEFFERNAN FAMILY, THE   see   CHICKEN EVERY
    SUNDAY

HEIDESCHULMEISTER UWE KARSTEN   (GER, 1933,
    source unlisted)
  HEIDESCHULMEISTER UWE KARSTEN   (GER, 1954)

HEIDI   (FOX, 1937, based on the book by Johanna Spyri)
  HEIDI   (SWI, 1952)
  HEIDI   (NBC--TV, 1955)
  HEIDI AND PETER   (SWI, 1955)
  GIFT FOR HEIDI, A   (RKO, 1959)
  HEIDI   (AUS, 1965)
  HEIDI   (NBC--TV, 1968)
  HEIDI   (WB, 1968)
  HEIDI   (series)   (GER--TV, 1976)
  HEIDI   (BRI--TV, 1976)
  HEIDI   (series)   (SWI--TV, 1978)
  NEW ADVENTURES OF HEIDI, THE   (NBC--TV, 1978)

HEIDI AND PETER   see   HEIDI

HEILIGE LUGE, DIE   (GER, 1927, source unlisted)
  HEILIGE LUGE, DIE   (GER, 1955)

HEILIGE UND IHR NARR, DIE   (GER, 1928, based on a
    story by Agnes Gunther)
  HEILIGE UND IHR NARR, DIE   (GER, 1935)
  HEILIGE UND IHR NARR, DIE   (AUS, 1957)

HEIMAT   (ITA, 1910, based on the book by Hermann Suder-
    mann)
  MAGDA   (SEZ, 1917)
  HEIMAT   (ITA, 1919)
  HEIMAT   (GER, 1938)

HEIMATLAND   see   KRAMBAMBULI

HEIMKEHR (HOMECOMING)   (GER, 1928, based on the
    book, "Karl und Anna," by Leonard Frank)
  HEIMKEHR (HOMECOMING)   (GER, 1941)

DESIRE ME   (MGM, 1947)

HEIN OCH SMALANNINGEN   (SWE, 1927, source unlisted)
  HEIN OCH SMALANNINGEN   (SWE, 1949)

HEINZELMANNCHEN, DIE   (short)   (GER, 1939, based on
    a story by August Kopisch)
  HEINZELMANNCHEN, DIE   (GER, 1956)

HEIR TO THE HOORAH, THE   (PAR, 1916, based on the play
    by Paul Armstrong)
  EVER SINCE EVE   (FOX, 1934)

HEIRESS, THE   (PAR, 1949, based on the book, "Washington
    Square," by Henry James and the play by Ruth and Augustus
    Goetz)
  HEIRESS, THE   (NBC--TV, 1954)
  HEIRESS, THE   (CBS--TV, 1961)

HELD MEINER TRAUME, DER   see   JOURS HEUREUX, LES

HELDEN   see   CHOCOLATE SOLDIER, THE

HELDINNEN   see   FRAULEIN VON BARNHELM, DAS

HELEN KELLER   see   DELIVERANCE

HELEN KELLER IN HER OWN STORY   see   DELIVERANCE

HELEN KELLER: THE WORLD I SEE   see   DELIVERANCE

HELEN MORGAN STORY, THE   (WB, 1957, based on the life
    of the noted popular singer)
  HELEN MORGAN STORY, THE   (CBS--TV, 1957)

HELEN OF TROY   see   CHUTE DE TROIE, LA

HELENA, DER UNTERGANG TROJAS   see   CHUTE DE
    TROIE, LA

HELENE WILLFUER   (GER, 1929, based on a book by Vicki
    Baum)
  HELENE   (FRA, 1936)

HELIOTROPE   (PAR, 1920, based on the book, "A Whiff of
    Heliotrope," by Richard Washburn Child)
  FORGOTTEN FACES   (PAR, 1928)
  FORGOTTEN FACES   (PAR, 1936)
  GENTLEMAN AFTER DARK, A   (UA, 1942)

HELLEVISION   see   DANTE'S INFERNO

HELLGATE   see   PRISONER OF SHARK ISLAND

HELLO, DOLLY!   see   MATCHMAKER, THE

HELLO, FRISCO, HELLO   see   KING OF BURLESQUE

HELLO, LOLA   see   SEVENTEEN

HELLO, SWEETHEART   see   BUTTER AND EGG MAN, THE

HELL'S HEROES   see   THREE GODFATHERS

HELL'S KITCHEN   see   MAYOR OF HELL

HELLZAPOPPIN'   (UN, 1941, based on a Broadway revue)
  HELLZAPOPPIN'   (ABC--TV, 1972)

HEMINGWAY'S ADVENTURES OF A YOUNG MAN (FOX,
  1962, based on the life and works of author Ernest
  Hemingway)
  HEMINGWAY (NBC–TV, 1965)
  HEMINGWAY'S SPAIN (ABC–TV, 1968)

HEMINGWAY'S ADVENTURES OF A YOUNG MAN see
  also WORLD OF NICK ADAMS, THE

HEMSOBORNA (SWE, 1919, source unlisted)
  HEMSOBORNA (SWE, 1944)
  HEMOSBORNA (SWE, 1955)

HENNES LILLA MAJESTAT (SWE, 1925, source unlisted)
  HENNES LILLA MAJESTAT (SWE, 1939)

HENRI DE TOULOUSE–LAUTREC see MOULIN ROUGE

HENRI MATISSE (short) (IND, 1946, based on the life and
  works of the noted artist)
  MATISSE – A SORT OF PARADISE (short) (FNC, 1969)
  MATISSE AND THE FAUVES (short) (IFB, 1970)
  HENRI MATISSE (short) (IFB, 1971)
  HENRI MATISSE CENTENNIAL AT THE GRAND PALAIS
  (short) (FRA, 1973)

HENRY FORD see AMERICAN ROAD, THE

HENRY MOORE (short) (RAD, 1948, based on the work
  of the noted artist)
  HENRY MOORE (short) (BRI, 1952)
  HENRY MOORE (short) (MHF, n.d.)
  SCULPTOR'S LANDSCAPE, A (BRI, n.d.)
  FACE TO FACE (short) (BRI–TV, 1967)
  HENRY MOORE: MAN OF FORM (short) (CBS–TV,
  1966)
  HENRY MOORE THE SCULPTOR (short) (EBE, 1969)
  HENRY MOORE, LONDON 1940–1942 (short) (BRI,
  1970)
  HENRY MOORE AT THE TATE GALLERY (short)
  (FNC, 1971)

HENRI IV (GER/ITA, 1926, based on the play Luigi Piran–
  dello)
  HENRI IV (ITA, 1943)

HENRY V (BRI, 1944, based on the play by William Shake–
  speare)
  LIFE OF HENRY V, THE (BRI–TV, 1957)
  AGE OF KINGS, AN (short) (BRI–TV, 1960)
  HENRY V (CBS–TV, 1966)

HENRY VI see AGE OF KINGS, AN

HENRY VIII (BRI, 1911, based on the life and the English
  monarch and the play by Wiliam Shakespeare)
  CARDINAL WOLSEY (VIT, 1912)
  ANNA BOLEYN (GER, 1920)
  PRIVATE LIFE OF HENRY VIII, THE (UA, 1934)
  WIVES OF HENRY VIII, THE (BRI–TV, 1971)

HER CARDBOARD LOVER see CARDBOARD LOVER

HER CONDONED SIN see JUDITH AND HOLOFERNES

HER FINAL RECKONING see PRINCE ZILAH, LE

HER HUSBAND LIES see STREET OF CHANCE

HER LITTLE MAJESTY see HENNES LILLA MAJESTAT

HER MAN (PAT, 1930, based on the song, "Frankie and
  Johnny"
  FRANKIE AND JOHNNY (RKO, 1935)
  CAFE HOSTESS (COL, 1940)
  ROOTY TOOT TOOT (short) (UPA, 1952)
  FRANKIE AND JOHNNY (UA, 1966)

HER MARRIAGE LINES (BRI, 1916, baeed on a story by
  Edith Banks)
  HER MARRIAGE LINES (BRI, 1921)

HER PRIVATE LIFE see DECLASSE

HER SACRIFICE see DOLL'S HOUSE, THE

HER SISTER FROM PARIS (FN, 1925, based on a play by
  Hans Kraely)
  MOULIN ROUGE (UA, 1934)
  TWO–FACED WOMAN (MGM, 1941)

HER SISTER'S SECRET see DARK ANGEL

HER WEDDING NIGHT see MISS BLUEBEARD

HER WONDERFUL LIE see VIE DE BOHEME, LA

HERBERT CLARK HOOVER (short) (NBC–TV, 1954,
  based on the life of President Herbert C. Hoover)
  HERBERT HOOVER (FNC, 1958)
  HERBERT CLARK HOOVER (short) (NBC–TV, 1959)
  HERBERT HOOVER (short) (WOL, 1964)
  TRIBUTE TO PRESIDENT HERBERT CLARK HOOVER,
  A (short) (NAV, 1964)

HERBSTMANOVER (GER, 1926, source unlisted)
  HERBSTMANOVER (GER, 1945)

HERE COME THE BRIDES see SEVEN BRIDES FOR
  SEVEN BROTHERS

HERE COMES KELLY see HE COULDN'T TAKE IT

HERE COMES MR. JORDAN (COL, 1941, based on the play,
  "Heaven Can Wait," by Harry Segall)
  DOWN TO EARTH (COL, 1947)
  HEAVEN CAN WAIT (PAR, 1978)

HERE COMES THE BANDWAGON see HALF WAY TO
  HEAVEN

HERE COMES THE GROOM (PAR, 1934, based on the play
  by Richard Flournoy)
  HERE COMES THE GROOM (PAR, 1951)
  HERE COMES THE GROOM (NBC–TV, 1956)

HERE IS MY HEART see LOST – A WIFE

HERITAGE OF THE DESERT (PAR, 1924, based on the book
  by Zane Grey)
  HERITAGE OF THE DESERT (PAR, 1933)
  HERITAGE OF THE DESERT (PAR, 1939)

HERNANI (FRA, 1910, based on a novel by Victor Hugo)
  HERNANI (ITA, 1910)
  HERNANI (ITA, 1920)

HERO, THE (IND, 1922, based on the play by Gilbert Emery)

SWELL GUY (UN, 1946)

HEROES see CHOCOLATE SOLDIER, THE

HEROES AND VILLAINS see CAUGHT

HEROES OF OUR TIME see BELLA

HEROES OF TELEMARK see OPERATION SWALLOW

HEROES OF THE WEST (serial) (UN, 1932, based on the
    story, "The Tie That Binds," by Peter B. Kyne)
    FLAMING FRONTIERS (UN, 1938)

HEROISM OF CLARA BARTON, THE see ANGEL OF
    MERCY

HERR OHNE WOHNUNG, DER (GER, 1925, based on a
    play (author unlisted)
    HERR OHNE WOHNUNG, DER (GER, 1934)
    WHO'S YOUR LADY FRIEND? (BRI, 1937)

HERREN VOM MAXIM, DIE (GER, 1920, source unlisted)
    HERREN VOM MAXIM, DIE (GER, 1920)

HERRIN DER WELT (GER, 1919, based on the book by
    Karl Figdor)
    HERRIN DER WELT (GER, 1960)

HERRSCHER, DER (GER, 1937, based on the noeel, "Vor
    Sonnenuntergant," by Gerhart Hauptmann)
    SONNENUNTERGAND. VOR (GER, 1956)

HERTZ BLEIBT ALLEIN, EIN see MEIN LEOPOLD

HET LEVENDE LIJK see LIVING CORPSE, THE

HEXER, DER see RINGER, THE

HEY, CINDERELLA see CINDERELLA AND THE FAIRY
    GODMOTHER

HI, BEAUTIFUL! see LOVE IN A BUNGALOW

HI, NELLIE! (WB, 1934, based on a story by Roy Chanslor)
    LOVE IS ON THE AIR (WB, 1937)
    YOU CAN'T ESCAPE FOREVER (WB, 1942)
    HOUSE ACROSS THE STREET, THE (WB, 1949)

HIAWATHA (BRI, 1903, based on the poem by Henry
    Wadsworth Longfellow)
    HIAWATHA (UN, 1909)
    HIAWATHA (BOS, 1909)
    HIAWATHA (IND, 1913)
    LITTLE HIAWATHA (short) (DIS, 1937)
    HIAWATHA (AA, 1952)
    HIAWATHA (NBC–TV, 1958)
    HIAWATHA (RAN, 1972)

HIBANA (JAP, 1922, source unlisted)
    BINANA (JAP, 1956)

HIDDEN LAND, THE see IT IS FOR ENGLAND

HIDEOUT (MGM, 1934, based on a story by Mauri Grashim)
    I'LL WAIT FOR YOU (MGM, 1941)
    I'LL WAIT FOR YOU (ITA, 1967)

HIGH BUTTON SHOES (NBC–TV, 1956, based on the musi-
    cal comedy by Jule Styne and Sammy Cahn)

HIGH BUTTON SHOES (CBS–TV, 1966)

HIGH PRESSURE (WB, 1932, based on a story by Aben Kand
    BLUFFEUR, LE (FRA, 1932)
    HOT MONEY (WB, 1936)

HIGH SEIRRA (WB, 1941, based on the book by W.R. Burnet
    COLORADO TERRITORY (WB, 1949)
    I DIED A THOUSAND TIMES (WB, 1955)

HIGH SOCIETY see PHILADELPHIA STORY, THE

HIGH TOR (NBC–TV, 1950, based on the play by Maxwell
    Anderson)
    HIGH TOR (CBS--TV, 1956)

HIGH WINDOW, THE see TIME TO KILL

HIGHWAY WEST see HEAT LIGHTNING

HIGHWAYMAN, THE (AA, 1951, based on the poem by Alfre
    Noyes)
    HIGHWAYMAN, THE (short) (MHF, 1959)

HIJA DEL REGIMENTO, LA see KING'S DAUGHTER, THE

HILL, THE (CAN–TV, 1956, based on a teleplay)
    HILL, THE (BRI–TV, 1959)
    HILL, THE (CAN–TV, 1960)

HILLBILLY, THE see HEART O' THE HILLS

HILLMAN, THE see IN THE BALANCE

HIMMEL AUF ERDEN (GER, 1926, based on the play by
    Wilhelm Jacobi and Arthur Lippschutz)
    HIMMEL AUF ERDEN (GER, 1935)

HINDLE WAKES (BRI, 1918, based on the play by Stanley
    Houghton)
    HINDLE WAKES (American Title: FANNY HAWTHORN)
    (BRI, 1927)
    HINDLE WAKES (BRI, 1931)
    HINDLE WAKES (American Title: HOLIDAY WEEK)
    (BRI, 1951)

HIP HIP HAPPY see GOOD NEWS

HIRED WIFE (UN, 1940, based on a story by George Beck)
    HIRED WIFE (NBC–TV, 1956)

HIROHITO (short) (MHF, 1963, based on the life of the
    Japanese emperor)
    EMPEROR HIROHITO (short) (MHF, 1964)

HIROKU KAIBYODEN see NABESHIMA KAIBYODEN

HIS CAPTIVE WOMAN see WOMAN GOD CHANGED, THE

HIS DOUBLE LIFE see GREAT ADVENTURE, THE

HIS FIGHTING BLOOD (SEL, 1915, based on the story by
    James Oliver Curwood)
    HIS FIGHTING BLOOD (AMB, 1935)

HIS GIRL FRIDAY see FRONT PAGE, THE

HIS GLORIOUS NIGHT (MGM, 1929, based on the play,
    "Olympia," by Ferenc Molnar)

SI L'EMPEREUR SAVAIT CA (FRA, 1929)
SI EL EMPERADOR LO SUPIERA (MEX,1929)
OLYMPIA (GER, 1929)
BREATH OF SCANDAL, A (PAR, 1960)

HIS GRACE GIVES NOTICE (BRI, 1924, based on the book
    by Lady Trowbirdge)
HIS GRAVE GIVES NOTICE (BRI, 1933)

HIS HOUSE IN ORDER (PAR, 1920, based on the play by
    Sir Arthur Wing Pinero)
HIS HOUSE IN ORDER (BRI, 1928)

HIS MAJESTY, BUNKER BEAN (PAR, 1918, based on the
    book by Harry Leon Wilson)
HIS MAJESTY, BUNKER BEAN (WB, 1925)
BUNKER BEAN (RKO, 1936)

HIS MAJESTY, THE SCARECROW OF OZ see DOROTHY
    AND THE SCARECROW OF OZ

HIS MEMORY WE CHERISH see MAHATMA GANDHI

HIS MUSICAL CAREER (short) (KEY, 1914, based on a
    screenplay by Mack Sennett; remakes uncredited)
HATS OFF (short) (MGM, 1927)
MUSIC BOX, THE (short) (MGM, 1932)
IT'S YOUR MOVE (short) (RKO, 1945)

HIS NIGHT OUT see OH, DOCTOR

HIS TIGER LADY see LOST – A WIFE

HIS WOMAN see SAL OF SINGAPORE

HISTOIRE D'UN PECHE, L' (POL, 1911, based on the book
    by Stefan Zeromski)
HISTOIRE D'UN PECHE, L' (ITA, 1917)
HISTOIRE D'UN PECHE, L' (POL, 1933)

HISTOIRES EXTRAORDINAIRES (FRA, 1949, based on
    stories by Edgar Allan Poe)
HISTOIRES EXTRAORDINAIRES (FRA/ITA, 1968)

HISTOIRES EXTRAORDINARIES see also AVENGING
    CONSCIENCE, THE and SEALED ROOM, THE

HIT MAN see GET CARTER

HIT THE DECK see SHORE LEAVE

HITLER see HITLER GANG, THE

HITLER GANG, THE (PAR, 1944, based on the life of the
    German dictator)
RISE OF A DICTATOR, THE (short) (TFC, 1952)
RISE AND FALL OF NAZI GERMANY, THE (short)
    (MOT, 1947)
RISE OF ADOLF HITLER, THE (short) (CBS–TV, 1953)
LAST DAYS OF HITLER, THE (ABC–TV, 1954)
TWISTED CROSS, THE (NBC–TV, 1958)
ADOLF HITLER: THE RISE OF POWER (short) (MFH,
    n.d.)
ADOLF HITLER: THE FALL OF THE THIRD REICH
    (short) (MHF, n.d.)
HITLER (AA, 1962)
SECRET LIFE OF ADOLF HITLER (TV, c1964)

PLOT TO MURDER HITLER, THE (ABC–TV, 1971)
HITLER -- THE LAST TEN DAYS (PAR, 1973)
SWASTIKA (BRI, 1973)
ADOLF HITLER: A PORTRAIT IN EVIL (ABC–TV,
    1975)
HITLER – A CAREER (GER, 1977)
HITLER: A FILM FROM GERMANY (BRI/FRA/GER,
    1977)

HOBBIT, THE (NBC–TV, 1977, based on "Lord of the Rings"
    by J.R.R. Tolkien)
LORD OF THE RINGS (UA, 1978)

HOBSON'S CHOICE (BRI, 1920, based on the play by Harold
    Brighouse; also the basis for the musical comedy, "Walking
    Happy," in 1966)
HOBSON'S CHOICE (BRI, 1931)
HOBSON'S CHOICE (BRI, 1954)

HOCHSTAPLERIN, DIE (GER, 1926, based on the book by
    Hans Land)
HOCHSTAPLERIN, DIE (GER, 1943)

HOCHTOURIST, DER (GER, 1931, based on the play by Curt
    Kraatz and Max Neal)
HOCHTOURIST, DER (GER, 1942)
HOCHTOURIST, DER (GER, 1961)

HOCHZEITSNACHT IN PARADIES (GER, 1950, source
    unlisted)
HOCHZEITSNACHT IN PARADIES (GER, 1962)

HOCHZEITREISE, DIE (GER, 1929, based on the play by
    Roderich Benedix)
HOCHZEITREISE, DIE (GER, 1969)

HOCHZEITSREISE ZU DRITT (GER, 1932, source unlited)
HOCHZEITSREISE ZU DRITT (GER, 1939)

HICUS POLUS (short) (COL, 1949, based on a screen play
    by Felix Adler)
FLAGPOLE JITTERS (short) (COL, 1956)

HOFFMANNS ERZAHLUNGEN (GER, 1914, baeed on the
    book, "Tales of Hoffmann," by Theodor Amadeus Hoff-
    mann and the opera by Jacques Offenbach)
HOFFMANS ERZAHLUNGEN (AUS, 1923)
TALES OF HOFFMAN (BRI, 1951)
TALES OF HOFFMANN (CZE, 1963)
NUTCRACKER, THE (POL, 1967)
VIOLIN DE CREMONE (short) (BEL, 1968)
ELIXIRS OF THE DEVIL, THE (GER, 1977)

HOG WILD (short) (MGM, 1930, based on a story by Leo
    McCarey)
PELE MELE (short) (FRA, 1930)
RADIO MANIA (short) (SPA, 1930)

HOKUSPOKUS (GER, 1930, based on the play by Kurt Goetz)
TEMPORARY WIDOW, THE (BRI, 1930)
HOKUSPOKUS (GER, 1953)

HOLD BACK THE DAWN (PAR, 1941, based on a story by
    Ketti Frings)
HOLD BACK THE DAWN (NBC–TV, 1954)

HOLD THAT BLONDE see PATHS TO PARADISE

HOLE IN THE HEAD see HEART IS A FORGOTTEN

HOLE IN THE WALL, THE (PAR, 1929, based on the play
 by Fred Jackson)
  HOLE IN THE WALL, THE (SWE, 1929)

HOLIDAY (PAT, 1930, based on the play by Philip Barry)
  HOLIDAY (COL, 1938)
  HOLIDAY (NBC--TV, 1956)

HOLIDAY FOR HENRIETTA (FRA, 1955, based on a screenplay by Julien Duvivier and Henri Jeanson)
  PARIS WHEN IT SIZZLES (PAR, 1964)

HOLIDAY WEEK see HINDLE WAKES

HOLLYWOOD REVUE OF 1929 (PAR, 1929, based on a
 screenplay by various authors)
  SCHALTEN UM AUF HOLLYWOOD, WIR (GER, 1930)

HOLY MATRIMONY see GREAT ADVENTURE, THE

HOLY NIGHT see PASSION PLAY, THE

HOLY TERROR, A see TRAILIN'

HOLY TERROR, THE see FLORENCE NIGHTINGALE

HOMAGE TO CHAGALL -- THE COLORS OF LOVE see
  GLIMPSE OF THE INNER LIFE OF MARC CHAGALL,
  A

HOMBRE MALO, EL see BAD ONE, THE

HOMBRE QUE ASESINO, EL see STAMBOUL

HOMBRE Y LA BESTIA, EL see DR. JEKYLL AND MR.
 HYDE

HOMBRES IN MI VIDA see MEN IN HER LIFE, THE

HOME AND BEAUTY see TOO MANY HUSBANDS

HOME IN INDIANA (FOX, 1944, based on the story, "The
 Phantom Filly," by George Agnew Chamberlain)
  APRIL LOVE (FOX, 1957)

HOME ON THE RANGE see CODE OF THE WEST

HOMECOMING see HEIMKEHR

HOMECOMING, THE see OLD HEIDELBERG and
  SPENCER'S MOUNTAIN

HOMER AND THE WACKY DOUGHNUT MACHINE see
  DOUGHNUTS

HOMER'S ODYSSEY see ULYSSES AND THE GIANT
  POLYPHEMUS

HOMETOWN (FURUSATO) (JAP, 1922, source unlisted)
  HOMETOWN (FURUSATO) (JAP, 1930)

HOMETOWNERS, THE (WB, 1928, based on a play by
 George M. Cohan)
  TIMES SQUARE PLAYBOY (WB, 1936)

HOMME A L'HISPANO, L' (FRA, 1926, based on the book
 by Pierre Frondale)

HOMME A L'HISPANO, L' (FRA, 1932)

HOMME AU CHAPEAU ROND, L' see GATTE, DER

HOMME DE LONDRES, L' (FRA, 1943, based on the book
 by Georges Simenon)
  TEMPTATION HARBOR (BRI, 1947)
  TEMPTATION HARBOR (FRA, 1947)

HOMME DE NULLE PART, L' see FEU MATHIAS PASCAL

HOMME EN HABIT, UN see EVENING CLOTHES

HOMME L' ORGUEIL ET LA VENGEANCE, L' see
  CARMEN

HOMME NI BON NI MAUVAIS, UN see DUEL, THE

HOMME QUI A PERDU SON OMBRE, L' see PETER
  SCHLEMIHL

HOMME QUI ASSASSINA, L' (FRA, 1914, based on a book
 by Claude Farrere)
  RIGHT TO LOVE, THE (PAR, 1920)
  MANN, DER DEN MORD BEGING, DER (GER, 1931)

HOMME QUI ASSASSINA, L' see also STAMBOUL

HOMME QUI REVIENT DE LOIN, L' (FRA, 1916, based on
 the book by Gaston Leroux)
  HOMME QUI REVIENT DE LOIN, L' (FRA, 1950)

HOMME QUI RIT, L' (FRA, 1909, based on the book by
 Victor Hugo)
  GRINSENDE GESICHT, DAS (AUS, 1921)
  MAN WHO LAUGHS, THE (UN, 1927)
  UOMO CHE RIDE (FRA/ITA, 1965)

HOMME QUI VENDIT SON AME AU DIABLE, L' (FRA,
 1920, based on the book by Pierre Veber)
  HOMME QUI VENDIT SON AME (FRA, 1943)

HOMMES NOUVEAUX, LES (FRA, 1922, based on a book
 by Claude Farrere)
  HOMMES NOUVEAUX, LES (FRA, 1936)

HONDO (WB, 1953, based on the book by Louis L'Amour)
  HONDO AND THE APACHES (MGM, 1966)
  HONDO (series) (ABC--TV, 1967)

HONDO AND THE APACHES see HONDO

HONEY see COME OUT OF THE KITCHEN

HONEY POT, THE see VOLPONE

HONEYMOON FOR THREE see GOODBYE AGAIN

HONEYMOON'S OVER, THE see SIX--CYLINDER LOVE

HONKY TONK (MGM, 1941, based on a screenplay by Marguerite Roberts and John Sanford)
  HONKY TONK (TV, 1974)

HONNEUR, L' (FRA, 1913, based on the book by Hermann
 Sudermann)
  VORDERHAUS UND HINTERHAUS (DEN/GER, 1913)
  VORDERHAUS UND HINTERHAUS (GER, 1926)

HONOR OF THE GAMILY   (FN, 1931, based on the story
     by Honore de Balzac)
   RABOUILLEUSE, LA   (FRA, 1943)
   ARRIVISTES, LES   (FRA/GER, 1960)

HONORABLE MURDER, AN   see   JULIUS CAESAR

HONORABLE SAM HOUSTON, THE   see   CONQUERER,
     THE

HOOP--LA   see   BARKER, THE

HOOSIER SCHOOLMASTER   (PAT, 1924, based on the book
     by Edward Eggleston)
   HOOSIER SCHOOLMASTER   (MON, 1935)
   HOOSIER SCHOOLMASTER   (NBC--TV, 1950)

HOP FROG   (FRA, 1910, based on a story, "The Masque
     of the Red Death," by Edgar Allan Poe)
   MASK OF THE RED DEATH   (ITA, 1911)
   SPECTER HAUNTS EUROPE, A   (RUS, 1922)
   MASQUE OF THE RED DEATH, THE   (AI, 1964)
   MASQUE OF THE RED DEATH, THE   (short)   (YUG,
     1969)

HOP O' MY THUMB   see   PETIT POUCET, LE

HORACE MANN   (short)   (EBE, 1951, based on the life and
     work of the noted educator)
   HORACE MANN, HUMANITARIAN   (short)   (IND,
     n.d.)

HORIZONTES NUEVOS, LE   see   BIG TRAIL, THE

HORN BLOWS AT MIDNIGHT, THE   (WB, 1945, based on an
     idea by Aubrey Weisberg)
   HORN BLOWS AT MIDNIGHT, THE   (CBS--TV, 1955)

HORNBLOWER   see   CAPTAIN HORATIO HORNBLOWER

HORRIBLE HYDE   see   DR. JEKYLL AND MR. HYDE

HORROR CHAMBER OF DR. FAUSTUS   see   EYES WITH--
     OUT A FACE

HORROR OF DRACULA   see   NOSFERATU

HORROR OF FRANKENSTEIN   see   FRANKENSTEIN

HOT MONEY   see   HIGH PRESSURE

HOT WIND   (JAP, 1934, source unlisted)
   HOT WIND   (JAP, 1943)

HOTEL DU LIBRE--ECHANGE, L'   (FRA, 1922, based on a
     play by Georges Feydeau and Maurice Desvallieres)
   HOTEL DU LIBRE--ECHANGE, L'   (FRA, 1934)
   HOTEL PARADISO   (BRI, 1966)

HOTEL IMPERIAL   (PAR, 1927, based on the play by Lajos
     Biro)
   HOTEL IMPERIAL   (PAR, 1939)

HOTTENTOT, THE   (FN, 1922, based on the play by Victor
     Mapes and William Collier)
   HOTTENTOT, THE   (WB, 1929)
   GOING PLACES   (WB, 1938)

HOUDINI   (PAR, 1953, based on the life of the noted magician)

GREAT HOUDINI, THE   (ABC--TV, 1976)

HOUND DOG MAN, THE   (CBS--TV, 1953, based on the book
     by Fred Gipson)
   HOUND DOG MAN, THE   (FOX, 1959)

HOUND OF THE BASKERVILLES, THE   (GER, 1914, based
     on the book by Sir Arthur Conan Doyle)
   HOUND OF THE BASKERVILLES, THE   (FRA, 1915)
   HUND VON BASKERVILLES, DER   (GER, 1917)
   HOUND OF THE BASKERVILLES, THE   (BRI, 1921)
   HOUND OF THE BASKERVILLES, THE   (FBO, 1922)
   HUND VON BASKERVILLES, DER   (GER, 1929)
   HOUND OF THE BASKERVILLES, THE   (BRI, 1931)
   HOUND OF THE BASKERVILLES, THE   (BRI, 1934)
   HUND VON BASKERVILLES, DER   (GER, 1936)
   HOUND OF THE BASKERVILLES, THE   (FOX, 1939)
   MURDER AT THE BASKERVILLES   (BRI, 1941)
   HOUND OF THE BASKERVILLES, THE   (BRI, 1959)
   HOUND OF THE BASKERVILLES, THE   (BRI--TV, 1968)
   HOUND OF THE BASKERVILLES, THE   (ABC--TV, 1972)

HOUNDS OF ZAROFF   see   MOST DANGEROUS GAME,
     THE

HOUR OF THE GUN   see   GUNFIGHT AT THE O. K. CORRAL

HOUR OF 13, THE   see   MYSTERY OF MR. X

HOUSE ACROSS THE STREET, THE   see   HI, NELLIE!

HOUSE IN MALTA, THE   (FRA, 1928, based on the book by
     Jean Vignaud)
   HOUSE IN MALTA, THE   (FRA, 1938)

HOUSE IN MONTEVIDEO, THE   (GER, 1951, based on the
     play by Curt Goetz)
   HOUSE IN MONTEVIDEO, THE   (GER, 1964)

HOUSE OF A THOUSAND CANDLES, THE   (SEL, 1915, based
     on the book by Meredith Nicholson)
   HAUNTING SHADOWS   (RC, 1919)
   HOUSE OF A THOUSAND CANDLES, THE   (REP, 1936)

HOUSE OF BAMBOO   see   STREET WITH NO NAME, THE

HOUSE OF DR. EDWARDES, THE   see   SPELLBOUND

HOUSE OF DRACULA   see   NOSFERATU

HOUSE OF ERRORS   see   BERTH MARKS

HOUSE OF FEAR   see   LAST WARNING, THE

HOUSE OF FRANKENSTEIN   see   FRANKENSTEIN

HOUSE OF FRIGHT   see   DR. JEKYLL AND MR. HYDE

HOUSE OF LYNCH   see   SCHOOL FOR WIVES

HOUSE OF MENACE   see   KIND LADY

HOUSE OF MYSTERY, THE   (MON, 1934, based on a play
     by Adam Hull Shirk)
   APE, THE   (MON, 1940)

HOUSE OF MYSTERY, THE   (FRA, 1922, based on the book
     by Jules Mary)
   HOUSE OF MYSTERY, THE   (FRA, 1934)

HOUSE OF ROTHSCHILD, THE (UA, 1934, based on his-
    torical characters and incidents; also the basis for the
    musical, "The Rothschilds")
    ROTHSCHILDS, THE (GER, 1940)

HOUSE OF SEC.ETS (CHE, 1929, based on the book by
    Sydney Horler)
    HOUSE OF SECRETS (CHE, 1936)

HOUSE OF STRANGERS (FOX, 1949, based on the book,
    "I'll Never Go There Anymore," by Jerome Weidman)
    BROKEN LANCE (FOX, 1954)
    LAST PATRIARCH, THE (CBS–TV, 1956)
    BIG SHOW, THE (FOX, 1961)

HOUSE OF THE ARROW (BRI, 1930, based on the book
    by A.E.W. Mason)
    HOUSE OF THE ARROW (BRI, 1940)
    HOUSE OF THE ARROW (BRI, 1952)

HOUSE OF THE SEVEN GABLES, THE (ED, 1910, based
    on the book by Nathaniel Hawthorne)
    HOUSE OF THE SEVEN GABLES, THE (UN, 1940)
    HOUSE OF THE SEVEN GABLES, THE (NBC–TV, 1951)
    HOUSE OF THE SEVEN GABLES, THE (NBC–TV, 1956)
    HOUSE OF THE SEVEN GABLES, THE (NBC–TV, 1960)
    HOUSE OF THE SEVEN GABLES, THE (AI, 1971)

HOUSE OF USHER, THE see FALL OF THE HOUSE OF
    USHER, THE

HOUSE OF WAX see MYSTERY OF THE WAX MUSEUM,
    THE

HOUSE OF WOMEN see CAGED

HOUSE OFF THE SQUARE, THE see BERKELEY SQUARE

HOUSE ON CEDAR HILL, THE (short) (MHF, 1953, based
    on the life of the noted black leader)
    FREDERICK DOUGLAS (SAU, 1966)
    FREDERICK DOUGLAS (short) (EBE, 1971)

HOUSE WITHOUT A KEY, THE (serial) (PAT, 1926, based
    on the book by Earl Derr Biggers)
    CHARLIE CHAN'S GREATEST CASE (FOX, 1933)

HOUSE WITHOUT WINDOWS OR DOORS, THE (GER,
    1914, source unlisted)
    HOUSE WITHOUT WINDOWS OR DOORS, THE (GER,
    1921)

HOW GREEN WAS MY VALLEY (FOX, 1941, based on the
    book by Richard Llewellyn)
    HOW GREEN WAS MY VALLEY (series) (BRI–TV, 1975)

HOW HIGH IS UP? see LIBERTY

HOW KITCHENER WAS BETRAYED see LIFE OF LORD
    KITCHENER

HOW MANY STARS? see STAR GAZERS

HOW SHE LIED TO HER HUSBAND (BRI, 1915, based on
    a play (author unlisted)
    HOW SHE LIED TO HER HUSBAND (BRI, 1931)

HOW THE STEEL WAS TEMPERED (RUS, 1942, based on
    the book by Nikolai Ostrovsky)

PAVEL KORCHAGIN (RUS, 1957)
HOW THE STEEL WAS TEMPERED (RUS–TV, 1973)

HOW THE WEST WAS WON see MACAHANS, THE

HOW TO BE VERY, VERY POPULAR see SHE LOVES
    ME NOT

HOW TO MARRY A MILLIONAIRE see GIRLS ABOUT
    TOWN and WORKING GIRLS

HOWDY STRANGER see COWBOY FROM BROOKLYN

HUCK AND TOM see TOM SAWYER

HUCK FINN see HUCKLEBERY FINN

HUCKLEBERRY FINN (PAR, 1920, based on the book by
    Mark Twain)
    HUCKLEBERRY FINN (PAR, 1931)
    ADVENTURES OF HUCKLEBERRY FINN, THE (MGM,
    1939)
    ADVENTURES OF HUCKLEBERRY FINN, THE (CBS–
    TV, 1955)
    HUCK FINN (CBS–TV, 1975)
    TOM AND HUCK (NBC–TV, 1960)
    ADVENTURES OF HUCKLEBERRY FINN, THE (MGM,
    1960)
    NEW ADVENTURES OF HUCKLEBERRY FINN, THE
    (series) (HB, 1968)
    LOST BOY (RUS, 1974)
    HUCKLEBERRY FINN (UA, 1974)
    ADVENTURES OF HUCKLEBERRY FINN, THE (series)
    (JAP–TV, 1976)

HUIS CLOS (FRA, 1954, based on the play by Jean–Paul
    Sartre)
    NO EXIT (NET–TV, 1961)
    NO EXIT (ARG, 1962)

HUMAN BEAST, THE see BETE HUMAINE, LA

HUMAN COMEDY, THE (MGM, 1943, based on the book by
    William Saroyan)
    HUMAN COMEDY, THE (CBS–TV, 1959)

HUMAN DESIRE see BESTIE IM MENSCHEN, DIE

HUMAN MONSTER see DARK EYES OF LONDON, THE

HUMANISM: JOHN DEWEY see DEMOCRACY IN EDU-
    CATION: JOHN DEWEY

HUMORESQUE (PAR' 1920, based on the story by Fannie
    Hurst)
    HUMORESQUE (WB, 1947)

HUMPBACKED HORSE, THE see MAGIC HORSE, THE

HUNCHBACK OF NOTRE DAME, THE see ESMERELDA

HUND VON BASKERVILLES, DER see HOUND OF THE
    BASKERVILLES, THE

HUNGARIAN RHAPSODY (GER, 1913, based on the book by
    Zsolt von Harsanyi)
    HUNGARIAN RHAPSODY (GER, 1928)

HUNT, THE see MOST DANGEROUS GAME, THE

HURRA, EIN JUNGE! (GER, 1931, based on the play by Franz Arnold and Ernst Bach)
HURRA, EIN JUNGE! (GER, 1953)

HURRA, ICH LEBE! (GER, 1928, based on the story, "Der Mutige Seefahrer," by Georg Kaiser)
MUTIGE SEEFAHRER, DER (GER, 1935)
GHOST COMES HOME, THE (MGM, 1939)

HUSARENLIEBE (GER, 1926, source unlisted)
HUSARENLIEBE (GER, 1932)

HUSN KA CHOR see ARABIAN NIGHTS

HUSTLER, THE (TV, n.d., based on the book by Walter S. Tevis)
HUSTLER, THE (FOX, 1961)

HYMENEE (RUS, 1909, based on a story by Nikolai Gogol)
HYMENEE (RUS, 1937)

HYPERBOLOIDE DE L'INGENIEUR GARINE, L' (RUS, 1966, based on the book by Alexei Tolstoy)
CRIME OF P. GARINE, THE (RUS–TV, 1973)

HYNOTIST, THE see LONDON AFTER MIDNIGHT

HYPOCRITE, THE see TARTUFFE

I.N.R.I. see PASSION PLAY, THE

I ACCUSE see AFFAIR DREYFUS, L'

I AM A CAMERA (UA, 1955, based on the book, "Berlin
     Stories," by Christopher Isherwood)
  CABARET (AA, 1973)

I AM A CRIMINAL (MON, 1938, based on a story by Harrison
     Jacobs)
  SMART GUY (MON, 1943)

I AM ALADDIN see ALADDIN

I AM LEGEND see LAST MAN ON EARTH

I AM THE GREATEST: THE ADVENTURES OF MUHAM-
     MAD ALI see FLOAT LIKE A BUTTERFLY, STING
     LIKE A BEE

I BEHELD THE GLORY see PASSION PLAY, THE

I CAN HARDLY WAIT see LEAVE 'EM LAUGHING

I, CLAUDIUS see EPIC THAT NEVER WAS, THE

I COVER THE WATERFRONT (UA, 1933, based on the book
     by Max Miller)
  SECRET OF DEEP HARBOR (UA, 1961)

I DIED A THOUSAND TIMES see HIGH SIERRA

I, DON QUIXOTE see DON QUIXOTE

I GIVE MY HEART see DUBARRY

I, HAMLET see HAMLET

I KILLED RASPUTIN see RASPUTIN, THE BLACK MONK

I KILLED THAT MAN see DEVIL'S MATE, THE

I LED THREE LIVES see I WAS A COMMUNIST FOR THE
     F.B.I.

I, LEONARDO VA VINCI see LEONARDO DA VINCI –
     MAN OF MYSTERY

I LIKE MONEY see TOPAZE

I MARRIED A DOCTOR see MAIN STREET

I, MONSTER see DR. JEKYLL AND MR. HYDE

I NEVER SAW ANOTHER BUTTERFLY (short) (NBC–TV,
     1966, based on drawings of children in Terezin Concen-
     tration Camp in Czechoslovakia during World War II)
  I NEVER SAW ANOTHER BUTTERLY (short) (CBS–TV,
     1967)

I PROMESSI SPOSI (ITA, 1909, source unlisted)
  I PROMESSI SPOSI (ITA, 1928)
  I PROMESSI SPOSI (ITA, 1943)

I REMEMBER MAMA (RKO, 1948, based on the book,
     "Mama's Bank Account," by Kathryn Forbes)
  MAMA (series) (CBS–TV, 1949)

I SHOT JESSE JAMES (SG, 1949, based on a newspaper

article)
  I SHOT JOHNNY RINGO (IND, 1965)

I SHOT JOHNNY RINGO see I SHOT JESSE JAMES

I . . . THE DOCTOR see KNOCK

I WAKE UP SCREAMING (FOX, 1941)
  VICKIE (FOX, 1953)

I WALKED WITH A ZOMBIE see JANE EYRE

I WAS A COMMUNIST FOR THE F.B.I. (WB, 1951, based on
     the book by Herbert Philbrick)
  I LED THREE LIVES (series) (TV, 1953)

I WAS A CRIMINAL see CAPTAIN FROM KOPENIK, THE

I WAS FRAMED see DUST BE MY DESTINY

ICEMAN COMETH, THE (NET–TV, 1960, based on the play
     by Eugene O'Neill)
  ICEMAN COMETH, THE (AFT, 1973)

ICH BEI TAG UND DU BEI NACHT (GER, 1932, based on a
     story by John Wells)
  MOI LE JOUR, A TOI NUIT, A (FRA, 1932)
  EARLY TO BED (BRI, 1933)
  RAFTER ROMANCE (RKO, 1934)
  LIVING ON LOVE (RKO, 1937)

ICH HAB MEIN HERZ IN HAIDBERG VERLOREN (GER,
     1926, source unlisted)
  ICH HAB MEIN HERZ IN HAIDBERG VERLOREN
     (GER, 1952)

ICH HEIRATE MEINE FRAU (GER, 1927, based on an
     original screenplay by Max Reichmann)
  ICH HEIRATE MEINE FRAU (GER, 1934)

ICH LIEBE ALLE FRAUEN (GER, 1935, source unlisted)
  J'AIME TOUT LES FEMMES (FRA, 1935)

ICH UND DIE KAISERIN (GER, 1933, based on story by
     Robert Liebman, Walter Reisch and Felix Salten)
  MOI ET L'EMPERATRICE (FRA, 1933)
  ONLY GIRL, THE (American Title: HEART SONG) (BRI,
     1933)

ICH WAR JACK MORTIMER (GER, 1935, based on the
     book by Alexander Lernet–Holenia)
  ADVENTURE IN VIENNA (AUS, 1952)

ICH WERDE DICH AUF HANDEN TRAGEN see SERE-
NADE

ICHABOD AND MR. TOAD see LEGEND OF SLEEPY-
HOLLOW, THE

I'D GIVE MY LIFE see NOOSE, THE

I'D RATHER BE RICH see IT STARTED WITH EVE

IDEAL HUSBAND, AN see IDEALER GATTE, EIN
     (GER, 1935, based on the play, "An Ideal Husband," by
     Oscar Wilde)
  IDEAL HUSBAND, AN (BRI, 1948)
  IDEAL HUSBAND, AN (PBS–TV, 1971)

IDIOT, THE   (ITA, 1907, based on the book by Feyodor
    Dostoyevsky)
    IDIOT, THE   (RUS, 1909)
    IDIOT, THE   (RUS, 1920)
    DUMMKOPF, DER   (GER, 1920)
    IDIOT, THE   (GER, 1921)
    IDIOT, THE   (GER, 1931)
    IDIOT, THE   (FRA, 1945)
    IDIOT, THE   (URU, 1947)
    IDIOT, THE (HAKUCHI)   (JAP, 1950)
    IDIOT, THE   (RUS, 1958)

IDIOT IN LOVE   (JAP, 1960, source unlisted)
    IDIOT IN LOVE   (JAP, 1967)

IDLE HANDS   see   RULING PASSION, THE

IDLE RICH   (MGM, 1929, based on the play by Edith Ellis)
    RICH MAN, POOR MAN   (MGM, 1938)

IDOL OF SEVILLE, THE   see   CARMEN

IF A BODY MEETS A BODY   see   LAUREL & HARDY
    MURDER CASE, THE

IF I WERE KING   (n.d., 1918, based on the play by Justin
    Huntly McCarthy and the operetta, "The Vagabond King,"
    by Rudolf Friml)
    IF I WERE KING   (FOX, 1920)
    BELOVED ROGUE, THE   (UA, 1927)
    VAGABOND KING, THE   (PAR, 1930)
    IF I WERE KING   (PAR, 1938)
    SWORD OF VILLON, THE   (short)   (TV, c1955)
    VAGABOND KING, THE   (PAR,1956)

IF I'M LUCKY   see   THANKS A MILLION

IF IT'S TUESDAY, THIS MUST BE BELGIUM   (CBS–TV,
    1966, based on a story by David Shaw)
    IF IT'S TUESDAY, THIS MUST BE BELGIUM   (UA, 1969)

IF WINTER COMES   (FOX, 1923, based on the book by A.S.M.
    Hutchinson)
    IF WINTER COMES   (MGM, 1947)

IF WOMEN ONLY KNEW   see   FEMME DE TRENTE ANS,
LA

IGLOO   (UN, 1932, the second film consists of stock footage
    from the first film)
    RED SNOW   (COL, 1952)

IHR LEIBHUSAR   see   AFFAIR OF YOUNG NOSZTY WITH
    MARI TOTH

IHRE DURCHLAUT, DIE VERKAUFERIN   see   MEINE
    SCHWESTER UND ICH

IHRE HOHEIT BEFIEHLT   see   ADORABLE

ILE DE CALYPSO, L'   (FRA, 1905, based on the novel, "The
    Odyssey," by Homer)
    RETOURE D'ULYSSE, LE   (FRA, 1908)
    ODYSSEY, THE   (ITA, 1911)
    ULYSSES   (ITA, 1954)

ILIAD, THE   see   CHUTE DE TROIE, LA

I'LL BE YOURS   see   GOOD FAIRY, THE

I'LL GET BY   see   TIN PAN ALLEY

I'LL NEVER FORGET YOU   see   BERKELEY SQUARE

I'LL NEVER GO THERE ANYMORE   see   HOUSE OF
    STRANGERS

I'LL TELL THE WORLD   (UN, 1934, based on a story by
    Lincoln Warberg and Lt. Com. Frank Wead)
    I'LL TELL THE WORLD   (UN, 1945)

I'LL WAIT FOR YOU   see   HIDEOUT

ILLEGAL   see   MOUTHPIECE, THE

ILLICIT   (WB, 1931, based on the play by Edith Fitzgerald
    and Robert Riskin)
    EX--LADY   (WB, 1933)

I'M A MONKEY'S UNCLE   (short)   (COL, 1948, based on a
    screenplay by Zion Myers)
    STONE--AGE ROMEOS   (short)   (COL, 1955)

IM WEISSEN ROSSL   (GER, 1926, based on the play by
    Oskar Blumenthal and Kadelburg)
    IM WEISSEN ROSSL   (GER, 1935)
    IM WEISSEN ROSSL   (GER, 1952)
    IM WEISSEN ROSSL   (GER, 1950)

IMAGINE ROBINSON   see   ROBINSON CRUSOE

IMITATION OF LIFE   (UN, 1934, based on the book by
    Fannie Hurst)
    IMITATION OF LIFE   (UN, 1959)

IMMEDIATE DISASTER   see   DAY THE EARTH STOOD
    STILL, THE

IMMELSEE   (SWE, nd., source unlisted)
    IMMELSEE   (SWE, 1956)

IMMENSEE   (GER, 1943, based on the book by Theodor
    Storm)
    UNSTERBLICHE LIEBE, WAS DIE SCHWALBE SANG
    (GER, 1956)

IMMORTAL MELODY   see   WALTZES FROM VIENNA

IMP IN THE BOTTLE, THE   see   IMP OF THE BOTTLE, THE

IMP OF THE BOTTLE, THE   (ED, 1909, based on the story,
    "The Bottle Imp," by Robert Lewis Stevenson)
    BOTTLE IMP, THE   (PAR, 1917)
    LOVE, DEATH AND THE DEVIL   (GER, 1934)
    IMP IN THE BOTTLE, THE   (PYR,1950)
    BOTTLE IMP, THE   (short)   (GER, 1952)
    BOTTLE IMP, THE   (CBS–TV, 1957)

IMPERFECT LADY, THE   (PAR, 1947, based on a story by
    Ladislas Fodor)
    IMPERFECT LADY, THE   (NBC–TV, 1954)

IMPORTANCE OF BEING EARNEST, THE   see   LIEBE,
    SCHERZ UND ERNST

IMPOSTER, EL   see   SCOTLAND YARD

IN DARKNESS WAITING   (NBC–TV, 1965, based on the
    teleplay by Robert L. Joseph)

STRATEGY OF TERROR   (UN, 1969)

IN DE VOETSPOREN VAN AUGUST VERMEYLEN see
AUGUST VERMEYLEN

IN HIS STEPS see MARTYRDOM OF PHILIP STRONG,
THE

IN OLD ARIZONA see CABALLERO'S WAY

IN OLD CHICAGO (FOX, 1938, based on the story, "We, the
O'Learys," by Niven Busch)
CITY IN FLAMES (FOX–TV, 1957)

IN OLD KENTUCKY (FN, 1920, based on the play by
Charles Dazey)
IN OLD KENTUCKY (MGM, 1927)
IN OLD KENTUCKY (FOX, 1935)

IN SEARCH OF ANCIENT ASTRONAUTS (TV, 1973,
based on the book, "Chariots of the Gods," by Erich von
Daniken)
CHARIOTS OF THE GODS (IND, 1974)
MIRACLES OF THE GODS (GER, 1976)

IN SEARCH OF THE CASTAWAYS (FRA, 1914, based on
the book by Jules Verne)
CHLDREN OF CAPTAIN GRANT, THE (RUS, 1936)
IN SEARCH OF THE CASTAWAYS (DIS, 1962)

IN THE ANTEROOM OF DEATH (INTERLUDE) (SWE,
1945, although the first two films are based on the story,
"Beyond," by Erich Maria Remarque and the third on the
book, "Heaven Has No Favorites," by the same author,
the two plots, with sexes reversed are similar)
OTHER LOVE, THE (UA, 1947)
BOBBY DEERFIELD (COL, 1977)

IN THE BALANCE (VIT, 1917, based on the book, "The
Hillman," by E. Philips Oppenheim)
BEHOLD THE WOMAN (VIT, 1924)

IN THE DAYS OF ROBIN HOOD see ROBIN HOOD AND
HIS MERRY MEN

IN THE GOOD OLD SUMMERTIME see SHOP AROUND
THE CORNER, THE

IN THE GRIP OF THE SPIDER see DANZA MACABRE, LA

IN THE NEXT ROOM (WB, 1930, based on the book, "Mystery
of the Boule Cabinet," by Burton E. Stevenson)
CASE OF THE BLACK PARROT, THE (WB, 1941)

IN THE PALACE OF THE KING (ESS, 1915, based on the
book by F. Marion Crawford)
IN THE PALACE OF THE KING (MGM, 1923)

IN THE TRACKS OF THE BREMEN MUSICIANS see FOUR
MUSICIANS OF BREMEN, THE

IN THE WAKE OF THE BOUNTY see MUTINY OF THE
BOUNTY

IN THE YEAR 2889 see DAY THE WORLD ENDED, THE

IN THIS CORNER -- JOE LOUIS see SPIRIT OF YOUTH

IN TIMES LIKE THESE see HAPPY DAYS

IN TWO HANDS (BRI–TV, n.d., based on a teleplay)
WEDNESDAY'S CHILD (BRI, 1972)

INCIDENT, THE see RIDE WITH TERROR

INCOMPARABLE BELLAIRS, THE (BRI, 1914, based on a
play by David Belasco and a book by Agnes and Egerton
Castle)
SWEET KITTY BELLAIRS (PAR, 1916)
SWEET KITTY BELLAIRS (WB, 1930)

INCONNUS DE LA MAISON, LES (FRA, 1942, based on the
book by Georges Simenon)
COP–OUT (STRANGER IN THE HOUSE) (BRI, 1967)

INCORREGIBLE, LA see MANSLAUGHTER

INCREDIBLE SARAH, THE see SARAH

INCREDIBLE TURK, THE see ATATURK, FOUNDER OF
MODERN TURKEY

INCREDIBLE WORLD OF HORACE FORD, THE (CBS–TV,
1955, based on a teleplay)
INCREDIBLE WORLD OF HORACE FORD, THE (TV,
1963)

INCREDIBLE WORLD OF MARK O'GULLIVER, THE see
GULLIVER'S TRAVELS

INDIAN RUBBER MAN, THE see RETURN OF THE FROG,
THE

INDIAN SCARF, THE see FRIGHTENED LADY

INDIAN TOMB, THE (GER, 1920, based on a story by Thea
von Harbou)
TIGER VON ESCHNAPUR (GER, 1921)
TIGER VON ESCHNAPUR (GER, 1934)
TIGER VON ESCHNAPUR (GER, 1959)
JOURNEY TO THE LOST CITY (AI, 1960)

INDIANAPOLIS SPEEDWAY see CROWD ROARS, THE

INDIANS (PBS--TV, n.d., based on the play by Arthur Kopit)
BUFFALO BILL AND THE INDIANS, or SITTING BULL'S
HISTORY LESSON (UA, 1976)

INDISCHE GRABMAL, DAS see INDIAN TOMB, THE

INDISCREET (NBC–TV, 1956, based on the play, "Kind Sir,"
by Norman Krasna)
INDISCREET (WB, 1958)

INFERNO (FOX, 1953, based on a screenplay by Francis
Cockrell)
ORDEAL (TV, 1973)

INFERNO see DANTE'S INFERNO

INFORMER, THE (BRI, 1928, based on the book by Liam
O'Flaherty)
INFORMER, THE (RKO, 1935)
UP TIGHT (PAR, 1968)

INHERIT THE WIND (UA, 1960, based on the play by
Jerome Lawrence and Robert E. Lee)
INHERIT THE WIND (NBC–TV, 1965)

INHERITANCE, THE   see   UNCLE SILAS

INN ON THE RIVER, THE   see   RETURN OF THE FROG, THE

INNOCENCE UNPROTECTED   (YUG, 1942, source unlisted)
INNOCENCE UNPROTECTED   (YUG, 1968)

INNOCENTS, THE   see   OTHERS, THE

INQUEST   (BRI, 1931, based on the play by Michael Barringer)
INQUEST   (BRI, 1940)

INSIDE STORY, THE   (REP, 1948, based on a story by Ernest Lehman and Geza Herczeg)
INSIDE STORY, THE   (NBC–TV, 1955)

INSOUMISE, L'   see   FAZIL

INSPECTOR CALLS, AN   (NBC–TV, 1948, based on the play by J.B. Priestley)
INSPECTOR CALLS, AN   (NBC–TV, 1951)
INSPECTOR CALLS, AN   (BRI, 1955)

INSPECTOR GENERAL, THE   see   REVIZOR

INSPIRATION   see   SAPHO

INSTINCT, L'   (FRA, 1916, based on a story by Henry Kistemaeckers)
INSTINCT, L'   (FRA, 1927)

INTERFERENCE   (PAR, 1929, based on the play by Roland Pertwee and Harold Dearborn)
WITHOUT REGRET   (PAR, 1935)

INTERLUDE   see   IN THE ANTEROOM OF DEATH and WHEN TOMORROW COMES

IMMEDIATE DISASTER   see   DAY THE EARTH STOOD STILL, THE

INSIDE CUBA TODAY   see   FIDEL CASTRO STORY, THE

INTERMEZZO   (SWE, 1936, based on a story by Gustav Molander)
INTERMEZZO   (UA, 1939)
INTERMEZZO   (NBC–TV, 1961)

INTERNATIONAL SQUADRON   see   CEILING ZERO

INTERNS, THE   (COL, 1962, based on stories by Richard Frede)
NEW INTERNS, THE   (COL, 1964)

INTIMATE LIFE OF MARK ANTHONY AND CLEOPATRA, THE   see   CLEOPATRA

INTIMATE RELATIONS   see   PARENTS TERRIBLES, LES

INTOLERANCE   see   WINTERSET

INTRODUCTION TO ERICA   see   MY GIRL TISA

INVADERS FROM MARS   (FOX, 1954, based on the book, "Counterspy Express," by A.S. Fleischman)
SPY IN THE SKY   (AA, 1958)

INVASION OF THE BODY SNATCHERS, THE   (AA, 1956, based on the story by Jack Finney)
INVASION OF THE BODY SNATCHERS, THE   (UA, 1978)

INVINCIBLE MR. DISRAELI, THE   see   DISRAELI

INVISIBLE AGENT, THE   see   INVISIBLE MAN, THE

INVISIBLE MAN, THE   (UN, 1933, based on the book by H.G. Wells)
INVISIBLE AGENT, THE   (UN, 1942)
INVISIBLE MAN'S REVENGE, THE   (UN, 1944)
ABBOTT AND COSTELLO MEET THE INVISIBLE MAN   (UN, 1951)
INVISIBLE MAN, THE   (series)   (TV, 1958)
NEW INVISIBLE MAN, THE   (MEX, 1962)
INVISIBLE MAN, THE   (series)   (TV, 1966)
INVISIBLE MAN, THE   (NBC–TV, 1975)
INVISIBLE MAN, THE   (series)   (NBC--TV, 1975)
GEMINI MAN, THE   (series)   (NBC–TV, 1975)

INVISIBLE MAN'S REVENGE   see   INVISIBLE MAN, THE

INVISIBLE MENACE, THE   (WB, 1937, based on a play by Ralph Spencer Zink)
MURDER ON THE WATERFRONT   (WB, 1943)

INVISIBLE MONSTER, THE   (serial)   (REP, 1950, based on a screenplay by various authors; the second version is an edited version of the serial)
SLAVES OF THE INVISIBLE MONSTER   (REP, 1966)

INVISIBLE SWORD   see   SIEGFRIED

IRENE   (FOX, 1926, based on the musical comedy by James Montgomery)
IRENE   (RKO, 1940)

IRIS   (PAT, 1917, based on the play by Sir Arthur Wing Pinero)
SLAVE OF VANITY, A   (RC, 1920)

IRMA LA DOUCE   (UA, 1963, based on the play, "Irma la Douce," by Alexandre Brefort)
RED LIGHT STREET   (TUR, 1968)

IRON HORSE, THE   (FOX, 1924, based on a historical incident)
UNION PACIFIC   (PAR, 1939)
UNION PACIFIC   (series)   (NBC–TV, 1958)

IRON MAN, THE   (UN, 1931, based on a book by W.R. Burnett)
SOME BLONDES ARE DANGEROUS   (UN, 1937)
IRON MAN, THE   (UN, 1950)

IRON MASK, THE   see   THREE MUSKETEERS, THE and MASQUE DE FER

IRON MASTER, THE   see   MAITRE DE FORGES, LE

IRON STAIR, THE (American Title: BRANDED SOUL, THE)   (BRI, 1920, based on the book, "Rita," author unlisted)
MY LORD CONCEIT   (BRI, 1921)
POINTING FINGER, THE   (BRI, 1922)
IRON STAIR, THE   (BRI, 1933)
POINTING FINGER, THE   (BRI, 1933)
DARBY AND JOAN   (BRI, 1937)

IRONSIDE   (NBC–TV, 1967, based on a teleplay)
IRONSIDE   (series)   (NBC–TV, 1967)

PRIEST KILLER, THE (NBC–TV, 1971)

IROQUOIS TRAIL, THE see LAST OF THE MOHICANS
and LEATHERSTOCKING

IS ANNA ANDERSON ANASTASIA? see ANASTASIA,
DIE FALSCHE ZARENTOCHTER

IS ZAT SO? (FOX, 1927, based on the play by James Gleason
and Richard Taber)
TWO FISTED (PAR, 1935)

ISADORA, THE BIGGEST DANCER IN THE WORLD (BRI–
TV, 1966, based on the life of the noted dancer)
LOVES OF ISADORA, THE (UN, 1969)

ISLAND OF DR. MOREAU, THE see ISLAND OF TERROR,
THE

ISLAND OF LOST MEN see WHITE WOMAN

ISLAND OF LOST SOULS see ISLAND OF TERROR

ISLAND OF TERROR, THE (BRI, 1913, based on the book,
"The Island of Dr. Moreau," by H.G. Wells)
ISLAND OF LOST SOULS (PAR, 1933)
TERROR IS A MAN (IND, 1959)
ISLAND OF DR. MOREAU, THE (AI, 1977)

ISLE OF DEAD SHIPS see ISLE OF LOST SHIPS

ISLE OF FURY see NARROW CORNER, THE

ISLE OF LIFE, THE (UN, 1916, based on a book by Stephen
French Whitman)
BLONDE SAINT (FN, 1926)

ISLE OF LOST SHIPS, THE (FN, 1923, based on the book,
"Isle of Dead Ships," by Crittenden Marriott)
ISLE OF LOST SHIPS, THE (FN, 1929)

ISLE OF THE DEAD (DEN, 1913, based on a painting,
"Island of the Dead," by Arnold Boecklin)
ISLE OF THE DEAD (RKO, 1945)
LITTLE PHANTASY ON A 19TH CENTURY PAINTING,
A (short) (CAN, 1946)

ISTANBUL see SINGAPORE

IT! see GOLEM, THE

IT AIN'T HAY see PRINCESS O'HARA

IT COMES UP MURDER see VOLPONE

IT CONQUERED THE WORLD (AI, 1956, based on a screen–
play by Lou Rusoff)
ZONTAR, THE THING FROM VENUS (AI, 1966)

IT GROWS ON TREES (UN, 1952, based on a story by Leonard
Praskins and Barney Slater)
IT GROWS ON TREES (NBC–TV, 1955)

IT HAD TO HAPPEN see DANGER SIGNAL

IT HAPPENED IN HOLLYWOOD see STAR IS BORN, A

IT HAPPENED ON FIFTH AVENUE (AA, 1947, based on a
story by Herbert Clyde Lewis and Frederick Stephani)

IT HAPPENED ON FIFTH AVENUE (NBC–TV, 1957)

IT HAPPENED ONE CHRISTMAS see IT'S A WONDERFUL
LIFE

IT HAPPEND ONE NIGHT (COL, 1934, based on the story,
"Night Bus," by Samuel Hopkins Adams; the Universal
film is an uncredited remake)
EVE KNEW HER APPLES (COL, 1945)
RUNAROUND, THE (UN, 1946)
YOU CAN'T RUN AWAY FROM IT (COL, 1956)

IT HAPPENED ONE SUMMER see STATE FAIR

IT PAYS TO ADVERTISE (PAR, 1919, based on a play by
Roi Megrue and Walter Hackett)
IT PAYS TO ADVERTISE (PAR, 1931)

IT STARTED WITH EVE (UN, 1941, based on a story by Hans
Kraly)
IT STARTED WITH EVE (NBC–TV, 1956)
I'D RATHER BE RICH (UN, 1964)
OH, JONATHAN, OH, JONATHAN (GER, 1973)

IT WAS AN EXCITING NIGHT (AUS, 1939, based on the
life of composer Peter Illytch Tchaikovsky)
SONG OF MY HEART (AA, 1947)
LIFE AND LOVES OF TCHAIKOVSKY, THE (GER, 1948)
PETER TCHAIKOVSKY STORY, THE (short) (DIS,
1961)
TCHAIKOVSKY (RUS, 1970)
MUSIC LOVERS, THE (BRI, 1970)

ITALIAN STRAW HAT, THE see CHAPEAU DE PAILLE
D'ITALIE

IT'S A DATE (UN, 1940, based on a story by Jane Hall,
Frederick Kohner and Ralph Block)
NANCY GOES TO RIO (MGM, 1950)

IT'S A DOG'S LIFE see ALMOST HUMAN

IT'S A GIFT see IT'S THE OLD ARMY GAME

IT'S A WONDERFUL LIFE (RKO, 1946, based on a story
by Frank Capra)
IT HAPPENED ONE CHRISTMAS (THE GREATEST
GIFT) (ABC–TV, 1977)

IT'S GREAT TO BE ALIVE see LAST MAN ON EARTH,
THE

IT'S IN THE BAG see TWELVE CHAIRS, THE

IT'S NEVER TOO LATE TO MEND (BRI, 1918, based on
the play by Charles Reade and Arthur Shilley)
IT'S NEVER TOO LATE TO MEND (short) (BRI, 1922)
IT'S NEVER TOO LATE TO MEND (BRI, 1937)

IT'S THE OLD ARMY GAME (PAR, 1926, based on the
play by Joseph McEvoy)
IT'S A GIFT (PAR, 1934)

IT'S YOUR MOVE see HIS MUSICAL CAREER

IVAN THE TERRIBLE (ITA, 1915, based on the life of the
Russian monarch and the opera by Rimsky–Korsakov)
PSKOVITYANKA (RUS, 1915)
WINGS OF THE SERF (RUS, 1926)

CZAR IVAN THE TERRIBLE (RUS, 1928)
IVAN THE TERRIBLE (RUS, 1943)
IVAN THE TERRIBLE II (RUS, 1947)
IVAN THE TERRIBLE (RUS, 1977)

IVANHOE (VIT, 1911, based on the book by Sir Walter
    Scott)
    IVANHOE (BRI, 1912)
    REBECCA THE JEWESS (BRI, 1913)

IVANHOE (MGM, 1952)
IVANHOE (series) (BRI–TV, 1957)
REVENGE OF IVANHOE, THE (ITA, 1964)
IVANHOE (series) (TV, 1971)

IVY (UN, 1947, based on the book, "The Story of Ivy," by
    Marie Belloc Lowndes)
    IVY (NBC–TV, 1956)

JFK: A THOUSAND DAYS . . . AND TEN YEARS see
    MAKING OF THE PRESIDENT – 1960, THE

J'ACCUSE! see AFFAIR DREYFUS, L'

JACK AND THE BEANSTALK (ED, 1902, based on the
    fairy tale)
    JACK AND THE BEANSTALK (LUB, 1903)
    JACK AND THE BEANSTALK (ED, 1904)
    JACK AND THE BEANSTALK (BRI, 1912)
    JACK AND THE BEANSTALK (ED, 1913)
    JACK AND THE BEANSTALK (THA, 1913)
    JACK AND THE BEANSTALK (FOX, 1917)
    JACK AND THE BEANSTALK (UN, 1924)
    JACK AND THE BEANSTALK (short) (PAR, 1931)
    MAGIC BEANS (short) (UN, 1939)
    JASPER AND THE BEANSTALK (short) (PAR, 1945)
    BEANSTALK JACK (short) (FOX, 1946)
    FUN AND FANCY FREE (sequence) (DIS, 1947)
    JACK AND THE BEANSTALK (WB, 1952)
    JACK AND THE BEANSTALK (short) (BRI, 1954)
    JACK AND THE BEANSTALK (NBC–TV, 1956)
    WOODY AND THE BEANSTALK (short) (UN, 1966)
    JACK AND THE BEANSTALK (NBC–TV, 1967)
    JACK AND THE BEANSTALK (JAP, 1976)

JACK FROST see MOROZKO

JACK JOHNSON see FUERZA Y NOBLEZA

JACK LONDON (UA, 1943, based on the life of the noted
    author)
    JACK LONDON: ADVENTURES IN THE GREAT
    NORTH (series) (ITA–TV, 1974)

JACK LONDON: ADVENTURES IN THE GREAT NORTH
    see JACK LONDON

JACK LONDON'S TALES OF THE FISH PATROL (UN,
    1923, based on a story by Jack London)
    HAUNTED SHIP, THE (TIF, 1927)
    STORM WATERS (TIF, 1928)

JACK THE RIPPER see LODGER, THE

JACK THE RIPPER OF LONDON see LODGER, THE

JACKALS, THE see YELLOW SKY

JACK'S RETURN HOME see GET CARTER

JADUI BANSARI see MAGIC FLUTE, THE

JAGD NACH DEM, DIE (GER, 1920, source unlisted)
    JAGD NACH DEM, DIE (GER, 1930)

JAGER VON FALL, DER (GER, 1918, based on a book by
    Ludwig Ganghofer)
    JAGER VON FALL, DER (GER, 1936)
    JAGERVON FALL, DER (GER, 1975)

JAILBREAK (WB, 1936, based on the story, "Murder in Sing
    Sing," by Jonathan Finn)
    SMASHING THE MONEY RING (WB, 1939)
    MURDER IN THE BIG HOUSE (WB, 1942)

J'AIME TOUT LES FEMMES see ICH LIEBE ALLE
    FRAUEN (GER, 1935)

JAKOMAN AND TETSU (JAP, 1949, source unlisted)
    JAKOMAN AND TETSU (JAP, 1964)

JALOUSIE see KREUTZER SONATA, THE

JAMES BOYS, THE (IND, c1908, based on historical events
    and characters)
    JESSE JAMES (IND, 1911)
    JESSE JAMES (PAR, 1927)
    JESSE JAMES (FOX, 1939)
    JESSE JAMES RIDES AGAIN (serial) (REP, 1947)
    ADVENTURES OF FRANK AND JESSE JAMES (serial)
        (REP, 1948)
    JAMES BROTHERS OF MISSOURI, THE (serial) (REP,
        1949)
    GREAT MISSOURI RAID, THE (PAR, 1950)
    TRUE STORY OF JESSE JAMES, THE (FOX, 1957)
    JESSE JAMES (ABC–TV, 1965)
    LEGEND OF JESSE JAMES (series) (ABC–TV, 1975)
    TIME FOR DYING, A (FRA, 1972)
    GREAT NORTHFIELD MINNESOTA RAID, THE (UN,
        1972)

JAMES BROTHERS OF MISSOURI, THE see JAMES BOYS,
    THE

JANE EYRE (ITA, 1909, based on the book by Charlotte
    Bronte; also the basis for the play, "Master of Thornfield,"
    in 1958 and a Canadian musical in 1970)
    JANE EYRE (THA, 1910)
    JANE EYRE (UN, 1914)
    JANE EYRE (BIO, 1915)
    WOMAN AND WIFE (IND, 1918)
    JANE EYRE (HOD, 1921)
    ORPHAN OF LOWOOD (GER, 1926)
    JANE EYRE (MON, 1934)
    I WALKED WITH A ZOMBIE (RKO, 1943)
    JANE EYRE (NBC–TV, 1957)
    JANE EYRE (CBS–TV, 1961)
    JANE EYRE (GRE, 1968)
    JANE EYRE (NBC–TV, 1971)

JANE SHORE (BRI, 1908, based on the play by Nicholas
    Rowe)
    JANE SHORE (BRI, 1911)
    JANE SHORE (BRI, 1915)
    JANE SHORE (short) (BRI, 1922)

JANOSIK (CZE, 1921, based on a historical characeer)
    JANOSIK (CZE, 1935)
    JANOSIK (POL, 1954)
    JANOSIK (CZE, 1962)
    JANOSIK (POL, 1974)

JANUSKOPF, DER see DR. JEKYLL AND MR. HYDE

JANSSON'S TEMPTATION (SWE, 1928, source unlisted)
    JANSSON'S TEMPTATION (SWE, 1936)

JASEI NO IN (JAP, 1920, source unlisted)
    UGETSU (JAP, 1953)

JASON AND THE ARGONAUTS see GIANTS OF
    THESSALY, THE

JAWAHARLAL NEHRU (short) (NBC–TV, 1958, based on
    the life of India's prime minister)
    CONVERSATION WITH JAWAHARLAL NEHRU, A
    (short) (IND, n.d.)

NEHRU ON WORLD RELATIONS (short) (IND, n.d.)
ESSENTIAL NEHRU, THE (short) (NET–TV, 1964)
NEHRU: MAN OF TWO WORLDS (short) (CBS–TV, 1966)
NEHRU (TIM, 1967)
NEHRU'S INDIA (short) (BRI–TV, n.d.)

JAWS OF HELL see CHARGE OF THE LIGHT BRIGADE, THE

JAZZ OF DAVE BRUBECK, THE (short) (CBS–TV, n.d., based on the life and works of the noted jazz pianist)
DAVE BRUBECK (BRI–TV, 1977)

JAZZ SINGER, THE (WB, 1927, based on the play by Samuel Raphaelson)
JAZZ SINGER, THE (WB, 1953)
JAZZ SINGER, THE (NBC–TV, 1959)

JEALOUSY see KREUTZER SONATA, THE

JEALOUSY (PAR, 1929, based on the play by Louis Verneuil)
DECEPTION (WB, 1946)

JEAN DE LA LUNE (FRA, 1931, based on a screenplay by Marcel Achard)
JEAN DE LA LUNE (FRA, 1948)

JEAN VALJEAN see CHEMINEAU, LE

JEANNE DORE (FRA, 1915, based on a book by Georges Bernanos)
JEANNE DORE (ITA, 1939)

JEANNIE (BRI, 1942, based on the play by Aimee Stuart)
LET'S BE HAPPY (BRI, 1956)

JEDE FRAU HAT ETWAS see COME OUT OF THE KIT–CHEN

JEDENACTE PRIKAZANI (THE 11TH COMMANDMENT) (CZE, 1925, based on the play by F.F. Samberk)
JEDENACTE PRIKAZANI (CZE, 1935)

JEDERMANN (GER, 1915, based on the play by Hugo von Hofmannsthal)
JEDERMANN (GER, 1918)
JEDERMANN (AUS, 1961)

JEFFERSON OF MONTICELLO (short) (IND, 1948, based on the life of U.S. President Thomas Jefferson)
THOMAS JEFFERSON (short) (EBE, 1949)
JEFFERSON THE ARCHITECT (short) (IFB, 1949)
THOMAS JEFFERSON (short) (HAN, 1967)
JEFFERSON'S MONTICELLO (NBC–TV, 1970)
1776 (COL, 1972)
THOMAS JEFFERSON'S MONTICELLO (short) (PAR, 1975)

JEKYLL'S INFERNO see DR. JEKYLL AND MR. HYDE

JENNY LIND see LADY'S MORALS, A

JEPHTHAH'S DAUGHTER (VIT, 1909, based on the Bible story)
VOW, THE (KLE, 1910)
JEPHTHAH'S DAUGHER (IND, 1913)
JEPHTHAH'S DAUGHER (CBS–TV, 1966)

JEPPE DU MONT (DEN, 1907, based on a novel by Ludvig Holberg)
JEPPE DU MONT (NOR, 1933)

JERRY see ALICE DOESN'T LIVE HERE ANYMORE

JERUSALEM DELIVERED (ITA, 1911, based on the book by Torquato Tasso)
JERUSALEM DELIVERED (ITA, 1918)
JERUSALEM DELIVERED (ITA, 1957)

JESSE JAMES see JAMES BOYS, THE

JESSE JAMES RIDES AGAIN see JAMES BOYS, THE

JESSICA'S FIRST PRAYER (BRI, 1908, based on the story by Hesba Stretton)
JESSICA'S FIRST PRAYER (BRI, 1922)

JESUS see PASSION PLAY, THE

JESUS CHRIST, SUPERSTAR see PASSION PLAY, THE

JESUS OF NAZARETH see PASSION PLAY, THE

JEUNES TIMIDES, LES see DEUX TIMIDES, LES

JEW SUSS see POWER

JEWELL (UN, 1915, based on a book by Clara Louise Burnham)
CHAPTER IN HER LIFE, A (UN, 1923)

JEZABEL (WB, 1938, based on the play by Owen David Sr.)
JEZABEL (NBC–TV, 1956)

JIGSAW see MIRAGE

JIM LA HOULETTE, ROI DES VOLEURS (FRA, 1926, based on a book by Jean Guitton)
JIM LA HOULETTE, ROI DES VOLEURS (FRA, 1935)

JIM THE PENMAN (PAR, 1915, based on the play by Sir Charles L. Young)
JIM THE PENMAN (FN, 1921)
JIM THE PENMAN (FRA, 1926)
JIM THE PENMAN (BRI, 1947)

JO see GAZEBO, THE

JO, THE CROSSING SWEEPER (BRI, 1910, based on the book, "Bleak House," by Charles Dickens)
JO, THE CROSSING SWEEPER (BRI, 1918)
BLEAK HOUSE (BRI, 1929)
BLEAK HOUSE (short) (BRI, 1922)

JOAN OF ARC (FRA, 1900, based on the life of the saint written by various authors and plays by Shaw and Anderson)
JOAN OF ARC (ITA, 1909)
JOAN OF ARC (FRA, 1909)
JOAN OF ARC (ITA, 1913)
JOAN OF ARC (FRA, 1914)
JOAN THE WOMAN (PAR, 1917)
PASSION OF JOAN OF ARC, THE (FRA, 1927)
SAINT JOAN (short) (BRI, 1927)
JOAN OF ARC (RKO, 1949)
DAUGHTERS OF DESTINY (sequence) (FRA, 1954)
JOAN OF ARC AT THE STAKE (ITA, 1954)
FINAL HOURS OF JOAN OF ARC, THE (short) (CBS–TV, 1955)

TRIAL OF ST. JOAN, THE   (CBS–TV, 1955)
SAINT JOAN   (UA, 1957)
LARK, THE   (NBC–TV, 1957)
TRIAL OF JOAN OF ARC, THE   (FRA, 1962)
SAINT JOAN   (NBC–TV, 1967)
ST. JOAN   (BRI, 1977)

JOAN OF ARC AT THE STAKE   see   JOAN OF ARC

JOAN THURSDAY   see   FOOTLIGHTS OF FATE

JOCELYN   (FRA, 1922, based on a book by Alphonse de
   Lamartine)
   JOCELYN   (FRA, 1933)
   JOCELYN   (FRA, 1951)

JOE FORRESTER   see   RETURN OF JOE FORRESTER,
   THE

JOE LOUIS STORY, THE   see   SPIRIT OF YOUTH

JOE MACBETH   see   MACBETH

JOE PALOOKA STORY, THE   see   PALOOKA

JOE SMITH, AMERICAN   (MGM, 1942, based on a story by
   Paul Gallico)
   BIG OPERATOR, THE   (MGM, 1959)

JOHAN ULFSTJERNA   (SWE, 1923, based on the story by
   T. Hedberg)
   JOHAN ULFSTJERNA   (SWE, 1936)

JOHANES DOKTOR FAUST   see   FAUST

JOHANN SEBASTIAN BACH   (short)   (BRI, 1961)
   CHRONICLE OF ANNA MAGDELENA BACH   (GER,
   1968)

JOHANNISNACHT   (GER, 1933, based on a play by Sir James
   M. Barrie)
   JOHANNISNACHT   (GER, 1956)

JOHN ADAMS   see   DECLARATION OF INDEPENDENCE,
   THE

JOHN F. KENNEDY   see   P. T. 109

JOHN F. KENNEDY   see   MAKING OF THE PRESIDENT –
   1960, THE

JOHN FITZGERALD KENNEDY   see   MAKING OF THE
   PRESIDENT – 1960, THE

JOHN GILPIN   (BRI, 1908, based on the poem by William
   Cowper)
   JOHN GILPIN'S RIDE   (BRI, 1908)

JOHN GILPIN'S RIDE   see   JOHN GILPIN

JOHN GLENN JR.   see   AMERICAN IN ORBIT, AN

JOHN GLENN STORY, THE   see   AMERICAN IN ORBIT,
   AN

JOHN HALIFAX, GENTLEMAN   (BRI, 1915, based on the
   book by Mrs. Craik)
   JOHN HALIFAX, GENTLEMAN   (BRI, 1938)

JOHN J. PERSHING   see   GENERAL PERSHING

JOHN L. LEWIS   (short)   (NBC–TV, 1951, based on the life
   of labor leader John L. Lewis)
   KING COAL   (MGM–TV, 1962)
   JOHN L. LEWIS   (short)   (WOL, 1962)
   JOHN L. LEWIS   (short)   (CBS–TV, 1964)
   JOHN L. LEWIS   (short)   (WOL, 1966)

JOHN MARSHALL   (EBE, 1951, based on the life of Chief
   Justice John Marshall)
   DECISION FOR JUSTICE: JOHN MARSHALL AND THE
   SUPREME COURT   (short)   (IND, 1963)
   JOHN MARSHALL: PROFILES IN COURAGE   (SAU,
   1965)

JOHN PAUL JONES   see   STARS AND STRIPES, THE

JOHN PETER ZENGER   see   STORY THAT COULDN'T BE
   PRINTED, THE

JOHN QUINCY ADAMS   (short)   (EBE, 1951, based on the
   life of the U.S. President)
   JOHN QUINCY ADAMS   (SAU, 1965)

JOHN YANKEE: JOHN ADAMS AND THE BOSTON
   MASSACRE   see   DECLARATION OF INDEPENDENCE,
   THE

JOHNNY ALLEGRO   see   MOST DANGEROUS GAME, THE

JOHNNY APPLESEED   (short)   (COR, 1954, based on an
   American legend)
   MELODY TIME   (sequence)   (DIS, 1948)
   JOHNNY APPLESEED   (RAN, 1972)

JOHNNY BELINDA   (WB, 1948, based on the play by Elmer
   Harris)
   JOHNNY BELINDA   (NBC–TV, 1958)
   JOHNNY BELINDA   (ABC–TV, 1967)
   JOHNNY BELINDA   (CAN–TV, 1977)

JOHNNY DARK   (UN, 1954, based on a screenplay by Franklin
   Coen)
   LIVELY SET, THE   (UN, 1964)

JOHNNY HAMLET   see   HAMLET

JOHNNY MINOTAUR   see   MINOTAUR, THE

JOHNNY NORTH   see   KILLERS, THE

JOHNNY TROUBLE   see   SOMEONE TO REMEMBER

JOLSON STORY, THE   (COL, 1946, based on the life of the
   noted entertainer)
   JOLSON SINGS AGAIN   (COL, 1949)

JOSEPH AND HIS BRETHREN   see   JOSEPH IN EGYPT

JOSEPH AND HIS BROTHERS   see   JOSEPH IN EGYPT

JOSEPH IN EGYPT   (KLE, 1912, based on the Bible stories)
   JOSEPH IN THE LAND OF EGYPT   (THA, 1914)
   JOSEPH AND HIS BRETHREN   (IND, 1915)
   JOSEPH IN THE LAND OF EGYPT   (IDE, 1930)
   JOSEPH IN THE LAND OF EGYPT   (BRI, 1932)
   JOSEPH IN EGYPT   (short)   (BRI, 1952)
   JOSEPH AND HIS BRETHREN   (ISR, 1962)

STORY OF JOSEPH AND HIS BRETHREN, THE (ITA, 1962)
JOSEPH AND HIS BROTHERS (ABC–TV, 1974)

JOSEPH IN THE LAND OF EGYPT see JOSEPH IN EGYPT

JOSEPH SCHMIDT STORY, THE see LIED GEHT UM DIE WELT, EIN

JOSIE AND THE PUSSYCATS (series) (CBS–TV, 1970, based on a teleplay)
JOSIE AND THE PUSSYCATS IN OUTER SPACE (series) (CBS–TV, 1972)

JOUEUR D'ECHECS, LE (FRA, 1927, based on a book by Henry Dupuy–Mazuel)
JOUEUR D'ECHECS, LE (FRA, 1938)

JOUR SE LEVE, LE (FRA, 1939, based on a story by Jacques Viot)
LONG NIGHT, THE (RKO, 1947)

JOURNALS OF LEWIS AND CLARK, THE see LEWIS AND CLARK

JOURNEY (JAP, 1953, source unlisted)
JOURNEY (JAP, 1967)

JOURNEY BACK TO OZ see DOROTHY AND THE SCARE–CROW OF OZ

JOURNEY INTO FEAR (RKO, 1942, based on the book by Eric Ambler)
JOURNEY INTO FEAR (NWP, 1976)

JOURNEY TO THE CENTER OF THE EARTH see VOY–AGE AU CENTRE DE LA TERRE

JOURNEY TO THE LOST CITY see INDIAN TOMB, THE

JOURNEY UNDER THE DESERT see ATLANTIDE, L'

JOURNEY'S END (TIF, 1930, based on a play by R.C. Sheriff)
ANDERE SEITE, DIE (GER, 1931)
ACES HIGH (BRI, 1976)

JOURS HEUREUX, LES (FRA, 1941, based on the book by Claude–Andre Puget)
HELD MEINER TRAUME, DER (GER, 1960)

JOYEUSE D'ORGUE, LA (FRA, 1925, based on a book by Xavier de Montepin)
JOYEUSE D'ORGUE, LA (FRA, 1936)

JOYLESS STREET, THE (GER, 1925, based on a book by Hugo Bettauer)
RUE SANS JOIE, LA (FRA, 1938)

JUANITA (FRA, 1935, based on a story by Alfred Rode)
GYPSY MELODY (BRI, 1936)

JUBAL see OTHELLO

JUDEMENT DE MINUIT, LE see RINGER, THE

JUDEX (serial) (FRA, 1916, based on material by Arthur Bernede and Louis Feuillade)
NEW MISSION OF JUDEX (serial) (FRA, 1917)

JUDEX (FRA, 1933)
JUDEX (FRA/ITA, 1963)

JUDGE AND HIS HANGMAN, THE (NBC--TV, 1956, based on the book by Friedrich Duerrenmatt)
END OF THE GAME (FOX, 1976)

JUDGE PRIEST (FOX, 1934, based on a story by Irwin S. Cobb)
SUN SHINES BRIGHT, THE (REP, 1953)

JUDGMENT AT NUREMBERG see TRIAL AT NUREMBERG

JUDGMENT: THE TRIAL OF JULIUS AND ETHEL ROSEN–BERG (ABC–TV, 1974, based on a historical incident)
UNQUIET DEATH OF ETHEL AND JULIUS ROSEN–BERG, THE (IND, 1974)
ROSENBERGS MUST NOT DIE, THE (FRA–TV, 1975)

JUDIN, DIE (GER, 1912, based on the novel, "Die Judin von Toledo," by Franz Grillparzer)
JUDIN, DIE (AUS, 1919)

JUDITH see JUDITH AND HOLOFERNES

JUDITH AND HOLOFERNES (ITA, 1908, based on the poem by Thomas Bailey Aldrich and a story in the Apocrypha)
JUDITH OF BETHULIA (GRI, 1913)
HER CONDONED SIN (GRI, 1917)
JUDITH AND HOLOFERNES (ITA, 1928)
HEAD OF A TYRANT (ITA, 1960)
JUDITH (short) (CBS–TV, 1960)

JUDITH OF BETHULIA see JUDITH AND HOLOFERNES

JUDO SAGA (JAP, 1945, source unlisted)
JUDO SAGA (JAP, 1965)

JUGEND (GER, 1920, based on a story by Joseph Conrad)
JUGEND (GER, 1938)

JUGEND (GER, 1920, based on a book by Max Halbe)
JUGEND (GER, 1922)
JUGEND (GER, 1938)

JUGEND (GER, 1929, based on the book, "Der Kampf der Tertia," by Wilhelm Speyer)
KAMPF DER TERTIA, DER (GER, 1952)

JUGENDRAUSCH see CIGALE ET LA FOURMI, LA

JUIF POLONAIS, LE see BELLS, THE

JUKA (FIN, 1935, source unlisted)
JUKA (FIN, 1950)

JULES VERNE'S MYSTERIOUS ISLAND see MYSTERIOUS ISLAND

JULIA, DU BIST ZAUBERHAFT (GER, 1961, based on a book by W. Somerset Maugham)
ADORABLE JULIA (FRA, 1964)

JULIUS CAESAR (FRA, 1907, based on the play by William Shakespeare)
SHAKESPEARE WRITING JULIUS CAESAR (FRA, 1907)
JULIUS CAESAR (LUB, 1908)
JULIUS CAESAR (VIT, 1908)

BRUTUS (ITA, 1909)
JULIUS CAESAR (BRI, 1911)
CAIUS JULIUS CAESAR (ITA, 1914)
JULIUS CAESAR (BRI, 1914)
JULIUS CAESAR (ITA, 1918)
JULIUS CAESAR (KLE, 1922)
JULIUS CAESAR (BRI, 1926)
JULIUS CAESAR (short) (BRI, 1945)
JULIUS CAESAR (IND, 1949)
JULIUS CAESAR (short) (BRI, 1951)
JULIUS CAESAR (MGM, 1953)
JULIUS CAESAR (short) (BRI, 1953)
JULIUS CAESAR (CBS–TV, 1955)
JULIUS CAESAR (BRI–TV, 1959)
HONORABLE MURDER, AN (BRI, 1960)
JULIUS CAESAR (CAN–TV, 1960)
JULIUS CAESAR (BRI–TV, 1962)
JULIUS CAESAR (BRI–TV, 1965)
HONORABLE MENTION, AN (CAN, 1969)
JULIUS CAESAR (BRI, 1969)
JULUS CAESAR (CAN–TV, 1970)

JUMPING FROG (IND, 1922, based on the story, "The Cele-
brated Jumping Frog of Calaveras County," by Mark
Twain)
BEST MAN WINS, THE (COL, 1948)
CELEBRATED JUMPING FROG (TV, 1951)

JUNE MOON (PAR, 1931, based on the play by Ring Lardner
and George S. Kaufman)
BLONDE TROUBLE, (PAR, 1937)

JUNGE BARON NEHAUS, DER (GER, 1934, based on a
screenplay by Gustav Ucicky)
NUIT DE MAI (FRA, 1934)

JUNGFRAU AUF DEM DACH, DIE see MOON IS BLUE,
THE

JUNGLE BOOK (UA, 1942, based on the books by Rudyard
Kipling)
JUNGLE BOOK (DIS, 1967)

MOWGLI'S BROTHERS (CBS–TV, 1976)

JUNGLE DRUMS OF AFRICA (serial) (REP, 1953, based on
a screenplay by various authors; the remake is a consensed
verion of the serial)
U–238 AND THE WITCH DOCTOR (REP, 1966)

JUNGLE GODDESS (serial) (IND, 1922, based on a screenplay by Frank Dazey and Agnes Johnson)
QUEEN OF THE JUNGLE (IND, 1935)

JUNGLE GOLD see TIGER WOMAN, THE

JUNGLE WOMAN see BIG CAGE, THE

JUNIOR MISS (FOX, 1945, based on stories by Sally Benson
and the play by Jerome Chorodov and Joseph Fields)
JUNIOR MISS (CBS–TV, 1957)

JUNO AND THE PAYCOCK (American Title: SHAME OF
MARY BOYLE, THE) (BRI, 1929, based on the play by
Sean O'Casey)
MONEY TREE, THE (CHN, 1937)
JUNO AND THE PAYCOCK (ABC–TV, 1960)
JUNO AND THE PAYCOCK (NET–TV, 1960)

JUPITER SMITTEN (n.d., 1910, based on a legend)

AMPHITRYON (FRA, 1937)
AMPHITRYON (GER, 1937)

JURIER DES ZAREN, DER see MICHAEL STROGOFF

JUST AN OLD SWEET SONG (CBS–TV, 1977, based on a
teleplay)
DOWN HOME (pilot) (CBS–TV, 1978)

JUSTINE AND JULIETTE see VICE AND VIRTUE

JUSTINE AND THE MISFORTUNES OF VIRTUE see VICE
AND VIRTUE

JUWELEN see FRAULEIN VON SCUDERI, DAS

KABALE UND LIEBE (GER, 1907, based on the play by
     Friedrich Schiller)
  LOUISA MILLER (FRA, 1911)
  ASCHERMITTWOCH (GER, 1920)
  TOCHTER DES ORGANISTEN, DIE (GER, 1921)
  LUISE MILLERIN (GER, 1922)
  ASCHERMITTWOCH (GER, 1925)
  ASCHERMITTWOCH (GER, 1930)
  KABALE UND LIEBE (GER, 1959)

KACHTANKA (RUS, 1926, based on the story by Anton
     Chekhov)
  KACHTANKA (RUS, 1952)

KAHU AND TSUNE (JAP, n.d., based on the book, "Jinsei
     Gekijo Zankyo–hen," by Shiro Ozaki)
  KAHU AND TSUNE (JAP, 1968)

KAIDAN KASANE--GA-FUCHI (JAP, 1957, source unlisted)
  KAIDAN KASANE–GA–FUCHI (JAP, 1960)
  KAIDAN KASANE--GA–FUCHI (JAP, 1970)

KAISERWALZER (GER, 1932, source unlisted)
  KAISERWALZER (GER, 1953)

KALIA MARDAN (IN, 1919, source unlisted)
  KALIA MARDAN (IN, 1934)

KALTE HERZ, DAS (GER, 1923, based on a story by Wil–
     helm Hauff)
  KALTE HERZ, DAS (GER, 1950)

KAMERADEN (GER, 1917, based on a play by August
     Strindberg)
  KAMERADEN (GER, 1919)
  KAMERADEN (GER, 1935)
  ALLES UM EINE FRAU (GER, 1941)

KAMPF DER TERTIA, DER see JUGEND

KARAMAZOV see BROTHERS KARAMAZOV, THE

KAREN see 90 BRISTOL COURT

KARL UND ANNA see HEIMKEHR

KARLEKEN SEGRAR (SWE, 1916, source unlisted)
  KARLEKEN SEGRAR (SWE, 1949)

KARRIERE IN PARIS see PERE GORIOT, LE

KARUSSEL DES LEBENS (GER, 1919, source unlisted)
  KARUSSEL DES KEBENS (GER, 1923)

KATE PLUS TEN (BRI, 1938, based on the book by Edgar
     Wallace)
  REIGN OF TERROR (BRI, 1967)

KATERINA IZMAILOVA (RUS, 1927, based on the book,
     "Lady Macbeth from Minsk," by Nikolai Lieskov and the
     opera by Dmitri Shostakovich)
  SIBERIAN LADY MACBETH (YUG, 1961)
  KATERINA IZMAILOVA (RUS, 1966)

KATHARINE KNIE (GER, 1929, based on the play by
     Carl Zuckmayer)
  MENSCHEN, DIE VORUBERZIEHEN (SWI, 1942)

KATHLEEN MAVOURNEEN (IND, 1911, based on the play

by Dion Boucicault)
  KATHLEEN MAVOURNEEN (ED, 1913)
  KATHLEEN MAVOURNEEN (FOX, 1919)
  KATHLEEN VAVOURNEEN (TIF, 1920)
  KATHLEEN MAVOURNEEN (BRI, 1937)

KATIA (KATJA) (FRA, 1938, based on the book by Princess
     Bibesco)
  KATIA (THE MAGNIFICENT SINNER) (FRA, 1960)

KATIOUCHA see RESURRECTION

KATIOUCHA MASLOVA see RESURRECTION

KATJA see KATIA

KATZENSTEG, DER (GER, 1915, based on the book by
     Herrmann Sudermann)
  KATZENSTEG, DER (GER, 1927)
  KATZENSTEG, DER (GER, 1937)

KAUFMANN VON VENEDIT, DER see MERCHANT OF
     VENICE, THE

KEAN (DEN, 1910, based on the book by Alexandre Dumas
     [pere])
  KEAN (ITA, 1916)
  LEICHTSINN UND GENIE (GER, 1918)
  KEAN (GER, 1921)
  KEAN (IND, 1922)
  KEAN (FRA, 1923)
  MANN, DER NICHT LIEBT, L'ETERNELLE IDOLE, DER
     (FRA/GER, 1929)
  KEAN (ITA, 1940)
  KEAN (ITA, 1956)

KEEP YOUR SEATS PLEASE see TWELVE CHAIRS, THE

KEEPER OF THE BEES (FBO, 1925, based on the book by
     Gene Stratton Porter)
  KEEPER OF THE BESS (MON, 1935)
  KEEPER OF THE BEES (COL, 1947)

KEEPER OF THE FLAME (MGM, 1942, based on a screenplay
     by Donald Ogden Stewart)
  SENATOR'S DAUGHTER, THE (TV, n.d.)

KEIN ENGEL IST SO REIN (GER, 1950, based on a screenplay
     by Hans Wilhelm)
  KEIN ENGEL IST SO REIN (GER, 1960)

KELLY GANG, THE (AUT, 1910, based on a historical inci–
     dent and characters; also appeared as an Australian rock
     musical in 1978)
  KELLY GANG, THE (AUT, 1917)
  KELLY GANG, THE (AUT, 1920)
  NED KELLY (BRI, 1970)

KENNEDY: THE MAN AND THE PRESIDENT see MAKING
     OF THE PRESIDENT -- 1960, THE

KENNEL MURDER CASE, THE (WB, 1933, based on the book
     by S.S. van Dine)
  CALLING PHILO VANCE (WB, 1940)

KEY LARGO (WB, 1948, based on the play by Maxwell
     Anderson)
  KEY LARGO (NBC–TV, 1956)

KEYHOLE, THE see DESERT BRIDE, THE

KHADJI MOURAT, THE WHITE DEVIL see WEISSE
    TEUFEL, DER

KHUN–E–NAHAK see HAMLET

KICK IN (PAR, 1922, based on the play by Willard Mack)
    KICK IN (PAR, 1931)

KID FROM BROOKLYN, THE see MILKY WAY, THE

KID GALAHAD (WB, 1937, based on a book by Frances
    Wallace)
    (TV TITLE: BATTLING BELLHOP, THE)
    WAGONS ROLL AT NIGHT, THE (WB, 1941)
    KID GALAHAD (UA, 1962)

KIDNAPPED (ED, 1917, based on the book by Robert Louis
    Stevenson; also the basis for the musical comedy, "The
    Silver Button," in 1969)
    KIDNAPPED (FOX, 1938)
    KIDNAPPED (MON, 1948)
    KIDNAPPED (NBC–TV, 1954)
    KIDNAPPED (DIS, 1959)
    ACHSUUSE UNTERM GALGEN (GER, 1969) (E. Ger.)
    DAVID AND CATRIONA (BRI, 1971)
    KIDNAPPED (BRI, 1971)
    KIDNAPPED (HB, 1973)

KIKI (FN, 1926, based on a play by Andre Picard and David
    Belasco)
    KIKI (UA, 1931)

KILL ME IF YOU CAN see CELL 2455 -- DEATH ROW

KILL OR BE KILLED see MOST DANGEROUS GAME,
    THE

KILLER, THE (PAR, 1921, based on the book by Stewart
    Edward White)
    MYSTERY RANCH (FOX, 1932)

KILLER McCOY see CROWD ROARS, THE

KILLERS, THE (UN, 1946, based on a story by Ernest Hem--
    ingway)
    KILLERS, THE (TV, 1959)
    KILLERS, THE (UN, 1964)

KIM (MGM, 1950, based on the book by Rudyard Kipling)
    KIM (NBC–TV, 1960)

KIND LADY (MGM, 1935, based on the play by Edward
    Chodorov and a story by Hugh Walpole)
    KIND LADY (MGM, 1951)
    KIND LADY (NET--TV, 1953)

KIND SIR see INDISCREET

KING: A FILMED RECORD, MONTGOMERY TO MEMPHIS
    see MARTIN LUTHER KING

KING AND I, THE see ANNA AND THE KING OF SIAM

KING COAL see JOHN L. LEWIS

KING IN SHADOW see DICTATOR, THE

KING IS DEAD, LONG LIVE THE QUEEN, THE (short)
    (WB, 1952, based on the life of the Queen of England)
    LIFE OF ELIZABETH (short) (PAT, 1953)
    ROYAL FAMILY, THE (short) (WB, n.d.)
    QUEEN ELIZABETH II (short) (WB, n.d.)
    ROYAL DESTINY (short) (BRI, n.d.)
    CORONATION CEREMONY (short) BRI, 1953)
    CORONATION OF QUEEN LIEZABETH OF ENGLAND
    (short) (WB, 1953)
    BRITAIN CROWNS A QUEEN (short) (PAT, 1953)
    QUEEN ELIZABETH II (short) (WOL, 1962)

KING KONG (RKO, 1933, based on an idea by Willis H.
    O'Brien)
    SON OF KONG (RKO, 1933)
    KING KONG SHOW, THE (series) (ABC–TV, 1966)
    KING KONG (PAR, 1976)

KING KONG SHOW, THE see KING KONG

KING LEAR (VIT, 1909, based on the play by William
    Shakespeare)
    KING LEAR (PAT, n.d.)
    KING LEAR (ITA, 1910)
    KING LEAR (ITA, 1910)
    KING LEAR (PAT, 1916)
    KING LEAR (THA, 1916)
    YIDDISH KING LEAR, THE (IND, 1935)
    FURIES, THE (PAR, 1950)
    KING LEAR (CBS--TV, 1953)
    KING LEAR (BRI, 1969)
    KING LEAR (RUS, 1970)

KING MIDAS (POL, n.d., based on a fairy tale)
    GOLDEN TOUCH, THE (short) (DIS, 1935)
    KING MIDAS AND THE GOLDEN TOUCH (short)
    (COR, 1949)
    STORY OF KING MIDAS, THE (short) (BFA, 1953)
    KING MIDAS (NBC–TV, 1961)
    TALE OF KING MIDAS, THE (short) (EBE, 1974)

KING MIDAS AND THE GOLDEN TOUCH see KING MIDAS

KING OEDIPUS see OPEDIPUS REX

KING OF BURLESQUE (FOX, 1935, based on a story by
    Vina Delmar; remake uncredited)
    HELLO, FRISCO, HELLO (FOX, 1943)

KING OF CHESS (JAP, 1948, source unlisted)
    KING OF CHESS (JAP, 1962)

KING OF KINGS see PASSION PLAY, THE

KING OF LIFE, THE see PICTURE OF DORIAN GRAY

KING OF THE KHYBER RIFLES see BLACK WATCH

KING OF THE LUMBERJACKS see TIGER SHARK

KING OF THE MONGOLS see GENGHIS KHAN

KING OF THE ROCKET MEN (serial) (REP, 1949, based on
    a screenplay by various authors; the remake is an abridged
    version of the serial)
    LOST PLANET AIRMEN (REP, 1966)

KING OF THE UNDERWORLD see DR. SOCRATES

KING ON MAIN STREET, THE (PAR, 1925, based on a story
    by Robert de Flers, Gaston Arman de Caillavet and
    Emmanuel Arene)
  ROI, LE (FRA, 1936)
  ROI, LE (FRA, 1949)

KING RICHARD AND THE CRUSADERS see RICHARD,
    THE LION-HEARTED

KING RICHARD II see RICHARD II

KING RICHARD III see RICHARD III

KING SOLOMON'S MINES (BRI, 1937, based on the book by
    H. Rider Haggard)
  KING SOLOMON'S MINES (MGM, 1950)
  WATUSI (MGM, 1959)

KING STEPS OUT, THE (COL, 1936, based on a story by
    Gustav Holm, Ernest and Hubert Mauscha and Ernest
    Decsey)
  CISSY (GER, c1955)

KINGDOM OF RAM, THE see SATI VIJAY

KING'S DAUGHTER, THE (BRI, 1917, based on the book
    by Alexandre Dumas and the opera by Gaetano Donizetti)
  REGIMENTSTOCHTER, DIE (GER, 1928)
  TOCHTER DES REGIMENTS, DIE (GER, 1933)
  REGIMENTSTOCHTER, DIE (GER, 1942)
  HIJA DEL REGIMENTO, LA (MEX, 1944)
  DAUGHTER OF THE REGIMENT (short) (PNX, 1973)

KING'S PIRATE, THE see AGAINST ALL FLAGS

KING'S ROW (WB, 1941, based on the book by Henry
    Belemann)
  KINGS ROW (series) (ABC--TV, 1955)

KING'S WALTZ, THE (GER, 1935, source unlisted)
  KING'S WALTZ, THE (GER, 1955)

KINGSTON: CONFIDENTIAL (NBC--TV, 1976, based on a
    teleplay)
  KINGSTON: CONFIDENTIAL (series) (NBC--TV, 1977)

KIPPS (BRI, 1920, based on the book by H.G. Wells)
  KIPPS (BRI, 1941)
  HALF A SIXPENCE (PAR, 1968)

KISMET (BRI, 1914, based on the play by Edward Knoblock;
    also the basis for the musical "Timbucktu," in 1978)
  KISMET (FRA, 1919)
  KISMET (RC, 1920)
  KISMET (FN, 1930)
  KISMET (GER, 1930)
  KISMET (TV Titles: ORIENTAL DREAM and HAREM
    DREAM) (MGM, 1944)
  KISMET (MGM, 1955)
  KISMET (ABC--TV, 1967)

KISS AND TELL (COL, 1945, based on the play by F. Hugh
    Herbert)
  KISS FOR CORLISS, A (TV Title: ALMOST A BRIDE)
    (UA, 1949)
  KISS AND TELL (CBS--TV, 1951)
  MEET CORLISS ARCHER (series) (CBS--TV, 1954)
  KISS AND TELL (NBC--TV, 1956)

KISS BEFORE THE MIRROR, A (UN, 1933, based on a
    play by Ladislas Fodor)
  WIVES UNDER SUSPICION (UN, 1938)

KISS FOR CORLISS, A see KISS AND TELL

KISS IN THE DARK, A (PAR, 1925, based on the play,
    "Aren't We All?," by Frederick Lonsdale)
  AREN'T WE ALL? (BRI, 1932)

KISS ME AGAIN see DIVORCONS and MADEMOISELLE
    MODISTE

KISS ME KATE see TAMING OF THE SHREW

KISS OF DEATH (FOX, 1947, based on a story by Eleazar
    Lipsky)
  FIEND WHO WALKED THE WEST, THE (FOX, 1958)

KISSES FOR BREAKFAST see MATRIMONIAL BED, THE

KISSING CUP'S RACE (BRI, 1920, based on the poem by
    Campbell Rae Brown)
  KISSING CUP'S RACE (BRI, 1930)

KIT CARSON (BIO, 1903, based on a legend, "Davy Crockett,
    Indian Scout" contains stock footage from the 1940
    version)
  KIT CARSON (PAR, 1928)
  KIT CARSON (UA, 1940)
  DAVY CROCKETT, INDIAN SCOUT (UA, 1950)
  ADVENTURES OF KIT CARSON, THE (series) (TV,
    1952)
  FRONTIER UPRISING (UA, 1961)

KITTY FOYLE (RKO, 1940, based on the book by Christopher
    Morley)
  KITTY FOYLE (NBC--TV, 1950)
  KITTY FOYLE (ABC--TV, 1954)
  KITTY FOYLE (CBS--TV, 1955)
  KITTY FOYLE (series) (NBC--TV, 1958)

KIZINO KIZI (JAP, 1964, the second is a re--edited version of
    the first with English dubbing by Woody Allen)
  WHAT'S UP, TIGER LILY? (AI, 1966)

KLARA MILITCH (RUS, 1915, based on the book by Ivan
    Turgenev)
  AFTER DEATH (RUS, 1915)

KLEIDER MACHEN LEUTE (GER, 1922, based on the book
    by Gottfried Keller)
  KLEIDER MACHEN LEUTE (GER, 1940)

KLEINE GRENZVERKEHR, DER (GER, 1943, based on the
    novel, "Georg und die Zwischenfalle," by Erich Kastner)
  SALZBURGER G'SCHICHTEN (GER, 1956)

KLEINE HERZOG, DER (GER, 1924, source unlisted)
  SARAJEVO (GER, 1955)

KLEINE MUTTER (GER, n.d., based on a story by Felix
    Jackson)
  BACHELOR MOTHER (RKO, 1939)
  BUNDLE OF JOY (RKO, 1956)

KLEINER MANN, GANZ GROSS (GER, 1938, source unlisted)
  KLEINER MANN, GANZ GROSS (GER, 1957)

KLEINER MANN – WAS NUN? (GER, 1933, based on a book by Hans Fallada)
   LITTLE MAN, WHAT NOW? (UN, 1934)

KLETTERMAXE (GER, 1926, based on the book by Hans Possendorf)
   KLETTERMAXE (GER, 1952)

KLONDIKE (MON, 1932, based on a story by Tristram Tupper)
   KLONDIKE FURY (MON, 1942)

KLONDIKE FURY see KLONDIKE

KLOSTER BEI SENDOMIR, DAS (GER, 1919, based on a novel by Franz Grillparzer)
   KLOSTER BEI SENDOMIR, DAS (SWE, 1919)
   KLOSTER BEI SENDOMIR, DAS (AUS, 1922)

KLOSTERJAEGER, DER (GER, 1935, based on the book by Ludwig Ganghofer)
   KLOSTERJAEGER, DER (GER, 1953)

KNICKERBOKER HOLIDAY (UA, 1944, based on the play by Maxwell Anderson and Kurt Weill)
   KNICKERBOKER HOLIDAY (ABC–TV, 1950)

KNIGHT OF THE QUEEN see THREE MUSKETEERS, THE

KNIGHT'S GAMBIT see TOMORROW

KNIGHTS OF THE ROUND TABLE (MGM, 1954, based on the book, "Le Morte d'Arthur," by Sir Thomas Malory)
   LANCELOT AND GUINEVERE (SWORD OF LANCELOT) (UN, 1963)

KNOCK (FRA, 1925, based on the play, "Dr. Knock," by Jules Romains)
   KNOCK (FRA, 1933)
   KNOCK (FRA, 1950)
   I . . . THE DOCTOR (EGY, 1968)

KNUTE ROCKNE, ALL–AMERICAN see SPIRIT OF NOTRE DAME

KNUTE ROCKNE – THE MAN AND THE LEGEND see SPIRIT OF NOTRE DAME

KOENIGSMARK (FRA, 1923, source unlisted)
   KOENIGSMARK (FRA, 1935)
   KOENIGSMARK (FRA, 1952)
   KOENIGSMARK (FRA–TV, 1968)

KOHLHEISEL'S DAUGHERS (GER, 1920, source unlisted)
   KOHLHEISEL'S DAUGHTERS (American Title: GRETEL AND LIESEL) (GER, 1930)
   KOHLHEISELS' DAUGHTERS (GER, 1943)
   KOHLHEISEL'S DAUGHTERS (GER, 1962)

KOLCHAK: THE NIGHT STALKER (ABC–TV, 1974, based on a teleplay)
   NIGHT STALKER, THE (series) (ABC–TV, 1974)

KOMET, DER see MY LIPS BETRAY

KOMM' ZU MIR ZUM RENDEZ–VOUS see AMOUR CHANTE, L'

KOMODIANTEN (GER, 1924, based on the book by Olly Boeheim)
   KOMODIANTEN (GER, 1941)

KONGO see WEST OF ZANZIBAR

KONGRESS TANZT, DER see CONGRESS DANCES

KONIG DER BERNINA DER see ETERNAL LOVE

KONIG VON PARIS, DER see ROI DE PARIS, LE

KONIGIN LUISE see LUISE, KONIGIN VON PREUSSEN

KONIGSLOGE, DIE see QUEEN OF THE NIGHTCLUBS

KONZERT, DAS see CONCERT, THE

KORKARLEN see PHANTOM CARRIAGE, THE

KRACH IM HINTERHAUS (GER, 1935, source unlisted)
   KRACH IM HINTERHAUS (GER, 1949)

KRACH UM JOLANTHE (GER, 1934, based on the play by August Hinrichs)
   KRACH UM JOLANTHE (GER, 1955)

KRAMBAMBULI (AUS/GER, 1940, based on the book by Marie von Ebner--Eschenbach)
   HEIMATLAND (AUS, 1955)
   WAS GESCHAH AUF SCHLOSS WILDBERG (GER, 1972)

KREUTZER SONATA, THE (RUS, 1911, based on the book by Leo Tolstoy)
   KREUTZER SONATA, THE (RUS, 1914)
   KREUTZER SONATA, THE (FOX, 1915)
   KREUTZERSONATE, DIE (GER, 1922)
   KREUTZER SONATA, THE (CZE, 1926)
   KREUTZER SONANTA, THE (RUS, 1928)
   KREUTZERSONATE, DIE (GER, 1937)
   NUITS BLANCHES DE SAINT–PETERSBOURG, LES (FRA, 1938)
   JALOUSIE (ARG, 1946)
   LOVERS WITHOUT LOVE (ITA, 1947)

KREUTZERSONATE, DIE see KREUTZER SONATA, THE

KRIEMHILD'S REVENGE see SIEGFRIED

KRISHNA LEELA (IN, 1935, based on a myth)
   KRISHNA LEELA (IN, 1945)

KRISHNA NARADI (IN, 1926, based on a myth)
   KRISHNA NARADI (IN, 1936)

KRISHNA SATYABHAMA (IN, 1921, based on a myth)
   KRISHNA SATYABHAMA (IN, 1951)

LA BOHEME see BOHEME, LA

LAB KUSH see SATI VIJAY

LACHE BAJAZZO see PAILLASSE

LAD AND THE LION, THE (SEL, 1917, based on the book
     by Edgar Rice Burroughs)
  LION MAN, THE (IND, 1936)

LADDIE (FBO, 1926, based on the book by Gene Stratton
     Porter)
  LADDIE (RKO, 1935)
  LADDIE (RKO, 1940)

LADIES IN RETIREMENT (COL, 1941, based on the play
     by Reginald Denham and Edward Percy)
  LADIES IN RETIREMENT (NBC--TV, 1951)
  LADIES IN RETIREMENT (NBC–TV, 1954)
  MAD ROOM, THE (COL, 1969)
  LADIES IN RETIREMENT (CAN--TV, 1978)

LAIDES OF LEISURE (COL, 1930, based on the play, "Ladies
     of the Evening," by David Belasco)
  WOMEN OF GLAMOUR (COL, 1937)

LADIES OF THE BIG HOUSE (PAR, 1931, based on the
     play by Ernst Booth)
  WOMEN WITHOUT NAMES (PAR, 1940)

LADIES OF THE EVENING see LADIES OF LEISURE

LADIES OF THE JURY (RKO, 1932, based on the play by
     John Frederick Ballard)
  WE'RE ON THE JURY (RKO, 1937)

LADIES OF THE MOB (PAR, 1928, based on the story by
     Ernst Booth)
  CITY STREETS (PAR, 1931)

LADRON DE AMOR see LOVE GAMBLER, THE

LADRONES see NIGHT OWLS

LADY, THE (FN, 1925, based on the play by Martin Brown)
  SECRET OF MADAME BLANCHE, THE (MGM, 1933)

LADY AND DEATH, THE see SUICIDE CLUB, THE

LADY AND GENT (PAR, 1932, based on a story by Grover
     Jones and William Slavens McNutt)
  UNMARRIED (PAR, 1939)

LADY AND THE BANDIT see DICK TURPIN

LADY AND THE MONSTER, THE (REP, 1944, based on the
     book, "Donovan's Brain," by Curt Siodmak)
  DONOVAN'S BRAIN (UA, 1953)
  DONOVAN'S BRAIN (CBS–TV, 1955)
  VENGEANCE (TV Title: BRAIN, THE) (BRI, 1962)

LADY AUDLEY'S SECRET (BRI, 1906, based on the play
     by Dorothy Braddon)
  LADY AUDLEY'S SECRET (BRI, 1920)

LADY BE CAREFUL see FLEET'S IN, THE

LADY BE GOOD (FN, 1928, based on the musical by George
     Gershwin, Guy Bolton and Fred Thompson)

LADY BE GOOD (MGM, 1941)

LADY CAROLINE LAMB see PRINCE OF LOVERS, THE

LADY CHATTERLEY'S LOVER (FRA, 1959, based on the
     book by D.H. Lawrence)
  YOUNG LADY CHATTERLEY (IND, 1977)

LADY CLARE (BRI, 1913, based on the poem by Alfred,
     Lord Tennyson)
  LADY CLARE (BRI, 1919)

LADY DANCES, THE see MERRY WIDOW, THE

LADY EVE, THE (PAR, 1941, based on a screenplay by Preston
     Sturges)
  BIRDS AND THE BEES, THE (PAR, 1956)

LADY FOR A DAY (COL, 1933, based on the story, "Madame
     La Gimp," by Damon Runyon)
  POCKETFUL OF MIRACLES (UA, 1961)

LADY FRANKENSTEIN see FRANKENSTEIN

LADY FROM LONGACRE, THE (FOX, 1922, based on a
     story by Victor Bridges)
  GREATER THAN A CROWN (FOX, 1925)

LADY GAMBLES, THE (UN, 1949, based on a story by Lewis
     Meltzer and Oscar Saul)
  LADY GAMBLES, THE (NBC–TV, 1955)

LADY HAMILTON see ROMANCE OF LADY HAMILTON,
     THE

LADY IN ERMINE, THE (FN, 1927, based on the operetta by
     Rudolph Schanzer and Ernst Welisch)
  BRIDE OF THE REGIMENT (FN, 1930)
  THAT LADY IN ERMINE (FOX, 1948)

LADY IN QUESTION, THE see HEART OF PARIS

LADY IN THE DARK (PAR, 1944, based on the musical
     comedy by Moss Hart and Kurt Weill)
  LADY IN THE DARK (NBC–TV, 1954)

LADY IN THE IRON MASK, THE see MAN IN THE IRON
     MASK, THE

LADY JANE GREY (BRI, 1923, based on the life of Lady Jane
     Grey)
  NINE DAYS A QUEEN (TUDOR ROSE) (BRI, 1936)
  LAST DAY OF AN ENGLISH QUEEN, THE (short)
     (CBS--TV, 1956)

LADY LIES, THE (PAR, 1929, based on the play by John
     Meehan)
  DONA MENTIRAS (SPA, 1930)
  UNE FEMME A MENTI (FRA, 1930)

LADY MACBETH FROM MINSK see KATERINA IZMAIL--
     OVA

LADY OF SHALOTT (BRI, 1912, based on the poem by
     Alfred, Lord Tennyson)
  LADY OF SHALOTT (VIT, 1915)

LADY OF THE CAMELIAS, THE see DAME AUX CAMI-
     LIAS, LA

LADY OF THE LAKE (VIT, 1912, based on the peem by Sir Walter Scott)
  LADY OF THE LAKE (BRI, 1928)

LADY OR THE TIGER, THE (short) (MGM, 1942, based on the story by Frank Stockton)
  LADY OR THE TIGER, THE (short) (TV, 1949)
  LADY OR THE TIGER, THE (TV, 1951)

LADY TO LOVE, A see SECRET HOUR, THE

LADY WHO DARES, THE (FN, 1931, based on the story, "The Devil's Playground," by Robert Hichens)
  DAMA ATREVIDA, LA (SPA, 1931)

LADY WINDERMERE'S FACHER see LADY WINDER-MERE'S FAN

LADY WINDERMERE'S FAN (RUS, 1913, based on the play by Oscar Wilde; also the basis for the musical, "After the Ball," in 1953)
  LADY WINDERMERE'S FAN (BRI, 1916)
  LADY WINDERMERE'S FAN (TRI, 1919)
  LADY WINDERMERE'S FAN (WB, 1925)
  LADY WINDERMERE'S FAN (GER 1935)
  LADY WINDERMERE'S FAN (MEX, 1944)
  STORY OF A WICKED WOMAN (ARG, 1948)
  FAN, THE (FOX, 1949)
  LADY WINDERMERE'S FAN (BRI–TV, 1967)
  LADY WINDERMERE'S FAN (BRI–TV, 1972)

LADY WITH THE LAMP see FLORENCE NIGHTINGALE

LADY'S MORALS, A (MGM, 1930, based on the life of singer Jenny Lind)
  JENNY LIND (FRA, 1930)
  P.T. BARNUM PRESENTS JENNY LIND (short) (CBS–TV, 1955)
  LEGEND OF JENNY LIND, THE (NBC–TV, 1956)

LAFAYETTE see SPIRIT OF LAFAYETTE, THE

LAFITTE, THE PIRATE see BUCCANEER, THE

LAMENT FOR A DEAD INDIAN see THIRD MAN, THE

LANCELOT OF THE LAKE see SWORD OF LANCELOT

LAND BEYOND THE LAW (FN, 1927, based on the story by Marion Jackson)
  BIG STAMPEDE, THE (WB, 1932)
  LAND BEYOND THE LAW (WB, 1937)

LAND DES LACHELNS, DAS (GER, 1930, source unlisted)
  LAND DES LACHELNS, DAS (GER, 1952)

LAND OF OZ see DOROTHY AND THE SCARECROW OF OZ

LAND OF RYE see RAGENS RIKE

LAND OF SMILES, THE (GER, 1930, based on the operetta by Viktor Leon)
  LAND OF SMILES, THE (AUS, 1952)

LAND WITHOUT MUSIC see FORBIDDEN MUSIC

LANDRU see MONSIEUR VERDOUX

LANDSTREICHER, DIE (GER, 1916, source unlisted)
  LANDSTREICHER, DIE (GER, 1937)

LANGTAN TIL HAVET see MARIUS

LANKA DAHAN (IN, 1917, based on a myth)
  LANKA DAHAN (IN, 1935)

LANTERN see SONG OF A LANTERN

LAREDO (series) (NBC–TV, 1966, based on a teleplay)
  BACKTRACK (UN, 1968)
  THREE GUNS FOR TEXAS (UN, 1969)

LARK, THE see JOAN OF ARC

LARSEN: WOLF OF THE SEVEN SEAS see SEA WOLVES, THE

LASCA see MAD STAMPEDE, THE

LASCA OF THE RIO GRANDE see MAD STAMPEDE, THE

LASSIE (series) (CBS–TV, 1957, based on characters created by Eric Knight) (TV TITLE: TIMMY AND LASSIE)
  LASSIE'S GREATEST ADVENTURE (FOX, 1963)
  LASSIE (series) (CBS–TV, 1964)
  LASSIE (series) (CBS–TV, 1968)
  LASSIE (series) (TV, 1971)
  LASSIE'S RESCUE RANGERS (series) (ABC–TV, 1973)
  MAGIC OF LASSIE, THE (IND, 1978)

LASSIE COME HOME (MGM, 1943, based on the book by Eric Knight)
  GYPSY COLT (MGM, 1954)
  GYPSY COLT (series) (ABC–TV, 1967)

LAST ANGRY MAN, THE (COL, 1959, based on the book by Gerald Green)
  LAST ANGRY MAN, THE (ABC–TV, 1974)

LAST BLAST, THE see GUNGA DIN

LAST CHARGE, THE see FRA DIAVOLO

LAST DAY, THE see WHEN THE DALTONS RODE

LAST DAY OF AN ENGLISH QUEEN, THE see LADY JANE GREY

LAST DAYS OF HITLER, THE see HITLER GANG, THE

LAST DAYS OF POMPEII, THE see ULTIMA GIORNO DE POMPEII, L'

LAST DETAIL, THE (COL, 1973, based on the book by Darryl Ponicsan)
  LAST DETAIL, THE (pilot) (ABC–TV, 1976)

LAST FLIGHT, THE see DAWN PATROL and L'EQUIPAGE

LAST FRONTIER, THE (PDC, 1926, based on stories by Courtney Ryley Cooper and Frank J. Wilstach; "Geronimo" (PAR, 1940) consists of stock footage from the 1937 film)
  LAST FRONTIER, THE (serial) (RKO, 1932)
  PLAINSMAN, THE (PAR, 1937)
  PLAINSMAN, THE (UN, 1966)

LAST HURRAH, THE (COL, 1958, based on the book by Edwin O'Connor)

LAST HURRAH, THE (NBC--TV, 1977)

LAST JOURNEY, THE see LEO TOLSTOY

LAST LEAF, THE (short) (BRO, 1912, based on a story
    by O. Henry (William Sidney Porter)
  LAST LEAF, THE (short) (IND, 1917)
  O. HENRY'S FULL HOUSE (sequence) (FOX, 1952)

LAST LAUGH, THE (DER LETZTE MANN) (GER, 1924,
    based on a screenplay by Carl Mayer)
  LETZTE MANN, DER (GER, 1955)

LAST LESSON, THE see PETIT CHOSE, LE

LAST MAN, THE see LAST LAUGH, THE

LAST MAN ON EARTH, THE (FOX, 1924, based on the
    story by John D. Swain)
  IT'S GREAT TO BE ALIVE (FOX, 1933)
  ULTIMO VARON SOBRE LA TIERRA (SPA, 1933)

LAST MAN ON EARTH, THE (AI, 1964, based on the book,
    "I Am Legend," by Richard Matheson)
  OMEGA MAN, THE (WB, 1971)

LAST MILE, THE (WW, 1930, based on the play by John
    Wexley)
  LAST MILE, THE (NBC--TV, 1952)
  LAST MILE, THE (UA, 1959)

LAST MOHICAN, THE see LAST OF THE MOHICANS, THE

LAST MUSKETEER, THE see THREE MUSKETEERS, THE

LAST NOTCH, THE (TV, n.d., based on a teleplay)
  FASTEST GUN ALIVE, THE (MGM, 1956)

LAST OF MRS. CHENEY, THE (MGM, 1929, based on the
    play by Frederick Lonsdale)
  LAST OF MRS. CHENEY, THE (MGM, 1937)
  LAW AND THE LADY, THE (MGM, 1951)
  LAST OF MRS. CHENEY, THE (PBS--TV, 1953)
  FRAU CHENEY'S ENDE (GER, 1961)

LAST OF THE BADMEN (AA, 1957, remake uncredited)
  GUNFIGHT AT COMANCHE CREEK (AA, 1963)

LAST OF THE COMANCHES, THE see THIRTEEN, THE

LAST OF THE DUANES, THE (FOX, 1919, based on the
    book by Zane Grey)
  LAST OF THE DUANES, THE (FOX, 1924)
  LAST OF THE DUANES, THE (FOX, 1930)
  ULTIMO DE LOS VARGAS, EL (SPA, 1930)
  LAST OF THE DUANES, THE (FOX, 1941)

LAST OF THE MOHICANS, THE (POW, 1911, based on the
    book by James Fenimore Cooper; the 1950 version con-
    sists of stock footage from the 1936 version)
  LAST OF THE MOHICANS, THE (THA, 1911)
  LAST OF THE MOHICANS (GER, 1920)
  LAST OF THE MOHICANS (GER, 1923)
  LAST OF THE MOHICANS, THE (serial) (IND, 1932)
  LAST OF THE MOHICANS, THE (UA, 1936)
  LAST OF THE REDMEN (COL, 1947)
  IROQUOIS TRAIL (UA, 1950)
  HAWKEYE (series) (TV, 1956)
  LETZE MOHIKANER, DER (GER, 1965)

LAST MOHICAN, THE (FRA--TV, 1968)
LAST OF THE MOHICANS, THE (series) (BRI--TV, 1972)

LAST OF THE REDMEN, THE see LAST OF THE MOHI-
    CANS, THE

LAST OUTPOST, THE (PAR, 1935, based on the story by
    F. Britten Austin)
  LAST OUTPOST, THE (APR, 1951)

LAST PATRIARCH, THE see HOUSE OF STRANGERS

LAST REMAKE OF BEAU GESTE, THE see BEAU GESTE

LAST ROUNDUP, THE see BORDER LEGION

LAST SUPPER, THE see PASSION PLAY, THE

LAST TRAIL, THE (FOX, 1921, based on the book by Zane
    Grey)
  LAST TRAIL, THE (FOX, 1927)
  LAST TRAIL, THE (FOX, 1933)

LAST TYCOON, THE (NBC--TV, 1951, based on the book by
    F. Scott Fitzgerald)
  LAST TYCOON, THE (CBS--TV, 1957)
  LAST TYCOON, THE (PAR, 1976)

LAST VOYAGE OF GULLIVER, THE see GULLIVER'S
    TRAVELS

LAST WALTZ, THE (FRA, 1926, source unlisted)
  LAST WALTZ, THE (GER, 1927)
  LAST WALTZ, THE (GER, 1934)
  LAST WALTZ, THE (GER, 1953)

LAST WARNING, THE (UN, 1929, based on the play by
    Thomas F. Fallon)
  LAST WARNING, THE (UN, 1938)
  HOUSE OF FEAR (UN, 1939)

LAST WILL OF DANIEL WEBSTER see DANIEL WEBSTER

LAST WILL OF DR. MABUSE, THE see TESTAMENT OF
    DR. MABUSE, THE

LATA LENA OCH GLAOGDA PER see HALTA LEAN OCH
    GINDOGEE PER

LATE CHRISTOPHER BEAN, THE see PRENEZ GARDE A
    LA PEINTURE

LATE GEORGE APLEY, THE (FOX, 1947, based on the
    book and play by John P. Marquand)
  BACK BAY ROMANCE (CBS--TV, 1955)

LATE MATTHEW PASCAL, THE see FEU MATHIAS
    PASCAL

LATIN QUARTER see QUARTIER LATIN

LAUDES EVANGELI see PASSION PLAY, THE

LAUGHING GRAVY see ANGORA LOVE

LAUGHING LADY, THE see SOCIETY SCANDAL, A

LAUGHING SINNERS (MGM, 1931, based on the play, "Torch
    Song," by Kenyon Nicholson)

TORCH SONG   (MGM, 1953)

LAUGHTER   (PAR, 1930, based on a story by Harry d'Abba–
   die d'Arrast and Douglas Doty)
   RIVE GAUCHE   (FRA, 1931)
   MANNER UM LUCIE, DIE   (GER, 1931)
   MEJOR ES REIR, LO   (SPA, 1931)

LAUNCHING THE NEW GOVERNMENT 1789–1800   see
   CHRONICLES OF AMERICA: ALEXANDER HAMIL-
   TON and DECLARATION OF INDEPENDENCE, THE

LAURA   (FOX, 1944, based on the story by Vera Caspary)
   PORTRAIT OF MURDER   (CBS–TV, 1955)
   LAURA   (GER–TV, 1962)
   LAURA   (ABC–TV, 1968)

LAUREL & HARDY MUDER CASE, THE   (short)   (MGM,
   1930, based on a screenplay by H.M. Walker)
   SPUK UM MITTERNACHT, DER   (short)   (GER, 1930)
   MAISON DE LA PEUR, LA   (short)   (FRA, 1930)
   NOCHE DE DUENDES   (short)   (SPA, 1930)
   IF A BODY MEETS A BODY   (short)   (COL, 1945)

LAURELS AND THE LADY   see   FOOLS' PARADISE

LAUSBUBENGESCHICHTEN   (GER, 1923, based on the
   book by Thoma Ludwig (OK)
   LAUSBUBENGESCHICHTEN   (GER, 1964)

LAVERNE AND SHIRLEY   see   LOVE AND THE HAPPY
   DAYS

LAW AND THE LADY, THE   see   LAST OF MRS.
   CHENEY, THE

LAW AND ORDER   (UN, 1932, based on the book "Saint
   Johnson," by W.R. Burnett)
   WILD WEST DAYS   (serial)   (UN, 1937)
   LAW AND ORDER   (UN, 1940)
   LAW AND ORDER,   (UN, 1953)

LAW OF THE TEXAN   see   BORDER LAW

LAW OF THE TROPICS   see   OIL FOR THE LAMPS OF
   CHINA

LAW OF THE UNDERWORLD   see   PAY--OFF, THE

LAW VS. GANGSTERS, THE   see   WHITE HEAT

LAWFUL LARCENY   (PAR, 1923, based on the play by
   Samuel Shipman)
   LAWFUL LARCENY   (RKO, 1930)

LAWGIVER, THE   see   LIFE OF MOSES, THE

LAWRENCE OF ARABIA   see   WITH LAWRENCE OF
   ARABIA

LAWYER QUINCE   (BRI, 1914, based on the story by W.W.
   Jacobs)
   LAWYER QUINCE   (BRI, 1924)

LAWYERS, THE   (PAR, 1969, based on a screenplay by Sidney
   J. Furie and Harold Buchman)
   NIGHT GAMES   (NBC–TV, 1974)
   PETROCELLI   (series)   (NBC–TV, 1974)

LAWYERS, THE   see   WHOLE WORLD IS WATCHING, THE

LEAH KLESCHNA   see   GIRL WHO CAME BACK, THE

LEAH THE FORSAKEN   (VIT, 1908, based on the Bible story)
   LEAH THE FORSAKEN   (UN, 1912)

LEATHER PUSHERS, THE   (serial)   (UN, 1922, based on the
   story by H.C. Witwer)
   LEATHER PUSHERS, THE   (serial)   (UN, 1930)

LEATHERNECKS HAVE LANDED, THE   (REP, 1936, based
   on a screenplay by Wellyn Totman and James Green)
   GIRL FROM HAVANA, THE   (REP, 1940)

LEATHERSTOCKING   (BIO, 1909, based on the book, "Lea-
   therstocking Tales," by James Fenimore Cooper)
   LEATHERSTOCKING TALES   (VIT, 1913)
   LEATHERSTOCKING   (serial)   (PAT, 1924)
   IROQUOIS TRAIL, THE   (British Title: TOMAHAWK
   TRAIL)   (UA, 1950)
   PATHFINDER, THE   (COL, 1952)
   LEATHERSTOCKING TALES   (FRA–TV, 1968)
   PATHFINDER, THE   (AUT–TV, 1973)

LEATHERSTOCKING TALES   see   LEATHERSTOCKING

LEAVE 'EM LAUGHING   (short)   (MGM, 1928)
   I CAN HARDLY WAIT   (short)   (COL, 1943)

LEAVE IT TO JANE   see   COLLEGE WIDOW

LEAVE US ALONE   see   LORD OF THE FLIES

LEAVENWORTH CASE, THE   (VIT, 1923, based on the
   book by Anna Katharine Green)
   LEAVENWORTH CASE, THE   (REP, 1936)

LEAVES FROM SATAN'S BOOK   see   SORROWS OF
   SATAN, THE

LEBEN BEGINNT UM 8, DAS   see   LIFE BEGINS AT 8:30

LEBEN UND TOD   (GER, 1919, based on the book, "Zwischen
   Himmel und Erde," by Otto Ludwig)
   LIEBE LASST SICH NICHT ERZWINGEN   (GER, 1934)
   ZWISCHEN HIMMEL UND ERDE   (GER, 1942)

LEBENDE LEICHNAM, DER   see   LIVING CORPSE, THE

LEE, THE VIRGINIAN   see   UNDER SOUTHERN STARS

LEFT–HANDED GUN, THE   see   BILLY THE KID

LEGACY   see   ADAM HAD FOUR SONS

LEGACY OF A DREAM   see   MARTIN LUTHER KING

LEGACY OF ALBERT SCHWEITZER, THE   see   DR.
   SCHWEITZER

LEGEND OF CAGLIOSTRO   see   CAGLIOSTRO

LEGEND OF CUSTER   see   CUSTER'S LAST STAND

LEGEND OF FAUST   see   FAUST

LEGEND OF FRA DIAVOLO   see   FRA DIAVOLO

LEGEND OF HORROR see AVENGING CONSCIENCE, THE

LEGEND OF JENNY LIND, THE see LADY'S MORALS, A

LEGEND OF JESSE JAMES see JAMES BOYS, THE

LEGEND OF JIMMY BLUE EYES (CBS–R, 1956, based on a radio play)
  LEGEND OF JIMMY BLUE EYES (short) (IND, 1967)

LEGEND OF LYLAH CLARE, THE (CBS–TV, 1963, based on the teleplay by Robert Thom and Edward de Blasio)
  LEGEND OF LYLAH CLARE, THE (MGM, 1968)

LEGEND OF MARILYN MONROE, THE see MARILYN

LEGEND OF ORPHEUS (FRA, 1909, based on a legend)
  ORPHEUS (FRA, 1950)
  BLACK ORPHEUS (FRA, 1960)

LEGEND OF ROBIN HOOD, THE see ROBIN HOOD AND HIS MERRY MEN

LEGEND OF SLEEPY HOLLOW, THE (KAL, 1908, based on the story by Washington Irving; also the basis for two musical comedies, "Sleepy Hollow," in 1948 and "Autumn's Here" in 1966)
  LEGEND OF SLEEPY HOLLOW, THE (FRA, 1912)
  HEADLESS HORSEMAN, THE (HOD, 1921)
  HEADLESS HORSEMAN, THE (short) (IND, 1934)
  ICHABOD AND MR. TOAD (DIS, 1949)
  LEGEND OF SLEEPY HOLLOW, THE (NBC–TV, 1958)
  TALES OF WASHINGTON IRVING (AUT–TV, 1970)
  LEGEND OF SLEEPY HOLLOW, THE (short) (IND, 1972)

LEGEND OF VALENTINO, THE see VALENTINO

LEGEND OF YOUNG DICK TURPIN see DICK TURPIN

LEGEND DES ONDINES (FRA, 1910, based on the legend)
  UNDINE (THA, 1912)
  UNDINE (UN, 1915)
  SEA SHADOW, THE (ABC–TV, 1965)
  ONDINE (GER, 1974)

LEGIONS OF THE NILE see CLEOPATRA

LEICHTE KAVALLERIE (GER, 1927, source unlisted)
  LEICHTE KAVALLERIE (GER, 1935)

LEMKES SEL. WITWE (GER, 1928, source unlisted)
  LEMKES SEL. WITWE (GER, 1957)

LEMON DROP KID, THE (PAR, 1934, based on the story by Damon Runyon)
  LEMON DROP KID, THE (PAR, 1951)

LEMONADE JOE (short) (CZE, 1940, based on the story by Jiri Brdeca)
  LEMONADE JOE (CZE, 1964)

LENA RIVERS (IND, 1914, based on the book by Mary J. Holmes)
  LENA RIVERS (IND, 1925)
  LENA RIVERS (TIF, 1932)

LENNY see DIRTYMOUTH

LENNY BRUCE ON TV see DIRTYMOUTH

LEO TOLSTOY (RUS, 1953, based on the life and works of Leo Tolstoy)

LEONARDO DA VINCI see LEONARDO DA VINCI – MAN OF MYSTERY

LEONARDA DA VINCI – MAN OF MYSTERY (ITA, 1952, based on the life of the noted artist)
  DRAWINGS OF LEONARDO DA VINCI, THE (BRI, 1953)
  LEONARDO DA VINCI AND HIS ART (short) (COR, 1957)
  LEONARDO DA VINCI – HIS INVENTIONS (short) (PIC, 1957)
  LEONARDO DA VINCI – HIS LIFE, HIS TIMES, HIS ART (short) (PIC, 1957)
  LEONARDO DA VINCI – HIS NOTEBOOKS (short) (PIC, 1957)
  LEONARDO DA VINCI -- THE QUEST FOR PERFECTION (short) (USC, 1963)
  I, LEONARDO DA VINCI (ABC–TV, 1965)
  LEONARDO DA VINCI (BRI, 1967)
  LEONARDO DA VINCI – TELL ME IF ANYTHING EVER WAS DONE (BRI, 1968)
  LEONARDO DA VINCI (ITA, 1970)
  LEONARDO DA VINCI (ITA–TV, 1971)
  LIFE OF LEONARDO DA VINCI, THE (BRI, 1971)
  LEONARDO DA VINCI -- THE FIRST MAN OF THE RENAISSANCE (short) (DIS, 1971)
  LIFE OF LEONARDO DA VINCI, THE (series) (CBS–TV, 1972)
  LEONARDO – TO KNOW HOW TO SEE (IND, 1972)
  LIFE OF LEONARDO DA VINCI (ITA--TV, 1973)

LEONARDO DA VINCI – TELL ME IF ANYTHING EVER WAS DONE see LEONARDO DA VINCI – MAN OF MYSTERY

LEONARDO – TO KNOW HOW TO SEE see LEONARDO DA VINCI – MAN OF MYSTERY

LEPKE see ENFORCER, THE

LES MISERABLES see MISERABLES, LES

LET US BE GAY (MGM, 1930, based on the play by Rachel Crothers)
  SOYONS GAIS (FRA, 1930)

LET'S BE HAPPY see JEANNIE

LET'S DO IT AGAIN see AWFUL TRUTH, THE

LET'S FACE IT see CRADLE SNATCHERS, THE

LET'S FALL IN LOVE (COL, 1934, based on a story by Herbert Fields)
  SLIGHTLY FRENCH (COL, 1949)

LET'S GET A DIVORCE see DIVORCONS

LET'S GET MARRIED see MAN FROM MEXICO, THE

LET'S PLAY KING see NEWLY RICH

LETTER, THE (PAR, 1929, based on the book by W. Somerset Maugham)
  LETTRE, LA (FRA, 1930)
  CARTA, LA (SPA, 1930)

WEIB IM DSCHUNGEL (GER, 1930)
LETTER, THE (WB, 1940)
UNFAITHFUL, THE (WB, 1947)
LETTER, THE (NBC–TV, 1950)
LETTER, THE (NET–TV, 1952)
LETTER, THE (CBS–TV, 1956)

LETTER FROM AN UNKNOWN WOMAN, A see NARKOSE

LETTRE, LA see LETTER, THE

LETTRE DE PARIS (short) (FRA, 1933, source unlisted)
LETTRE DE PARIS (short) (FRA, 1945)

LETZE KOMPANIE, DAS (GER, 1930, source unlisted)
LETZE KOMPANIE, DAS (GER, 1967)

LETZE MOHIKANER, DER see LAST OF THE MOHICANS, THE

LETZTE MANN, DER see LAST LAUGH, THE

LEUCHTER DES KAISERS, DIE (AUS, 1936, based on the story by Baroness Orczy)
EMPEROR'S CANDLESTICKS, THE (MGM, 1937)

LEVRES CLOSES see LIEBELEI

LEWIS AND CLARK (short) (EBE, 1950, based on the lives of the noted explorers)
U.S. EXPANSION: THE OREGON COUNTRY (short) (COR, 1956)
LEWIS AND CLARK AT THE GREAT DIVIDE (short) (BFA, n.d.)
JOURNALS OF LEWIS AND CLARK, THE (NBC–TV, 1965)
LEWIS AND CLARK JOURNEY (short) (COR, 1968)

LEY DEL HAREN, LA see FAZIL

LIBELED LADY (MGM, 1936, based on a story by Wallace Sullivan)
EASY TO WED (MGM, 1946)

LIBERTY (short) (MGM, 1929, based on a screenplay by Leo McCarey)
HOW HIGH IS UP? (short) (COL, 1940)

LIEBE see DUKE FROM LANGEAIS, THE

LIEBE AUGUSTIN, DER (GER, 1940, source unlisted)
LIEBE AUGUSTIN, DER (GER, 1960)

LIEBE GEHT SELLSAME WEGE (GER, 1926, source unlisted)
LIEBE GEHT SELLSAME WEGE (GER, 1937)

LIEBE LASST SICH NICHT ERZWINGEN see LEBEN UND TOD

LIEBE, SCHERZ UND ERNST (GER, 1932, based on the play, "The Importance of Being Earnest," by Oscar Wilde; also the basis for two musical comedies: "Oh, Earnest," in 1927 and "Earnest in Love," in 1960)
IMPORTANCE OF BEING EARNEST, THE (NBC–TV, 1950)
IMPORTANCE OF BEING EARNEST, THE (BRI–TV, 1952)
IMPORTANCE OF BEING EARNEST, THE (BRI, 1952)
WHO'S EARNEST? (CBS–TV, 1957)

LIEBE, TOD UND TEUFEL see BOTTLE IMP, THE

LIEBE UND TROMPETENBLASEN (GER, 1925, source unlisted)
LIEBE UND TROMPETENBLASEN (GER, 1954)

LIEBELEI (AUS, 1911, based on the book by Arthur Schnitzler)
LOVE GAMES (DEN, 1913)
LIEBELEI (GER, 1925)
LEVRES CLOSES (SWE, 1927)
LIEBELEI (GER, 1933)
LIEBELEI (FRA, 1933)
CHRISTINE (FRA/ITA, 1958)

LIEBELIST UND LUST see DECAMERON, THE

LIEBESGESCHICTEN see MAEDELS VON HEUTE

LIEBESLIED (GER, 1931, source unlisted)
LIEBESLIED (GER, 1935)

LIEBESERWACHEN (GER, 1936, source unlisted)
LIEBESERWACHEN (GER, 1953)

LIEBESKARUSELL, DAS see REIGEN, DER

LIEBESWALZER (GER, 1930, source unlisted)
LOVE WALTZ, THE (BRI, 1930)

LIEBLING DEN GOTTER (GER, 1930, source unlisted)
LIEBLING DEN GOTTER (GER, 1960)

LIED EINER NACHT, DAS see TELL ME TONIGHT

LIED GEHT UM DIE WELT, EIN (GER, 1933, based on the play by Ernst Neubach and Heinz Goldberg)
JOSEPH SCHMIDT STORY, THE (GER, 1958)

LIED VON DER GLOCKE, DAS see GLOCKE I, DIE

LIERMONTOV (RUS, 1912, based on the book by Mikhail Liermontov)
LIERMONTOV (RUS, 1943)

LIESE FLEHEN MEINE LIEDER see SCHUBERT'S FRUH– LINGSTRAUM

LT. ROBIN CRUSOE, USN see ROBINSON CRUSOE

LIFE AND LEGEND OF WYATT EARP see FRONTIER MARSHAL

LIFE AND LOVES OF MOZART, THE see LITTLE NIGHT MUSIC, A

LIFE AND LOVES OF TCHAIKOVSKY, THE see IT WAS AN EXCITING NIGHT

LIFE AND TIMES OF BARNEY MILLER (ABC–TV, 1974, based on a teleplay)
BARNEY MILLER (series) (ABC–TV, 1975)
FISH (series) (ABC–TV, 1977)

LIFE AND TIMES OF BERTRAND RUSSELL, THE see BERTRAND RUSSELL

LIFE AND TIMES OF JUDGE ROY BEAN see ADVEN– TURES OF JUDGE ROY BEAN

LIFE AND TIMES OF TEDDY ROOSEVELT, THE see
    TEDDY, THE ROUGH RIDER

LIFE AND TIMES OF XAVIERA HOLLANDER, THE (IND,
    1975, based on the book, "The Happy Hooker," by
    Xaviera Hollander)
  HAPPY HOOKER, THE (IND, 1975)
  HAPPY HOOKER IN WASHINGTON, THE (IND, 1977)

LIFE AND TIMES OF WILLIAM SHAKESPEARE, THE
    see LIFE OF SHAKESPEARE

LIFE BEGINS (FRA, 1931, based on the play by Mary
    McDougal Axelson)
  LIFE BEGINS (WB, 1932)
  CHILD IS BORN, A (WB, 1940)

LIFE BEGINS AT 8:30 (FOX, 1942, based on the play, "Light
    of Heart," by Emlyn Williams)
  LEBEN BEGINNT UM 8, DAS (GER, 1962)

LIFE DRAMA OF NAPOLEON BONAPARTE AND EMPRESS
    JOSEPHINE OF FRANCE, THE see NAPOLEON --
    MAN OF DESTINY

LIFE IN THE COUNTRY see LIVET PA LANDET

LIFE IN THE LATIN QUARTER see BOHEME, LA

LIFE OF A RICHSHAW MAN see RICKSHAW MAN

LIFE OF A WOMAN see ONE LIFE

LIFE OF A WOMAN IN THE MEIJI (JAP, 1935, source
    unlisted)
  LIFE OF A WOMAN IN THE MEIJI (JAP, 1955)

LIFE OF CHARLES PEACE, THE (BRI, 1905, based on a
    historical incident)
  LIFE OF CHARLES PEACE, KING OF CRIMINALS (BRI,
    1914)
  CASE OF CHARLES PEACE, THE (BRI, 1949)

LIFE OF CHARLES PEACE, KING OF CRIMINALS see
    LIFE OF CHARLES PEACE, THE

LIFE OF CHOPIN (short) (BRI, 1938, based on the life of
    the composer)
  SONG TO REMEMBER, A (COL, 1944)
  FREDERIC CHOPIN (short) (BRI, 1961)
  CHOPIN (short) (IFB, 1975)

LIFE OF CHRIST, THE see PASSION PLAY, THE

LIFE OF ELIZABETH, THE see KING IS DEAD, LONG
    LIVE THE QUEEN, THE

LIFE OF EMILE ZOLA, THE (WB, 1937, based on the life
    of the noted French writer)
  ZOLA (FRA, 1954)
  LIFE OF EMILE ZOLA, THE (NBC–TV, 1955)

LIFE OF HENRY V, THE see HENRY V

LIFE OF JIMMY DOLAN, THE (WB, 1933, based on the
    play by Bertram Milhauser and Beulah Marie Dix)
  THEY MADE ME A CRIMINAL (WB, 1939)

LIFE OF LEONARDO DA VINCI, THE see LEONARDO

DA VINCI -- MAN OF MYSTERY

LIFE OF LORD KITCHENER (BRI, 1917, based on a histor-
    ical incident)
  HOW KITCHENER WAS BETRAYED (BRI, 1921)

LIFE OF MOSES, THE (VIT, 1909, based on Bible stories)
  TEN COMMANDMENTS, THE (PAR, 1923)
  FORGOTTEN COMMANDMENTS (PAR, 1932)
  MOSES AND HIS PEOPLE (short) (BRI, 1952)
  MOSES AND THE 10 COMMANDMENTS (short) (BRI,
    1952)
  MOSES IN EGYPT (short) (BRI, 1952)
  TEN COMMANDMENTS, THE (PAR, 1956)
  MOSES, LEADER OF GOD'S PEOPLE (short) (IND, 1958)
  MOSES STORY, THE (short) (BRI, 1961)
  MOSES: THE LAWGIVER (short) (NBC–TV, 1964)
  MOSES: THE LEARNER (short) (NBC–TV, 1964)
  LAWGIVER, THE (ITA–TV, 1974)

LIFE OF MOZART, THE see WHOM THE GODS LOVE

LIFE OF RILEY, THE (UN, 1949, based on a radio series)
  LIFE OF RILEY, THE (series) (IND–TV, 1949)
  LIFE OF RILEY, THE (series) (NBC–TV, 1953)

LIFE OF ROBERT BURNS, THE (BRI, 1926, based on the
    life of the noted poet)
  AULD LANG SYNE (BRI, 1937)
  ROMANCE OF ROBERT BURNS, THE (short) (WB, 1937)
  SCOTLAND: BACKGROUND FOR LITERATURE (short)
    (COR, 1947)
  COMIN' THRU THE RYE (BRI, 1947)

LIFE OF SHAKESPEARE (BRI, 1914, based on the life and
    works of the noted playwright)
  MASTER WILL SHAKESPEARE (short) (IND, 1936)
  OUR MR. SHAKESPEARE (short) (IND, n.d.)
  WILLIAM SHAKESPEARE: BACKGROUND FOR HIS
    WORKS (short) (COR, 1951)
  WILLIAM SHAKESPEARE (short) (EBE, 1955)
  SHAKESPEARE: SOUL OF AN AGE (NBC--TV, 1963)
  WILL SHAKESPEARE – GENT (short) (TIM, 1967)
  LIFE AND TIMES OF WILLIAM SHAKESPEARE, THE
    (series) (ABC–TV, 1974)
  WILL SHAKESPEARE (series) (BRI–TV, 1978)

LIFE OF THE PARTY see TWIN BEDS

LIFE OF VILLA (short) (FA, 1912, based on the life of the
    Mexican bandit)
  VIVA VILLA! (FOX, 1934)
  PANCHO VILLA RETURNS (MEX, 1951)
  SECRET OF PANCHO VILLA, THE (MEX, 1954)
  HEAD OF PANCHO VILLA, THE (MEX, 1955)
  VILLA! (FOX, 1958)
  PANCHO VILLA (SPA, 1972)

LIFE STORY OF JOHN LEE – THE MAN THEY COULD NOT
    HANG see MAN THEY COULD NOT HANG, THE

LIFE WITH FATHER (WB, 1947, based on the play by Howard
    Lindsay and Russell Crouse)
  LIFE WITH FATHER (series) (CBS–TV, 1953)

LIFE WITHOUT SOUL see FRANKENSTEIN

LIFE'S WHIRLPOOL (WOR, 1915, based on the book,
    "McTeague," by Frank Norris)

GREED (MGM, 1924)

LIGHT OF WESTERN STARS, THE (IND, 1918, based
    on the book by Zane Grey)
LIGHT OF WESTERN STARS, THE (PAR, 1925)
LIGHT OF WESTERN STARS, THE (PAR, 1930)
LIGHT OF WESTERN STARS, THE (PAR, 1940)

LIGHT THAT FAILED, THE (ITA, 1914, based on the book
    by Rudyard Kipling)
LIGHT THAT FAILED, THE (PAT, 1916)
LIGHT THAT FAILED, THE (PAR, 1923)
LIGHT THAT FAILED, THE (PAR, 1939)
LIGHT THAT FAILED, THE (ABC–TV, 1961)

LIGHTNIN' (FOX, 1925, based on the play by Frank Bacon)
LIGHTNIN' (FOX, 1930)

LIGHTNING EXPRESS see WHISPERING SMITH

LIGHTNING STRIKES TWICE (WB, 1951, based on the
    book by Margaret Echard)
LIGHTNING STRIKES TWICE (NBC–TV, 1955)

LIGHTS OUT (RC, 1923, based on the play by Paul Dickey
    and Mann Page)
CRASHING HOLLYWOOD (RKO, 1937)

LIKES OF 'ER, THE see SALLY IN OUR ALLEY

LIGHTS OUT (series) (NBC–TV, 1949, based on the radio
    anthology series by Arch Obler)
LIGHTS OUT (NBC–TV, 1972)

LI'L ABNER (RKO, 1940, based on the comic strip by Al
    Capp)
LI'L ABNER (PAR, 1960)
LI'L ABNER (ABC–TV, 1971)

LILA AKAC (HUN, 1934, based on the book by Erno Szep)
LILA AKAC (HUN, 1972)

LILI MARLENE see TRUE STORY OF LILI MARLENE,
    THE

LILIES OF THE FIELD (FN, 1924, based on the play by
    William Hurlburt)
LILIES OF THE FIELD (FN, 1930)

LILIOM see TRIP TO PARADISE, A

LILY CZEPANEK (n.d., based on the book by Hermann
    Sudermann)
LILY OF THE DUST (PAR, 1924)
SONG OF SONGS (PAR, 1933)

LILY OF KILLARNEY see COLLEEN BAWN, THE

LILY OF THE DUST see LILY CZEPANEK

LIMEHOUSE NIGHTS see BROKEN BLOSSOMS

LIMPING MAN, THE see CREEPING SHADOWS

LINCOLN see ABRAHAM LINCOLN

LINCOLN CONSPIRACY, THE see MAN IN THE BARN,
    THE

LINCOLN: TRIAL BY FIRE see ABRAHAM LINCOLN

LINCOLN'S LAST DAY see ABRAHAM LINCOLN

LINDBERG VS. THE ATLANTIC see SPIRIT OF ST. LOUIS,
    THE

LINE CAMP, THE (NBC–TV, 1960, based on a teleplay from
    "The Westerner" series by Tom Gries)
WILL PENNY (PAR, 1966)

LINE–UP, THE (series) (CBS–TV, 1954, based on a teleplay)
LINE–UP, THE (COL, 1958)

LION AND THE MOUSE, THE (VIT, 1919, based on the
    play by Charles Klein)
LION AND THE MOUSE, THE (WB, 1928)

LION MAN, THE see LAD AND THE LION, THE

LIOUBOV IAROVAIA (RUS, 1953, based on the book by
    Constantin Treniov)
LIOUBOV IAROVAIA (RUS, 1970)

LISA AND LOTTIE see TWICE UPON A TIME

LISOLETTE VON DER PFALZ (GER, 1935, source unlisted)
LISOLETTE VON DER PFALZ (GER, 1966)

LISZT AND HIS MUSIC see DREAM OF LOVE

LISZTOMANIA see DREAM OF LOVE

LITTLE ACCIDENT (UN, 1930, based on the play by Floyd
    Dell and Thomas Mitchell; the last also used the book, "An
    Ummarried Father," by Floyd Dell)
PAPA SANS LE SAVOIR (FRA, 1931)
LITTLE ACCIDENT (UN, 1939)
CASANOVA BROWN (RKO, 1944)

LITTLE ADVENTURESS, THE (PDC, 1927, based on the
    book, "The Dover Road," by A.A. Milne)
WHERE SINNERS MEET (RKO, 1934)

LITTLE BIGHORN (LIP, 1951, based on a historical incident)
LITTLE BIG HORN (GER, 1973)

LITTLE BIT OF FLUFF (BRI, 1919, based on the play by
    Walter Ellis)
LITTLE BIT OF FLUFF (BRI, 1928)

LITTLE BOY BLUE (short) (UN, 1916, based on the poem
    by Eugene Field)
LITTLE BOY BLUE (short) (MGM, 1936)

LITTLE BROTHER OF THE RICH, A (UN, 1915, based on
    the book by Joseph Medill Patterson)
LITTLE BROTHER OF THE RICH, A (UN, 1919)

LITTLE DAMOZEL (BRI, 1916, based on the play by Monck–
    ton Hoffe)
LITTLE DAMOZEL (BRI, 1933)

LITTLE DORRIT (THA, 1913, based on the book by Charles
    Dickens)
LITTLE DORRIT (BRI, 1920)
LITTLE DORRIT (DEN, 1924)
LITTLE DORRIT (BRI, 1926)
LITTLE DORRIT (GER, 1934)

LITTLE EMILY (BRI, 1911, based on the book, "David
   Copperfield," by Charles Dickens)
  EARLY LIFE OF DAVID COPPERFIELD, THE (THA,
   1911)
  DAVID COPPERFIELD (FRA, 1912)
  DAVID COPPERFIELD (BRI, 1913) (2 versions)
  DAVID COPPERFIELD (DEN, 1922)
  DAVID COPPERFIELD (AE, 1923)
  DAVID COPPERFIELD (MGM, 1935)
  DAVID COPPERFIELD (CBS--TV, 1954)
  DAVID AND MR. MICAWBER (short) (BRI–TV, 1963)
  DAVID COPPERFIELD (NBC–TV, 1970)
  CHARLES DICKENS SHOW, THE (BRI, 1973)
  DAVID COPPERFIELD (series) (PBS–TV, 1976)

LITTLE FOXES, THE (RKO, 1941, based on the play by
   Lillian Hellman)
  LITTLE FOXES, THE (NBC–TV, 1956)

LITTLE GYPSY, THE (SPA, 1914, source unlisted)
  LITTLE GYPSY, THE (FRA, 1923)
  LITTLE GYPSY, THE (SPA, 1940)

LITTLE HIAWATHA see HIAWATHA

LITTLE HORSE, THE see SENTIMENTAL JOURNEY

LITTLE HOUSE ON THE PRAIRIE, THE (NBC–TV, 1974,
   based on books by Laura Ingals Wilder)
  LITTLE HOUSE ON THE PRAIRIE, THE (series) (NBC–
   TV, 1975)

LITTLE HUMPBACKED HORSE (RUS, 1939, based on a
   Russian folk tale)
  LITTLE HUMPBACKED HORSE (RUS, 1948)
  LITTLE HUMPBACKED HORSE (RUS, 1961)

LITTLE JOHNNY JONES (WB, 1923, based on the musical
   comedy by George M. Cohan)
  LITTLE JOHNNY JONES (WB, 1930)

LITTLE LORD FAUNTLEROY (BRI, 1914, based on the
   book by Frances Hodgson Burnett)
  LITTLE LORD FAUNTLEROY (UA, 1921)
  LITTLE LORD FAUNTLEROY (SEZ, 1936)

LITTLE MATCH GIRL (BRI, 1902, based on the story by
   Hans Christian Andersen)
  LITTLE MATCHSELLER'S CHRISTMAS (FRA, 1910)
  LITTLE MATCH GIRL (BRI, 1914)
  LITTLE MATCH GIRL (RUS, 1919)
  LITTLE MATCH GIRL FRA, 1927)
  LITTLE MATCH GIRL (short) (COL, 1937)
  MATCH GIRL (IND, 1966)
  FABLES FROM HANS CHRISTIAN ANDERSEN (JAP,
   1968)
  MATCH GIRL (RUM, 1968)

LITTLE MATCHSELLER'S CHRISTMAS see LITTLE
  MATCH GIRL

LITTLE MEN (MAS, 1934, based on the book by Louisa May
   Alcott)
  LITTLE MEN (RKO, 1940)
  LITTLE MEN (NBC–TV, 1960)

LITTLE MINISTER, THE see STORY OF THE LITTLE
  MINISTER, THE

LITTLE MISS BIG see THREE KIDS AND A QUEEN

LITTLE MISS BLUEBEARD see MISS BLUEBEARD

LITTLE MISS MARKER (PAR, 1934, based onthe story by
   Damon Runyan; the Universal film is an uncredited remake)
  SORROWFUL JONES (PAR, 1949)
  40 POUNDS OF TROUBLE (UN, 1962)

LITTLE MISS NOBODY see BLUE SKIES

LITTLE MOOK (RUS, 1938, source unlisted)
  LITTLE MOOK (GER, 1954)

LITTLE MOON OF ALBAN, THE (NBC--TV, 1958, based on
   the teleplay by James Costigan)
  LITTLE MOON OF ALBAN, THE (NBC–TV, 1964)

LITTLE NELL see OLD CURIOUSITY SHOP, THE

LITTLE NIGHT MUSIC, A see SMILES OF A SUMMER
  NIGHT

LITTLE OLD NEW YORK (MGM, 1923, based on the play
   by Rida Johnson Young)
  LITTLE OLD NEW YORK (FOX, 1939)

LITTLE ORPHAN ANNIE (IND, 1919, based on the comic
   strip by Harold Gray)
  LITTLE ORPHAN ANNIE (RKO, 1932)
  LITTLE ORPHAN ANNIE (PAR, 1938)

LITTLE PHANTASY ON A 19TH CENTURY PAINTING, A
  see ISLE OF THE DEAD

LITTLE PRINCE, HE (RUS, 1967, based on the book, "Le
   Petit Prince" by Antoine de Saint--Exupery)
  LITTLE PRINCE, THE (PAR, 1975)

LITTLE PRINCESS, THE (ART, 1917, based on the book by
   Frances Hodgson Burnett)
  LITTLE PRINCESS, THE (FOX, 1939)
  LITTLE PRINCESS, THE (AUT–TV, 1973)

LITTLE RED RIDING HOOD see PETIT CHAPERON
  ROUGE, LE

LITTLE SHEPHERD OF KINGDOM COME (MGM, 1920,
   based on the book by John Fox Jr.)
  LITTLE SHEPHERD OF KINGDOM COME (FBO, 1928)
  LITTLE SHEPHERD OF KINGDOM COME (FOX, 1961)

LITTLE SISTER (TV, n.d., based on the book by Raymond
   Chandler)
  MARLOWE (MGM, 1969)

LITTLE SNOW WHITE see SNOW WHITE

LITTLE TOM THUMB see HOP O' MY THUMB

LITTLE WILDCAT, THE (VIT, 1922, based on a story by
   Gene Wright)
  LITTLE WILDCAT, THE (WB, 1928)

LITTLE WOMEN (BRI, 1917, based on the book by Louisa
   May Alcott; also the basis for two musicals, "A Girl Named
   Jo" in England and "Jo" in America)
  LITTLE WOMEN (PAR, 1919)
  LITTLE WOMEN (RKO, 1933)

LITTLE WOMEN   (MGM, 1949)
LITTLE WOMEN   (CBS–TV, 1950)
LITTLE WOMEN   (NBC–TV, 1958)
LITTLE WOMEN   (CBS–TV, 1958)
LITTLE WOMEN   (NBC–TV, 1969)
LITTLE WOMEN   (series) (BRI–TV, 1970)
LITTLE WOMEN   (CAN–TV, 1977)

LITTLEST ANGEL, THE   (short) (COR, 1950, based on the
      story by Charles Taswell)
LITTLEST ANGEL, THE   (short) (STE, 1963)
LITTLEST ANGEL, THE   (NBC–TV, 1970)

LITTLEST HOBO, THE   (AA, 1958, based on a screenplay by
      Dorrell MacGowan)
LITTLEST HOBO, THE   (series) (TV, 1963)

LIVE GHOST, THE   see   SHANGHAIED

LIVELY SET, THE   see   JOHNNY DARK

LIVES OF A BENGAL LANCER   (PAR, 1935, based on the
      book by Francis Yeats Brown)
GERONIMO   (PAR, 1939)

LIVET PA LANDET   (SWE, 1924, source unlisted)
LIVET PA LANDET   (SWE, 1943)

LIVING CORPSE, THE   (RUS, 1911, based on the book by
      Leo Tolstoy)
LIVING CORPSE, THE   (JAP, 1912)
LIVING CORPSE, THE   (SAV, 1913)
LIVING CORPSE, THE   (UN, 1915)
WEAKNESS OF MAN, THE   (WOR, 1916)
SHADOWS OF MY LIFE   (STG, 1917)
LEBENDE LEICHNAM, DER   (GER, 1918)
LIVING CORPSE, THE   (RUS, 1918)
LIVING CORPSE, THE   (JAP, 1918)
LIVING CORPSE, THE   (PIO, 1919)
BIGAMIE   (GER, 1922)
LEBENDE LEICHNAM, DER   (GER, 1927)
LIVING CORPSE, THE   (RUS, 1928)
REDEMPTION   (MGM, 1929)
LIVING CORPSE, THE   (GER, 1930)
NUITS DE FEU   (FRA, 1936)
LIVING CORPSE, THE   (FRA, 1939)
LIVING CORPSE, THE   (RUS, 1952)
LIVING CORPSE, THE   (RUS, 1968)
HET LEVENDE LIJK   (HOL–TV, 1972)

LIVING DEAD, THE   see   EERIE TALES and FEU MATHIAS
      PASCAL

LIVING DEAD AT THE MANCHESTER MORGUE, THE   see
      NIGHT OF THE LIVING DEAD

LIVING IT UP   see   NOTHING SACRED

LIVING ON LOVE   see   ICH BEI TAG UND DU BEI NACHT

LIVINGSTONE   (BRI, 1925, based on a historical incident and
      characters)
DAVID LIVINGSTONE   (BRI, 1936)
STANLEY AND LIVINGSTONE   (FOX, 1939)
TRAIL OF STANLEY AND LIVINGSTONE, THE   (TV,
      1967)

LLAMA SEGRADE, LA   see   SACRED FLAME, THE

LLANO KID, THE   see   DOUBLE–DYED DECEIVER, THE

LLORONA, LA   (MEX, 1933, based on a Mexican legend)
LLORONA, LA   (MEX, 1946)
CURSE OF THE CRYING WOMEN   (MEX, 1961)

LOCAL BOY MAKES GOOD   see   POOR NUT, THE

LOCANDIERA, LA   (ITA, 1928, based on a story by Carlo
      Goldoni)
LOCANDIERA, LA   (ITA, 1943)

LOCATAIRE, LA   (FRA, 1938, source unlisted)
DERNIER REFUGE   (ITA, 1947)

LOCKED DOOR, THE   see   SIGN ON THE DOOR, THE

LODGER, THE   (BRI, 1926, based on historical events and
      the book by Marie Belloc Lowndes)
PHANTOM FIEND, THE   (BRI, 1932)
LODGER, THE   (FOX, 1944)
ROOM TO LET   (BRI, 1950)
MAN IN THE ATTIC, THE   (FOX, 1953)
JACK THE RIPPER   (BRI, 1960)
STUDY IN TERROR, A   (BRI, 1965)
HANDS OF THE RIPPER   (BRI, 1971)
JACK THE RIPPER OF LONDON   (ITA/SPA, 1971)
JACK THE RIPPER   (BRI–TV, 1973)

LOGAN'S RUN   (MGM, 1976, based on the book by William
      F. Nolan)
LOGAN'S RUN   (series) (CBS–TV, 1977)

LOHENGRIN   (GER, 1907, based on the German legend and
      the opera by Richard Wagner)
LOHENGRIN   (ITA, 1936)

LOI ET LE DEVOIR, LA   (RUS, 1927, based on the book,
      "Amok," by Stefan Zweig)
AMOK   (FRA, 1934)
AMOK   (MEX, 1944)

LOKIS   see   MARRIAGE OF THE BEAR

LOLA MONTES   see   PALACE OF PLEASURE

LONDON AFTER MIDNIGHT   (MGM, 1927, based on the
      story, "The Hypnotist," by Tod Browning)
MARK OF THE VAMPIRE   (MGM, 1935)

LONE COWBOY, THE   (PAR, 1933, based on the book by
      Will James)
SHOOT OUT   (UN, 1971)

LONE RIDER, THE   (COL, 1930, based on a story by Frank H.
      Clark; remakes uncredited)
MAN TRAILER, THE   (COL, 1934)
THUNDERING WEST, THE   (COL, 1939)

LONE STAR RANGER, THE   (FOX, 1919, based on the book
      by Zane Grey)
LONE STAR RANGER, THE   (FOX, 1923)
LONE STAR RANGER, THE   (FOX, 1929)
LONE STAR RANGER, THE   (FOX, 1942)

LONE WOLF   see   BEZHIN MEADOW

LONEDALE OPERATOR, THE   (BIO, 1911, based on a screen–
      play by D.W. Griffith)

GIRL AND HER TRUST, A (BIO, 1912)

LONELY VILLA, THE (BIO, 1909, based on a screenplay by
    D.W. Griffith)
  ONE EXCITING NIGHT (UA, 1922)

LONG CHANCE, THE (UN, 1915, based on the book by Peter
    B. Kyne)
  LONG CHANCE, THE (UN, 1918)
  LONG CHANCE, THE (UN, 1922)

LONG DAY'S JOURNEY INTO NIGHT (EMB, 1962, based
    on the play by Eugene O'Neill)
  LONG DAY'S JOURNEY INTO NIGHT (ABC--TV, 1973)

LONG GOODBYE, THE (CBS–TV, 1954, based on the book
    by Raymond Chandler)
  LONG GOODBYE, THE (UA, 1973)

LONG HOT SUMMER, THE (FOX, 1958, based on the book
    by William Faulkner)
  LONG HOT SUMMER, THE (series) (ABC–TV, 1965)

LONG JOHN SILVER (AUT, 1955, based on characters in
    the book, "Treasure Island," by Robert Louis Stevenson)
  ADVENTURES OF LONG JOHN SILVER, THE (series)
    (AUT--TV, 1955)

LONG JOHN SILVER see also PIRATE'S TREASURE

LONG, LONG TRAIL, THE see RAMBLIN' KID, THE

LONG NIGHT, THE see JOUR SE LEVE, LE

LONG SWIFT SWORD OF SIEGFRIED, THE see
    SIEGFRIED

LONGSTREET (ABC–TV, 1971, based on a teleplay)
  LONGSTREET (series) (ABC–TV, 1971)

LOOK FOR THE SILVER LINING see SALLY

LOOK WHAT'S HAPPENED TO ROSEMARY'S BABY see
    ROSEMARY'S BABY

LOOT see GRAY GHOST, THE

LOPEZ LE BANDIT see BAD MAN, THE

LORD ARTHUR SAVILLE'S CRIME (RUS, 1916, based on the
    story by Oscar Wilde)
  HALLUCINATION (HUN, 1919)
  CRIME DE LORD ARTHUR SAVILLE, LE (FRA, 1921)
  FLESH AND FANTASY (sequence) (UN, 1943)
  LORD ARTHUR SAVILLE'S CRIME (NBC–TV, 1958)
  WORLD OF HORROR (sequence) (POL, 1968)

LORD CHUMLEY (KE, 1914, based on the play by David
    Belasco and Henry C. DeMille)
  FORTY WINKS (PAR, 1925)

LORD JIM (PAR, 1925, based on the book by Joseph Conrad)
  LORD JIM (COL, 1965)

LORD OF THE FLIES (BRI, 1962, based on the book by
    William Golding)
  LEAVE US ALONE (DEN, 1975)

LORD OF THE RINGS see HOBBIT, THE

LORNA DOONE (THA, 1911, based on the book by R.D.
    Blackmore)
  LORNA DOONE (BRI, 1912)
  LORNA DOONE (BIO, 1915)
  LORNA DOONE (BRI, 1920)
  LORNA DOONE (INC, 1922)
  LORNA DOONE (FN, 1923)
  LORNA DOONE (BRI, 1935)
  LORNA DOONE (COL, 1951)

LOS QUE DANZAN see THOSE WHO DANCE

LOST – A WIFE (PAR, 1925, based on the book, "The Grand
    Duchess and the Waiter," and the play, "Super of the
    Gaiety," by Alfred Savoir)
  GRAND DUCHESS AND THE WAITER, THE (PAR, 1926)
  HIS TIGER LADY (PAR, 1928)
  HERE IS MY HEART (PAR, 1934)

LOST ATLANTIS see ATLANTIDE, L'

LOST BOY see HUCKLEBERRY FINN

LOST CANYON see RUSTLER'S VALLEY

LOST CONTINENT, THE see ATLANTIDE, L'

LOST GOD see SEA GOD, THE

LOST HORIZON (COL, 1937, based on the book by James
    Hilton)
  SHANGRI–LA (NBC–TV, 1960)
  LOST HORIZON (COL, 1973)

LOST IN SPACE see PERILS OF THE WILD

LOST IN THE STARS see CRY THE BELOVED COUNTRY

LOST ISLAND OF KIOGA see HAWK OF THE WILDERNESS

LOST KINGDOM, THE see ATLANTIDE, L'

LOST LADY, A (WB, 1924, based on the book by Willa
    Cather)
  LOST LADY, A (WB, 1934)

LOST MAN, THE see ODD MAN OUT

LOST MOMENT, THE (UN, 1947, based on the book, "The
    Aspern Papers," by Henry James)
  GARDEN IN THE SEA, A (ABC–TV, 1954)

LOST ONE, THE see DAME AUX CAMELIAS, LA

LOST PATROL, THE (BRI, 1929, based on the story, "Patrol,"
    by Philip MacDonald)
  LOST PATROL, THE (RKO, 1934)

LOS PLANET AIRMEN see KING OF THE ROCKET MEN

LOST WEEKEND, THE (PAR, 1945, based on the book by
    Charles R. Jackson)
  LOST WEEKEND, THE (NBC–TV, 1955)

LOST WORLD, THE (FN, 1925, based on the book by Sir
    Arthur Conan Doyle)
  LOST WORLD, THE (FOX, 1960)

LOTSA LUCK see ON THE BUSES

LOTTA CRABTREE see GOLDEN GIRL

LOU GEHRIG STORY, THE see PRIDE OF THE YANKEES

LOU GRANT see MARY TYLER MOORE SHOW, THE

LOUEUR, LE (FRA, 1938, based on a book by Feyodor
    Dostoyevsky)
  SPIELER, DER (GER, 1938)
  GREAT SINNER, THE (MGM, 1949)
  LOUEUR, LE (FRA/ITA, 1958)

LOUIS BRAILLE (short) (WB, n.d., based on the life and
    work of the noted teacher of the blind)
  TRIUMPH OF LOUIS BRAILLE, THE (short) (CBS–TV,
  1956)

LOUISA MILLER see KABALE UND LIEBE

LOUISIANA PURCHASE (PAR, 1941, based on a musical
    comedy by Morrie Ryskind, B.G. de Silva and Irving
    Berlin)
  LOUISIANA PURCHASE (NBC–TV, 1951)

LOUVE, LA (ITA, 1917, based on the book by Giovanni
    Verga)
  LOUVE, LA (ITA, 1953)

LOVE see ANNA KARENINA

LOVE AFFAIR (RKO, 1939, based on a story by Mildred
    Cram and Leo McCarey)
  AFFAIR TO REMEMBER, AN (FOX, 1956)

LOVE AFFAIR: THE ELEANOR AND LOU GEHRIG
    STORY, A see PRIDE OF THE YANKEES

LOVE AND THE HAPPY DAYS (ABC–TV, 1974, based on
    a teleplay first aired as an episode of "Love American
    Style")
  HAPPY DAYS (series) (ABC–TV, 1974)
  LAVERNE AND SHIRLEY (series) (ABC–TV, 1976)

LOVE BEGINS AT 20 see TOO YOUNG TO MARRY

LOVE BIRDS, THE (JAP, 1955, based on a book by Sakuno–
    suke Oda)
  LOVE BIRDS, THE (JAP, 1968)

LOVE BOAT, THE (ABC–TV, 1976, based on a teleplay)
  LOVE BOAT, THE (series) (ABC–TV, 1977)

LOVE, DEATH AND THE DEVIL see IMP OF THE BOTTLE,
    THE

LOVE 'EM AND LEAVE 'EM (PAR, 1926, based on the
    play by John Van Alstyne Weaver and George Abbott)
  SATURDAY NIGHT KID, THE (PAR, 1929)

LOVE 'EM AND WEEP (short) (PAT, 1927, based on a
    screenplay by Hal Roach)
  CHICKENS COME HOME (short) (MGM, 1931)
  POLITIQUERIAS, LOS (short) (SPA, 1931)

LOVE FROM A STRANGER (UA, 1937, based on the book,
    "Philomel Cottage," by Agatha Christie and the play by
    Frank Vosper)
  LOVE FROM A STRANGER (EL, 1947)

LOVE GAMBLER, THE (FOX, 1922, based on a story by
    Lillian Bennet Thompson and George Hubbard)
  LADRON DE AMOR (SPA, 1930)

LOVE GAMES see LIEBELEI

LOVE IN A BUNGALOW (UN, 1937, based on a story by
    Eleanore Griffin and William Rankin)
  HI, BEAUTIFUL! (UN, 1944)

LOVE IN A WOOD see AS YOU LIKE IT

LOVE IN THE AFTERNOON see ARIANE

LOVE IN THE ROUGH see SPRING FEVER

LOVE INSURANCE (PAR, 1919, based on a story by Earl
    Derr Biggers)
  RECKLESS AGE, THE (UN, 1924)
  ONE NIGHT IN THE TROPICS (UN, 1940)

LOVE IS A MANY–SPLENDORED THING (FOX, 1955,
    based on the book by Han Suyin)
  LOVE IS A MANY–SPLENDORED THING (series) (CBS–
  TV, 1967)

LOVE IS NEWS (FOX, 1937, based on a story by William R.
    Lipman and Frederick Stephani)
  SWEET ROSIE O'GRADY (FOX, 1943)
  THAT WONDERFUL URGE (FOX, 1948)

LOVE IS ON THE AIR see HI, NELLIE!

LOVE LETTERS (PAR, 1945, based on the book by Chris
    Massie)
  LOVE LETTERS (NBC–TV, 1955)

LOVE OF ANDREI, THE see TARAS BULBA

LOVE OF CAMILLE, THE (WB, 1924, based on a story by
    Sacha Guitry)
  DEBURAU (FRA, 1950)

LOVE OF SUNYA, THE see EYES OF YOUTH

LOVE THAT BRUTE see DRESSED TO KILL

LOVE WALTZ, THE see LIEBESWALZER

LOVE WATCHES (VIT, 1918, based on a story, "L'Amour
    Veille," by Robert de Flers and Gaston Arman de
    Caillavet)
  AMOUR VEILLE, L' (FRA, 1937)

LOVE WILL CONQUER see KARLEKEN SEGRAR

LOVELY LADIES, KIND GENTLEMEN see TEAHOUSE
    OF THE AUGUST MOON, THE

LOVELY TO LOOK AT see ROBERTA

LOVER OF CAMILLE, THE see DAME AUX CAMELIAS,
    LA

LOVER'S DUET (JAP, 1939, based on a screenplay by Ryo–
    suke Saito and Kihan Nagase)
  LOVER'S DUET (JAP, 1967)

LOVER'S QUARREL WITH THE WORLD, A see ROBERT

FROST

LOVERS WITHOUT LOVE see KREUTZER SONATA, THE

LOVES AND TIMES OF SCARAMOUCHE, THE see
   SCARAMOUCHE

LOVES OF A DICTATOR see DICTATOR, THE

LOVES OF CARMEN, THE see CARMEN

LOVES OF CASANOVA see CASANOVA

LOVES OF ISADORA, THE see ISADORA, THE BIGGEST
   DANCER IN THE WORLD

LOVES OF MANON LESCAUT, THE see MANON LESCAUT

LOVES OF MARY, QUEEN OF SCOTS (BRI, 1923, based on
   historical incidents and characters)
   MARY, QUEEN OF SCOTS (short) (BRI, 1922)
   MARY OF SCOTLAND (RKO, 1936)
   MARY, QUEEN OF SCOTS (UN, 1971)

LOVES OF SALAMBO, THE see SALAMBO

LOVE'S SURPRISES ARE FUTILE see SACRIFICE, THE

LOWER DEPTHS, THE (RUS, 1912, based on the play by
   Maxim Gorky)
   LOWER DEPTHS, THE (GER, 1919)
   BAS–FONDS, LES (FRA, 1936)
   LOWER DEPTHS, THE (RUS, 1947)
   LOWER DEPTHS, THE (JAP, 1957)
   LOWER DEPTHS, THE (NET–TV, 1966)

LOYAL 47 RONIN (JAP, 1932, source unlisted)
   LOYAL 47 RONIN (JAP, 1934)
   LOYAL 47 RONIN (JAP, 1939)
   LOYAL 47 RONIN (JAP, 1954)
   LOYAL 47 RONIN (JAP, 1958)
   LOYAL 47 RONIN (JAP, 1962)
   LOYAL 47 RONIN OF THE GENROKU (JAP, 1963)

LOYAL 47 RONIN OF THE GENROKU see LOYAL 47
   RONIN

LOYAL REBEL, THE see EUREKA STOCKADE

LUCIA DI LAMMERMOOR (ITA, 1908, based on the book,
   "The Bride of Lammermoor" by Sir Walter Scott and the
   opera by Gaetano Donizetti)
   BRIDE OF LAMMERMOOR (IND, 1914)
   BRIDE OF LAMMERMOOR (short) (BRI, 1922)

LUCK OF ROARING CAMP, THE (ED, 1909, based on the
   story by Bret Harte)
   LUCK OF ROARING CAMP, THE (AUT, 1911)
   LUCK OF ROARING CAMP, THE (ED, 1917)
   LUCK OF ROARING CAMP, THE (MON, 1937)
   OUTCASTS OF POKER FLAT, THE (RKO, 1937)

LUCK OF THE NAVY (BRI, 1927, based on the play by
   Clifford Mills)
   LUCK OF THE NAVY (BRI, 1938)

LUCKY DAMAGE see SKIN DEEP

LUCRETIA BORGIA (ITA, 1909, based on historical char–

acters)
   ETERNAL SIN, THE (IND, 1917)
   LUCRETIA BORGIA (GER, 1922)
   LUCRETIA BORGIA (MUT, 1929)
   LUCRETIA BORGIA (FRA, 1936)
   LUCRETIA BORGIA (IND, 1949)
   BRIDE OF VENGEANCE (PAR, 1949)
   LUCRETIA BORGIA (FRA, 1952)
   NIGHTS OF LUCRETIA BORGIA (ITA, 1960)
   LUCRETIA, THE DEVIL'S LOVER (AUS/ITA, 1968)

LUISE, KONIGIN VON PREUSSEN (GER, 1931, based on
   the book by Walter von Molo)
   KONIGIN LUISE (GER, 1957)

LUISE MILLERIN see KABALE UND LIEBE

LULU (GER, 1917, based on the plays by Frank Wedekind
   "Earth Spirit" and "Pandora's Box;" also the basis for the
   opera by Alban Berg)
   LULU (HUN, 1917)
   BUCHSE DER PANDORA, DIE (GER, 1919)
   ERDGEIST (GER, 1922)
   BUCHSE DER PANDORA, DIE (GER, 1928)
   LULU (GER, 1952)
   LULU (AUS, 1962)
   NO ORCHIDS FOR LULU (GER, 1967)

LUMMEL VONDER ERSTEN BANK II, DIE (GER, 1968, source
   unknown)
   LUMMEL VON DER ERSTEN BANK III, DIE (GER, 1969)

LUMPACI THE VAGABOND (GER, 1922, source unlisted)
   LUMPACI THE VAGABOND (GER, 1937)

LUMPAZIVAGABUNDUS (DEN, 1911, based on the book by
   Johann Nestroy)
   LUMPAZIVAGABUNDUS (GER, 1922)
   LUMPAZIVAGABUNDUS (SWE, 1923)
   LUMPAZIVAGABUNDUS (AUS, 1937)
   LUMPAZIVAGABUNDUS (GER, 1956)

LURE OF THE WILDERNESS see SWAMP WATER

LUST FOR A VAMPIRE see STRANGE CASE OF DAVID
   GRAY, THE

LUST FOR LIFE see VAN GOGH

LUSTIGEN VAGABUNDEN (GER, 1928, source unlisted)
   LUSTIGEN VAGABUNDEN (GER, 1940)
   LUSTIGEN VAGABUNDEN (GER, 1963)

LUTHER see MARTIN LUTHER, THE NIGHTINGALE OF
   WITTENBERG

LYDA SSANIN (GER, 1922, based on a book by Mikhail
   Artsybachev)
   SSANIN (AUS, 1924)

LYDIA see CARNET DU BAL, UN

LYNCH MOB see OX–BOW INCIDENT, THE

LYONS MAIL (BRI, 1916, based on the play by Charles Reade)
   LYONS MAIL (BRI, 1931)

LYSISTRATA see WARRIOR'S HUSBAND, THE

M   (GER, 1931, based on a screenplay by Thea von Harbou)
  M   (COL, 1951)
  VAMPIRE OF DUSSELDROF, THE   (FRA, 1965)

M*A*S*H   (FOX, 1970, based on the book by Richard
    Hooker)
  M*A*S*H   (series)   (CBS–TV, 1972)

M*A*S*H   see also   BATTLE CIRCUS

MacARTHUR   see   GENERAL DOUGLAS MacARTHUR

McCLOUD: WHO KILLED MISS USA?   see   COOGAN'S
    BLUFF

McCOY   see   BIG RIPOFF, THE

McFADDEN'S PLATS   (FN, 1927, based on the play by Gus
    Hill)
  McFADDEN'S FLATS   (PAR, 1935)

McHALE'S NAVY   (series)   (ABC–TV, 1962, based on a
    teleplay)
  McHALE'S NAVY   (UN, 1964)
  McHALE'S NAVY JOINS THE AIR FORCE   (UN, 1965)

McTEAGUE   see   LIFE'S WHIRLPOOL

MA AND PA   (short)   (CBS–TV, 1974, based on the play,
    "Twigs," by George Furth)
  TWIGS   (CBS–TV, 1975)

MA COUSINE DE VARSOVIE   see   MEINE COUSINE AUS
    WARSCHAU

MA TANTE D'HONFLEUR   (FRA, 1923, based on a book by
    Paul Gavault)
  MA TANTE D'HONFLEUR   (FRA, 1948)

MACAHANS, THE   (ABC–TV, 1976, based on a teleplay)
  HOW THE WEST WAS WON   (ABC–TV, 1977)
  HOW THE WEST WAS WON   (series)   (ABC–TV, 1978)

MACBETH   (BIO, 1905, based on the play by William Shake–
    speare)
  MACBETH   (VIT, 1908)
  MACBETH   (FRA, 1909)
  MACBETH   (ITA, 1910)
  MACBETH   (BRI, 1911)
  MACBETH   (BRI, 1913)
  MACBETH   (GER, 1913)
  MACBETH   (FRA, 1916)
  MACBETH   (TRI, 1916)
  REAL THING AT LAST, THE   (BRI, 1916)
  MACBETH   (BRI, 1917)
  MACBETH   (GER, 1920)
  MACBETH   (short)   (BRI, 1922)
  MACBETH   (GER, 1922)
  MACBETH   (short)   (BRI, 1945)
  MACBETH   (BRA, 1946)
  MACBETH   (IND, 1946)
  MACBETH   (REP, 1948)
  MACBETH   (NBC–TV, 1950)
  MACBETH   (BJU, 1950)
  MACBETH   (CBS–TV, 1951)
  RIDEAU ROUGE, LE   (FRA, 1952)
  MACBETH   (short)   (BRI, 1953)
  MACBETH   (NBC–TV, 1953)
  MACBETH   (NBC–TV, 1954)

JOE MACBETH   (COL, 1956)
THRONE OF BLOOD   (JAP, 1958)
MACBETH   (BRI, 1960)
MACBETH   (CBS–TV, 1961)
MACBETH   (CAN–TV, 1962)
SIBERIAN LADY MACBETH   (YUG, 1962)
MACBETH   (series)   (BRI–TV, c1965)
TRAGEDY OF MACBETH, THE   (NET–TV, 1968)
MACBETH   (BRI, 1971)

MACHINE A REFAIRE LA VIE, LA   (FRA, 1924, source
    unlisted)
  MACHINE A REFAIRE LA VIE, LA   (FRA, 1933)

MACHT DER FINSTERNIS   see   PUISSANCE DES TENE–
    BRES, LA

MACISTE IN HELL   see   DANTE'S INFERNO

MAD ABOUT MUSIC   (UN, 1938, based on a story by Marcella
    Burke and Frederick Kolmer)
  TOY TIGER   (UN, 1956)

MAD EMPEROR, THE   see   PATRIOT, THE

MAD HOUR, THE   see   MAN AND THE MOMENT, THE

MAD LOVE   see   HANDS OF ORLAC, THE

MAD NIGHT   see   REVIZOR

MAD ROOM, THE   see   LADIES IN RETIREMENT

MAD STAMPEDE, THE   (UN, 1917, based on a poem by Frank
    Desprez)
  LASCA   (UN, 1919)
  LASCA OF THE RIO GRANDE   (UN, 1931)

MADAME   see   MADAME SANS–GENE

MADAME BOVARY   see   UNHOLY LOVE

MADAME BUTTERFLY   (BRA, 1910, based on the play by
    David Belasco and the opera by Giocomo Puccini)
  MADAME BUTTERFLY   (PAR, 1915)
  HARA KIRI   (GER, 1919)
  TOLL OF THE SEA   (IND, 1922)
  MADAME BUTTERFLY   (PAR, 1932)
  DREAM OF BUTTERFLY, THE   (GER/ITA, 1939)
  MADAME BUTTERFLY   (NBC–TV, 1950)
  MADAME BUTTERFLY   (NBC–TV, 1955)
  MADAME BUTTERFLY   (ITA/JAP, 1955)
  MADAME BUTTERFLY   (ITA, 1970)

MADAME CURIE   (MGM, 1943, based on the lives and work
    of scientists Eve and Pierre Curie)
  MONSIEUR ET MADAME CURIE   (short)   (FRA, 1953)
  DISCOVERY OF RADIUM, THE   (short)   (CBS–TV, 1956)
  MARIE CURIE – A LOVE STORY   (short)   (CEN, 1977)
  MARIE CURIE   (PBS-TV, 1978)

MADAME DUBARRY   see   DUBARRY

MADAME LA GIMP   see   LADY FOR A DAY

MADAME LA PRESIDENTE   see   PRESIDENT, LA

MADAME SANS–GENE (DUCHESSE DE DANTZIG, LA
    (DEN, 1909, based on the play by Victorien Sardou and
    Emile Moreau)

MADAME SANS–GENE (FRA, 1911)
MADAME SANS–GENE (ITA, 1917)
NAPOLEON UND DIE KLEINE WACSHERIN (GER, 1920)
DAUGHTERS OF MADAME SANS–GENE, THE (ITA, 1921)
MADAME SANS–GENE (IND, 1922)
MADAME SANS–GENE (FRA, 1924)
MADAME SANS–GENE (PAR, 1925)
MADAME SANS–GENE (FRA, 1941)
MADAME SANS–GENE (ARG, 1945)
MADAME (FRA, 1963)

MADAME SPY see UNTER FALSCHEN FLAGGEN

MADAME TALLIEN (FRA, 1911, based on the book by Victorien Sardou)
MADAME TALLIEN (ITA, 1916)

MADAME WUNSCHT KEINE KINDER (GER, 1926, based on the book by Clement Vautel)
MADAME WUNSCHT KEINE KINDER (GER, 1933)

MADAME X (PAT, 1915, based on the play by Alexandre Bisson)
MADAME X (MGM, 1920)
MADAME X (TV Title: ABSINTHE) (MGM, 1929)
MUJER X, LA (MEX, 1931)
MADAME X (MGM, 1937)
TRIAL OF MADAME X, THE (BRI, 1948)
MADAME X (GRE, 1960)
MADAME X (UN, 1966)

MADELEINE (UN, 1950, based on a story by Stanley Haynes and Nicholas Phipps)
MADELEINE (NBC–TV, 1960)

MLLE. FIFI see WOMAN DISPUTED, A

MLLE. JOSETTE, MA FEMME (FRA/GER, 1926, based on a story by Paul Gavault and Robert Charvay)
MLLE. JOSETTE, MA FEMME (FRA, 1932)
MLLE. JOSETTE, MA FEMME (FRA, 1950)

MADEMOISELLE LA PRESIDENTE see PRESIDENT, LA

MADEMOISELLE MODISTE (FN, 1926, based on the musical by Henry Blossom and Victor Herbert)
KISS ME AGAIN (WB, 1931)
FIFI (short) (WB, 1933)
MLLE. MODISTE (NBC–TV, 1951)

MLLE. NITOUCHE see MAM'ZELLE NITOUCHE

MADIGAN (UN, 1968, based on a screenplay by Abraham Polonsky and Henri Simoun)
MADIGAN (series) (NBC–TV, 1972)

MADMAN'S HOLIDAY see CRACK–UP

MADMEN OF EUROPE see ENGLISHMEN'S HOME, AN

MADONE DES SLEEPINGS, LA (FRA, 1927, based on a story by Maurice Dekobra)
MADONE DES SLEEPINGS, LA (FRA, 1955)

MADONNA OF THE STREETS (FN, 1924, based on the play, "The Ragged Messenger," by W.C. Maxwell)
MADONNA OF THE STREETS (COL, 1930)

MAEDCHEN AUS DER FREMDE, DAS (GER, 1921, source unlisted)
MAEDCHEN AUS DER FREMDE, DAS (GER, 1926)

MAEDCHEN IN UNIFORM (GER, 1931, based on the play, "Gestern und Heute," by Christa Winsloe)
YOUNG GIRLS IN PERU (FRA, 1939)
MAECHEN IN UNIFORM (GER, 1958)
MAEDCHEN IN UNIFORM (GER, 1965)
GIRLS IN UNIFORM (BRI–TV, 1967)

MAEDCHEN VOM MOORHOF, DAS see FILLE DE LA TOURBIERE, LA

MAEDCHEN VOM PFARRHOF, DAS see PFARRER VON KIRCHENFELD, DER

MAEDCHENJAHRE EINER KONIGIN (GER, 1936, source unlisted)
MAEDCHENJAHRE EINER KONIGIN (GER, 1954)

MAEDEL VOM BALLETT (GER, 1918, source unlisted)
MAEDEL VOM BALLETT (GER, 1936)

MAEDEL VON DER REEPERBAHN see MENSCHEN IM RAUSCH

MAEDELS VON HEUTE (GER, 1925, source unlisted)
MAEDELS VON HEUTE (GER, 1933)
LIEBESGESCHICTEN (GER, 1943)

MAENNER MUESSEN SO SEIN (GER, 1939, based on the book by Heinrich Seidel)
MAENNER MUESSEN SO SEIN (GER, 1959)

MAENNER VON DER EHE (GER, 1927)
MAENNER CON DER EHE (GER, 1936)

MAESTRO FRANZ LISZT AT WEIMAR see DREAM OF LOVE

MAGDA see HEIMAT

MAGIC BOW, THE see PAGANINI

MAGIC CLOAK OF OZ, THE see DOROTHY AND THE SCARECROW OF OZ

MAGIC FIRE see RICHARD WAGNER

MAGIC FLUTE, THE (IN, 1934, based on the opera by Wolfgang Amadeus Mozart)
PAPAGENO (GER, 1935)
FLUTE MAGIQUE, LA (FRA, 1946)
JADUI BANSARI (IN, 1948)
MAGIC FLUTE, THE (IND, 1962)
MAGIC FLUTE, THE (DEN/SWE, 1975)

MAGIC HORSE, THE (RUS, 1948, based on a story by Pytor Yershov)
HUMPBACKED HORSE, THE (RUS, 1976)

MAGIC MIRROR OF ALOISE, THE (short) (IND, 1977, based on the life of painter Aloise)
ALOISE (FRA, 1975)

MAGIC OF LASSIE, THE see LASSIE COME HOME

MAGIC SKIN, THE see PEAU D'ANE

MAGIC SLIPPERS, THE see CINDERELLA AND THE
    FAIRY GODMOTHER

MAGIC SWORD, THE see ST. GEORGE AND THE
    DRAGON

MAGNETIC MONSTER, THE see GOLD

MAGNIFICENT AMBERSONS, THE see PAMPERED
    YOUTH

MAGNIFICENT CONCUBINE see EMPRESS YANG KWEI
    FEI

MAGNIFICENT LIE, THE see FOOL'S PARADISE

MAGNIFICENT OBSESSION (UN, 1935, based on the book
    by Lloyd C. Douglas)
    MAGNIFICENT OBSESSION (UN, 1954)

MAGNIFICENT SEVEN, THE see SEVEN SAMURAI

MAGNIFICENT SINNER, THE see KATIA

MAGNIFICENT 6–½, THE (short) (BRI, 1968, based on a
    teleplay)
    DOUBLE–DECKERS, THE (series) (BRI–TV, 1971)

MAGNIFICENT YANKEE, THE (MGM, 1950, based on the
    life of Supreme Court justice Oliver Wendell Holmes and a
    play by Emmet Lavery)
    OLIVER WENDELL HOLMES (short) (EBE, 1950)
    MAGNIFICENT YANKEE, THE (NBC–TV, 1965)

MAGNOLIA see FIGHTING COWARD, THE

MAGNOLIA LADY, THE see COME OUT OF THE KITCHEN

MAGOO AT SEA see PIRATE'S TREASURE and SEA
    BEAST, THE

MAGOO IN THE KING'S SERVICE see CYRANO and
    THREE MUSKETEERS, THE

MAHABHARET (IN, 1919, based on an Indian myth)
    MAHABHARET (IN, 1936)
    MAHABHARET (IN, 1944)

MAHATMA see MAHATMA GANDHI

MAHATMA GANDHI (short) (IDE, n.d., based on the life
    and teachings of the noted Indian spiritual leader)
    MAHATMA GANDHI (short) (EBE, 1955)
    HIS MEMORY WE CHERISH (short) (IN, n.d.)
    GANDHI (short) (CBS–TV, 1959)
    MAHATMA GANDHI – THE STILL SMALL VOICE
        WITHIN (short) (USC, 1962)
    MAHATMA, THE GREAT SOUL (short) (MGM–TV,
        1963)
    MAHATMA GANDHI (short) (MHF, 1964)
    MAHATMA GANDHI – THE SILENT REVOLUTION (short)
        (IFB, 1969)

MAHATMA, THE GREAT SOUL see MAHATMA GANDHI

MAHATMA GANDHI – THE SILENT REVOLUTION see
    MAHATMA GANDHI

MAHATMA GANDHI – THE STILL SMALL VOICE WITHIN

see MAHATMA GANDHI

MAID OF CEFN YDFA (BRI, 1908, based on the play by
    James Haggar Jr.)
    MAID OF CEFN YDFA (BRI, 1914)

MAIN STREET (WB, 1923, based on the book by Sinclair
    Lewis)
    I MARRIED A DOCTOR (WB, 1936)

MAINLY ON THE PLAINS see DON QUIXOTE

MAISON CERNEE, LA (SWE, 1922, based on a novel, "La
    Route Imperiale," by Pierre Frondaie)
    ROUTE IMPERIALE, LA (FRA, 1935)

MAISON DANS LA DUNE, LA (FRA, 1933, baeed on the
    book by Maxence van der Meersch)
    MAISON DANS LA DUNE, LA (FRA, 1951)

MAISON DE LA PEUR, LA see LAUREL & HARDY
    MURDER CASE, THE

MAITRE BOLBEC ET SON MARI (n.d., based on a book
    by Georges Berr and Louis Verneuil)
    WORLD AT HER FEET, THE (PAR, 1927)
    MAITRE BOLBEC AT SON MARI (FRA, 1934)

MAITRE DE FORGES, LE (FRA, 1913, based on the book
    by Georges Ohnet)
    VIEILLE HISTOIRE, LA (DEN, 1913)
    MAITRE DE FORGES, LE (ITA, 1918)
    IRON MASTER, THE (IND, 1932)
    MAITRE DE FORGES, LE (FRA, 1933)
    MAITRE DE FORGES (LE, 1947)
    MAITRE DE FORGES, LE (ITA/SPA, 1959)

MAJESTAT AUF ABWEGEN see NEWLY RICH

MAJOR AND THE MINOR, THE (PAR, 1942, based on a
    story by Fannie Kilbourne and a play by Edward Childs
    Carpenter)
    YOU'RE NEVER TOO YOUNG (PAR, 1955)

MAKE ME A STAR see MERTON OF THE MOVIES

MAKE MINE MUSIC see PETER AND THE WOLF

MAKE ROOM FOR DADDY (series) (CBS–TV, 1953, based
    on a teleplay)
    MAKE ROOM FOR GRANDADDY (series) (ABC–TV,
    1970)

MAKE ROOM FOR GRANDADDY see MAKE ROOM FOR
    DADDY

MAKE WAY FOR TOMORROW (PAR, 1937, based on the
    book by Josephine Lawrence and the play by Helen and
    Nolan Leary)
    MAKE WAY FOR TOMORROW (NBC–TV, 1955)

MAKING OF A MURAL, THE (short) (EBE, 1947, based on
    the life and work of the noted artist)
    THOMAS HART BENTON: PROFILES IN COURAGE
    (SAU, 1957)

MAKING OF O'MALLEY, THE (FN, 1925, based on a story
    by Gerald Beaumont)
    GREAT O'MALLEY, THE (WB, 1937)

MAKING OF THE PRESIDENT – 1960, THE (XEX, 1961, based on the life of U.S. President John F. Kennedy)
P. T. 109 (WB, 1963)
DEATH OF PRESIDENT KENNEDY, THE (short) (IND, 1963)
JOHN FITZGERALD KENNEDY (short) (FOX, n.d.)
JOHN F. KENNEDY (TV, 1964)
JOHN F. KENNEDY: YEARS OF LIGHTNING, DAYS OF DRUMS (EMB, 1964)
BURDEN AND GLORY OF JOHN F. KENNEDY, THE (CBS–TV, 1964)
KENNEDY: THE MAN AND THE PRESIDENT (short) (UNI, 1964)
JOHN F. KENNEDY REMEMBERED (NBC–TV, 1964)
YOUNG MAN FROM BOSTON, THE (ABC–TV, 1965)
JOHN FITZGERALD KENNEDY -- A HISTORY OF OUR TIMES (short) (CFD, n.d.)
KENNEDY -- WHAT IS REMEMBERED IS NEVER LOST (short) (NBC–TV, 1966)
JOHN FITZGERALD KENNEDY: A HISTORY OF OUR TIME (IND, 1967)
AGE OF KENNEDY, THE (NBC–TV, 1967)
JFK: A THOUSAND DAYS . . . AND TEN YEARS (CBS–TV, 1973)
JFK: A TIME TO REMEMBER (ABC–TV, 1974)

MAKING OF THE PRESIDENT – 1960, THE (FNC, 1964, based on the life of the U.S. president)
NIXON–KENNEDY DEBATES (IND, 1960)
NIXON: CHECKERS TO WATERGATE (short) (PYR, 1976)

MALARPRIRATER (SWE, 1923, source unlisted)
MALARPIRATER (SWE, 1959)

MALE AND FEMALE see BACK TO NATURE

MALE ANIMAL, THE (WB, 1942, based on the play by Elliott Nugent and James Thurber)
SHE'S WORKING HER WAY THROUGH COLLEGE (WB, 1952)

MALE SIERENA see QUEEN OF THE SEA

MALEDICTION DE BELPHEGOR, LA (series) (FRA–TV, 1966, based on a teleplay by Georges Combret and Michel Dubosc)
MALEDICTION DE BELPHEGOR, LA (FRA, 1967)

MALTESE FALCON, THE (TV Title: DANGEROUS FEMALE) (WB, 1931, based on the book by Dashiell Hammett)
SATAN MET A LADY (HARD LUCK DAME) (WB, 1936)
MALTESE FALCON, THE (WB, 1941)
OLD, THE NEW AND THE DEADLY, THE (ABC–TV, 1971)
BLACK BIRD, THE (COL, 1975)
CHEAP DETECTIVE, THE (COL, 1978)

MAMA see I REMEMBER MAMA

MAMAN COLIBRI (FRA, 1929, based on a book by Henri Bataille)
MAMAN COLIBRI (FRA, 1937)

MAME see AUNTIE MAME

MAM'ZELLE NITOUCHE (SANTARELLINA) (ITA, 1911, based on the play by Henri Meilhac and Arthur Millaud)
MAM'ZELLE NITOUCHE (FRA, 1931)

MAM'ZELLE NITOUCHE (GER, 1931)
MAM'ZELLE NITOUCHE (FRA, 1953)

MAN (JAP, 1925, source unlisted)
MAN (JAP, 1962)

MAN, THE (TV, n.d., based on the play by Mel Dinelli)
BEWARE MY LOVELY (RKO, 1952)

MAN ABOUT THE HOUSE (series) (BRI–TV, n.d., based on a teleplay)
THREE'S COMPANY (ABC–TV, 1977)

MAN AND SUPERMAN see DON JUAN IN HELL

MAN AND THE MOMENT, THE (AE, 1922, based on a story by Elinor Glyn)
MAD HOUR, THE (FN, 1928)

MAN AT SIX, THE see GABLES MYSTERY, THE

MAN BEAST see ABOMINABLE SNOWMAN, THE

MAN BETRAYED, A (REP, 1937, based on a story by Dorrell and Stuart McGowan)
MAN BETRAYED, A (REP, 1941)

MAN CALLED GANNON, A see MAN WITHOUT A STAR

MAN CALLED EDISON, THE see YOUNG TOM EDISON

MAN FRIDAY see ROBINSON CRUSOE

MAN FROM ATLANTIS (NBC–TV, 1977, based on a teleplay)
MAN FROM ATLANTIS (series) (NBC–TV, 1977)

MAN FROM BLANKLEY'S, THE see FOURTEENTH MAN, THE

MAN FROM GALVESTON, THE (WB, 1964, based on a screenplay by Dean Riesner and Michael Zagor)
TEMPLE HOUSTON (series) (NBC–TV, 1964)

MAN FROM HOME, THE (PAR, 1914, based on the play by Booth Tarkington and Harry Leon Wilson)
MAN FROM HOME, THE (PAR, 1922)

MAN FROM MEXICO, THE (PAR, 1914, based on the play by Henry A. DuSouchet)
LET'S GET MARRIED (PAR, 1926)

MAN IN DRESS CLOTHES, THE see EVENING CLOTHES

MAN IN HALF--MOON STREET, THE (PAR, 1944, based on the play by Barre Lyndon)
MAN IN HALF–MOON STREET, THE (NBC–TV, 1953)
MAN WHO COULD CHEAT DEATH, THE (BRI, 1959)

MAN IN POSSESSION, THE (MGM, 1931, based on the play by H.M. Harwood)
PERSONAL PROPERTY (MGM, 1937)

MAN IN THE ATTIC, THE see LODGER, THE

MAN IN THE BARN, THE (short) (MGM, 1937, based on information regarding the assassination of Abraham Lincoln and the death of John Wilkes Booth)
LINCOLN CONSPIRACY, THE (IND, 1977)

MAN IN THE DARK   see   MAN WHO LIVED TWICE, THE

MAN IN THE IRON MASK, THE   (short)   (BRI, 1928, based
   on the book by Alexandre Dumas)
IRON MASK, THE   (UA, 1929)
MAN IN THE IRON MASK   (UA, 1939)
LADY IN THE IRON MASK   (FOX, 1952)
PRISONER OF THE IRON MASK   (FRA/ITA, 1961)
MAN IN THE IRON MASK, THE   (NBC--TV, 1977)
BEHIND THE IRON MASK   (AUS, 1977)

MAN IS TEN FEET TALL, A   (NBC–TV, 1955, based on a
   teleplay by Robert Alan Aurthur)
EDGE OF THE CITY   (MGM, 1957)

MAN NAMED JOHN, A   see   AND THERE CAME A MAN

MAN NOBODY KNOWS, THE   see   PASSION PLAY, THE

MAN OF CONQUEST   see   CONQUERER, THE

MAN OF HER CHOICE, A   see   BACK TO NATURE

MAN OF LA MANCHA   see   DON QUIXOTE

MAN OF THE FOREST   (HOD, 1921, based on the book by
   Zane Grey)
MAN OF THE FOREST   (PAR, 1926)
MAN OF THE FOREST   (PAR, 1933)

MAN ON FIRE   (NBC–TV, 1956, based on the teleplay by
   Malvin Wald and Jack Jacobs)
MAN ON FIRE   (MGM, 1957)

MAN ON THE BOX, THE   (PAR, 1914, based on the book and
   play by Harold McGrath)
MAN ON THE BOX, THE   (WB, 1925)

MAN ON THE EIFFEL TOWER, THE   see   TETE D'UN
   HOMME, LA

MAN ON THE LEDGE   see   14 HOURS

MAN SPIELT NICHT MIT DER LIEBE   (GER, 1926, source
   unlisted)
MAN SPIELT NICHT MIT DER LIEBE   (GER, 1949)

MAN THEY COULD NOT HANG   (AUT, 1917, source unlisted)
MAN THEY COULD NOT HANG   (AUT, 1921)

MAN TO REMEMBER, A   see   ONE MAN'S JOURNEY

MAN TRAILER, THE   see   LONE RIDER, THE

MAN WHO CAME BACK, THE   (FOX, 1924, based on the
   story by John Fleming Wilson)
MAN WHO CAME BACK, THE   (FOX, 1930)
CAMINO DEL INFIERNO   (SPA, 1931)

MAN WHO CAME TO DINNER, THE   (WB, 1941, based on
   the play by George S. Kaufman and Moss Hart; also the
   basis for the musical comedy, "Sherry," in 1967)
MAN WHO CAME TO DINNER, THE   (CBS--TV, 1954)
MAN WHO CAME TO DINNER, THE   (NBC--TV, 1972)

MAN WHO CHANGED HIS NAME, THE   (BRI, 1928, based
   on the book by Edgar Wallace)

MAN WHO CHANGED HIS NAME, THE   (BRI, 1934)

MAN WHO CHEATED DEATH, THE   see   STUDENT OF
   PRAGUE, THE

MAN WHO CORRUPTED HADLEYSBURG, THE   see   MAN
   WITH A MILLION

MAN WHO COULD CHEAT DEATH, THE   see   MAN IN
   HALF–MOON STREET, THE

MAN WHO DARED, THE   see   STAR WITNESS

MAN WHO DEMORALIZED HADLEYSBURG, THE   see
   MAN WITH A MILLION

MAN WHO KILLED BILLY THE KID, THE   see   BILLY THE
   KID

MAN WHO KNEW TOO MUCH, THE   (BRI, 1935, based on
   a screenplay by Edwin Greenwood and A.R. Rawlinson)
MAN WHO KNEW TOO MUCH, THE   (PAR, 1956)

MAN WHO LAUGHS, THE   see   HOMME QUI RIT, L'

MAN WHO LOST HIMSELF, THE   (SEZ, 1920, based on the
   book by H. DeVere Stackpole)
MAN WHO LOST HIMSELF, THE   (UN, 1941)

MAN WHO NEVER WAS, THE   (FOX, 1956, based on the
   book by Ewen Montagu)
MAN WHO NEVER WAS, THE   (series)   (ABC–TV, 1966)

MAN WHO PLAYED GOD, THE   (UA, 1922, based on the
   play by Jules Eckert Goodman)
MAN WHO PLAYED GOD, THE   (WB, 1932)
SINCERELY YOURS   (WB, 1955)
MAN WHO PLAYED GOD, THE   (CBS--TV, 1957)

MAN WHO RECLAIMED HIS HEAD, THE   (UN,1935, based on
   a play by Jean Bart)
STRANGE CONFESSION   (UN, 1945)

MAN WHO SOLD HIS SOUL, THE   see   MAN WHO SOLD HIS
   SOUL TO THE DEVIL, THE

MAN WHO SOLD HIS SOUL TO THE DEVIL, THE   (FRA,
   1920, source unknown)
MAN WHO SOLD HIS SOUL, THE   (FRA, 1943)

MAN WHO TALKED TOO MUCH, THE   see   MOUTHPIECE,
   THE

MAN WHO WON, THE   see   TWINS OF SUFFERING CREEK

MAN WHO WOULDN'T TALK, THE   see   VALIANT, THE

MAN WITH A MILLION, THE   see   MILLION POUND NOTE,
   THE

MAN WITH A TWISTED LIP, THE   (short)   (BRI, 1921,
   based on the story by Sir Arthur Conan Doyle)
MAN WITH THE TWISTED LIP, THE   (short)   (BRI, 1951)

MAN WITH TWO HEADS, THE   see   DR. JEKYLL AND MR.
   HYDE

MAN WITHIN, THE   see   ANDERE, DER

MAN WITHOUT A COUNTRY, THE see DEATH OF
    NATHAN HALE, THE

MAN WITHOUT A FACE see PSYCHO CIRCUS

MAN WITHOUT A STAR (UN, 1955, based on a book by Dee
    Linford)
  MAN CALLED GANNON, A (UN, 1968)

MAN, WOMAN AND SIN (MGM, 1927, based on a story by
    Monta Bell)
  UP FOR MURDER (UN, 1931)

MANDRAKE see ALRAUNE

MANEGE (GER, 1927, source unlisted)
  MANEGE (GER, 1937)

MANFISH see AVENGING CONSCIENCE, THE and
    SCARABEE D'OR, LE

MANHATTAN HEARTBEAT see BAD GIRL

MANHATTAN MELODRAMA (MGM, 1934, based on a story
    by Arthur Caesar)
  NORTHWEST RANGERS (MGM, 1942)

MANHUNT (FOX, 1941, based on the book, "Rogue Male,"
    by Geoffrey Householder)
  ROGUE MALE (BRI–TV, 1976)

MANHUNT OF MYSTERY ISLAND (serial) (REP, 1945,
    based on a screenplay by various authors; the remake is a
    condensation of the serial)
  CAPTAIN MEPHISTO AND THE TRANSFORMATION
    MACHINE (REP, 1966)

MANIA see BODY SNATCHER, THE

MANN IM SATTEL, DER (GER, 1925, source unlisted)
  MANN IN SATTEL, DER (GER, 1945)

MANOLESCU (GER, 1929, based on the book by George
    Manolescu)
  MANOLESCU, DER FURST DER DIEBE (GER, 1933)

MANOLESCU, DER FURST DER DIEBE see MANOLESCU

MANOLETE (SPA, 1949, based on the life of the noted bull–
    fighter)
  DEATH OF MANOLETE (CBS–TV, 1957)
  DAY MANOLETE WAS KILLED, THE (short) (GO, 1964)

MANON LESCAUT (ITA, 1908, based on the book by Antoine–
    Francois Prevost d'Exiles and the opera by Giacommo
    Puccini)
  MANON LESCAUT (FRA, 1910)
  MANON LESCAUT (FRA, 1911)
  MANON LESCAUT (IND, 1914)
  MANON LESCAUT (GER, 1919)
  MANON LESCAUT (GER, 1926)
  WHEN A MAN LOVES (WB, 1927)
  MANON LESCAUT (ITA, 1939)
  MANON LESCAUT (FRA, 1948)
  LOVES OF MANON LESCAUT, THE (FRA/ITA, 1954)
  MANON '70 (FRA/GER/ITA, 1968)

MANON '70 see MANON LESCAUT

MANPOWER see TIGER SHARK

MANSLAUGHTER (PAR, 1922, based on a story by Alice
    Duer Miller)
  MANSLAUGHTER (PAR, 1930)
  INCORREGIBLE, LA (SPA, 1930)
  REQUISITOIRE, LE (FRA, 1930)

MANTEAU, LA see OVERCOAT, THE

MANTEAU PARLANT, LE (HUN, 1941, based on the book
    by Kalman Mikszath)
  MANTEAU PARLANT, LE (HUN, 1967)

MANTRAP (PAR, 1926, based on the book by Sinclair Lewis)
  UNTAMED (PAR, 1940)

MANXMAN (BRI, 1916, based on the book by Hall Caine)
  MANXMAN (BRI, 1929)

MANY LOVES OF DOBIE GILLIS, THE see AFFAIRS OF
    DOBIE GILLIS, THE

MANY MOONS (ABC--TV, 1954, based on the story by James
    Thurber)
  MANY MOONS (MHF, 1962)
  ALICE IN WONDERLAND IN PARIS (sequence) (CHI, 196◗

MANY SAPPY RETURNS see FAST WORK

MAO TSE TUNG see RED CHINA

MAQUILLAGE see BEHIND THE MAKE–UP

MARAT/SADE (UA, 1967, based on the play by Peter Weiss)
  MARAT/SADE (PBS–TV, 1970)

MARCH AU SOLEIL, LE (FRA, 1934, source unlisted)
  CHILDREN OF THE SUN (UN, 1934)

MARCH OF THE WOODEN SOLDIERS see BABES IN
    TOYLAND

MARCHAND DE VENISE, LE see MERCHANT OF VENICE,
    THE

MARCO see ADVENTURES OF MARCO POLO, THE

MARCO POLO see ADVENTURES OF MARCO POLO

MARCO POLO JR. see ADVENTURES OF MARCO POLO,
    THE

MARCO THE CLOWN see CAMP VOLANT

MARCO THE MAGNIFICENT see ADVENTURES OF
    MARCO POLO, THE

MARCUS--NELSON MURDERS, THE (CBS--TV, 1972, based
    on a teleplay by Abby Mann)
  KOJAK (series) (CBS–TV, 1973)

MARE NOSTRUM (MGM, 1926, based on the book by
    Vicente Blasco–Ibanez)
  MARE NOSTRUM (SPA, 1948)
  DU SANG L'AUBE (ITA/SPA, 1953)

MARGIE (FOX, 1946, based on stories by Ruth McKenney
    and Richard Bransten)

MARGIE (series) (ABC–TV, 1961)

MARGUERITE OF THE NIGHT see FAUST

MARIA CHAPDELAINE (FRA, 1934, based on a novel by
Louis Hemon)
MARIA CHAPDELAINE (BRI, 1949)
NAKED HEART, THE (FRA, 1949)

MARIA MAGDALENE (GER, 1918, based on a story by
Christian Friedrich Hebbel)
INTRIGANT, DER (GER, 1919)

MARIA MARTEN see MARIA MARTEN: OR THE MUR–
DER IN THE RED BARN

MARIA MARTEN: OR THE MURDER IN THE RED BARN
(BRI, 1902, based on a news story)
RED BARN CRIME: OR THE MARIA MARTEN STORY
(BRI, 1908)
MARIA MARTEN: OR THE MURDER IN THE RED BARN
(BRI, 1913)
MARIA MARTEN (BRI, 1928)
MARIA MARTEN (BRI, 1935)

MARIA ROSA (PAR, 1916, based on the play by Guido
Marburg and Wallace Gillpatrick)
MARIA ROSA (SPA, 1965)

MARIA STUART see MARY STUART

MARIA WALEWSKA (GER, 1936, based on a book by Waclaw
Gasiorowski)
CONQUEST (MGM, 1937)
MARIA WALEWSKA AND NAPOLEON (POL, 1966)

MARIAGE DE MADEMOISELLE BEULEMANS, LE (BEL/
FRA, 1926, based on a story by Jean–Francois Fonson and
Fernand Wicheler)
MARIAGE DE MADEMOISELLE BEULEMANS, LE
(BEL/FRA, 1932)
MARIAGE DE MADEMOISELLE BEULEMANS, LE
(BEL/FRA, 1950)

MARIDA Y MUJER see BAD GIRL

MARIE ANTOINETTE (GER, 1922, based on a historical
character and historical events)
MARIE ANTOINETTE (IND, 1929)
MARIE ANTOINETTE (MGM, 1938)
SHADOW OF THE GUILLOTINE (FRA, 1953)
MARIE ANTOINETTE (BRI/ITA, 1960)

MARIE CURIE see MADAME CURIE

MARIE CURIE -- A LOVE STORY see MADAME CURIE

MARIES (SWE, 1926, based on the play by August Strindberg)
MARIES (SWE, 1955)

MARILYN (FOX, 1963, based on the life of actress Marilyn
Monroe)
MARILYN MONROE SPECIAL (ABC–TV, 1963)
LEGEND OF MARILYN MONROE, THE (ABC–TV, 1966)
MARILYN REMEMBERED (ABC–TV, 1974)

MARILYN MONROE SPECIAL see MARILYN

MARILYN REMEMBERED see MARILYN

MARION DELORME (FRA, 1912, based on a novel by Victor
Hugo)
MARION DELORME (FRA, 1918)

MARIONS–NOUS see MISS BLUEBEARD

MARITANA (short) (BRI, 1922, based on the opera by H.V.
Wallace)
MARITANA (short) (BRI, 1927)

MARIUS (FRA, 1930, based on a screenplay by Marcel Pagnol)
ZUM GOLDENEN ANKER (GER, 1931)
LANGTAN TILL HAVET (SWE, 1931)
MARIUS (ITA, 1931)

MARIUS see also FANNY

MARK OF THE FROG, THE (BRI, 1928, based on the book
by Edgar Wallace)
FROG, THE (BRI, 1931)
FROG, THE (BRI, 1937)
FACE OF THE FROG, THE (GER, 1959)

MARK OF THE VAMPIRE see LONDON AFTER MIDNIGHT

MARK OF ZORRO, THE (UA, 1920, based on a legend)
BOLD CABALLERO, THE (REP, 1936)
MARK OF ZORRO, THE (FOX, 1940)
MARK OF ZORRO, THE (FOX–TV, 1974)
ZORRO (ITA, 1975)

MARK SABER MYSTERY THEATER (series) (ABC–TV,
1951, based on a teleplay)
SABER OF LONDON (series) (TV Title: UNCOVERED)
(NBC–TV, 1957)

MARK TWAIN see ADVENTURES OF MARK TWAIN, THE

MARKED MAN see THREE GODFATHERS

MARLOWE see LITTLE SISTER

MARQUISE VON POMPADOUR (GER, 1922, source
unlisted)
MARQUISE VON POMPADOUR (GER, 1930)

MARRAINE DE CHARLEY, LA see CHARLEY'S AUNT

MARRIAGE BROKER, THE see MODEL AND THE
MARRIAGE BROKER, THE

MARRIAGE CIRCLE, THE (WB, 1923, based on the play by
Lothar Schmidt [Goldschmidt])
ONE HOUR WITH YOU (PAR, 1932)
UNE HEURE PRES DE TOI (FRA, 1932)

MARRIAGE--GO--ROUND, THE (FOX, 1960, based on the
play by Leslie Stevens)
MY WIFE, THE SWEDE AND I (ARG, 1967)

MARRIAGE ITALIAN STYLE see FILUMENA MATURANO

MARRIAGE OF ESTHER, THE see ESTHER AND MORDE-
CAI

MARRIAGE OF FIGARO, THE see FIGARO'S WEDDING

MARRIAGE OF KITTY, THE (PAR, 1915, based on the book,
"La Passerelle," by Francis de Croisset and Fred Gresac)

AFRAID TO LOVE (PAR, 1927)

MARRIAGE OF KRIETCHINSKI, THE (sequence) (RUS, 1908, based on the book by Alexandre Soukhovo-Kobyline)
MARRIAGE OF KRIETCHINSKI, THE (RUS, 1953)

MARRIAGE OF RAMUNTCHO, THE see RAMUNTCHO

MARRAIGE OF THE BEAR (NIGHT OF THE BEARS, THE) (RUS, 1926, based on the book, "Lokis," by Prosper Merimee)
LOKIS (POL, 1969)

MARRIED LIFE see GIFTAS

MARSHAL OF MESA CITY see ARIZONIAN, THE

MARTHA (short) (BRI, 1922, based on the opera by Friederich von Flothow)
MARTHA (GER, 1936)

MARTHA GRAHAM DANCE COMPANY, THE see DANCER'S WORLD, A

MARTIN CHUZZLEWIT (IND, 1912, based on a book by Charles Dickens)
MARTIN CHUZZLEWIT (BIO, 1914)

MARTIN EDEN (FOX, 1914, based on a book by Jack London)
CREATION CAN'T BE BOUGHT (RUS, 1918)
ADVENTURES OF MARTIN EDEN, THE (COL, 1942)
STORY OF JACK LONDON, THE (UA, 1943)

MARTIN KANE, PRIVATE EYE (series) (NBC–TV, 1949, based on a teleplay)
NEW ADVENTURES OF MARTIN KANE (series) (NBC–TV, 1953)

MARTIN LUTHER see MARTIN LUTHER, THE NIGHTINGALE OF WITTENBERG

MARTIN LUTHER, THE NIGHTINGALE OF WITTENBERG (IND, 1913, based on the life and work of reformer and clergyman Martin Luther)
MARTIN LUTHER (GER, 1925)
MARTIN LUTHER (IND, 1953)
REFORMATION, THE (short) (COR, 1955)
WORLD OF MARTIN LUTHER, THE (short) (IND, 1965)
REFORMATION, THE (short) (MHF, 1967)
MARTIN LUTHER AND THE PROTESTANT REFORMA-TION: THE MOMENT AND THE MAN (short) (BRI–TV, 1968)
LUTHER (ABC–TV, 1968)
MARTIN LUTHER (short) (TFC, 1971)
REFORMATION – AGE OF REVOLT, THE (short) (EBE, 1973)
LUTHER (AFT, 1973)

MARTIN LUTHER KING (short) (NBC–TV, 1960, based on the life of the noted civil rights leader)
LEGACY OF A DREAM (short) (RAD, n.d.)
MARTIN LUTHER KING 1929–1968 (short) (TIM, 1968)
MARTIN LUTHER KING: THE MAN AND THE MARCH (NET–TV, 1968)
MARTIN LUTHER KING JR.: A MAN OF PEACE (short) (JOU, 1968)
MARTIN LUTHER KING JR. -- FROM MONTGOMERY TO MEMPHIS (short) (BFA, 1969)

KING: A FILMED RECORD, MONTGOMERY TO MEMPHIS (RAD, 1970)
MARTIN LUTHER KING JR. (short) (EBE, 1971)
KING (NBC–TV, 1978)

MARTIN, THE COBBLER see WHERE LOVE IS, GOD IS

MARTY (NBC–TV, 1953, based on a teleplay by Paddy Chayevsky)
MARTY (UA, 1955)

MARTYRDOM OF PHILIP STRONG, THE (PAR, 1916, based on the books, "The Crucifixion of Philip Strong" and "In His Steps," by Charles Sheldon)
IN HIS STEPS (SINS OF THE CHILDREN) (GN, 1936)

MARTYRDOM OF THOMAS A BECKET (BRI, 1908, based on historical incidents and characters as well as plays by Eliot and Tennyson)
BECKET (VIT, 1910)
BECKET (BRI, 1923)
MURDER IN THE CATHEDRAL (BRI, 1952)
BECKET (PAR, 1964)

MARVELOUS VOYAGE OF NILS HOLGERSSON, THE see GARCON ENSORCELE, LE

MARY see MURDER

MARY JANE'S PA (VIT, 1917, based on the play by Ruth Ellis)
MARY JANE'S PA (FN, 1935)

MARY MAGDELENE (IND, 1914, based on the Bible)
MARY MAGDELENE (GER, 1919)

MARY OF SCOTLAND see LOVES OF MARY, QUEEN OF SCOTS

MARY POPPINS (CBS–TV, 1949, based on the book by P.L. Travers)
MARY POPPINS (DIS, 1964)

MARY, QUEEN OF SCOTS see LOVES OF MARY, QUEEN OF SCOTS

MARY STUART (ED, 1913, based on the play by Friedrich Schiller)
MARIA STUART (GER, 1921)
MARIA STUART (GER, 1927)
MARIA STUART (AUS, 1959)
MARY STUART (NET–TV, 1960)

MARY TYLER MOORE SHOW, THE (series) (CBS–TV, 1971, based on a teleplay)
RHODA (series) (CBS–TV, 1974)
PHYLLIS (series) (CBS–TV, 1975)
LOU GRANT (series) (CBS–TV, 1977)

MASK OF THE MUSKETEERS see THREE MUSKETEERS, THE

MASK OF THE RED DEATH see HOP FROG

MASKE FAELLT, DIE see WAY OF ALL MEN, THE

MASKE IN BLAU (GER, 1942, based on a story by Heinz Hentschke)
MASKE IN BLAU (GER, 1953)

MASKED MARVEL, THE (serial) (REP, 1943, based on a screenplay by various authors; the second film is a con--densed version of the serial)
SAKIMA AND THE MASKED MARVEL (REP, 1966)

MASKEE see SHIPMATES

MASKERADE (GER, 1934, based on a screenplay by Walter Reisch)
ESCAPADE (MGM, 1935)
MASQUERADE IN VIENNA (AUS, 1938)

MASKS AND FACES, (BIO, 1914, based on the book, "Peg Woffington," by Charles Blade)
MASKS AND FACES (BRI, 1917)
PEG OF OLD DRURY (BRI, 1936)

MASQUE DE FER (ITA, 1910, based on the book by Alex--andre Dumas (pere)
MANN MIT DER EISERNEN MASKE, DER (GER, 1922)
IRON MASK, THE (UA, 1929)
MAN IN THE IRON MASK, THE (UA, 1939)
LADY IN THE IRON MASK, THE (FOX, 1952)
VICOMTE DE BRAGELONNE, LE (FRA/ITA, 1954)
PRISONNIER DU ROI, LE (FRA/ITA, 1954)
VENGEANCE OF THE MASK OF IRON (FRA/ITA, 1961)
MASQUE DE FER (FRA, 1962)

MASQUE D'HOLLYWOOD, LE see SHOW GIRL

MASQUE OF THE RED DEATH, THE see HOP FROG

MASQUERADE (RUS, 1910, based on the book by Mikhail Liermontov)
MASQUERADE (RUS, 1914)
MASQUERADE (RUS, 1919)
MASQUERADE (RUS, 1941)

MASQUERADE IN MEXICO see MIDNIGHT

MASQUERADE IN VIENNA see MASKERADE

MASQUERADER, THE (GN, 1922, based on the book by Katherine Cecil Thurston)
MASQUERADER, THE (MGM, 1933)

MASTER AND MAN see BACK TO NATURE

MASTER BUILDER, THE (NBC-TV, 1957, based on the play by Hendrick Ibsen)
MASTER BUILDER, THE (NET-TV, 1960)

MASTER DETECTIVE, THE (GER, 1933, source unlisted)
MASTER DETECTIVE, THE (GER, 1944)

MASTER GUNFIGHTER, THE see GOYO--KIN

MASTER MIND, THE (PAR, 1914, based on the story by Daniel D. Carter)
MASTER MIND, THE (PAR, 1920)

MASTER OF HORROR see AVENGING CONSCIENCE, THE and SEALED ROOM, THE

MASTER OF THE WORLD (AI, 1961, based on the book by Jules Verne)
MASTER OF THE WORLD (AUT--TV, 1976)

MASTERPIECE see GENTLEMAN AT HEART

MATA HARI see SPIONIN

MATA HARI: THE RED DANCER see SPIONIN

MATCH GIRL see LITTLE MATCH GIRL

MATCHMAKER, THE (PAR, 1958, based on the play, "The Merchant of Yonkers," by Thornton Wilder)
HELLO, DOLLY! (FOX, 1969)

MATER DOLOROSA (FRA, 1917, source unlisted)
MATER DOLOROSA (FRA, 1932)

MATERNELLE, LA (FRA, 1925, based on a book by Leon Frapie)
MATERNELLE, LA (FRA, 1933)
MATERNELLE, LA (FRA, 1948)

MATHIAS SANDORF (FRA, 1920, based on the book by Jules Verne)
MATHIAS SANDORF (FRA/ITA/SPA, 1962)

MATISSE see HENRI MATISSE

MATRIMONIAL BED, THE (WB, 1930, based on a story by Harvey Thew)
KISSES FOR BREAKFAST (WB, 1940)

MATRON'S REPORT, THE see BLUE SKIES

MATTER OF CONSCINECE, A see RESURRECTION

MATTER OF WIFE . . . AND DEATH see SHAMUS

MATTHEW BRADY: PHOTOGRAPHER OF AN ERA (short) (IND, n.d., based on the work of photographer Matthew Brady)
TRUE STORY OF THE CIVIL WAR, THE (short) (MHF, 1956)

MATURA see GIRL'S DORMITORY

MAUD MULLER (ESS, 1909, based on the poem by John Greenleaf Whittier)
MAUD MULLER (PAT, 1924)

MAUDE see ALL IN THE FAMILY

MAULKORB, DER (GER, 1938, based on the book by Hein--rich Spoerl)
MAULKORB, DER (GER, 1958)

MAUVAISE GRAINE (FRA, 1934, based on a screenplay by Stafford Dickens)
FIRST OFFENSE (BRI, 1936)

MAX UND MORITZ see SPUK MIT MAX UND MORITZ

MAXIME MAXIMYTCH see BELLA

MAY NIGHT (RUS, 1918, based on a story by Nikolai Gogol)
MAY NIGHT (RUS, 1941)
MAY NIGHT (RUS, 1952)

MAYA (MGM, 1966, based on a screenplay by John Fante)
MAYA (series) (NBC-TV, 1967)

MAYA AND BRENDA see MEDEA

MAYA BAZAR (IN, 1939, based on an Indian myth)
  MAYA BAZAR (IN, 1949)
  MAYA BAZAR (IN, 1959)

MAYBE IT'S LOVE see SATURDAY'S CHILDREN

MAYBERRY R.F.D. see ANDY GRIFFITH SHOW, THE

MAYERLING (RUS, 1915, based on the book, "Idyl's End,"
    by Claude Anet)
  DRAMA VON MAYERLING (GER, 1924)
  VETSERA, DIE (GER, 1928)
  MAYERLING (FRA, 1937)
  MAYERLING TO SARAJEVO (FRA, 1940)
  SECRET OF MAYERLING, THE (FRA, 1951)
  RIDDLE OF MAYERLING, THE (CBS–TV, 1953)
  MAYERLING (CBS–TV, 1957)
  MAYERLING (AUS, 1958)
  MAYERLING (BRI, 1968)

MAYERLING TO SARAJEVO see MAYERLING

MAYTIME (PRE, 1923, based on the play by Rida Johnson
    Young)
  MAYTIME (MGM, 1937)

MAZURKA (GER, 1935, based on a screenplay by Hans
    Rameau)
  CONFESSION (WB, 1937)

MAZURKA DER LIEBE see BETTEL–STUDENT, DER

ME AND MY GAL (FOX, 1932, based on a story by Philip
    Klein and Barry Connors)
  PIER 13 (FOX, 1940)

ME AND THE MAFIA see OH, YOU'RE AWFUL

MEANEST MAN IN THE WORLD, THE (IND, 1923,
    based on the play by George M. Cohan)
  MEANEST MAN IN THE WORLD, THE (FOX, 1942)
  MEANEST MAN IN THE WORLD, THE (CBS–TV, 1955)

MEASURE FOR MEASURE (LUB, 1909, based on the play
    by William Shakespeare)
  DENTE PER DENTE (ITA, 1942)
  ZWEIERLEI MASS (GER, 1963)

MEDAL FOR BENNY, A (PAR, 1945, based on a story by
    John Steinbeck and Jack Wagner)
  MEDAL FOR BENNY, A (NBC–TV, 1951)
  MEDAL FOR BENNY, A (NBC–TV, 1954)

MEDEA (GER, 1911, based on a play by Euripides, a book by
    Franz Grillparzer and an opera by Cherubini)
  MEDEA (GER, 1920)
  MEDEA (NET–TV, 1959)
  MEDEA (ITA, 1971)
  DREAM OF PASSION, A (GRE, 1977)

MEDIUM, THE (CBS–TV, 1948, based on an opera by Gian–
    Carlo Menotti)
  MEDIUM, THE (ITA, 1951)
  MEDIUM, THE (NBC–TV, n.d.)
  MEDIUM, THE (FRA, 1969)

MEET CORLISS ARCHER see KISS AND TELL

MEET ME IN ST. LOUIS (MGM, 1944, based on the book by

Sally Benson)
  MEET ME IN ST. LOUIS (CBS–TV, 1959)
  MEET ME IN ST. LOUIS (short) (ABC–TV, 1966)

MEET ME TONIGHT see WE WERE DANCING

MEET MR. KRINGLE see MIRACLE ON 34TH STREET,
    THE

MEET MR. LINCOLN see ABRAHAM LINCOLN

MEET NERO WOLFE (COL, 1936, based on books by Rex
    Stout)
  NERO WOLFE (pilot) (ABC–TV, n.d.)

MEIN HERZ RUFT NACH DIR (GER, 1934, source unlisted)
  MON COEUR T'APPELLE (FRA, 1934)

MEIN LEOPOLD (GER, 1924, based on the play by L'Arronge)
  MEIN LEOPOLD (GER, 1931)
  HERTZ BLEIBT ALLEIN, EIN (GER, 1955)

MEINE COUSINE AUS WARSCHAU (GER, 1931, based on
    the book "Ma Cousine de Varsovie," by Louis Verneuil)
  MA COUSINE DE VARSOVIE (FRA, 1932)

MEINE SCHWESTER UND ICH (GER, 1929, based on the
    play, "My Sister and I," by Louis Verneuil)
  IHRE DURCHLAUT, DIE VERKAUFERIN (GER, 1933)
  MEINE SCHWESTER UND ICH (GER, 1954)

MEINE TANTE, DEINE TANTE (GER, 1926, based on a play
    by Walter Supper based on the opera, "Don Pasquale," by
    Donizetti)
  MEINE TANTE, DEINE TANTE (GER, 1939)
  MEINE TANTE, DEINE TANTE (GER, 1956)

MEINEIDBAUER, DER (GER, 1926, based on the play by
    Ludwig Anzengruber)
  MEINEIDBAUER, DER (GER, 1941)
  MEINEDIBAUER, DER (GER, 1956)

MEJOR ES REIR, LO see LAUGHTER

MELO (FRA, 1932, based on a book by Henry Bernstein)
  DREAMING LIPS (BRI, 1937)
  TRAUMENDE MUND, DER (GER, 1952)
  DREAMING LIPS (DCA, 1958)

MELODIE DES HERZENS (GER, 1929, source unlisted)
  MELODIE DES HERZENS (GER, 1950)

MELODY TIME see JOHNNY APPLESEED

MELVILLE GOODWIN, U.S.A. (ABC–TV, 1952, based on
    the book by John P. Marquand)
  TOP SECRET AFFAIR (WB, 1957)

MEMBER OF THE WEDDING, A (COL, 1952, based on the
    play by Carson McCullers)
  MEMBER OF THE WEDDING, A (CBS–TV, 1958)

MEN AGAINST SPEED see RACERS, THE

MEN ARE LIKE THAT see ARIZONA and SHOW–OFF, THE

MEN ARE NOT GODS see OTHELLO

MEN IN HER LIFE, THE (COL, 1931, based on a story by
    Warner Fabian)
    HOMBRES IN MI VIDA (SPA, 1932)

MEN IN HER LIFE, THE see REMEMBER THE DAY

MEN IN WHITE (MGM, 1934, based on the play by Sidney
    Kingsley)
    MEN IN WHITE (CBS–TV, 1958)
    MEN IN WHITE (CBS–TV, 1960)

MEN OF IRON (UN, n.d., based on a book by Howard Pyle)
    BLACK SHIELD OF FALWORTH, THE (UN, 1954)

MEN OF SHERWOOD FOREST see ROBIN HOOD AND
    HIS MERRY MEN

MEN OF SHILOH, THE see VIRGINIAN, THE

MEN OF THE NORTH (MGM, 1930, based on a story by
    Willard Mack)
    MONSIEUR LE FOX (FRA, 1930)
    MONSIEUR LE FOX (SPA, 1930)

MEN OF THE SEA see MIDSHIPMAN EASY

MENACE, THE see SQUEAKER, THE

MENDEL -- FATHER OF GENETICS see MENDEL'S
    EXPERIMENTS

MENDEL'S EXPERIMENTS (short) (NET–TV, 1960, based
    on the work of scientist Gregory Mendel)
    MAENDEL'S RECOMBINATION (short) (MHF, 1960)
    MENDEL'S SEGREGATION (short) (MHF, 1960)
    MENDEL – FATHER OF GENETICS (short) (FNC, 1972)

MENSCHEN, DIE VORUBERZIEHEN see KATHARINE
    KNIE

MENSCHEN HINTER GETTERN see BIG HOUSE, THE

MENSCHEN IM HOTEL see GRAND HOTEL

MENSCHEN IM KAFIG LE CAP PERDU see CAPE FOR–
    LORN

MENSCHEN IM RAUSCH (GER, 1920, based on the book by
    Benno Vigny)
    MAEDEL VON DER REEPERBAHN (GER, 1930)

MENSONAGE DE NINA PETROVNA see WONDERFUL LIE
    OF NINA PETROVNA, THE

MEOTO ZENZAI (JAP, 1955, based on the book, "Love Birds,"
    by Sakunosuke Oda)
    MEOTO ZENZAI (JAP, 1968)

MERCHANT OF VENICE, THE see MIRROR OF VENICE

MERCHANT OF YONKERS, THE see MATCHMAKER, THE

MERELY MARY ANN (FOX, 1916, based on the play by
    Israel Zangwill)
    MERELY MARY ANN (FOX, 1920)
    MERELY MARY ANN (FOX, 1931)

MERRILY WE LIVE see WHAT A MAN

MERRY–GO–ROUND see REIGEN

MERRY MEN OF SHERWOOD, THE see ROBIN HOOD
    AND HIS MERRY MEN

MERRY WIDOW, THE (FRA, 1913, based on the operetta
    by Franz Lehar)
    MERRY WIDOW (short) (ESS, 1913)
    MERRY WIDOW, THE (MGM, 1925)
    MERRY WIDOW, THE (TV Title: LADY DANCES, THE)
        (MGM, 1934)
    MERRY WIDOW, THE (NBC–TV, 1950)
    MERRY WIDOW, THE (MGM, 1952)
    MERRY WIDOW, THE (CBS–TV, 1954)
    MERRY WIDOW, THE (NBC–TV, 1955)
    MERRY WIDOW, THE (AUS/FRA, 1962)
    VEUVE JOYEUSE, LA (FRA, 1934)

MERRY WIVES OF WINDSOR, THE (SEL, 1910, based on
    the play by William Shakespeare; also the basis of an opera
    by Otto Nicolai)
    MERRY WIVES OF WINDSOR (FALSTAFF) (FRA, 1911)
    MERRY WIVES OF WINDSOR, THE (GER, 1917)
    FALSTAFF, THE TAVERN KNIGHT (BRI, 1923)
    MERRY WIVES OF WINDSOR, THE (GER, 1935)
    MERRY WIVES OF WINDSOR, THE (GER, 1950)
    MERRY WIVES OF WINDOSR, THE (GER, 1962)
    MERRY WIVES OF WINDSOR, THE (GER, 1965)
    CHIMES AT MIDNIGHT (FALSTAFF) (SPA/SWI, 1965)

MERTON OF THE MOVIES (PAR, 1924, based on the book
    by Harry Leon Wilson and a play by George S. Kaufman
    and Marc Connelly)
    MAKE ME A STAR (PAR, 1932)
    MERTON OF THE MOVIES (MGM, 1947)

MERVEILLEUSE JOURNEE, LA (FRA, 1928, based on the
    play by Yves Mirande and Gustave Quinson)
    MERVEILLEUSE JOURNEE, LA (FRA, 1932)

MERVEILLEUX VOYAGE DE NILS HOLGERSSON, LE
    see GARCON ENSORCELE, LE

MESSAGE FROM MARS (AUT, 1909, based on the play by
    Richard Ganthony)
    MESSAGE FROM MARS (BRI, 1913)
    MESSAGE FROM MARS (MGM, 1921)

MESSAGE TO GARCIA, A (ED, 1916, based on an essay by
    Elbert Hubbard)
    MESSAGE TO GARCIA, A (FOX, 1936)

MESSALINA (ITA, 1923, based on a historical figure)
    AFFAIRS OF MESSALINA (ITA, 1954)

MESSIEURS LES RONDS–DE–CUIR (FRA, 1937, based on
    a book by Georges Courteline)
    MESSIEURS LES RONDS–DE–CUIR (FRA, 1959)

METAMORPHOSIS (IND, 1948, based on the story by Franz
    Kafka)
    METAMORPHOSIS (short) (BRI, 1953)
    METAMORPHOSIS (short) (IND, 1972)
    FORVANDLINGEN (SWE, 1975)
    METAMORPHOSIS (GER–TV, 1975)

METRO MAN see RETURN OF JOE FORRESTER, THE

MEUNIERE DEBAUCHEE, LA (SPA, 1935, based on the

book, "Le Tricorne," by Pedro Antonio de Alarcon)
MEUNIERE MALICIEUSE, LA (FRA/SPA, 1954)
BELLE MEUNIERE, LA (ITA, 1955)

MEUNIERE MALICIEUSE, LA see MEUNIERE DEBAU–
CHEE, LA

MEXICAN, THE (MEX, 1944, based on the book by Jack
London)
MEXICAN, THE (RUS, 1956)

MIARKA, LA FILLE A L'OURSE (FRA, 1920, based on the
book by Jean Richepin)
MIARKA, LA FILLE A L'OURSE (FRA, 1937)

MICHAEL see MIKAEL

MICHAEL HAS COMPANY FOR COFFEE see WHERE
LOVE IS, GOD IS

MICHAEL O'HALLERAN (HOD, 1923, based on the book
by Gene Stratton Porter)
MICHAEL O'HALLERAN (ANY MAN'S WIFE) (REP,
1937)
MICHAEL O'HALLERAN (MON, 1948)

MICHAEL STROGOFF (ED, 1910, based on the book by
Jules Verne)
MICHAEL STROGOFF (PPL, 1914)
MICHAEL STROGOFF (RUS, 1925)
MICHAEL STROGOFF (FRA, 1926)
MICHAEL STROGOFF (FRA, 1936)
JURIER DES ZAREN, DER (GER, 1936)
SOLDIER AND THE LADY, THE (RKO, 1937)
MICHAEL STROGOFF (MEX, 1944)
MICHAEL STROGOFF (FRA/ITA/YUG, 1956)
TARTARS OF THE NORTH (REVOLT OF THE TARTARS)
(ITA, 1961)
TRIUMPH OF MICHAEL STROGOFF, THE (FRA/ITA,
1961)
STROGOFF (FRA/GER/ITA, 1970)

MICHELANGELO (GER, 1940, based on the life and works
of the noted Renaissance artist)
TITAN, THE (IND, 1950)
MICHELANGELO AND HIS ART (short) (COR, 1963)
MICHELANGELO – THE MEDICI CHAPEL (short) (RAD,
1964)
MICHELANGELO (short) (EBE, 1965)
MICHELANGELO: THE LAST GIANT (NBC–TV, 1966)
SECRET OF MICHELANGELO, THE (ABC–TV, 1968)
MICHELANGELO 1475–1564 (TIM, 1970)
MICHELANGELO (series) (ITA–TV, 1975)

MICHELANGELO: THE LAST GIANT see MICHELANGELO

MI–CHEMIN DU CIEL, A see HALF WAY TO HEAVEN

MICHIGAN KID, THE (UN, 1928, based on the book by Rex
Beach)
MICHIGAN KID, THE (UN, 1947)

MIDDLE OF THE NIGHT (NBC–TV, 1954, based on a tele--
play by Paddy Chayevsky)
MIDDLE OF THE NIGHT (COL, 1959)

MIDDLE WATCH (BRI, 1930, based on the play by Ian Hay
and Stephen King--Hall)
MIDDLE WATCH (BRI, 1940)

GIRLS AT SEA (BRI, 1958)

MIDNIGHT (PAR, 1939, based on a story by Edwin Justus
Mayer and Franz Schulz)
MASQUERADE IN MEXICO (PAR, 1945)

MIDNIGHT ALIBI (FN, 1937, based on the story, "The Old
Doll's House," by Damon Runyan)
AT THE STROKE OF TWELVE (WB, 1941)

MIDNIGHT BELL, A (SEL, 1913, based on the play by Charles
H. Hoyt)
MIDNIGHT BELL, A (SEL, 1917)
MIDNIGHT BELL, A (FN, 1921)

MIDNIGHT EPISODE see MONSIEUR LA SOURIS

MIDNIGHT RIDE OF PAUL REVERE, THE (short) (ED,
1914, based on a historical incident and the poem by Henry
Wadsworth Longfellow)
PAUL REVERE'S RIDE (short) (CBS–TV, 1955)
PAUL REVERE'S RIDE (short) (MLA, 1955)
MIDNIGHT RIDE OF PAUL REVERE, THE (short)
(EBE, 1957)
MIDNIGHT RIDE OF PAUL REVERE, THE (short)
(COR, 1957)
PAUL REVERE'S RIDE (short) (BFA, 1964)
PAUL REVERE (short) (MAC, 1965)
PAUL REVERE'S RIDE (short) (MHF, 1967)
PAUL REVERE'S RIDE (CBS–TV, 1971)

MIDNIGHT WARNING (MAY, 1932, based on a book by
Anthony Thorne)
SO LONG AT THE FAIR (BRI, 1950)

MIDSHIPMAN EASY (BRI, 1915, based on the book by Capt.
Frederick Marryat)
MIDSHIPMAN EASY (BRI, 1935)
MEN OF THE SEA (AST, 1951)

MIDSUMMER NIGHT'S DREAM, A (BRI, 1909, based on the
play by William Shakespeare; also the basis for the musical
comedy, "Swingin' the Dream," in 1939)
MIDSUMMER NIGHT'S DREAM, A (FRA, 1909)
MIDSUMMER NIGHT'S DREAM, A (VIT, 1910)
MIDSUMMER NIGHT'S DREAM, A (IND, 1912)
MIDSUMMER NIGHT'S DREAM, A (ITA, 1913)
MIDSUMMER NIGHT'S DREAM, A (GER, 1913)
MIDSUMMER NIGHT'S DREAM, A (GER, 1917)
MIDSUMMER NIGHT'S DREAM, A (GER, 1925)
MIDSUMMER NIGHT'S DREAM, A (IND, 1928)
MIDSUMMER NIGHT'S DREAM, A (WB, 1935)
MIDSUMMER NIGHT'S DREAM, A (GER, 1935)
MIDSUMMER NIGHT'S DREAM, A (short) (BRI, 1953)
MIDSUMMER NIGHT'S DREAM, A (CZE, 1959)
MIDSUMMER NIGHT'S DREAM, A (BRI–TV, 1959)
MIDSUMMER NIGHT'S DREAM, A (BRI--TV, 1961)
MR. MAGOO'S STORY BOOK (UPA, 1964)
MIDSUMMER NIGHT'S DREAM, A (COL, 1967)
MIDSUMMER NIGHT'S DREAM, A (BRI, 1968)
MIDSUMMER NIGHT'S DREAM, A (BRI--TV, 1968)
MIDSUMMER NIGHT'S DREAM, A (CBS–TV, 1669)

MIDWICH CUCKOOS, THE see VILLAGE OF THE DAMNED

MIGNON (FRA, 1906, based on the story by Goethe and the
opera by Ambroise Thomas)
WILHELM MEISTER (GER, 1909)
WILHELM MESITER (GER, 1912)
ROMAN DE MIGNON, LE (ITA, 1914)
MIGNON (GER, 1919)
MIGNON (GER, 1922)

MIKADO, THE see FAN–FAN

MIKAEL (SWE, 1916, based on the book by Herman Bang)
  MICHAEL (DEN, 1924)
  MICHAEL (GER, 1924)

MILADY see THREE MUSKETEERS, THE

MILADY AND THE MUSKETEERS see THREE MUSKE–
  TEERS, THE

MILDRED PIERCE (WB, 1945, based on the book by James
  M. Cain)
  MILDRED PIERCE (CBS–TV, 1956)

MILKY WAY, THE (PAR, 1936, based on the play by Lynn
  Root and Harry Clark)
  KID FROM BROOKLYN, THE (UA, 1946)

MILL ON THE FLOSS, THE (MUT, 1915, based on the
  book by George Eliot)
  MILL ON THE FLOSS, THE (THA, 1916)
  MILL ON THE FLOSS, THE (BRI, 1939)

MILLE DE DEUXIEME NUIT, LA see ARABIAN NIGHTS

MILLION DOLLAR MYSTERY, THE (MUT, n.d., based on
  a story by Lloyd Lonergan)
  MILLION DOLLAR MYSTERY, THE (RAY, 1927)

MILLION POUND BANK NOTE, THE see MILLION POUND
  NOTE, THE

MILLION POUND NOTE, THE (HUN, 1916, based on the
  story, "The Million Pound Bank Note," by Mark Twain)
  MILLION POUND NOTE, THE (NBC–TV, 1951)
  MAN WITH A MILLION, THE (BRI, 1953)

MILLIONAIRE, THE (series) (CBS–TV, 1954, based on a
  teleplay)
  MILLIONAIRE, THE (CBS–TV, 1979)

MILLIONAIRE, THE see RULING PASSION, THE

MILLIONERBSCHAFT, DIE (GER, 1920, source unlisted)
  MILLIONERBSCHAFT, DIE (GER, 1937)

MILLS OF GOD, THE see ACT OF MURDER, AN

MIMI see VIE DE BOHEME, LA

MIMI PINSON (FRA,1923, based on a story by Alfred de
  Musset)
  MIMI PINSON (FRA, 1958)

MIN AND BILL (MGM, 1930, based on the book, "Dark Star,"
  by Lorna Moon)
  FRUTA AMARGA, LA (SPA, 1931)

MINE WITH THE IRON DOOR, THE (PRI, 1924, based on
  the book by Harold Bell Wright)
  MINE WITH THE IRON DOOR, THE (COL, 1936)

MINICK see EXPERT, THE

MINISTER, THE see VICAR OF WAKEFIELD

MINNA VON BERNHELM (GER, 1922, based on the book
  by Gotthold Ephriam Lessing)

FRAULEIN VON BARNHELM, DAS (GER, 1940)
HELDINNEN (GER, 1960)
MINNA VON BARNHELM (GER, 1962)

MINNIE, THE YOUNG LIBERTINE (FRA, 1929, source
  unlisted)
  MINNIE, THE YOUNG LIBERTINE (FRA, 1950)

MINOTAUR, THE (VIT, 1910, based on a Greek legend)
  THESEUS VS. THE MINOTAUR (ITA, 1960)
  JOHNNY MINOTAUR (GRE, n.d.)

MIOCHE, LE (FRA, 1938, based on a screenplay by Jean
  Guitton)
  40 LITTLE MOTHERS (MGM, 1940)

MIQUETTE ET SA MERE (FRA, 1914, based on a story by
  Robert de Flers and Gaston Arman de Caillavet)
  MIQUETTE ET SA MERE (FRA, 1933)
  MIQUETTE ET SA MERE (FRA, 1939)
  MIQUETTE ET SA MERE (FRA, 1949)

MIRACLE, THE (AUS, 1912, based on the play by Karl
  Vollmoeller)
  MIRACLE, THE (GER, 1914)
  MIRACLE, THE (GER, 1917)
  MIRACLE, THE (WB, 1959)

MIRACLE DES LOUPS, LE (FRA, 1924, based on a book by
  Henry Dupuy–Mazuel)
  MIRACLE DES LOUPS, LE (FRA/ITA, 1961)

MIRACLE MAN, THE (PAR, 1919, based on a story by Frank
  Lucius Packard and a play by George M. Cohan)
  MIRACLE MAN, THE (PAR, 1932)

MIRACLE OF MORGAN'S CREEK, THE (PAR, 1944, based
  on a screenplay by Preston Sturges)
  ROCK–A–BYE BABY (PAR, 1958)

MIRACLE ON 34TH STREET, THE (FOX, 1947, based on a
  story by Valentine Davies; also the basis for the musical
  comedy, "Here's Love")
  MIRACLE ON 34TH STREET, THE (CBS–TV, 1955)
  MEET MR. KRINGLE (CBS–TV, 1957)
  MIRACLE ON 34TH STREET, THE (NBC–TV, 1959)
  MIRACLE ON 34TH STREET, THE (CBS–TV, 1973)

MIRACLE WORKER, THE see DELIVERANCE

MIRAGE (UN, 1964, based on the book, "Fallen Angels," by
  Howard Fast)
  JIGSAW (UN, 1968)

MIRAGE, THE (PDC, 1924, based on the play by Edgar Selwyn)
  POSSESSED (MGM, 1931)

MIREILLE (FRA, 1906, based on the book by Frederic
  Mistral and the opera by Charles Gounod)
  MIREILLE (FRA, 1920)
  MIREILLE (FRA, 1934)

MIRROR OF VENICE, THE (FRA, 1905, based on the play
  by William Shakespeare; also the basis of the 1977 musical,
  "Fire Angel")
  MERCHANT OF VENICE, THE (VIT, 1908)
  MERCHANT OF VENICE, THE (RUS, 1909)
  MERCHANT OF VENICE, THE (ITA, 1910)
  MERCHANT OF VENICE, THE (MUT, 1912)

SHYLOCK (FRA, 1913)
MERCHANT OF VENICE, THE (UNI, 1914)
MERCHANT OF VENICE, THE (BRI, 1916)
MERCHANT OF VENICE (short) (BRI, 1922)
KAUFMANN VON VENEDIG, DER (GER, 1923)
MERCHANT OF VENICE, THE (short) (BRI, 1927)
MARCHAND DE VENISE, LA (FRA, 1933)
MERCHAND DE VENISE, LE (FRA, 1952)
STRANGE DESIRE OF MONSIEUR BARD, THE (FRA, 1953)
MERCHANT OF VENICE, THE (PBS–TV, 1962)
MERCHANT OF VENICE (ABC–TV, 1973)

MISERABLE ONES, THE see CHEMINEAU, LE

MISERABLES, LES see CHEMINEAU, LE

MISLEADING LADY, THE (ESS, 1916, based on the play by Charles Goddard and Paul Dickey)
MISLEADING LADY, THE (MGM, 1921)
MISLEADING LADY, THE (PAR, 1932)

MISS BLUEBEARD (PAR, 1925, based on the play, "Little Miss Bluebeard," by Avery Hopwood)
HER WEDDING NIGHT (PAR, 1930)
SU NOCHE DE BODAS (SPA, 1930)
MARIONS–NOUS (FRA, 1931)

MISS BRACEGIRDLE DOES HER DUTY (short) (BRI, 1926, based on a story by Stacy Aumonier)
MISS BRACEGIRDLE DOES HER DUTY (short) (BRI, 1936)

MISS BREWSTER'S MILLIONS see BREWSTER'S MILLIONS

MISS JULIE (SWE, 1912, based on the play by August Strindberg)
PLEBIAN (RUS, 1915)
MISS JULIE (SWE, c1920)
FRAULEIN JULIE (GER, 1921)
PECHE DE JULIE (ARG, 1947)
MISS JULIE (SWE, 1951)
MISS JULIE (NET–TV, 1960)
MISS JULIE (CAN–TV, 1966)
MISS JULIE (DEN, 1970)
MISS JULIE (BRI, 1972)

MISS LONELYHEARTS see ADVICE TO THE LOVELORN

MISS PINKERTON (FN, 1932, based on the book by Mary Roberts Rinehart)
NURSE'S SECRET, THE (WB, 1941)

MISS ROBIN CRUSOE see ROBINSON CRUSOE

MISS ROBIN HOOD see ROBIN HOOD AND HIS MERRY MEN

MISS SADIE THOMPSON see MISS SADIE THOMPSON

MISS SUSIE SLAGLE'S (PAR, 1945, based on the book by Augusta Tucker)
MISS SUSIE SLAGLE'S (NBC–TV, 1955)

MISS THOMPSON see SADIE THOMPSON

MISSED FORTUNE, A see HEALTHY, WEALTHY AND DUMB

MISSILE BASE AT TANIAK see CANADIAN MOUNTIES VS. ATOMIC INVADERS

MISSILE TO THE MOON see CAT WOMEN OF THE MOON

MISSING GUEST, THE see SECRET OF THE BLUE ROOM

MISSING HUSBANDS see ATLANTIDE, L'

MISSING WITNESSES see BUREAU OF MISSING PERSONS

MISSION: IMPOSSIBLE see CALL TO DANGER

MISSIONS (short) (IND, 1977, based on the book, "Heart of Darkness," by Joseph Conrad)
APOCALYPSE NOW (UA, 1978)

MISSISSIPPI see FIGHTING COWARD, THE

MISSISSIPPI GAMBLER (UN, 1929, based on a story by Karl Brown and Leonard Fields)
MISSISSIPPI GAMBER (TV Title: DANGER ON THE RIVER) (UN, 1942)
MISSISSIPPI GAMBLER (UN, 1953)

MR. AND MRS. NORTH (MGM, 1941, based on the radio series and stories by Frances and Richard Lockridge)
MR. AND MRS. NORTH (series) (NBC–TV, 1949)
MR. AND MRS. NORTH (series) (CBS–TV, 1952)
MR. AND MRS. NORTH (series) (NBC–TV, 1954)

MR. BARRY'S ETCHINGS see MR. 880

MR. BELVEDERE see SITTING PRETTY

MR. BELVEDERE RINGS THE BELL (FOX, 1951, based on the play, "The Silver Whistle," by Robert McEnroe)
SILVER WHISTLE, THE (CBS–TV, 1959)

MR. BILLION see MR. DEEDS GOES TO TOWN

MR. BISBEE'S PRINCESS see SO'S YOUR OLD MAN

MR. DEEDS GOES TO TOWN (COL, 1936, based on a story by Clarence Buddington Kelland; the Fox film is an uncredited remake)
MR. DEEDS GOES TO TOWN (series) (ABC–TV, 1969)
MR. BILLION (FOX, 1977)

MR. DODD TAKES THE AIR see CROONER, THE

MR. 880 (FOX, 1950, based on a story, "Old 880," by St. Clair McKelway and the play, "Mr. Barry's Etchings")
MONEY MAKER, THE (CBS–TV, 1956)

MR. FANTOMAS see FANTOMAS

MR. FROG WENT A'COURTIN' see FROG WENT A' COURTIN'

MR. JUSTICE RAFFLES see RAFFLES, THE AMATEUR CRACKSMAN

MR. LUCKY (RKO, 1943, based on a story by Milton Holmes)
GAMBLING HOUSE (RKO, 1950)
MR. LUCKY (series) (CBS–TV, 1959)

MR. MAGOO IN SHERWOOD FOREST see ROBIN HOOD AND HIS MERRY MEN

MR. MAGOO – MAN OF MYSTERY see FRANKENSTEIN, DICK TRACY and SHERLOCK HOLMES

MR. MAGOO'S CHRISTMAS CAROL see CHRISTMAS CAROL, A

MR. MAGOO'S FAVORITE HEROES see GUNGA DIN, RIP VAN WINKLE and WILLIAM TELL

MR. MAGOO'S SNOW WHITE see SNOW WHITE

MR. MAGOO'S STORY BOOK see DON QUIXOTE, MID–SUMMER NIGHT'S DREAM, and SNOW WHITE

MR. MOTO ON DANGER ISLAND see MURDER IN TRINIDAD

MR. MUSIC see ACCENT ON YOUTH

MR. PEEK–A–BOO (FRA, 1950, based on the book, "The Man Who Walked Through Walls," by Marcel Ayme)
MAN WHO WALKED THROUGH WALLS, THE (GER, 1960)

MR. QUILP see OLD CURIOUSITY SHOP, THE

MR. ROBERTS (WB, 1955, based on the book by Thomas Heggen and the play by Heggen and Joshua Logan)
ENSIGN PULVER (WB, 1964)
MR. ROBERTS (series) (NBC–TV, 1965)

MR. ROBINSON CRUSOE see ROBINSON CRUSOE

MR. SMITH GOES TO WASHINGTON (COL, 1939, based on a story by Lewis R. Foster)
MR. SMITH GOES TO WASHINGTON (series) (ABC–TV, 1963)
BILLY JACK GOES TO WASHINGTON (IND, 1977)

MRS. SUNDANCE see THREE OUTLAWS

MR. TVARDOVSKI (RUS, 1916, source unlisted)
MR. TVARDOVSKI (RUS, 1937)

MR. WONG, DETECTIVE (MON, 1938, based on a story by Hugh Wiley)
DOCKS OF NEW ORLEANS (MON, 1948)

MR. WONG IN CHINATOWN (MON, 1939, based on a story by Hugh Wiley)
CHINESE RING, THE (MON, 1947)

MR. WU (BRI, 1919, based on the play by Harry M. Vernon and Harold Owen)
MR. WU (MGM, 1927)
WU–LI–CHANG (MEX, 1930)

MISTLETOE BOUGH, THE (BRI, 1904, based on a poem by E.T. Bayley)
MISTLETOE BOUGH, THE (BRI, 1923)
MISTLETOE BOUGH, THE (BRI, 1926)
MISTLETOE BOUGH, THE (BRI, 1938)

MRS. ANDERSSON'S CHARLIE see ANDERSSONSSKANS KALLE

MRS. MIKE (UA, 1949, based on the book by Benedict and Nancy Freedman)
MRS. MIKE (NBC–TV, 1950)

MRS. MINIVER (MGM, 1942, based on the book by Jan Struther)
MRS. MINIVER (CBS–TV, 1960)

MRS. WIGGS OF THE CABBAGE PATCH (IND, 1914, based on the book by Alice Hegan Rice)
MRS. WIGGS OF THE CABBAGE PATCH (PAR, 1919)
MRS. WIGGS OF THE CABBAGE PATCH (PAR, 1934)
MRS. WIGGS OF THE CABBAGE PATCH (PAR, 1942)

M'LISS (WOR, 1915, based on the story by Bret Harte)
M'LISS (PAR, 1918)
GIRL WHO RAN WILD, THE (UN, 1922)
M'LISS (RKO, 1936)
M'LISS (NBC––TV, 1952)

MOBY DICK see SEA BEAST, THE

MODEL AND THE MARRIAGE BROKER, THE (FOX, 1951, based on a screenplay by Charles Brackett, Walter Reisch and Richard Breen)
MARRIAGE BROKER, THE (CBS––TV, 1957)

MODERN SALOME, A see SALOME

MOGAMBO see RED DUST

MOI ET L'IMPERATRICE see ICH UND DIE KAISERIN

MOI LE JOUR, A TOI NUIT, A see ICH BEI TAG UND DU BEI NACHT

MOITIE D'UN GARS, LA (HUN, 1924, based on the book by Kalman Mikszath)
MOITIE D'UN GARS, LA (HUN, 1944)

MOLLY see GOLDBERGS, THE

MOLLY AND I see MY UNMARRIED WIFE

MOLLY MOO–COW AND RIP VAN WINKLE see RIP VAN WINKLE

MON AMI TIM see FIFTY FATHOMS DEEP

MON COEUR T'APPELLE see MEIN HERZ RUFT NACH DIR

MON CRIME see TRUE CONFESSION

MON CURE CHEZ LES PAUVRES (FRA, 1925, based on the book by Clement Vautel)
MON CURE CHEZ LES PAUVRES (FRA, 1956)

MON CURE CHEZ LES RICHES (FRA, 1925, based on the book by Clement Vautel)
MON CURE CHEZ LES RICHES (FRA, 1931)
MON CURE CHEZ LES RICHES (FRA, 1938)
MON CURE CHEZ LES RICHES (FRA, 1952)

MON GOSSE DE PERE (FRA, 1930, based on the book by Leopold Marchand)
MON GOSSE DE PERE (FRA, 1952)

MONEY MAKER, THE see MR. 880

MONEY TREE, THE see JUNO AND THE PAYCOCK

MONKEY'S PAW, THE (BRI, 1915, based on the story by

W.W. Jacobs)
MONKEY'S PAW, THE (SEZ, 1923)
MONKEY'S PAW, THE (BRI, 1923)
MONKEY'S PAW, THE (RKO, 1932)
MONKEY'S PAW, THE (BRI, 1948)
SPIRITISM (MEX, 1961)
MONKEY'S PAW, THE (NBC–TV, 1965)
TALES FROM THE CRYPT (sequence) (BRI, 1972)

MONNA VANNA (ITA, 1915, based on the book by Maurice
Maeterlinck)
MONNA VANNA (UN, 1916)
MONNA VANNA (GER, 1922)
MONNA VANNA (FOX, 1923)

MONROE DOCTINE, THE (short) (WB, 1939, based on the
life and times of the president)
OUR MONROE DOCTRINE (short) (IND, 1940)
JAMES MONROE: THE BOY, THE MAN, THE PRESIDENT
(short) (IND, 1962)

MONSIEUR BEAUCAIRE (VIT, 1905, based on the book by
Booth Tarkington)
MONSIEUR BEAUCAIRE (IND, 1909)
MONSIEUR BEAUCAIRE (PAR, 1924)
MONTE CARLO (PAR, 1930)
MONSIEUR BEAUCAIRE (PAR, 1946)

MONSIEUR CHASSE (FRA, 1912, based on a play by Georges
Feydeau)
MONSIEUR CHASSE (FRA, 1946)

MONSIEUR ET MADAME CURIE see MADAME CURIE

MONSIEUR LA SOURIS (FRA, 1943, based on a book by
George Simenon)
MIDNIGHT EPISODE (BRI, 1951)

MONSIEUR LE FOX see MEN OF THE NORTH

MONSIEUR VERDOUX (UA, 1947, based on the life and
crimes of M. Landru)
BLUEBEARD (GER, 1951)
BLUEBEARD (FRA, 1951)
BLUEBEARD'S TEN HONEYMOONS (AA, 1960)
LANDRU (BLUEBEARD) (FRA/ITA, 1963)

MONSTER AND THE GIRL, THE see GO AND GET IT

MONSTER OF FATE see GOLEM, THE

MONTANA BELLE see BELLE STARR

MONTE CARLO see MONSIEUR BEAUCAIRE

MONTE CARLO MADNESS (GER, 1931, source unlisted)
MONTE CARLO MADNESS (GER, 1960)

MONTE CRISTO see COUNT OF MONTE CRISTO, THE

MONUMENT OF MAIDEN'S LILY (JAP, 1953, based on a
screenplay by Motonari Wakai and Shiro Ishimari)
MONUMENT OF MAIDEN'S LILY (JAP, 1968)

MOON AND SIXPENCE, THE (UA, 1942, based on the book
by W. Somerset Maugham)
MOON AND SIXPENCE, THE (NBC–TV, 1951)
MOON AND SIXPENCE, THE (NBC–TV, 1959)

MOON IS BLUE, THE (UA, 1953, based on the play by F.
Hugh Herbert)
JUNGFRAU AUF DEM DACH, DIE (GER, 1953)

MOON OVER MIAMI see WORKING GIRLS

MOONLIGHT WITNESS see ABRAHAM LINCOLN

MOONSTONE, THE (SEL, 1909, based on the book by Wilkie
Collins)
MOONSTONE, THE (BRI, 1911)
MOONSTONE, THE (WOR, 1915)
MOONSTONE, THE (MON, 1934)
MOONSTONE, THE (NBC–TV, 1952)
MOONSTONE, THE (ABC–TV, 1964)
MOONSTONE, THE (BRI–TV, 1971)

MOOR, THE see OTHELLO

MOOR'S PAVANE, THE see OTHELLO

MORAL (GER, 1927, based on the book by Thoma Ludwig)
MORAL (GER, 1936)

MORAL SINNER, THE see GIRL WHO CAME BACK, THE

MORALS see MORALS OF MARCUS, THE

MORALS OF MARCUS, THE (ED, 1915, based on the play,
"The Morals of Marcus Ordeyne," by William John Locke)
MORALS (REA, 1921)
MORALS OF MARCUS, THE (BRI, 1935)

MORALS OF MARCUS ORDEYNE, THE see MORALS OF
MARCUS, THE

MORDPROZESS MARY DUGAN see TRAIL OF MARY
DUGAN, THE

MORE THE MERRIER, THE (COL, 1943, based on a screen--
play by Robert Russell and Frank Ross)
WALK, DON'T RUN (COL, 1966)

MOREL, DER MEISTER DER KETTE (GER, 1920, based on
the story, "Splendeurs et Miseres des Courtisanes" by
Honore de Balzac)
GLANZ UND ELEND DER KURTISANEN (GER, 1927)

MORGAN! see MORGAN – A SUITABLE CASE FOR
TREATMENT

MORGAN – A SUITABLE CASE FOR TREATMENT (BRI--
TV, 1966, based on a teleplay by David Mercer)
MORGAN! (BRI, 1966)

MORGAN THE PIRATE (serial) (FRA, 1909, based on
historical incidents)
MORGAN THE PIRATE (MGM, 1961)

MORNING GLORY (RKO, 1933, based on the play by Zoe
Atkins)
STAGE STRUCK (DIS, 1958)

MORNING'S AT SEVEN (NBC–TV, 1956, based on the play
by Paul Osborn)
MORNING'S AT SEVEN (NET–TV, 1960)

MOROK see WANDERING JEW, THE

MOROZKO (RUS, 1924, based on the fairy tale)
   JACK FROST (short) (IND, 1934)
   JACK FROST (CHI, 1965)

MORT AUX VACHES see CRAINQUEBILLE

MORTE DU CYGNE, LE see BALLERINA, THE

MORTE EN FUITE, LE (FRA, 1936, based on the book by
   Loic le Gouriadec)
   BREAK THE NEWS (BRI, 1937)
   DEUX FONT LA PAIRE, LES (FRA, 1954)

MOSAIC – FRANKENSTEIN 1980 see FRANKENSTEIN

MOSCOW NIGHTS (FRA, 1934, based on a book by Pierre
   Benoit)
   I STAND CONDEMNED (BRI, 1935)

MOSES see LIFE OF MOSES, THE

MOST DANGEROUS GAME, THE (RKO, 1932, based on a
   story by Richard Connell)
   GAME OF DEATH, THE (RKO, 1945)
   JOHNNY ALLEGRO (COL, 1949)
   KILL OR BE KILLED (EL, 1950)
   BLACK FOREST (IND, 1954)
   RUN FOR THE SUN (UA, 1956)
   BLOODLUST (CRO, 1961)
   MOST DANGEROUS GAME, THE (FRA, 1958)
   HUNT, THE (short) (EBE, 1975)

MOST DANGEROUS SIN, A see CRIME AND PUNISHMENT

MOTHER (RUS, 1919, based on a book by Maxim Gorky)
   MOTHER (RUS, 1926)
   MOTHER (RUS, 1955)

MOTHER (JAP, 1929, source unlisted)
   MOTHER (JAP, 1963)

MOTHER CAREY'S CHICKENS (RKO, 1938, based on the
   book by Kate Douglas Wiggin)
   SUMMER MAGIC (DIS, 1963)

MOTHER JOAN OF THE ANGELS see JOAN OF THE
   ANGELS

MOTHER, JUGS AND SPEED (FOX, 1976, based on a story
   by Stephen Manes and Tom Mankiewicz)
   MOTHER, JUGS AND SPEED (pilot) (ABC–TV, 1978)

MOTHER KUSTERS GOES TO HEAVEN see MUTTERS
   KRAUSENS FAHRT IN GLUCK

MOTOR MADNESS see SPEED DEMON

MOULIN ROUGE (UA, 1952, based on the life and works of
   artist Henri de Toulouse–Lautrec)
   TOULOUSE–LAUTREC (short) (MAC, 1952)
   HENRI DE TOULOUSE–LAUTREC (short) (PIC, 1953)
   TOULOUSE–LAUTREC 1864–1901 (short) (TIM, 1970)

MOULIN ROUGE see HER SISTER FROM PARIS

MOUMOU see GUERASSIM AND MOUMOU

MOUNT VERNON IN VIRGINIA (short) (MHF, 1950,
   based on the life and times of President George Washington)

GEORGE WASHINGTON (short) (EBE, 1951)
VALLEY FORGE (short) (MHF, 1955)
WASHINGTON'S FAREWELL TO HIS OFFICERS (short)
   (CBS–TV, 1955)
WASHINGTON CROSSES THE DELAWARE (short)
   (CBS–TV, 1956)
WASHINGTON IN VIRGINIA (short) (IND, n.d.)
BOYHOOD OF GEORGE WASHINGTON, THE (short)
   (COR, 1957)
GEORGE WASHINGTON AT VALLEY FORGE (short)
   (IND, 1971)
GEORGE WASHINGTON'S GREATEST VICTORY (short)
   (COR, 1966)
GEORGE WASHINGTON (short) (HAN, 1968)
VALLEY FORGE (short) (EBE, 1972)
GEORGE WASHINGTON'S INAUGURATION (short)
   (HAN, 1972)
GEORGE WASHINGTON AT THE WHISKEY REBELLION
   (short) (LCA, 1974)

MOUNTED STRANGER, THE see RIDIN' KID FROM POW–
   DER RIVER, THE

MOUSQUETAIRES DE LA REINE, LE see THREE MUSKE–
   TEERS, THE

MOUTHPIECE, THE (WB, 1932, based on a play by Frank
   Collins)
   MAN WHO TALKED TOO MUCH, THE (WB, 1940)
   ILLEGAL (WB, 1955)

MOVE OVER, DARLING see MY FAVORITE WIFE

MOWGLI'S BROTHERS see JUNGLE BOOK

MOZART see WHOM THE GODS LOVE

MOZART: A CHILDHOOD CHRONICLE see WHOM THE
   GODS LOVE

MOZART AND SALIERI see SYMPHONY OF LOVE AND
   DEATH, THE

MOZART -- REICH MIR DIE HAND, MEIN LEBEN see
   WHOM THE GODS LOVE

MUCH ADO ABOUT NOTHING (SATY DELAJI CLOVEKA)
   (CZE, 1912, based on the play by William Shakespeare)
   WET PAINT (PAR, 1926)
   MUCH ADO ABOUT NOTHING (NBC–TV, 1955)
   MUCH ADO ABOUT NOTHING (RUS, 1956)
   MUCH ADO ABOUT NOTHING (NBC–TV, 1958)
   MUCH ADO ABOUT NOTHING (GER, 1963)
   MUCH ADO ABOUT NOTHING (CBS–TV, 1973)
   MUCH ADO ABOUT NOTHING (RUS, 1973)

MUCHACHOS DE ANTES NO USABAN GOMINA, LOS
   (ARG, 1938, based on a story by Manuel Romero)
   MUCHACHOS DE ANTES NO USABAN GOMINA, LOS
   (ARG, 1969)

MUDE THEODOR, DER (GER, 1936, source unlisted)
   MUDE THEODOR, DER (GER, 1957)

MUDLARK, THE (FOX, 1950, based on the life and times
   of Queen Victoria of England)
   QUEEN VICTORIA AND DISRAELI (short) (TFC, 1955)

MUHAMMAD ALI – SKILL, BRAINS AND GUTS see

FLOAT LIKE A BUTTERFLY, SING LIKE A BEE

MUJER DE LAS CAMELLIAS, LA see DAME AUX
   CAMELIAS, LA

MUJER X, LA see MADAME X

MULLIGAN'S STEW (NBC–TV, 1977, based on a teleplay)
   MULLIGAN'S STEW (series) (NBC–TV, 1977)

MUMMY'S HAND, THE (UN, 1940, based on a story by Nina
   Wilcox Putnam and Richard Schayer)
   MUMMY, THE (UN, 1959)

MUNCHAUSEN see BARON DE CRAC

MUNCHAUSEN IN AFRICA see BARON DE CRAC

MUNSTERS, THE (series) (CBS–TV, 1964, based on a tele--
   play)
   MUNSTER, GO HOME (UN, 1966)

MUPPET MUSICIANS OF BREMEN see FOUR MUSICIANS
   OF BREMEN

MURDER (BRI, 1930, based on the play, "Enter Sir John,"
   by Clemence Dane and Helen Simpson)
   MARY (GER, 1930)

MURDER AT THE BASKERVILLES see HOUND OF THE
   BASKERVILLES, THE and SILVER BLAZE, THE

MURDER IN A PRIVATE CAR see RED LIGHTS

MURDER IN PEYTON PLACE see PEYTON PLACE

MURDER IN THE BIG HOUSE see JAILBREAK

MURDER IN THE BLUE ROOM see SECRETS OF THE
   BLUE ROOM

MURDER IN THE CATHEDRAL see MARTYRDOM OF
   THOMAS A BECKET

MURDER IN THORNTON SQUARE see GASLIGHT

MURDER IN TRINIDAD (FOX, 1934, based on a book by
   John W. Vandercook)
   MR. MOTO ON DANGER ISLAND (FOX, 1939)
   CARIBBEAN MYSTERY (FOX, 1945)

MURDER INC. see ENFORCER, THE

MURDER MY SWEET see FALCON TAKES OVER, THE

MURDER ON DIAMOND ROW see SQUEAKER, THE

MURDER ON THE WATERFRONT see INVISIBLE MENACE,
   THE

MURDER, SHE SAID see LADY ON A TRAIN

MURDER WILL OUT (WB, 1930, based on the story, "Purple
   Hieroglyph, The," by Murray Leinster)
   TORCHY BLANE IN CHINATOWN (WB, 1939)

MURDERER, THE see CRIME AND PUNISHMENT

MURDERS IN THE RUE MORGUE, THE see SHERLOCK

HOLMES AND THE GREAT MURDER MYSTERY

MURPHY'S WAKE (BRI, 1903, based on the play, "Conn the
   Shaugraun," by Dion Boucicault)
   MURPHY'S WAKE (BRI, 1906)

MUSGRAVE RITUAL, THE (short) (BRI, 1912, based on
   the story by Sir Arthur Conan Doyle)
   MUSGRAVE RITUAL, THE (short) (BRI, 1922)
   SHERLOCK HOLMES FACES DEATH (UN, 1943)

MUSIC BOX, THE see HIS MUSICAL CAREER

MUSIC LOVERS, THE see IT WAS AN EXCITING NIGHT

MUSICA PROIBITA see FORBIDDEN MUSIC

MUSIK IM BLUT (GER, 1934, source unlisted)
   MUSIK IM BLUT (GER, 1955)

MUSS MAN SICH GLEICH SCHEIDEN LASSEN? (GER, 1932,
   source unlisted)
   MUSS MAN SICH GLEICH SCHEIDEN LASSEN? (GER,
   1953)

MUSSOLINI see BENITO MUSSOLINI

MUSTERGATTE, DER (GER, 1927, source unlisted)
   MUSTERGATTE, DER (GER, 1956)

MUTINES DE L'ELSENEUR, LES see MUTINY, THE

MUTINY, THE (MGM, 1920, based on the book, "Mutiny on
   the Elsinore," by Jack London)
   MUTINES DE L'ELSENEUR, LES (FRA, 1935)
   MUTINY ON THE ELSINORE (BRI, 1937)

MUTINY OF THE BOUNTY (AUT, 1916, based on the book,
   "Mutiny on the Bounty," by Charles Nordhoff and James
   Norman Hall)
   IN THE WAKE OF THE BOUNTY (AUT, 1933)
   MUTINY ON THE BOUNTY (MGM, 1935)
   BOUNTY COURT MARTIAL (CBS–TV, 1955)
   MUTINY ON THE BOUNTY (MGM, 1961)

MUTINY ON THE BLACKHAWK see SUTTER'S GOLD

MUTINY ON THE BOUNTY see MUTINY OF THE
   BOUNTY

MUTINY ON THE ELSINORE see MUTINY, THE

MUTTERS KRAUSENS FAHRT IN GLUCK (GER, 1929,
   based on a screenplay by Berthold Brecht)
   MOTHER KUSTERS GOES TO HEAVEN (GER, 1976)

MUTTER UND KIND (GER, 1915, based on a story by
   Christian Friedrich Hebbel)
   MUTTER UND KIND (GER, 1924)
   MUTTER UND KIND (GER, 1933)

MUTTERLIEBE (GER, 1929, based on a screenplay by Henny
   Porten)
   MUTTERLIEBE (GER, 1939)

MY BILL see COURAGE

MY BOY, OLIVER TWIST see OLIVER TWIST

144

MY CLIENT CURLEY see ONCE UPON A TIME

MY DARLING CLEMENTINE see FRONTIER MARSHAL

MY DAUGHTER JOY see DAVID GOLDER

MY DREAM IS YOURS see 20 MILLION SWEETHEARTS

MY FAIR LADY see PYGMALION

MY FAVORITE MARTIAN (series) (CBS--TV, 1963, based
    on a teleplay)
    MY FAVORITE MARTIAN (series) (CBS–TV, 1973)

MY FAVORITE WIFE (RKO, 1940, based on a story by Sam
    and Bela Spewack)
    MOVE OVER, DARLING (FOX, 1963)

MY FIRST GIRL FRIEND see ADOLESCENCE

MY FRIEND FLICKA (FOX, 1943, based on the book by
    Mary O'Hara)
    THUNDERHEAD, SON OF FLICKA (FOX, 1945)
    MY FRIEND FLICKA (series) (CBS--TV, 1956)

MY FRIEND IRMA (PAR, 1949, based on the radio series by
    Cy Howard)
    MY FRIEND IRMA GOES WEST (PAR, 1950)
    MY FRIEND IRMA (series) (CBS--TV, 1952)

MY FRIEND IRMA GOES WEST see MY FRIEND IRMA

MY FRIEND JEKYLL see DR. JEKYLL AND MR. HYDE

MY GIRL TISA (WB, 1948, based on the play, "Ever the
    Beginning," by Lucille Frumbs and Sara Smith)
    INTRODUCTION TO ERICA (WB–TV, 1956)

MY LADY'S SLIPPER see STARS AND STRIPES, THE

MY LIPS BETRAY (FOX, 1922, based on the play, "Der
    Komet," by Attila Orbok)
    THIN ICE (FOX, 1937)

MY LORD CONCEIT see IRON STAIR, THE

MY MAN GODFREY, (UN, 1936, based on a book by
    Eric Harch)
    ESCUELA DE VAGABUNDOS (MEX, 1954)
    MY MAN GODFREY (UN, 1957)

MY NAME IS JULIA ROSS (COL, 1945, based on the book,
    "The Woman in Red," by Anthony Gilbert)
    MY NAME IS JULIA ROSS (NBC–TV, 1955)

MY OLD DUTCH (VIT, 1911, based on a play by Albert
    Chevalier and Arthur Shirley)
    OLD DUTCH (BRI, 1915)
    OLD DUTCH (WOR, 1917)
    MY OLD DUTCH (UN, 1926)
    OLD DUTCH (BRI, 1934)

MY OLD MAN see UNDER MY SKIN

MY SISTER AND I see IHRE DURCHLAUT, DIE VERKAU--
    FERIN

MY SISTER EILEEN (COL, 1942, based on the play by Joseph
    Fields and Jerome Chodorov)

MY SISTER EILEEN (COL, 1955)
    WONDERFUL TOWN (CBS--TV, 1958)
    MY SISTER EILEEN (series) (CBS--TV, 1960)

MY SISTER, MY LOVE (SWE, 1966, based on the play, " 'Tis
    a Pity She's a Whore," by John Ford)
    'TIS A PITY SHE'S A WHORE (ADDIO, FRATELLO
    CRUDELE) (ITA, 1971)

MY THREE ANGELS see WE'RE NO ANGELS

MY UNCLE BENJAMIN (FRA, 1923, based on the book by
    Claude Tillier)
    NE PLEURE PAS (RUS, 1969)
    MY UNCLE BENJAMIN (FRA/ITA, 1969)

MY UNMARRIED WIFE (UN, 1917, based on the story,
    "Molly and I," by Frank R. Adams)
    MOLLY AND I (FOX, 1920)

MY WIFE, THE SWEDE AND I see MARRIAGE--GO--
    ROUND

MY WIFE'S FAMILY (BRI, 1931, based on the play by Fred
    Duprez)
    MY WIFE'S FAMILY (BRI, 1941)
    MY WIFE'S FAMILY (BRI, 1956)

MY WORLD AND WELCOME TO IT (series) (NBC–TV,
    1969, based on the writings of James Thurber)
    WAR BETWEEN MEN AND WOMEN, THE (NGP, 1972)

MYSTERE DE LA CHAMBRE JAUNE, LE (FRA, 1913,
    based on the book by Gaston Leroux)
    MYSTERY OF THE YELLOW ROOM, THE (REA, 1919)
    MYSTERE DE LA CHAMBRE JAUNE, LE (FRA, 1931)
    MYSTERY OF THE YELLOW ROOM (ARG, 1947)
    MYSTERE DE LA CHAMBRE JAUNE, LE (FRA, 1949)

MYSTERIES OF PARIS (FRA, 1911, based on the book by
    Eugene Sue)
    MYSTERIES OF PARIS (BRI, 1912)
    CHILD OF FATE (IND, 1913)
    MYSTERIES OF PARIS (ITA, 1917)
    PRINCE RODOLPHE, LE (ITA, 1917)
    SECRETS OF PARIS (FRA, 1921)
    SECRETS OF PARIS (IND, 1922)
    MYSTERIES OF PARIS (FRA, 1935)
    MYSTERIES OF PARIS (FRA, 1943)
    MYSTERIES OF PARIS (FRA/ITA, 1957)
    MYSTERIES OF PARIS (FRA/ITA, 1962)

MYSTERIES OF THE BLACK JUNGLE, THE (ITA, 1954,
    based on the book by Emilio Salgari)
    MYSTERIES OF THE BLACK JUNGLE, THE (GER/ITA,
    1964)

MYSTERIOUS AVENGER, THE (COL, 1936, based on a
    story by Peter B. Kyne; remake uncredited)
    STRANGER FROM TEXAS, THE (COL, 1939)

MYSTERIOUS DR. SATAN (serial) (REP, 1940, based on a
    screenplay by various authors; the remake is a condensa--
    tion of the serial)
    DR. SATAN'S ROBOT (REP, 1966)

MYSTERIOUS HOUSE OF DR. COPPELIUS, THE see
    COPPELIA OU LA POUPEE ANIMEE

MYSTERIOUS ISLAND (MGM, 1929, based on the book by

Jules Verne)
MYSTERIOUS ISLAND (RUS, 1941)
MYSTERIOUS ISLAND (serial) (COL, 1951)
JULES VERNE'S MYSTERIOUS ISLAND (COL, 1961)
MYSTERIOUS ISLAND (FRA/ITA/SPA, 1973)

MYSTERIOUS ISLAND OF CAPTAIN NEMO see 20,000
    LEAGUES UNDER THE SEA

MYSTERIOUS MAGICIAN, THE see RINGER, THE

MYSTERIOUS MR. REEDER, THE (BRI, 1937, based on a
    book by Edgar Wallace)
    ROOM 13 (GER, 1964)

MYSTERIOUS RIDER, THE (HOD, 1921, based on a book
    by Zane Grey)
    MYSTERIOUS RIDER, THE (PAR, 1927)
    MYSTERIOUS RIDER, THE (PAR, 1933)
    MYSTERIOUS RIDER, THE (PAR, 1938)

MYSTERIOUS UNCLE SILAS, THE see UNCLE SILAS

MYSTERY AT THE VILLA ROSE see AT THE VILLA
    ROSE

MYSTERY OF AMELIA EARHART, THE see FLIGHT FOR
    FREEDOM

MYSTERY OF EDWIN DROOD, THE (BRI, 1909, based on
    the book by Charles Dickens)

MYSTERY OF EDWIN DROOD, THE (BRI, 1914)
MYSTERY OF EDWIN DROOD, THE (UN, 1935)
MYSTERY OF EDWIN DROOD, THE (CBS–TV, 1952)

MYSTERY OF MR. X (MGM, 1934, based on a book by Philip
    MacDonald)
    HOUR OF 13, THE (MGM, 1953)

MYSTERY OF THE BOULE CABINET, THE see IN THE
    NEXT ROOM

MYSTERY OF THE CATACOMBS (ITA, 1913, based on
    the book, "Fabiola," by Cardinal Nicholas Wiseman)
    FABIOLA (ITA, 1917)
    FABIOLA (ITA, 1922)
    FABIOLA (FRA/ITA, 1948)
    REVOLT OF THE SLAVES (GER/ITA/SPA, 1960)
    FABIOLA (EMB, 1963)

MYSTERY OF THE THIRTEENTH GUEST, THE see THIR-
    TEENTH GUEST, THE

MYSTERY OF THE WAX MUSEJM (WB, 1933, based on a
    play by Charles S. Belden)
    HOUSE OF WAX (WB, 1953)
    CHAMBER OF HORRORS (WB, 1966)

MYSTERY OF THE YELLOW ROOM see MYSTERE DE
    LA CHAMBRE JAUNE, LE

MYSTERY RANCH see KILLER, THE

NABESHIMA KAIBYODEN (JAP, 1949, based on a
    Japanese legend)
  HIROKU KAIBYODEN (JAP, 1969)

NACHT DER ENTSCHEIDUNG, DIE (GER, 1931, based on
    the book by Lajos Zilahy)
  NACHT DER ENTSCHEIDUNG, DIE (GER, 1938)
  NACHT DER ENTSCHEIDUNG, DIE (GER, 1956)

NACHT DES GRAUENS, DIE (GER, 1912, source unlisted)
  NACHT DES GRAUENS, DIE (GER, 1916)

NACHT GEHORT UNS, DIE (GER, 1929, based on a story
    by Henry Kistemaeckers)
  NUIT EST A NOUS, LA (FRA, 1953)

NACHT VON PORT SAID, DIE see PORT SAID NIGHTS

NACKTE WAHREIT, DIE see NOTHING BUT THE
    TRUTH

NACHTGESTALTEN (GER, 1920, based on the book by
    Anthony Carlyle)
  NACHTGESTALTEN (GER, 1928)

NAKED CITY (UN, 1948, based on a story by Malvin Wald)
  NAKED CITY (series) (ABC--TV, 1958)

NAKED HEART, THE see MARIA CHAPDELAINE

NAKED MAJA, THE see GLORY OF GOYA

NALA DAMYANTI (IN, 1917, based on an Indian myth)
  NALA DAMYANTI (IN, 1945)

NANA (DEN, 1912, based on the book by Emile Zola)
  NANA (ITA, 1913)
  NANA (GER, 1923)
  NANA (FRA, 1926)
  NANA (UA, 1934)
  NANA (MEX, 1944)
  NANA (FRA/ITA, 1955)
  NANA (FRA/SWE, 1970)
  NANA (series) (BRI--TV, 1973)

NANCY GOES TO RIO see IT'S A DATE

NANON (GER, 1923, source unlisted)
  NANON (GER, 1938)

NAPLES AU BAISER DE FEU (FRA, 1925, based on a book
    by Auguste Bailly)
  NAPLES AU BASIER DE FEU (FRA/ITA, 1937)
  FLAME AND THE FLESH (MGM, 1954)

NAPOLEON -- MAN OF DESTINY (VIT, 1909, based on the
    life of the Emperor of France)
  LIFE DRAMA OF NAPOLEON BONAPARTE AND
    EMPRESS JOSEPHINE OF FRANCE, THE (VIT, 1909)
  CHECKMATED (BRI, 1910)
  NAPOLEON ON ST. HELENA (FRA, c1911)
  BATTLE OF WATERLOO (BRI, 1913)
  HIS LIFE FOR THE EMPEROR (VIT, 1913)
  ROYAL DIVORCE, A (BRI, 1923)
  NAPOLEON (FRA, 1927)
  NAPOLEON ON STE. HELENE (GER, 1929)
  NAPOLEON (MGM, 1929)
  CONQUEST (MGM, 1937)
  ROYAL DIVORCE, A (BRI, 1938)

NAPOLEON (FRA, 1945)
NAPOLEON (FRA, 1954)
NAPOLEONIC ERA, THE (short) (COR, 1957)
EAGLE IN A CAGE (NBC--TV, 1967)
NAPOLEON'S RETURN FROM ELBA (short) (CBS--TV,
    1965)
NAPOLEON (short) (LCA, 1970)
WATERLOO (COL, 1971)
EAGLE IN A CAGE (BRI, 1971)
NAPOLEON AND LOVE (series) (BRI--TV, 1974)

NAPOLEON OF BROADWAY see TWENTIETH CENTURY

NAPOLEON UND DIE KLEINE WACSHERIN see
    MADAME SANS--GENE

NAPOLEON'S BARBER (short) (FOX, 1928, based on a
    story by Arthur Caesar)
  BARBERO DE NAPOLEON (short) (SPA, 1930)

NAR BENGT OCH ANDERS BYTTE HUSTRUR (SWE,
    1925, source unknown)
  NAR BENGT OCH ANDERS BYTTE HUSTRUR (SWE,
    1950)

NARA NARAYAN (IN, 1937, based on an Indian myth)
  NARA NARAYAN (IN, 1939)

NARAYANA see PEAU DE CHAGRIN, LA

NARKOSE (GER, 1929, based on the book, "Brief einer
    unbekannten," by Stefan Zweig)
  BRIEF EINER UNBEKANNTEN (FIN, 1943)
  LETTER FROM AN UNKNOWN WOMAN, A (UN, 1948)
  LETTER FROM AN UNKNOWN WOMAN, A (CBS--TV,
    1952)

NARROW CORNER, THE (WB, 1933, based on the book by
    W. Somerset Maugham)
  ISLE OF FURY (WB, 1936)

NARROW STREET, THE (WB, 1924, based on a book by
    Edwin Bateman Morris)
  WIDE OPEN (WB, 1930)

NATACHA ROSTOVA see WAR AND PEACE

NATHAN HALE see DEATH OF NATHAN HALE, THE

NATIONAL VELVET (MGM, 1944, based on the book by
    Enid Bagnold)
  NATIONAL VELVET (series) (NBC--TV, 1960)

NE PLEURE PAS see MY UNCLE BENJAMIN

NEAREST AND DEAREST (series) (BRI--TV, 1971, based on
    a teleplay)
  THICKER THAN WATER (series) (ABC--TV, 1973)

NEBO ZOWET (RUS, 1959, remake based on stock footage
    from the former film)
  BATTLE BEYOND THE SUN (AI, 1963)

NED KELLY see KELLY GANG, THE

NED McCOBB'S DAUGHTER (PAT, 1928, based on the play
    by Sidney Howard)
  NED McCOBB'S DAUGHTER (TV, 1950)

NEEDLES AND PINS see RAG TRADE, THE

NE'ER--DO--WELL, THE (SEL, 1915, based on the book by
    Rex Beach)
   NE'ER--DO--WELL, THE (PAR, 1923)

NEF, LA (ITA, 1911, based on a book by Gabriele
    D'Annunzio)
   NEF, LA (ITA, 1920)

NELL GWYNNE see NELL GWYNNE, THE ORANGE
    GIRL

NELL GWYNNE, THE ORANGE GIRL (BRI, 1911, based
    on the life of the British courtesan)
   NELL GWYNNE (BRI, 1926)
   NELL GWYNNE (BRI, 1934)

NELSON (BRI, 1918, based on historical characters and
    incidents)
   NELSON (BRI, 1926)
   NELSON AFFAIR, THE (BRI, 1973)

NELSON AFFAIR, THE see NELSON and ROMANCE OF
    LADY HAMILTON, THE

NELSON--MARCUS MURDERS, THE (CBS--TV, 1973, based
    on a teleplay)
   KOJAK (series) (CBS--TV, 1973)

NERO WOLFE see MEET NERO WOLFE

NERVOUS WRECK, THE (PDC, 1926, based on the book,
    "The Wreck," by Owen Davis and the play by E.J. Rath)
   WHOOPEE (UA, 1930)
   UP IN ARMS (UA, 1944)
   NERVOUS WRECK, THE (TV, 1952)

NEVADA (PAR, 1927, based on the book by Zane Grey)
   NEVADA (PAR, 1935)
   NEVADA (RKO, 1944)

NEVADA SMITH see CARPETBAGGERS, THE

NEVER SAY DIE (AE, 1924, based on the play by William
    H. Post)
   NEVER SAY DIE (PAR, 1939)

NEVER SAY GOODBYE see THIS LOVE OF OURS

NEVER TAKE NO FOR AN ANSWER (ITA, 1951, based on
    a story by Paul Gallico)
   SMALL MIRACLE, THE (NBC--TV, 1973)

NEVER THE TWAIN SHALL MEET (MGM, 1925, based on a
    story by Peter B. Kyne)
   NEVER THE TWAIN SHALL MEET (MGM, 1931)

NEVER TO LOVE see BILL OF DIVORCEMENT, A

NEVER WAVE AT A WAC (CBS--TV, 1951, based on a tele--
    play by Frederick Kohner and Fred Brady)
   NEVER WAVE AT A WAC (RKO, 1952)

NEW ADVENTURES OF HEIDI, THE see HEIDI

NEW ADVENTURES OF HUCKLEBERRY FINN, THE see
    HUCKLEBERRY FINN

NEW ADVENTURES OF MARTIN KANE see MARTIN
    KANE, PRIVATE EYE

NEW ADVENTURES OF PINOCCHIO, THE see
    PINOCCHIO

NEW ADVENTURES OF ROBIN HOOD, THE see ROBIN
    HOOD AND HIS MERRY MEN

NEW ADVENTURES OF SPIN AND MARTY, THE see
    SPIN AND MARTY

NEW AVENGERS, THE see AVENGERS, THE

NEW GULLIVER, THE see GULLIVER'S TRAVELS

NEW INVISIBLE MAN, THE see INVISIBLE MAN, THE

NEW LAND, THE (SWE, 1973, based on the book by Vilhelm
    Moberg)
   NEW LAND, THE (series) (ABC--TV, 1974)

NEW MAGDALEN, THE (IND, 1910, based on a book by
    Wilkie Collins)
   NEW MAGDALEN, THE (IND, 1913)

NEW MISSION OF JUDEX see JUDEX

NEW SALEM see ABRAHAM LINCOLN

NEW WINE see SCHUBERT'S FRUHLINGSTRAUM

NEW YEAR SACRIFICE see PEASANT HSIANG LIN'S
    WIFE, THE

NEWLY RICH (PAR, 1931, based on the book, "Let's Play
    King," by Sinclair Lewis)
   MAJESTAT AUF ABWEGEN (GER, 1958)

NICHEE DE GENTILSHOMMES, UNE (RUS, 1915, based on
    the book by Ivan Turgenev)
   NICHEE DE GENTILSHOMMES, UNE (RUS, 1969)

NICHOLAS AND ALEXANDRA see RASPUTIN, THE
    BLACK MONK

NICHOLAS NICKELBY (BIO, 1903, based on the book by
    Charles Dickens)
   DOTHBOY'S HALL (BRI, 1903)
   NICHOLAS NICKELBY (THA, 1912)
   NICHOLAS NICKELBY (BRI, 1947)

NICHTS ALS ARGER MIT DER LIEBE see CONCERT, THE

NIE WIEDER LIEBE (GER, 1931, source unlisted)
   CALAIS--DOUVRE (FRA, 1931)

NIGHT BEFORE CHRISTMAS, THE (ED, 1905, based on the
    poem by Clement Moore)
   NIGHT BEFORE CHRISTMAS, THE (short) (DIS, 1933)
   NIGHT BEFORE CHRISTMAS, THE (short) (MGM, 1941)
   NIGHT BEFORE CHRISTMAS, THE (short) (RUS, 1951)
   'TWAS THE NIGHT BEFORE CHRISTMAS (CBS--TV,
    1974)

NIGHT BUS see IT HAPPENED ONE NIGHT

NIGHT CLUB, THE see AFTER FIVE

NIGHT CLUB SCANDAL   see   GUILTY AS HELL

NIGHT CREATURES   see   DR. SYN

NIGHT GAMES   see   LAWYERS, THE

NIGHT IN PARADISE   see   PEACOCK'S FEATHER

NIGHT IN VENICE, A   (GER, 1934, based on the operetta
    by Johann Strauss, Jr.)
  NIGHT IN VENICE, A   (GER, 1942)
  NIGHT IN VENICE, A   (GER, 1953)

NIGHT MUST FALL   (MGM, 1937, based on the play by
    Emlyn Williams)
  NIGHT MUST FALL   (NET–TV, 1952)
  NIGHT MUST FALL   (NBC–TV, 1956)
  NIGHT MUST FALL   (MGM, 1964)

NIGHT OF ADVENTURE, A   see   HAT, COAT AND GLOVE

NIGHT OF JANUARY 16TH, THE   (PAR, 1941, based on
    the play by Ayn Rand)
  NIGHT OF JANUARY 16TH, THE   (TV, 1952)

NIGHT OF MYSTERY   see   GREENE MURDER CASE, THE

NIGHT OF THE BEARS, THE   see   MARRIAGE OF THE
    BEAR

NIGHT OF THE GARTER, A   see   GETTING GERTIE'S
    GARTER

NIGHT OF THE LIVING DEAD   (CON, 1968, based on a
    screenplay by John A. Russo)
  LIVING DEAD AT THE MANCHESTER MORGUE, THE
    (BRI, 1974)

NIGHT OF THE VAMPIRE   see   NOSFERATU

NIGHT OWLS   (short)   (MGM, 1930, based on a story by
    Leo McCarey)
  LADRONES   (short)   (MGM, 1930)
  NIGHT OWLS   (FRA, 1930)
  NIGHT OWLS   (ITA, 1930)
  NIGHT OWLS   (GER, 1930)

NIGHT PLANE FROM CHUNKING   see   SHANGHAI
    EXPRESS

NIGHT STALKER, THE   see   KOLCHAK: THE NIGHT
    STALKER

NIGHT STRIKE: JOHN PAUL JONES   see   WAR OF
    INDEPENDENCE 1775–1783

NIGHT THE ANIMALS TALKED, THE   see   PASSION
    PLAY, THE

NIGHT THEY KILLED RASPUTIN, THE   see   RASPUTIN,
    THE BLACK MONK

NIGHT TO REMEMBER, A   see   ATLANTIC

NIGHT WATCH, THE   (FN, 1928, based on the play by
    Lajos Biro)
  GIRL FROM MONTE CARLO, THE   (FN, 1932)

NIGHTCOMERS, THE   see   OTHERS, THE

NIGHTINGALE, THE   see   EMPEROR'S NIGHTINGALE,
    THE

NIGHTMARE   see   FEAR IN THE NIGHT

NIGHTS OF CABIRIA   (ITA, 1957, based on a screenplay by
    Federico Fellini)
  SWEET CHARITY   (UN, 1969)

NIGHTS OF DRACULA   see   NOSFERATU

NIGHTS OF LUCRETIA BORGIA   see   LUCRETIA BORGIA

NIGHTSTICK   see   ALIBI

NIKKI, WILD DOG OF THE NORTH   see   NOMADS OF THE
    NORTH

NINA PETROVNA   see   WONDERFUL LIE OF NINA
    PETROVNA, THE

NINE DAYS A QUEEN   see   LADY JANE GREY

NINETY AND NINE, THE   (VIT, 1916, based on the play by
    Ramsay Morris)
  NINETY AND NINE, THE   (VIT, 1922)

90 BRISTOL COURT   (series)   (NBC–TV, based on a teleplay)
  KAREN   (series)   (NBC–TV, 1965)

NINETY DEGREES SOUTH   see   SCOTT ANTARCTIC
    EXPEDITION

NINOTCHKA   (MGM, 1939, based on a story by Melchior
    Lengyel)
  SILK STOCKINGS   (MGM, 1957)
  NINOTCHKA   (ABC–TV, 1960)

NITCHEVO!   (FRA, 1926, based on a screen play by Jacques
    de Baroncelli)
  NITCHEVO!   (FRA, 1936)

NIXON: CHECKERS TO WATERGATE   see   MAKING OF
    THE PRESIDENT – 1960, THE

NO DEJAS LA PUERTA ABIERTA   see   PLEASURE CRUISE

NO EXIT   see   HUIS CLOS

NO FOOD FOR THOUGHT   (TV, n.d., based on a teleplay by
    Robert M. Fresco)
  TARANTULA   (UN, 1955)

NO GREATER GLORY   see   PAUL STREET BOYS, THE

NO HARD FEELINGS   see   SMART BLONDE

NO, NO, NANETTE   (WB, 1930, based on the musical comedy
    by Vincent Youmans)
  NO, NO, NANETTE   (RKO, 1940)
  TEA FOR TWO   (WB, 1950)

NO ORCHIDS FOR LULU   see   LULU

NO ORCHIDS FOR MISS BLANDISH   (BRI, 1948, based on
    the book by James Hadley Chase)
  GRISSOM GANG, THE   (CIN, 1971)
  FLESH FOR THE ORCHID   (FRA, 1975)

NO PLACE LIKE HOMICIDE see GHOUL, THE

NO PLACE TO GO see WELCOME HOME

NO SAD SONGS FOR ME (COL, 1950, based on the book by
    Ruth Southard)
  NO SAD SONGS FOR ME (NBC–TV, 1955)

NO TIME FOR COMEDY (WB, 1940, based on the play by
    S.N. Behrman)
  NO TIME FOR COMEDY (ABC–TV, 1951)
  NO TIME FOR COMEDY (NBC–TV, 1957)

NO TIME FOR SERGEANTS (CBS–TV, 1955, based on the
    book by Mac Hyman and the play by Ira Levin)
  NO TIME FOR SERGEANTS (WB, 1958)
  NO TIME FOR SERGEANTS (series) (ABC–TV, 1964)

NOAH AND HIS FAMILY see NOAH'S ARK

NOAH AND THE ARK see NOAH'S ARK

NOAH AND THE FLOOD see NOAH'S ARK

NOAH'S ARK (BRI, 1909, based on the Bible story)
  TALE OF THE ARK (short) (BRI, 1909)
  SINFLUT (GER, 1927)
  NOAH'S ARK (WB, 1929)
  NOAH'S ARK (FRA, 1950)
  NOAH AND HIS FAMILY (short) (IND, n.d.)
  NOAH AND THE ARK (short) (IND, 1955)
  NOAH'S ARK (short) (DIS, 1959)
  NOAH AND THE FLOOD (CBS–TV, 1962)
  BIBLE, THE (sequence) (FOX, 1966)
  NOAH AND THE FLOOD (IND, 1968)
  BIBLE, LA (FRA, 1977)

NOCHE DE DUENDAS see LAUREL & HARDY MURDER
  CASE, THE

NOMADS OF THE NORTH (FN, 1920, based on the book by
    James Oliver Curwood)
  NORTHERN PATROL (BRI, 1954)
  NIKKI, WILD DOG OF THE NORTH (DIS, 1961)

NOMBRE DE LA AMISTAD, EN see FRIENDSHIP

NOOSE, THE (WB, 1928, based on the play by Willard Mack
    and H.H. van Loan)
  I'D GIVE MY LIFE (PAR, 1937)

NOOSE HANGS HIGH, THE see FOR LOVE OR MONEY

NORA see DOLL'S HOUSE, A

NORLA, LA see DIARY OF A MADMAN

NORTH OF '36 (PAR, 1924, based on a story by Emerson
    Hough)
  CONQUERING HORDE, THE (PAR, 1931)
  TEXANS, THE (PAR, 1938)

NORTH POLE EXPLORATION see EXPEDITION TO
  ANTARCTICA

NORTHERN PATROL see NOMADS OF THE NORTH

NORTHWEST PASSAGE (MGM, 1940, based on the book by
    Kenneth Roberts)

NORTHWEST PASSAGE (series) (NBC–TV, 1957)

NORTHWEST RANGERS see MANHATTAN MELODRAMA

NOSE, THE (short) (FRA, 1963, based on the story by
    Nicolai Gogol)
  NOSE, THE (short) (IND, 1966)

NOSFERATU (DRACULA) (GER, 1922, based on the book
    by Bram Stoker)
  DRACULA (UN, 1931)
  DRACULA (SPA, 1931)
  DRACULA'S DAUGHTER (UN, 1936)
  HOUSE OF DRACULA (UN, 1945)
  HORROR OF DRACULA (BRI, 1958)
  BRIDES OF DRACULA (BRI, 1960)
  BAD FLOWER, THE (KOR, 1961)
  NIGHT OF THE VAMPIRES (GER/YUG, 1965)
  DRACULA HAS RISEN FROM THE GRAVE (BRI, 1969)
  NIGHTS OF DRACULA (FRA/GER/SPA, 1969)
  TASTE THE BLOOD OF DRACULA (BRI, 1970)
  HANNON CAMBIATO FACCIA (ITA, 1971)
  SCARS OF DRACULA (BRI, 1971)
  TWINS OF DRACULA (BRI, 1971)
  COUNT DRACULA (GER/SPA, 1971)
  DRACULA TODAY (BRI, 1971)
  RETURN OF DRACULA (SWE, 1972)
  BLACULA (AI, 1972)
  DRACULA VS. FRANKENSTEIN (SPA, 1972)
  BLOOD FOR DRACULA (FRA/ITA, 1973)
  DRACULA (CAN–TV, 1973)
  DRACULA (CBS–TV, 1974)

NOSTALGIE see POSTMASTER, THE

NOT EXACTLY GENTLEMEN see THREE BAD MEN

NOT SO DUMB see DULCY

NOT SO DUSTY (BRI, 1936, based on a story by Wally
    Patch and Frank Atkinson)
  NOT SO DUSTY (BRI, 1956)

NOTHING BUT THE TRUTH (PAR, 1920, based on the book
    by Frederic S. Isham; also the basis for two musical
    comedies, "Tell Her the Truth" in 1916 and "Yes, Yes,
    Yvette" in 1927)
  NOTHING BUT THE TRUTH (PAR, 1929)
  NACKE WAHREIT, DIE (GER, 1930)
  RIEN QUE LA VERITE (FRA, 1931)
  PURA VERDAD, LA (SPA, 1932)
  NOTHING BUT THE TRUTH (PAR, 1941)
  NOTHING BUT THE TRUTH (TV, 1952)

NOTHING BUT THE TRUTH see BARON DE CRAC

NOTHING SACRED (UA, 1937, based on a book by James
    H. Street; also the basis for the musical comedy, "Hazel
    Flagg," in 1953)
  LIVING IT UP (PAR, 1954)

NOTORIOUS (RKO, 1946, based on a screenplay by Ben
    Hecht)
  NOTORIOUS (NBC–TV, 1961)

NOTORIOUS GENTLEMAN, A (UN, 1935, based on a story
    by Florence Ryerson and Colin Clements)
  SMOOTH AS SILK (UN, 1946)

NOTRE DAME   see   ESMERELDA

NOTRE DAME DE PARIS   see   ESMERELDA

NOUVELLE AURORE, LA   see   CHERI--BIBI

NOVEMBER 22 AND THE WARREN REPORT   (CBS–TV,
     1964, based on incidents in the assassination of President
     John F. Kennedy)
  WARREN REPORT, THE   (CBS–TV, 1967)
  REPORT   (short)   (IND, 1967)
  RUSH TO JUDGMENT   (NYF, 1967)
  AMERICAN ASSASSINS, THE   (CBS–TV, 1975)
  RUBY AND OSWALD   (CBS–TV, 1977)
  TRIAL OF LEE HARVEY OSWALD, THE   (ABC–TV,
     1977)

NOW I'LL TELL   see   STREET OF CHANCE

NOW, VOYAGER   (WB, 1942, based on the book by Olive
     Higgins Prouty)
  NOW, VOYAGER   (NBC–TV, 1956)

NUISANCE, THE   (MGM, 1933, based on a story by
     Chandler Sprague and Howard Emmett Rogers)
  CHASE, THE   (MGM, 1938)

NUIT D'ESPAGNE   see   TRANSGRESSION

NUIT DE MAI   see   JUNGLE BARON NEUHAUS, DER

NUIT DE NOCES, SA   (SWE, 1916, based on a story, "La
     Belle Aventure," by Robert de Flers, Gaston Arman de
     Caillavet and Etienne Rey)
  SHONE ABENTEUER, DAS   (GER, 1932)
  BELLE AVENTURE, LA   (FRA, 1942)

NUIT EST A NOUS, LE   see   NACHT GEHORT UNS, DIE

NUITS EXTRAVAGANTE, UNE   see   THEIR PURPLE
     MOMENT

NUITS BLANCHES DE SAINT–PETERSBOURG, LES   see
     KREUTZER SONATA, THE

NUITS DE FUE   see   LIVING CORPSE, THE

NUITS DE PRINCES   (FRA, 1929, based on a novel by Joseph
     Kessel)
  NUITS DE PRINCES   (FRA, 1938)

NUMBER 17   (BRI, 1928, based on the play by J. Jefferson
     Farjeon)

NUMBER 17   (BRI, 1932)

NO. 96   (series)   (AUT–TV, 1972)
  NO. 96   (AUT, 1974)

NUN OF MONZA, THE   (ITA, 1947, based on the book, "La
     Religieuse de Monza," by Mario Mazzucchelli)
  NUN OF MONZA, THE   (ITA/FRA, 1962)
  NUN OF MONZA, THE   (ITA, 1968)

NUREMBERG TRIALS, THE   (RUS, 1947, based on the trial
     of Nazi war criminals)
  NUREMBERG TRIALS, THE   (IND, 1949)
  NUREMBERG TRIAL, THE   (GER, 1958)

NUREMBERG TRIALS, THE   see also   JUDGMENT AT
     NUREMBERG

NURSE CAVELL   (BRI, 1915, based on the book, "Dawn,"
     by Reginald Berkeley)
  EDITH CAVELL   (AUT, 1916)
  DAWN   (BRI, 1917)
  WOMEN THE GERMANS SHOT, THE   (PLC, 1918)
  DAWN   (PAT, 1919)
  DAWN   (COL, 1928)
  NURSE EDITH CAVELL   (RKO, 1939)

NURSE EDITH CAVELL   see   NURSE CAVELL

NURSES, THE   (series)   (CBS--TV, 1962, based on a teleplay)
  DOCTORS AND NURSES   (series)   (CBS-TV, 1965)
  NURSES, THE   (series)   (ABC-TV, 1965)

NURSE'S SECRET, THE   see   MISS PINKERTON

NUTCRACKER, THE   (CBS--TV, 1958, based on the ballet by
     Peter Illytch Tchaikovsky)
  ENCHANTED NUTCRACKER, THE   (ABC--TV, 1961)
  NUTCRACKER SUITE, THE   (TV, 1964)
  NUTCRACKER, THE   (GER, 1965)
  NUTCRACKER, THE   (NBC-TV, 1966)
  NUTCRACKER, THE   (short)   (POL, 1967)
  NUTCRACKER, THE   (CBS--TV, 1968)
  NUTCRACKER, THE   (short)   (RUS, 1975)

NUTCRACKER, THE   see   HOFFMANNS ERZAHLUNGEN

NUTCRACKER SUITE, THE   see   NUTCRACKER, THE

NUTTY PROFESSOR, THE   see   DR. JEKYLL AND MR.
     HYDE

NYOKA AND THE LOST SECRETS OF HIPPOCRATES   see
     PERILS OF NYOKA, THE

O. HENRY'S FULL HOUSE   (FOX, 1952, based on stories
   by O. Henry (William Sidney Porter)
   BELLE ETOILE, LA   (FRA, 1966)

O. HENRY'S FULL HOUSE   see also   THE COP AND THE
   ANTHEM, GIFT OF THE MAGI, THE LAST LEAF,
   RANSOM OF RED CHIEF, and THE SACRIFICE

O, PROMISE ME   see   BUCKAROO KID, THE

OBSESSION   see   OSSESSIONE

OCCUPE--TOI D'AMELIE!   (FRA, 1912, based on a play by
   Georges Feydeau)
   OCCUPE--TOI D'AMELIE!   (FRA, 1933)
   OCCUPE--TOI D'AMELIE!   (FRA, 1949)

OCCURENCE AT OWL CREEK, AN   see   OCCURENCE AT
   OWL CREEK BRIDGE, AN

OCCURENCE AT OWL CREEK BRIDGE, AN   (IND, n.d.,
   based on the story by Ambrose Bierce)
   OCCURENCE AT OWL CREEK   (SA, n.d.)
   SPY, THE   (IND, 1930)
   OCCURENCE AT OWL CREEK BRIDGE, AN   (CBS--TV,
   1959)
   RIVIERE DU HIBOU, LA   (FRA, 1961)
   BRIDGE, THE   (POL, 1962)
   AU COEUR DE LA VIE   (sequence)   (FRA, 1968)

OCHSENKRIEG, DER   (GER, 1919, based on the book by
   Ludwig Ganghofer)
   OCHSENKRIEG, DER   (GER, 1942)

8 MAEDELS IN BOOT   (GER, 1932, based on a story by
   Helmut Brandis)
   EIGHT GIRLS IN A BOAT   (PAR, 1934)
   8 MAEDELS IN BOOT   (GER, 1959)

OCTAROON, THE   (AUT, 1912, based on the play by Dion
   Boucicault)
   OCTAROON, THE   (AUT, 1919)

ODD COUPLE, THE   (PAR, 1968, based on the play by Neil
   Simon)
   ODD COUPLE, THE   (series)   (ABC--TV, 1970)
   ODDBALL COUPLE, THE   (series)   (ABC--TV, 1975)

ODD FREAK   (short)   (BRI, 1916, based on a story by W.
   W. Jacobs)
   ODD FREAK   (short)   (BRI, 1923)

ODD MAN OUT   (BRI, 1947, based on a book by F. L. Green)
   LOST MAN, THE   (UN, 1969)

ODDBALL COUPLE, THE   see   ODD COUPLE, THE

ODETTE   (ITA, 1916, based on the book by Victorien Sardou)
   ODETTE   (GER, 1927)
   ODETTE   (ITA, 1935)
   DESARROI   (FRA, 1946)

ODYSSEY, THE   see   ULYSSES AND THE GIANT POLY--
   PHEMUS

OEDIPUS REX   (ITA, c1909, based on the play by Sophocles)
   OEDIPUS REX   (FRA, 1912)
   OEDIPUS REX   (IND, 1914)
   OEDIPUS REX   (CAN, 1957)

OEDIPUS THE KING   (ABC--TV, 1957)
OEDIPUS THE KING   (UN, 1967)
OEDIPUS THE KING   (BRI, 1967)
EDIPO RE   (ITA, 1967)
KING OEDIPUS   (BRI--TV, 1974)
RISE OF GREEK TRAGEDY, THE   (FFH, 1975)

OEDIPUS THE KING   see   OEDIPUS REX

O'ER THE RAMPARTS WE WATCHED   see   SONG OF A
   NATION

OF HUMAN BONDAGE   (RKO, 1934, based on the book by
   W. Somerset Maugham)
   OF HUMAN BONDAGE   (WB, 1946)
   FUERZA DEL DESEO, LA   (MEX, 1955)
   OF HUMAN BONDAGE   (UA, 1964)

OF MICE AND MEN   (UA, 1939, based on the book by John
   Steinbeck; also the basis of an opera in 1958)
   OF MICE AND MEN   (ABC--TV, 1968)

OFFICE GIRL, THE   see   SUNSHINE SUSIE

OFFICER 666   (KLE, 1914, based on the play by Augustin
   MacHugh)
   OFFICER 666   (AUT, 1916)
   OFFICER 666   (MGM, 1920)

OH, DOCTOR   (UN, 1924, based on the book by Harry Leon
   Wilson)
   HIS NIGHT OUT   (UN, 1935)
   OH, DOCTOR   (UN, 1937)

OH; JONATHAN, OH, JONATHAN   see   IT STARTED WITH
   EVE

OH, MR. PORTER   (BRI, 1938, based on a story by Frank
   Launder)
   UP THE CREEK   (BRI, 1958)

OH, PROMISE ME   see   BUCCAROO KID, THE

OH, ROSALINDA!   see   FLEDERMAUS, DIE

OH, SAILOR BEWARE   (WB, 1931, based on the play by
   Elmer Rice)
   SEE NAPLES AND DIE   (BRI, 1950)

OH, YOU'RE AWFUL   (BRI, 1971, source unlisted)
   ME AND THE MAFIA   (DEN, 1973)

O'HARA, UNITED STATES TREASURY   (CBS–TV, 1971,
   based on a teleplay)
   O'HARA, UNITED STATES TREASURY   (series)   (CBS–
   TV, 1971)

OIL FOR THE LAMPS OF CHINA   (WB, 1935, based on the
   book by Alice Tisdale Hobart)
   LAW OF THE TROPICS   (WB, 1941)

OKAY, AMERICA   (UN, 1932, based on a story by William
   Anthony McGuire)
   RISKY BUSINESS   (UN, 1939)

OKLAHOMA RAIDERS   see   COME ON, DANGER

OLD ACQUAINTANCE   (WB, 1943, based on the play by
   John Van Druten)

OLD ACQUAINTANCE (ABC--TV, 1951)
OLD ACQUAINTANCE (NBC--TV, 1956)

OLD CURIOSITY SHOP, THE (THA, 1911, based on the
    book by Charles Dickens)
  LITTLE NELL (FRA, 1912)
  OLD CURIOSITY SHOP, THE (BRI, 1913)
  OLD CURIOSITY SHOP, THE (BRI, 1914)
  OLD CURIOSITY SHOP, THE (BRI, 1921)
  OLD CURIOSITY SHOP, THE (BRI, 1934)
  OLD CURIOSITY SHOP, THE (BRI--TV, 1962)
  CHARLES DICKENS SHOW, THE (BRI, 1973)
  MR. QUILP (BRI, 1975)

OLD DARK HOUSE, THE (UN, 1932, based on the book
    by J. B. Priestley)
  OLD DARK HOUSE, THE (COL, 1963)

OLD DOLL'S HOUSE, THE see MIDNIGHT ALIBI

OLD DUTCH see MY OLD DUTCH

OLD--FASHIONED WAY, THE (sequence) (PAR, 1934,
    based on the play, "The Drunkard," by W. H. Smith)
  VILLAIN STILL PURSUED HER, THE (RKO, 1940)

OLD FATHERS AND YOUNG SONS see FATHER'S SON

OLD HEIDELBERG (TRI, 1915, based on the book by
    Wilhelm Meyer--Foerster and the operetta by Sigmund
    Romberg)
  OLD HEIDELBERG (IND, 1916)
  STUDENT PRINCE, THE (GER, 1923)
  STUDENT PRINCE, THE (GER, 1926)
  STUDENT PRINCE, THE (MGM, 1927)
  HOMECOMING (PAR, 1929)
  STUDENT'S ROMANCE, A (BRI, 1936)
  STUDENT PRINCE, THE (MGM, 1954)
  OLD HEIDELBERG (GER, 1959)

OLD HICKORY (short) (WB, 1939, based on the life of U.S.
    president Andrew Jackson)
  ANDREW JACKSON (short) (EBE, 1951)
  YOUNG ANDY JACKSON (short) (TFC, 1964)
  ANDREW JACKSON AT THE HERMITAGE (short) (COR,
  1964)

OLD HOMESTEAD, THE (PAR, 1915, based on the play by
    Denman Thompson)
  OLD HOMESTEAD, THE (PAR, 1922)
  OLD HOMESTEAD, THE (IND, 1935)

OLD LADY SHOWS HER MEDALS, THE see SEVEN DAYS'
  LEAVE

OLD MAID, THE (WB, 1939, based on the book by Edith
    Wharton)
  OLD MAID, THE (ABC--TV, 1954)
  OLD MAID, THE (NBC--TV, 1956)

OLD PLAY OF EVERYMAN see EVERYMAN

OLD SOAK, THE (UN, 1926, based on the play by Don
    Marquis)
  GOOD OLD SOAK, THE (MGM, 1937)

OLD SOLDIER see GENERAL DOUGLAS Mac ARTHUR

OLD SWIMMIN' HOLE, THE (FN, 1921, based on the poem

by James Whitcomb Riley)
OLD SWIMMIN' HOLE, THE (MON, 1940)

OLD TESTAMENT, THE see CAIN AND ABEL

OLD, THE NEW AND THE DEADLY, THE see MALTESE
  FALCON, THE

OLIVER! see OLIVER TWIST

OLIVER AND THE ARTFUL DODGER see OLIVER TWIST

OLIVER CROMWELL see CROMWELL

OLIVER TWIST (VIT, 1909, based on the book by Charles
    Dickens)
  OLIVER TWIST (PAT, 1910)
  OLIVER TWIST (FRA, 1910)
  OLIVER TWIST (DEN, 1910)
  OLIVER TWIST (BRI, 1912)
  OLIVER TWIST (IND, 1912)
  OLIVER TWIST (PAR, 1916)
  DEHEIMNISSE VON LONDON, DIE (GER, 1920)
  OLIVER TWIST JR. (FOX, 1921)
  OLIVER TWIST (BRI, 1922)
  FAGIN (short) (BRI, 1922)
  MY BOY, OLIVER TWIST (FN, 1922)
  OLIVER TWIST (MON, 1933)
  OLIVER TWIST (IND, 1940)
  OLIVER TWIST (BRI, 1948)
  OLIVER TWIST (CBS--TV, 1959)
  OLIVER! (COL, 1968)
  OLIVER AND THE ARTFUL DODGER (ABC--TV, 1972)
  CHARLES DICKENS SHOW, THE (BRI, 1973)

OLIVER WENDELL HOLMES see MAGNIFICENT YANKEE

OLTRE L'AMORE, L' see VANINA VANINI

OLYMPIA see HIS GLORIOUS NIGHT

O'MALLEY OF THE MOUNTED (PAR, 1921, based on a
    book by William S. Hart)
  O'MALLEY OF THE MOUNTED (FOX, 1936)

OMBRE, L' (ITA, 1916, based on the book by Dario
    Niccodemi)
  OMBRE, L' (ITA, 1919)
  OMBRE, L' (ITA, 1923)
  OMBRE, L' (ITA, 1954)

OMEGA MAN, THE see LAST MAN ON EARTH, THE

OMOO--OMOO, THE SHARK GOD (SG, 1949, based on the
    book, "Omoo," by Herman Melville)
  ENCHANTED ISLAND (WB, 1958)

ON A DESERT ISLAND see VICTORY

ON APPROVAL (BRI, 1930, based on the play by Frederick
    Lonsdale)
  ON APPROVAL (BRI, 1944)

ON BORROWED TIME (MGM, 1939, based on the book by
    Lawrence Edward Watkins and the play by Paul Osborne)
  ON BORROWED TIME (ABC-TV, 1952)
  ON BORROWED TIME (NBC-TV, 1957)

ON MOONLIGHT BAY see PENROD

ON NE BADINE PAS AVEC L'AMOUR (FRA, 1908, based
    on a story by Alfred de Musset)
  ON NE BADINE PAS AVEC L'AMOUR (FRA, 1924)
  ON NE BADINE PAS AVEC L'AMOUR (FRA, 1954)

ON THE BUSES (series) (BRI–TV, 1971, based on a teleplay)
  LOTSA LUCK (series) (NBC–TV, 1973)

ON THE RIVIERA see FOLIES BERGERE

ON THE ROCKS see PORRIDGE

ON THE TWELFTH DAY (short) (BRI, 1954, based on the
    folk song, "The 12 Days of Christmas")
  TWELVE DAYS OF CHRISTMAS, THE (short) (FNC,
    1977)

ON TRIAL (ESS, 1916, based on the play by Elmer Rice)
  ON TRIAL (WB, 1928)
  ON TRIAL (WB, 1939)
  ON TRIAL (NBC–TV, 1955)

ON YOUR BACK (FOX, 1930, based on a story by Rita
    Weiman)
  ESCALVAS DE LA MODA (SPA, 1931)

ONCE A LADY see THREE SINNERS

ONCE A WOMAN see FIRST A GIRL

ONCE AND FUTURE KING, THE see SWORD IN THE
    STONE, THE

ONCE UPON A BROTHERS GRIMM see WONDERFUL
    WORLD OF THE BROTHERS GRIMM, THE

ONCE UPON A MATRESS (CBS–TV, 1964, based on a
    musical comedy by Jay Thompson, Dean Fuller and Mary
    Rodgers from the story, "The Princess and the Pea")
  ONCE UPON A MATRESS (CBS–TV, 1972)

ONCE UPON A TIME (COL, 1944, based on a radio play by
    Norman Corwin and Lucille Fletcher)
  CATERPILLAR (short) (CZE, 1970)

ONCE YOU KISS A STRANGER see STRANGERS ON A
    TRAIN

ONDINE see LEGENDE DES ONDINES

ONE ARABIAN NIGHT see ALADDIN

ONE DAY IN THE LIFE OF IVAN DENISOVICH (NBC–TV,
    1963, based on the book by Alexander Solzhenitzen)
  ONE DAY IN THE LIFE OF IVAN DENISOVICH (CIN,
    1971)

ONE EXCITING ADVENTURE see WAS FRAUEN
    TRAUMEN

ONE EXCITING NIGHT see LONELY VILLA, THE

ONE FOOT IN HEAVEN (WB, 1941, based on the book by
    Hartzell Spence)
  ONE FOOT IN HEAVEN (NBC–TV, 1955)

ONE FOR ALL see THREE MUSKETEERS, THE

ONE HAMLET LESS see HAMLET

ONE HORSE TOWN see SMALL TOWN GIRL

ONE HOUR WITH YOU see MARRIAGE CIRCLE, THE

100 MEN AND A GIRL (UN, 1937, based on a story by Hans
    Kraly)
  SABINE UND THRE 100 MANNER (GER, n.d.)

ONE LIFE (FIN, 1947, based on the book, "Une Vie," by
    Guy de Maupassant)
  WOMAN'S LIFE, A (JAP, 1953)
  ONE LIFE (FRA, 1958)
  LIFE OF A WOMAN (JAP, 1962)
  ONE LIFE (JAP, 1967)

ONE MAD KISS (FOX, 1930, based on a play by Adolph
    Paul)
  PRECIO DE UN BESO, EL (SPA, 1930)

ONE MAN'S JOURNEY (RKO, 1933, based on the book
    "Failure," by Katherine Haviland–Taylor)
  MAN TO REMEMBER, A (RKO, 1938)

ONE MILLION B. C. (UA, 1940, based on a screenplay by
    various authors)
  ONE MILLION YEARS B. C. (FOX, 1966)

ONE MILLION B. C. see also TWO LOST WORLDS

ONE MORE TOMORROW see ANIMAL KINGDOM, THE

ONE NIGHT IN THE TROPICS see LOVE INSURANCE

ONE NIGHT, THREE WOMEN see PHAEDRA

ONE NIGHT WITH YOU see FUGA A DUE VOCI

ONE OF OUR OWN (NBC–TV, 1975, based on a teleplay)
  DOCTOR'S HOSPITAL (series) (NBC–TV, 1975)

ONE ROMANTIC NIGHT see SWAN, THE

ONE STOLEN NIGHT see ARAB, THE

ONE SUNDAY AFTERNOON (PAR, 1933, based on the play
    by James Hagan)
  STRAWBERRY BLONDE (WB, 1941)
  ONE SUNDAY AFTERNOON (WB, 1948)
  ONE SUNDAY AFTERNOON (CBS–TV, 1951)
  ONE SUNDAY AFTERNOON (NBC–TV, 1957)
  STRAWBERRY BLONDE (NBC–TV, 1959)

1001 NIGHTS see ALADDIN

ONE TOUCH OF VENUS (UN, 1948, based on the musical
    comedy by Ogden Nash and Kurt Weill)
  ONE TOUCH OF VENUS (NBC–TV, 1955)

ONE––WAY PASSAGE (WB, 1932, based on a story by Robert
    Lord)
  TIL WE MEET AGAIN (WB, 1940)

ONE WEEK (short) (MGM, 1920, based on a screenplay by
    Buster Keaton and elaborated upon in the remakes)
  SMITHY (short) (PAT, 1924)
  FINISHING TOUCH, THE (short) (MGM, 1928)

ONE WOMAN'S STORY see PASSIONATE FRIENDS, THE

ONE WORK OF ART (RUS, 1914, based on the story by
    Anton Chekhov)
  ONE WORK OF ART (RUS, 1960)

ONKEL BRASIG see UT MINE STROMTID

ONKEL TOMS HUTTE see UNCLE TOM'S CABIN

ONLY A DREAM see MARRIAGE CIRCLE, THE

ONLY A WOMAN see WHEN A MAN SEES RED

ONLY GIRL, THE see ICH UND DIE KAISERIN

ONLY SAPS WORK see EASY COME, EASY GO

ONLY WAY, THE see TALE OF TWO CITIES, A

ONLY YESTERDAY (UN, 1933, based on the book by
    Frederick Lewis Allen)
  ONLY YESTERDAY (NBC--TV, 1956)

OP HOOP VAN ZEGEN (HOL, 1918, based on a story by
    Herman Heijermans)
  OP HOOP VAN ZEGEN (HOL, 1934)

OPERA DE QUAT'SOUS see THREE--PENNY OPERA, THE

OPENING OF MISTY BEETHOVEN, THE see PYGMALION

OPERATION CICERO see FIVE FINGERS

OPERATION PETTICOAT (UN, 1959, based on a story by
    Paul King and Joseph Stone)
  OPERATION PETTICOAT (series) (ABC--TV, 1977)

OPERATION SWALLOW (NOR/FRA, 1947, based on a
    historical incident during World War II)
  HEROES OF TELEMARK (COL, 1965)
  SABOTEURS OF TELEMARK (PBS--TV, 1976)

OPERATION THUNDERBOLT see VICTORY AT ENTEBBE

OPERATION X see DAVID GOLDER

OPERETTE see WALTZES FROM VIENNA

OPERNBALL (GER, 1939, source unlisted)
  OPERNBALL (GER, 1956)

OPHELIA see HAMLET

OPPOSITE SEX, THE see WOMEN, THE

OPTIMISTIC TRAGEDY, AN (RUS, 1963, based on the book
    by Vsavolod Vichnievski)
  OPTIMISTISCHE TRAGODIE (GER--TV, 1971)

OPTIMISTISCHE TRAGODIE see OPTIMISTIC TRAGEDY,
    AN

OR, L' see GOLD

ORAGE (FRA, 1937, based on a book by Henry Bernstein)
  DELIRE, LE (ITA, 1952)

ORAGE, L' (RUS, 1912, based on the play by Alexandre
    Ostrovsky)
  ORAGE, L' (RUS, 1934)

ORDEAL see INFERNO

ORDEAL OF WOODROW WILSON, THE see WILSON

ORDERS ARE ORDERS see ORDERS IS ORDERS

ORDERS IS ORDERS (BRI, 1933, based on the play by Ian
    Hay and Anthony Armstrong)
  ORDERS IS ORDERS (BRI, 1954)

ORDET (SWE, 1921, source unlisted)
  ORDET (SWE, 1943)
  ORDET (DEN, 1955)

ORDONNANCE, L' (FRA, 1921, based on a book by Guy de
    Maupassant)
  ORDONNANCE, L' (FRA, 1933)

ORIENT EXPRESS (GER, 1927, source unlisted)
  ORIENT EXPRESS (GER, 1944)
  ORIENT EXPRESS (GER, 1955)

ORIENTAL DREAM see KISMET

ORIENTE Y OCCIDENTE see EAST IS WEST

ORPHAN OF LOWOOD see JANE EYRE

ORPHANS OF THE STORM see TWO ORPHANS, THE

ORPHEUS see LEGEND OF ORPHEUS

OSCAR WILDE (BRI, 1930, based on the life of the noted
    writer and playwright)
  OSCAR WILDE (BRI, 1959)
  GREEN CARNATION, THE (TRIALS OF OSCAR WILDE,
    THE) (BRI, 1960)

OSSESSIONE see DERNIER TOURNANT, LE

OTHELLO (ITA, 1907, based on the play by William Shake--
    speare; also the basis for the opera by Giuseppe Verdi in
    1887)
  OTHELLO (GER, 1907)
  OTHELLO (DEN, 1908)
  OTHELLO (ITA, 1909) (2 versions)
  UP IN DESDEMONA'S ROOM (IND, 1910)
  DESDEMONA (SWE, 1912)
  OTHELLO (KLE, 1914)
  OTHELLO (FRA, 1915)
  OTHELLO (GER, 1918)
  OTHELLO (BRI, 1921)
  MOOR, THE (GER, 1922)
  OTHELLO (EPI, 1923)
  MEN ARE NOT GODS (BRI, 1936)
  MURDER ON LENNOX AVENUE (IND, 1941)
  OTHELLO (short) (BRI, 1946)
  DOUBLE LIFE, A (excerpts) (UN, 1947)
  MOOR'S PAVANE, THE (short) (IND, 1950)
  OTHELLO (MOR, 1951)
  OTHELLO (short) (BRI, 1953)
  OTHELLO (NBC--TV, 1953)
  OTHELLO (RUS, 1955)
  OTHELLO (UA, 1955)
  JUBAL (COL, 1956)
  OTHELLO (RUS, 1960)
  ALL NIGHT LONG (BRI, 1962)
  OTHELLO (BRI, 1965)

OTHELLO   (RUS, 1967)
CATCH MY SOUL   (CIN, 1974)

OTHER, THE   (MEX, 1946, based on a story by Rian James)
DEAD RINGER   (WB, 1964)

OTHER, THE   see   ANDERE, DER

OTHER LOVE, THE   see   IN THE ANTEROOM OF DEATH

OTHER WORLD OF WINSTON CHURCHILL, THE   see
CHURCHILL – MAN OF THE CENTURY

OTHERS, THE   (NBC–TV, 1959, based on the book, "Turn
of the Screw," by Henry James; also the basis for Sir
Benjamin Britten's opera in 1954)
TURN OF THE SCREW   (CBS–TV, 1955)
TURN OF THE SCREW   (NBC–TV, 1959)
INNOCENTS, THE   (FOX, 1961)
NIGHTCOMERS, THE   (BRI, 1971)
TURN OF THE SCREW   (ABC–TV, 1974)

OTRA, LA   see   STOLEN LIFE, THE

OUR BILL OF RIGHTS   (short)   (IND, 1940, based on the
life of stateman Benjamin Franklin)
BENJAMIN FRANKLIN'S ALBANY PLAN   (short)   (IND–
TV, 1947)
BENJAMIN FRANKLIN   (short)   (EBE, 1949)
BENJAMIN FRANKLIN, FIRST AMERICAN   (IND–TV,
1947)
BENJAMIN FRANKLIN AND THE MID--ATLANTIC
SIGNERS   (IND, n.d.)
POOR RICHARD: BENJAMIN FRANKLIN   (short)   (TFC,
1965)
BENJAMIN FRANKLIN – SCIENTIST, STATESMAN,
SCHOLAR AND SAGE   (short)   (HAN, 1970)
1776   (COL, 1973)

OUR CONSTITUTION   see   DECLARATION OF INDEPEN–
DENCE, THE

OUR COUNTRY'S SONG   see   SONG OF A NATION

OUR GIRL FRIDAY   see   BACK TO NATURE

OUR HEARTS WERE YOUNG AND GAY   (PAR, 1944, based
on the book by Cornelia Otis Skinner and Emily
Kimbrough)
OUR HEARTS WERE GROWING UP   (PAR, 1946)
YOUNG AND GAY   (series)   (CBS--TV, 1950)
OUR HEARTS WERE YOUNG AND GAY   (NBC–TV, 1954)

OUR INHERITANCE FROM HISTORIC GREECE   (short)
(sequence)   (COR, 1952, based on the life and work of
the noted scientist)
ARISTOTLE AND THE SCIENTIFIC METHOD   (short)
(COR, 1959)
ARISTOTLE'S ETHICS: THEORY OF HAPPINESS   (short)
(IND, n.d.)

OUR MISS BROOKS   (series)   (CBS--TV, 1952, based on
a radio series)
OUR MISS BROOKS   (WB, 1956)

OUR MR. SHAKESPEARE   see   LIFE OF SHAKESPEARE

OUR TOWN   (UA, 1940, based on the play by Thornton
Wilder)

OUR TOWN   (ABC–TV, 1950)
OUR TOWN   (NBC–TV, 1955)
OUR TOWN   (NBC–TV, 1977)

OUT OF THE FRYING PAN   see   YOUNG AND WILLING

OUT OF THE REACH OF THE DEVIL   see   FAUST

OUT OF THE STORM   see   WRONG ROAD, THE

OUTCAST, THE   (EMP, 1917, based on the play by Hubert
Henry Davies)
OUTCAST, THE   (PAR, 1922)
OUTCAST, THE   (FN, 1928)
GIRL FROM TENTH AVENUE, THE   (WB, 1935)

OUTCASTS OF POKER FLAT, THE   (UN, 1919, based on the
story by Bret Harte)
OUTCASTS OF POKER FLAT, THE   (RKO, 1937)
OUTCASTS OF POKER FLAT, THE   (FOX, 1952)

OUTCASTS OF POKER FLAT   see also   LUCK OF ROARING
CAMP, THE

OUTPOST IN MALAYA   (UA, 1952, based on the book,
"Planter's Wife," by S. C. George)
PLANTER'S WIFE, THE   (BRI, 1959)

OUTRAGE, THE   see   RASHOMON

OUTSIDE THE LAW   (UN, 1921, based on a story by Tod
Browning)
OUTSIDE THE LAW   (UN, 1930)

OUTSIDER, THE   (FOX, 1926, based on the play by Dorothy
Brandon)
OUTSIDER, THE   (BRI, 1931)
OUTSIDER, THE   (MGM, 1933)
OUTSIDER, THE   (BRI, 1939)

OUTWARD BOUND   (WB, 1930, based on the play by Sutton
Vane)
BETWEEN TWO WORLDS   (WB, 1944)
OUTWARD BOUND   (TV, 1952)
HAUNTS OF THE VERY RICH   (TV, 1972)

OVER THE BORDER   see   HEART OF THE WILDS and
THREE BAD MEN

OVER THE HILL   see   OVER THE HILL TO THE POOR--
HOUSE

OVER THE HILL TO THE POORHOUSE   (BIO, 1908, based
on poems by Will Carleton)
OVER THE HILL   (PAT, 1917)
OVER THE HILL   (FOX, 1920)
OVER THE HILL   (FOX, 1931)

OVER 21   (COL, 1945, based on the play by Ruth Gordon)
OVER 21   (CBS--TV, 1950)

OVERCOAT, THE (THE CLOAK)   (RUS, 1926, based on the
story by Nikolai Gogol)
OVERCOAT, THE (IL CAPPOTTO)   (ITA, 1952)
OVERCOAT, THE   (FRA, 1955)
CLERK AND THE COAT, THE   (IN, 1955)
BESPOKE OVERCOAT, THE   (BRI, 1956)
OVERCOAT, THE   (RUS, 1958)
OVERCOAT, THE   (RUS, 1965)

OVERLAND BOUND   see   RIDIN' DOUBLE

OVERLAND WITH KIT CARSON   (serial)   (COL, 1939, based on a screenplay by various authors)
   BLAZING THE OVERLAND TRAIL   (serial)   (COL, 1956)

OVERNIGHT HAUL   see   THIEVES' HIGHWAY

OVERTHROW OF THE TWEED RING, THE   (short)   (CBS--TV, 1957, based on the life and work of cartoonist Thomas Nast)
   TIGER'S TAIL -- THOMAS NAST VS. BOSS TWEED, THE   (short)   (TFC, 1965)
   ERIE WAR, THE   (short)   (FNC, 1976)

OWD BOB   (BRI, 1924, based on the book by Alfred Olivant)

OWD BOB (TO THE VICTOR)   (BRI, 1938)
   THUNDER IN THE VALLEY   (FOX, 1947)

OWEN MARSHALL, COUNSELOR--AT--LAW   (ABC--TV, 1971, based on a teleplay)
   OWEN MARSHALL   (series)   (ABC--TV, 1971)

OWL AND THE PUSSYCAT, THE   (COL, 1970)
   OWL AND THE PUSSYCAT, THE   (NBC--TV, 1975)

OX--BOW INCIDENT, THE   (FOX, 1943, based on a book by Walter van Tilberg Clark)
   LYNCH MOB   (CBS--TV, 1955)

OZ   see   DOROTHY AND THE SCARECROW OF OZ

P.J. AND THE PRESIDENT'S SON see PRINCE AND THE
    PAUPER, THE

P. T. BARNUM PRESENTS JENNY LIND see LADY'S
    MORALS, A

P. T. 109 see MAKING OF THE PRESIDENT -- 1960, THE

PA LIVETS ODEVAGAR (SWE, 1913, source unlisted)
    HAVSGAMAR (SWE, 1916)
    ROSEN PA SISTELON (SWE, 1945)

PAARUNGER see DANCE OF DEATH

PACIFIC RENDEZVOUS see RENDEZVOUS

PACT WITH THE DEVIL see DR. JEKYLL AND MR.
    HYDE

PADDLE TO THE SEA see PEOPLE ALONG THE
    MISSISSIPPI

PADDY--THE--NEXT--BEST--THING (BRI, 1923, based on
    the book and play by Gertrude Page)
    PADDY--THE--NEXT--BEST--THING (FOX, 1933)

PAGANINI (GER, 1923, based on the life of the noted
    violinist and composer, Niccolo Paganini)
    GERN HAB' ICH DIE FRAU'N GEHUSST (GER, 1934)
    MAGIC BOW, THE (BRI, 1947)
    PAGANINI (ITA, 1970)
    PAGANINI (series) (ITA--TV, 1975)

PAGES FROM LIFE see CRASH, THE

PAGLIACCI see PAILLASSE

PAGLIACCI SWINGS IT see PAILLASSE

PAGODE, DIE (GER, 1914, source unlisted)
    PAGODE, DIE (GER, 1923)

PAID see WITHIN THE LAW

PAID TO LOVE (FOX, 1927, based on a story by Harry Carr)
    HAY QUE CASAR AL PRINCIPE (SPA, 1931)

PAILLASSE (FRA, 1900, based on the opera by Ruggerio
    Leoncavallo)
    VENEGEANCE DE PAGLIACCI, LA (ITA, 1907)
    PAILLASSE (FRA, 1910)
    LACHE BAJAZZO (GER, 1914)
    PAGLIACCI (short) (IND, 1914)
    PAGLIACCI (ITA, 1914)
    PAGLIACCI (DEN, 1918)
    PAGLIACCI (ITA, 1918)
    PAGLIACCI (BRI, 1923)
    PAGLIACCI (ITA, 1931)
    PAGLIACCI (BRI, 1936)
    PAGLIACCI (GER, 1936)
    PAGLIACCI (NBC--TV, 1940)
    LACHE BAJAZZO (GER, 1943)
    PAGLIACCI SWINGS IT (short) (UN, 1944)
    PAGLIACCI (ITA, 1948)
    PAGLIACCI (IND, 1951)

PAINTED DAUGHTERS (AUT, 1925, based on a biography)
    FLORADORA GIRL, THE (MGM, 1930)

PAINTED LADY, THE see WHEN A MAN SEES RED

PAINTED VEIL, THE (MGM, 1934, based on the book by
    W. Somerset Maugham)
    SEVENTH SIN, THE (MGM, 1957)

PAINTING THE CLOUDS WITH SUNSHINE see GOLD
    DIGGERS, THE

PAIR OF SIXES, A (ESS, 1918, based on the play by Edward
    Peple)
    QUEEN HIGH (PAR, 1930)

PALACE OF PLEASURE (FOX, 1926, based on a story by
    Adolf Paul)
    LOLA MONTES (FRA, 1952)
    LOLA MONTES (short) (TV, 1954)
    LOLA MONTES (NBC--TV, 1959)

PALEFACE, THE (PAR, 1948, based on a screenplay by
    Edmund Hartman and Frank Tashlin)
    SHAKIEST GUN IN THE WEST, THE (UN, 1968)

PALMETTO CONSPIRACY, THE see ABRAHAM LINCOLN

PALOMA, LA (GER, 1934, source unlisted)
    GROSSE FREIHEIT (GER, 1944)
    PALOMA, LA (GER, 1959)

PALS FIRST (MGM, 1918, based on the book by Francis
    Perry Elliott and a play by Lee Wilson Dodd)
    PALS FIRST (FN, 1926)

PAMPAS BARBERA (ARG, 1946, based on the book by
    Homero Manzi and Ulises Petit de Murat)
    SAVAGE PAMPAS (SPA, 1966)

PAMPERED YOUTH (VIT, 1925, based on the book, "The
    Magnificent Ambersons," by Booth Tarkington)
    MAGNIFICENT AMBERSONS, THE (RKO, 1942)
    MAGNIFICENT AMBERSONS, THE (ABC--TV, 1950)

PAN (NOR, 1921, based on a book by Knut Hamsun)
    PAN (GER, 1937)

PAN TWARDOWSKI see FAUST

PAN WOLODYJOWSKI (POL, 1969, based on the book by
    Henryk Sienkiewicz)
    PAN WOLODYJOWSKI (POL-TV, 1969)

PANAMA FLO (RKO, 1932, based on a story by Garret Fort)
    PANAMA LADY (RKO, 1939)

PANAMA HATTIE (MGM, 1942, based on the musical comedy
    by Cole Porter)
    PANAMA HATTIE (CBS-TV, 1954)

PANAMA LADY see PANAMA FLO

PANAMERICANA see TRAUMSTRASSE DER WELT

PANCHO VILLA RETURNS see LIFE OF VILLA

PANDORA AND THE FLYING DUTCHMAN see FLYING
    DUTCHMAN, THE

PANDORA'S BOX see LULU

PANTALOONS see DON JUAN

PANTHER GIRL OF THE KONGO (serial) (REP, 1955,
    based on a screenplay by various authors; the remake is
    a condensation of the serial)
  CLAW MONSTER, THE (REP, 1966)

PAPA SANS LE SAVOIR see LITTLE ACCIDENT, THE

PAPAGENO see MAGIC FLUTE, THE

PAPER MOON (PAR, 1973, based on the book, "Addie Pray,"
    by Joe David Brown)
  PAPER MOON (series) (ABC--TV, 1974)

PAPRIKA (GER, 1932, based on an operetta by Max Reimann
    and Otto Schwartz)
  PAPRIKA (GER, 1959)
PARABLE OF THE PRODIGAL SON, THE (FRA, 1911,
    based on the Bible)
  ENFANT PRODIGUE, L' (FRA, 1916)
  PRODIGAL SON, THE (BRI, 1923)
  PRODIGAL SON, THE (PAT, 1927)
  PRODIGAL, THE (MGM, 1955)

PARADINE CASE, THE (SRO, 1948, based on the book by
    Robert Hitchens)
  PARADINE CASE, THE (NBC--TV, 1962)

PARADISE see TOO MUCH CHAMPAGNE

PARADISE LAGOON see BACK TO NATURE

PARAMOUNT ON PARADE (PAR, 1930, based on a screen--
    play by various authors)
  PARAMOUNT ON PARADE (FRA, 1930)
  GALAS DE LA PARAMOUNT (SPA, 1930)

PARDAILLAN see CHEVALIER DE PARDAILLAN, LE

PARDNERS see RHYTHM ON THE RANGE

PARDON US (MGM, 1931, based on a screenplay by H. M.
    Walker)
  PARDON US (FRA, 1931)
  PARDON US (SPA, 1931)
  PARDON US (ITA, 1931)
  PARDON US (GER, 1931)

PAREE, PAREE see FIFTY MILLION FRENCHMEN

PARENT TRAP, THE see DOPPELTE LOTTCHEN, DAS

PARENTS TERRIBLES, LES (STORM WITHIN, THE) (FRA,
    1949, based on the play by Jean Cocteau)
  INTIMATE RELATIONS (BRI, 1954)

PARFUM DE LA DAME EN NOIR, LE (FRA, 1914, based
    on the book by Gaston Leroux)
  PARFUM DE LA DAME EN NOIR, LE (FRA, 1931)
  PERFUM DE LA DAME EN NOIR, LE (FRA, 1949)

PARIS AT MIDNIGHT see PERE GORIOT

PARIS WHEN IT SIZZLES see HOLIDAY FOR HENRIETTA

PARISIAN BELLE, THE see NEW MOON, THE

PARLOR, BEDROOM AND BATH (MGM, 1920, based on
    the play by C. W. Bell and Mark Swan)
  PARLOR, BEDROOM AND BATH (MGM, 1931)

PAROLE, LA (SWE, 1943, based on the book by Kaj Munk)
  PAROLE, LA (DEN, 1955)

PARSHURAN (IN, 1929, source unlisted)
  PARSHURAN (IN, 1935)

PARSIFAL (ED, 1904, based on a legend and the opera by
    Richard Wagner)
  PARSIFAL (ITA, 1912)
  EVIL FOREST, THE (SPA, 1951)

PARSON AND THE OUTLAW, THE see BILLY THE KID

PARSON OF PANAMINT, THE (PAR, 1916, based on the
    book by Peter B. Kyne)
  WHILE SATAN SLEEPS (PAR, 1922)
  PARSON OF PANAMINT, THE (PAR, 1941)

PARTON TEVEDTEM see SCANDAL IN BUDAPEST

PARTRIDGE FAMILY, THE (series) (ABC--TV, 1970,
    based on a teleplay)
  PARTRIDGE FAMILY: 2200 A.D., THE (series) (CBS--
    TV, 1974)

PARTRIDGE FAMILY: 2200A.D., THE see PARTRIDGE
    FAMILY, THE

PASADA ACUSA, EL see GOOD BAD GIRL

PASCAL see UNIVERSE OF NUMBERS

PASSAGE FROM HONG KONG see BLIND ADVENTURE

PASSE MURAILLE, LE see MR. PEEK--A--BOO

PASSING OF THE THIRD FLOOR BACK, THE (BRI, 1918,
    based on the play by Jerome K. Jerome)
  PASSING OF THE THIRD FLOOR BACK, THE (BRI,
    1935)

PASSION see DU BARRY

PASSION, LA see PASSION PLAY, THE

PASSION ACCORDING TO MATTHEW see PASSION PLAY,
    THE

PASSION FIRE (JAP, 1947, source unlisted)
  TORMENTED FLAME (JAP, 1959)
  AFFAIR (JAP, 1967)

PASSION OF ANDREW, THE see ANDREI RUBLEV

PASSION OF CAROL, THE see CHRISTMAS CAROL, A

PASSION OF JESUS, THE see PASSION PLAY, THE

PASSION OF JOAN OF ARC, THE see JOAN OF ARC

PASSION PLAY, THE (KE, 1897, based on the Bible and
    accounts on the life of Jesus)
  PASSION, LA (FRA, 1897)
  PASSION, LA (FRA, 1898)
  PASSION PLAY, THE (LUB, 1898)

VIE DU CHRIST, LA (FRA, 1906)
PASSION OF JESUS, THE (FRA, 1907)
VIE DU CHRIST, LA (FRA, 1910)
JESUS (FRA, 1911)
JESUS OF NAZARETH (FROM THE MANGER TO THE
  CROSS) (KAL, 1911)
BIRTH OF OUR SAVIOR, THE (ED, 1914)
LAST SUPPER, THE (ARC, 1914)
CHRISTUS (ITA, 1916)
BEHOLD THE MAN (short) (PAT, 1921)
I.N.R.I. (GER, 1923)
MAN NOBODY KNOWS, THE (ISR, 1925)
KING OF KINGS (PAT, 1927)
JESUS OF NAZARETH (IDE, 1928)
PRINCE OF PEACE (BRI, 1939)
WESTMINSTER PASSION PLAY (BRI, 1951)
DAY OF TRIUMPH (BRI, 1954)
SILENT NIGHT (TV, 1954)
SON OF MAN (ITA, 1955)
GREAT COMMANDMENT, THE (IND, 1956)
I BEHELD HIS GLORY (IND, 1957)
COMING OF CHRIST, THE (short) (NBC--TV, 1960)
STAR OF BETHLEHEM (TV, 1961)
KING OF KINGS (MGM, 1961)
HE IS RISEN (NBC--TV, 1962)
KING OF KINGS (SPA, 1962)
LAUDES EVANGELI (CBS--TV, 1962)
HOLY NIGHT (IND, 1965)
GREATEST STORY EVER TOLD, THE (UA, 1965)
GOSPEL ACCORDING TO ST. MATTHEW, THE (ITA,
  1966)
PRINCE OF PEACE (series) (TV, 1967)
SON OF MAN (BRI--TV, 1969)
NIGHT THE ANIMALS TALKED, THE (ABC--TV, 1970)
CRUCIFIXION OF JESUS (CBS--TV, 1972)
GODSPELL (COL, 1973)
GOSPEL ROAD, THE (F)X, 1973)
JESUS CHRIST, SUPERSTAR (UN, 1973)
LIFE OF CHRIST, THE (ITA, 1974)
PASSION ACCORDING TO MATTHEW (YUG, 1975)
THREE WISE MEN (MEX, 1976)
JESUS OF NAZARETH (NBC--TV, 1977)
LAST SUPPER, THE (CUB, 1978)

PASSION PLAY, THE see also STAR OF BETHLEHEM

PASSIONATE FRIENDS, THE see DON QUIXOTE

PASSIONATE PLUMBER, THE see CARDBOARD LOVER

PASSPORT TO HEAVEN see CAPTAIN FROM KOPENIK,
  THE

PAST OF MARY HOLMES, THE see GOOSE WOMAN

PASTEUR see STORY OF LOUIS PASTEUR, THE

PAT GARRETT AND BILLY THE KID see PAT GARRETT'S
  SIDE OF IT

PAT GARRETT'S SIDE OF IT (short) (TV, 1956, based on
  historical characters and incidents)
  PAT GARRETT AND BILLY THE KID (MGM, 1973)

PATCHWORK GIRL OF OZ, THE see DOROTHY AND THE
  SCARECROW OF OZ

PATHFINDER, THE see LEATHERSTOCKING

PATHS TO PARADISE (PAR, 1925, based on the play, "The
  Heart of the Thief," by Paul Armstrong)
  HOLD THAT BLONDE (PAR, 1945)

PATIENT VANISHES, THE see THIS MAN IS DANGEROUS

PATRIE (FRA, 1913, based on the book by Victorien Sardou)
  PATRIE (FRA, 1945)

PATRIOT, THE (PAR, 1928, based on a play by Alfred
  Neumann)
  PATRIOTE, LE (THE MAD EMPEROR) (FRA, 1938)

PATRIOTE, LE see PATRIOT, THE

PATROL see LOST PATROL

PATTERNS (NBC--TV, 1955, based on the teleplay by Rod
  Serling)
  PATTERNS (PATTERNS OF POWER) (UA, 1956)

PATTERNS OF POWER see PATTERNS

PAUL GAUGHIN (short) (PIC, 1953, based on the life of
  painter Paul Gaughin)
  GAUGHIN IN TAHITI -- SEARCH FOR PARADISE (CBS--
  TV, 1968)

PAUL GAUGHIN see also MOON AND SIXPENCE, THE

PAUL REVERE'S RIDE see MIDNIGHT RIDE OF PAUL
  REVERE, THE

PAUL STREET BOYS, THE see BOYS OF PAUL STREET,
  THE

PAUVRES MILLIONNAIRES (SWE, 1936, based on the
  novel, "Drei Manner in Schnee," by Erich Kastner)
  PARADISE FOR THREE (MGM, 1938)
  DREI MANNER IM SCHNEE (AUS, 1955)

PAVEL KORCHAGIN see HOW THE STEEL WAS TEM--
  PERED

PAX DOMINE (FRA, 1924, based on the play, "The Man I
  Killed," by Maurice Rostand)
  BROKEN LULLABY (PAR, 1932)

PAY--OFF, THE (RKO, 1930, based on a story by Samuel
  Shipman)
  LAW OF THE UNDERWORLD (RKO, 1938)

PAYSANS, LES (POL, 1922, based on the book by Wladyslaw
  Stanislaw Reymont)
  PAYSANS, LES (POL--TV, 1972)

PEACE OF THE WORLD (JAP, 1928, source unlisted)
  PEACE OF THE WORLD (JAP, 1955)

PEACOCK ALLEY (MGM, 1921, based on a story by Ouida
  Berger)
  PEACOCK ALLEY (TIF, 1930)

PEACOCK'S FEATHER (PAR, 1934, based on a book by
  George S. Hellman)
  NIGHT IN PARADISE, A (UN, 1946)

PEARL, THE (RKO, 1948, based on the story by John Stein--
  beck)

PEARL, THE (NBC--TV, 1953)

PEARL NECKLACE, THE see DIAMOND NECKLACE,
THE

PEASANT HSIANG LIN'S WIFE, THE (CHN, 1947, source
unlisted)
NEW YEAR SACRIFICE, THE (CHN, 1956)

PEAU D'ANE (FRA, 1908, based on the story by Charles
Perrault)
WILD ASS'S SKIN, THE (FRA, 1909)
MAGIC SKIN, THE (UN, 1913)
CHAGRINLIEDER, DAS (ITA, 1913)
MAGIC SKIN, THE (ED, 1915)
SAGRENSKA KOZA (short) (YUG, 1960)
DONKEY SKIN (FRA, 1975)

PEAU DE CHAGRIN, LA (FRA, 1912, based on the story
by Honore de Balzac)
DESIRE (BRI, 1920)
NARAYANA (FRA, 1921)
SLAVE OF DESIRE (GOL, 1923)
UNHEIMLICHEN WUNSCHE, DIE (GER, 1939)
PEAU DE CHAGRIN (short) (MHF, 1970)
PEAU DE CHAGRIN (short) (YUG, 1974)
PEAU DE CHAGRIN (short) (IND, 1976)

PEBBLE BY THE WAYSIDE (JAP, 1938, source unlisted)
WAYSIDE PEBBLE (JAP, 1960)

PEBBLES AND BAM BAM see FLINTSTONES, THE

PECHE DE JULIE see MISS JULIE

PECHE IVRESSE, LE see RAUSCH

PECHEUR D'ISLANDE (FRA, 1916, based on the book by
Pierre Loti)
PECHEUR D'ISLANDE (FRA, 1924)
PECHEUR D'ISLANDE (FRA, 1934)
PECHEUR D'ISLANDE (FRA, 1959)

PECK'S BAD BOY (FN, 1921, based on a story by George W.
Peck)
PECK'S BAD BOY (FOX, 1934)

PEDAGOGICAL POEM, A see ROAD TO LIFE

PEEP BEHIND THE SCENES (BRI, 1918, based on the book
by Mrs. O. F. Walton)
PEEP BEHIND THE SCENES (BRI, 1929)

PEER GYNT (PAR, 1915, based on the play by Henrick Ibsen)
PEER GYNT (GER, 1918)
PEER GYNT (GER, 1934)
PEER GYNT (IND, 1941)
PEER GYNT (NBC--TV, 1952)
GIRL ON THE GREEN MOUNTAIN, THE (BRI, 1971)
PEER GYNT (BRI--TV, 1974)

PEG O' MY HEART (MGM, 1923, based on the play by J.
Hartley Manners; also the basis for the musical, "Peg," in
1967)
PEG O' MY HEART (MGM, 1933)

PEG OF OLD DRURY see MASKS AND FACES

PEG WOFFINGTON see MASKS AND FACES

PEKING EXPRESS see SHANGHAI EXPRESS

PELE MELE see HOG WILD

PENITENTIARY see CRIMINAL CODE, THE

PENNY SERENADE (COL, 1941, based on a book by Martha
Cheavens)
PENNY SERENADE (NBC--TV, 1955)

PENROD (FN, 1922, based on stories by Booth Tarkington)
PENROD AND SAM (FN, 1923)
ADVENTURES OF PENROD AND SAM, THE (FN, 1931)
PENROD'S DOUBLE TROUBLE (WB, 1936)
PENROD AND SAM (WB, 1937)
PENROD AND HIS TWIN BROTHER (WB, 1938)
ON MOONLIGHT BAY (WB, 1951)
BY THE LIGHT OF THE SILVERY MOON (WB, 1953)

PENROD AND HIS TWIN BROTHER see PENROD

PENROD AND SAM see PENROD

PENROD'S DOUBLE TROUBLE see PENROD

PENSION SCHOLLER (GER, 1930, based on the play by
Wilhelm Jacoby and Carl Lauff)
PENSION SCHOLLER (GER, 1952)
PENSION SCHOLLER (GER, 1960)

PENSIONNAIRE, LE see SECRET DE LA MAISON
SEIGNEURIALE, LE

PENTHOUSE (MGM, 1933, based on a story by Arthur
Somers Roche)
SOCIETY LAWYER (MGM, 1939)

PEOPLE ALONG THE MISSISSIPPI (short) (EBE, 1953,
based on an idea of a toy boat taking a trip)
PADDLE TO THE SEA (short) (CAN, 1967)

PEOPLE NEXT DOOR, THE (CBS--TV, 1968, based on the
teleplay by J. P. Miller)
PEOPLE NEXT DOOR, THE (EMB, 1970)

PEOPLE OF HEMSO see HEMSOBORNA

PEOPLE OF SIMLANGEN VALLEY see FOLKET I
SIMLANGSDALEN

PEOPLE OF THE VARMLAND see VARMLANNINGARNA

PEOPLE WILL TALK see DR. PRAETORIUS

PEPE LE MOKO (FRA, 1937, based on a book by Detective
Ashelbe (Henry La Barthe)
ALGIERS (UA, 1938)
CASBAH (UN, 1948)

PERE CELIBATAIRE, LE see BACHELOR FATHER

PERE GORIOT, LE (BIO, 1915, based on the book by Honore
de Balzac)
PERE GORIOT, LE (FRA, 1919)
PERE GORIOT, LE (ITA, 1919)
PERE GORIOT, LE (FRA, 1922)
PARIS AT MIDNIGHT (PDC, 1926)
PERE GORIOT, LE (FRA, 1944)
KARRIERE IN PARIS (GER, 1951)

PERE GORIOT, LE   (GER, 1954)
PERE GORIOT, LE   (BRI--TV, 1972)

PERE SERGE   see   FATHER SERGIUS

PERFECT CRIME, THE   (FBO, 1928, based on the book,
    "The Big Bow Mystery," by Israel Zangwill)
  CRIME DOCTOR, THE   (RKO, 1934)
  VERDICT, THE   (WB, 1946)
  BIG BOW MYSTERY, THE   (CBS--TV, 1953)

PERILS OF NYOKA, THE   (serial)   (REP, 1942, based on
    a screenplay by various authors; the remake is a condensed
    version of the serial)
  NYOKA AND THE LOST SECRETS OF HIPPOCRATES
    (REP, 1966)

PERILS OF PAULINE, THE   (serial)   (IND, 1914, based on
    the story, "Les Mysteres de New York," by Pierre
    Decourcelle)
  AGONIES OF AGNES, THE   (short)   (IND, 1918)
  PERILS OF PAULINE, THE   (serial)   (UN, 1933)
  PERILS OF PAULINE, THE   (PAR, 1947)
  PERILS OF PAULINE, THE   (UN, 1967)

PERILS OF THE JUNGLE   (serial)   (ART, 1927, the second
    film consists of stock footage from the first)
  WHITE PONGO   (PRC, 1945)

PERILS OF THE WILD   (serial)   (UN, 1925, based on the
    book, "Swiss Family Robinson," by Johan David Wyss)
  SWISS FAMILY ROBINSON   (RKO, 1940)
  SWISS FAMILY ROBINSON   (NBC--TV, 1958)
  SWISS FAMILY ROBINSON   (DIS, 1960)
  LOST IN SPACE   (series)   (FOX--TV, 1965)
  SWISS FAMILY ROBINSON   (RAN, 1972)
  SWISS FAMILY ROBINSON   (AUT--TV, 1973)
  SWISS FAMILY ROBINSON   (HB, 1973)
  SWISS FAMILY ROBINSON   (series)   (CAN--TV, 1974)
  SWISS FAMILY ROBINSON   (series)   (ABC--TV, 1975)

PERILS OF THE WILD   see   CARYL OF THE MOUNTAINS

PERON AND EVITA   (short)   (CBS--TV, 1958, based on the
    life of the wife of the South American dictator)
  EVA PERON   (short)   (WOL, 1963)

PERSHING STORY, THE   see   GENERAL PERSHING

PERSONAL PROPERTY   see   MAN IN POSSESSION, THE

PETE AND GLADYS   see   DECEMBER BRIDE

PETE 'N' TILLIE   (UN, 1973, based on the novella, "Witch's
    Milk," by Peter de Vries)
  PETE 'N' TILLIE   (CBS--TV, 1974)

PETE KELLY'S BLUES   (WB, 1955, based on a radio series
    by Jack Webb)
  PETE KELLY'S BLUES   (series)   (NBC--TV, 1959)

PETER AND THE WOLF   (short taken from "Make Mine
    Music")   (DIS, 1946, based on music by Serge Prokofiev)
  ART CARNEY MEETS PETER AND THE WOLF   (ABC--
    TV, 1958)
  PETER AND THE WOLF   (short)   (TV, 1967)
  PETER AND THE WOLF   (NET--TV, 1970)
  SAND, OR PETER AND THE WOLF   (IR, 1972)

PETER GUNN   (series)   (NBC--TV, 1958, based on a teleplay)
  GUNN   (PAR, 1967)

PETER IBBETSON   (PAR, 1914, based on the book by George
    du Maurier)
  FOREVER   (PAR, 1921)
  PETER IBBETSON   (PAR, 1935)
  PETER IBBETSON   (CBS--TV, 1951)

PETER PAN   (PAR, 1925, based on the play by Sir James M.
    Barrie)
  PETER PAN   (DIS, 1953)
  PETER PAN   (NBC--TV, 1955)

PETER SCHLEMIHL   (GER, 1915, based on the book by
    Adalbert von Chamisso)
  VERLORENE SCHATTEN, DER   (GER, 1920)
  HOMME QUI A PERDU SON OMBRE, L'   (FRA--TV, 1966)

PETER TCHAIKOVSKY STORY, THE   see   IT WAS AN
    EXCITING NIGHT

PETER VOSS, THE MILLIONAIRE   (GER, 1932, based on the
    book by Ewald Gerhard Seeliger)
  PETER VOSS, THE MILLIONAIRE   (GER, 1945)
  PETER VOSS, THE MILLIONAIRE   (GER, 1958)

PETERSBURG NIGHTS   see   DARK EYES

PETERSBURGER NACHTE   see   DARK EYES

PETIT CAFE, LA   see   PLAYBOY OF PARIS

PETIT CAFE, LE   (FRA, 1919, based on a book by Georges
    Bernanos)
  PETIT CAFE, LE   (FRA, 1930)

PETIT CHAPERON ROUGE, LE   (FRA, 1901, based on the
    fairy tale by Charles Perrault)
  PETIT CHAPERON ROUGE, LE   (FRA, 1907)
  LITTLE RED RIDING HOOD   (BRI, 1911)
  LITTLE RED RIDING HOOD   (ESS, 1911)
  LITTLE RED RIDING HOOD   (MAJ, 1911)
  LITTLE RED RIDING HOOD   (ED, 1917)
  LITTLE RED RIDING HOOD   (IND, 1921)
  LITTLE RED RIDING HOOD   (SEZ, 1922)
  LITTLE RED RIDING HOOD   (GRI, 1922)
  LITTLE RED RIDING HOOD   (DIS, 1923)
  LITTLE RED RIDING HOOD   (UN, 1925)
  LITTLE RED RIDING HOOD   (IND, 1925)
  PETIT CHAPERON ROUGE, LE   (FRA, 1928)
  STORY OF LITTLE RED RIDING HOOD, THE   (BFA,
    1949)
  LITTLE RED RIDING HOOD   (YUG, 1954)
  LITTLE RED RIDING HOOD   (GER, 1955)
  LITTLE RED RIDING HOOD   (MEX, 1959)
  DANGEROUS CHRISTMAS OF RED RIDING HOOD
    (ABC--TV, 1965)

PETIT CHOSE, LE   (FRA, 1911, based on a book by Alphonse
    Daudet)
  PETIT CHOSE, LE   (FRA, 1913)
  PETIT CHOSE, LE   (FRA, 1923)
  PETIT CHOSE, LE   (FRA, 1938)
  LAST LESSON, THE   (IND, 1942)

PETIT JACQUES, LE   (FRA, 1912, based on a book by Jules
    Claretie)
  PETIT JACQUES, LE   (FRA, 1923)

PETIT JACQUES, LE (FRA, 1934)
PETIT JACQUES, LE (FRA, 1953)

PETIT POUCET, LE (FRA, 1905, based on the fairy tale by
Charles Perrault)
PETIT POUCET, LE (FRA, 1908)
PULGARCITO (SPA, 1910)
HOP O' MY THUMB (FRA, 1912)
TOM THUMB (MGM, 1958)
LITTLE TOM THUMB (MEX, 1958)
TOM THUMB (MEX, 1967)
PETIT POUCET, LE (FRA, 1972)
TOM THUMB (PAR, 1976)

PETITE CHOCOLATIERE, LA (FRA, 1913, based on a book
by Paul Gavault)
PETITE CHOCOLATIERE, LA (FRA, 1927)
PETITE CHOCOLATIERE, LA (FRA, 1931)
PETITE CHOCOLATIERE, LA (FRA, 1949)

PETRIFIED FOREST, THE (WB, 1936, based on the play by
Robert E. Sherwood)
ESCAPE IN THE DESERT (WB, 1945)
PETRIFIED FOREST, THE (ABC--TV, 1952)
PETRIFIED FOREST, THE (NBC--TV, 1955)

PETROCELLI see LAWYERS, THE

PETTIGREW'S GIRL (PAR, 1919, based on a story by Dana
Burnet)
SHOPWORN ANGEL, THE (PAR, 1929)
SHOPWORN ANGEL, THE (MGM, 1938)

PEYTON PLACE (FOX, 1957, based on the book by Grace
Metalious)
RETURN TO PEYTON PLACE (FOX, 1961)
PEYTON PLACE (series) (ABC--TV, 1964)
PEYTON PLACE (series) (NBC--TV, 1972)
PEYTON PLACE REVISITED (series) (ABC--TV, 1975)
MURDER IN PEYTON PLACE (NBC--TV, 1977)

PEYTON PLACE REVISITED see PEYTON PLACE

PFARRER VON KIRCHFELD, DER (AUS, 1918, based on a
book by Ludwig Anzengruber)
PFARRER VON KIRCHFELD, DER (GER, 1926)
PFARRER VON KIRCHFELD, DER (AUS, 1937)
PFARRER VON KIRCHFELD, DER (GER, 1955)
MAEDCHEN VOM PFARRHOF, DAS (AUS, 1955)

PHAEDRA (FRA, 1909, based on a legend and writings by
Seneca and Racine)
COUEUR DE LA CASBAH, AU (FRA, 1951)
DEVIL'S DAUGHTER (SPA, 1956)
PHAEDRA (GER, 1962)
PHEDRE (FRA, 1968)
FEDRA WEST (SPA/ITA, 1968)
ONE NIGHT, THREE WOMEN (PHI, 1975)

PHANTOM BARON, THE see BARON FANTOME, LE

PHANTOM BUCCANEER, THE (ESS, 1916, based on the
book, "Another Man's Shoes," by Victor Bridges)
ANOTHER MAN'S SHOES (UN, 1922)

PHANTOM CHARIOT, THE (SWE, 1920, based on the book
by Selma Lagerlof)
PHANTOM CHARIOT, THE (FRA, 1928)
PHANTOM CHARIOT, THE (SWE, 1958)

PHANTOM CITY (FN, 1928, based on a story by Adele
Buffington)
HAUNTED GOLD (WB, 1932)

PHANTOM FIEND, THE see LODGER, THE

PHANTOM FILLY, THE see HOME IN INDIANA

PHANTOM KILLER, THE see SPHINX, THE

PHANTOM LADY (UN, 1944, based on a screenplay by
Bernard C. Schoenfeld)
PHANTOM LADY (NBC--TV, 1950)

PHANTOM MELODY see VENDETTA

PHANTOM OF HOLLYWOOD, THE see PHANTOM OF THE
OPERA, THE

PHANTOM OF PARIS see CHERI--BIBI

PHANTOM OF THE CATACOMBS, THE see WANDERING
JEW, THE

PHANTOM OF THE OPERA, THE (UN, 1925, based on the
book by Gaston Leroux)
SONG AT MIDNIGHT (CHN, 1935)
PHANTOM OF THE OPERA, THE (UN, 1943)
FANTASMA DE LA OPERETTA, EL (ARG, 1955)
PHANTOM OF THE OPERA, THE (BRI, 1962)
SHANTO AGAINST THE STRANGLER (MEX, 1964)
PHANTOM OF THE PARADISE, THE (FOX, 1974)
PHANTOM OF HOLLYWOOD, THE (CBS--TV, 1974)

PHANTOM OF THE PARADISE, THE see PHANTOM OF
THE OPERA, THE

PHANTOM OF THE RUE MORGUE, THE see SHERLOCK
HOLMES AND THE GREAT MURDER MYSTERY

PHANTOM STRIKES, THE see RINGER, THE

PHEDRE see PHAEDRA

PHILADELPHIA STORY, THE (MGM, 1940, based on the
play by Philip Barry)
PHILADELPHIA STORY, THE (NBC--TV, 1950)
PHILADELPHIA STORY, THE (CBS--TV, 1954)
HIGH SOCIETY (MGM, 1956)
PHILADELPHIA STORY, THE (NBC--TV, 1959)

PHILOMEL COTTAGE see LOVE FROM A STRANGER

PHILOSOPHY OF THE BOUDOIR see BEYOND LOVE
AND EVIL

PHONE CALL FROM A STRANGER (FOX, 1952, based
on a story by I. A. R. Wylie)
CRACK--UP (CBS--TV, 1956)

PHOTOGRAPHER, THE (short) (NAV, 1948, based on the
life and work of photographer Edward Weston)
DAYBOOKS OF EDWARD WESTON, THE (short) (IND,
n.d.)

PHYLLIS see MARY TYLER MOORE SHOW, THE

PICASSO: LE PEINTRE ET SON MODELE (short) (FRA,
n.d., based on the life of the noted artist)

GUERNICA – PABLO PICASSO (short) (PIC, 1953)
PICASSO (API, 1956)
PICASSO – HIS LIFE AND ART (BRI--TV, n.d.)
CHICAGO PICASSO, THE (short) (NET--TV, 1968)
PICASSO – JOIE DE VIVRE (short) (TIM, 1970)
PICASSO – A PORTRAIT (FRA, 1970)
PICASSO AT 90 (CBS--TV, 1971)
PICASSO THE SCULPTOR (short) (FNC, 1971)
PICASSO – WAR, PEACE AND LOVE (UNI, 1973)
PICASSO – PAINTER OF THE CENTURY (FRA, 1973)
PICASSO, THE MAN AND HIS WORK (FRA, 1974)
ADVENTURES OF PICASSO, THE (SWE, 1978)

PICCADILLY JIM (SEZ, 1919, based on the book by P. G.
    Wodehouse)
    PICCADILLY JIM (MGM, 1936)

PICK--UP ON SOUTH STREET (FOX, 1952, based on a story
    by Dwight Taylor)
    ESCAPE ROUTE CAPE TOWN (CAPE TOWN AFFAIR)
    (SA, 1967)

PICKWICK see PICKWICK PAPERS, THE

PICKWICK PAPERS, THE (ADVENTURES OF MR. PICKWICK,
    THE (BRI, c1900, based on the book by Charles Dickens)
    GABRIEL GRUB, THE SURLY SEXTON (BRI, 1904)
    PICKWICK PAPERS, THE (BRI, 1913)
    PICKWICK PAPERS, THE (VIT, 1913)
    PICKWICK PAPERS, THE (ED, 1914)
    ADVENTURES OF MR. PICKWICK, THE (BRI, 1921)
    PICKWICK PAPERS, THE (BRI, 1952)
    TRIAL OF MR. PICKWICK, THE (CBS--TV, 1952)
    CHARLES DICKENS CHRISTMAS, A (short) (EBE,
    1956)
    PICKWICK PAPERS, THE (ITA--TV, 1968)
    PICKWICK! (BRI--TV, 1968)
    PICKWICK (TIM, 1970)
    PICKWICK (BRI--TV, 1972)

PICTURE OF DORIAN GRAY, THE (DEN, 1910, based on
    the book by Oscar Wilde)
    PICTURE OF DORIAN GRAY, THE (DEN, 1913)
    PICTURE OF DORIAN GRAY, THE (MUT, 1913)
    PICTURE OF DORIAN GRAY, THE (RUS, 1915)
    PICTURE OF DORIAN GRAY, THE (THA, 1915)
    PICTURE OF DORIAN GRAY, THE (BRI, 1916)
    PICTURE OF DORIAN GRAY, THE (GER, 1917)
    PICTURE OF DORIAN GRAY, THE (HUN, 1917)
    PICTURE OF DORIAN GRAY, THE (MGM, 1945)
    PICTURE OF DORIAN GRAY, THE (ABC--TV, 1953)
    PICTURE OF DORIAN GRAY, THE (CBS--TV, 1961)
    SECRET OF DORIAN GRAY, THE (AI, 1970)
    PICTURE OF DORIAN GRAY, THE (ABC--TV, 1973)
    PICTURE OF DORIAN GRAY, THE (IND, 1975)
    TAKE OFF (IND, 1978)

PICTURE SNATCHER (WB, 1933, based on a story by Danny
    Ahearn)
    ESCAPE FROM CRIME (WB, 1942)

PIED PIPER (BRI, 1907, based on a story by Robert Browning)
    PIED PIPER (THA, 1911)
    PIED PIPER (FRA, 1911)
    PIED PIPER (ED, 1913)
    PIED PIPER (ED, 1917)
    PIED PIPER OF HAMELIN (RATCATCHER) (GER,
    1918)
    PIED PIPER OF HAMELIN (short) (BRI, 1926)

PIED PIPER (short) (DIS, 1933)
PIED PIPER OF HAMELIN (NBC--TV, 1956)
PIED PIPER, THE (BUL/USA, 1967)
HAMELIN (SPA, 1968)
PIED PIPER, THE (PAR, 1972)
PIED PIPER OF HAMELIN, THE (FRA, 1972)

PIED PIPER OF HAMELIN see PIED PIPER

PIER 13 see ME AND MY GAL

PIERNAS DE SEDA see SILK LEGS

PIERRE ET JEAN (FRA, 1924, based on a story by Guy de
    Maupassant)
    PIERRE ET JEAN (FRA, 1943)

PIERRE OF THE PLAINS see HEART OF THE WILD, THE

PIES AND GUYS see HALF WIT'S HOLIDAY

PIGS IS PIGS (short) (VIT, 1914, based on the story by
    Ellis Parker Butler)
    PIGS IS PIGS (short) (WB, 1937)
    PIGS IS PIGS (short) (DIS, 1954)

PILLAR OF FIRE (short) (FRA, 1899, based on the book,
    "She," by H. Rider Haggard)
    SHE (ED, 1908)
    SHE (THA, 1911)
    SHE (BRI, 1912)
    SHE (FRA, 1916)
    SHE (BRI, 1916)
    SHE (FOX, 1917)
    SHE (BRI, 1925)
    SHE (RKO, 1935)
    MALIKA SALOMI (IN, 1953)
    SHE (BRI, 1965)
    VENGEANCE OF SHE (BRI, 1967)

PILLARS OF SOCIETY (THA, 1911, based on a play by
    Henrik Ibsen)
    STUTZE DER GESELLSCHAFT (GER, 1935)

PIMPERNELL SMITH see SCARLET PIMPERNELL, THE

PINCH HITTER, THE (TRI, 1917, based on the story by C.
    Gardner Sullivan)
    PINCH HITTER, THE (AE, 1926)

PINOCCHIO (ITA, 1911, based on the book by Collodi)
    PINOCCHIO (ITA, 1935)
    ADVENTURES OF PINOCCHIO (ITA, 1940)
    PINOCCHIO (DIS, 1941)
    ADVENTURES OF CUCURUCHITO AND PINOCCHIO
    (serial) (MEX, 1942)
    CUCURUCHITO AND PINOCCHIO (MEX, 1944)
    PINOCCHIO (NBC--TV, 1957)
    NEW ADVENTURES OF PINOCCHIO, THE (series)
    (TV, 1961)
    PINOCCHIO IN OUTER SPACE (BEL, 1965)
    TURLIS ADVENTURE (GER, 1967)
    PINOCCHIO (NBC--TV, 1968)
    PINOCCHIO (GER, 1969)
    PINOCCHIO (IND, 1971)
    PINOCCHIO (ITA--TV, 1971)
    ADVENTURES OF PINOCCHIO, THE (ABC--TV, 1976)
    PINOCCHIO (series) (GER--TV, 1976)
    SPINNOLIO (short) (CAN, 1977)

PINOCCHIO (IND, 1978)

PIQUE DAME (RUS, 1910, based on the story, "Dame de Pique," by Alexander Pushkin)
  QUEEN OF SPADES (GER, 1910)
  PIQUE DAME (ITA, 1911)
  QUEEN OF SPADES (ITA, 1913)
  PIQUE DAME (RUS, 1916)
  QUEEN OF SPADES (HUN, 1920)
  QUEEN OF SPADES (AYW, 1925)
  PIQUE DAME (GER, 1927)
  PIQUE DAME (FRA, 1937)
  PIQUE DAME (FRA, 1937)
  PIQUE DAME (RUS, 1937)
  QUEEN OF SPADES (BRI, 1948)
  QUEEN OF SPADES (NBC--TV, 1950)
  QUEEN OF SPADES (short) (DYN, 1954)
  QUEEN OF SPADES (CAN–TV, 1956)
  PIQUE DAME (FIN, 1959)
  QUEEN OF SPADES (RUS, 1960)
  PIQUE DAME (FRA, 1965)
  PIQUE DAME (GER, 1965)
  QUEEN OF SPADES (NET–TV, 1971)

PIRATES OF LAKE MALAR, THE (SWE, 1923, based on the book by Sigfrid Siwertz)
  PIRATES OF LAKE MALAR, THE (SWE, 1959)

PIRATE'S TREASURE (VIT, 1908, based on the book by Robert Louis Stevenson)
  TREASURE ISLAND (BRI, 1908)
  TREASURE ISLAND (ED, 1911)
  TREASURE ISLAND (FOX, 1915)
  TREASURE ISLAND (PAR, 1920)
  TREASURE ISLAND (MGM, 1934)
  TREASURE ISLAND (RUS, 1938)
  TREASURE ISLAND (CBS--TV, 1942)
  TREASURE ISLAND (DIS, 1950)
  LONG JOHN SILVER (BRI, 1954)
  LONG JOHN SILVER (series) (AUT--TV, 1956)
  TREASURE ISLAND (CBS--TV, 1960)
  TREASURE ISLAND (NBC--TV, 1960)
  MAGOO AT SEA (UPA, 1964)
  TREASURE ISLAND (series) (BRI/FRA--TV, 1967)
  EVEN IN THE WEST THERE WAS GOD ONCE UPON A TIME (ITA/SPA, 1968)
  TREASURE ISLAND (CC, 1970)
  TREASURE ISLAND (AUT--TV, 1970)
  TREASURE ISLAND (RUS, 1971)
  TREASURE ISLAND (HB, 1971)
  DOBUTSU TAKARAJIMA (JAP, 1971)
  TREASURE ISLAND (BRI, 1972)
  SCALAWAG (PAR, 1973)
  TREASURE ISLAND (BRI, 1975)

PISTE DES GEANTS, LA see BIG TRAIL, THE

PIT, THE see CORNER IN WHEAT, A and PIT AND THE PENDULUM, THE

PIT AND THE PENDULUM, THE (FRA, 1910, based on the story by Edgar Allan Poe)
  PIT AND THE PENDULUM, THE (SOL, 1913)
  PIT AND THE PENDULUM, THE (AI, 1961)
  PIT AND THE PENDULUM, THE (BRI, 1962)
  PIT, THE (short) (BRI, 1962)
  PIT AND THE PENDULUM, THE (short) (FRA, 1963)
  PIT AND THE PENDULUM, THE (FRA--TV, 1963)
  BLOOD DEMON, THE (GER, 1967)

PIT AND THE PENDULUM, THE (CAN, 1967)

PLACE IN THE SUN, A see AMERICAN TRAGEDY, AN

PLAINSMAN, THE see LAST FRONTIER, THE and WILD BILL HICKOCK

PLANET OF THE APES (FOX, 1968, based on the book by Pierre Boule)
  PLANET OF THE APES (series) (CBS--TV, 1974)

PLANET OUTLAWS see BUCK ROGERS

PLANTER'S WIFE, THE see OUTPOST IN MALAYA

PLATINUM HIGH SCHOOL see BAD DAY AT BLACK ROCK

PLATO'S CAVE (short) (PYR, 1974, based on a story by Plato)
  CAVE, THE (short) (IND, 1974)

PLAYBOY OF PARIS, THE (PAR, 1930, adapted from the book, "Petit Cafe, Le," by Tristan Bernard)
  PETIT CAFE, LE (FRA, 1930)

PLAYBOY OF THE WESTERN WORLD, THE (BRI, 1963, based on the play by John Millington Synge)
  PLAYBOY OF THE WESTERN WORLD, THE (series) (BRI--TV, c1965)

PLEASE DON'T EAT THE DAISIES (MGM, 1960, based on the book by Jean Kerr)
  PLEASE DON'T EAT THE DAISIES (series) (NBC--TV, 1965)

PLEASURE CRUISE (FOX, 1933, based on a play by Austen Allen)
  NO DEJAS LA PUERTA ABIERTA (SPA, 1933)

PLEASURE SEEKERS, THE see THREE COINS IN THE FOUNTAIN

PLEBIAN see MISS JULIE

PLEIN CIEL (short) (IND, n.d., based on the life of author Antoine de Saint--Exupery)
  ST. EXUPERY (short) (IND, n.d.)
  SAINT--EXUPERY (short) (MHF, 1964)

PLOMBIER AMOUREUX, LE see CARDBOARD LOVER, THE

PLOT TO MURDER HITLER, THE see HITLER GANG, THE

POCHARDE, LA (FRA, 1921, based on the book by Jules Mary)
  POCHARDE, LA (FRA, 1936)
  POCHARDE, LA (FRA, 1952)

POCKETFUL OF MIRACLES see LADY FOR A DAY

POE: A VISIT WITH THE AUTHOR see EDGAR ALLAN POE: BACKGROUND FOR HIS WORKS

POETRY OF ADALEN see ADALANS POESI

POIL DE CAROTTE (FRA, 1925, based on the book by Jules

Renard)
POIL DE CAROTTE (FRA, 1932)
POIL DE CAROTTE (FRA, 1952)
POIL DE CAROTTE (FRA, 1973)

POINT OF VIEW see ANSEL ADAMS, PHOTOGRAPHER

POINTING FINGER, THE see IRON STAIR, THE

POKPOONGEA UHUNDUCK see WUTHERING HEIGHTS

POLE POPPENSPALER (GER, 1935, based on the book by
    Theodor Storm)
PUPPENSPIELER, DER (GER, 1945)
DORF IN DER HEIMAT, DAS (GER, 1956)

POLICE SURGEON see DR. SIMON LOCKE

POLICHE (FRA, 1929, based on a book by Henry Bataille)
POLICHE (FRA, 1934)

POLIKOUCHKA (RUS, 1919, based on the book by Leo
    Tolstoy)
POLIKOUCHKA (FRA/GER/ITA, 1958)

POLISH JEW, THE see BELLS, THE

POLITIQUERIAS, LOS see LOVE 'EM AND WEEP

POLLY OF THE CIRCUS (MGM, 1917, based on the play
    by Margaret Mayo)
POLLY OF THE CIRCUS (MGM, 1932)

POLLYANNA (UA, 1920, based on the book by Eleanor H.
    Porter)
POLLYANNA (DIS, 1960)

PONT DES SOUPIRS, LE (ITA, 1919, based on the book by
    Michel Zevaco)
PONT DES SOUPIRS, LE (ITA, 1940)
PONT DES SOUPIRS, LE (ITA/SPA, 1964)

PONY EXPRESS (PAR, 1925, based on a story by Henry
    James Forman and Walter Woods)
PONY EXPRESS (PAR, 1953)

POOR COW see CATHY COME HOME

POOR NUT, THE (FN, 1927, based on the play by J. C. and
    Elliott Nugent)
LOCAL BOY MAKES GOOD (FN, 1931)
ATHLETE INCOMPLET, L' (FRA, 1931)

POOR RICHARD: BENJAMIN FRANKLIN see OUR BILL
    OF RIGHTS

POPI (UA, 1969, based on a screenplay by Tim and Lester
    Pine)
POPI (series) (CBS--TV, 1975)

POPPY see SALLY OF THE SAWDUST

PORRIDGE (series) (BRI--TV, 1973, based on a teleplay)
ON THE ROCKS (series) (ABC--TV, 1975)

PORT ARTHUR (GER, 1934, source unlisted)
PORT ARTHUR (FRA, 1934)
PORT ARTHUR (CZE, 1934)

PORT OF THE SEVEN SEAS see FANNY

PORT SAID NIGHTS (FRA, 1930, source unlisted)
NACHT VON PORT SAID, DIE (GER, 1930)

PORTEUSE DE PAIN, LA (FRA, 1924, based on a book by
    Xavier de Montepin)
PORTEUSE DE PAIN, LA (FRA, 1933)
PORTEUSE DE PAIN, LA (FRA/ITA, 1949)
PORTEUSE DE PAIN, LA (FRA/ITA, 1963)

PORTRAIT OF DAG HAMMARSKJOLD, A (short) (MHF,
    1961, based on the life of the United Nations secretary)
DAG HAMMARSKJOLD (short) (STE, 1963)
THREE MEN (sequence) (NET--TV, 1965)

PORTRAIT OF MURDER see LAURA

POSSESSED see GAMBLER, THE and MIRAGE, THE

POSTMAN, THE see WOZZECK

POSTMAN ALWAYS RINGS TWICE, THE see DERNIER
    TOURNANT, LE

POSTMASTER, THE (RUS, 1925, based on the story by
    Alexander Pushkin)
NOSTALGIE (FRA, 1937)
POSTMEISTER, DER (GER, 1940)
DUNJA (AUS, 1955)

POSTMEISTER, DER see POSTMASTER, THE

POTEMKIN (RUS, 1925, second film consists of stock footage
    from the first)
SEEDS OF FREEDOM (RUS, 1943)

POUCHKINE (RUS, 1949, documentaries on the life of the
    noted Russian writer)
POUCHKINE AND MIKHAILOVSKOIE (RUS, 1950)
POUCHKINE IN ST. PETERSBERG (RUS, 1950)

POUCHKINE AND MIKHAILOVSKOIE see POUCHKINE

POUCHKINE IN ST. PETERSBURG see POUCHKINE

POUPEE, LA (FRA, 1899, based on the play by Edmond
    Audran)
POUPEE, LA (BRI, 1920)

POUPEES, LES see DECAMERON, THE

POUR CONSTRUIRE UN FEU (FRA, 1925, based on a story
    by Jack London)
TO BUILD A FIRE (IND, 1971)
TO BUILD A FIRE (short) (BFA, 1975)

POUR UN NUIT D'AMOUR, JUSTICE D'ABORD see PUBLIC
    PROSECUTOR

POUR UNE NUIT D'AMOUR (FRA, 1922, based on the book
    by Emile Zola)
POUR UNE NUIT D'AMOUR (FRA, 1947)

POWDER RIVER see FRONTIER MARSHAL

POWER (BRI, 1934, based on the book, "Jew Suss," by Leon
    Feuchtwanger)
JEW SUSS (GER, 1938)

POWER AND THE GLORY, THE see FUGITIVE, THE

PRANKS ON BOARD (ARG, 1936, based on the play by
    Manuel Romero)
  PRANKS ON BOARD (ARG, 1967)
PRECIEUSES RIDICULES, LES (FRA, 1900, based on the
    play by Moliere)
  PRECIEUSES RIDICULES, LES (FRA, 1935)

PRECIO DE UN BESO, EL see ONE MAD KISS

PREDICTION, THE see CLAIRVOYANT, THE

PRELUDE (BRI, 1927, based on the story, "Premature
    Burial," by Edgar Allan Poe)
  CRIME OF DR. CRESPI, THE (LIB, 1935)
  PREMATURE BURIAL (NBC--TV, 1961)
  PREMATURE BURIAL (AI, 1962)
  BLANCHEVILLE MONSTER (ITA/SPA, 1963)

PREMATURE BURIAL see PRELUDE

PREMIERES ARMES DE ROCAMBOLE, LES see
    ROCAMBOLE

PRENZ GARDE A LA PEINTURE (FRA, 1932, based on the
    play, "The Late Christopher Bean," by Sidney Howard
    from an original play, "Prenez Garde a la Peinture," by
    Rene Fauchois)
  CHRISTOPHER BEAN (MGM, 1933)
  LATE CHRISTOPHER BEAN, THE (NBC--TV, 1949)
  LATE CHRISTOPHER BEAN, THE (ABC--TV, 1950)
  LATE CHRISTOPHER BEAN, THE (CBS--TV, 1955)
  CHRISTOPHER BEAN (BRI, 1956)

PRESIDENT, LA (FRA, 1938, based on the play, "Madame
    la presidente," by Pierre Veber and Maurice Hennequin)
  MADEMOISELLE LA PRESIDENTE (ITA, 1952)

PRESIDENT VANISHES, THE (PAR, 1934, author unlisted)
  PRESIDENT VANISHES, THE (CBS--TV, 1964)

PRESIDO, EL see BIG HOUSE, THE

PRETTY BABY (WB, 1960, based on a story by Jules Furthman)
  GIRL ON THE SUBWAY (ABC--TV, 1955)

PRETTY BOY FLOYD (CON, 1960, based on the life of the
    gangster)
  BULLET FOR PRETTY BOY, A (AI, 1970)
  STORY OF PRETTY BOY FLOYD, THE (ABC--TV, 1974)

PRICE OF A SOUL see CHEMINEAU, LE

PRICE SHE PAID, THE (SEZ, 1917, based on the book by
    David Graham Phillips)
  PRICE SHE PAID, THE (COL, 1924)

PRIDE AND PREJUDICE (MGM, 1940, based on the book
    by Jane Austen; also the basis for the musical "First
    Impressions," in 1959)
  PRIDE AND PREJUDICE (NBC--TV, 1949)
  PRIDE AND PREJUDICE (CAN--TV, 1958)

PRIDE OF THE YANKEES, THE (RKO, 1942, based on the
    life of the noted baseball player)
  LOU GEHRIG STORY, THE (CBS--TV, 1956)
  LOVE AFFAIR: THE ELEANOR AND LOU GEHRIG
    STORY, A (NBC--TV, 1977)

PRIEST KILLER, THE see IRONSIDE

PRIMAVERA, DIE KAMELIENDAME see DAME AUX
    CAMELIAS, LA

PRIME MINISTER, THE see DISRAELI

PRIME OF MISS JEAN BRODIE, THE (FOX, 1969, based
    on the book by Muriel Spark and the play by Jay Presson
    Allen)
  PRIME OF MISS JEAN BRODIE, THE (BRI--TV, 1977)
  PRIME OF MISS JEAN BRODIE, THE (FOX--TV, 1978)

PRIMROSE PATH, THE see BURNT WINGS

PRINCE AND THE PAUPER THE (ED, 1909, based on the
    book by Mark Twain)
  PRINCE AND THE PAUPER, THE (BRI, 1909)
  PRINCE AND THE PAUPER, THE (PAR, 1915)
  SEINE MAJESTAT, DAS BETTELKIND (AUS, 1920)
  PRINCE AND THE PAUPER, THE (ARC, 1922)
  PRINCE AND THE PAUPER, THE (AUS, 1923)
  PRINCE AND THE PAUPER, THE (WB, 1937)
  PRINCE AND THE PAUPER, THE (RUS, 1943)
  PRINCE AND THE PAUPER, THE (CBS--TV, 1957)
  PRINCE AND THE PAUPER, THE (NBC--TV, 1960)
  PRINCE AND THE PAUPER, THE (DIS, 1962)
  RAJA AUR RUNK (IN, 1968)
  PRINCE AND THE PAUPER, THE (CHI, 1966)
  PRINCE AND THE PAUPER, THE (HB, 1972)
  P. J. AND THE PRESIDENT'S SON (ABC--TV, 1976)
  PRINCE AND THE PAUPER, THE (SWI, 1977)
  CROSSED SWORDS (BRI, 1978)
  RINGO (NBC--TV, 1978)

PRINCE AU MASQUE ROUGE, LE see CHEVALIER DE
    MAISON--ROUGE, LE

PRINCE CHAP, THE (SEL, 1916, based on the play by Edward
    Peple)
  PRINCE CHAP, THE (PAR, 1920)

PRINCE IGOR (RUS, 1970, based on the opera by Alexander
    Borodin)
  PRINCE IGOR (BRI--TV, 1975)

PRINCE JEAN, LE (FRA, 1928, based on the book by Charles
    Mere)
  PRINCE JEAN, LE (FRA, 1934)

PRINCE OF LOVERS, THE (BRI, 1922, based on the life of
    the poet Lord Byron)
  PRINCE OF LOVERS, THE (BRI, 1927)
  BAD LORD BYRON (BRI, 1949)
  LADY CAROLINE LAMB (BRI, 1972)

PRINCE OF PEACE see PASSION PLAY, THE

PRINCE OF PLAYERS see HAMLET and RICHARD III

PRINCE OF THIEVES see ROBIN HOOD AND HIS MERRY
    MEN

PRINCE RUDOLPHE, LE see MYSTERIES OF PARIS

PRINCE WHO WAS A THIEF, THE (UN, 1951, based on a
    story by Theodore Dreiser)
  SWORD OF ALI BABA, THE (UN, 1965)

PRINCE ZILAH, LE   (ITA, 1918, based on a book by Jules Claretie)
   HER FINAL RECKONING   (PAR, 1918)
   PRINCE ZILAH, LE   (FRA, 1927)

PRINCESS A VOUS ORDRES   see   ADORABLE

PRINCESS AND THE PEA, THE   see   ONCE UPON A MATTRESS

PRINCESS MARY, THE   see   BELLA

PRINCESS O'HARA   (UN, 1935, based on a story by Damon Runyon)
   IT AIN'T HAY   (UN, 1943)

PRINCESS O'ROURKE   (WB, 1943, based on a story by Norman Krasna)
   PRINCESS O'ROURKE   (NBC–TV, 1956)

PRINCESS ROMANOFF   see   FEDORA

PRINCESSE TSIGANE, LE   see   ZIGEUNERBARON, DER

PRISON DE FEMMES   (FRA, 1938, based on a book by Francis Carco)
   PRISON DE FEMMES   (FRA, 1958)

PRISON SANS BARREAUX   (FRA, 1936, based on a play by E. and O. Eis, Gina Kaus and Hans Wilhelm)
   PRISON WITHOUT BARS   (UA, 1938)

PRISON WITHOUT BARS   see   PRISON SANS BARREAUX

PRISONER OF SHARK ISLAND, THE   (FOX, 1936, based on the assassination of President Abraham Lincoln)
   HELLGATE   (LIP, 1953)
   CASE FOR DR. MUDD, THE   (CBS–TV, 1958)

PRISONER OF THE IRON MASK   see   MAN IN THE IRON MASK, THE

PRISONER OF ZENDA, THE   (IND, 1913, based on the book by Sir Anthony Hope; also the basis for two musical comedies, "Princess Flavia" in 1925, and "Zenda" in 1963)
   ROMAN D'UN ROI, LA   (ITA, 1913)
   PRISONER OF ZENDA, THE   (BRI, 1915)
   PRISONER OF ZENDA, THE   (MGM, 1922)
   PRISONER OF ZENDA, THE   (UA, 1937)
   PRISONER OF ZENDA, THE   (MGM, 1952)
   PRISONER OF ZENDA, THE   (CBS–TV, 1961)

PRIVATE AFFAIRS OF BEL AMI, THE   see   BEL AMI

PRIVATE LIFE OF HELEN OF TROY, THE   see   CHUTE DE TROIE, LA

PRIVATE LIFE OF HENRY VIII, THE   see   HENRY VIII

PRIVATE LIVES   (MGM, 1931, based on the play by Noel Coward)
   AMANTS TERRIBLES, LES   (FRA, 1936)

PRIVATE LIVES OF ELIZABETH AND ESSEX, THE   see   QUEEN ELIZABETH

PRIVATE NUMBER   see   COMMON CLAY

PRIVATE PETTIGREW'S GIRL   see   PETTIGREW'S GIRL

PRIVATE POTTER   (BRI–TV, n.d., based on a teleplay by Ronald Harwood)
   PRIVATE POTTER   (BRI, 1963)

PRIVATE WORLDS   (PAR, 1935, based on the book by Phyllis Bottome)
   PRIVATE WORLDS   (CBS–TV, 1955)

PRIVATESEKRATARIN, DIE   (GER, 1931, based on the operetta by William Thiele and Paul Abraham)
   SUNSHINE SUSIE   (BRI, 1931)
   PRIVATSEKRATARIN, DIE   (GER, 1953)

PRIX DE BEAUTE   (FRA, 1930, source unlisted)
   GREAT AMERICAN BEAUTY CONTEST, THE   (ABC–TV, 1972)

PROCES DE MARY DUGAN, LE   see   TRIAL OF MARY DUGAN, THE

PROCESO DE MARY DUGAN, EL   see   TRIAL OF MARY DUGAN, THE

PRODIGAL, THE   see   PARABLE OF THE PRODIGAL SON, THE

PRODIGAL SON, THE   see   PARABLE OF THE PRODIGAL SON, THE

PRODIGAL SON, THE   (JAP, 1949, source unlisted)
   PRODIGAL SON, THE   (JAP, 1958)

PROFESSOR DE MI MUJER, EL   see   AMOUR CHANTE, L'

PROFESSOR MAMLOCK   (RUS, 1938, based on the book by Dr. Friedrich Wolf)
   PROFESSOR MAMLOCK   (GER, 1961)

PROF. UNRATH   see   BLUE ANGEL, THE

PROMESSI SPOSI, I   see   BETROTHED, THE

PROMOTER, THE   see   CARD, THE

PSKOVITYANKA   see   IVAN THE TERRIBLE

PSYCHO–CIRCUS   (CIRCUS OF FEAR)   (BRI, 1966, based on a story by Peter Welbeck)
   RATSEL DES SILBERNEN DREIECKS, DAS   (GER, 1967)

PUBLIC ENEMY'S WIFE   (WB, 1936, based on a story by P.J. Wolfson)
   BULLETS FOR O'HARA   (WB, 1941)

PUBLIC HERO NO. 1   (MGM, 1935, based on a story by J. Walter Rubin and Wells Root)
   GETAWAY, THE   (MGM, 1941)

PUBLIC PIGEON NO. 1   (CBS–TV, 1955, based on a teleplay by Devery Freeman)
   PUBLIC PIGEON NO. 1   (UN, 1957)

PUBLIC PROSECUTOR   (RUS, 1917, source unlisted)
   POUR UN NUIT D'AMOUR, JUSTICE D'ABORD   (FRA, n.d.)

PUISSANCE DES TENEBRES, LA   (RUS, 1909, based on the

book by Leo Tolstoy)
PUISSANCE DES TENEBRES, LA (RUS, 1918)
MACHT DER FINSTERNIS (GER, 1923)

PULGARCITO see PETIT POUCET, LE

PUPPENSPIELER, DER see POLE POPPENSPALER

PURA VERDAD, LA see NOTHING BUT THE TRUTH

PURGATORY see TOO MUCH CHAMPAGNE

PURITAN PASSIONS see LORD FEATHERTOP

PURPLE AND FINE LINEN see THREE HOURS

PURPLE GANG, THE (AA, 1960, based on historical
    incidents and characters)
  PURPLE GANG, THE (ABC–TV, 1960)

PURPLE HIEROGLYPH, THE see MURDER WILL OUT

PURPLE LILACS see GIRL WHO LIKED PURPLE
    FLOWERS, THE

PURSUED see WHEN A MAN SEES RED

PURSUIT AND LOVES OF QUEEN VICTORIA see SIXTY
    YEARS A QUEEN

PUSHKIN see POUCHKINE

PUSS IN BOOTS (FRA, 1902, based on the fairy tale)

PUSS IN BOOTS (LUB, 1903)
PUSS IN BOOTS (FRA, 1908)
PUSS IN BOOTS (ED, 1917)
PUSS IN BOOTS (SWE, 1919)
PUSS IN BOOTS (COL, 1932)
PUSS IN BOOTS (IND, 1934)
PUSS IN BOOTS (GER, 1934)
PUSS IN BOOTS (GER, 1938)
PUSS IN BOOTS (RUS, 1938)
PUSS IN BOOTS (BRI, 1954)
PUSS IN BOOTS (EBE, 1958)
PUSS IN BOOTS (MEX, 1961)
PUSS IN BOOTS (RAN, 1972)
PUSS 'N BOOTS TRAVELS AROUND THE WORLD (JAP,
    1977)

PUTTING PANTS ON PHILIP (short) (MGM, 1927, based
    on a screenplay by Leo McCarey)
SOCK AND FUN (short) (ART, 1927)

PYGMALION (GER, 1935, based on the play by George
    Bernard Shaw)
PYGMALION (HOL, 1936)
PYGMALION (MGM, 1938)
PYGMALION (NBC–TV, 1963)
MY FAIR LADY (WB, 1964)
OPENING OF MISTY BEETHOVEN, THE (IND, 1975)

PYGMALION AND GALATEA (FRA, 1898, based on a
    legend)
PYGMALION AND GALATEA (BRI, 1912)

QUALITY STREET (MGM, 1927, based on the play by Sir
James M. Barrie)
QUALITY STREET (RKO, 1937)
QUALITY STREET (NBC--TV, 1949)

QUANT ON EST BELLE see EASIEST WAY, THE

QUARANTE ET UNIEME, LE (RUS, 1927, based on the book
by Boris Lavreniov)
QUARANTE ET UNIEME, LE (RUS, 1956)

QUARRY, THE see CITY OF SILENT MEN

QUARTIER LATIN (FRA, 1929, based on a story by
Maurice Dekobra)
QUARTIER LATIN (FRA, 1939)

QUASIMODO see HUNCHBACK OF NOTRE DAME, THE

QUATRE PAS DANS LES NUAGES (ITA, 1942, based on the
story by Paolo Zappa)
SOUS LE SOLEIL DE PROVENCE (FRA/ITA, 1956)

QUEEN ELIZABETH (PAR, 1912, based on historical
incidents in the life of Elizabeth of England)
VIRGIN QUEEN, THE (BRI, 1923)
PRIVATE LIVES OF ELIZABETH AND ESSEX, THE
(WB, 1939) (TV title: ELIZABETH THE QUEEN)
VIRGIN QUEEN, THE (FOX, 1955)
ELIZABETH THE QUEEN (NBC--TV, 1968)
ELIZABETH R (series) (BRI--TV, 1971)

QUEEN ELIZABETH II see KING IS DEAD, LONG LIVE
THE QUEEN, THE

QUEEN FOR CAESAR, A see CLEOPATRA

QUEEN HIGH see PAIR OF SIXES, A

QUEEN LUISE (GER, 1927, based on the book by Walther
von Molo)
QUEEN LUISE (GER, 1957)

QUEEN OF ATLANTIS see ATLANTIDE, L'

QUEEN OF SPADES see PIQUE DAME

QUEEN OF THE JUNGLE see JUNGLE GODDESS

QUEEN OF THE NIGHTCLUBS (WB, 1929, based on a
screenplay by Murray Roth and Addison Buckhart)
KONIGSLOGE, DIE (GER, 1929)

QUEEN OF THE SEA (FOX, 1918, based on the story "The
Little Mermaid," by Hans Christian Andersen)
LITTLE MERMAID, THE (NBC--TV, 1961)
DAYDREAMER, THE (EMB, 1966)
FANTASY . . . 3 (SPA, 1966)
MALE SIRENA (short) (YUG, 1968)
LITTLE MERMAID, THE (RUS, 1976)
LITTLE MERMAID, THE (CZE, 1977)

QUEEN VICTORIA AND DISRAELI see MUDLARK, THE

QUEEN WAS IN THE PARLOR, THE (BRI, 1927, based on
the play by Sir Noel Coward)
FORBIDDEN LOVE (PAT, 1928)
TONIGHT IS OURS (PAR, 1932)

QUEEN'S HUSBAND, THE see ROYAL BED, THE

QUEEN'S SECRET, THE see THREE WEEKS

QUENTIN DURWARD (FRA, 1911, based on the book by Sir
Walter Scott)
QUENTIN DURWARD (MGM, 1955)

QUICK (GER, 1932, source unlisted)
QUICK (FRA, 1932)

QUICK MILLIONS (FOX, 1931, based on a screenplay by
Rowland Brown and Courtenay Terrett)
QUICK MILLIONS (FOX, 1939)

QUIET WEDDING (BRI, 1942, based on the play by Esther
McCracken)
HAPPY IS THE BRIDE (BRI, 1958)

QUINNEYS, THE (BRI; 1919, based on the play by Horace
Annesley Vachell)
QUINNEYS, THE (BRI, 1927)

QUO VADIS? (FRA, 1901, based on the book by Henryk
Sienkiewicz)
AU TEMPS DES PREMIERS CRETIENS (FRA, 1910)
QUO VADIS? (ITA, 1912)
QUO VADIS? (ITA, 1924)
QUO VADIS? (MGM, 1951)

RCMP AND THE TREASURE OF GENGHIS KHAN see
DANGERS OF THE CANADIAN MOUNTED

RABBIT TRAP, THE (NBC–TV, 1955, based on a teleplay
by J.P. Miller)
RABBIT TRAP, THE (UA, 1959)

RACERS, THE (FOX, 1955, based on a book by Hans Ruesch)
MEN AGAINST SPEED (CBS–TV, 1956)

RACHEL: A JEWISH TRAGEDY (IND, 1914, based on a
Bible story)
RACHEL, THE OUTCAST (POL, 1922)

RACHEL, THE OUTCAST see RACHEL: A JEWISH
TRAGEDY

RACK, THE (ABC–TV, 1955, based on a teleplay by Rod
Serling)
RACK, THE (MGM, 1956)

RACKET, THE (PAR, 1928, based on the play by Bartlett
Cormack)
RACKET, THE (RKO, 1951)

RADAR MEN FROM THE MOON (serial) (REP, 1952,
based on a screenplay by various authors; the remake is a
condensation of the serial)
RETIK, THE MOON MENACE (REP, 1966)

RADHA KRISCHNA (IN, 1930, based on an Indian legend)
RADHA KRISCHNA (IN, 1948)

RADIO MANIA see HOG WILD

RADIO PATROL (serial) (UN, 1937, stock footage from
the serial was used in the 1940 feature)
ENEMY AGENT (UN, 1940)

RAFFLES see RAFFLES, THE AMATEUR CRACKSMAN

RAFFLES, GENTLEMAN BURGLAR see RAFFLES, THE
AMATEUR CRACKSMAN

RAFFLES, LADRA GENTILUOMO see RAFFLES, THE
AMATEUR CRACKSMAN

RAFFLES MEXICANO, EL see RAFFLES, THE AMATEUR
CRACKSMAN

RAFFLES, THE AMATEUR CRACKSMAN (VIT, 1905, based
on the stories of E.W. Hornung)
RAFFLES (DEN, 1910)
RAFFLES (serial) (ITA, 1911)
RAFFLES, GENTLEMAN BURGLAR (KEY, 1914)
RAFFLES, THE AMATEUR CRACKSMAN (IND, 1917)
RAFFLES, LADRA GENTILUOMO (ITA, 1920)
MR. JUSTICE RAFFLES (BRI, 1921)
RAFFLES, THE AMATEUR CRACKSMAN (UA, 1925)
RAFFLES (UA, 1930)
RETURN OF RAFFLES (BRI, 1932)
RAFFLES (UA, 1940)
RAFFLES MEXICANO, EL (MEX, c1960)

RAFTER ROMANCE see ICH BEI TAG UND DU BEI
NACHT

RAG TRADE, THE (series) (BRI––TV, n.d., based on a
teleplay)
NEEDLES AND PINS (series) (NBC–TV, 1973)

RAGAMUFFIN (PAR, 1915, based on a story by William
C. DeMille)
SPLENDID CRIME, THE (PAR, 1925)

RAGENS RIKE (SWE, 1929, source unlisted)
RAGENS RIKE (SWE, 1951)

RAGGED GIRL OF OZ, THE see DOROTHY AND THE
SCARECROW OF OZ

RAGGED MESSENGER, THE see MADONNA OF THE
STREETS

RAGGEDY ANN AND ANDY see RAGGEDY ANN AND
RAGGEDY ANDY

RAGGEDY ANN AND RAGGEDY ANDY (short) (PAR,
1936, based on stories and characters by Johnny Gruelle)
RAGGEDY ANN AND ANDY (FOX, 1976)

RAID ON ENTEBBE see VICTORY AT ENTEBBE

RAILROADED (EL, 1947, based on a news item)
CALL NORTHSIDE 777 (FOX, 1948)
FALSE WITNESS (CALLING NORTHSIDE 777) (CBS–
TV, 1957)

RAIN see SADIE THOMPSON

RAINBOW TRAIL, THE (FOX, 1918, based on the book,
"The Desert Crucible," by Zane Grey)
RAINBOW TRAIL, THE (FOX, 1925)
RAINBOW TRAIL, THE (FOX, 1932)

RAINMAKER, THE (NBC–TV, 1953, based on a teleplay by
N. Richard Nash; also the basis for the musical, "110 in
the Shade")
RAINMAKER, THE (PAR, 1956)

RAINS CAME, THE (FOX, 1939, based on the book by Louis
Bromfield)
RAINS OF RANCHIPUR, THE (FOX, 1955)

RAINS OF RANCHIPUR, THE see RAINS CAME, THE

RAJA AUR RANK see PRINCE AND THE PAUPER, THE

RAJA HARISCHANDRA (IN, 1913, based on an Indian
legend)
RAJA HARISCHANDRA (IN, 1923)
RAJA HARISCHANDRA (IN, 1927)

RAMAYANA see SATI VIJAY

RAMBLIN' KID, THE (UN, 1923, based on a book by Earl
Wayland Bowman)
LONG, LONG TRAIL, THE (UN, 1929)

RAMONA (BIO, 1910, based on a novel by Helen Hunt
Jackson)
RAMONA (IND, 1916)
RAMONA (UA, 1928)
RAMONA (FOX, 1936)

RAMUNTCHO (FRA, 1919, based on the book by Pierre
Loti)
RAMUNTCHO (FRA, 1937)
MARRIAGE OF RAMUNTCHO, THE (FRA, 1946)
RAMUNTCHO (FRA, 1958)

RANGE COURAGE see BLINKY

RANSOM OF RED CHIEF, THE (IND, 1911, based on a
    story by O. Henry)
  DUMB LUCK (short) (EDU, 1935)
  GRAND CHEF (FRA/ITA, 1959)
  O. HENRY'S FULL HOUSE (FOX, 1952)

RANSOM'S FOLLY (ED, 1915, based on a story by Richard
    Harding Davis)
  RANSOM'S FOLLY (FN, 1926)

RAPUNZEL (short) (BFA, 1951, based on the fairy tale)
  RAPUNZEL (NBC--TV, 1958)

RASHOMON (JAP, 1950, based on a story by Ryunosuke
    Akutagawa)
  OUTRAGE, THE (MGM, 1964)
  RASHOMON (NET--TV, 1960)
  RASHOMON (NET--TV, 1966)

RASKOLNIKOV see CRIME AND PUNISHMENT

RASPOUTINE see RASPUTIN, THE BLACK MONK

RASPUTIN see RASPUTIN, THE BLACK MONK

RASPUTIN AND THE EMPRESS see RASPUTIN, THE
  BLACK MONK

RASPUTIN, THE BLACK MONK (PEE, 1917, based on the
    biography of the historical figure)
  RASPUTIN (GER, 1917)
  FALL OF THE ROMANOFFS (IND, 1917)
  GRIGORI RASPUTIN AND THE GREAT RUSSIAN
    REVOLUTION (RUS, 1917)
  RASPUTIN'S LIEBESABENTEUER (AUS, 1925)
  RASPUTIN (GER, 1929)
  RASPUTIN, THE HOLY SINNER (IND, 1929) (re--edited
    version of RASPUTIN)
  RASPUTIN, THE HOLY DEVIL (GER, 1930)
  RASPUTIN, DER DAEMON DER FRAUEN (GER, 1932)
  RASPUTIN AND THE EMPRESS (MGM, 1932)
  RASPUTIN (FRA, 1938)
  RASPOUTINE (FRA, 1953)
  DERNIER TSAR, LE (FRA/ITA, 1960)
  NIGHT THEY KILLED RASPUTIN, THE (ITA, 1964)
  RASPUTIN, THE MAD MONK (BRI, 1965)
  I KILLED RASPUTIN (FRA/ITA, 1967)
  RASPUTIN (BRI, 1970)
  NICHOLAS AND ALEXANDRA (COL, 1971)

RASPUTIN, THE HOLY SINNER see RASPUTIN, THE
  BLACK MONK

RASPUTIN, THE MAD MONK see RASPUTIN, THE BLACK
  MONK

RASPUTIN'S LIEBESABENTEUER see RASPUTIN, THE
  BLACK MONK

RAT, THE (BRI, 1925, based on the play by Ivor Novello and
    Constance Collier)
  TRIUMPH OF THE RAT (BRI, 1926)
  RETURN OF THE RAT (BRI, 1929)
  RAT, THE (BRI, 1937)

RATNAKA (IN, 1921, based on an Indian legend)
  RATNAKA (IN, 1922)

RATNAKA (IN, 1935)
RATNAKA (IN, 1946)

RATSEL DES SILBERNEN DREIECKS, DAS see PSYCHO--
  CIRCUS

RATTEN, DIE (GER, 1921, based on a novel by Gerhart
    Hauptmann)
  RATTEN, DIE (GER, 1955)

RAUB DER SABINERINNEN (GER, 1928, based on the
    play by Paul and Franz Schonthan)
  RAUB DER SABINERINNEN (GER, 1936)
  RAUB DER SABINERINNEN (GER, 1954)

RAUSCH (GER, 1919, based on the play, "Crime and Crime,"
    by August Strindberg)
  PECHE IVRESSE, LE (SWE, 1928)

RAVEN, THE see EDGAR ALLAN POE

REAL THING AT LAST, THE see MACBETH

REAR CAR see RED LIGHTS

REBECCA (UA, 1940, based on the book by Daphne du
    Maurier)
  REBECCA (NBC--TV, 1948)
  REBECCA (NBC--TV, 1950)
  REBECCA (NBC--TV, 1952)

REBECCA OF SUNNYBROOK FARM (PAR, 1917, based on
    the book by Kate Douglas Wiggin)
  REBECCA OF SUNNYBROOK FARM (FOX, 1932)
  REBECCA OF SUNNYBROOK FARM (FOX, 1938)

REBECCA THE JEWESS see IVANHOE

REBELLE, LE see VIRTUOUS SIN, THE

REBELLIOUS NOVICE, THE see SOUND OF MUSIC, THE

REBEL'S SON, THE see TARAS BULBA

RECHT AUF LIEBE, DAS (GER, 1929, source unlisted)
  RECHT AUF LIEBE, DAS (GER, 1939)

RECITS DE L'ENSEIGNE STAL, LES (SWE, 1909, based on
    the book by Johan Ludvig Runeberg)

RECKLESS AGE, THE see LOVE INSURANCE

RECREATION OF BRIAN KENT, THE see WILD BRIAN
  KENT

RED AND THE BLACK, THE (ITA, 1925, based on the book
    by Stendhal)
  GEHEIME KURIER, DER (GER, 1928)
  COURRIER OF THE KING (ITA, 1947)
  RED AND THE BLACK, THE (FRA/ITA, 1954)

RED BADGE OF COURAGE, THE (MGM, 1951, based on the
    book by Stephen Crane)
  RED BADGE OF COURAGE, THE (NBC--TV, 1974)

RED BARN CRIME: OR THE MARIA MARTEN STORY see
    MARIA MARTEN: OR THE MURDER IN THE RED
    BARN

RED CANYON see WHEN ROMANCE RIDES

RED CHINA (short) (NBC–TV, 1962, based on the life and
    times of Red China's leader, Mao Tse Tung)
  MAO TSE TUNG (short) (WOL, 1964)
  MAO TSE TUNG'S IDEALOGICAL CONTRIBUTIONS
  (short) (IND, 1964)
  MAO VS. CHIANG (short) (WOL, 1964)
  RED CHINA DIARY WITH MORLEY SAFER (CBS–TV,
  1967)
  CHINA: THE SOCIAL REVOLUTION (short) (MHF,
  1967)
  RED CHINA – MAO TSE TUNG'S SYSTEM (BRI–TV,
  1971)
  CHINA: CENTURY OF REVOLUTION (FNC, 1972)

RED CIRCLE, THE see CRIMSON CIRCLE

RED DUST (MGM, 1932, based on a play by Wilson Collison)
  CONGO MAISIE (MGM, 1940)
  MOGAMBO (MGM, 1953)

RED HORSES, THE (DEN, 1950, source unlisted)
  RED HORSES, THE (DEN, 1968)

RED INN, THE see AUBERGE ROUGE, L'

RED LIGHT STREET see IRMA LA DOUCE

RED LIGHTS (MGM, 1923, based on a story by Edward E.
  Rose)
  MURDER IN A PRIVATE CAR (MGM, 1934)

RED MILL, THE (MGM, 1927, based on the operetta by
  Victor Herbert and Henry Blossom)
  RED MILL, THE (CBS–TV, 1958)

RED PEACOCK, THE see DAME AUX CAMELIAS, LA

RED PONY, THE (REP, 1949, based on the story by John
  Steinbeck)
  RED PONY, THE (NBC–TV, 1973)

RED SHADOW, THE see DESERT SONG, THE

RED SHOES, THE (BRI, 1948, based on a fairy tale by Hans
  Christian Andersen)
  GIRL WHO DANCED INTO LIFE, THE (HUN, 1964)
  FABLES FROM HANS CHRISTIAN ANDERSEN (JAP,
  1968)

RED SNOW see IGLOO

RED SUNDAY see CUSTER'S LAST STAND

REDEEMING SIN, THE (VIT, 1925, based on the story by
  L.V. Jefferson)
  REDEEMING SIN, THE (WB, 1929)

REDEMPTION see LIVING CORPSE, THE

REDHEAD (MON, 1934, based on a book by Vera Brown)
  REDHEAD (MON, 1941)

REDHEAD AND THE COWBOY see WELLS FARGO

REDIGO see EMPIRE

REFLECTIONS ON MURDER see DIABOLIQUE

REFLUX OU L'ENFER AU PARADIS, LE see EBB TIDE

REFORMATION, THE see MARTIN LUTHER, THE
  NIGHTINGALE OF WITTENBERG

REGIMENTSTOCHTER, DIE see KING'S DAUGHTER,
  THE

REGINE (GER, 1927, based on a novel by Gottfried Keller)
  REGINE (GER, 1934)
  REGINE (GER, 1955)

REIFENDE JUGEND (GER, 1933, based on a book by Max
  Dreyer)
  REIFENDE JUGUND (GER, 1955)

REIGEN, DER (GER, 1920, based on the play by Arthur
  Schnitzler; also the basis of a musical comedy, "Rondelay,"
  in 1969)
  RONDE, LA (FRA, 1950)
  INVITATION TO THE DANCE (sequence) (MGM, 1956)
  GROSSE LIEBESSPIEL, DAS (AUS/GER, 1963)
  CIRCLE OF LOVE (FRA/ITA, 1964)
  LIEBESKARUSELL, DAS (GER, 1965)
  REIGEN (GER, 1973)
  MERRY–GO–ROUND (NLC, 1976)

REIGN OF TERROR see KATE PLUS TEN

REINE MARGOT, LA (FRA, 1910, based on a book by
  Alexandre Dumas [pere])
  REINE MARGOT, LA (FRA, 1914)
  REINE MARGOT, LA (FRA/ITA, 1954)

REISE UM DIE WELT, DIE see 'ROUND THE WORLD IN
  80 DAYS

REISENRAD, DAS see FOURPOSTER, THE

RELIGIEUSE DE MONZA, LA see NUN OF MONZA, THE

RELUCTANT DRAGON, THE (DIS, 1941, based on the book
  by Kenneth Grahame)
  RELUCTANT DRAGON, THE (ABC–TV, 1955)
  RELUCTANT DRAGON, THE (NBC–TV, 1960)

REMBRANDT (BRI, 1936, based on the life and works of
  the noted artist Rembrandt van Rijn)
  REMBRANDT (GER, 1942)
  REMBRANDT: POET OF LIGHT (short) (IFB, 1953)
  REMBRANDT (short) (MAC, n.d.)
  REMBRANDT VAN RIJN – A SELF–PORTRAIT (short)
  (EBE, 1955)
  REMBRANDT: PAINTER OF MAN (short) (COR, 1958)
  REMBRANDT AND THE BIBLE (short) (ABC--TV, 1968)
  REMBRANDT'S CHRIST (short) (TIM, 1970)
  REMBRANDT'S THREE CROSSES (short) (FNC, 1971)
  REMBRANDT (short) (GRA, 1972)
  REMBRANDT -- FECIT 1669 (HOL, 1978)

REMEMBER THE ALAMO (short) (TFC, 1950, based on a
  historical incident)
  ALAMO, THE (UA, 1960)
  SIEGE OF THE ALAMO, THE (CBS–TV, 1971)

REMEMBER THE DAY (FOX, 1941, based on a play by Philo
  Higley and Phillip Dunning)
  MEN IN HER LIFE, THE (CBS–TV, 1957)

REMEMBER THE NIGHT   (PAR, 1940, based on a screenplay
   by Preston Sturges)
   REMEMBER THE NIGHT   (NBC–TV, 1955)

RENDEZVOUS   (MGM, 1935, based on a book by Herbert O.
   Yardley)
   PACIFIC RENDEZVOUS   (MGM, 1942)

RENEGADE RANGER   see   COME ON, DANGER

REPORT   see   NOVEMBER 22 AND THE WARREN
   REPORT

REQUIEM FOR A HEAVYWEIGHT   (CBS–TV, 1956, based
   on the teleplay by Rod Serling)
   REQUIEM FOR A HEAVYWEIGHT   (BRI–TV, 1957)
   REQUIEM FOR A HEAVYWEIGHT   (COL, 1962)

REQUISITOIRE, LE   see   MANSLAUGHTER

RESCUE OF DR. BEANES: FRANCIS SCOTT KEY AND
   THE STAR–SPANGLED BANNER   see   SONG OF A
   NATION

RESERVED FOR LADIES   see   SERVICE FOR LADIES

REST IS SILENCE, THE   see   HAMLET

RESURECCION   see   RESURRECTION

RESURRECTION   (FRA, 1907, based on the book by Leo
   Tolstoy)
   RESURRECTION   (BIO, 1909)
   RESURRECTION   (RUS, 1909)
   RESURRECTION   (FRA, 1910)
   RESURRECTION   (IND, 1912)
   RESURRECTION   (RUS, 1912)
   KATIOUCHA   (JAP, 1914)
   WOMAN'S RESURRECTION, A   (FOX, 1915)
   KATIOUCHA MASLOVA   (RUS, 1915)
   RESURRECTION   (ITA, 1916)
   RESURRECTION   (ITA, 1917)
   RESURRECTION   (PAR, 1918)
   RESURRECTION   (GER, 1923)
   RESURRECTION   (UA, 1927)
   RESURRECTION   (UA, 1931)
   RESURRECCION   (MEX, 1931)
   WE LIVE AGAIN   (UA, 1934)
   RESURRECTION   (JAP, 1937)
   RESURRECTION   (CHN, 1940)
   RESURRECCION   (MEX, 1943)
   RESURRECTION   (ITA, 1943)
   RESURRECTION   (JAP, 1950)
   AUFERSTEHUNG   (FRA/GER/ITA, 1958)
   RESURRECTION   (RUS, 1960)
   MATTER OF CONSCIENCE, A   (BRI–TV, 1962)

RETIK, THE MOON MENACE   see   RADAR MEN FROM
   THE MOON

RETURN OF DRACULA   see   NOSFERATU

RETURN OF JIMMY VALENTINE, THE   (REP, 1936,
   based on a play, "Paul Armstrong")
   AFFAIRS OF JIMMY VALENTINE, THE   (REP, 1941)
      (TV title: UNFORGOTTEN CRIME)

RETURN OF JOE FORRESTER, THE   (NBC–TV, 1975,
   based on a teleplay)
   JOE FORRESTER   (series) (NBC–TV, 1975) (original

title: METRO MAN)

RETURN OF MONTE CRISTO   see   COUNT OF MONTE
   CRISTO, THE

RETURN OF PETER GRIMM, THE   (FOX, 1926, based on a
   play by David Belasco)
   RETURN OF PETER GRIMM, THE   (FOX, 1935)

RETURN OF RAFFLES   see   RAFFLES, THE AMATEUR
   CRACKSMAN

RETURN OF THE CISCO KID   see   CABALLERO'S WAY

RETURN OF THE FROG, THE   (BRI, 1939, based on the book,
   "The Indian Rubber Man," by Edgar Wallace)
   INN ON THE RIVER, THE   (GER, 1962)

RETURN OF THE RAT   see   RAT, THE

RETURN OF THE SCARLET PIMPERNEL, THE   see
   SCARLET PIMPERNEL, THE

RETURN OF THE TERROR   see   TERROR, THE

RETURN TO FANTASY ISLAND   (ABC–TV, 1977, based on
   a teleplay)
   FANTASY ISLAND   (series) (ABC–TV, 1978)

RETURN TO PARADISE   (UA, 1953, based on a book by
   James Mitchener)
   UNTIL THEY SAIL   (MGM, 1957)

RETURN TO PEYTON PLACE   see   PEYTON PLACE

RETURNING HOME   see   BEST YEARS OF OUR LIVES,
   THE

REUNION   see   REUNION IN VIENNA

REUNION IN VIENNA   (MGM, 1933, based on the play by
   Robert E. Sherwood)
   REUNION   (MGM, 1942)
   REUNION   (ABC–TV, 1952)
   REUNION IN VIENNA   (NBC–TV, 1955)
   REUNION IN VIENNA   (CBS–TV, 1958)

REVE, LE   (FRA, 1921, based on the book by Emile Zola)
   REVE, LE   (FRA, 1931)

REVE BLONDE, UNE   see   BLONDER TRAUM, EIN

REVENGE OF FRANKENSTEIN   see   FRANKENSTEIN

REVENGE OF IVANHOE, THE   see   IVANHOE

REVENGE OF THE MUSKETEERS   see   THREE MUSKE-
   TEERS, THE

REVENGE RIDER, THE   (COL, 1935, based on a screenplay
   by Ford Beebe)
   RIDERS OF BLACK RIVER   (COL, 1939)

REVIZOR   (RUS, 1915, based on the book, "The Inspector
   General," by Nicolai Gogol)
   INSPECTOR GENERAL, THE   (CZE, 1933)
   MAD NIGHT   (CHN, 1936)
   INSPECTOR GENERAL, THE   (CZE, 1937)
   INSPECTOR GENERAL, THE   (WB, 1949)

REVIZOR   (RUS, 1952)
CALZONIN INSPECTOR   (MEX, 1974)

REVOLT OF THE SLAVES   see   MYSTERY OF THE
   CATACOMBS

REVOLT OF THE TARTARS   see   MICHAEL STROGOFF

REVOLUTIONSCHOCHZEIT   (GER, 1928, based on the play
   by Sophus Michaelis)
   REVOLUTIONSCHOCHZEIT   (GER, 1937)

RHINOCEROS   (short)   (GER/POL, 1963, based on the play
   by Eugene Ionesco)
   RHINOCEROS   (AFT, 1973)

RHODA   see   MARY TYLER MOORE SHOW, THE

RHYTHM ON THE RANGE   (PAR, 1936, based on a story
   by Merwin J. Houser)
   PARDNERS   (PAR, 1956)

RICH MAN, POOR GIRL   see   IDLE RICH

RICH MAN, POOR MAN   (series)   (ABC--TV, 1976, based on
   the book by Irwin Shaw)
   RICH MAN, POOR MAN   (series)   (ABC--TV, 1976)

RICH MAN'S FOLLY   see   DOMBEY AND SON

RICHARD E. BYRD   see   EXPEDITION TO ANTARCTICA

RICHARD THE LION HEART   see   RICHARD, THE LION--
   HEARTED

RICHARD, THE LION--HEARTED   (IND, 1923, based on the
   book, "The Talisman," by Sir Walter Scott)
   KING RICHARD AND THE CRUSADERS   (WB, 1954)
   RICHARD THE LION HEART   (series)   (TV, 1963)

RICHARD II   (NBC--TV, 1954, based on the play by William
   Shakespeare)
   AGE OF KINGS, AN   (BRI--TV, 1960)

RICHARD III   (VIT, 1908, based on the play by William
   Shakespeare)
   RICHARD III   (BRI, 1911)
   KING RICHARD III   (STE, 1913)
   KING RICHARD III   (GER, 1922)
   SHOW OF SHOWS, THE   (sequence)   (WB, 1929)
   TOWER OF LONDON   (UN, 1939)
   RICHARD III   (NBC--TV, 1950)
   RICHARD III   (BRI, 1955)
   PRINCE OF PLAYERS   (sequence)   (FOX, 1955)
   AGE OF KINGS, AN   (BRI--TV, 1960)
   WAR OF THE ROSES, THE   (BRI--TV, 1964)
   TOWER OF LONDON   (UA, 1964)

RICHARD WAGNER   (GER, 1912, based on the life of the
   noted German composer)
   MAGIC FIRE   (REP, 1956)

RICHELIEU   (VIT, 1909, based on a historical figure and
   incidents)
   RICHELIEU   (FRA, c1911)
   CARDINAL'S EDICT, THE   (ED, 1911)
   RICHELIEU   (BIS, 1914)
   CARDINAL RICHELIEU   (UA, 1935)

RICHELIEU, OR THE CARDINAL'S CONSPIRACY   see
   THREE MUSKETEERS, THE

RICHEST GIRL IN THE WORLD, THE   (RKO, 1934, based
   on a screenplay by Norman Krasna)
   BRIDE BY MISTAKE   (RKO, 1944)
   RICHEST GIRL IN THE WORLD, THE   (DEN, 1960)

RICHIAMO DEL CUORE, IL   see   SARAH AND SON

RICHTER VON ZALAMEA, DER   see   ALCADE DE
   ZALAMEA, L'

RICKSHAW MAN   (JAP, 1958, source unlisted)
   LIFE OF A RICKSHAW MAN   (JAP, 1963)

RIDDLE ME THIS   see   GUILTY AS HELL

RIDDLE OF MAYERLING, THE   see   MAYERLING

RIDE HIM COWBOY   see   UNKNOWN CAVALIER

RIDE THE PINK HORSE   (UN, 1947, based on a book by
   Dorothy B. Hughes)
   HANGED MAN, THE   (UN, 1964)

RIDE TO HANGMAN'S TREE, THE   see   BLACK BART

RIDE WITH TERROR   (NBC--TV, 1963, based on a teleplay
   by Nicholas E. Baehr)
   INCIDENT, THE   (FOX, 1967)

RIDEAU ROUGE, LE   see   MACBETH

RIDERS OF BLACK RIVER   see   REVENGE RIDER, THE

RIDERS OF THE PURPLE SAGE   (FOX, 1918, based on the
   book by Zane Grey)
   RIDERS OF THE PURPLE SAGE   (FOX, 1925)
   RIDERS OF THE PURPLE SAGE   (FOX, 1931)
   RIDERS OF THE PURPLE SAGE   (FOX, 1941)

RIDERS OF THE ROCKIES   see   BORDER LAW

RIDIN' DOUBLE   (IND, 1924, based on a screenplay by Ford
   Beebe)
   OVERLAND BOUND   (UN, 1929)

RIDING HIGH   see   BROADWAY BILL and HEARTS OF
   THE WEST

RIDIN' KID FROM POWDER RIVER, THE   (UN, 1924, based
   on a book by Henry Herbert Knibbs)
   MOUNTED STRANGER   (UN, 1930)

RIEN QUE LA VERITE   see   NOTHING BUT THE TRUTH

RIGHT OF WAY   (MGM, 1915, based on the book by Sir
   Gilbert Parker)
   RIGHT OF WAY   (MGM, 1920)
   RIGHT OF WAY   (FN, 1931)

RIGHT TO BE HAPPY, THE   see   CHRISTMAS CAROL, A

RIGHT TO LIVE, THE   see   SACRED FLAME, THE

RIGHT TO THE HEART   see   WOMAN POWER

RIGOLETTO   see   FOOL'S REVENGE, A

RIKKI–TIKKI–TAVI (RUS, 1966, based on a story from "The Jungle Book" by Rudyard Kipling)
  RIKKI–TIKKI–TAVI (short) (WWS, 1973)
  RIKKI–TIKKI–TAVI (CBS–TV, 1974)

RIME OF THE ANCIENT MARINER, THE see ANCIENT MARINER, THE

RINALDO RINALDINI (GER, 1926, based on the book by Christian August Vulpius)
  RINALDO RINANDINI (GER/YUG–TV, 1967)

RING FOR CATTY see CARRY ON, NURSE

RING OF PASSION see SPIRIT OF YOUTH

RINGER, THE (BRI, 1928, based on the book, "The Gaunt Stranger," by Edgar Wallace)
  RINGER, THE (BRI, 1931)
  HEXER, DER (GER, 1932)
  JUDEMENT DE MINUIT, LE (FRA, 1933)
  GAUNT STRANGER, THE (PHANTOM STRIKES, THE) (BRI, 1938)
  GAUNT STRANGER, THE (BRI, 1952)
  MYSTERIOUS MAGICIAN, THE (HEXER, DER) (GER, 1964)

RINGO see PRINCE AND THE PAUPER, THE

RIO BRAVO (WB, 1959, remake, uncredited)
  EL DORADO (PAR, 1967)

RIO RITA (RKO, 1929, based on the musical by Guy Bolton, Fred Thompson and Harry Tierney)
  RIO RITA (MGM, 1942)
  RIO RITA (NBC–TV, 1950)

RIP VAN WINKLE (IND, 1895, based on the story by Washington Irving)
  RIP VAN WINKLE (BIO, 1896)
  RIP VAN WINKLE (LUB, 1903)
  RIP VAN WINKLE (BRI, 1903)
  RIP VAN WINKLE (FRA, 1905)
  RIP VAN WINKLE (BOS, 1908)
  RIP VAN WINKLE (SEL, 1908)
  RIP VAN WINKLE (COL, 1910)
  RIP VAN WINKLE (THA, 1910)
  RIP VAN WINKLE (REL, 1912)
  RIP VAN WINKLE (AUT, 1912)
  RIP VAN WINKLE (IND, 1912)
  RIP VAN WINKLE (VIT, 1912)
  RIP VAN WINKLE (FRA, 1912)
  RIP VAN WINKLE (BRI, 1914)
  RIP VAN WINKLE (IND, 1914)
  RIP VAN WINKLE (HOD, 1921)
  RIP VAN WINKLE (UN, 1924)
  RIP VAN WINKLE (short) (EDU, 1934)
  MOLLY MOO–COW AND RIP VAN WINKLE (short) (RKO, 1935)
  RIP VAN WINKLE (CBS–TV, 1942)
  RIP VAN WINKLE (NBC–TV, 1950)
  RIP VAN WINKLE (NBC–TV, 1953)
  RIP VAN WINKLE (NBC–TV, 1958)
  MR. MAGOO'S FAVORITE HEROES (UPA, 1964)
  TALES OF WASHINGTON IRVING (AUT–TV, 1970)

RIPOIS AND HIS NEMESIS see KNAVE OF HEARTS

RISE AND FALL OF BENITO MUSSOLINI, THE see
BENITO MUSSOLINI

RISE AND FALL OF NAZI GERMANY, THE see HITLER GANG, THE

RISE OF A DICTATOR, THE see HITLER GANG, THE

RISE OF ADOLF HITLER, THE see HITLER GANG, THE

RISE OF GREEK TRAGEDY, THE see OEDIPUS REX

RISKY BUSINESS see OKAY, AMERICA

RITA see IRON STAIR, THE

RIVALS, THE (IND, 1913, based on the play by Richard Brinsley Sheridan)
  RIVALS, THE (NBC–TV, 1950)
  RIVALS, THE (NBC–TV, 1952)
  RIVALS, THE (BRI–TV, n.d.)

RIVE GAUCHE see LAUGHTER

RIVER BOY (short) (ABC–TV, 1967, source unlisted)
  SON OF THE NILE (EGY, n.d.)

RIVER OF ROMANCE see FIGHTING COWARD, THE

RIVER'S END (FN, 1920, based on the book by James Oliver Curwood)
  RIVER'S END (WB, 1931)
  RIVER'S END (WB, 1940) (TV title: DOUBLE IDENTITY)

RIVIERE DU HIBOU, LA see OCCURRENCE AT OWL CREEK BRIDGE, AN

ROAD TO GLORY see CROIX DU BOIS

ROAD TO LIFE (RUS, 1932, based on a screenplay by Nicolai Ekk)
  WILD BOYS OF THE ROAD (WB, 1933)
  PEDAGOGICAL POEM, A (RUS, 1956)

ROAD TO PARADISE see CORNERED AND ULICKA V RAJI

ROAD WEST, THE (series) (NBC–TV, 1966, based on a teleplay)
  THIS SAVAGE LAND (UN, 1969)

ROADS OF DESTINY see FOURTH IN SALVADOR, THE

ROB ROY (BRI, 1911, based on the book by Sir Walter Scott)
  ROB ROY (FRA, 1913)
  ROB ROY (BRI, 1922)
  ROB ROY, THE HIGHLAND ROGUE (DIS, 1953)

ROB ROY, THE HIGHLAND ROGUE see ROB ROY

ROBBER, THE (GER, 1907, based on the book by Friedrich von Schiller)
  ROBBERS, THE (IND, 1913)
  ROBBER, THE (GER, 1913)

ROBBER SYMPHONY see THREEPENNY OPERA, THE

ROBBERS, THE see ROBBER, THE

ROBBER'S ROOST (FOX, 1932, based on the story by Zane Grey)
ROBBER'S ROOST (UA, 1955)

ROBBERY UNDER ARMS (AUT, 1907, based on the book by Rolf Boldrewood)
ROBBERY UNDER ARMS (AUT, 1920)
ROBBERY UNDER ARMS (BRI, 1957)

ROBERT E. LEE see UNDER SOUTHERN STARS

ROBERT FROST (short) (NBC–TV, 1958, based on the life and works of poet Robert Frost)
CONVERSATION WITH ROBERT FROST, A (short) (EBE, 1958)
LOVER'S QUARREL WITH THE WORLD, A (IND–TV, 1962)
ROBERT FROST (short) (PAR, 1972)

ROBERT UND BERTRAM (GER, 1915, source unlisted)
ROBERT UND BERTRAM (GER, 1928)
ROBERT UND BERTRAM (GER, 1939)

ROBERTA (RKO, 1935, based on the musical by Jerome Kern and Otto Harbach)
LOVELY TO LOOK AT (MGM, 1952)
ROBERTA (NBC–TV, 1955)
ROBERTA (NBC–TV, 1958)
ROBERTA (NBC–TV, 1969)

ROBIN AND MARIAN see ROBIN HOOD AND HIS MERRY MEN

ROBIN HOOD see ROBIN HOOD AND HIS MERRY MEN

ROBIN HOOD AND HIS MERRY MEN (BRI, 1908, based on a legend; also the basis for the British musical comedy, "Twang!" in 1965)
ROBIN HOOD -- OUTLAWED (BRI, 1912)
ROBIN HOOD (FRA, 1912)
ROBIN HOOD (UN, 1912)
ROBIN HOOD (THA, 1913)
IN THE DAYS OF ROBIN HOOD (BRI, 1913)
ROBIN HOOD (UA, 1922)
MERRY MEN OF SHERWOOD, THE (BRI, 1931)
ADVENTURES OF ROBIN HOOD, THE (WB, 1938)
BANDIT OF SHERWOOD FOREST (COL, 1946)
ROGUES OF SHERWOOD FOREST (COL, 1946)
PRINCE OF THIEVES (COL, 1948)
TALES OF ROBIN HOOD (LIP, 1952)
MISS ROBIN HOOD (IND, 1952)
STORY OF ROBIN HOOD, THE (RKO, 1953)
MEN OF SHERWOOD FOREST (BRI, 1954)
ROBIN HOOD (series) (CBS–TV, 1955)
SON OF ROBIN HOOD (BRI, 1959)
SWORD OF SHERWOOD FOREST (COL, 1961)
TRIUMPH OF ROBIN HOOD (ITA, 1962)
MR. MAGOO IN SHERWOOD FOREST (UPA, 1964)
ROBIN HOOD AND THE PIRATES (ITA, 1964)
ROBIN HOOD (IND, 1966)
ROCKET ROBIN HOOD AND HIS MERRY SPACE MEN (series) (TV, 1967)
LEGEND OF ROBIN HOOD, THE (NBC–TV, 1968)
CHALLENGE FOR ROBIN HOOD (BRI, 1968)
ROBIN HOOD (AUT--TV, 1970)
ROBIN HOOD, THE INVISIBLE ARCHER (ITA, 1971)
LEGEND OF ROBIN HOOD, THE (HB, 1971)
ROBIN HOOD JR. (BRI, n.d.)
ROBIN HOOD (RAN, 1972)

ROBIN HOOD (DIS, 1973)
WHEN THINGS WERE ROTTEN (series) (ABC–TV, 1975)
ROBIN HOODNIK (HB, 1975)
ROBIN AND MARION (COL, 1976)
NEW ADVENTURES OF ROBIN HOOD, THE (CBS–TV, 1977)

ROBIN HOOD AND THE PIRATES see ROBIN HOOD AND HIS MERRY MEN

ROBIN HOOD -- OUTLAWED see ROBIN HOOD AND HIS MERRY MEN

ROBIN HOOD, THE INVISIBLE ARCHER see ROBIN HOOD AND HIS MERRY MEN

ROBIN HOODNIK see ROBIN HOOD AND HIS MERRY MEN

ROBINSON CRUSOE (FRA, 1902, based on the book by Daniel Defoe)
ROBINSON CRUSOE (LUB, 1903)
ROBINSON CRUSOE (NOR, 1910)
ROBINSON CRUSOE (REX, 1913)
ROBINSON CRUSOE (UN, 1915)
ROBINSON CRUSOE (IND, 1916)
ROBINSON CRUSOE (UN, 1917)
ADVENTURES OF ROBINSON CRUSOE, THE (FRA, 1921)
ROBINSON CRUSOE (serial) (UN, 1922)
ROBINSON CRUSOE (short) (UN, 1924)
ROBINSON CRUSOE (BRI, 1927)
ADVENTURES OF ROBINSON CRUSOE (FBO, 1928)
ROBINSON CRUSOE (BRI, 1929)
MR. ROBINSON CRUSOE (UA, 1932)
ROBINSON CRUSOE (IND, 1936)
ROBINSON CRUSOE (GER, 1940)
ROBINSON CRUSOE (RUS, 1946)
ROBINSON CRUSOE (FRA, 1950)
ROBINSON CRUSOE (ITA, 1951)
ADVENTURES OF ROBINSON CRUSOE (MEX, 1954)
MISS ROBINSON CRUSOE (FOX, 1954)
ROBINSON ET LE TRIPORTEUR (FRA/SPA, 1960)
ROBINSON CRUSOE (short) (RUM, n.d.)
LEGEND OF ROBINSON CRUSOE, THE (GER, 1962)
ROBINSON CRUSOE (series) (TV, 1964)
ROBINSON CRUSOE ON MARS (PAR, 1964)
LT. ROBIN CRUSOE U.S.N. (DIS, 1966)
IMAGINE ROBINSON (FRA, 1968)
ROBINSON CRUSOE ON ICE (ABC–TV, 1972)
ROBINSON CRUSOE (RAN, 1972)
ROBINSON CRUSOE (HB, 1972)
ROBINSON CRUSOE AND THE TIGER (SPA, 1972)
ROBINSON CRUSOE (MEX, 1972)
ROBINSON CRUSOE (NBC–TV, 1974)
MAN FRIDAY (BRI, 1975)
ROBINSON CRUSOE (BRI–TV, 1975)

ROBINSON CRUSOE AND THE TIGER see ROBINSON CRUSOE

ROBINSON CRUSOE OF CLIPPER ISLAND (serial) (REP, 1936, based on a screenplay by various authors; remake is condensation of serial)
ROBINSON CRUSOE OF MYSTERY ISLAND (REP, 1955)

ROBINSON CRUSOE OF MYSTERY ISLAND see ROBINSON CRUSOE OF CLIPPER ISLAND

ROBINSON CRUSOE ON MARS   see   ROBINSON CRUSOE

ROBINSON ET LE TRIPORTEUR   see   ROBINSON CRUSOE

ROCAMBOLE   (FRA, 1913, based on a story by Ponson du
     Terrail)
   PREMIERES ARMES DE ROCAMBOLE, LES   (FRA,
     1924)
   AMOURS DE ROCAMBOLE, LES   (FRA, 1924)
   ROCAMBOLE   (FRA, 1933)
   ROCAMBOLE   (FRA/ITA, 1947)
   ROCAMBOLE   (FRA/ITA, 1962)
   ROCAMBOLE   (FRA--TV, n.d.)

ROCK--A--BYE BABY   see   MIRACLE OF MORGAN'S
     CREEK, THE

ROCKET ROBIN HOOD AND HIS MERRY SPACE MEN
     see   ROBIN HOOD AND HIS MERRY MEN

ROCKET TO THE MOON   see   TRIP TO THE MOON, A

ROCKING HORSE WINNER, THE   (BRI, 1950, based on the
     story by D.H. Lawrence)
   ROCKING HORSE WINNER, THE   (short)   (LCA, 1976)

ROCKS OF VALPRE   (BRI, 1919, based on the book by
     Ethel M. Dell)
   ROCKS OF VALPRE   (BRI, 1934)

ROCKY MOUNTAIN MYSTERY   see   GOLDEN DREAMS

ROGER--LA--HONTE   (FRA, 1922, based on the book by
     Jules Mary)
   ROGER--LA--HONTE   (FRA, 1932)
   REVANCHE DE ROGER--LA--HONTE, LA   (FRA, 1946)
   ROGER--LA--HONTE   (FRA/ITA, 1966)

ROGUE IN LOVE   (BRI, 1916, based on the book by Tom
     Gallon)
   ROGUE IN LOVE   (BRI, 1922)

ROGUE MALE   see   MANHUNT

ROGUES OF SHERWOOD FOREST   see   ROBIN HOOD
     AND HIS MERRY MEN

ROI DE PARIS, LE   (FRA, 1922, based on the book by
     Georges Ohnet)
   KONIG VON PARIS, DER   (FRA/GER, 1930)

ROI DES AULNES, LE   (FRA, 1909, based on the story,
     "Der Erlkonig," by Goethe)
   ERLKONIGS TOCHTER   (GER, 1915)
   ERLKONIG, DER   (FRA/GER, 1931)

ROI S'AMUSE, LE   (ITA, 1908, based on the novel by Victor
     Hugo and the opera by Giuseppe Verdi)
   RIGOLETTO   (FRA, 1909)
   RIGOLETTO   (ITA, 1910)
   RIGOLETTO   (GER, 1928)
   RIGOLETTO   (ITA, 1941)
   RIGOLETTO   (ITA, 1946)
   RIGOLETTO ET SA TRAGEDIE, L'ESCLAVE DU ROI
     (ITA, 1954)

ROLE OF THE WEAK, THE   see   ERIC HOFFER, THE
     PASSIONATE STATE OF MIND

ROLL ALONG COWBOY   see   DUDE RANGER

ROLLENDE KUGEL, DIE   (GER, 1919, source unlisted)
   ROLLENDE KUGEL, DIE   (GER, 1927)

ROMAN AVEC LA CONTREBASSE, LE   (RUS, 1911, based
     on the story by Anton Chekhov)
   ROMAN AVEC LA CONTREBASSE, LE   (CZE, 1949)

ROMAN DE MIGNON, LE   see   MIGNON

ROMAN DE RENARD, LE   (FRA, 1939, based on the story
     by Goethe)
   BLACK FOX, THE   (IND, 1963)

ROMAN D'UN JEUNE HOMME PAUVRE, LE   (FRA, 1911,
     based on the book by Octave Feuillet)
   DERNIER DE FRONTIGNAC, LE   (ITA, 1911)
   ROMAN D'UN JEUNE HOMME PAUVRE, LE   (ITA, 1920)
   ROMAN D'UN JEUNE HOMME PAUVRE, LE   (FRA/GER,
     1927)
   PARISIAN ROMANCE, A   (ALL, 1932)
   ROMAN D'UN JEUNE HOMME PAUVRE, LE   (FRA,
     1935)
   ROMAN D'UN JEUNE HOMME PAUVRE, LE   (ITA, 1943)
   ROMAN D'UN JEUNE HOMME PAUVRE, LE   (ITA/SPA,
     1958)

ROMAN D'UN ROI, LA   see   PRISONER OF ZENDA, THE

ROMAN D'UN SPAHI, LE   (FRA, 1914, based on a story by
     Pierre Loti)
   ROMAN D'UN SPAHI, LE   (FRA, 1936)

ROMANCE   (UA, 1920, based on the book by Edward
     Brewster Sheldon)
   ROMANCE   (MGM, 1930)

ROMANCE AND RICHES   see   AMAZING QUEST OF MR.
     ERNEST BLISS, THE

ROMANCE OF ANNIE LAURIE   see   ANNIE LAURIE

ROMANCE OF LADY HAMILTON, THE   (BRI, 1919, based
     on historical characters and incidents)
   AFFAIRS OF LADY HAMILTON, THE   (GER, 1921)
   DIVINE LADY, THE   (FN, 1929)
   THAT HAMILTON WOMAN   (UA, 1941)
   EMMA HAMILTON   (FRA/GER/ITA, 1969)
   NELSON AFFAIR, THE   (BRI, 1973)

ROMANCE OF OLD BILL, THE   see   BETTER 'OLE, THE

ROMANCE OF ROBERT BURNS, THE   see   LIFE OF
     ROBERT BURNS, THE

ROMANCE OF THE LIMBERLOST   see   GIRL OF THE
     LIMBERLOST

ROMANCE OF THE REDWOODS, A   (ART, 1918, based on
     the story, "The White Silence," by Jack London)
   ROMANCE OF THE REDWOODS, A   (COL, 1939)

ROMANCE OF THE RIO GRANDE   (FOX, 1929, based on
     the book, "Conquistador," by Katherine Fullerton
     Gerould)
   ROMANCE OF THE RIO GRANDE   (FOX, 1941)

ROMANCE ON THE HIGH SEAS   see   DESERT BRIDE, THE

ROMANCE WITH A DOUBLE BASS   see   BASS FIDDLE,
   THE

ROME EXPRESS   (BRI, 1933, based on a story by Clifford
   Grey)
   SLEEPING CAR TO TRIESTE   (BRI, 1948)

ROMEO AND JULIET   (FRA, 1900, based on the play by
   William Shakespeare; also the basis for the musical
   comedy, "Sensations," in 1970)
   ROMEO AND JULIET   (VIT, 1908)
   ROMEO AND JULIET   (ITA, 1908)
   ROMEO AND JULIET   (BRI, 1908)
   ROMEO AND JULIET   (THA, 1911)
   ROMEO AND JULIET   (ITA, 1911)
   ROMEO AND JULIET   (FRA, 1912)
   ROMEO AND JULIET   (BIO, 1914)
   ROMEO AND JULIET   (MGM, 1916)
   ROMEO AND JULIET   (FOX, 1916)
   ROMEO AND JULIET   (short)   (IND, 1917)
   ROMEO AND JULIET   (short)   (BRI, 1919)
   ROMEO AND JULIET   (FRA, n.d.)
   DOUBLING FOR ROMEO   (GOL, 1921)
   ROMEO AND JULIET   (short)   (PAT, 1924)
   TRIUMPH   (sequences)   (PAT, 1924)
   ROMEO AND JULIET   (MGM, 1936)
   SHUHADDAA EL GHARAM   (EGY, 1942)
   ROMEO AND JULIET   (MEX, 1943)
   ANJUMAN   (IN, 1948)
   AMANTS DE VERONE, LES   (FRA, 1951)
   ROMEO AND JULIET   (BRI/ITA, 1954)
   ROMEO AND JULIET   (NBC–TV, 1954)
   BALLET OF ROMEO AND JULIET, THE   (BRI, 1955)
   PRINCE OF PLAYERS   (sequence)   (FOX, 1955)
   ROMEO AND JULIET   (NBC–TV, 1957)
   ROMANOFF AND JULIET   (UN, 1961)
   WEST SIDE STORY   (UA, 1961)
   TARANTOS, LOS   (SPA, 1964)
   ROMEO AND JULIET   (ITA/SPA, 1964)
   ROMEO AND JULIET   (series)   (BRI––TV, 1965)
   ROMEO AND JULIET   (BRI, 1965)
   ROMEO AND JULIET   (BRI, 1966)
   ROMEO AND JULIET   (BRI/ITA, 1968)
   SECRET SEX LIVES OF ROMEO AND JULIET, THE
      (IND, 1969)
   SEVEN FRECKLES   (E. GER, 1978)

ROMMEL   see   DESERT VICTORY

RONDE, LA   see   REIGEN, DER

ROOM AT THE TOP   (BRI, 1959, based on the book by
   John Braine)
   ROOM AT THE TOP   (series)   (BRI––TV, 1972)

ROOM FOR ONE MORE   (WB, 1952, based on the book by
   Anna Perrot Rose)
   ROOM FOR ONE MORE   (series)   (ABC––TV, 1962)

ROOM SERVICE   (RKO, 1938, based on the play by John
   Murray and Allan Boretz)
   STEP LIVELY   (RKO, 1944)
   ROOM SERVICE   (CBS–TV, 1950)
   ROOM SERVICE   (TV, 1954)

ROOM 13   see   MYSTERIOUS MR. REEDER, THE

ROOM TO LET   see   LODGER, THE

ROOSEVELT STORY, THE   see   FIGHTING PRESIDENT,
   THE

ROOTY TOOT TOOT   see   HER MAN

ROQUEVILLARD, LES   (FRA, 1922, based on a book by
   Henry Bordeaux)
   ROQUEVILLARD, LES   (FRA, 1943)

ROSALINDA   see   FLEDERMAUS, DIE

ROSARY, THE   (SEL, 1915, based on the play by Edward E.
   Rose)
   ROSARY, THE   (SEL, 1922)

ROSE BERND   (GER, 1919, based on the book by Gerhart
   Hauptmann)
   SINS OF ROSE BERND   (GER, 1957)

ROSE EFFEUILLEE, LA   (FRA, 1925, based on the book by
   Claude Revol)
   ROSE EFFEUILLEE, LA   (FRA, 1935)

ROSE–MARIE   (MGM, 1928, based on the operetta by Rudolph
   Friml, Otto Harbach and Arthur Hammerstein)
   ROSE–MARIE   (MGM, 1936)
   ROSE–MARIE   (MGM, 1953)

ROSE OF THE RANCHO   (PAR, 1914, based on the play by
   Richard Walton Tully and David Belasco)
   ROSE OF THE RANCHO   (PAR, 1936)

ROSE OF THISTLE ISLAND, THE   see   PA LIVETS
   ODEVAGAR

ROSE OF TRALEE   (BRI, 1937, based on the story by Oswald
   Mitchell)
   ROSE OF TRALEE   (BRI, 1942)

ROSE OF WASHINGTON SQUARE   (FOX, 1939, based on
   the life of entertainer Fanny Brice)
   FUNNY GIRL   (COL, 1968)
   FUNNY LADY   (COL, 1975)

ROSE TATTOO, THE   (PAR, 1955, based on the play by
   Tennessee Williams)
   ROSE TATTOO, THE   (CAN–TV, 1964)

ROSEANNA McCOY   (GOL, 1949, based on the lives of the
   feuding families)
   HATFIELDS AND THE McCOYS, THE   (TV, 1975)

ROSEMARY'S BABY   (PAR, 1968, based on the book by
   Ira Levin)
   LOOK WHAT'S HAPPENED TO ROSEMARY'S BABY
   (ABC––TV, 1976)

ROSEN IM HERBST   see   SCHRITT VOM WEGE, DER

ROSEN IN TIROL   see   VOGELHANDLER, DER

ROSEN PA SISTELON   see   PA LIVETS ODEVAGAR

ROSENKAVALIER, DER   (AUS/GER, 1925, based on the
   story by Hugo von Hofmannsthal and the operetta by
   Richard Strauss)
   ROSENKAVALIER, DER   (AUS, 1960)

ROSENMONTAG   (GER, 1924, based on a novel by Otto

Erich Hartleben)
ROSENMONTAG (GER, 1930)
ROSENMONTAG (GER, 1955)

ROSES FROM THE SOUTH (GER, 1925, source unlisted)
ROSES FROM THE SOUTH (GER, 1934)
ROSES FROM THE SOUTH (GER, 1954)

ROSES NOIRES see SCHWARZE ROSEN

ROSETTI AND RYAN (NBC–TV, 1977, based on a teleplay)
ROSETTI AND RYAN (series) (NBC–TV, 1977)

ROSIE O'GRADY (APO, 1917, based on a story by Jo
Swerling)
AROUND THE CORNER (COL, 1930)

ROSIER DE MADAME HUSSON, LE (FRA, 1931, based on
a story by Guy de Maupassant)
ROSIER DE MADAME HUSSON, LE (FRA, 1950)

ROSITA see DON CESAR DE BAZAN

ROSS see WITH LAWRENCE IN ARABIA

ROTE HERGERGE, DIE (FRA, 1909, source unlisted)
ROTE HERGERGE, DIE (FRA, 1922)
ROTE HERGERGE, DIE (FRA, 1951)

ROTE KREIS, DER see CRIMSON CIRCLE

ROTE MUHLE, DIE (GER, 1921, source unlisted)
ROTE MUHLE, DIE (GER, 1940)

ROTE REITER, DER (GER, 1923, based on the book by
Franz Xavier Kappus)
ROTE REITER, DER (GER, 1935)

ROTHSCHILDS, THE see HOUSE OF ROTHSCHILD, THE

ROUE, LA (FRA, 1922, based on a screenplay by Abel Gance)
ROUE, LE (WHEELS OF FATE) (FRA, 1956)

ROUGE AND TEARS see STREET ANGEL

'ROUND THE WORLD IN 80 DAYS (IND, 1914, based on
the book, "Around the World in 80 Days," by Jules
Verne)
REISE UM DIE WELT, DIE (GER, 1919)
AROUND THE WORLD IN 80 DAYS (series) (UN, 1922)
AROUND THE WORLD IN 80 MINUTES (UA, 1931)
AROUND THE WORLD IN 80 DAYS (UA, 1956)
AROUND THE WORLD IN 18 MINUTES (short) (GO,
1960)
THREE STOOGES GO AROUND THE WORLD IN A
DAZE, THE (COL, 1963)
AROUND THE WORLD IN 79 DAYS (series) (ABC–TV,
1969)
AROUND THE WORLD IN 80 DAYS (RAN, 1972)
AROUND THE WORLD IN 80 DAYS (series) (AUT–TV,
1972)

ROUND–UP, THE (PAR, 1920, based on the play by Edmund
Day)
ROUND–UP, THE (PAR, 1941)

ROXIE HART see CHICAGO

ROYAL BED, THE (UA, 1930, based on the play, "The
Queen's Husband," by Robert E. Sherwood)
ECHEC AU ROI (FRA, 1931)

ROYAL BOX, THE (SEL, 1914, based on a play by Charles
Coghlan)
ROYAL BOX, THE (WB, 1930)

ROYAL DESTINY see KING IS DEAD, LONG LIVE THE
QUEEN, THE

ROYAL DIVORCE see NAPOLEON – MAN OF DESTINY

ROYAL FAMILY, THE see KING IS DEAD, LONG LIVE
THE QUEEN, THE and ROYAL FAMILY OF BROAD–
WAY, THE

ROYAL FAMILY OF BROADWAY, THE (PAR, 1930, based
on the play by Edna Ferber and George S. Kaufman)
ROYAL FAMILY, THE (ABC–TV, 1951)
ROYAL FAMILY, THE (CBS–TV, 1954)
ROYAL FAMILY, THE (PBS–TV, 1977)

ROYAL SCANDAL, A see FORBIDDEN PARADISE

RUBY AND OSWALD see NOVEMBER 22 AND THE
WARREN REPORT

RUDDIGORE (BRI–TV, 1965, based on the operetta by
Gilbert and Sullivan)
RUDDIGORE (BRI, 1967)

RUDOLPH, THE RED--NOSED REINDEER (short) (IND,
1948, based on a story by Robert L. May)
RUDOLPH, THE RED--NOSED REINDEER (NBC--TV,
1967)

RUGGLES OF RED GAP (ESS, 1918, based on the book by
Harry Leon Wilson)
RUGGLES OF RED GAP (PAR, 1923)
RUGGLES OF RED GAP (PAR, 1935)
FANCY PANTS (PAR, 1950)
RUGGLES OF RED GAP (CBS–TV, 1951)
RUGGLES OF RED GAP (NBC–TV, 1957)

RUISSEAU, LE see VIRTUOUS MODEL, THE

RUKMANI HARAN (IN, 1934, based on an Indian legend)
RUKMANI HARAN (IN, 1937)

RULING PASSION, THE (UA, 1922, based on the story,
"Idle Hands," by Earl Derr Biggers)
MILLIONAIRE, THE (WB, 1931)
THAT WAY WITH WOMEN (WB, 1947)

RUMPELSTILTSKIN (INC, 1915, based on the fairy tale)
RUMPELSTILTSKIN (short) (EBE, 1952)
RUMPELSTILTSKIN (NBC–TV, 1958)
TALE OF RUMPELSTILTSKIN (short) (EBE, 1974)
RUMPELSTILTSKIN (IND–TV, 1978)

RUN FOR THE SUN see MOST DANGEROUS GAME, THE

RUNAROUND, THE see IT HAPPENED ONE NIGHT

RUNWAY ZERO 8 see FLIGHT INTO DANGER

RUPERT OF HENTZAU (FRA, 1915, based on the novel by
Sir Anthony Hope)

RUPERT OF HENTZAU   (BRI, 1915)
RUPERT OF HENTZAU   (SEZ, 1923)

RUSH TO JUDGMENT   see   NOVEMBER 22 AND THE
     WARREN REPORT

RUSLAN AND LUDMILLA   (RUS, 1914, based on the story
     by Alexander Pushkin and the opera by Mikhail Glinka)
RUSLAN AND LUDMILLA   (RUS, 1939)
RUSLAN AND LUDMILLA   (RUS, 1972)

RUSTLER'S VALLEY   (PAR, 1937, based on the book by

Clarence E. Mulford)
LOST CANYON   (UA, 1942)

RUTH   see   BOOK OF RUTH, THE

RUY BLAS   (IND, 1909, based on the book by Victor Hugo)
RUY BLAS   (FRA, 1912)
RUY BLAS   (MUT, 1914)
RUY BLAS   (FRA, 1944)
DELUSIONS OF GRANDEUR   (FRA, 1971)

RUY BLAS   see also   DON CESAR DE BAZAN

S.O.S. EISBERG see ATLANTIC

SABBATH OF THE BLACK CAT see EERIE TALES

SABER OF LONDON see MARK SABER MYSTERY
 THEATER

SABINE UND THRE 100 MANNER see 100 MEN AND A
 GIRL

SABOTEURS OF TELEMARK see OPERATION
 SWALLOW

SABRINA, THE TEEN–AGE WITCH see ARCHIE'S FUN
 HOUSE

SABU AND THE MAGIC RING see ARABIAN NIGHTS

SACCO AND VANZETTI see WINTERSET

SACCO AND VANZETTI STORY, THE see WINTERSET

SACRED FLAME, THE (WB, 1929, based on the play by
 W. Somerset Maugham)
 SACRED FLAME, THE (GER, 1930)
 LLAMA SEGRADA, LA (SPA, 1932)
 RIGHT TO LIVE, THE (WB, 1935)

SACRIFICE, THE (BIO, 1909, based on the story, "Gift of
 the Magi," by O. Henry)
 GIFT OF THE MAGI, THE (LOVE'S SURPRISES ARE
 FUTILE) (RUS, 1916)
 GIFT OF THE MAGI, THE (IND, 1917)
 O. HENRY'S FULL HOUSE (sequence) (FOX, 1952)
 GIFT OF THE MAGI (CBS–TV, 1958)
 GIFT OF LOVE, THE (NBC–TV, 1978)

SADIE THOMPSON (UA, 1928, based on the story, "Miss
 Thompson," by W. Somerset Maugham; also appeared as
 a musical comedy, "Sadie Thompson," in 1944)
 RAIN (UA, 1932)
 DIRTY GERTIE FROM HARLEM, USA (IND, 1946)
 MISS SADIE THOMPSON (COL, 1954)
 RAIN (BRI–TV, 1970)

SADKO see SINBAD THE SAILOR

SAGA OF BILLY THE KID, THE see BILLY THE KID

SAGRENSKA KOZA see PEAU D'ANE

SAHARA see THIRTEEN, THE

SAILOR BEWARE see FLEET'S IN, THE

SAILOR OF THE KING see BROWN ON 'RESOLUTION'

SAILOR'S LADY see SHE LEARNED ABOUT SAILORS

ST. ELMO (IND, 1914, based on the book by Auguste J.
 Evans)
 ST. ELMO (BRI, 1923)

ST. EXUPERY see PLEIN CIEL

ST. FRANCIS OF ASSISI (MEX, 1943, based on the life of
 the Saint)
 ST. FRANCIS OF ASSISI (ITA, c1955)
 FRANCIS OF ASSISI (FOX, 1961)

BROTHER FRANCIS AND SISTER EARTH (BRI–TV,
 1972)
 BROTHER SUN, SISTER MOON (PAR, 1973)

SAINT IN PALM SPRINGS, THE (RKO, 1941, based on a
 novel by Leslie Charteris)
 SAINT MENE LA DANSE, LE (FRA, 1960)

SAINT JOAN see JOAN OF ARC

SAINT JOHNSON see LAW AND ORDER

ST. VALENTINE'S DAY MASSACRE, THE see SEVEN
 AGAINST THE WALL

SAINTE PECHERESSE, LA see CONVERSION OF FERDYS
 PISTORA, THE

SAKIMA AND THE MASKED MARVEL see MASKED
 MARVEL, THE

SAL OF SINGAPORE (PAT, 1929, based on the book, "The
 Sentimentalist," by Dale Collins)
 HIS WOMAN (PAR, 1931)

SALAMBO (ITA, 1913, based on the book by Gustave
 Flaubert)
 SALAMMBO (AUS, 1924)
 SALAMMBO (FRA, 1925)
 LOVES OF SALAMBO, THE (ITA, 1960)

SALAMMBO see SALAMBO

SALGA DE LA COCINA see COME OUT OF THE KITCHEN

SALLY BISHOP (BRI, 1916, based on the book by Ernest
 Temple Thurston)
 SALLY BISHOP (BRI, 1923)
 SALLY BISHOP (BRI, 1932)

SALLY IN OUR ALLEY (BRI, 1916, based on the book by
 Ernest Temple Thurston)
 SALLY IN OUR ALLEY (BRI, 1931)

SALLY, IRENE AND MARY (MGM, 1925, based on the play
 by Edward Dowling and Cyrus Wood)
 SALLY, IRENE AND MARY (FOX, 1938)

SALLY OF THE SAWDUST (UA, 1925, based on the play,
 "Poppy," by Dorothy Donnelly)
 POPPY (PAR, 1936)

SALOME (GER, 1902, based on the play by Oscar Wilde and
 the opera by Richard Strauss)
 SALOME (VIT, 1908)
 SALOME (ITA, 1909)
 SALOME (ITA, 1913)
 SALOME (VIT, 1913)
 SALOME (FOX, 1918)
 MODERN SALOME, A (MGM, 1920)
 SALOME (GER, 1922)
 SALOME (ALL, 1922)
 SALOME (IND, 1923)
 SALOME (COL, 1953)
 SALOME (CBS–TV, 1955)
 SALOME (ITA, 1972)
 SALOME (PBS–TV, 1972)
 SALOME (SPA–TV, 1977)

SALOMY JANE   (IND, 1914, based on the story, "Salome Jane's Kiss," by Bret Harte)
  SALOMY JANE   (PAR, 1923)
  WILD GIRL   (FOX, 1932)

SALTO MORTALE   (GER, 1931, based on the book by Alfred Machard)
  SALTO MORTALE   (GER, 1953)

SALVATION NELL   (WOR, 1915, based on the book by Edward Brewster Sheldon)
  SALVATION NELL   (FN, 1921)
  SALVATION NELL   (TIF, 1931)

SALZBURG EVERYMAN, THE   see   EVERYMAN

SAM HOUSTON   see   CONQUERER, THE

SAM "LIGHTNIN' " HOPKINS   see   BLUES ACCORDING TO LIGHTNIN' HOPKINS, THE

SAMMY   see   EDDIE

SAMSON   see   SAMSON AND DELILAH

SAMSON AND DELILAH   (FRA, 1903, based on the Bible story)
  SAMSON AND DELILAH   (FRA, 1908)
  SAMSON'S BETRAYAL   (short)   (KLE, 1910)
  SAMSON   (UN, 1914)
  SAMSON   (UN, 1915)
  SAMSON AND DELILAH   (AUS, 1922)
  SAMSON AND DELILAH   (short)   (BRI, 1922)
  SAMSON AND DELILAH   (GER, 1922)
  SAMSON AND DELILAH   (short)   (BRI, 1927)
  SAMSON AND DELILAH   (PAR, 1949)

SAN LAISSER D'ADRESSE   (FRA, n.d., based on a screenplay by Jean Paul la Chanois)
  TAXI   (FOX, 1953)

SAN QUENTIN STORY, THE   see   DUFFY OF SAN QUENTIN

SANCTUARY   see   STORY OF TEMPLE DRAKE, THE

SAND, OR PETER AND THE WOLF   see   PETER AND THE WOLF

SANDERS OF THE RIVER   (BRI, 1935, based on the book by Edgar Wallace)
  DEATH DRUMS ALONG THE RIVER   (BRI, 1963)
  COAST OF SKELETONS   (BRI, 1964)

SANFORD AND SON   see   STEPTOE AND SON

SANFORD ARMS   see   STEPTOE AND SON

SANGEN OM DEN ELDRODA BLOMMAN   (SWE, 1919, source unlisted)
  SANGEN OM DEN ELDRODA BLOMMAN   (SWE, 1934)
  SANGEN OM DEN ELDRODA BLOMMAN   (SWE, 1956)

SANS DOT   (RUS, 1912, based on the play by Alexandre Ostrovsky)
  SANS DOT   (RUS, 1937)

SANS FAMILLE   (FRA, 1913, based on the book by Hector Malot)

SANS FAMILLE   (FRA, 1926)
SANS FAMILLE   (FRA, 1934)
SENZA FAMIGLIA   (ITA, 1944)
SENZA FAMIGLIA   (FRA/ITA, 1958)

SANT TUKARAM   (IN, 1936, based on an Indian legend)
  SANT THUKARAM   (IN, 1963)

SANTARELLINA   see   MAM'ZELLE NITOUCHE

SANTO AGAINST THE STRANGLER   see   PHANTOM OF THE OPERA, THE

SAP, THE   (WB, 1926, based on the play by William A. Grew)
  SAP, THE   (WB, 1929)

SAPHEAD, THE   see   LAMB, THE

SAPHO   (LUB, 1900, based on the book by Alphonse Daudet)
  SAPHO   (ITA, 1908)
  SAPHO   (MAJ, 1913)
  SAPHO   (FRA, 1913)
  ETERNAL SAPHO, THE   (FOX, 1916)
  SAPHO   (PAR, 1917)
  SAPHO   (GER, 1920)
  INSPIRATION   (MGM, 1931)
  SAPHO   (FRA, 1934)
  SAPHO   (ARG, 1943)

SARAH   (CAN–TV, 1976, based on the life of the noted French actress, Sarah Bernhardt)
  INCREDIBLE SARAH, THE   (IND, 1976)

SARAH AND SON   (PAR, 1930, based on the book by Timothy Shea)
  CANCAO DO BERCO   (POR, 1930)
  TODA UNA VIDA   (SPA, 1931)
  RICHIAMO DEL CUORE, IL   (ITA, 1931)
  TOUTE SA VIE   (FRA, 1930)

SARAJEVO   see   KLEINE HERZOG, DER

SARATI LE TERRIBLE   (FRA, 1923, based on the book by Jean Vignaud)
  SARATI LE TERRIBLE   (FRA, 1938)

SARGE: THE BADGE OR THE CROSS   (NBC–TV, 1971, based on a teleplay)
  SARGE   (series)   (NBC–TV, 1971)

SATAN   see   SATAN'S SISTER

SATAN MET A LADY   see   MALTESE FALCON, THE

SATAN'S FIVE WARNINGS   (SPA, 1938, source unlisted)
  SATAN'S FIVE WARNINGS   (MEX, 1945)
  SATAN'S FIVE WARNINGS   (POR/SPA, 1969)

SATAN'S SATELLITES   see   ZOMBIES OF THE STRATOSPHERE

SATAN'S SISTER   (BRI, 1925, based on the play, "Satan," by Henry de Vere Stacpoole)
  TRUTH ABOUT SATAN, THE   (UN, 1965)

SATCHMO THE GREAT   (UA, 1957, based on the life of the noted jazz musician)
  BOY FROM NEW ORLEANS: A TRIBUTE TO LOUIS ARMSTRONG   (TV, 1971)

SATI SAVITRI (IN, 1926, based on an Indian legend)
  SATI SAVITRI (IN, 1932)
  SATI SAVITRI (IN, 1933)
  SATI SAVITRI (IN, 1934)

SATI SULOCHANA (IN, 1920, based on an Indian legend)
  SATI SULOCHANA (IN, 1934)
  SATI SULOCHANA (IN, 1936)
  SATI SULOCHANA (IN, 1937)

SATI VIJAY (IN, 1930, based on the book, "Ramayana,"
    by Valmiki)
  SATI VIJAY (IN, 1948)
  LAB KUSH (IN, 1967)
  KINGDOM OF RAM, THE (IN, 1967)

SATURDAY AFTERNOON (short) (PAT, 1926, based on a
    screenplay)
  HALF HOLIDAY (short) (EDU, 1931)

SATURDAY NIGHT AT FORT APACHE (short) (NBC–
    TV, 1972, based on documentary material from the
    Bronx police station)
  FORT APACHE, THE BRONX (BRY, 1976)

SATURDAY NIGHT FEVER (PAR, 1977, based on a screen--
    play by Norman Wexler)
  STAYING ALIVE (series) (ABC--TV, 1979)

SATURDAY NIGHT KID see LOVE 'EM AND LEAVE 'EM

SATURDAY'S CHILDREN (FN, 1929, based on the play by
    Maxwell Anderson)
  MAYBE IT'S LOVE (FN, 1934)
  SATURDAY'S CHILDREN (WB, 1940)
  SATURDAY'S CHILDREN (CBS--TV, 1950)
  SATURDAY'S CHILDREN (ABC--TV, 1952)

SATY DELAJI CLOVEKA see MUCH ADO ABOUT
    NOTHING

SATYRICON (ITA, 1968, based on stories by Petrone)
  SATYRICON (ITA, 1969)

SAUL (FRA, 1907, based on the Bible story)
  SAUL AND DAVID (VIT, 1909)
  SAUL AND DAVID (KLE, 1911)
  SAUL AND DAVID (VIT, 1911)
  SAUL AND DAVID (BRI, 1911)
  SAUL AND DAVID (PAT, 1912)
  SAUL AND DAVID (FRA, 1912)
  SAUL AND DAVID (ITA/SPA, 1968)

SAUL AND DAVID see SAUL

SAVAGE PAMPAS see PAMPA BARBERA

SAY GOODBYE AGAIN see NEXT TIME WE LOVE

SCALAWAG see PIRATE'S TREASURE

SCAMPOLO (ITA, 1928, based on the book by Dario
    Niccodemi)
  SCAMPOLO (AUS/GER, 1932)
  SCAMPOLO (ITA, 1941)
  SCAMPOLO '53 (FRA/ITA, 1953)
  SCAMPOLO (GER, 1957)

SCAMPOLO '53 see SCAMPOLO

SCANDAL, THE (FRA, 1916, based on a book by Henry
    Bataille)
  SCANDAL, THE (BRI/FRA, 1923)
  SCANDAL, THE (FRA, 1936)

SCANDAL IN BUDAPEST (GER, 1933, source unlisted)
  PARTON TEVEDTEM (HUN, 1933)

SCANDALS OF CLOCHEMERLE, THE (FRA, 1950, source
    unlisted)
  EASIEST PROFESSION, THE (FRA, 1960)
  CLOCHEMERLE (BRI–TV, 1972)

SCARABEE D'OR, LE (FRA, 1911, based on the story, "The
    Gold Bug," by Edgar Allan Poe)
  MANFISH (UA, 1956)

SCARAMOUCHE (MGM, 1923, based on the book by Rafael
    Sabatini)
  SCARAMOUCHE (MGM, 1952)
  SCARAMOUCHE (FRA/ITA/SPA, 1963)
  LOVES AND TIMES OF SCARAMOUCHE, THE (EMB,
    1976)

SCARECROW see LORD FEATHERTOP

SCARED STIFF see GHOST BREAKER, THE

SCARLET ANGEL see FLAME OF NEW ORLEANS, THE

SCARLET CAR, THE (UN, 1917, based on the book by
    Richard Harding Davis)
  SCARLET CAR, THE (UN, 1923)

SCARLET DAREDEVIL, THE see SCARLET PIMPERNEL,
    THE

SCARLET EMPRESS, THE see ADVENTUROUS LIFE OF
    CATHERINE I OF RUSSIA

SCARLET LETTER, THE (FOX, 1917, based on the book by
    Nathaniel Hawthorne)
  SCARLET LETTER, THE (SEZ, 1920)
  SCARLET LETTER, THE (short) (BRI, 1922)
  SCARLET LETTER, THE (MGM, 1926)
  SCARLET LETTER, THE (MAJ, 1934)
  SCARLET LETTER, THE (CBS–TV, 1950)
  SCARLET LETTER, THE (CBS–TV, 1952)
  SCARLET LETTER, THE (NBC–TV, 1954)
  SCARLET LETTER, THE (GER, 1973)

SCARLET PEN, THE see CORBEAU, LE

SCARLET PIMPERNEL, THE (FOX, 1917, based on the story
    by Baroness Orczy)
  ELUSIVE PIMPERNELL, THE (BRI, 1919)
  SCARLET DAREDEVIL, THE (WW, 1928) (British title:
    TRIUMPH OF THE SCARLET PIMPERNEL, THE)
  SCARLET PIMPERNEL, THE (UA, 1935)
  RETURN OF THE SCARLET PIMPERNEL, THE (BRI,
    1938)
  PIMPERNEL SMITH (BRI, 1942)
  ELUSIVE PIMPERNEL, THE (BRI, 1950)
  SCARLET PIMPERNEL, THE (CBS--TV, 1960)

SCARLET STREET see CHIENNE, LA

SCARS OF DRACULA see NOSFERATU

SCENES FROM A MARRIAGE (series) (SWE–TV, 1974,
    based on a screenplay by Ingmar Bergman)
  SCENES FROM A MARRIAGE (SWE, 1975)

SCHALTEN UM AUF HOLLYWOOD, WIR see HOLLY–
    WOOD REVUE OF 1929

SCHATTEN, DER see VIOLANTHA

SCHATZE DES TEUFELS, DIE see FRAULEIN VON
    SCUDERI, DAS

SCHELME IM PARADIES, DIE see GUEUX AU PARADIS,
    LES

SCHEMING SCHEMERS see A–PLUMBING WE WILL GO

SCHICKSAL (GER, 1924, based on the book by Guido
    Kreutzer)
  SCHICKSAL (GER, 1942)

SCHIFF, DAS (ITA, 1911, based on a play by Gabriele
    d'Annunzio)
  SCHIFF, DAS (ITA, 1921)

SCHIFF IN NOT (GER, 1928, source unlisted)
  SCHIFF IN NOT (GER, 1932)

SCHINDERHANNES (GER, 1927, based on the play by Carl
    Zuckmayer)
  SCHINDERHANNES (GER, 1958)

SCHLOSS HUBERTUS (GER, 1934, based on a book by Lud--
    wig Ganghofer)
  SCHLOSS HUBERTUS (GER, 1954)
  SCHLOSS HUBERTUS (GER, 1974)

SCHLOSS VOGELOD see VOGELOD CASTLE

SCHLUSSAKKORD (GER, 1936, source unlisted)
  SCHLUSSAKKORD (GER, 1960)

SCHNEIDER WIBBEL (GER, 1931, based on the book by
    Hans Mueller--Schlosser)
  SCHNEIDER WIBBEL (GER, 1939)
  SONNTAGSKIND, DAS (GER, 1956)

SCHONE ABENTEUER, DAS (GER, 1924, based on the book
    by Antonia Ridge)
  SCHONE ABENTEUER, DAS (GER, 1932)
  SCHONE ABENTEUER, DAS (GER, 1959)

SCHONEN TAGE IN ARANJUEZ, DIE (GER, 1933, based
    on a play by Hans Szekely and R.A. Stemmle)
  ADIEU, LES BEAUX JOURS (FRA, 1933)
  DESIRE (PAR, 1936)

SCHOOL FOR SCANDAL (KAL, 1914, based on the play by
    Richard Brinsley Sheridan; also the basis for a musical
    comedy, "Lady Teazle," in 1904)
  SCHOOL FOR SCANDAL (BRI, 1923)
  SCHOOL FOR SCANDAL (BRI, 1930)
  SCHOOL FOR SCANDAL (CBS--TV, 1950)
  SCHOOL FOR SCANDAL (TV, 1966)

SCHOOL FOR WIVES (VIC, 1925, based on the book, "The
    House of Lynch," by Leonard Merrick)
  SCHOOL FOR WIVES (ABC--TV, 1956)

SCHRITT VOM WEGE, DER (GER, 1939, based on a novel
    by Theodor Fontane)
  ROSEN IM HERBST (GER, 1955)
  EFFI BRIEST (GER–TV, 1970)

SCHUBERT, THE MELODY MASTER see SCHUBERT'S
    FRUHLINGSTRAUM

SCHUBERT'S FRUHLINGSTRAUM (GER, 1931, based on
    the life of composer Franz Schubert; also the basis for
    two operettas, "Blossom Time" and "Das Dreimaederl–
    haus")
  LIESE FLEHEN MEINE LIEDER (GER, 1933)
  UNFINISHED SYMPHONY (BRI, 1934)
  SERENADE (FRA, 1940)
  NEW WINE (SCHUBERT, THE MELODY MASTER) (UA,
    1941)
  SCHUBERT AND HIS MUSIC (short) (COR, 1954)

SCHULD, DIE (GER, 1918, based on the play by Adolph
    Muellner)
  SCHULD, DIE (GER, 1924)

SCHULDIG! (GER, 1913, based on the book by Richard
    Voss)
  SCHULDIG! (GER, 1927)

SCHUSSE UNTERM GALGEN see KIDNAPPED

SCHUTZENLIESL (GER, 1926, source unlisted)
  SCHUTZENLIESL (GER, 1954)

SCHWACHE STUNDE, DIE (GER, 1919, source unlisted)
  SCHWACHE STUNDE, DIE (GER, 1943)

SCHWARZE AUGEN see DARK EYES

SCHWARZE ROSEN (GER, 1935, based on a story by Paul
    Martin, Curt Braun and Salter Supper)
  ROSES NOIRES (FRA, 1935)
  DID I BETRAY? (BRI, 1936)

SCHWARZE SCHAF, DAS (GER, 1943, based on a book by
    G.K. Chesterton)
  SCHWARZE SCHAF, DAS (GER, 1960)

SCHWARZE WALFISCH, DER see FANNY

SCHWARTZWALDMADEL (GER, 1929, based on an opera
    by August Neidhard)
  SCHWARTZWALDMADEL (GER, 1933)
  SCHWARTZWALDMADEL (GER, 1950)

SCHWEIGEN IM WALDE, DAS (GER, 1923, based on a book
    by Ludwig Ganghofer)
  SCHWEIGEN IM WALDE, DAS (GER, 1937)
  SCHWEIGEN IM WALDE, DAS (GER, 1955)

SCHWEJKS FLEGELJAHRE see GOOD SOLDIER
    SCHWEIK, THE

SCHWEIK'S NEW ADVENTURE see GOOD SOLDIER
    SCHWEIK, THE

SCOTLAND: BACKGROUND FOR LITERATURE see
    LIFE OF ROBERT BURNS, THE

SCOTLAND YARD (FOX, 1930, based on a screenplay by
    Garrett Fort)

IMPOSTER, EL (SPA, 1931)

SCOTT ANTARCTIC EXPEDITION (WITH CAPTAIN
    SCOTT, R.N., TO THE SOUTH POLE) (BRI, 1911,
    based on the exploits of the noted explorer)
  GREAT WHITE SILENCE, THE (BRI, 1911)
  NINETY DEGREES SOUTH (BRI, 1930)
  SCOTT OF THE ANTARCTIC (BRI, 1949)
  SCOTT'S LAST JOURNEY (MHF, 1962)
  TRIO (sequence) (MGM–TV, 1963)

SCOTT JOPLIN (short) (PYR, 1977, based on the life and
    works of the noted jazz composer)
  SCOTT JOPLIN – KING OF RAGTIME (UN, 1977)

SCOTT OF THE ANTARCTIC see SCOTT'S ANTARCTIC
    EXPEDITION

SCOTT'S LAST JOURNEY see SCOTT'S ANTARCTIC
    EXPEDITION

SCREENTEST see BELOVED INFIDEL

SCROOGE see CHRISTMAS CAROL, A

SCULPTOR'S LANDSCAPE, A see HENRY MOORE

SEA BEAST, THE (WB, 1925, based on the book, "Moby
    Dick," by Herman Melville)
  MOBY DICK (WB, 1930)
  DAMON DES MEERS, DER (GER, 1931)
  MOBY DICK (NBC–TV, 1954)
  STORY OF MOBY DICK, THE (short) (MHF, 1954)
  MOBY DICK (WB, 1956)
  MAGOO AT SEA (UPA, 1964)
  MOBY DICK (CBS–TV, n.d.)

SEA GOD, THE (PAR, 1930, based on the story, "Lost God,"
    by John Russell)
  SEA GOD, THE (FRA, 1930)
  DIOS DEL MAR, EL (MEX, 1930)

SEA GULL, THE (VIT, 1914, based on the play by Anton
    Chekhov)
  WOMAN FROM THE SEA (unreleased) (UA, 1926)
  SEA GULL, THE (WB, 1968)
  SEA GULL, THE (RUS, 1971)
  CHAIKA (RUS, 1973)
  SEA GULL, THE (ITA–TV, 1977)

SEA GYPSIES, THE see TUNDRA

SEA HAWK, THE (FN, 1924, based on the book by Rafael
    Sabatini)
  SEA HAWK, THE (WB, 1940)

SEA SHADOW, THE see LEGENDE DES ONDINES

SEA WOLF, THE see SEA WOLVES, THE

SEA WOLVES, THE (IND, 1910, based on the book, "The
    Sea Wolf," by Jack London)
  SEA WOLF, THE (BOS, 1913)
  SEA WOLF, THE (PAR, 1920)
  SEA WOLF, THE (INC, 1925)
  SEA WOLF, THE (FOX, 1930)
  SEA WOLF, THE (WB, 1941)
  BARRICADE (WB, 1950)
  WOLF LARSEN (AA, 1958)

LARSEN: WOLF OF THE SEVEN SEAS (ITA, 1975)

SEALED ROOM, THE (n.d., 1909, based on the story, "The
    Cask of Amontillado," by Edgar Allan Poe)
  CASK OF AMONTILLADO (BRA, 1954)
  TALES OF TERROR (sequence) (AI, 1962)
  MASTER OF HORROR (MEX, 1965)
  HISTOIRES EXTRAORDINAIRES (SPIRITS OF THE
    DEAD) (FRA, 1969)

SEASON IN SALZBURG see UND DIE MUSIK SPIELT
    DAZU

SECOND BEST BED see TAMING OF THE SHREW, THE

SECOND FLOOR MYSTERY see BLIND ADVENTURE

SECOND GREATEST SEX, THE see WARRIOR'S HUS--
    BAND, THE

SECOND HUNDRED YEARS, THE see ADVENTURER,
    THE

SECOND LIFE, THE see THREE SINNERS

SECOND MRS. TANQUERAY, THE (BRI, 1916, based on the
    play by Sir Arthur Wing Pinero)
  SECOND MRS. TANQUERAY, THE (VIT, 1917)
  SECOND MRS. TANQUERAY, THE (ITA, 1922)
  SECOND MRS. TANQUERAY, THE (BRI, 1952)
  SECOND MRS. TANQUERAY, THE (BRI–TV, n.d.)

SECOND WIFE (RKO, 1930, based on the play, "All the
    King's Men," by Fulton Oursler)
  SECOND WIFE (RKO, 1936)

SECRET AGENT X--9 (serial) (UN, 1936, based on a screen--
    play by various authors)
  SECRET AGENT X--9 (serial) (UN, 1945)

SECRET CALL see TELEPHONE GIRL

SECRET DE LA MAISON SEIGNEURIALE, LE (RUS, 1913,
    based on the book, "Le Pensionnaire," by Ivan Turgenev)
  PENSIONNAIRE, LE (RUS, 1953)

SECRET DU DOCTEUR, LE see DOCTOR'S SECRET, THE

SECRET FOUR, THE see FOUR JUST MEN

SECRET GARDEN, THE (PAR, 1919, based on the book by
    Frances Hodgson Burnett)
  SECRET GARDEN, THE (MGM, 1949)

SECRET HOUR, THE (PAR, 1928, based on the play, "They
    Knew What They Wanted," by Sidney Howard; also the
    basis for the musical drama, "The Most Happy Fella," in
    1956)
  LADY TO LOVE, A (MGM, 1930)
  SEHNSUCHT JEDER FRAU, DIE (GER, 1930)
  THEY KNEW WHAT THEY WANTED (RKO, 1940)
  THEY KNEW WHAT THEY WANTED (ABC–TV, 1952)
  UNHOLY WIFE, THE (UN, 1957)

SECRET LIFE OF ADOLF HITLER, THE see HITLER
    GANG, THE

SECRET MARK OF D'ARTAGNAN, THE see THREE
    MUSKETEERS, THE

SECRET OF DEEP HARBOR see I COVER THE WATER-
FRONT

SECRET OF DORIAN GRAY, THE see PICTURE OF
DORIAN GRAY, THE

SECRET OF MADAME BLANCHE, THE see LADY, THE

SECRET OF MAYERLING, THE see MAYERLING

SECRET OF MICHELANGELO, THE see MICHELANGELO

SECRET OF MONTE CRISTO, THE see COUNT OF
MONTE CRISTO, THE

SECRET OF PANCHO VILLA, THE see LIFE OF VILLA

SECRET OF POLICHINELLE, THE (FRA, 1913, based on
the book, "Le Secret de Polichinelle," by Pierre Wolff)
SECRET OF POLICHINELLE, THE (ITA, 1913)
SECRET OF POLICHINELLE, THE (FRA, 1922)
SECRET OF POLICHINELLE, THE (FRA, 1936)
FAMILY SECRET, THE (SWE, 1936)

SECRET OF SIGMUND FREUD, THE (series) (CBS–TV,
1953, based on the life of the noted psychiatrist)
FREUD (UN, 1962)

SECRET OF THE BLUE ROOM, THE (UN, 1933, based on a
story by Erich Philippi)
MISSING GUEST, THE (UN, 1938)
MURDER IN THE BLUE ROOM (UN, 1944)

SECRET SERVICE (PAR, 1919, based on the play by William
Gillette)
SECRET SERVICE (RKO, 1931)

SECRET SERVICE IN DARKEST AFRICA, THE (serial)
(REP, 1943, based on a screenplay by various authors; the
remake is a condensation of the serial)
BARON'S AFRICAN WAR, THE (REP, 1966)

SECRET SEX LIVES OF ROMEO AND JULIET, THE see
ROMEO AND JULIET

SECRETO DEL DOCTOR, EL see DOCTOR'S SECRET,
THE

SECRETS (FN, 1924, based on the play by Rudolph Bessier
and May Edgington)
SECRETS (UA, 1933)

SECRETS OF PARIS, THE see MYSTERIES OF PARIS

SECRETS OF THE PURPLE REEF see BENEATH THE
12--MILE REEF

SEDUCTION OF MIMI, THE (ITA, 1974, based on a story
by Lina Wertmuller)
WHICH WAY IS UP? (UN, 1977)

SEE NAPLES AND DIE see OH, SAILOR BEWARE

SEEDS OF FREEDOM see POTEMKIN

SEETA (IN, 1934, based on an Indian legend)
SEETA (IN, 1935)

SEHNSUCHT EINER FRAU, DIE see SECRET HOUR, THE

SEIN BESTER FREUND (GER, 1929, source unlisted)
SEIN BESTER FREUND (GER, 1937)
SEIN BESTER FREUND (GER, 1962)

SEINE EXZELLENZ DER REVISOR (GER, 1922, based on a
story by Nikolai Gogol)
EINE STADT STEHT KOPF (GER, 1932)
INSPECTOR GENERAL, THE (WB, 1949)
REVIZOR (RUS, 1952)

SEINE MAJESTAT, DAS BETTELKIND see PRINCE AND
THE PAUPER, THE

SEINE TOCHTER IST DER PETER (GER, 1936, source
unlisted)
SEINE TOCHTER IST DER PETER (GER, 1955)

SEISHUN TARO (series) (JAP--TV, 1966, based on a teleplay
by Yasuo Tanami)
YOUTHFUL TARO (JAP, 1967)

SEITENSPRUNGE (GER, 1930, source unlisted)
SEITENSPRUNGE (GER, 1940)

SELFISH GIANT, THE (short) (IND, 1971, based on the
story by Oscar Wilde)
SELFISH GIANT, THE (short) (TV, 1972)
SELFISH GIANT, THE (short) (PYR, 1972)

SELIGE EXZELLENZ, DIE (GER, 1926, based on the book
by Rudolph Presber)
SELIGE EXZELLENZ, DIE (GER, 1935)

SENATOR'S DAUGHTER, THE see KEEPER OF THE
FLAME

SENDUNG DER LYSISTRATA, DIE see WARRIOR'S
HUSBAND, THE

SENIOR YEAR (CBS--TV, 1973, based on a teleplay)
SONS AND DAUGHTERS (series) (CBS--TV, 1974)

SENSATION HUNTERS (MON, 1934, based on the story,
"Cabaret," by Whitman Chambers)
SENSATION HUNTERS (MON, 1946)

SENTIMENTAL JOURNEY (FOX, 1946, based on the story,
"The Little Horse," by Nelia Gardner White)
GIFT OF LOVE, THE (FOX, 1958)

SENTIMENTALIST, THE see SAL OF SINGAPORE

SENZA FAMIGLIA see SANS FAMILLE

SEPTEMBER AFFAIR (PAR, 1950, based on a screenplay by
Robert Thoeren)
SEPTEMBER AFFAIR (NBC--TV, 1954)
SEPTEMBER AFFAIR (NBC--TV, 1956)

SERENADE (GER, 1937, based on the book, "Viola
Tricolor," by Theodor Storm)
ICH WERDE DICH AUF HANDEN TRAGEN (GER, 1943)
ICH WERDE DICH AUF HANDEN TRAGEN (GER, 1958)

SERENADE see SCHUBERT'S FRUHLINGSTRAUM

SERGE PANINE (FRA, 1913, based on the book by Georges
Ohnet)
VIE POUR VIE (RUS, 1916)

SERGE PANINE (AUS/FRA, 1923)
SERGE PANINE (FRA, 1938)

SERGEANT RYKER see CASE AGAINST PAUL RYKER,
THE

SERGEANT WAS A LADY, THE see FRANCIS JOINS
THE WACS

SERGEANT YORK (WB, 1941, based on the biography of
the World War I soldier)
SERGEANT YORK (CBS–TV, n.d.)

SERGEANTS 3 see GUNGA DIN

SERPENT OF THE NILE see CLEOPATRA

SERPICO (PAR, 1973, based on the book by Peter Maas)
SERPICO (NBC–TV, 1976)
SERPICO (series) (NBC––TV, 1976)

SERVICE FOR LADIES (PAR, 1927, based on the story,
"Head Waiter," by Ernst Vajda)
RESERVED FOR LADIES (BRI, 1932)

SEUL AMOUR, UN see GRANDE BRETECHE, LA

SEVEN AGAINST THE WALL (CBS–TV, 1959, based on a
historical event)
ST. VALENTINE'S DAY MASSACRE, THE (FOX, 1967)

SEVEN BRIDES FOR SEVEN BROTHERS (MGM, 1954,
based on the book, "Sobbin' Women," by Ben Ames
Williams)
HERE COME THE BRIDES (series) (ABC–TV, 1969)

SEVEN DAYS' LEAVE (PAR, 1930, based on the story, "The
Old Lady Shows Her Medals," by Sir James M. Barrie)
OLD LADY SHOWS HER MEDALS, THE (CBS––TV, 1956)
OLD LADY SHOWS HER MEDALS, THE (NBC–TV, 1963)

SEVEN FRECKLES see ROMEO AND JULIET

SEVEN IN ONE BLOW see BRAVE LITTLE TAILOR

7 INTO SNOWY see SNOW WHITE

SEVEN KEYS TO BALDPATE (AUT, 1915, based on the
book by Earl Derr Biggers and the play by George M.
Cohan)
SEVEN KEYS TO BALDPATE (ART, 1917)
SEVEN KEYS TO BALDPATE (PAR, 1925)
SEVEN KEYS TO BALDPATE (RKO, 1929)
SEVEN KEYS TO BALDPATE (RKO, 1935)
SEVEN KEYS TO BALDPATE (RKO, 1947)
SEVEN KEYS TO BALDPATE (TV, 1952)
SEVEN KEYS TO BALDPATE (NBC––TV, 1962)

SEVEN LITTLE FOYS, THE (PAR, 1955, based on the
biography of vaudevillian Eddie Foy)
SEVEN LITTLE FOYS, THE (NBC––TV, 1964)

SEVEN RAVENS, THE see SEVEN SWANS, THE

SEVEN SAMURAI (JAP, 1954, based on a screenplay by
Shinobu Hashimoto, Hideo Oguni and Akira Kurosawa)
MAGNIFICENT SEVEN, THE (UA, 1960)

SEVEN SINNERS (UN, 1940, based on a story by Ladislaus
Fodor and Laslo Vadnai)
SOUTH SEA SINNER (UN, 1950)

SEVEN SINNERS see WRECKER, THE

SEVEN SWANS, THE (PAR, 1917, based on a story by
J. Searle Dawley)
SEVEN RAVENS, THE (GER, 1952)
SEVEN RAVENS, THE (short) (GER, 1969)

SEVENTEEN (PAR, 1916, based on the story by Booth
Tarkington; also the basis for two musical comedies,
"Hello, Lola," in 1926 and "Seventeen" in 1951)
SEVENTEEN (PAR, 1940)

1776 see DECLARATION OF INDEPENDENCE, THE,
JEFFERSON OF MONTICELLO and OUR BILL OF
RIGHTS

SEVENTH HEAVEN (FOX, 1927, based on the play by Austin
Strong)
WILD GRASS (CHN, 1930)
SEVENTH HEAVEN (FOX, 1937)
SEVENTH HEAVEN (TV, 1953)

SEVENTH SIN, THE see PAINTED VEIL, THE

SEVENTH VEIL, THE (BRI, 1946, based on a story by Muriel
and Sidney Box)
SEVENTH VEIL, THE (CBS––TV, 1955)

SEVILLA DE MIS AMORES see CALL OF THE FLESH

SEX ADVENTURES OF THE THREE MUSKETEERS, THE
see THREE MUSKETEERS, THE

SHADA KALO see DR. JEKYLL AND MR. HYDE

SHADOW OF A DOUBT (UN, 1943, based on a story by
Gordon McDonell)
SHADOW OF A DOUBT (NBC––TV, 1955)
STEP DOWN TO TERROR (UN, 1958)
STRANGE HOMECOMING (TV, n.d.)

SHADOW OF THE GUILLOTINE see MARIE ANTOIN––
ETTE

SHADOW OF THE LAW see CITY OF SILENT MEN

SHADOWMAN see EYES WITHOUT A FACE

SHADOWS (MGM, 1919, based on the play, "Ching, Ching,
Chinaman," by Perry Walsh)
BOAT FROM SHANGHAI (BRI, 1932)

SHADOWS OF FEAR see THERESE RAQUIN

SHADOWS OF MY LIFE see LIVING CORPSE, THE

SHAKESPEARE: SOUL OF AN AGE see LIFE OF
SHAKESPEARE

SHAKESPEARE WRITING JULIUS CAESAR see JULIUS
CAESAR

SHAKIEST GUN IN THE WEST, THE see PALEFACE, THE

SHAKUNTALA (IN, 1945, based on an Indian legend)
SHAKUNTALA (IN, 1947)

SHALOM OF SAFED (short) (CBS--TV, 1961, based on the work of the noted artist Israeli Shalom Moskowitz)
WORLD OF SHALOM OF SAFED, THE (ABC--TV, 1968)
SHALOM OF SAFED (short) (IND, 1969)

SHAME OF MARY BOYLE, THE see JUNO AND THE PAYCOCK

SHAMUS (COL, 1974, based on a screenplay by Barry Beckerman)
MATTER OF WIFE . . . AND DEATH, A (NBC--TV, 1975)

SHANE (PAR, 1953, based on the book by Jack Schaefer)
SHANE (series) (ABC--TV, 1966)

SHANGHAI EXPRESS (PAR, 1932, based on a story by Harry Hervey)
SOUTH TO KARANGA (UN, 1940)
NIGHT PLANE FROM CHUNKING (PAR, 1943)
PEKING EXPRESS (PAR, 1951)

SHANGHAI LADY see DRIFTING

SHANGHAIED (short) (ESS, 1915, based on a screenplay)
LIVE GHOST, THE (short) (MGM, 1934)

SHANGRI--LA see LOST HORIZON

SHANNONS OF BROADWAY, THE (UN, 1929, based on the play by James Gleason)
GOODBYE BROADWAY (UN, 1938)

SHARAD OF ATLANTIS see UNDERSEAS KINGDOM

SHAZAM! (series) (CBS--TV, 1974, based on the comic strip by Charles C. Beck)
CAPTAIN MARVEL (series) (CBS--TV, 1976)

SHE see PILAR OF FIRE

SHE CAME, SHE SAW, SHE CONQUERED (KAL, 1916, based on a story by Carroll Fleming and Edward P. Kidder)
SIS HOPKINS (MGM, 1919)
SIS HOPKINS (REP, 1941)

SHE COULDN'T SAY NO (WB, 1930, based on a screenplay by Robert Lord and Arthur Caesar)
SHE COULDN'T SAY NO (WB, 1940)

SHE CREATURE, THE (AI, 1956, source unlisted)
CREATURE OF DESTRUCTION (IND, 1967)

SHE FREAK see FREAKS

SHE LEARNED ABOUT SAILORS (FOX, 1934, based on a story by Randall H. Faye)
SAILOR'S LADY (FOX, 1940)

SHE LOVES ME NOT (PAR, 1934, based on the book by Edward Hope and the play by Howard Lindsay)
TRUE TO THE ARMY (PAR, 1942)
HOW TO BE VERY, VERY POPULAR (FOX, 1955)

SHEIKH CHILLI (IN, 1937, based on an Indian legend)
SHEIKH CHILLI (IN, 1956)

SHEPHERD OF THE HILLS (IND, 1919, based on the book by Harold Bell Wright)

SHEPHERD OF THE HILLS (FN, 1928)
SHEPHERD OF THE HILLS (PAR, 1941)
SHEPHERD OF THE HILLS (IND, 1963)

SHERLOCK HOLMES (ESS, 1916, based on the play by William Gillette)
SHERLOCK HOLMES (BRI, 1920)
SHERLOCK HOLMES (MGM, 1922)
SHERLOCK HOLMES (FOX, 1932)
SHERLOCK HOLMES (NBC--TV, 1950)
SHERLOCK HOLMES (series) (NBC--TV, 1954)

SHERLOCK HOLMES AND THE GREAT MURDER MYSTERY (DEN, 1908, based on the book, "Murders in the Rue Morgue," by Edgar Allan Poe)
MURDERS IN THE RUE MORGUE (IND, 1914)
MURDERS IN THE RUE MORGUE (UN, 1932)
PHANTOM OF THE RUE MORGUE (WB, 1954)
MURDERS IN THE RUE MORGUE (AI, 1971)

SHERLOCK HOLMES AND THE SILVER BLAZE see SILVER BLAZE, THE

SHERLOCK HOLMES FACES DEATH see MUSGRAVE RITUAL, THE

SHE'S WORKING HER WAY THROUGH COLLEGE see MALE ANIMAL, THE

SHINBONE ALLEY (PBS--TV, 1960, based on the "Archie and Mehitabel" stories by Don Marquis)
SHINBONE ALLEY (AA, 1971)

SHINING HOUR, THE (MGM, 1928, based on the play by Keith Winter)
SHINING HOUR, THE (ABC--TV, 1951)

SHINING VICTORY (WB, 1941, based on a book, "Jupiter Laughs," by A.J. Cronin)
ICH SUCHE DICH (GER, 1956)

SHIPMATES FOREVER (WB, 1935, based on a story by Delmer Daves)
DEAD END KIDS ON DRESS PARADE (WB, 1939)

SHIPWRECKED see BACK TO NATURE

SHIV LEELA (IN, 1922, based on an Indian legend)
SHIV LEELA (IN, 1951)

SHOCK WAVE see CHAIN LIGHTNING

SHOEMAKER AND THE ELVES, THE (short) (COL, 1934, based on a fairy tale)
SHOEMAKER AND THE ELVES, THE (short) (COR, 1962)
WONDERFUL WORLD OF THE BROTHERS GRIMM, THE (sequence) (MGM, 1963)

SHOEMAKERS OF PROVINCE, THE (FIN, 1926, source unlisted)
SHOEMAKERS OF PROVINCE, THE (FIN, 1948)

SHOOT OUT see LONE COWBOY, THE

SHOOT THE WORLD (PAR, 1934, based on a play by Ben Hecht and Gene Fowler)
SOME LIKE IT HOT (PAR, 1939)

SHOOTING OF DAN MCGREW, THE   (MGM, 1915, based on the poem by Robert W. Service)
    SHOOTING OF DAN MCGREW, THE   (MGM, 1924)

SHOOTING STAR   see   GREAT GAME

SHOP AROUND THE CORNER, THE   (MGM, 1940, based on a play by Niklaus Lazlo; also the basis for the musical comedy, "She Loves Me," in 1963)
    IN THE GOOD OLD SUMMERTIME   (MGM, 1949)

SHOPWORN ANGEL, THE   see   PETTIGREW'S GIRL

SHORE LEAVE   (FN, 1925, based on the play by Hubert Osborne)
    HIT THE DECK   (RKO, 1930)
    FOLLOW THE FLEET   (RKO, 1936)
    HIT THE DECK   (NBC–TV, 1950)
    HIT THE DECK   (MGM, 1955)

SHORT CUT TO HELL   see   THIS GUN FOR HIRE

SHOT IN THE DARK, A   see   SMART BLONDE

SHOW GIRL   (FN, 1928, based on a book by J.P. McEvoy)
    SHOW GIRL IN HOLLYWOOD   (FN, 1930)
    MASQUE D'HOLLYWOOD, LE   (FRA, 1931)

SHOW GIRL IN HOLLYWOOD   see   SHOW GIRL

SHOW OF SHOWS, THE   see   RICHARD III

SHOWBOAT   (UN, 1929, based on the book by Edna Ferber and the musical by Jerome Kern and Oscar Hammerstein II)
    SHOWBOAT   (UN, 1936)
    SHOWBOAT   (MGM, 1951)

SHOWDOWN AT ABILENE   (UN, 1956, based on the book, "Gun Shy," by Clarence Upson Young)
    GUNFIGHT AT ABILENE   (UN, 1967)

SHOWDOWN AT THE O.K. CORRAL   see   GUNFIGHT AT THE O.K. CORRAL

SHOW–OFF, THE   (PAR, 1926, based on the play by George Kelly)
    MEN ARE LIKE THAT   (PAR, 1929)
    SHOW–OFF, THE   (MGM, 1934)
    SHOW–OFF, THE   (MGM, 1946)
    SHOW–OFF, THE   (CBS–TV, 1955)

SHUHADDAA EL GHARAM   see   ROMEO AND JULIET

SHYLOCK   see   MIRROR OF VENICE

SI EL EMPERADOR LO SUPIERA   see   HIS GLORIOUS NIGHT

SI L'EMPEREUR SAVAIT CA   see   HIS GLORIOUS NIGHT

SIBERIAN LADY MACBETH   see   KATERINA IZMAILOVA

SIDEKICKS   see   SKIN GAME, THE

SIE UND DIE DREI   (GER, 1922, source unlisted)
    SIE UND DIE DREI   (GER, 1935)

SIEG DER LIEBE   (GER, 1932, based on a story, "An Heiligen Wassern," by Jakob Christoph Heer)

AN HEILIGEN WASSERN   (SWI, 1960)

SIEGE OF THE ALAMO, THE   see   REMEMBER THE ALAMO

SIEGFRIED   (ITA, 1912, based on the opera by Richard Wagner and the Nibelungen saga and legend)
    SIEGFRIED   (GER, 1923)
    KRIEMHILD'S REVENGE   (GER, 1924)
    SIEGFRIED   (ITA, 1957)
    SIEGFRIED   (GER, 1958)
    INVISIBLE SWORD, THE   (ITA, 1962)
    SIEGFRIED   (PHI, c1963)
    DRAGON'S BLOOD   (ITA, 1963)
    SIEGFRIED OF ZANTEN   (GER, 1967)
    WHOM THE GODS WISH TO DESTROY   (GER, 1969)
    LONG SWIFT SWORD OF SIEGFRIED, THE   (GER, 1971)

SIEGFRIED OF ZANTEN   see   SIEGFRIED

SIEGNEUR BOITEUX, LE   (RUS, 1915, based on the book by Alexei Tolstoy)
    SIEGNEUR BOITEUX, LE   (RUS, 1929)

SIERRA   see   FORBIDDEN VALLEY

SIGFRIDO   see   KRIEMHELD'S REVENGE

SIGN OF FOUR, THE   (BRI, 1923, based on the book by Sir Arthur Conan Doyle)
    SIGN OF FOUR, THE   (BRI, 1932)

SIGN OF THE CROSS, THE   (BRI, 1904, based on the play by Wilson Barrett)
    SIGN OF THE CROSS, THE   (PAR, 1914)
    SIGN OF THE CROSS, THE   (PAR, 1932)

SIGN OF THE PAGAN   see   ATTILA

SIGN ON THE DOOR, THE   (FN, 1921, based on the story by Channing Pollock)
    LOCKED DOOR, THE   (UA, 1929)

SIGNORA SENZA CAMELIE, LA   see   DAME AUX CAMELIAS, LA

SILAS MARNER   see   FAIR EXCHANGE, A

SILENCE   (PDC, 1926, based on the play by Max Marcin)
    SILENCE   (PAR, 1931)

SILENT NIGHT   see   PASSION PLAY, THE

SILK LEGS   (FOX, 1927, based on a story by Frederica Sagar)
    PIERNAS DE SEDA   (SPA, 1935)

SILK STOCKINGS   see   NINOTCHKA

SILVER BLAZE, THE   (BRI, 1912, based on a book by Sir Arthur Conan Doyle)
    SILVER BLAZE, THE   (FRA, 1913)
    SILVER BLAZE, THE   (short)   (BRI, 1922)
    SHERLOCK HOLMES AND THE SILVER BLAZE   (BRI, 1936)
    SILVER BLAZE, THE   (short)   (BRI–TV, 1976)

SILVER CORD, THE   (RKO, 1933, based on the play by Sidney Howard)

SILVER CORD, THE   (ABC–TV, 1951)

SILVER HORDE, THE   (MGM, 1920, based on the book by
   Rex Beach)
   SILVER HORDE, THE   (RKO, 1930)

SILVER WHISTLE, THE   see   MR. BELVEDERE RINGS
   THE BELL

SIN FLOOD   see   WAY OF ALL MEN, THE

SINBAD, ALI BABA AND ALADDIN   see   ALADDIN, ALI
   BABA and SINBAD

SINBAD THE SAILOR   (UN, 1919, based on a legend)
   SINDBAD THE SAILOR   (IN, 1930)
   POPEYE THE SAILOR MEETS SINBAD THE SAILOR
   (short)   (PAR, 1936)
   SINDBAD THE SAILOR   (IN, 1939)
   SINDBAD THE SAILOR   (IN, 1946)
   SINBAD THE SAILOR   (RKO, 1946)
   THIEF OF DAMASCUS   (COL, 1951)
   SINDBAD THE SAILOR   (IN, 1952)
   MAGIC VOYAGE OF SINBAD   (RUS, 1952)
   SON OF SINBAD   (RKO, 1953)
   INVITATION TO THE DANCE   (sequence)   (MGM, 1956)
   SINBAD THE SAILOR   (short)   (IND, 1955)
   SEVENTH VOYAGE OF SINBAD   (COL, 1958)
   JACK THE GIANT KILLER   (UA, 1962)
   ADVENTURES OF SINBAD   (JAP, 1962)
   CAPTAIN SINBAD   (MGM, 1963)
   SINBAD, ALI BABA AND ALADDIN   (IN, 1963)
   LOST WORLD OF SINBAD, THE   (JAP, 1963)
   SINBAD AGAINST THE SARACENS   (ITA, 1964)
   ADVENTURES OF SINBAD, JR.   (series)   (TV, 1965)
   ADVENTURES OF SINBAD, THE   (JAP, 1968)
   GOLDEN VOYAGE OF SINBAD, THE   (COL, 1974)
   ADVENTURES OF SINDBAD THE NAVIGATOR, THE
   (POL–TV, 1969)
   SINDBAD   (series)   (GER–TV, 1976)
   SINBAD AND THE EYE OF THE TIGER   (COL, 1977)

SINCERELY YOURS   see   MAN WHO PLAYED GOD, THE
   and SPRING IS HERE

SINFLUT   see   NOAH'S ARK

SINGAPORE   (UN, 1947, based on a story by Seton I.
   Miller)
   ISTANBUL   (UN, 1957)

SINGAPORE WOMAN   see   DANGEROUS

SINGIN' IDOL, THE   (NBC–TV, 1957, based on a teleplay by
   Paul Monash)
   SING, BOY, SING   (FOX, 1958)

SINGLE STANDARD, THE   see   BATTLE OF THE SEXES

SINISTER STORIES   see   SUICIDE CLUB, THE

SINS OF CASANOVA   see   CASANOVA

SINS OF ROSE BERND   see   ROSE BERND

SINS OF THE CHILDREN   see   MARTYRDOM OF PHILIP
   STRONG, THE

SIR ARNE'S TREASURE   see   TREASURE OF ARNE, THE

SIR FRANCIS DRAKE   see   DRAKE'S LOVE STORY

SIRE DE MALETROIT'S DOOR   (CBS–TV, 1951, based on
   the story by Robert Louis Stevenson)
   STRANGE DOOR, THE   (UN, 1951)

SIREN OF ATLANTIS   see   ATLANTIDE, L'

SIS HOPKINS   see   SHE CAME, SHE SAW, SHE
   CONQUERED

SISTER TO ASSIST'ER, A   (BRI, 1922, based on the play by
   John le Breton)
   SISTER TO ASSIST'ER, A   (BRI, 1927)
   SISTER TO ASSIST'ER, A   (BRI, 1930)
   SISTER TO ASSIST'ER, A   (BRI, 1938)
   SISTER TO ASSIST'ER, A   (BRI, 1947)

SITTING BULL   (UA, 1954, based on historical events and
   characters)
   DEATH OF SITTING BULL   (CBS–TV, 1963)

SITTING PRETTY   (FOX, 1948, based on a book by Gwen
   Davenport)
   GENIUS, THE   (MR. BELVEDERE)   (CBS–TV, 1956)

SIX–CYLINDER LOVE   (FOX, 1923, based on a play by
   William Anthony McGuire)
   SIX–CYLINDER LOVE   (FOX, 1931)
   HONEYMOON'S OVER, THE   (FOX, 1939)

SIXTEEN FATHOMS DEEP   (MON, 1934, based on a story by
   Eustace L. Adams)
   16 FATHOMS DEEP   (MON, 1948)

SIXTY GLORIOUS YEARS   see   SIXTY YEARS A QUEEN

SIXTY YEARS A QUEEN   (BRI, 1913, based on historical
   events and characters. Television presentations based on
   the play by Laurence Houseman)
   SIXTY GLORIOUS YEARS   (BRI, 1938)
   VICTORIA REGINA   (NBC–TV, 1951)
   VICTORIA REGINA   (NBC–TV, 1957)
   PURSUIT AND LIVES OF QUEEN VICTORIA   (GER,
   1958)
   VICTORIA REGINA   (NBC–TV, 1961)

SKANDAL UM DR. VLIMMEN   see   TIERARZT DR.
   VLIMMEN

SKI PATROL   see   DOOMED BATALLION

SKIN DEEP   (FN, 1922, based on the story, "Lucky Damage,"
   by Marc Edmund Jones)
   SKIN DEEP   (WB, 1929)

SKIN GAME, THE   (BRI, 1920, based on the play by John
   Galsworthy)
   SKIN GAME, THE   (BRI, 1931)

SKIN GAME, THE   (WB, 1971, based on a story by Richard
   A. Simmons)
   SIDEKICKS   (CBS–TV, 1974)

SKIN OF OUR TEETH   (ABC–TV, 1951, based on the play by
   Thornton Wilder)
   SKIN OF OUR TEETH   (NBC–TV, 1955)
   SKIN OF OUR TEETH   (IND, 1968)

SKINNER'S DRESS SUIT   (ESS, 1917, based on the book by
   Henry Irving Dodge)
   SKINNER'S DRESS SUIT   (UN, 1925)
   SKINNER STEPS OUT   (UN, 1929)

SKINNER STEPS OUT   see   SKINNER'S DRESS SUIT

SKIPPY   (PAR, 1931, based on the comic strip by Percy
   Crosby)
   SOOKY   (PAR, 1931)
   SKIPPY   (short)   (UA, 1938)

SKYLARK   (PAR, 1941, based on the play by Samson
   Raphaelson)
   SKYLARK   (CBS–TV, 1951)
   SKYLARK   (NBC–TV, 1956)

SKYLINE   see   EAST SIDE, WEST SIDE

SLAVE OF DESIRE   see   PEAU DE CHAGRIN, LA

SLAVE OF VANITY, A   see   IRIS

SLAVES OF THE INVISIBLE MONSTER   see   INVISIBLE
   MONSTER, THE

SLEEPERS EAST   (FOX, 1934, based on a book by Frederick
   Nebel)
   SLEEPERS WEST   (FOX, 1941)

SLEEPERS WEST   see   SLEEPERS EAST

SLEEPING BEAUTY   (FRA, 1902, based on the story by
   Charles Perrault)
   SLEEPING BEAUTY   (LUB, 1903)
   SLEEPING BEAUTY   (FRA, 1908)
   SLEEPING BEAUTY   (BRI, 1912)
   SLEEPING BEAUTY   (IND, 1913)
   SLEEPING BEAUTY   (RUS, 1914)
   SLEEPING BEAUTY   (RUS, c1920)
   SLEEPING BEAUTY   (GER, 1922)
   SLEEPING BEAUTY   (FRA, 1935)
   SLEEPING BEAUTY   (HOL, 1937)
   SLEEPING BEAUTY   (ITA, 1942)
   SLEEPING BEAUTY   (IND, 1947)
   SLEEPING BEAUTY   (short)   (COR, 1950)
   SLEEPING BEAUTY   (short)   (EBE, 1952)
   SLEEPING BEAUTY   (short)   (GER, 1954)
   SLEEPING BEAUTY   (NBC–TV, 1955)
   SLEEPING BEAUTY   (NBC–TV, 1958)
   SLEEPING BEAUTY   (DIS, 1958)
   SLEEPING BEAUTY   (BRI–TV, 1959)
   SLEEPING BEAUTY   (GER, 1963)
   SLEEPING BEAUTY   (RUS, 1964)
   EVENING WITH ROYAL BALLET, AN   (BRI, 1965)
   SLEEPING BEAUTY   (GER, 1970)
   SLEEPING BEAUTY   (RAN, 1972)

SLEEPING CAR TO TRIESTE   see   ROME EXPRESS

SLEEPING PARTNERS   (BRI, 1930, based on a story,
   "Faisons un Reve," by Sacha Guitry)
   FAISONS UN REVE   (FRA, 1936)

SLIGHT CASE OF MURDER, A   see   AMAZING DR.
   CLITTERHOUSE, THE

SLIGHTLY FRENCH   see   LET'S FALL IN LOVE

SLIGHTLY SCARLET   (PAR, 1930, based on a screenplay by
   Howard Estabrook and Joseph L. Mankiewicz)
   ENIGMATIQUE MR. PARKES, L'   (FRA, 1930)
   AMOR AUDAZ   (SPA, 1930)

SLIM PRINCESS, THE   (ESS, 1914, based on the story by
   George Ade)
   SLIM PRINCESS, THE   (MGM, 1920)

SLIPPER AND THE ROSE, THE   see   CINDERELLA AND
   THE FAIRY GODMOTHER

SLIPPING WIVES   (short)   (PAR, 1927, based on an idea by
   Hal Roach and elaborated upon in the remakes)
   FIXER--UPPERS, THE   (short)   (MGM, 1935)
   BOOBS IN ARMS   (short)   (COL, 1941)

SLIPPY McGEE   (FN, 1923, based on the book by Marie
   Conway Oemler)
   SLIPPY McGEE   (REP, 1948)

SLITHER   (MGM, 1973, based on a screenplay by W.D. Richter)
   SLITHER   (short)   (CBS--TV, 1974)

SLOPE IN THE SUN, A   (JAP, n.d., based on the book, "Hi No
   Ataru Sakamichi," by Yojiro Ishizaka)
   STREET IN THE SUN, A   (JAP, 1967)

SMALL MIRACLE, THE   see   NEVER TAKE NO FOR AN
   ANSWER

SMALL TOWN GIRL   (MGM, 1936, based on the book by
   Ben Ames Williams)   (TV title: ONE HORSE TOWN)
   SMALL TOWN GIRL   (MGM, 1953)

SMALL WORLD OF SAMMY LEE, THE   see   EDDIE

SMART BLONDE   (WB, 1936, based on a story by Frederick
   Nebel)
   SHOT IN THE DARK, A   (WB, 1941)

SMART GUY   see   I AM A CRIMINAL

SMASHING THE MONEY RING   see   JAILBREAK

SMILE, PLEASE   (short)   (PAT, 1924, based on a screenplay
   and elaborated upon in the remakes)
   FAMILY GROUP, THE   (short)   (MGM, 1928)
   WILD POSES   (short)   (MGM, 1933)

SMILES OF A SUMMER NIGHT   (SWE, 1957, based on a
   screenplay by Ingmar Bergman)
   LITTLE NIGHT MUSIC, A   (AUS, 1977)

SMILING LIEUTENANT, THE   see   WALTZ DREAM, THE

SMILING THROUGH   (FN, 1922, based on the play by Jane
   Cowl and Jane Murfin; also the basis for two musicals,
   "Through the Years" in 1932 and "When You're Young"
   in 1966)
   SMILIN' THROUGH   (MGM, 1932)
   SMILIN' THROUGH   (MGM, 1941)
   SMILIN' THROUGH   (ABC--TV, 1953)

SMITHY   see   ONE WEEK

SMOKY   (FOX, 1933, based on the book by Will James)
   SMOKY   (FOX, 1946)
   SMOKY   (FOX, 1966)

SMOOTH AS SATIN (FBO, 1925, based on the play, "The Chatterbox," by Bayard Veillier)
    ALIAS FRENCH GERTIE (RKO, 1930)

SMOOTH AS SILK see NOTORIOUS GENTLEMEN, A

SMUGGLER'S CIRCUIT see LAW AND DISORDER

SNAKE PRINCESS, THE (JAP, 1940, source unlisted)
    SNAKE PRINCESS, THE (JAP, 1949)

SNAVELY see FAWLTY TOWERS

SNIEGOUROTCHKA (RUS, 1914, based on the play by Alexandre Ostrovsky)
    SNIEGOUROTCHKA (RUS, 1952)
    SNIEGOUROTCHKA (RUS, 1969)

SNOOP SISTERS, THE see DO NOT FOLD, SPINDLE OR MUTILATE

SNOW BEAUTY, THE see SNOW MAIDEN, THE

SNOW CREATURE see ABOMINABLE SNOWMAN, THE

SNOW MAIDEN (ITA, 1911, based on a fairy tale)
    SNOW MAIDEN (RUS, 1914)
    SNOW MAIDEN (RUS, 1953)
    SNOW BEAUTY (RUS, 1969)

SNOW QUEEN, THE (UN, 1958, based on a fairy tale)
    SNOW QUEEN, THE (RUS, c1968)
    SNOW QUEEN, THE (BRI, 1975)

SNOW WHITE (LUB, 1903, based on a fairy tale)
    LITTLE SNOW WHITE (FRA, 1910)
    SNOW WHITE (POW, 1913)
    SNOW WHITE (EDU, 1916)
    SNOW WHITE (IND, 1916)
    SNOW WHITE (UN, 1917)
    SNOW WHITE (short) (PAR, 1933)
    SNOW WHITE AND THE SEVEN DWARFS (DIS, 1937)
    CHINESE PRINCESS WHITE SNOW (CHN, 1940)
    SNOW WHITE AND ROSE RED (short) (BRI, 1953)
    SNOW WHITE AND THE SEVEN DWARFS (GER, 1955)
    SNOW WHITE AND THE 3 STOOGES (FOX, 1961)
    MR. MAGOO'S SNOW WHITE (UPA, 1964)
    SNOW WHITE AND ROSE RED (CHI, 1967)
    SNOW WHITE (RAN, 1972)
    7 INTO SNOWY (IND, 1977)

SNOW WHITE AND ROSE RED see SNOW WHITE

SNOW WHITE AND THE SEVEN DWARFS see SNOW WHITE

SNOW WHITE AND THE 3 STOOGES see SNOW WHITE

SNOWS OF KILIMANJARO, THE (FOX, 1952, based on the story by Ernest Hemingway)
    SNOWS OF KILIMANJARO, THE (CBS–TV, 1960)

SO BIG (FN, 1925, based on the book by Edna Ferber)
    SO BIG (WB, 1932)
    SO BIG (WB, 1953)

SO DARK THE NIGHT (COL, 1946, based on a screenplay by Martin Berkeley and Dwight Babcock)
    SO DARK THE NIGHT (NBC–TV, 1955)

SO EVIL MY LOVE (PAR, 1948, based on a book by Joseph Shearing)
    SO EVIL MY LOVE (NBC–TV, 1955)

SO LONG AT THE FAIR see MIDNIGHT WARNING

SO LONG LETTY (RC, 1920, based on the musical comedy by Oliver Morosco and Earl Carroll)
    SO LONG LETTY (WB, 1930)

SO THIS IS LONDON (FOX, 1930, based on the play by Arthur Goodrich)
    SO THIS IS LONDON (FOX, 1939)

SOCIETY LAWYER see PENTHOUSE

SOCIETY SCANDAL, A (PAR, 1924, based on the play, "The Laughing Lady," by Alfred Sutro)
    LAUGHING LADY, THE (PAR, 1929)

SOCK AND FUN see PUTTING PANTS ON PHILIP

SODOM AND GOMORRAH (GER, 1920, based on a story in the Bible)
    SODOM AND GOMORRAH (AUS, 1923)
    SODOM AND GOMORRAH (FRA/ITA, 1961)

SODOM'S END (GER, 1913, based on the book by Hermann Sudermann)
    SODOM'S END (GER, 1922)

SOFI see DIARY OF A MADMAN

SOGNO DE KRI KRI, UN see THREE MUSKETEERS, THE

SOHN DER GOTTER, DER JUNGE GOETHE, DER see DICHTUNG UND WAHRHEIT

SOLDIER AND THE LADY, THE see MICHAEL STROGOFF

SOLDIER MAN (PAT, 1927, based on a screenplay and elaborated upon in the remakes)
    UNACCUSTOMED AS WE ARE (short) (MGM, 1929)
    BLOCKHEADS (UA, 1938)
    WAKE ME WHEN THE WAR IS OVER (ABC–TV, 1970)

SOLOMON AND SHEBA (UA, 1959, based on the Bible story)
    SOLOMON AND SHEBA (short) (TV, 1961)

SOMBRA, THE SPIDER WOMAN see BLACK WIDOW, THE

SOMBRAS DE GLORIA see BLAZE O'GLORY

SOMBRAS DEL CIRCO see HALF WAY TO HEAVEN

SOME BLONDES ARE DANGEROUS see IRON MAN, THE

SOME LIKE IT HOT see FIRST A GIRL and SHOOT THE WORKS

SOME MUST WATCH see SPIRAL STAIRCASE, THE

SOMEONE AT THE DOOR (BRI, 1936, based on the play by Dorothy and Campbell Christie)
    SOMEONE AT THE DOOR (BRI, 1950)

SOMEONE TO LOVE see CHARM SCHOOL

SOMEONE TO REMEMBER (REP, 1943, based on a story by

Ben Ames Williams)
JOHNNY TROUBLE (WB, 1957)

SOMEWHERE IN SONORA (FN, 1927, based on the book,
"Somewhere South in Sonora," by Will Livingston
Confort)
SOMEWHERE IN SONORA (WB, 1933)

SOMEWHERE SOUTH IN SONORA see SOMEWHERE IN
SONORA

SOMMERLIEBE (GER, 1942, based on the book, "Die
Serenyi," by Otto Erich Hartleben)
SOMMERLIEBE (GER, 1955)

SON OF ALI BABA see ALI BABA

SON OF CAPTAIN BLOOD see CAPTAIN BLOOD

SON OF D'ARTAGNAN see THREE MUSKETEERS, THE

SON OF FRANKENSTEIN see FRANKENSTEIN

SON OF FURY (FOX, 1942, based on the book, "Benjamin
Blake," by Edison Marshall)
TREASURE OF THE GOLDEN CONDOR (FOX, 1953)

SON OF KONG see KING KONG

SON OF MAN see PASSION PLAY, THE

SON OF MONTE CRISTO see COUNT OF MONTE
CRISTO, THE

SON OF ROBIN HOOD see ROBIN HOOD AND HIS
MERRY MEN

SON OF THE NILE see RIVER BOY

SON OF THE SHEIK (UA, 1926, based on the book, "Sons
of the Sheik," by E.M. Hull)
SON OF THE SHEIK (SPA, n.d.)
SON OF THE SHEIK (TUR, 1969)

SONG AND DANCE MAN, THE (PAR, 1925, based on a
musical by George M. Cohan)
SONG AND DANCE MAN, THE (FOX, 1936)

SONG AT MIDNIGHT see PHANTOM OF THE OPERA,
THE

SONG IS BORN, A see BALL OF FIRE

SONG OF A FLOWER BASKET, THE (JAP, 1937, source
unlisted)
SONG OF A FLOWER BASKET, THE (JAP, 1946)

SONG OF A LANTERN (JAP, 1943, source unlisted)
LANTERN (JAP, 1960)

SONG OF A NATION (short) (WB, 1945, based on the life
of composer Francis Scott Key)
OUR COUNTRY'S SONG (short) (COR, 1953)
RESCUE OF DR. BEANES: FRANCIS SCOTT KEY AND
THE STAR–SPANGLED BANNER (short) (CBS–TV,
1956)
O'ER THE RAMPARTS WE WATCHED (short) (MHF,
n.d.)
EARLY LIGHT OF DAWN, THE (short) (NBC–TV, 1967)

SONG OF BERNADETTE, THE (FOX, 1943, based on a
legend and the novel by Franz Wuerfel)
BERNADETTE (CBS--TV, 1958)
BERNADETTE OF LOURDES (FRA, 1960)

SONG OF BUTTERFLY, THE see MADAME BUTTERFLY

SONG OF LOVE (MGM, 1947, based on the life of the noted
musician)
CLARA SCHUMANN STORY, THE (NBC–TV, 1954)

SONG OF LOVE TRIUMPHANT, THE (RUS, 1915, based on
the book by Ivan Turgenev)
CHANT DE L'AMOUR TRIOMPHANT, LE (FRA, 1923)
SONG OF LOVE TRIUMPHANT, THE (POL, 1967)

SONG OF MYSELF see WALT WHITMAN

SONG OF SHEHERAZADE see ARABIAN NIGHTS

SONG OF SONGS see LILY CZEPANEK

SONG OF THE SCARLET FLOWER see SANGEN ON
DEN FLORODEN BLOMMAN

SONG OF THE SOUTH see UNCLE REMUS – BR'ER
RABBIT

SONG TO REMEMBER, A (COL, 1945, based on the life of
the noted writer)
GEORGE SAND (short) (FRA, n.d.)

SONG TO REMEMBER, A see also LIFE OF CHOPIN, THE

SONG WITHOUT END see DREAM OF LOVE

SONNE VON ST. MORITZ, DIE (GER, 1923, based on the
book by Paul Oscar Hoecker)
SONNE VON ST. MORITZ, DIE (GER, 1954)

SONNTAGSKIND, DAS see SCHNEIDER WIBBEL

SONS AND DAUGHTERS see SENIOR YEAR

SONS OF THE BLACK EAGLE, THE see DOUBROVSKY

SONS OF THE DESERT see AMBROSE'S FIRST FALSE–
HOOD

SONS OF THE SHEIK see SON OF THE SHEIK

SONTAG DES LEBENS see DEVIL'S HOLIDAY

SONYA AND THE MADMAN see CRIME AND PUNISH–
MENT

SOOKY see SKIPPY

SORCERER, THE see WAGES OF FEAR, THE

SORCERER'S APPRENTICE, THE see WIZARD'S
APPRENTICE, THE

SOROCHINSK FAIR (RUS, 1918, based on a story by
Nikolai Gogol)
SOROCHINSK FAIR (RUS, 1927)
SOROCHINSK FAIR (RUS, 1939)

SORRELL AND SON (UA, 1927, based on the book by

George Warwick Deeping)
SORRELL AND SON (BRI, 1934)

SORROWFUL JONES see LITTLE MISS MARKER

SORROWS OF SATAN (BRI, 1917, based on the book by
Marie Corelli)
LEAVES FROM SATAN'S BOOK (DEN, 1918)
SORROWS OF SATAN (PAR, 1925)

SORRY, WRONG NUMBER (PAR, 1948, based on the radio
play by Lucille Fletcher)
SORRY, WRONG NUMBER (NBC--TV, 1954)

SO'S YOUR OLD MAN (PAR, 1926, based on a story, "Mr.
Bisbee's Princess," by Julian Street)
YOU'RE TELLING ME (PAR, 1934)

SOULIERS DE CENDRILLON, LES see CINDERELLA
AND THE FAIRY GODMOTHER

SOUND AND THE FURY, THE (NBC–TV, 1955, based on
the book by William Faulkner)
SOUND AND THE FURY, THE (FOX, 1959)

SOUND OF HUNTING, A see EIGHT IRON MEN

SOUND OF MUSIC, THE see TRAPP FAMILE, DIE

SOUS LE SOLEIL DE PROVENCE see QUATRE PAS
DANS LES NUAGES

SOUTH OF THE SLOT see TWO SOULS

SOUTH SEA SINNER see SEVEN SINNERS

SOUTH TO KARANGA see SHANGHAI EXPRESS

SOUTH WIND (JAP, 1939, source unlisted)
SOUTH WIND (JAP, 1942)

SOVIET CHALLENGE, THE see STALIN ERA, THE

SOYONS GAIS see LET US BE GAY

SPANISCHE FLIEGE, DIE (GER, 1931, based on the play
by Franz Arnold and Ernst Bach)
SPANISCHE FLIEGE, DIE (GER, 1955)

SPANISH DANCER, THE see DON CESAR DE BAZAN

SPARK (JAP, 1922, source unlisted)
SPARK (JAP, 1956)

SPARTACUS (ITA, 1914, based on a legend)
SPARTACUS (UN, 1960)

SPAWN OF THE NORTH (PAR, 1938, based on a book by
Barrett Willoughby; see also "The Virginian" for similar
plot)
ALASKA SEAS (PAR, 1954)

SPECIAL AGENT (WB, 1935, based on a story by Martin
Mooney)
GAMBLING ON THE HIGH SEAS (WB, 1940)

SPECKLED BAND, THE (short) (BRI, 1912, based on the
story by Sir Arthur Conan Doyle)
SPECKLED BAND, THE (short) (BRI, 1923)

SPECKLED BAND, THE (BRI, 1931)

SPECTER HAUNTS EUROPE, A see HOP FROG

SPECTRE VERT, LE see UNHOLY NIGHT, THE

SPEED DEMON (COL, 1932, based on a story by Charles R.
Condon)
MOTOR MADNESS (COL, 1937)

SPEED OF LIGHT, THE see STAR GAZERS

SPELL OF THE YUKON, THE see SHOOTING OF DAN
McGREW, THE

SPELLBOUND (UA, 1945, based on the book, "The House of
Dr. Edwardes," by Francis Belding)
SPELLBOUND (NBC--TV, 1962)

SPENCER'S MOUNTAIN (WB, 1963, based on the book by
Earl Hamner Jr.)
HOMECOMING, THE (CBS–TV, 1970)
WALTONS, THE (series) (CBS–TV, 1972)

SPHINX, THE (ITA, 1918, based on a book by Octave
Feuillet)
SPHINX, THE (ITA, 1919)

SPHINX, THE (MON, 1933, based on a story by Albert
Demond)
PHANTOM KILLER, THE (MON, 1943)

SPIEL MIT DEM FEUER, DAS (GER, 1921, based on a
screenplay by Julius Horst and Alexander Engel)
SPIEL MIT DEM FEUER, DAS (GER, 1934)

SPIELERIN, DIE (GER, 1920, based on the play by Henry A.
Jones)
SPIELERIN, DIE (GER, 1927)

SPIN AND MARTY (series) (ABC–TV, c1956, based on a
teleplay)
NEW ADVENTURES OF SPIN AND MARTY, THE (series)
(ABC--TV, c1957)

SPINNOLIO see PINOCCHIO

SPIONIN (FWE, 1921, based on the life of the notorious
spy; also the basis for the 1967 musical comedy, "Ballad
for a Firing Squad")
MATA HARI (GER, 1927)
MATA HARI: THE RED DANCER (BRI, 1928)
MATA HARI (MGM, 1932)
MATA HARI (CBS--TV, 1955)
MATA HARI (FRA, 1961)

SPIRAL STAIRCASE, THE (RKO, 1946, based on the book,
"Some Must Watch," by Ethel Lina White)
SPIRAL STAIRCASE, THE (ABC--TV, 1961)

SPIRIT AND THE FLESH see I PROMESSI SPOSI

SPIRIT OF CULVER see TOM BROWN AT CULVER

SPIRIT OF LAFAYETTE, THE (IND, 1919, based on the life
of the Revolutionary War hero)
LAFAYETTE, CHAMPION OF LIBERTY (short) (TFC,
1946)
LAFAYETTE, SOLDIER OF LIBERTY (short) (EBE,

1955)
LAFAYETTE (FRA, 1962)
LAFAYETTE AND WASHINGTON (short) (MAC, 1965)

SPIRIT OF NOTRE DAME (UN, 1931, based on the life of
the noted athletic coach)
KNUTE ROCKNE, ALL AMERICAN (WB, 1940)
KNUTE ROCKNE -- THE MAN AND THE LEGEND
(MGM--TV, 1962)

SPIRIT OF ST. LOUIS, THE (WB, 1957, based on the
exploits of the noted aviator)
CROWDED IDOL, THE (MGM--TV, 1962)
LINDBERG VS. THE ATLANTIC (short) (WOL, 1964)

SPIRIT OF YOUTH (GN, 1937, documentaries and
dramatic films based on the life of the champion prize--
fighter)
BROWN BOMBER, THE (IND, 1940)
JOE LOUIS STORY, THE (UA, 1953)
IN THIS CORNER -- JOE LOUIS (TV, 1963)
RING OF PASSION (NBC--TV, 1978)

SPIRITISM see MONKEY'S PAW, THE

SPIRITS OF THE DEAD see SEALED ROOM, THE and
STUDENT OF PRAGUE, THE

SPITE MARRIAGE (MGM, 1929, based on a story by Lew
Lipton)
BUSTER SE MARIE (FRA, 1929)

SPLENDEURS ET MISERES DES COURTISANES see
MOREL, DER MEISTER DER KETTE

SPLENDID CRIME, THE see RAGAMUFFIN

SPOEGELSESTOGET see GHOST TRAIN, THE

SPOILERS, THE (SEL, 1914, based on the book by Rex
Beach)
SPOILERS, THE (GOL, 1923)
SPOILERS, THE (PAR, 1930)
SPOILERS, THE (UN, 1942)
SPOILERS, THE (UN, 1955)

SPOKBARONEN (SWE, 1927, source unlisted)
FLOTTANS KAVALJERER (SWE, 1949)

SPOOK LOUDER see GREAT PIE MYSTERY, THE

SPORCKSCHEN JAGER, DIE (GER, 1926, based on the book
by Richard Skowroneck)
SPORCKSCHEN JAGER, DIE (GER, 1934)

SPORTING BLOOD (MGM, 1930, based on a story by
Frederick Hazlitt Brennan)
SPORTING BLOOD (MGM, 1939) (TV title: STERLING
METAL)

SPORTING GOODS see TRAVELING SALESMAN, THE

SPORTING LIFE (PAR, 1918, based on the play by Sir
Seymour Hicks and Cecil Raleigh)
SPORTING LIFE (UN, 1925)

SPORTSMAN'S SKETCHES, A see BEZHIN MEADOW

SPOTLIGHT, THE see FOOTLIGHTS

SPRING FEVER (MGM, 1927, based on a play by Vincent
Lawrence)
LOVE IN THE ROUGH (MGM, 1930)

SPRING IN PARK LANE see COME OUT OF THE
KITCHEN

SPRING IS HERE (WB, 1930, based on the musical by Owen
David, Richard Rodgers and Lorenz Hart)
SINCERELY YOURS (WB, 1933)

SPRING REUNION (NBC--TV, 1954, based on a teleplay by
Robert Alan Aurthur)
SPRING REUNION (UA, 1957)

SPUK MIT MAX UND MORITZ (GER, 1951, based on a book
by Wilhelm Busch)
MAX UND MORITZ (GER, 1956)

SPUK UM MITTERNACHT, DER see LAUREL AND
HARDY MURDER CASE, THE

SPURS see FREAKS

SPY, THE see OCCURENCE AT OWL CREEK BRIDGE, AN

SPY IN THE SKY see INVADERS FROM MARS

SPY SHIP see CAUGHT IN THE FOG

SPY SMASHER RETURNS see SPY SMASHERS

SPY SMASHERS (serial) (REP, 1942, based on a screenplay
by various authors; the remake is a condensed version of
the serial)
SPY SMASHER RETURNS (REP, 1966)

SQUARE CROOKS (FOX, 1928, based on the play by James
P. Judge)
BABY TAKE A BOW (FOX, 1935)

SQUAW MAN, THE (PAR, 1913, based on the book by Edwin
Milton Royle; also the basis for the 1927 operetta, "The
White Eagle," by Rudolph Friml)
SQUAW MAN, THE (PAR, 1919)
SQUAW MAN, THE (MGM, 1931)

SQUEAKER, THE (BRI, 1930, based on a book by Edgar
Wallace)
ZINKER, DER (GER, 1931)
MENACE, THE (COL, 1932)
FEATHERED SERPENT, THE (BRI, 1934)
MURDER ON DIAMOND ROW (BRI, 1937)
ZINKER, DER (GER, 1963)

SQUIBS (BRI, 1921, based on the play by Clifford Seyler)
SQUIBS (BRI, 1935)

STAGE DOOR (RKO, 1937, based on the play by Edna Ferber
and George S. Kaufman)
STAGE DOOR (NBC--TV, 1939)
STAGE DOOR (CBS--TV, 1955)

STAGE STRUCK see MORNING GLORY

STAGE OF LORDSBURY see STAGECOACH

STAGECOACH (UA, 1939, based on the book, "Stage to
Lordsbury," by Ernest Haycox)

STAGECOACH (FOX, 1966)

STAIRS OF SAND (PAR, 1929, based on a book by Zane
    Grey)
  ARIZONA MAHONEY (PAR, 1936)

STAIRWAY TO HEAVEN see AMAZING QUEST OF MR.
    ERNEST BLISS, THE

STALIN see STALIN ERA, THE

STALIN ERA, THE (short) (NET–TV, 1960, based on the
    life of the Soviet dictator)
  GREAT DESIGN, THE (short) (NET–TV, 1960)
  DECLINE AND FALL OF JOSEF STALIN, THE (short)
    (IND, n.d.)
  SOVIET CHALLENGE, THE (short) (EBE, 1962)
  DEATH OF STALIN, THE (short) (NBC–TV, 1963)
  STALIN (short) (MHF, 1963)

STALK THE WILD CHILD see WILD CHILD, THE

STAMBOUL (BRI, 1931, based on the play, "L'Homme qui
    assassina," by Pierre Frondale)
  HOMBRE QUE ASESINO (SPA, 1932)

STAMPEDE see STORMY TRAIL

STANDARD BEARER OF THE JEWISH PEOPLE, THE see
    WANDERING JEW, THE

STANLEY AND LIVINGSTONE see LIVINGSTONE

STAR GAZERS (short) (IND, 1946, based on the life and
    work of the noted astronomer and scientist, Galileo)
  GALILEO'S LAWS OF FALLING BODIES (short) (EBE,
    1953)
  HOW MANY STARS? (short) (IND, 1954)
  SPEED OF LIGHT, THE (short) (EBE, 1955)
  GALILEO (short) (COR, 1959)
  GALILEO (FRA/ITA, 1968)
  GALILEO -- THE CHALLENGE OF REASON (short)
    (LCA, 1969)
  GALILEO AND HIS UNIVERSE (short) (BFA, 1972)
  GALILEO (AFT, 1975)

STAR IS BORN, A see WHAT PRICE HOLLYWOOD?

STAR OF BETHLEHEM (ED, 1908, based on a Bible story)
  STAR OF BETHLEHEM (THA, 1912)
  STAR OF BETHLEHEM (BRI, 1956)

STAR OF BETHLEHEM see also PASSION PLAY, THE

STAR TREK (series) (NBC–TV, 1966, based on a teleplay)
  STAR TREK (series) (NBC–TV, 1973)

STAR WITNESS (WB, 1932, based on a story by Lucien
    Hubbard)
  MAN WHO DARED, THE (WB, 1939)

STARDUST ON THE SAGE see GIT ALONG LITTLE
    DOGIES

STARS AND STRIPES, THE (ED, 1910, based on the life of
    the noted military hero, John Paul Jones)
  MY LADY'S SLIPPER (VIT, 1916)
  WAR OF INDEPENDENCE 1775–1783 (short) (NAV,
    1952)

JOHN PAUL JONES (WB, 1959)
  NIGHT STRIKES: JOHN PAUL JONES (short) (TFC,
    1964)
  JOHN PAUL JONES (IND, 1967)

STARS OF THE RUSSIAN BALLET see SWAN LAKE

STARSKY AND HUTCH (ABC–TV, 1975, based on a teleplay)
  STARSKY AND HUTCH (series) (ABC–TV, 1975)

START THE REVOLUTION WITHOUT ME see
    CORSICAN BROTHERS, THE

STATE FAIR (FOX, 1933, based on the book by Philip
    Strong and the musical version by Richard Rodgers and
    Oscar Hammerstein II)
  STATE FAIR (FOX, 1945) (TV title: IT HAPPENED
    ONE SUMMER)
  STATE FAIR (FOX, 1961)
  STATE FAIR (CBS–TV, 1976)

STATE OF THE UNION (TV, 1945, based on the play by
    Howard Lindsay and Russell Crouse)
  STATE OF THE UNION (MGM, 1948)
  STATE OF THE UNION (NBC–TV, 1954)

STATE'S ATTORNEY (RKO, 1932, based on a story by
    Louis Stevens)
  CRIMINAL LAWYER (RKO, 1937)

STAYING ALIVE see SATURDAY NIGHT FEVER

STEEL CAGE, THE see DUFFY OF SAN QUENTIN

STELLA DALLAS (UA, 1925, based on the book by Olive
    Higgins Prouty)
  STELLA DALLAS (UA, 1937)

STELLA MARIS (ART, 1918, based on the play by William
    John Locke)
  STELLA MARIS (UN, 1926)

STEN STENSSON STEEN FRAN ESLOV (SWE, 1924, source
    unlisted)
  STEN STENSSON STEEN FRAN ESLOV (SWE, 1932)
  STEN STENSSON KOMMER TILL STAM (SWE, 1945)
  STEN STENSSON KOMMER TILLBAKA (SWE, 1963)

STENKA RAZIN see VOLGA VOLGA

STEP DOWN TO TERROR see SHADOW OF A DOUBT

STEP LIVELY see ROOM SERVICE

STEP LIVELY, JEEVES see THANK YOU, JEEVES

STEPHEN FOSTER AND HIS SONGS see SWANEE RIVER

STEPTOE AND SON (series) (BRI–TV, n.d., based on a
    British teleplay)
  SANFORD AND SON (series) (NBC–TV, 1972)
  STEPTOE AND SON RIDE AGAIN (BRI, 1973)
  GRADY (series) (NBC–TV, 1975)
  SANFORD ARMS (NBC–TV, 1977)

STEPTOE AND SON RIDE AGAIN see STEPTOE AND SON

STERLING METAL see SPORTING BLOOD

STERN VON RIO   (GER, 1940, source unlisted)
  STERN VON RIO   (GER, 1955)

STILL TRUMPET, THE   see   TWO FLAGS WEST

STIMME DES HERZENS, DIE   (GER, 1924, source unlisted)
  STIMME DES HERZENS, DIE   (GER, 1937)
  STIMME DES HERZENS, DIE   (GER, 1924)

STINE IRRUNGEN, WIRRUNGEN   see   ALTE LIED, DAS

STINGAREE   (IND, 1915, based on a book by Ernest William
    Hornung)
  STINGAREE   (RKO, 1934)

STINGIEST MAN IN TOWN, THE   see   CHRISTMAS
    CAROL, A

STJENKA RAZIN   see   VOLGA VOLGA

STOLEN AIRSHIP, THE   see   20,000 LEAGUES UNDER
    THE SEA

STOLEN HEAVEN   (PAR, 1931, based on a story by Dana
    Burnet)
  STOLEN HEAVEN   (PAR, 1938)

STOLEN HOURS   see   DARK VICTORY

STOLEN LIFE, A   (BRI, 1939, based on a book by Karel J.
    Benes)
  STOLEN LIFE, A   (WB, 1946)

STONE--AGE ROMEOS   see   I'M A MONKEY'S UNCLE

STONECUTTER, THE   see   TARA, THE STONECUTTER

STOP, LOOK AND LOVE   see   FAMILY UPSTAIRS, THE

STOP, YOU'RE KILLING ME   see   AMAZING DR.
    CLITTERHOUSE, THE

STORM, THE   (GER, 1922, based on a book by Max Halbe)
  STORM, THE   (GER, 1942)

STORM, THE   (UN, 1922, based on the play by Langdon
    McCormick)
  STORM, THE   (UN, 1930)
  STORM, THE   (UN, 1938)

STORM CLOUDS OF VENUS   (RUS, c1964, second film
    based on stock footage from the first, put together by
    Peter Bogdanovich)
  VOYAGE TO THE PLANET OF PREHISTORIC WOMEN,
    THE   (AI, 1967)

STORM IN A TEACUP   see   BLUMENFRAU VON LINDEN-
    AU, DIE

STORM OVER ASIA   (RUS, 1930, source unlisted)
  STORM OVER ASIA   (GER, 1938)
  TEMPETE SUR L'ASIE   (FRA, 1938)

STORM OVER THE ANDES   (UN, 1935, based on a story
    by Eliot Gibbons and La Clade Christy)
  ALAS SOBRE EL CHACO   (MEX, 1935)

STORM OVER THE NILE   see   FOUR FEATHERS

STORM WATERS   see   JACK LONDON'S TALES OF THE
    FISH PATROL

STORM WITHIN, THE   see   PARENTS TERRIBLES, LES

STORMY TRAIL   (GN, 1937, based on a book by Edward
    Beverly Mann)
  STAMPEDE   (AA, 1949)

STORY OF A BAD WOMAN, THE   see   LADY WINDER-
    MERE'S FAN

STORY OF A LIGHTER, THE   see   TINDERBOX, THE

STORY OF A POOR YOUNG MAN, THE   (ARG, 1942,
    based on the book by Octave Feuillet)
  STORY OF A POOR YOUNG MAN, THE   (ARG, 1972)

STORY OF A NIGHT   (ARG, 1941, source unlisted)
  STORY OF A NIGHT   (ARG, 1961)

STORY OF A VILLAGE, THE   see   TESTAMENT OF A MAN

STORY OF A WICKED WOMAN   see   LADY WINDERMERE'S
    FAN

STORY OF ALEXANDER GRAHAM BELL, THE   (FOX,
    1939, based on the life of the teacher and inventor)
  ALEXANDER GRAHAM BELL   (short)   (IND, n.d.)
  MR. BELL   (short)   (IND, 1947)
  HERE IS TOMORROW -- THE STORY OF ALEXANDER
    GRAHAM BELL   (NET-TV, n.d.)

STORY OF CHRISTOPHER COLUMBUS, THE   see   COMING
    OF COLUMBUS, THE

STORY OF DR. CARVER, THE   (short)   (MGM, 1938, based
    on the life and work of the noted scientist)
  GEORGE WASHINGTON CARVER   (short)   (IND, 1959)
  DR. GEORGE WASHINGTON CARVER   (short)   (IND,
    1966)
  GEORGE WASHINGTON CARVER   (short)   (BFA, 1967)
  BOYHOOD OF GEORGE WASHINGTON CARVER   (short)
    (COR, 1973)

STORY OF FLOATING WEEDS, A   (JAP, 1934, source
    unlisted)
  FLOATING WEEDS   (JAP, 1959)

STORY OF HANSEL AND GRETEL, THE   see   HANSEL
    AND GRETEL

STORY OF IVY, THE   see   IVY

STORY OF JACK LEE, THE MAN THEY COULD NOT
    HANG   see   MAN THEY COULD NOT HANG, THE

STORY OF JACK LONDON, THE   see   MARTIN EDEN

STORY OF JOSEPH AND HIS BRETHREN, THE   see
    JOSEPH IN EGYPT

STORY OF KING MIDAS, THE   see   KING MIDAS

STORY OF LITTLE RED RIDING HOOD, THE   see   LITTLE
    RED RIDING HOOD

STORY OF LOUIS PASTEUR, THE   (WB, 1935, based on the

life of the noted scientist)
PASTEUR   (FRA, 1935)
PASTEUR   (FRA, 1947)
TRIAL OF LOUIS PASTEUR, THE   (IND, 1958)

STORY OF MOBY DICK, THE   see   SEA BEAST, THE

STORY OF NATHAN HALE, THE   see   DEATH OF
NATHAN HALE, THE

STORY OF PRETTY BOY FLOYD, THE   see   PRETTY
BOY FLOYD

STORY OF ROBIN HOOD, THE   see   ROBIN HOOD AND
HIS MERRY MEN

STORY OF RUTH, THE   see   BOOK OF RUTH

STORY OF TEMPLE DRAKE, THE   (PAR, 1933, based on
the book, "Sanctuary," by William Faulkner)
SANCTUARY   (FOX, 1961)

STORY OF THE FISHERMAN AND THE LITTLE FISH, THE
(RUS, 1911, based on the story by Alexander Pushkin)
STORY OF THE FISHERMAN AND THE LITTLE FISH,
THE   (RUS, 1913)
STORY OF THE FISHERMAN AND THE LITTLE FISH,
THE   (RUS, 1937)
STORY OF THE FISHERMAN AND THE LITTLE FISH,
THE   (CZE, 1951)
STORY OF THE FISHERMAN AND THE LITTLE FISH,
THE   (RUS, 1951)

STORY OF THE LAST CHRYSANTHEMUMS, THE   (JAP,
1939, source unlisted)
STORY OF THE LAST CHRYSANTEHMUMS, THE
(JAP, 1956)

STORY OF THE LITTLE MINISTER, THE   (VIT, 1912,
based on the play, "The Little Minister," by Sir James M.
Barrie)
LITTLE MINISTER, THE   (BRI, 1915)
LITTLE MINISTER, THE   (VIT, 1921)
LITTLE MINISTER, THE   (PAR, 1922)
LITTLE MINISTER, THE   (RKO, 1934)
LITTLE MINISTER, THE   (NBC--TV, 1957)

STORY OF TOSCA, THE   see   TOSCA, LA

STORY OF TSAR SULTAN, THE   (RUS, 1943, based on the
story by Alexander Pushkin)
STORY OF TSAR SULTAN, THE   (RUS, 1967)

STORY OF WILL ROGERS, THE   (WB, 1952, based on the
life of the noted humorist)
WILL ROGERS   (short)   (STE, 1960)
WILL ROGERS   (NBC–TV, 1961)

STORY THAT COULDN'T BE PRINTED, THE   (short)
(MGM, 1939, based on the life of publisher John Peter
Zenger)
JOHN PETER ZENGER   (short)   (IND, n.d.)

STRAIGHT IS THE WAY   see   FOUR WALLS

STRANGE AFFAIR OF UNCLE HARRY, THE   (UN, 1945,
based on the play, "Uncle Harry," by Thomas Job)
UNCLE HARRY   (CBS–TV, 1950)
UNCLE HARRY   (ABC–TV, 1954)

UNCLE HARRY   (NET–TV, 1960)

STRANGE CASE OF DAVID GRAY, THE   (FRA/GER, 1932,
based on the book, "Carmilla," by Sheridan le Fanu)
BLOOD AND ROSES   (FRA/ITA, 1960)
TERROR IN THE CRYPT   (CURSE OF THE KARN--
STEINS)   (ITA/SPA, 1963)
CARMILLA   (JAP/SWE, 1968)
VAMPIRE LOVERS, THE   (BRI, 1970)
TWINS OF EVIL   (DAUGHTERS OF DARKNESS)   (BRI,
1971)
LUST FOR A VAMPIRE   (BRI, 1971)
BLOODY BRIDE, THE   (SPA, 1972)
DAUGHTER OF DRACULA, THE   (FRA/POR/SPA, 1972)

STRANGE CASE OF DR. FAUSTUS, THE   see   FAUST

STRANGE CASE OF DR. JEKYLL AND MR. HYDE   see
DR. JEKYLL AND MR. HYDE

STRANGE CASE OF THE MAN AND THE BEAST   see   DR.
JEKYLL AND MR. HYDE

STRANGE CONFESSION   see   MAN WHO RECLAIMED HIS
HEAD, THE

STRANGE CONQUEST   see   CRIME OF DR. HALLET, THE

STRANGE DESIRE OF MONSIEUR BARD, THE   see
MERCHANT OF VENICE, THE

STRANGE DOOR, THE   see   SIRE DE MALETROIT'S
DOOR

STRANGE HOMECOMING   see   SHADOW OF A DOUBT

STRANGE ILLUSION   see   HAMLET

STRANGE SKIRTS   see   WHEN LADIES MEET

STRANGER, THE   (PAR, 1924, based on a book, "The First
and the Last," by John Galsworthy)
TWENTY--ONE DAYS   (BRI, 1940)
LETZTEN WERDEN DIE ERSTEN SEIN, DIE   (GER,
1957)

STRANGER FROM TEXAS, THE   see   MYSTERIOUS
AVENGER, THE

STRANGER IN THE HOUSE   see   INCONNUS DANS LA
MAISON, LES

STRANGERS IN THE NIGHT   (MGM, 1923, based on the
play, "Captain Applejack," by Walter Hackett)
CAPTAIN APPLEJACK   (WB, 1931)

STRANGER IN THE NIGHT   see   GHOST AND MRS. MUIR,
THE

STRANGERS ON A TRAIN   (WB, 1951, based on a book by
Patricia Highsmith)
ONCE YOU KISS A STRANGER   (WB, 1969)

STRANGLER OF THE SWAMP   see   FAHRMANN MARIA

STRATEGY OF TERROR   see   IN DARKNESS WAITING

STRAUSS FAMILY, THE   see   WALTZES FROM VIENNA

STRAW HAT, THE see CHAPEAU DE PAILLE D'ITALIE

STRAWBERRY BLONDE see ONE SUNDAY AFTERNOON

STREET ANGEL (FOX, 1928, based on a play by Monckton
    Hoffe)
  STREET ANGEL (CHN, 1935)
  ROUGE AND TEARS (CHN, 1938)

STREET GIRL (RKO, 1929, based on the book, "Viennese
    Charmer," by W. Carey Wonderly)
  THAT GIRL FROM PARIS (RKO, 1937)
  FOUR JACKS AND A JILL (RKO, 1941)

STREET IN THE SUN, A see SLOPE IN THE SUN, A

STREET OF CHANCE (PAR, 1930, based on a story by
    Oliver H.P. Garrett)
  NOW I'LL TELL (FOX, 1934)
  HER HUSBAND LIES (PAR, 1937)

STREET SCENE (UA, 1931, based on the play by Elmer
    Rice; also the basis of an opera by Kurt Weill)
  STREET SCENE (NBC–TV, 1948)
  STREET SCENE (ABC–TV, 1952)

STREET WITH NO NAME, THE (FOX, 1948, based on a
    screenplay by Harry Kleiner)
  HOUSE OF BAMBOO (FOX, 1955)

STREETS OF LAREDO see TEXAS RANGERS, THE

STRICTLY DISHONORABLE (UN, 1931, based on the play
    by Preston Sturges)
  STRICTLY DISHONORABLE (MGM, 1951)

STRICTLY MODERN see COUSIN KATE

STRICTLY UNCONVENTIONAL see CIRCLE, THE

STROGOFF see MICHAEL STROGOFF

STROM, DER (GER, 1922, source unlisted)
  STROM, DER (GER, 1942)

STRONGER, THE (TV, 1960, based on a play by August
    Strindberg)
  STRONGER, THE (short) (IND, 1970)
  STRONGER, THE (short) (AFI, 1976)

STRONGER THAN DESIRE see EVELYN PRENTICE

STRONGER THAN LOVE see VANINA VANINI

STUDENT CHEMIST HELENE WILLFUR (GER, 1929,
    source unlisted)
  STUDENT CHEMIST HELENE WILLFUR (FRA, 1936)

STUDENT OF PRAGUE (GER, 1913, based on the book by
    Hanns Heinz Ewers)
  MAN WHO CHEATED DEATH, THE (GER, 1926)
  STUDENT OF PRAGUE (AUS, 1935)
  HELP! (ITA, 1954)
  WILLIAM WILSON (short) (NBC–TV, 1961)
  SPIRITS OF THE DEAD (sequence) (AI, 1969)

STUDENT PRINCE, THE see OLD HEIDELBERG

STUDENT'S ROMANCE, A see OLD HEIDELBERG

STUDIO OF DR. FAUST see FAUST

STUDS LONIGAN (UA, 1960, based on the book by James T.
    Farrell)
  STUDS LONIGAN (NBC–TV, 1978)

STUDY IN SCARLET, A (BRI, 1914, based on the book by
    Sir Arthur Conan Doyle)
  STUDY IN SCARLET, A (BRI, 1933)

STUDY IN TERROR, A see LODGER, THE and SHERLOCK
  HOLMES series

STURM IN WASSERGLAS see BLUMENFRAU VON
  LINDENAU, DIE

STURME DER LEIDENSCHAFT (GER, 1931, based on the
    play by Robert Liebmann and Hans Mueller)
  TUMULTES (FRA, 1931)

STURMFLUT (GER, 1917, based on a book by Heinrich
    Sienkiewicz)
  STURMFLUT (GER, 1942)

STYRMAN KARLSSONS FLAMMOR (SWE, 1925, source
    unlisted)
  STYRMAN KARLSSONS FLAMMOR (SWE, 1938)

SU NOCHE DE BODAS see MISS BLUEBEARD

SU ULTIMA NOCHE see GAY DECEIVER, THE

SUBMARINE (COL, 1929, based on a story by Norman
    Springer)
  DEVIL'S PLAYGROUND, THE (UA, 1946)

SUBMARINE D–1 (WB, 1937, based on a story by Frank
    Wead)
  DIVE BOMBER (WB, 1941)

SUCH A BOOR (THE FIRE–TONGUE BOWL) (GER, 1932,
    based on the book, "Die Feuerzangenbowle," by Heinrich
    Spoerl)
  FEUERZANGENBOWLE, DIE (GER, 1944)
  FEUERZANGENBOWLE, DIE (GER, 1970)

SUCH A LITTLE QUEEN (PAR, 1914, based on the play by
    Channing Pollock)
  SUCH A LITTLE QUEEN (REA, 1921)

SUGARFOOT (WB, 1951, based on a story
    by Clarence Buddington Kelland)
  SUGARFOOT (series) (ABC–TV, 1957)

SUGATO SANSHIRO (JAP, 1945, source unlisted)
  SUGATO SANSHIRO (JAP, 1955)
  SUGATO SANSHIRO (JAP, 1965)

SUICIDE CLUB, THE (BIO, 1909, based on stories by
    Robert Louis Stevenson)
  AMERICAN SUICIDE CLUB (FRA, 1910)
  SUICIDE CLUB, THE (BRI, 1914)
  FIVE SINISTER STORIES (sequence) (GER, 1919)
  SUICIDE CLUB, THE (ITA, 1922)
  SUICIDE CLUB, THE (BRI, 1932)
  SINISTER STORIES (sequence) (GER, 1932)
  TROUBLE FOR TWO (MGM, 1936)
  FEMME DE LA MORT, LA (CHL, 1945)
  LADY AND DEATH, THE (CHN, 1946)
  SUICIDE CLUB, THE (NBC–TV, 1960)

SUICIDE CLUB, THE (BRI–TV, 1970)
SUICIDE CLUB, THE (ABC–TV, 1973)

SULTAN ROUGE, LE see ABDUL THE DAMNED

SUMMER AND SMOKE (PAR, 1961, based on the play by
    Tennessee Williams)
SUMMER AND SMOKE (BRI–TV, 1972)

SUMMER HOLIDAY see AH, WILDERNESS

SUMMER MAGIC see MOTHER CAREY'S CHICKENS

SUMMONING OF EVERYMAN see EVERYMAN

SUMURUN (GER, 1908, based on a pantomime by
    Friedrick Freksa and Victor Hollaender)
SUMURUN (GER, 1912)
SUMURUN (GER, 1920)

SUN SHINES BRIGHT, THE see JUDGE PRIEST

SUNDIGE DORF, DAS (GER, 1940, based on the play by
    Max Neal)
SUNDIGE DORF, DAS (GER, 1954)

SUNDOWN SLIM (UN, 1920, based on a story by H.H. Knibbs)
BURNING TRAIL, THE (UN, 1925)

SUNNY (FN, 1930, based on the musical comedy by Jerome
    Kern, Otto Harbach and Oscar Hammerstein II)
SUNNY (RKO, 1941)

SUNNY GOES HOME see MAJOR AND THE MINOR, THE

SUNRISE (FOX, 1927, based on the book, "A Trip to
    Tilsit," by Hermann Sudermann)
TRIP TO TILSIT, A (GER, 1939)
TRIP TO TILSIT, A (GER, 1969)

SUNRISE AT CAMPOBELLO see FIGHTING PRESIDENT,
    THE

SUNSET AT APPOMATTOX see UNDER SOUTHERN
    STARS

SUNSET BOULEVARD (PAR, 1950, based on a story, "A
    Can of Beans," by Billy Wilder and Charles Brackett)
SUNSET BOULEVARD (NBC–TV, 1955)

SUNSET PASS (PAR, 1929, based on a story by Zane Grey)
SUNSET PASS (PAR, 1933)
SUNSET PASS (RKO, 1946)

SUNSHINE BOYS, THE (MGM, 1975, based on the play by
    Neil Simon)
SUNSHINE BOYS, THE (series) (NBC–TV, 1977)

SUNSHINE SUSIE see PRIVATSEKRATARIN, DIE

SUNSTROKE (DEN, n.d., source unlisted)
SUNSTROKE AT THE BEACH RESORT (DEN, 1973)

SUNSTROKE AT THE BEACH RESORT see SUNSTROKE

SUPER OF THE GAIETY see LOST -- A WIFE

SURROUNDED BY WOMEN see BETWEEN TWO WOMEN

SUSAN AND GOD (MGM, 1940, based on the play by
    Rachel Crothers)
SUSAN AND GOD (ABC--TV, 1951)
SUSAN AND GOD (NBC–TV, 1956)

SUSAN B. ANTHONY (short) (EBE, 1951, based on the life
    of the American suffragist)
SUSAN B. ANTHONY IS TRIED FOR VOTING (short)
    (CBS--TV, 1955)
SUSAN B. ANTHONY AND WOMEN'S RIGHTS (short)
    (BFA, n.d.)

SUSPECT, THE (UN, 1944, based on a book by James Ronald)
SUSPECT, THE (NBC–TV, 1955)

SUTTER'S GOLD (UN, 1936, the second film consists of
    stock footage from the first film)
MUTINY ON THE BLACKHAWK (UN, 1939)

SVARTA ROSAR (SWE, 1932, source unlisted)
SVARTA ROSAR (SWE, 1945)

SVENGALI see TRILBY AND LITTLE BILLEE

SVENGALI AND THE BLONDE see TRILBY AND
    LITTLE BILLEE

SWAMP WATER (FOX, 1941, based on a story by Vereen
    Bell)
LURE OF THE WILDERNESS (FOX, 1952)

SWAN, THE (PAR, 1925, based on the play by Ferenc Molnar)
ONE ROMANTIC NIGHT (UA, 1930)
SWAN, THE (CBS–TV, 1950)
SWAN, THE (MGM, 1956)

SWAN LAKE (short) (FRA, 1949, based on the ballet by
    Peter Tchaikovsky)
STARS OF THE RUSSIAN BALLET (RUS, 1953)
SWAN LAKE (RUS, 1957)
SWAN LAKE (BRI, 1960)
SWAN LAKE (GER, 1964)
SWAN LAKE (short) (BUL, 1965)
SWAN LAKE (GER–TV, 1967)
SWAN LAKE (RUS, 1968)
SWAN LAKE (ITA, n.d.)
SWAN LAKE (SWI, n.d.)

SWANEE RIVER (FOX, 1939, based on the life and work of
    composer Stephen Foster)
BEAUTIFUL DREAMER (short) (IND, 1947)
STEPHEN COLLINS FOSTER (short) (IND, n.d.)
STEPHEN FOSTER AND HIS SONGS (short) (COR,
    1960)

SWASTIKA see HITLER GANG, THE

SWEATER GIRL see COLLEGE SCANDAL

SWEDENHEILM FAMILY, THE (DEN, n.d., source unlisted)
SWEDENHEILM FAMILY, THE (DEN, 1947)

SWEENEY TODD (BRI, 1928, based on the play by George
    Dibden Pitt and C. Hazelton)
DEMON BARBER OF FLEET STREET (BRI, 1936)
BLOODTHIRSTY BUTCHERS (BRI, 1969)
SWEENEY TODD (BRI--TV, 1970)

SWEEPINGS (RKO, 1933, based on the book by Lester Cohen)

THREE SONS   (RKO, 1939)

SWEET CHARITY   see   NIGHTS OF CABIRIA

SWEET KITTY BELLAIRS   see   INCOMPARABLE
    BELLAIRS, THE

SWEET LAVENDER   (BRI, 1915, based on the play by
    Arthur Wing Pinero)
  SWEET LAVENDER   (REA, 1920)

SWEET ROSIE O'GRADY   see   LOVE IS NEWS

SWEETHEART OF SIGMA CHI   (MON, 1933, based on a
    story by George Waggner)
  SWEETHEART OF SIGMA CHI   (MON, 1946)

SWELL GUY   see   HERO, THE

SWING HIGH, SWING LOW   see   DANCE OF LIFE, THE

SWING OPERA, A   see   BOHEMIAN GIRL, THE

SWISS FAMILY ROBINSON   see   PERILS OF THE WILD

SWITCH   (CBS–TV, 1975, based on a teleplay)
  SWITCH   (series)   (CBS–TV, 1975)

SWORD AND THE ROSE, THE   see   WHEN KNIGHTHOOD
    WAS IN FLOWER

SWORD AND THE SUMO RING, THE   (JAP, 1931, source
    unlisted)
  SWORD AND THE SUMO RING, THE   (JAP, 1934)
  SWORD AND THE SUMO RING, THE   (JAP, 1960)

SWORD IN THE STONE, THE   (DIS, 1963, based on the
    book, "The Once and Future King," by T.H. White)
  CAMELOT   (WB, 1967)

SWORD OF ALI BABA, THE   see   PRINCE WHO WAS A
    THIEF, THE

SWORD OF LANCELOT   (UN, 1962, based on a legend)
  ADVENTURES OF SIR LANCELOT   (series)   (NBC–TV,
    1955)
  LANCELOT OF THE LAKE   (FRA, 1974)

SWORD OF SHERWOOD FOREST   see   ROBIN HOOD AND
    HIS MERRY MEN

SWORD OF VILLON, THE   see   IF I WERE KING

SYLPHIDES, LES   (short)   (BRI–TV, 1958, based on the
    ballet by Frederic Chopin)
  CHOPINIANA   (RUS, 1958)
  EVENING WITH THE ROYAL BALLET, AN   (BRI, 1965)
  SYLPHIDES, LA   (PBS–TV, 1972)

SYLVESTER   see   YOU KNOW WHAT SAILORS ARE

SYMPHONIE PASTORALE, LA   (JAP, 1935, based on a
    story by Andre Gide)
  SYMPHONIE PASTORALE, LA   (FRA, 1946)

SYMPHONY OF LOVE AND DEATH, THE   (RUS, 1914,
    based on the story, "Mozart and Salieri," by Alexander
    Pushkin and the opera by Nicholai Rimsky–Korsakov)
  MOZART AND SALIERI   (RUS, 1952)

SYNNOVE SOLBAKKEN   (NOR/SWE, 1919, source unlisted)
  SYNNOVE SOLBAKKEN   (NOR/SWE, 1934)
  SYNNOVE SOLBAKKEN   (NOR/SWE, 1956)

SYSTEM, THE   see   SYSTEM OF DOCTOR TARR AND
    PROFESSOR FETHER, THE

SYSTEM OF DOCTOR TARR AND PROFESSOR FETHER,
    THE   (FRA, 1912, based on the story by Edgar Allan
    Poe)
  SYSTEM OF DOCTOR TARR AND PROFESSOR
    FETHER, THE   (GER, 1920)
  SYSTEM, THE   (POL, 1971)

THX--1138 (short) (IND, 1967, based on a screenplay by
Francis Ford Coppola)
THX--1138 (WB, 1969)

T--MEN (EL, 1948, based on a story by Virginia Kellog)
FILE OF THE GOLDEN GOOSE, THE (UA, 1969)

TABITHA see BEWITCHED

TAGEBUCH EINER VERLORENEN, DAS (GER, 1920,
based on a book by Margarete Bohme)
TAGEBUCH EINER VERLORENEN, DAS (DIARY OF
A LOST GIRL) (GER, 1929)

TAGORE (IN, 1961, based on the life and works of
Rabindranath Tagore)
TAGORE (RUS, 1961)

TAIFUN see TYPHOON

TAILOR--MADE MAN, A (UA, 1922, based on the play by
Harry James Smith)
TAILOR--MADE MAN, A (MGM, 1931)

TAKE OFF see PICTURE OF DORIAN GRAY, THE

TAL DES LEBENS, DAS (GER, 1914, based on the play by
Max Dreyer)
AMMENKONIG, DER (GER, 1935)

TALE OF GENJI (JAP, 1951, source unlisted)
TALE OF GENJI (JAP, 1966)

TALE OF KING MIDAS, THE see KING MIDAS

TALE OF RUMPELSTILTSKIN see RUMPELSTILTSKIN

TALE OF THE ARK see NOAH'S ARK

TALE OF TWO CITIES, A (VIT, 1911, based on the book by
Charles Dickens; also the basis for the musical, "Two
Cities" in 1969)
TALE OF TWO CITIES, A (VIT, 1913)
TALE OF TWO CITIES, A (FOX, 1917)
ONLY WAY, THE (short) (BRI, 1922)
ONLY WAY, THE (BRI, 1925)
TALE OF TWO CITIES, A (MGM, 1935)
TALE OF TWO CITIES, A (ABC--TV, 1953)
TALE OF TWO CITIES, A (CBS--TV, 1958)
TALE OF TWO CITIES, A (BRI, 1958)

TALES FROM THE CRYPT see MONKEY'S PAW, THE

TALES OF A THOUSAND AND ONE NIGHTS see
ARABIAN NIGHTS

TALES OF BEATRIX POTTER see WORLD OF BEATRIX
POTTER, THE

TALES OF HOFFMANN see HOFFMANNS ERZAHLUNGEN

TALES OF 1001 ARABIAN NIGHTS see ARABIAN
NIGHTS

TALES OF ROBIN HOOD see ROBIN HOOD AND HIS
MERRY MEN

TALES OF TERROR see EERIE TALES and SEALED
ROOM, THE

TALES OF WASHINGTON IRVING see LEGEND OF
SLEEPY HOLLOW, THE and RIP VAN WINKLE

TALISMAN, THE see RICHARD THE LION--HEARTED

TALL, DARK AND HANDSOME see DRESSED TO KILL

TAMAGNE see BELLA

TAMING OF THE SHREW, THE (BIO, 1908, based on the
play by William Shakespeare and the musical comedy by
Cole Porter)
TAMING OF THE SHREW, THE (ITA, 1908)
TAMING OF THE SHREW, THE (BRI, 1911)
TAMING OF THE SHREW, THE (FRA, 1911)
TAMING OF THE SHREW, THE (ITA, 1913)
TAMING OF THE SHREW, THE (NOR, 1914)
TAMING OF THE SHREW, THE (BRI, 1915)
TAMING OF THE SHREW, THE (BRI, 1923)
TAMING OF THE SHREW, THE (UA, 1929)
TAMING OF THE SHREW, THE (ITA, 1941)
SECOND BEST BED (BRI, 1944)
TAMING OF THE SHREW, THE (CBS--TV, 1950)
KISS ME KATE (MGM, 1953)
TAMING OF THE SHREW, THE (NBC--TV, 1954)
TAMING OF THE SHREW, THE (FRA/SPA, 1955)
TAMING OF THE SHREW, THE (NBC--TV, 1956)
TAMING OF THE SHREW, THE (NBC--TV, 1958)
KISS ME KATE (NBC--TV, 1958)
TAMING OF THE SHREW, THE (RUS--TV, 1961)
KISS ME KATE (BRI--TV, 1963)
TAMING OF THE SHREW, THE (COL, 1966)
KISS ME KATE (ABC--TV, 1967)
TAMING OF THE SHREW, THE (PBS--TV, 1976)

TAMPICO (MGM, 1930, based on the book, "The Woman I
Stole," by Joseph Hergesheimer)
WOMAN I STOLE, THE (COL, 1933)

TANGLED LIVES see WOMAN IN WHITE, THE

TANZ GEHT WEITER, DER see THOSE WHO DANCE

TARA, THE STONECUTTER (short) (IND, 1955, based on
the Japanese folk tale)
STONECUTTER, THE (short) (IND, 1965)
STONECUTTER, THE (short) (IND, 1975)

TARAKANOVA (FRA/GER, 1930, based on the book by
Andre Lang and Rene Lehmann)
TARAKANOVA (FRA/ITA, 1938)

TARANTOS, LOS see ROMEO AND JULIET

TARANTULA see NO FOOD FOR THOUGHT

TARAS BULBA (LOVE OF ANDREI, THE) (RUS, 1909,
based on the story by Nikolai Gogol; stock footage from
the 1936 film was used in the 1939 film)
TARAS BULBA (GER, 1923)
TARAS BULBA (POL, 1927)
TARAS BULBA (FRA, 1936)
BARBARIAN AND THE LADY, THE (BRI, 1939) (TV
title: REBEL'S SON, THE)
TARAS BULBA (FRA/ITA, 1961)
TARAS BULBA (UA, 1962)

TARASS CHEVTCHENKO (RUS, 1926, based on the life of
Tarass Chevtchenko)

TARASS CHEVTCHENKO (RUS, 1951)

TARGET, SEA OF CHINA see TRADER TOM OF THE CHINA SEAS

TARTARIN DE TARASCON (FRA, 1908, based on a book by Alphonse Daudet)
TARTARIN DE TARASCON (FRA, 1934)
TARTARIN DE TARASCON (FRA, 1962)

TARTARS OF THE NORTH see MICHAEL STROGOFF

TARTUFFE (ITA, 1908, based on the play by Moliere)
TARTUFFE (FRA, 1910)
TARTUFFE (GER, 1925)
HYPOCRITE, THE (CHN, 1926)
TARTUFFE, THE HYPOCRITE (GER, 1927)
TARTUFFE (PBS--TV, 1978)

TARTUFFE, THE HYPOCRITE see TARTUFFE

TARZAN OF THE APES (FN, 1918, based on the book by Edgar Rice Burroughs)
TARZAN, THE APE MAN (MGM, 1932)
TARZAN, THE APE MAN (MGM, 1959)

TARZAN, THE APE MAN see TARZAN OF THE APES

TASTE THE BLOOD OF DRACULA see NOSFERATU

TAUGENICHTS, DER (GER, 1922, based on the book by Joseph von Eichendorff)
AUS DEM LEBEN EINES TAUGENICHTS (GER, 1973)

TAXI see SAN LAISSER D'ADRESSE

TCHAIKOVSKY see IT WAS AN EXCITING NIGHT

TEA FOR TWO see NO, NO, NANETTE

TEAHOUSE OF THE AUGUST MOON, THE (MGM, 1956, based on the book by Vern Snider and the play by John Patrick; also the basis for the musical comedy, "Lovely Ladies, Kind Gentlemen," in 1970)
TEAHOUSE OF THE AUGUST MOON, THE (NBC--TV, 1962)

TECHNIQUE see ANSEL ADAMS, PHOTOGRAPHER

TEDDY BEARS, THE (ED, 1907, based on the fairy tale)
GOLDILOCKS AND THE 3 BEARS (PP, 1917)
GOLDILOCKS AND THE THREE BEARS (short) (MGM, 1939)
GOLDILOCKS AND THE THREE BEARS (short) (COR, 1953)
GOLDILOCKS (short) (CZE, 1954)
GOLDILOCKS AND THE THREE BEARS (short) (IND, 1957)
GOLDILOCKS AND THE THREE BEARS (short) (TV, 1967)
GOLDILOCKS (NBC--TV, 1970)

TEDDY, THE ROUGH RIDER (short) (WB, 1940, based on the life of President Theodore Roosevelt)
ATTEMPT TO ASSASSINATE THEODORE ROOSEVELT, THE (short) (CBS--TV, 1957)
THEODORE ROOSEVELT, AMERICAN (short) (NAV, 1958)
LIFE AND TIMES OF TEDDY ROOSEVELT, THE (short)

(CBS--TV, 1959)
THEODORE ROOSEVELT (short) (MHF, 1963)

TENDERFOOT: THEODORE ROOSEVELT, THE (short) (TFC, 1965)
THEODORE ROOSEVELT'S SAGAMORE HILL (short) (IND, 1972)
TEDDY ROOSEVELT -- THE RIGHT MAN AT THE RIGHT TIME (short) (LCA, 1974)

TELEPHONE GIRL (PAR, 1927, based on the play, "The Woman," by William C. DeMille)
SECRET CALL (PAR, 1931)

TELEVISION (FRA, 1930, source unlisted)
TELEVISION (RUM, 1930)

TELL see GUILLAUME TELL ET LE CLOWN

TELL ME TONIGHT (BE MINE TONIGHT) (BRI, 1932, based on a story by Irma von Cube and A. Joseph)
LIED EINER NACHT, DAS (GER, 1932)
CHANSON D'UNE NUIT, LES (FRA, 1932)

TELL--TALE HEART, THE see AVENGING CONSCIENCE, THE

TEMPEST, THE (BRI, 1905, based on the play by William Shakespeare)
TEMPEST, THE (BRI, 1908)
TEMPEST, THE (THA, 1911)
TEMPEST, THE (FRA, 1912)
TEMPEST, THE (IND, 1913)
TEMPEST, THE (BRI, 1919)
TEMPEST, THE (FRA, 1921)
FORBIDDEN PLANET (MGM, 1956)
TEMPEST, THE (NBC--TV, 1960)
TEMPEST, THE (NBC--TV, 1963)
TEMPEST, THE (BRI--TV, 1969)

TEMPETE SUR L'ASIE see STORM OVER ASIA

TEMPLE HOUSTON see MAN FROM GALVESTON, THE

TEMPLE TOWER (FOX, 1930, based on the book by Sapper [Herman Cyril McNeile])
BULLDOG DRUMMOND'S SECRET POLICE (PAR, 1939)

TEMPORARY WIDOW, THE see HOKUSPOKUS

TEMPTATION (JAP, 1948, source unlisted)
TEMPTATION (JAP, 1957)

TEMPTATION see BELLA DONNA

TEMPTATION HARBOR see HOMME DE LONDRES, L'

TEMPTATION OF ST. ANTHONY, THE (FRA, 1898, source unlisted)
TEMPTATION OF ST. ANTHONY, THE (BIO, 1902)
TEMPTATION OF ST. ANTHONY, THE (FRA, 1905)
TEMPTATION OF ST. ANTHONY, THE (ITA, 1911)

TEN CENTS A DANCE (COL, 1931, based on a song by Richard Rodgers and Lorenz Hart)
CARNET DE CABARET (SPA, 1931)

TEN COMMANDMENTS, THE see LIFE OF MOSES, THE

TEN DOLLAR RAISE   (AP, 1921, based on the story by Peter
   B. Kyne)
   TEN DOLLAR RAISE   (FOX, 1935)
   HE HIRED THE BOSS   (FOX, 1943)

TEN LITTLE INDIANS   see   AND THEN THERE WERE
   NONE

TEN NIGHTS IN A BARROOM   (BIO, 1903, based on the
   book by T.S. Arthur and the play by William W. Pratt)
   TEN NIGHTS IN A BARROOM   (LUB, 1903)
   TEN NIGHTS IN A BARROOM   (ESS, 1909)
   TEN NIGHTS IN A BARROOM   (THA, 1910)
   TEN NIGHTS IN A BARROOM   (SEL, 1911)
   TEN NIGHTS IN A BARROOM   (IND, 1913)
   TEN NIGHTS IN A BARROOM   (IND, 1921)
   TEN NIGHTS IN A BARROOM   (CPC, 1926)
   TEN NIGHTS IN A BARROOM   (IND, 1930)

TENDER IS THE NIGHT   (CBS--TV, 1955, based on the book
   by F. Scott Fitzgerald)
   TENDER IS THE NIGHT   (FOX, 1962)

TENDERFOOT, THE   see   BUTTER AND EGG MAN, THE

TENDERFOOT: THEODORE ROOSEVELT, THE   see
   TEDDY, THE ROUGH RIDER

TENNESSEE JOHNSON   (MGM, 1942, based on the life of
   President Andrew Johnson)
   CIVIL WAR: POSTWAR PERIOD   (short)   (COR, 1964)
   ANDREW JOHNSON   (short)   (EBE, n.d.)
   ANDREW JOHNSON   (SAU, 1966)

TENNESSEE'S PARDNER   (PAR, 1916, based on the book
   by Bret Harte)
   GOLDEN PRINCESS, THE   (PAR, 1925)
   FLAMING FORTIES   (PDC, 1925)
   TENNESSEE'S PARTNER   (RKO, 1955)

TENTATION, LA   (FRA, 1929, based on the book by Charles
   Mere)
   TENTATION, LA   (FRA, 1936)

TEREZIN   see   GHETTO TEREZIN

TEREZIN REQUIEM   see   GHETTO TEREZIN

TERRES DEFRICHEES   (RUS, 1939, based on a book by
   Mikhail Cholokhov)
   TERRES DEFRICHEES   (RUS, 1961)

TERREUR DES DAMES, LA   see   CE COCHON DE MORIN

TERRIBLE PEOPLE, THE   (serial)   (PAT, 1928, based on the
   book by Edgar Wallace)
   TERRIBLE PEOPLE, THE   (GER, 1960)
   TERRIBLE PEOPLE, THE   (BRI, 1965)

TERROR, THE   (WB, 1928, based on the play by Edgar
   Wallace)
   RETURN OF THE TERROR   (FN, 1934)
   TERROR, THE   (BRI, 1938)
   TERROR, THE   (AI, 1963)

TERROR IN THE CRYPT   see   STRANGE CASE OF DAVID
   GRAY, THE

TERROR IN THE SKY   see   FLIGHT INTO DANGER

TERROR IS A MAN   see   ISLAND OF TERROR

TERRORS OF RUSSIA, THE   see   BLACK 107, THE

TESS OF THE STORM COUNTRY   (PAR, 1914, based on the
   book, "Tess of the d'Ubervilles," by Grace Miller White)
   TESS OF THE STORM COUNTRY   (UA, 1922)
   TESS OF THE D'UBERVILLES   (MGM, 1924)
   TESS OF THE STORM COUNTRY   (FOX, 1932)
   TESS OF THE STORM COUNTRY   (FOX, 1960)
   BRIDE FOR A SINGLE NIGHT   (IN, 1967)

TESS OF THE D'UBERVILLES   see   TESS OF THE STORM
   COUNTRY

TESTAMENT OF A MAN   (SWE, 1940, source unlisted)
   STORY OF A VILLAGE, THE   (SWE, 1941)

TESTAMENT OF DR. CORDELIER, THE   see   DR. JEKYLL
   AND MR. HYDE

TESTAMENT OF DR. MABUSE, THE   (GER, 1932, based on
   a screenplay by Thea von Harbou)
   LAST WILL OF DR. MABUSE, THE   (GER, 1962)

TESTAMENT OF MONTE CRISTO, THE   see   COUNT OF
   MONTE CRISTO, THE

TESTING OF SAM HOUSTON   see   CONQUERER, THE

TETE D'UN HOMME, LA   (FRA, 1932, based on the book by
   Georges Simenon)
   MAN ON THE EIFFEL TOWER, THE   (RKO, 1949)

TEVYA   (IND, 1939, based on stories by Scholem Aleichem)
   TEVYE AND HIS SEVEN DAUGHTERS   (GER/ISR, 1967)
   TEVYA   (short)   (ISR, 1968)
   FIDDLER ON THE ROOF   (UA, 1971)

TEVYA AND HIS SEVEN DAUGHTERS   see   TEVYA

TEXAN, THE   see   DOUBLE--DYED DECEIVER, THE

TEXANS, THE   see   NORTH OF '36

TEXAS RANGERS, THE   (PAR, 1936, based on the book by
   Walter Prescott Webb)
   STREETS OF LAREDO   (PAR, 1949)

TEXAS STAMPEDE   see   DAWN TRAIL, THE

TEXAS STEER, A   (SEL, 1915, based on the play by
   Charles H. Hoyt)
   TEXAS STEER, A   (FN, 1927)

THAIS   (FRA, 1911, based on a story by Anatole France)
   THAIS   (GOL, 1917)

THANK YOU, JEEVES   (FOX, 1936, based on the books by
   P.J. Wodehouse)
   STEP LIVELY, JEEVES   (FOX, 1937)
   THANK YOU, JEEVES   (series)   (NBC--TV, c1956)

THANKS A MILLION   (FOX, 1935, based on a screenplay by
   Nunnally Johnson)
   IF I'M LUCKY   (FOX, 1946)

THANKS FOR THE MEMORY   see   UP POPS THE DEVIL

THAT CERTAIN WOMAN see TRESPASSER, THE

THAT FORSYTE WOMAN (MGM, 1949, based on the book,
    "The Forsyte Saga," by John Galsworthy)
  FORSYTE SAGA, THE (series) (BRI--TV, 1966)

THAT GIRL FROM PARIS see STREET GIRL

THAT HAMILTON WOMAN see ROMANCE OF LADY
    HAMILTON, THE

THAT LADY IN ERMINE see LADY IN ERMINE, THE

THAT MAN'S HERE AGAIN see YOUNG NOWHERES

THAT NIGHT IN RIO see FOLIES BERGERE

THAT OBSCURE OBJECT OF DESIRE see WOMAN
    AND THE PUPPET, THE

THAT UNCERTAIN FEELING see DIVORCONS

THAT WAY WITH WOMEN see RULING PASSION, THE

THAT WONDERFUL URGE see LOVE IS NEWS

THEIR PURPLE MOMENT (short) (MGM, 1928, based on a
    story by Leo McCarey and elaborated upon in the remake)
  BLOTTO (short) (MGM, 1930)
  VIDA NOCTURNA, LA (short) (SPA, 1930)
  NUITE EXTRAVAGANTE, UNE (short) (FRA, 1930)

THEODORA see THEODORA, EMPRESS OF BISANZIO

THEODORA, EMPRESS OF BISANZIO (ITA, 1909, based
    on the book, "Theodora," by Victorien Sardou)
  THEODORA (FRA, 1912)
  THEODORA (ITA, 1913)
  THEODORA (ITA, 1919)
  THEODORA (FRA, 1921)
  THEODORA (FRA/ITA, 1954)

THERE GOES KELLY see UP IN THE AIR

THEODORE ROOSEVELT see TEDDY, THE ROUGH
    RIDER

THERE'S ALWAYS TOMORROW (UN, 1934, based on the
    book by Ursula Parrott)
  THERE'S ALWAYS TOMORROW (UN, 1956)

THERESE (FRA, 1962, based on the book, "Therese
    Desqueyroux," by Francois Mauriac)
  THERESE DESQUEYROUX (FRA, 1965)

THERESE DESQUEYROUX see THERESE

THERESE RAQUIN (ITA, 1915, based on the book by Emile
    Zola)
  THERESE RAQUIN (FRA, 1927)
  THERESE RAQUIN, DU SOLLST NICHT EHEBRECHEN
    (SHADOWS OF FEAR) (GER, 1927)
  THERESE RAQUIN (FRA, 1953)
  ADULTRESS, THE (FRA, 1957)
  THERESE RAQUIN (NET--TV, 1961)

THERESE RAQUIN, DU SOLLST NICHT EHERBRECHEN
    see THERESE RAQUIN

THESE THREE (UA, 1936, based on the play, "The
    Children's Hour," by Lillian Hellman)
  CHILDREN'S HOUR, THE (UA, 1961)

THESEUS VS. THE MINOTAUR see MINOTAUR, THE

THEY ALL DO IT see CHUANG--TSE TESTS HIS WIFE

THEY ALSO SERVE see MASTER SPY

THEY CALLED HIM DEATH see THIS MAN IS
    DANGEROUS

THEY DIED WITH THEIR BOOTS ON see CUSTER'S
    LAST STAND

THEY DRIVE BY NIGHT see BORDERTOWN

THEY LIVE BY NIGHT (RKO, 1948, based on the book,
    "Thieves Like Us," by Edward Anderson)
  THIEVES LIKE US (UA, 1974)

THEY MADE ME A CRIMINAL see LIFE OF JIMMY
    DOLAN, THE

THEY'VE KILLED PRESIDENT LINCOLN! see ABRAHAM
    LINCOLN

THICKER THAN WATER see NEAREST AND DEAREST

THIEF, THE (FRA, 1914, based on the play by Henri
    Bernstein)
  THIEF, THE (FOX, 1914)
  THIEF, THE (FOX, 1920)

THIEF, THE (RUS, 1916, based on the book, "The Three
    Thieves," by Umberto Notari)
  THREE THIEVES, THE (RUS, 1918)
  CANDIDATE FOR PRESIDENT (RUS, 1923)
  TRIAL OF THE THREE MILLION, THE (RUS, 1926)
  THREE THIEVES, THE (ITA, 1954)

THIEF OF BAGDAD, THE (UA, 1924, based on the fairy
    tale)
  FLYING BANDIT, THE (CHN, 1928)
  THIEF OF BAGDAD (IN, 1934)
  THIEF OF BAGDAD, THE (UA, 1940)
  THIEF OF BAGDAD, THE (IN, 1957)
  BAGDAD THIRUDAN (IN, 1960)
  THIEF OF BAGDAD, THE (IN, c1965)
  THIEF OF BAGDAD, THE (ITA, 1961)
  THIEF OF BAGDAD, THE (TUR, 1968)

THIEF OF DAMASCUS see ALADDIN and ALI BABA

THIEVES' HIGHWAY (FOX, 1949, based on a screenplay by
    Z.I. Bezzerides)
  OVERNIGHT HAUL (CBS--TV, 1956)

THIEVES LIKE US see THEY LIVE BY NIGHT

THIN ICE see MY LIPS BETRAY

THIRD ALARM, THE (FBO, 1922, based on a story by Emilie
    Johnson)
  THIRD ALARM, THE (TIF, 1926)

THIRD DEGREE, THE (VIT, 1919, based on a play by

Charles Klein)
THIRD DEGREE, THE   (WB, 1926)

THIRD MAN, THE   (SEZ, 1950, based on the book by Graham
     Greene)
THIRD MAN, THE   (series)   (BRI--TV, 1960)
LAMENT FOR A DEAD INDIAN   (ABC--TV, 1961)

THIRD NUMBER III, THE   (HUN, 1919, source unlisted)
THIRD NUMBER III, THE   (HUN, 1937)

THIRD ROUND, THE   see   BULLDOG DRUMMOND'S
     THIRD ROUND

THIRD STRING, THE   (BRI, 1914, based on a story by
     W. W. Jacobs)
THIRD STRING, THE   (BRI, 1932)

THIRTEEN, THE   (RUS, 1937, based on an original screenplay)
SAHARA   (COL, 1943)
LAST OF THE COMANCHES   (COL, 1952)

THIRTEEN CLOCKS, THE   (ABC--TV, 1953, based on the
     story by James Thurber)
THIRTEEN CLOCKS, THE   (CAN--TV, 1968)

THIRTEENTH CHAIR, THE   (PAT, 1919, based on the play
     by Bayard Veiller)
THIRTEENTH CHAIR, THE   (MGM, 1929)
THIRTEENTH CHAIR, THE   (MGM, 1937)
THIRTEENTH CHAIR, THE   (CBS--TV, 1954)

THIRTEENTH GUEST, THE   (MON, 1932, based on the
     book by Armitage Trail)
MYSTERY OF THE THIRTEENTH GUEST, THE   (MON,
     1943)

THIRTEENTH LETTER, THE   see   CORBEAU, LE

39 STEPS, THE   (BRI, 1935, based on a book by John Buchan)
39 STEPS, THE   (BRI, 1960)
39 STEPS, THE   (BRI, 1978)

33.333   (SWE, 1924, source unlisted)
33.333   (SWE, 1936)

THIS AGONY, THIS TRIUMPH   see   WINTERSET

THIS GUN FOR HIRE   (PAR, 1942, based on the book by
     Graham Greene)
SHORT CUT TO HELL   (PAR, 1957)

THIS HAPPY BREED   (BRI, 1947, based on the play by Noel
     Coward)
THIS HAPPY BREED   (CBS--TV, 1956)

THIS IS EDWARD STEICHEN   see   FAMILY OF MAN, THE

THIS IS THE NIGHT   see   GOOD AND NAUGHTY

THIS LOVE OF OURS   (UN, 1945, based on the play, "Comme
     Maglio de Prima," by Luigi Pirandello)
NEVER SAY GOODBYE   (UN, 1956)

THIS MAD WORLD   (MGM, 1930, based on the book, "Terre
     Inhumaine," by Francois de Curel)
BOIS DE AMANTS, LE   (FRA/ITA, 1960)

THIS RECKLESS AGE   see   GOOSE HANGS HIGH, THE

THIS SAVAGE LAND   see   ROAD WEST, THE

THIS THING CALLED LOVE   (PAR, 1929, based on the play
     by Edwin Burke)
THIS THING CALLED LOVE   (COL, 1941)

THOMAS HART BENTON: PROFILES IN COURAGE   see
     MAKING OF A MURAL, THE

THOMAS JEFFERSON   see   JEFFERSON OF MONTICELLO

THOSE WHO DANCE   (FN, 1924, based on a story by George
     Kibbe Turner)
THOSE WHO DANCE   (WB, 1930)
LOS QUE DANZAN   (SPA, 1930)
TANZ GEHT WEITER, DER   (GER, 1930)
CONTRE--ENQUETE   (FRA, 1930)

THOU SHALL NOT STEAL   see   FILE NO. 113

THOUSAND AND ONE NIGHTS, A   see   ARABIAN NIGHTS

THOUSAND CRANES, A   (JAP, 1953, source unlisted)
THOUSAND CRANES, A   (JAP, 1969)

THOUSAND SHALL FALL, A   see   CROSS OF LORAINE

3--1/2 MUSKETEERS   see   THREE MUSKETEERS, THE

THREE BAD MEN   (FOX, 1925, based on the book, "Over
     the Border," by Herman Whittaker)
NOT EXACTLY GENTLEMEN   (FOX, 1931)

THREE BLIND MICE   see   WORKING GIRLS

THREE COINS IN THE FOUNTAIN   (FOX, 1954, based on
     a book by John H. Secondari)
PLEASURE SEEKERS, THE   (FOX, 1964)

THREE DAYS IN THE GUARDHOUSE   (GER, 1930, source
     unlisted)
THREE DAYS IN THE GUARDHOUSE   (GER, 1955)

THREE FACES EAST   (PDC, 1926, based on a story by
     Anthony Paul Kelly)
THREE FACES EAST   (WB, 1930)
BRITISH INTELLIGENCE   (WB, 1940)

THREE FOR THE SHOW   see   TOO MANY HUSBANDS

THREE GODFATHERS   (UN, 1916, based on the book by
     Peter B. Kyne)
MARKED MEN   (UN, 1919)
HELL'S HEROES   (UN, 1929)
THREE GODFATHERS   (MGM, 1936)
THREE GODFATHERS   (MGM, 1949)
GODCHILD, THE   (ABC--TV, 1974)

THREE GUNS FOR TEXAS   see   LAREDO

THREE HOURS   (FN, 1927, based on the story, "Purple and
     Fine Linen," by May Edgington)
ADVENTURE IN MANHATTAN   (COL, 1936)

THREE KIDS AND A QUEEN   (UN, 1935, based on a story
     by Harry Poppe, Chester Beecroft and Mary Marlind)
LITTLE MISS BIG   (UN, 1946)

THREE LITTLE GIRLS IN BLUE   see   WORKING GIRLS

THREE LITTLE PIGS (short) (DIS, 1933, based on the fairy tale)
  BIG BAD WOLF, THE (CHI, 1966)

THREE LIVE GHOSTS (PAR, 1922, based on the play by Frederic S. Isham)
  THREE LIVE GHOSTS (UA, 1929)
  THREE LIVE GHOSTS (MGM, 1935)

THREE MEN see PORTRAIT OF DAG HAMMARSKJOLD, A

THREE MEN IN A BOAT (BRI, 1920, based on the book by Jerome K. Jerome)
  THREE MEN IN A BOAT (BRI, 1933)
  THREE MEN IN A BOAT (BRI, 1956)

THREE MEN ON A HORSE (WB, 1936, based on the play by John Cecil Holm and George Abbott; also the basis for two musical comedies, "Banjo Eyes" in 1942 and "Let It Ride" in 1961)
  THREE MEN ON A HORSE (NBC--TV, 1939)
  THREE MEN ON A HORSE (CBS--TV, 1950)
  THREE MEN ON A HORSE (TV, 1952)
  DREI MANN AUF EINEM PFERD (GER, 1957)
  THREE MEN ON A HORSE (CBS--TV, 1957)
  TROIS HOMMES SUR UN CHEVAL (FRA/ITA, 1969)

THREE MUSKETEERS, THE (FRA, 1903, based on the book by Alexandre Dumas)
  THREE MUSKETEERS, THE (ITA, 1908)
  RICHELIEU, OR THE CARDINAL'S CONSPIRACY (INC, 1909)
  MOUSQUETAIRES DE LA REINE, LE (FRA, 1909)
  THREE MUSKETEERS, THE (ED, 1911)
  THREE MUSKETEERS, THE (FRA, 1912)
  THREE MUSKETEERS, THE (IND, 1913)
  D'ARTAGNAN THE BRAVE (n.d., 1913)
  SOGNO DE KRI KRI, UN (short) (ITA, 1913)
  THREE MUSKETEERS, THE (IND, 1914)
  D'ARTAGNAN (TRI, 1916)
  THREE MUST--GET--THEIR'S, THE (RC, 1919)
  THREE MUSKETEERS, THE (FRA, 1921)
  THREE MUSKETEERS, THE (UA, 1921)
  THREE MUST--GET--THEIRS, THE (UA, 1922)
  MILADY (IND, 1923)
  GAY MUSKETEER, THE (short) (IND, 1928)
  IRON MASK, THE (UA, 1929)
  THREE MUSKETEERS, THE (FRA, 1932)
  THREE MUSKETEERS, THE (serial) (MAS, 1933)
  THREE MUSKETEERS, THE (short) (RUS, 1934)
  THREE MUSKETEERS, THE (RKO, 1935)
  THREE MUSKETEERS, THE (short) (RUS, 1938)
  THREE MUSKETEERS, THE (ONE FOR ALL) (FOX, 1939)
  THREE MUSKETEERS, THE (MEX, 1942)
  THREE MUSKETEERS, THE (ARG, 1946)
  THREE MUSKETEERS, THE (MGM, 1948)
  GAY SWORDSMAN, THE (SON OF D'ARTAGNAN) (ITA, 1950)
  MILADY AND THE MUSKETEERS (ITA, 1951)
  SWORD OF D'ARTAGNAN (TV, 1952)
  AT SWORD'S POINT (RKO, 1952)
  FOUR MUSKETEERS, THE (FRA, 1953)
  THREE MUSKETEERS, THE (ARG, 1953)
  KNIGHTS OF THE QUEEN (ITA, 1954)
  LAST MUSKETEER, THE (ITA, 1955)
  THREE MUSKETEERS, THE (series) (TV, 1956)
  MASK OF THE MUSKETEERS (ITA, 1960)

  THREE MUSKETEERS, THE (CBS--TV, 1960)
  VENGEANCE OF THE THREE MUSKETEERS, THE (FRA/ITA, 1961)
  3--1/2 MUSKETEERS, THE (ITA, 1961)
  CYRANO AND D'ARTAGNAN (FRA, 1962)
  SECRET MARK OF D'ARTAGNAN, THE (FRA/ITA, 1962)
  MASQUE DE FER, LE (FRA, 1962)
  ZORRO AND THE THREE MUSKETEERS (ITA, 1963)
  D'ARTAGNAN AGAINST THE THREE MUSKETEERS (ITA, 1963)
  FIGHTING MUSKETEERS, THE (FRA, 1963)
  REVENGE OF THE MUSKETEERS (ITA, 1964)
  MAGOO IN THE KING'S SERVICE (UPA, 1964)
  ADVENTURES OF THE 3 MUSKETEERS, THE (ITA, 1964)
  THREE MUSKETEERS, THE (CAN--TV, 1969)
  SEX ADVENTURES OF THE THREE MUSKETEERS, THE (GER, 1970)
  THREE MUSKETEERS, THE (HB, 1973)
  THREE MUSKETEERS, THE (FRA, 1973)
  THREE MUSKETEERS, THE (FOX, 1974)
  FOUR MUSKETEERS, THE (FOX, 1975)

THREE MUSKETEERS, THE see also MASQUE DE FER, LE

THREE MUST--GET--THEIR'S, THE see THREE MUSKE-- TEERS, THE

3 NUTS FOR CINDERELLA see CINDERELLA AND THE FAIRY GODMOTHER

THREE ON A MATCH (WB, 1932, based on a story by Kubee Glasmon and John Bright)
  BROADWAY MUSKETEERS (WB, 1938)

3 ON A SPREE see BREWSTER'S MILLIONS

THREE OUTLAWS (AFR, 1956, based on historical incidents and characters)
  BADMAN'S COUNTRY (WB, 1958)
  BUTCH CASSIDY AND THE SUNDANCE KID (FOX, 1969)
  MRS. SUNDANCE (FOX--TV, 1973)
  WANTED -- THE SUNDANCE WOMAN (ABC--TV, 1976)

THREE ROGUES see HEART OF THE WILD, THE

THREE RUSSIAN GIRLS see GIRL FROM LENINGRAD, THE

THREE SAILORS AND A GIRL see BUTTER AND EGG MAN, THE

THREE SINNERS (PAR, 1928, based on the play, "The Second Life," by Rudolf Bernauer and Rudolf Osterreicher)
  ONCE A LADY (PAR, 1931)

THREE SISTERS (RUS, 1964, based on the play by Anton Chekhov)
  THREE SISTERS (BRI, 1970)
  THREE SISTERS (AFT, 1974)

THREE SONS see SWEEPINGS

THREE STOOGES GO AROUND THE WORLD IN A DAZE, THE see ROUND THE WORLD IN 80 DAYS

THREE THIEVES, THE   see   THIEF, THE

THREE WEEKS   (REL, 1915, based on the book by Elinor
   Glyn)
   QUEEN'S SECRET, THE   (RUS, 1919)
   THREE WEEKS   (MGM, 1924)

THREE WISE FOOLS   (MGM, 1923, based on the book by
   Austin Strong)
   THREE WISE FOOLS   (MGM, 1946)

THREE WISE MEN   see   PASSION PLAY, THE

THREE WORLDS OF GULLIVER, THE   see   GULLIVER'S
   TRAVELS

THREEPENNY OPERA, THE   (GER, 1931, based on a story
   which became the basis for two operas: "The Beggar's
   Opera" by John Gay, and "The Threepenny Opera" by
   Bertoldt Brecht and Kurt Weill)
   OPERA DE QUAT'SOUS, L'   (FRA, 1931)
   ROBBER SYMPHONY, THE   (AUS, 1935)
   BEGGAR'S OPERA, THE   (BRI, 1953)
   THREEPENNY OPERA, THE   (GER, 1964)
   BEGGAR'S OPERA, THE   (TV, 1972)
   BEGGAR'S OPERA, THE   (PBS--TV, 1967)
   BEGGAR'S OPERA, THE   (TV, 1973)

THREE'S COMPANY   see   MAN ABOUT THE HOUSE

THRILL OF BRAZIL, THE   see   FRONT PAGE, THE

THRONE OF BLOOD   see   MACBETH

THROUGH THE YEARS   see   SMILIN' THROUGH

THROW ME TO THE VAMPIRE   see   DANZA MACABRE,
   LA

THUMBELINA   see   HANS CHRISTIAN ANDERSEN

THUNDER IN THE EAST   see   BATTLE, THE

THUNDER IN THE VALLEY   see   OWD BOB

THUNDER MOUNTAIN   see   TO THE LAST MAN

THUNDER OF BATTLE   see   CORIOLANUS

THUNDER ON THE HILL   (UN, 1951, based on the play,
   "Bonaventure," by Charlotte Hastings)
   THUNDER ON THE HILL   (NBC--TV, 1955)

THUNDERGAP OUTLAWS   see   BAD MEN OF THUNDER
   GAP

THUNDERHEAD, SON OF FLICKA   see   MY FRIEND
   FLICKA

THUNDERING HERD   (PAR, 1925, based on the book by
   Zane Grey)
   THUNDERING HERD   (PAR, 1934)

THUNDERING HOOFS   (FBO, 1924, based on a story by
   Marion Jackson)
   THUNDERING HOOFS   (RKO, 1941)

THUNDERING WEST, THE   see   LONE RIDER, THE

THY NAME IS WOMAN   (MGM, 1924, based on the book,
   "Weibsteufel, Der," by Karl Schoenherr)
   WEIBSTEUFEL, DER   (AUS, 1951)
   WEIBSTEUFEL, DER   (AUS, 1966)

TICKET OF LEAVE MAN   (AUS, 1913, based on a story by
   Tom Taylor)
   TICKET OF LEAVE MAN   (BRI, 1918)
   TICKET OF LEAVE MAN   (BRI, 1937)

TIE THAT BINDS, THE   see   HEROES OF THE WEST

TIEFLAND   (GER, 1922, based on the opera by Eugen
   D'Albert)
   TIEFLAND   (GER, 1945)

TIEMBA Y TITUBEA   see   BELOW ZERO

TIERARZT DR. VLIMMEN   (GER, 1944, based on the book
   by Antonius)
   SKANDAL UM DR. VLIMMEN   (GER, 1956)

TIGER ROSE   (WB, 1923, based on the play by Willard Mack)
   TIGER ROSE   (WB, 1929)

TIGER SHARK   (WB, 1932, based on a story, "Tuna," by
   Houston Branch and material by Bryan Foy)
   BENGAL TIGER   (WB, 1936)
   KING OF THE LUMBERJACKS   (WB, 1940)
   MANPOWER   (WB, 1941)

TIGER VON ESCHNAPUR   see   INDIAN TOMB, THE

TIGER WOMAN, THE   (serial)   (REP, 1944, based on a
   screenplay by various authors; the remake is a condensation
   of the serial)
   JUNGLE GOLD   (REP, 1966)

TIGER'S TAIL – THOMAS NAST VS. BOSS TWEED, THE
   see   OVERTHROW OF THE TWEED RING, THE

TIL EULENSPIEGEL   (GER, 1922, based on a legend)
   BOLD ADVENTURE   (n.d.)
   ADVENTURES OF TIL L'ESPIEGLE   (FRA, 1956)

TIL WE MEET AGAIN   see   ONE--WAY PASSAGE

TILL DEATH US DO PART   (series)   (BRI--TV, 1967, based
   on a teleplay)
   ALL IN THE FAMILY   (series)   (CBS--TV, 1971)

TILLIE THE TOILER   (MGM, 1927, based on the comic
   strip by Russ Westover)
   TILLIE THE TOILER   (COL, 1941)

TILLIE'S PUNCTURED ROMANCE   (KEY, 1914, based on a
   play by Monte Brice)
   TILLIE'S TOMATO SURPRISE   (LUB, 1915)
   TILLIE'S PUNCTURED ROMANCE   (PAR, 1927)

TILLIE'S TOMATO SURPRISE   see   TILLIE'S PUNCTURED
   ROMANCE

TILLY OF BLOOMSBURY   (BRI, 1921, based on the play by
   Ian Hay)
   TILLY OF BLOOMSBURY   (BRI, 1931)
   TILLY OF BLOOMSBURY   (BRI, 1940)

TIME FOR BEANY, A   (series)   (IND--TV, 1949, based on

characters created by Bob Clampett)
BEANY AND CECIL (series) (IND--TV, 1961)

TIME FOR DYING, A see JAMES BOYS, THE

TIME OF YOUR LIFE, THE (UA, 1948, based on the play
by William Saroyan)
TIME OF YOUR LIFE, THE (CBS--TV, 1958)

TIME TO KILL (FOX, 1942, based on the book, "The High
Window," by Raymond Chandler)
BRASHER DOUBLOON, THE (FOX, 1947)

TIMES SQUARE PLAYBOY see HOMETOWNERS, THE

TIMOTHY'S QUEST (IND, 1922, based on the book by Kate
Douglas Wiggin)
TIMOTHY'S QUEST (PAR, 1936)

TIN BADGE, THE see TIN STAR, THE

TIN LIZZIE TYCOON, THE see AMERICAN ROAD, THE

TIN PAN ALLEY (FOX, 1940, based on a story by Pamela
Harris)
I'LL GET BY (FOX, 1950)

TIN STAR, THE (PAR, 1957, based on the book, "The
Tin Badge," by Barney Slater)
DEPUTY, THE (series) (NBC--TV, 1959)

TINDERBOX, THE (DEN, 1907, based on a fairy tale)
TINDERBOX, THE (DEN, 1948)
STORY OF A LIGHTER, THE (DEN, 1969)

TINGEL--TANGEL (GER, 1922, source unlisted)
TINGEL--TANGEL (GER, 1930)

TIRE AU FLANC (FRA, 1928, based on the play by Andre
Mouezy--Eon and Andre Sylvane)
TIRE AU FLANC (FRA, 1933)
TIRE AU FLANC (FRA, 1949)
TIRE AU FLANC (FRA, 1961)

TIRED THEODORE see TROTTE TEODOR

'TIS A PITY SHE'S A WHORE see MY SISTER, MY LOVE

TITAN, THE see MICHELANGELO

TITANIC see ATLANTIC

TO BUILD A FIRE see POUR CONSTRUIRE UN FEU

TO EACH HIS OWN (PAR, 1946, based on a story by
Charles Brackett)
TO EACH HIS OWN (NBC--TV, 1954)

TO HAVE AND HAVE NOT (WB, 1944, based on the book
by Ernest Hemingway)
BREAKING POINT, THE (WB, 1950)
TO HAVE AND HAVE NOT (NBC--TV, 1957)
GUN RUNNERS, THE (UA, 1958)
WOMEN PREFER THE MAMBO (DISHONORABLE
DISCHARGE) (FRA, 1958)

TO HAVE AND TO HOLD (PAR, 1916, based on a book by
Mary Johnston)
TO HAVE AND TO HOLD (PAR, 1922)

TO THE LAST MAN (PAR, 1923, based on a book by Zane
Grey)
TO THE LAST MAN (PAR, 1933)
THUNDER MOUNTAIN (FOX, 1935)
THUNDER MOUNTAIN (RKO, 1947)

TO THE VICTOR see OWD BOB

TOBY TYLER see CIRCUS DAYS

TOCHTER DES ORGANISTEN, DIE see KABALE UND
LIEBE

TOCHTER DES REGIMENTS, DIE see KING'S DAUGHTER,
THE

TODA UNA VIDA see SARAH AND SON

TODLICHEN TRAUME, DIE see FRAULEIN VON
SCUDERI, DAS

TOILERS OF THE SEA, THE see TRAVAILLEURS DE LA
MER, LES

TOL'ABLE DAVID (FN, 1921, based on a story by Joseph
Hergesheimer)
TOL'ABLE DAVID (COL, 1930)

TOLL OF THE SEA see MADAME BUTTERFLY

TOLLE BOMBERG, DER (GER, 1932, based on the book by
Josef Winckler)
TOLLE BOMBERG, DER (GER, 1957)

TOLLE LOLA, DIE (GER, 1927, based on the play by Gustav
Kadelburg)
TOLLE LOLA, DIE (GER, 1953)

TOLLE NACHT (GER, 1943, based on the play by Freund
and Mannstaedt)
TOLLE NACHT (GER, 1957)

TOM AND HUCK see TOM SAWYER

TOM BROWN AT CULVER (UN, 1932, based on a story by
George Green, Tom Buckingham and Clarence Marks)
SPIRIT OF CULVER (UN, 1939)

TOM BROWN'S SCHOOL DAYS (BRI, 1910, based on the
book by Thomas Hughes; also the basis for the British
musical in 1972)
TOM BROWN'S SCHOOL DAYS (BRI, 1916)
TOM BROWN'S SCHOOL DAYS (RKO, 1940) (TV title:
ADVENTURES AT RUGBY)
TOM BROWN'S SCHOOL DAYS (BRI, 1951)
TOM BROWN'S SCHOOL DAYS (BRI--TV, 1971)

TOM, DICK AND HARRY (RKO, 1941, based on a story by
Paul Jerico)
GIRL MOST LIKELY, THE (UN, 1957)

TOM JONES (BRI, 1917, based on the book by Henry
Fielding)
TOM JONES (UA, 1963)
TOM JONES (CAN--TV, 1968)
BAWDY ADVENTURES OF TOM JONES, THE (UN, 1975)

TOM SAWYER (PAR, 1917, based on the book by Mark
Twain)

HUCK AND TOM   (PAR, 1918)
TOM SAWYER   (PAR, 1930)
TOM SAWYER, DETECTIVE   (PAR, 1938)
ADVENTURES OF TOM SAWYER, THE   (UA, 1938)
TOM SAWYER   (CBS--TV, 1956)
TOM AND HUCK   (NBC--TV, 1960)
ADVENTURES OF TOM SAWYER, THE   (RUM, 1967)
BACHPAN   (IN, 1972)
TOM SAWYER   (RAN, 1972)
TOM SAWYER   (CBS--TV, 1972)
TOM SAWYER   (UA, 1973)

TOM SAWYER, DETECTIVE   see   TOM SAWYER

TOM THUMB   see   PETIT POUCET, LE

TOMA   (ABC--TV, 1973, based on a teleplay)
BARETTA   (ABC--TV, 1975)

TOMAHAWK TRAIL, THE   see   LEATHER--STOCKING

TOMMY ATKINS   (BRI, 1910, based on the play by Arthur
      Shurley and Ben Landeck)
TOMMY ATKINS   (BRI, 1915)
TOMMY ATKINS   (BRI, 1928)
TOMMY ATKINS   (BRI, 1930)

TOMORROW   (CBS--TV, 1960, based on a short story by
      William Faulkner, adapted by Horton Foote)
TOMORROW   (IND, 1972)

TOMORROW IS FOREVER   (RKO, 1946, based on the book
      by Gwen Bristow)
TOMORROW IS FOREVER   (NBC--TV, 1966)

TONIGHT AT 8:30   see   WE WERE DANCING

TONIGHT IS OURS   see   QUEEN WAS IN THE PARLOR,
      THE

TONS OF MONEY   (BRI, 1928, based on the play by Will
      Evans and Arthur Valentine)
TONS OF MONEY   (BRI; 1931)

TOO BUSY TO WORK   see   AFTER HIS OWN HEART and
      DOUBTING THOMAS

TOO MANY CROOKS   (VIT, 1919, based on the book by
      E.J. Rath)
TOO MANY CROOKS   (PAR, 1927)

TOO MANY HUSBANDS   (COL, 1940, based on a play by
      W. Somerset Maugham)
THREE FOR THE SHOW   (COL, 1955)

TOO MUCH CHAMPAGNE   (VIT, 1908, source unlisted)
PURGATORY   (ITA, 1911)
PARADISE   (ITA, 1912)

TOO YOUNG TO MARRY   (WB, 1931, based on the play,
      "Broken Dishes," by Martin Flavin)
LOVE BEGINS AT 20   (WB, 1936)

TOOMAI OF THE ELEPHANTS   see   ELEPHANT BOY

TOP SECRET AFFAIR   see   MELVILLE GOODWIN, U.S.A.

TOPAZE   (FRA, 1932, based on the play by Marcel Pagnol)
TOPAZE   (RKO, 1933)

GOLD AND SILVER WORLD   (CHN, 1939)
TOPAZE   (FRA, 1936)
TOPAZE   (FRA, 1950)
TOPAZE   (CBS--TV, 1957)
I LIKE MONEY   (BRI, 1961)

TOPS IS THE LIMIT   see   ANYTHING GOES

TOPSY AND EVA   see   UNCLE TOM'S CABIN

TORCH, THE   see   ENAMORADA

TORCH BEARERS, THE   see   DOUBTING THOMAS

TORCH SONG   see   LAUGHING SINNERS

TORCHY BLANE IN CHINATOWN   see   MURDER WILL
      OUT

TORMENT OF BEETHOVEN   see   BEETHOVEN UND DAS
      VOLK

TORMENTED FLAME   see   PASSION FIRE

TORPEDO OF DOOM, THE   see   FIGHTING DEVIL DOGS,
      THE

TORQUATO TASSO   (FRA, 1910, based on the book by
      Goethe)
TORQUATO TASSO   (ITA, 1913)
TORQUATO TASSO   (GER, 1914)

TORTOISE AND THE HARE   (short)   (UA, 1934, based on
      the folk tale)
TORTOISE AND THE HARE   (FRA, n.d.)

TOSCA, LA   (FRA, 1908, based on the story by Victorien
      Sardou and the opera by Giaccomo Puccini)
TOSCA, LA   (FRA, 1910)
TOSCA, LA   (ITA, 1918)
TOSCA, LA   (PAR, 1918)
ENFANTS DE LA SCENE, LES   (DEN, 1919)
TOSCA, LA   (short)   (BRI, 1922)
STAR--PLUCKING GIRL, THE   (CHN, 1925)
TOSCA, LA   (ITA, 1940)
STORY OF TOSCA, THE   (ITA, 1947)
TOSCA, LA   (ITA, 1956)
TOSCA, LA   (ITA, 1973)

TOSEN FRAN STORMYRTORPET   (SWE, 1917, source
      unlisted)
TOSEN FRAN STORMYRTORPET   (GER, 1935)
TOSEN FRAN STORMYRTORPET   (FIN, 1940)
TOSEN FRAN STORMYRTORPET   (SWE, 1947)
TOSEN FRAN STORMYRTORPET   (GER, 1958)

TOTENTANZ, DER   see   DANCE OF DEATH

TOTO   see   GAY DECEIVER, THE

TOUCH OF GRACE, A   see   FOR THE LOVE OF ADA

TOULOUSE--LAUTREC   see   MOULIN ROUGE

TOUR DE NESLE, LA   (FRA, 1912, based on the book by
      Alexandre Dumas [pere] and Frederic Gaillardet)
BURIDAN   (FRA, 1922)
TOUR DE NESLE, LA   (FRA, 1937)
BURIDAN, LE HEROES DE LA TOUR DE NESLE

(FRA, 1951)
    TOUR DE NESLE, LA (FRA/ITA, 1954)

TOUT PETIT FAUST, LE see FAUST

TOUTE SA VIE see SARAH AND SON

TOVARICH (FRA, 1935, based on the play by Jacques
    Deval)
    TOVARICH (WB, 1937)

TOWER OF LIES, THE (MGM, 1925, based on the book,
    "Emperor of Portugal, The," by Selma Lagerlof)
    EMPEROR OF PORTUGAL, THE (SWE, 1944)

TOWER OF LONDON see RICHARD III

TOWN HAS BURNED TO DUST, A (TV, 1960, based on a
    teleplay)
    TOWN HAS TURNED TO DUST, A (BRI--TV, 1961)

TOWN MUSICIANS, THE see FOUR MUSICIANS OF
    BREMEN

TOWN RAT AND THE COUNTRY RAT, THE see
    COUNTRY MOUSE, THE

TOY TIGER see MAD ABOUT MUSIC

TOY WIFE, THE see FROU--FROU

TRADER HORN (MGM, 1931, based on the book by
    Ethelreda Lewis)
    TRADER HORN (MGM, 1972)

TRADER TOM OF THE CHINA SEAS (serial) (REP, 1954,
    based on a screenplay by various authors; the remake is a
    condensation of the serial)
    TARGET: SEA OF CHINA (REP, 1966)

TRAGEDIA ALLA CORTE DI SICILIA, UNA see
    WINTER'S TALE, A

TRAGEDY OF MACBETH, THE see MACBETH

TRAGEDY OF THE KOROSKO see FIRES OF FATE

TRAGEDY OF THE STREET see DIRNENTRAGODIE

TRAIL BEYOND see WOLF HUNTERS

TRAIL OF STANLEY AND LIVINGSTONE, THE see
    LIVINGSTONE

TRAIL OF THE LONESOME PINE, THE (PAR, 1916, based
    on the book by John William Fox Jr.)
    TRAIL OF THE LONESOME PINE, THE (PAR, 1923)
    TRAIL OF THE LONESOME PINE, THE (PAR, 1936)

TRAIL OF THE YUKON (MON, 1949, based on the book,
    "The Gold Hunters," by James Oliver Curwood)
    YUKON GOLD (MON, 1952)

TRAILIN' (FOX, 1921, based on a book by Max Brand)
    HOLY TERROR, A (FOX, 1931)

TRAILIN' TROUBLE see HARD HOMBRE

TRAIN DE 8 H. 47, LE (FRA, 1925, based on a book by

Georges Courteline)
    TRAIN DE 8 H. 47, LE (FRA, 1935)

TRAITOR, THE see BORDER LAW

TRAITOR'S GATE (BRI, 1965, based on the book by Edgar
    Wallace)
    VERRATERTOR, DAS (GER, 1965)

TRANSATLANTIC TUNNEL see TUNNEL, DER

TRANSGRESSION (UA, 1931, based on the book by Kate
    Jordan)
    NUIT D'ESPAGNE (FRA, 1931)

TRANSLATION OF A SAVAGE, THE see BEHOLD MY
    WIFE

TRAPP FAMILY, DIE (GER, 1956, based on the life of the
    singing family)
    TRAPP--FAMILE IN AMERIKA, DIE (GER, 1958)
    SOUND OF MUSIC, THE (FOX, 1964)
    REBELLIOUS NOVICE, THE (ARG, 1968)

TRAPP--FAMILE IN AMERIKA, DIE see TRAPP--FAMILIE,
    DIE

TRAUMENDE MUND, DER see DREAMING LIPS

TRAUMSTRASSE DER WELT (GER, 1958, based on a
    screenplay by Hans Domnick)
    PANAMERICANA (GER, 1968)

TRAVAILLEURS DE LA MER, LES (FRA, 1918, based on a
    story by Victor Hugo)
    TOILERS OF THE SEA (BRI, 1923)

TRAVELING MUSICIANS, THE see FOUR MUSICIANS
    OF BREMEN

TRAVELING SALESMAN, THE (PAR, 1916, based on the
    play by James Forbes)
    TRAVELING SALESMAN, THE (PAR, 1921)
    SPORTING GOODS (PAR, 1928)

TRAVIATA, LA see DAME AUX CAMELIAS, LA

TREASURE ISLAND see PIRATE'S TREASURE

TREASURE OF ARNE, THE (SWE, 1919, source unlisted)
    TREASURE OF ARNE, THE (SWE, 1954)

TREASURE OF THE GOLDEN CONDOR see SON OF
    FURY

TREE GROWS IN BROOKLYN, A (FOX, 1945, based on the
    book by Betty Smith)
    TREE GROWS IN BROOKLYN, A (NBC--TV, 1974)

TRELAWNY OF THE 'WELLS' (BRI, 1916, based on the
    play by Sir Arthur Wing Pinero)
    ACTRESS, THE (MGM, 1928)

TRENT'S LAST CASE (BRI, 1920, based on the book by
    E.C. Bentley)
    TRENT'S LAST CASE (FOX, 1929)
    TRENT'S LAST CASE (BRI, 1952)

TRESPASSER, THE (UA, 1929, based on a screenplay by

Edmund Goulding)
THAT CERTAIN WOMAN   (WB, 1937)

TRIAL AND ERROR   see   DOCK BRIEF

TRIAL AT NUREMBERG   (CBS--TV, 1959, based on
      historical incidents during and after World War II)
   JUDGMENT AT NUREMBERG   (UA, 1961)
   TRIAL AT NUREMBERG   (UA--TV, 1964)

TRIAL OF CAPTAIN KIDD   see   CAPTAIN KIDD

TRIAL OF JOAN OF ARC, THE   see   JOAN OF ARC

TRIAL OF LEE HARVEY OSWALD, THE   see   NOVEMBER
      22 AND THE WARREN REPORT

TRIAL OF LOUIS PASTEUR, THE   see   STORY OF LOUIS
      PASTEUR, THE

TRIAL OF MADAME X, THE   see   MADAME X

TRIAL OF MARY DUGAN, THE   (MGM, 1929, based on the
      play by Bayard Veiller)
   PROCES DE MARY DUGAN, LE   (FRA, 1929)
   MORDPROZESS MARY DUGAN   (GER, 1929)
   TRIAL OF MARY DUGAN, THE   (MGM, 1941)
   TRIAL OF MARY DUGAN, THE   (TV, 1952)

TRIAL OF MR. PICKWICK, THE   see   PICKWICK PAPERS,
   THE

TRIAL OF ST. JOAN, THE   see   JOAN OF ARC

TRIAL OF THE THREE MILLION, THE   see   THIEF, THE

TRIALS OF CHARLES DE GAULLE, THE   (CBS--TV, 1961,
      based on the life of the premiere of France)
   ENIGMA OF CHARLES DE GAULLE, THE   (short)
      (IND, n.d.)
   CHARLES DE GAULLE   (short)   (IND, n.d.)
   CHARLES DE GAULLE   (short)   (MHF, 1964)
   CHARLES DE GAULLE 1890--1970   (short)   (IND, 1970)

TRIALS OF OSCAR WILDE   see   GREEN CARNATION,
   THE

TRIBUTE TO PRESIDENT HERBERT CLARK HOOVER, A
   see   HERBERT CLARK HOOVER

TRIFLING WOMEN   see   BLACK ORCHIDS

TRILBY   see   TRILBY AND LITTLE BILLEE

TRILBY AND LITTLE BILLEE   (BIO, 1896, based on the
      book by Georges du Maurier)
   TRILBY   (DEN, 1908)
   TRILBY   (BRI, 1912)
   TRILBY   (AUS/HUN, 1912)
   TRILBY   (PAR, 1913)
   TRILBY   (BRI, 1914)
   TRILBY   (WOR, 1915)
   TRILBY   (WOR, 1917)
   TRILBY   (short)   (BRI, 1922)
   TRILBY   (FN, 1923)
   SVENGALI   (GER, 1927)
   SVENGALI   (WB, 1931)
   TRILBY   (CBS--TV, 1950)
   SVENGALI   (BRI, 1955)

SVENGALI AND THE BLONDE   (CBS--TV, 1955)

TRIP TO CHINATOWN, A   (SEL, 1917, based on the play by
      Charles Hoyt)
   TRIP TO CHINATOWN, A   (FOX, 1926)

TRIP TO PARADISE, A   (MGM, 1921, based on the play,
      "Liliom," by Ferenc Molnar and the musical drama by
      Richard Rodgers and Oscar Hammerstein II)
   LILIOM   (FOX, 1930)
   LILIOM   (GER, 1934)
   LILIOM   (FRA, 1935)
   LILIOM   (HUN, 1956)
   CAROUSEL   (FOX, 1956)
   CAROUSEL   (ABC--TV, 1967)

TRIP TO THE MOON, A   (FRA, 1902, based on "Voyage to
      the Moon" by Jules Verne)
   FROM THE EARTH TO THE MOON   (WB, 1958)
   ROCKET TO THE MOON   (BRI, 1967)

TRIP TO TILSIT, A   see   SUNRISE

TRISTAN AND ISOLDE   see   ETERNAL RETURN, THE

TRIUMPH OF ALEXANDER THE GREAT   see   ALEXAN--
      DER THE GREAT

TRIUMPH OF LOUIS BRAILLE, THE   see   LOUIS BRAILLE

TRIUMPH OF MICHAEL STROGOFF, THE   see   MICHAEL
      STROGOFF

TRIUMPH OF ROBIN HOOD   see   ROBIN HOOD AND
      HIS MERRY MEN

TRIUMPH OF THE RAT   see   RAT, THE

TRIUMPH OF THE SCARLET PIMPERNEL, THE   see
      SCARLET PIMPERNEL, THE

TROIS MASQUES, LES   (FRA, 1921, based on the book by
      Charles Mere)
   TROIS MASQUES, LES   (FRA, 1929)

TROIS VOLEURS, LES   see   THIEF, THE

TROPENNACHTE   see   VICTORY

TROTTE TEODOR   (SWE, 1931, source unlisted)
   TROTTE TEODOR   (SWE, 1945)

TROU DANS LE MUR, LE   (FRA, 1931, based on the book
      by Yves Mirande)
   TROU DANS LE MUR, LE   (FRA, 1950)

TROUBLE AT TRES CRUCES   (NBC--TV, 1958, based on a
      teleplay by Sam Peckinpah)
   WESTERNER, THE   (series)   (NBC--TV, 1960)

TROUBLE FOR TWO   see   SUICIDE CLUB, THE

TROUBLESOME DOUBLE, THE   see   EGGHEAD'S ROBOT

TROVATORE, IL   (short)   (ITA, 1908, based on the opera
      by Giuseppe Verdi)
   TROVATORE, IL   (short)   (GRI, 1910)
   TROVATORE, IL   (short)   (BRI, 1922)
   TROVATORE, IL   (short)   (BRI, 1927)

TROVATORE, IL   (ITA, 1948)

TRUE AND THE FALSE, THE   see   GRANDE BRETECHE, LA

TRUE CONFESSION   (PAR, 1937, based on the book, "Mon Crime," by Louis Verneuil and the play by Verneuil and Georges Barr)
CROSS MY HEART   (PAR, 1947)

TRUE STORY OF JESSE JAMES, THE   see   JAMES BOYS, THE

TRUE STORY OF LILI MARLENE   (BRI, 1944, based on a poem by Hans Leip)
LILI MARLENE   (BRI, 1951)
. . . WIE EINST, LILI MARLEEN   (GER, 1956)

TRUE STORY OF THE CIVIL WAR, THE   see   MATTHEW BRADY: PHOTOGRAPHER OF AN ERA

TRUE TO THE ARMY   see   SHE LOVES ME NOT

TRUMAN YEARS, THE   see   FROM PRECINCT TO PRESIDENT

TRUTH ABOUT SPRING, THE   see   SATAN'S SISTER

TRUTH ABOUT YOUTH, THE   see   WHEN WE WERE 21

TRUTH GAME   see   BUT THE FLESH IS WEAK

TSAR SULTAN   see   STORY OF TSAR SULTAN, THE

TSAREVITCH, LE   see   ZAREWITSCH, DER

TUDOR ROSE   see   LADY JANE GREY

TUGBOAT ANNIE   (MGM, 1922, based on stories by Norman Reilly Raine)
TUGBOAT ANNIE SAILS AGAIN   (WB, 1940)

TUGBOAT ANNIE SAILS AGAIN   see   TUGBOAT ANNIE

TUMULTES   see   STURME DER LEIDENSCHAFT

TUNA   see   TIGER SHARK

TUNDRA   (BTZ, 1936, the second film consists of stock footage from the first film)
ARCTIC FURY   (PLY, 1949)

TUNNEL, DER   (GER, 1933, based on a story by Bernhard Kellerman)
TUNNEL, THE   (FRA, 1933)
TRANSATLANTIC TUNNEL   (BRI, 1934)

TUO VIZIO E UNA STANZA CHIUSA E SOLO IO NE NO LA CHIARE, IL   see   EERIE TALES

TURLIS ADVENTURE   see   PINOCCHIO

TURMOIL, THE   (MGM, 1916, based on the book by Booth Tarkington)
TURMOIL, THE   (UN, 1924)

TURN OF THE SCREW   see   OTHERS, THE

TURNING POINT OF JIM MALLOY, THE   (NBC--TV, 1975, based on a teleplay by Frank Gilroy)
GIBBSVILLE   (series)   (NBC--TV, 1976)

'TWAS THE NIGHT BEFORE CHRISTMAS   see   NIGHT BEFORE CHRISTMAS, THE

TWELFTH NIGHT   (VIT, 1910, based on the play by William Shakespeare; also the basis for two musical comedies, "Your Own Thing" in 1967 and "Music Is" in 1976)
TWELFTH NIGHT   (NBC-TV, 1949)
TWELFTH NIGHT   (short)   (BRI, 1953)
TWELFTH NIGHT   (RUS, 1955)
TWELFTH NIGHT   (NBC-TV, 1957)
TWELFTH NIGHT   (GER, 1962)
TWELFTH NIGHT   (GER-TV, 1963)
TWELFTH NIGHT   (NET-TV, 1969)
TWELFTH NIGHT   (BRI-TV, 1969)
VIOLA AND SEBASTIAN   (GER, 1973)

12 ANGRY MEN   (CBS--TV, 1954, based on the teleplay by Reginald Rose)
12 ANGRY MEN   (UA, 1957)
DOCE HOMBRES SIN PIEDAD   (SPA--TV, 1973)

TWELVE CHAIRS, THE   (RUS, n.d., based on the play by Elie Ilf and Eugene Petrov)
TWELVE CHAIRS, THE   (CUB, n.d.)
KEEP YOUR SEATS PLEASE   (BRI, 1936)
IT'S IN THE BAG   (UA, 1945)
TWELVE CHAIRS, THE   (UMC, 1970)
TWELVE CHAIRS, THE   (RUS, 1971)

TWELVE DAYS OF CHRISTMAS, THE   see   ON THE TWELFTH DAY

12 O'CLOCK HIGH   (FOX, 1949, based on the book by Bernie Lay Jr. and Sy Bartlett)
12 O'CLOCK HIGH   (series)   (ABC--TV, 1964)

TWENTIETH CENTURY   (COL, 1934, based on a play, "Napoleon of Broadway," by Charles Bruce Millholland and a play by Ben Hecht and Charles MacArthur)
TWENTIETH CENTURY   (TV, 1953)
TWENTIETH CENTURY   (CBS--TV, 1956)

20TH CENTURY OZ   see   DOROTHY AND THE SCARE-- CROW OF OZ

21 DAYS TOGETHER   see   STRANGER, THE

24 HOURS IN THE LIFE OF A WOMAN   see   VIERUND-- ZWANZIG STUNDEN AUS DEM LEBEN EINER FRAU

20 MILLION SWEETHEARTS   (WB, 1934, based on a story by Paul Finder Moss and Jerry Wald)
MY DREAM IS YOURS   (WB, 1949)

20,000 LEAGUES UNDER THE SEA   (FRA, 1907, based on the book by Jules Verne)
20,000 LEAGUES UNDER THE SEA   (UN, 1916)
20,000 LEAGUES UNDER THE SEA   (TV, 1949)
20,000 LEAGUES UNDER THE SEA   (DIS, 1954)
RETURN OF CAPTAIN NEMO, THE   (CBS--TV, 1968)
STOLEN AIRSHIP, THE   (CZE, 1969)
CAPTAIN NEMO AND THE UNDERWATER CITY   (BRI, 1969)
20,000 LEAGUES UNDER THE SEA   (RAN, 1972)
20,000 LEAGUES UNDER THE SEA   (HB, 1973)
MYSTERIOUS ISLAND OF CAPTAIN NEMO, THE

(SPA, 1974)

20,000 YEARS IN SING SING (WB, 1933, based on the
    book by Warden Lewis E. Lawes)
    CASTLE ON THE HUDSON (WB, 1940)

23--1/2 HOURS LEAVE (PAR, 1919, based on the story by
    Mary Roberts Rinehart)
    23--1/2 HOURS LEAVE (GN, 1937)

TWICE AROUND THE DAFFODILS see CARRY ON,
    NURSE

TWICE TOLD TALES see DR. HEIDEGGER'S EXPERI--
    MENT

TWICE UPON A TIME see DOPPELTE LOTTCHEN, DAS

TWIGS see MA AND PA

TWIN BEDS (FN, 1920, based on the play by Margaret Mayo
    and Salisbury Field)
    TWIN BEDS (FN, 1929)
    LIFE OF THE PARTY (BRI, 1934)
    TWIN BEDS (UA, 1942)

TWIN PAWNS see WOMAN IN WHITE, THE

TWINS OF DRACULA see NOSFERATU

TWINS OF EVIL see STRANGE CASE OF DAVID GRAY,
    THE

TWINS OF SUFFERING CREEK (FOX, 1920, based on a
    story by Ridgewell Callum)
    MAN WHO WON, THE (FOX, 1923)

TWISTED CROSS, THE see HITLER GANG, THE

TWO AGAINST THE WORLD see 5--STAR FINAL

TWO--FACED WOMAN see HER SISTER FROM PARIS

TWO FACES OF DR. JEKYLL, THE see DR. JEKYLL AND
    MR. HYDE

TWO FISTED see IS ZAT SO?

TWO FLAGS WEST (FOX, 1950, based on a story by Frank
    S. Nugent)

STILL TRUMPET, THE (CBS--TV, 1957)

TWO GIRLS ON BROADWAY see BROADWAY MELODY

TWO GUYS FROM TEXAS see COWBOY FROM
    BROOKLYN

TWO IN THE DARK (RKO, 1936, based on a book by Gelett
    Burgess)
    TWO O'CLOCK COURAGE (RKO, 1945)

TWO LOST WORLDS (EL, 1950, based on footage from
    CAPTAIN CAUTION (UA, 1940); CAPTAIN FURY
    (UA, 1939); and ONE MILLION B.C. (UA, 1940))

TWO MRS. CARROLLS, THE (WB, 1947, based on the play
    by Martin Vale)
    TWO MRS. CARROLLS, THE (TV, 1952)
    TWO MRS. CARROLLS, THE (NBC--TV, 1958)

TWO O'CLOCK COURAGE see TWO IN THE DARK

TWO OF US, THE see VI TVA

TWO ORPHANS (FRA, 1910, based on the play by Adolphe
    Philippe and Eugene Corman)
    TWO ORPHANS (IND, 1911)
    TWO ORPHANS (FOX, 1915)
    TWO ORPHANS (SEL, 1916)
    ORPHANS OF THE STORM (UA, 1921)
    DEUX ORPHELINES, LES (FRA, 1933)
    DUE ORFANELLE, LE (ITA, 1942)
    DUE ORFANELLE, LE (FRA/ITA, 1954)
    DUE ORFANELLE, LE (FRA/ITA, 1965)

TWO--SOUL WOMAN (UN, 1918, based on a book by Gelett
    Burgess)
    UNTAMEABLE, THE (UN, 1923)

TWO SOULS (RUS, 1920, source unlisted)
    WHO ARE YOU? (RUS, 1927)

TWO WORLDS OF CHARLY GORDON, THE (CBS--TV,
    1961, based on the story, "Flowers for Algernon," by
    Daniel Keyes)
    CHARLY (CIN, 1968)

TYPHOON (INC, 1914, based on the story by Melchior
    Lengyel)
    TAIFUN (GER, 1933)

U–238 AND THE WITCH DOCTOR   see   JUNGLE DRUMS
   OF AFRICA

U.S. GRANT: AN IMPROBABLE HERO   see   SUNSET AT
   APPOMATTOX

UGETSU   see   JASEI NO IN

UGLY DUCKLING, THE   (short)   (DIS, 1939, based on the
   story by Hans Christian Andersen)
   HANS CHRISTIAN ANDERSEN   (RKO, 1952)
   UGLY DUCKLING, THE   (short)   (EBE, 1953)

UGLY DUCKLING, THE   see   DR. JEKYLL AND MR,
   HYDE

ULICKA V RAJI   (ROAD TO PARADISE)   (CZE, 1936,
   based on a screenplay by Hugo Haas and Otakar Vavia)
   GASSCHEN ZUM PARADIES, DAS   (GER, 1936)

ULTIMO DE LOS VARGAS, EL   see   LAST OF THE DUANES,
   THE

ULTIMO GIORNO DE POMPEII, L'   (ITA, 1898, based on
   the book by Edward George Bulwer Lytton)
   LAST DAYS OF POMPEII, THE   (BRI, 1901)
   ULTIMO GIORNO DE POMPEII, L'   (ITA, 1908)
   ULTIMO GIORNO DE POMPEII, L'   (ITA, 1913)
   (3 productions)
   ULTIMO GIORNO DE POMPEII, L'   (ITA, 1924)
   ULTIMO GIORNO DE POMPEII, L'   (ITA, 1926)
   LAST DAYS OF POMPEII, THE   (RKO, 1935)
   ULTIMO GIORNO DE POMPEII, L'   (ITA, 1937)
   DERNIERS JOURS DE POMPEII, LES   (FRA/ITA, 1948)
   LAST DAYS OF POMPEII, THE   (GER/ITA/SPA, 1959)

ULTIMO VARON SOBRE LA TIERRA   see   LAST MAN
   ON EARTH, THE

ULTRA MAN, THE   (series)   (JAP–TV, 1966, the second is
   re--edited from the series footage)
   ULTRA MAN, THE   (JAP, 1967)

ULYSSES   see   ODYSSEY, THE

ULYSSES AND THE GIANT POLYPHEMUS   (FRA, 1905,
   based on the book by Homer; James Joyce's modern–
   day book on the same subject, "Ulysses," was released in
   1967)
   ODYSSEY, THE   (IND, 1909)
   HOMER'S ODYSSEY   (ITA, 1911)
   ULYSSES   (PAR, 1955)
   ODYSSEY, THE   (AUT, 1963)
   ODYSSEY, THE   (ITA–TV, 1968)

UM EINE NASENLANGE   (GER, 1931, source unlisted)
   UM EINE NASENLANGE   (GER, 1949)

UM THRON UND LIEVE   see   KLEINE HERZOG, DER

UMBRELLA OF SAINT PETER, THE   (HUN, 1917, based
   on the book by Kalman Mikszath)
   UMBRELLA OF SAINT PETER, THE   (HUN, 1935)
   UMBRELLA OF SAINT PETER, THE   (HUN, 1958)

UNACCUSTOMED AS WE ARE   see   SOLDIER MAN

UNCENSORED DECAMERON   see   DECAMERON, THE

UNCLE HARRY   see   STRANGE AFFAIR OF UNCLE HARRY

UNCLE REMUS – BR'ER RABBIT   (n.d., 1919, based on
   stories by Joel Chandler Harris)
   SONG OF THE SOUTH   (DIS, 1946)

UNCLE SILAS   (BRI, 1947, based on the book by Sheridan
   le fanu)
   MYSTERIOUS UNCLE SILAS   (ARG, 1947)
   INHERITANCE, THE   (BRI, 1951)

UNCLE TOM'S CABIN   (ED, 1903, based on the book by
   Harriett Beecher Stowe)
   UNCLE TOM'S CABIN   (LUB, 1903)
   UNCLE TOM'S CABIN   (THA, 1910)
   UNCLE TOM'S CABIN   (VIT, 1910)
   UNCLE TOM'S CABIN   (PAT, 1910)
   UNCLE TOM'S CABIN   (UN, 1913)
   UNCLE TOM'S CABIN   (KAL, 1913)
   UNCLE TOM'S CABIN   (WOR, 1914)
   UNCLE TOM'S CABIN   (PAR, 1918)
   UNCLE TOM WITHOUT THE CABIN   (short)   (PAR,
   1919)
   UNCLE TOM'S CABIN   (IND, 1922)
   DINKY DOODLE IN UNCLE TOM'S CABIN   (short)   (IND,
   1926)
   UNCLE TOM'S CABIN   (UN, 1927)
   TOPSY AND EVA   (UA, 1927)
   UNCLE TOM'S CABIN   (CBS–TV, 1955)
   ONKEL TOMS HUTTE   (GER/ITA/YUG, 1965)
   CURIOUS CASE OF "UNCLE TOM'S CABIN,"THE   (IND–
   TV, 1977)

UNCLE TOM WITHOUT THE CABIN   see   UNCLE TOM'S
CABIN

UNCLE VANYA (NBC–TV, 1950, based on the play by Anton
   Chekhov)
   UNCLE VANYA   (CON, 1958)
   UNCLE VANYA   (BRI, 1964)
   UNCLE VANYA   (NET–TV, 1968)
   UNCLE VANYA   (RUS, 1971)

UND DER REGEN VERWISCHT JEDE SPUR   see   BOUR–
   RASQUE DE NEIGE, LA

UND DIE MUSIK SPIELT DAZU   (GER, 1943, based on the
   play by Max Wallner and Kurt Feltz)
   SEASON IN SALZBURG   (AUS, 1952)
   SEASON IN SALZBURG   (GER, 1961)

UNDER MILK WOOD   (CAN–TV, 1959, based on the play by
   Dylan Thomas)
   UNDER MILK WOOD   (BRI, 1972)

UNDER MY SKIN   (FOX, 1950, based on the story, "My Old
   Man," by Ernest Hemingway)
   MY OLD MAN   (short)   (EBE, 1968)

UNDER SOUTHERN STARS   (short)   (WB, 1939, based on
   the life of General Ulysses S. Grant)
   SUNSET AT APPOMATTOX   (short)   (TFC, 1953)
   GRANT AND LEE AT APPOMATTOX   (short)   (CBS–TV,
   1956)
   U.S. GRANT: AN IMPROBABLE HERO   (short)   (NBC–TV,
   1962)

UNDER SOUTHERN STARS   (short)   (WB, 1939, based on the
   life of American General Thomas Jonathan Jackson)

DEATH OF STONEWALL JACKSON, THE (short) (CBS–TV, 1955)

UNDER SOUTHERN STARS (short) (WB, 1939, based on the life of Gen. Robert E. Lee)
ROBERT E. LEE (short) (COR, 1953)
LEE, THE VIRGINIAN (short) (TFC, 1963)

UNDER THE RED ROBE (BRI, 1915, based on the book by Stanley J. Weyman)
UNDER THE RED ROBE (MGM, 1923)
UNDER THE RED ROBE (FOX, 1937)

UNDER THE SIGN OF MONTE CRISTO see COUNT OF MONTE CRISTO, THE

UNDER THE TONTO RIM (PAR, 1928, based on the book by Zane Grey)
UNDER THE TONTO RIM (PAR, 1933)
UNDER THE TONTO RIM (RKO, 1947)

UNDER THE YUM YUM TREE (COL, 1963, based on the play by Lawrence Roman)
UNDER THE YUM YUM TREE (ABC–TV, 1969)

UNDER TWO FLAGS (FOX, 1916, based on the book by Ouida)
UNDER TWO FLAGS (FOX, 1922)
UNDER TWO FLAGS (FOX, 1936)

UNDERGROUND MAN (NBC–TV, 1974, based on characters by Ross McDonald)
ARCHER (series) (NBC–TV, 1975)

UNDERSEA KINGDOM (serial) (REP, 1936, based on a screen-play by various authors; the remake is a condensation of the serial)
SHARAD OF ATLANTIS (REP, 1966)

UNDINE see LEGENDE DES ONDINES

UNE FEMMEN A MENTI see LADY LIES, THE

UNE HEUR PRES DE TOI see ONE HOUR WITH YOU

UNENTSCHULDIGTE, DIE (GER, 1937, based on the play, "Die Unentschuldigte Stunde," by Stefan Bekeffi and Adorjan Stella)
UNENTSCHULDIGTE, DIE (GER, 1957)

UNENTSCHULDIGTE STUNDE, DIE see UNENTSCHULDIG-TE, DIE

UNFAITHFUL, THE see LETTER, THE

UNFINISHED BUSINESS (UN, 1941, based on the screenplay by Eugene Thackery)
UNFINISHED BUSINESS (ABC–TV, 1951)

UNFINISHED DANCE, THE see BALLERINA, THE

UNFINISHED SYMPHONY see SCHUBERT'S FRUHLING-STRAUM

UNFORGOTTEN CRIME see RETURN OF JIMMY VALEN-TINE, THE

UNGETREUE ECKEHART, DER (GER, 1931, based on the book by Hans Sturm)
UNGETREUE ECKEHART, DER (GER, 1940)

UNHEIMLICHE GESCHICHTEN see SUICIDE CLUB, THE

UNHEIMLICHEN WUNSCHE, DIE see PEAU DE CHAGRIN, LA

UNHOLY LOVE (HOD, 1932, based on the book, "Madame Bovary," by Gustave Flaubert)
MADAME BOVARY (IND, 1934)
MADAME BOVARY (GER, 1937)
MADAME BOVARY (ARG, 1947)
MADAME BOVARY (MGM, 1949)
MADAME BOVARY (series) (PBS–TV, 1976)
MADAME BOVARY (series) (ITA–TV, 1977)

UNHOLY LOVE see ALRAUNE

UNHOLY NIGHT, THE (MGM, 1929, based on a story by Ben Hecht)
SPECTRE VERT, LE (FRA, 1930)

UNHOLY THREE, THE (MGM, 1925, based on the book by Clarence Aaron Robbins)
UNHOLY THREE, THE (MGM, 1930)

UNHOLY WISH, THE see WILD ASS'S SKIN, THE

UNION PACIFIC see IRON HORSE, THE

U. S. EXPANSION: THE OREGON COUNTRY see LEWIS AND CLARK
UNIVERSE OF NUMBERS (short) (NET–TV, 1962, based on the life and work of the noted mathematician)
BLAISE PASCAL (short) (FRA, n.d.)
PASCAL (ITA, 1973)

UNKEIMLICHE GESCHICHTEN (GER, 1919, based on short stories by Edgar Allan Poe and Robert Louis Stevenson)
UNKEIMLICHE GESCHICHTEN (GER, 1932)

UNKNOWN BLONDE (MAJ, 1934, based on a play by lenore Coffee)
AGE OF INDISCRETION (MGM, 1935)

UNKNOWN CAVALIER (FN, 1926, based on the book, "Ride Him Cowboy," by Kenneth Perkins)
RIDE HIM COWBOY (THE HAWK) (WB, 1932)

UNMAN, WITTERING AND ZIGO (BRI–TV, 1957, based on a radio play by Giles Cooper)
UNMAN, WITTERING AND ZIGO (BRI, 1971)

UNMARRIED see LADY AND GENT

UNMARRIED FATHER, AN see LITTLE ACCIDENT

UNNATURAL see ALRAUNE

UNQUIET DEATH OF ETHEL AND JULIUS ROSENBERG, THE see JUDGMENT: THE TRIAL OF JULIUS AND ETHEL ROSENBERG

UNSCHULD VOM LANDE, DIE (GER, 1933, source un-listed)
UNSCHULD VOM LANDE, DIE (GER, 1957)

UNSER TAGLICH BROT (GER, 1925, source unlisted)
UNSER TAGLICH BROT (GER, 1949)

UNSINKABLE MRS. BROWN, THE (short) (IND–TV, 1952,

based on the story by Richard Morris)
UNSINKABLE MRS. BROWN, THE   (CBS–TV, 1957)
UNSINKABLE MOLLY BROWN, THE   (MGM, 1964)

UNSINKABLE MOLLY BROWN, THE   see   UNSINKABLE
MRS. BROWN, THE

UNSTERBLICHE LIEBE, WAS DIE SCHWALBE SANG   see
IMMENSEE

UNSTERBLICHE MELODIEN   see   WALTZES FROM VI–
ENNA

UNTAMEABLE, THE   see   TWO–SOUL WOMAN

UNTAMED   see   MANTRAP

UNTER FALSCHEN FLAGGEN   (GER, 1932, based on the
book by Max Kimmich)
MADAME SPY   (UN, 1934)
MADAME SPY   (UN, 1942)

UNTIL THEY SAIL   see   RETURN TO PARADISE

UOMO CHE RIDE   see   HOMME QUI RIT, L'

UP FOR MURDER   see   MAN, WOMAN AND SIN

UP FOR THE CUP   (BRI, 1931, based on the story by Con
West)
UP FOR THE CUP   (BRI, 1950)

UP IN ARMS   see   NERVOUS WRECK, THE

UP IN DESDEMONA'S ROOM   see   OTHELLO

UP IN MABEL'S ROOM   (PDC, 1926, based on the play by
Wilson Collinson and Otto Harbach)
UP IN MABEL'S ROOM   (UA, 1944)

UP IN THE AIR   (MON, 1941, based on a screenplay by Ed–

mond Kelso)
THERE GOES KELLY   (MON, 1945)

UP POPS THE DEVIL   (PAR, 1930, based on the play by
Albert Hackett and Frances Goodrich; also the basis
for the 1931 musical comedy, "Everybody's Welcome")
THANKS FOR THE MEMORY   (PAR, 1938)

UP THE CREEK   see   OH, MR. PORTER

UP THE JUNCTION   (BRI–TV, 1965, based on the book by
Nell Dunn)
UP THE JUNCTION   (BRI, 1968)

UP THE RIVER   (FOX, 1930, based on a story by Maurine
Watkins)
UP THE RIVER   (FOX, 1938)

UP TIGHT   see   INFORMER, THE

UPSTAIRS AND DOWNSTAIRS   (series)   (BRI–TV, 1974)
based on a teleplay)
BEACON HILL   (series)   (CBS–TV, 1975)

URLAUB AUF EHRENWORT   (GER, 1937, source unlisted)
URLAUB AUF EHRENWORT   (GER, 1955)

UT MINE STROMTID   (GER, 1920, based on the book by
Fritz Reuter)
VIE A LA CAMPAGNE, LA   (SWE, 1924)
ONKEL BRASIG   (GER, 1936)
VIE A LA COMPAGNE, LA   (SWE, 1943)

UTAMARO AND HIS FIVE WOMEN   (JAP, 1946, based on
the life and work of the noted printmaker)
UTAMARO'S WORLD   (JAP, 1977)

UTAMARO'S WORLD   see   UTAMARO AND HIS FIVE
WOMEN

VA BANQUE   (GER, 1920, source unlisted)
  VA BANQUE   (GER, 1930)

VACANCES DU DIABLE, LES   see   DEVIL'S HOLIDAY,
  THE

VADERTJE LANGBEEN   see   DADDY LONG LEGS

VAGABOND, THE   (FRA/ITA, 1916, based on a book by
  Anthony W. Coldeway)
  VAGABOND, THE   (FRA, 1930)

VAGABOND KING, THE   see   IF I WERE KING

VALENTINO   (COL, 1951, based on the life of the movie
    star)
  LEGEND OF VALENTINO, THE   (short)   (STE, 1960)
  LEGEND OF VALENTINO, THE   (ABC–TV, 1975)
  VALENTINO   (BRI, 1977)

VALIANT, THE   (FOX, 1929, based on the play by Holworthy
    Hall and Robert M. Middlemass)
  VALIENTE, EL   (SPA, 1930)
  VALIANT, THE   (NBC–TV, 1939)
  MAN WHO WOULDN'T TALK, THE   (FOX, 1940)
  VALIANT, THE   (CBS–TV, 1950)

VALIANT YEARS, THE   see   CHURCHILL – MAN OF THE
  CENTURY

VALIENTE, EL   see   VALIANT, THE

VALLEY FORGE   see   MOUNT VERNON IN VIRGINIA

VALLEY OF DECISION   (MGM, 1945, based on the book by
    Marcia Davenport)
  VALLEY OF DECISION   (NBC–TV, 1960)

VALLEY OF SILENT MEN, THE   (IND, 1915, based on a
    story by James Oliver Curwood)
  VALLEY OF SILENT MEN, THE   (PAR, 1922)

VALLEY OF THE GIANTS   (PAR, 1919, based on the book
    by Peter B. Kyne)
  VALLEY OF THE GIANTS   (FN, 1927)
  VALLEY OF THE GIANTS   (WB, 1938)
  BIG TREES, THE   (WB, 1952)

VALMIKI   (IN, 1946, based on an Indian legend)
  VALMIKI   (IN, 1963)

VALSE DE L'ADIEU, LA   (FRA, 1926, based on a book by
    Henry Dupuy--Mazuel)
  ABSCHIEDSWALZER   (GER, 1934)

VAMPIRE LOVERS, THE   see   STRANGE CASE OF DAVID
  GRAY, THE

VAMPIRE OF DUSSELDORF, THE   see   M

VAN GOGH   (short)   (IND, 1949, based on the life and
    works of the noted artist)
  VINCENT VAN GOGH   (NBC–TV, 1950)
  VAN GOGH   (short)   (PIC, 1953)
  VAN GOGH -- FROM DARKNESS INTO LIGHT   (short)
    (MGM, 1956)
  LUST FOR LIFE   (MGM, 1956)
  VINCENT VAN GOGH 1853--1890   (short)   (COR, 1959)
  VINCENT VAN GOGH -- TO THEO, WITH LOVE   (USC,
    1962)

VAN GOGH – A SELF–PORTRAIT   (NBC–TV, 1962)
  VAN GOGH   (short)   (TIM, 1967)
  VAN GOGH   (short)   (BFA, 1969)

VANINA VANINI   (VANINA)   (GER, 1922, based on the
    short story by Stendhal)
  OLTRE L'AMORE, L'   (STRONGER THAN LOVE)
    (ITA, 1940)
  BETRAYER, THE   (VANINA VANINI)   (FRA/ITA, 1961)

VANISHING AMERICAN, THE   (PAR, 1926, based on the
    book by Zane Grey)
  VANISHING AMERICAN, THE   (REP, 1955)

VANITY FAIR   (VIT, 1911, based on the book by William
    Makepeace Thackery)
  VANITY FAIR   (ED, 1915)
  VANITY FAIR   (short)   (BRI, 1922)
  VANITY FAIR   (GOL, 1923)
  VANITY FAIR   (IND, 1932)
  BECKY SHARP   (RKO, 1935)
  BECKY SHARP   (NBC–TV, 1949)
  VANITY FAIR   (CBS–TV, 1961)
  VANITY FAIR   (BRI–TV, 1967)
  VANITY FAIR   (BRI–TV, 1972)

VARIETY   (GER, 1925, based on a screenplay by E.A. Dupont
    and a book by Felix Hollaender)
  VARIETE   (FRA, 1935)
  VARIETY   (GER, 1935)

VARMLANNINGARNA   (SWE, 1910, based on an opera
    [composer unlisted])
  VARMLANNINGARNA   (SWE, 1911)
  VARMLANNINGARNA   (SWE, 1921)
  VARMLANNINGARNA   (SWE, 1932)
  VARMLANNINGARNA   (SWE, 1957)

VAUTRIN   (ITA, 1917, based on a story by Honore de Balzac)
  GALEERENSTRAFLING, DER   (GER, 1919)
  VAUTRIN   (FRA, 1943)
  BAGNOSTRAFLING, DER   (GER, 1949)

VEGAS   (ABC–TV, 1978, based on a teleplay)
  VEGAS   (series)   (ABC–TV, 1978)

VEILLE D'ARMES   (BRI/FRA, 1925, based on a story by
    Claude Farrere and Lucien Nepoty)
  WOMAN FROM MONTE CARLO, THE   (FN, 1932)
  VEILLE D'ARMES   (FRA, 1935)

VEINE D'OR, LA   (ITA, 1928, based on the book by
    Guglielmo Zorzi)
  VEINE D'OR, LA   (ITA, 1955)

VELASQUEZ   (short)   (PIC, n.d., based on the life and works
    of the noted artist)
  VELASQUEZ   (short)   (IFB, 1955)

VENDETTA   (FRA, 1914, based on a book by F. McGraw
    Willis)
  PHANTOM MELODY, THE   (UN, 1919)

VENDETTA   see   CAVALLERIA RUSTICANNA and
  COLOMBA

VENGEANCE   see   LADY AND THE MONSTER, THE

VENGEANCE DE PAGLIACCI, LA   see   PAILLASSE

VENGEANCE OF DR. CALIGARI, THE see CABINET OF DR. CALIGARI

VENGEANCE OF RANNAH (SEL, 1915, source unlisted)
  VENGEANCE OF RANA (n.d.)

VENGEANCE OF THE BLACK EAGLE, THE see DOUBROVSKY

VENGEANCE OF THE THREE MUSKETEERS see THREE MUSKETEERS, THE

VERA THE MEDIUM (IND, 1910, based on the book by Richard Harding Davis)
  VERA THE MEDIUM (SEZ, 1916)

VERDI see GIUSEPPE VERDI

VERDICT, THE see PERFECT CRIME, THE

VERKAUFTE GROSSVATER, DER (GER, 1942, based on the play by Anton Hamik)
  VERKAUFTE GROSSVATER, DER (GER, 1962)

VERLORENE SCHATTEN, DER see PETER SCHLEMIHL

VERLORENE SCHUH, DER see CINDERELLA AND THE FAIRY GODMOTHER

VERLORENE SOHN, DER (GER, 1917, based on the play by Johann Heinrich de Noel)
  VERLORENE SOHN, DER (GER, 1934)

VERRATERTOR, DAS see TRAITOR'S GATE

VERRE D'EAU, LE see GLAS WASSER, EIN

VERSCHWENDER, DER (AUS, 1917, based on the book by Yordan Raditchkov)
  VERSCHWENDER, DER (AUS, 1952)
  VERSCHWENDER, DER (GER, 1964)

VERSCHWORUNG DES FIESCO ZU GENUA, DIE see FIESCO

VERSCHWORUNG ZU GENUA, DIE see FIESCO

VERTAGE HOCHZEITSNACHT, DIE (GER, 1924, source unlisted)
  VERTAGE HOCHZEITSNACHT, DIE (GER, 1953)

VERTIGE, LE (FRA, 1927, based on the book by Charles Mere)
  VERTIGE, LE (FRA, 1935)

VERTIGE D'UN SOIR see ANGST, DIE SCHWACHE STUNDE EINER FRAU

VERY HONORABLE GUY, A (WB, 1934, based on a story by Damon Runyan)
  GUYS AND DOLLS (MGM, 1955)
  GUYS AND DOLLS (TV, n.d.)

VERY YOUNG LADY, A see GIRL'S DORMITORY

VESSEL OF WRATH see BEACHCOMBER, THE

VETSERA, DIE see MAYERLING

VETTER AUS DINGSDA, DER (GER, 1934, based on the operetta by Eduard Kuennecke)
  VETTER AUS DINGSDA, DER (GER, 1953)

VEUVE JOYEUSE, LA see MERRY WIDOW, THE

VI TVA (SWE, 1930, source unlisted)
  VI TVA (SWE, 1939)

VIA MALA see VIA MALA, DIE STRASSE DES BOSEN

VIA MALA, DIE STRASSE DES BOSEN (GER, 1944, based on a story by John Knittel)
  VIA MALA (FRA/GER, 1961)

VIAJE EL CENTRO DE LA TIERRA see VOYAGE AU CENTRE DE LA TERRE

VICAR OF WAKEFIELD, THE (BRI, 1912, based on the book by Oliver Goldsmith)
  VICAR OF WAKEFIELD, THE (BRI, 1913)
  VICAR OF WAKEFIELD, THE (BRI, 1914)
  MINISTER, THE (EAS, 1915)
  VICAR OF WAKEFIELD, THE (BRI, 1916)
  VICAR OF WAKEFIELD, THE (PAR, 1917)

VICE AND VIRTUE (FRA/ITA, 1962, based on "Justine and Juliette" by Marquis de Sade)
  JUSTINE AND THE MISFORTUNES OF VIRTUE (FRA/GER/ITA, 1968)

VICE–PRESIDENT'S STORY, THE see DECLARATION OF INDEPENDENCE, THE

VICE VERSA (BRI, 1916, based on the book by F. Anstey)
  VICE VERSA (BRI, 1947)

VICKIE see I WAKE UP SCREAMING

VICTOR FRANKENSTEIN see FRANKENSTEIN

VICTOIRE INUTILE, LA see CARRIERE D'UNE CHANTEUSE DES RUES, LA

VICTORIA AND HER HUSSAR (GER, 1931, based on the operetta by Paul Abraham)
  VICTORIA AND HER HUSSAR (GER, 1954)

VICTORIA REGINA see SIXTY YEARS A QUEEN

VICTORIA THE GREAT see SIXTY YEARS A QUEEN

VICTORY (PAR, 1919, based on the book by Joseph Conrad)
  DANGEROUS PARADISE (PAR, 1930)
  DANS UNE ILE PERDUE (FRA, 1930)
  TROPENNACHTE (GER, 1930)
  VICTORY (PAR, 1940)
  VICTORY (NBC–TV, 1952)
  VICTORY (NBC–TV, 1960)

VICTORY AT ENTEBBE (ABC--TV, 1976, based on an actual airline hijacking incident)
  RAID ON ENTEBBE (FOX, 1977)
  ENTEBBE COUNTDOWN (OPERATION THUNDERBOLT) (ISR, 1977)

VIDA NOCTURNA, LA see THEIR PURPLE MOMENT

VIE A LA CAMPAGNE, LA see UT MINE STROMTID

VIE COMMENCE DEMAIN, LA (FRA, 1950, documentaries based on the life and works of the noted French writer)
AVEC ANDRE GIDE (FRA, 1951)

VIE DE BOHEME, LA (FRA, 1913, based on the book, "Scenes de la vie de Boheme," by Henri Murger and the opera "La Boheme," by Giacomo Puccini)
BOHEME, LA (WOR, 1916)
VIE DE BOHEME, LA (ITA, 1923)
BOHEME, LA (MGM, 1926)
MIMI (BRI, 1934)
CHARM OF LA BOHEME, THE (GER, 1937)
VIE DE BOHEME, LA (FRA, 1942)
HER WONDERFUL LIE (COL, 1950)
BOHEME, LA (NBC–TV, 1956)
BOHEME, LA (FRA/ITA, 1965)
BOHEME, LA (AUT–TV, 1976)

VIE DU CHRIST, LA see PASSION PLAY, THE

VIE POUR VIE see SERGE PANINE

VIEILLE HISTOIRE, LA see MAITRE DE FORGES, LE

VIENNESE CHARMER see STREET GIRL

VIERGE FOLLE, LA (ITA, 1918, based on a book by Henri Bataille)
VIERGE FOLLE, LA (FRA, 1928)
VIERGE FOLLE, LA (FRA, 1938)

VIERTE GEBOT, DAS (GER, 1920, based on the play by Ludwig Anzen Gruber)
VIERTE GEBOT, DAS (GER, 1950)

VIERUNDZWANZIG STUNDEN AUS DEM LEBEN EINER FRAU (GER, 1931, based on the book by Stephen Zweig)
24 HOURS IN THE LIFE OF A WOMAN (FRA, 1931)
24 HOURS IN THE LIFE OF A WOMAN (ARG, 1944)
AFFAIR IN MONTE CARLO (BRI, 1952)
24 HOURS IN A WOMAN'S LIFE (CBS–TV, 1961)
24 HOURS IN THE LIFE OF A WOMAN (FRA/GER, 1968)

VIEUX TRICHEUR, LE (HUN, 1924, based on the book by Kalman Mikszath)
ALTE GAUNER, DER (GER/HUN, 1932)

VIGILANTES ARE COMING, THE see EAGLE, THE

VIGNES DU SEIGNEUR, LES (FRA, 1932, based on a story by Robert de Flers and Francis de Croisset)
VIGNES DU SEIGNEUR, LES (FRA, 1958)

VII see BLACK SUNDAY

VILLA! see LIFE OF VILLA

VILLAGE BLACKSMITH, THE (BRI, 1905, based on the poem by Henry Wadsworth Longfellow)
VILLAGE BLACKSMITH, THE (BRI, 1908)
VILLAGE BLACKSMITH, THE (BRI, 1917)
VILLAGE BLACKSMITH, THE (FOX, 1922)

VILLAGE PERFORMANCE OF HAMLET, A see HAMLET

VILLAIN STILL PURSUED HER, THE see OLD–FASHIONED WAY, THE

VINCENT VAN GOGH see VAN GOGH

VINCENT VAN GOGH – A SELF PORTRAIT see VAN GOGH

VINDICATORE see EAGLE, THE

VINYL (IND, 1965, based on the book, "A Clockwork Orange," by Anthony Burgess)
CLOCKWORK ORANGE, A (WB, 1971)

VIOLA AND SEBASTIAN see TWELFTH NIGHT

VIOLA TRICOLOR see SERENADE

VIOLANTHA (GER, 1927, based on the book, "Der Schatten," by Ernst Zahn)
VIOLANTHA (GER, 1942)

VIOLETTES IMPERIALES (FRA, 1923, based on a screen-play by Pierre Marodon and Henry–Roussell)
VIOLETTES IMPERIALES (FRA, 1928)
VIOLETTES IMPERIALES (FRA, 1932)

VIOLIN MAKER OF CREMONA, THE (GRI, 1909, based on a book by Francois Coppee)
VIOLIN MAKER OF CREMONA, THE (FRA, 1909)

VIOLON DE CREMONE see HOFFMANNS ERZAHLUNGEN

VIRAGO OF THE OSTERMAN BROTHERS see BRODERNA OSTERMANS HUSKORS

VIRGIN, THE see WOMAN DISPUTED, A

VIRGIN OF GUADALUPE, THE (MEX, 1942, based on a legend)
VIRGIN OF GUADALUPE, THE (MEX, 1950)

VIRGIN QUEEN, THE see QUEEN ELIZABETH

VIRGINIAN, THE (PAR, 1914, based on the book by Owen Wister)
VIRGINIAN, THE (PRE, 1923)
VIRGINIAN, THE (PAR, 1929)
VIRGINIAN, THE (PAR, 1946)
VIRGINIAN, THE (series) (NBC–TV, 1962)
MEN OF SHILOH, THE (series) (NBC–TV, 1970)

VIRGINIAN, THE see also SPAWN OF THE NORTH

VIRGINIA'S HUSBAND (BRI, 1928, based on the play by Florence Kilpatrick)
VIRGINIA'S HUSBAND (BRI, 1934)

VIRTUOSO FRANZ LISZT AS COMPOSER see DREAM OF LOVE

VIRTUOUS BIGAMIST, THE see FOUR STEPS IN THE CLOUDS

VIRTUOUS MODEL, THE (PAR, 1919, based on "Ruisseau, Le," by Pierre Wolff)
RUISSEAU, LE (FRA, 1929)
RUISSEAU, LE (FRA, 1938)

VIRTUOUS SIN, THE (PAR, 1930, based on the story, "The General," by Lajos Zilahy)
VIRTUOUS SIN, THE (GER, 1931)

REBELLE, LE (FRA, 1930)

VISIT TO A SMALL PLANET, A (NBC--TV, 1955, based on
the play by Gore Vidal)
VISIT TO A SMALL PLANET, A (PAR, 1960)

VISIT WITH CARL SANDBURG, A see CARL SANDBURG

VIVA KNIEVEL! see EVEL KNIEVEL

VIVA VILLA! see LIFE OF VILLA

VIVA ZAPATA (FOX, 1952, based on historical incidents
and a book by John Steinbeck)
EMILIANO ZAPATA (MEX, 1970)

VOGELHANDLER, DER (GER, 1935, based on the operetta,
"Rosen in Tirol," by Carl Zeller)
ROSEN IN TIROL (GER, 1940)
VOGELHANDLER, DER (GER, 1953)

VOGELOD CASTLE (GER, 1921, based on the book,
"Schloss Vogelod," by Rudolf Stratz)
VOGELOD CASTLE (GER, 1936)

VOILE BLEU, LE (FRA, 1942, based on the book by
Francois Campaux)
BLUE VEIL, THE (RKO, 1951)

VOILE DU BONHEUR, LE (FRA, 1910, based on a book by
Georges Clemenceau)
VOILE DU BONHEUR, LE (FRA, 1923)

VOLGA VOLGA (GER, 1928, based on the book by Kurt
Heynicke)
STJENKA RAZIN (GER, 1936)

VOLPONE (FRA, 1938, based on the play by Ben Jonson;
also the basis for the musical comedy, "Foxy," in 1964)
VOLPONE (FRA, 1947)
VOLPONE (NET--TV, 1960)
HONEY POT, THE (IT COMES UP MURDER) (UA,
1967)

VOLUNTAD DEL MUERTO, LA see CAT AND THE
CANARY, THE

VOM NIEDERRHEIN, DIE (GER, 1926, based on a novel
by Rudolf Herzog)

VOM NIEDERRHEIN, DIE (GER, 1933)

VOR SONNENUNTERGANG see HERRSCHER, DER

VORDERHAUS UND HINTERHAUS see HONNEUR, L'

VOUS N'AVEZ RIEN A DECLARER? (FRA, 1937, based on
a story by Maurice Hennequin and Pierre Veber)
VOUS N'AVEZ RIEN A DECLARER? (FRA, 1959)

VOW, THE see JEPHTHAH'S DAUGHTER

VOX POPULI (SWE, n.d., source unlisted)
VOX POPULI (SWE, 1932)

VOYAGE AU CENTRE DE LA TERRE (FRA, 1909, based
on the book by Jules Verne)
JOURNEY TO THE CENTER OF THE EARTH (FOX,
1959)
ADVENTURE TO THE CENTER OF THE EARTH (MEX,
1966)
JOURNEY TO THE CENTER OF THE EARTH (series)
(ABC--TV, 1967)
VIAJE AL CENTRO DE LA TIERRA (SPA, 1977)

VOYAGE DE LA FAMILLE BOURSICHON, LE (FRA, 1913,
based on the play, "Voyage de Monsieur Perrichon," by
Eugene Labiche and Edouard Martin)
VOYAGE DE MONSIEUR PERRICHON, LE (FRA, 1934)

VOYAGE DE MONSIEUR PERRICHON, LE see VOYAGE
DE LA FAMILLE BOURSICHON, LE

VOYAGE OF FRIENDSHIP 7 see AMERICAN IN ORBIT,
AN

VOYAGE OF GULLIVER TO LILLIPUT AND THE HOUSE
OF GIANTS see GULLIVER'S TRAVELS

VOYAGE TO THE BOTTOM OF THE SEA (FOX, 1961,
based on the book by Irwin Allen)
VOYAGE TO THE BOTTOM OF THE SEA (series) (ABC--
TV, 1964)

VOYAGE TO THE MOON see TRIP TO THE MOON, A

VOYAGE TO THE PLANET OF PREHISTORIC WOMEN,
THE see STORM CLOUDS OF VENUS

W.B. YEATS – A TRIBUTE (short) (MAC, 1950, based on the life and work of the noted poet)
    YEATS COUNTRY (short) (IFB, 1965)

WABASH AVENUE see CONEY ISLAND

WACKIEST SHIP IN THE ARMY, THE (COL, 1960, based on a story by Herbert Carlson)
    WACKIEST SHIP IN THE ARMY, THE (series) (NBC–TV, 1965)

WAGES OF FEAR, THE (FRA, 1953, based on the book by Georges Arnaud)
    SORCERER (PAR/UN, 1977)

WAGNER see RICHARD WAGNER

WAGON WHEELS see FIGHTING CARAVANS

WAGONMASTER (RKO, 1950, based on a story by Frank S. Nugent and Patrick Ford)
    FLAME OVER INDIA (BRI, 1960)

WAGONS ROLL AT NIGHT, THE see KID GALAHAD

WAHRE JAKOB, DER (GER, 1931, source unlisted)
    WAHRE JAKOB, DER (GER, 1960)

WAITING FOR GODOT see CEKAJI NA GODOTA

WAKE ME WHEN THE WAR IS OVER see SOLDIER MAN

WALDRAUSCH (GER, 1939, based on a book by Ludwig Ganghofer)
    WALDRAUSCH (GER, 1961)

WALDWINTER (GER, 1936, based on the book by Paul Keller)
    WALDWINTER (GER, 1956)

WALK, DON'T RUN see MORE THE MERRIER, THE

WALK THE PROUD LAND see GERONIMO

WALKING DOWN BROADWAY see HELLO, SISTER

WALLENSTEIN (GER, 1911, based on the play by Friedrich von Schiller)
    WALLENSTEIN (GER, 1916)
    WALLENSTEINS LAGER (GER, 1921)
    WALLENSTEIN (GER, 1925)

WALLENSTEINS LAGER see WALLENSTEIN

WALPURGIS NIGHT see FAUST

WALT WHITMAN: BACKGROUND FOR HIS WORKS (short) (COR, 1957, based on the life and works of poet Walt Whitman)
    WALT WHITMAN'S "LEAVES OF GRASS" (short) (IND, 1965)
    WALT WHITMAN'S WESTERN JOURNEY (short) (IND, 1965)
    FACE TO FACE: WALT WHITMAN 100 YEARS HENCE (short) (IND, 1968)
    WALT WHITMAN'S CIVIL WAR (short) (CHU, 1970)
    WALT WHITMAN: POET FOR A NEW AGE (short) (EBE, 1971)
    WALT WHITMAN (short) (PAR, 1972)

SONG OF MYSELF (short) (BFA, 1976)

WALTER GROPIUS (short) (NBC–TV, 1958, interviews with the noted German architect)
    CONVERSATION WITH WALTER GROPIUS, A (short) (EBE, n.d.)

WALTONS, THE see SPENCER'S MOUNTAIN

WALTZ DREAM, THE (BRA, 1910, based on the operetta by Oscar Straus)
    WALTZ DREAM, THE (MGM, 1926)
    SMILING LIEUTENANT, THE (PAR, 1931)
    WALTZ DREAM, THE (CBS–TV, 1951)

WALTZ KING, THE see WALTZES FROM VIENNA

WALTZ OF THE TOREADORS (NET–TV, 1959, based on the play by Jean Anouilh)
    WALTZ OF THE TOREADORS (BRI, 1962)

WALTZ TIME see FLEDERMAUS, DIE

WALTZES FROM VIENNA (BRI, 1933, based on the lives and works of composers Johann Strauss Sr. and Jr.)
    WALTZKREIG (GER, 1933)
    GUERRE DES VALSES, LA (FRA, 1933)
    UNSTERBLICHE MELODIEN (GER, 1935)
    IMMORTAL MELODY (AUS, 1935)
    GREAT WALTZ, THE (MGM, 1938)
    OPERETTE (GER, 1940)
    WEIN TANZT (GER, 1954)
    EWIGER WALZER (GER, 1935)
    GREAT WALTZ, THE (NBC–TV, 1955)
    WALTZ KING, THE (short) (DIS, 1964)
    GREAT WALTZ, THE (MGM, 1972)
    STRAUSS FAMILY, THE (series) (BRI–TV, 1972)
    FAREWELL TO ST. PETERSBURG, A (RUS, 1973)

WANDERER OF THE WASTELAND (PAR, 1924, based on the book by Zane Grey)
    WANDERER OF THE WASTELAND (PAR, 1935)
    WANDERER OF THE WASTELAND (RKO, 1945)

WANDERING (JAP, 1927, source unlisted)
    WANDERING (JAP, 1960)

WANDERING JEW, THE (FRA, 1904, based on the book by Eugene Sue)
    WANDERING JEW, THE (ITA, 1913)
    PHANTOM OF THE CATACOMBS, THE (ITA, 1915)
    AHASUERUS (CZE, 1915)
    MOROK (ITA, 1918)
    STANDARD BEARER OF THE JEWISH PEOPLE, THE (IND, 1921)
    WANDERING JEW, THE (BRI, 1923)
    WANDERING JEW, THE (FRA, 1926)
    WANDERING JEW, THE (BRI, 1933)
    WANDERING JEW, THE (ITA, 1949)

WANTED – THE SUNDANCE WOMAN see THREE OUTLAWS

WAR AND PEACE (RUS, 1915, based on the book by Leo Tolstoy; also the basis for the opera by Serge Prokofiev in 1944)

NATACHA ROSTOVA (RUS, 1915)
WAR AND PEACE (JAP, 1947)
WAR AND PEACE (PAR, 1956)
WAR AND PEACE (NBC–TV, 1957)
WAR AND PEACE (RUS, 1964)
WAR AND PEACE (BRI–TV, 1972)

WAR BETWEEN MEN AND WOMEN see MY WORLD AND
   WELCOME TO IT

WAR OF THE BUTTONS see GENERALS WITHOUT
   BUTTONS

WAR OF THE ROSES, THE see AGE OF KINGS, AN

WARE CASE, THE (BRI, 1917, based on the story by George
   Pleydell Bancroft)
   WARE CASE, THE (BRI, 1928)
   WARE CASE, THE (FN, 1929)
   WARE CASE, THE (FOX, 1939)

WARLORDS OF ATLANTIS see ATLANTIDE, L'

WARM CURRENT (JAP, 1939, source unlisted)
   WARM CURRENT (JAP, 1957)

WARPATH see GREAT MISSOURI RAID, THE

WARREN REPORT, THE see NOVEMBER 22 AND THE
   WARREN REPORT

WARRENS OF VIRGINIA, THE (PAR, 1915, based on the
   play by David Belasco)
   WARRENS OF VIRGINIA, THE (FOX, 1924)

WARRIOR'S HUSBAND, THE (FOX, 1933, based on the
   play by Julian Thompson; also the basis for three
   musical comedies – "By Jupiter" (1942), "Happiest Girl
   in the World" (1961) and "Coldest War of All" (1969),
   and original source can be traced back to the "Lysistrata"
   by Aristophanes)
   LYSISTRATA (AUS, 1948)
   DAUGHTERS OF DESTINY (ITA, 1954)
   SECOND GREATEST SEX, THE (UN, 1955)
   SENDUNG DER LYSISTRATA, DIE (GER, 1961)
   WHEN WOMEN PLAYED DING–DONG (ITA, 1971)
   LYSISTRATA (GRE, 1972)

WARSAW GHETTO, THE (short) (CBS–TV, 1959, based on
   incidents in Warsaw, Poland, during the Nazi regime in
   World War II)
   WARSAW GHETTO, THE (BRI–TV, 1966)

WARSCHAUER ZITADELLE, DIE see CELUI–LA

WAS FRAUEN TRAUMEN (GER, 1931, based on a screenplay
   by Billy Wilder)
   ONE EXCITING ADVENTURE (UN, 1934)

WAS GESCHAH AUF SCHLOSS WILDBERG see KRAM–
   BAMBULI

WASHINGTON see MOUNT VERNON IN VIRGINIA

WASHINGTON IRVING (short) (EBE, 1949, based on the
   life of the American author)
   WASHINGTON IRVING'S WORLD (short) (COR, 1966)

WATCH THE BIRDIE see CAMERAMAN, THE

WATERLOO see NAPOLEON -- MAN OF DESTINY

WATERLOO BRIDGE (UN, 1931, based on the play by
   Robert E. Sherwood)
   WATERLOO BRIDGE (MGM, 1940)
   GABY (MGM, 1956)

WATUSI see KING SOLOMON'S MINES

WAY DOWN EAST (IND, 1909, based on the play by Lottie
   Blair Parker)
   WAY DOWN EAST (UA, 1920)
   WAY DOWN EAST (FOX, 1935)

WAY FOR A SAILOR (MGM, 1930, based on the book by
   Albert Richard Wetjen)
   CADA PUERTO UN AMOR, EN (MEX, 1931)

WAY OF ALL FLESH, THE (PAR, 1927, based on a story by
   Lajos Biro and Jules Furthman)
   WAY OF ALL FLESH, THE (PAR, 1940)

WAY OF ALL MEN, THE (WB, 1930, based on the story, "Sin
   Flood," by Henning Berger)
   MASKE FAELLT, DIE (GER, 1930)

WAY OUT, THE see DIAL 999

WAY TO LOVE, THE (PAR, 1933, based on a screenplay by
   Gene Fowler and Benjamin Glazer)
   AMOUR GUIDE, L' (FRA, 1933)

WAYSIDE PEBBLE see PEBBLE BY THE WAYSIDE

WE FAW DOWN see AMBROSE'S FIRST FALSEHOOD

WE LIVE AGAIN see RESURRECTION

WE, THE O'LEARYS see IN OLD CHICAGO

WE WERE DANCING (MEET ME TONIGHT) (MGM, 1942,
   based on the plays by Sir Noel Coward)
   TONIGHT AT 8:30 (BRI, 1953)
   TONIGHT AT 8:30 (CBS–TV, 1954)

WEAKNESS OF MAN, THE see LIVING CORPSE, THE

WEBSTER'S SACRIFICE TO SAVE THE UNION see
   DANIEL WEBSTER

WEDDING MARCH, THE (ITA, 1915, based on a book by
   Henry Bataille)
   WEDDING MARCH, THE (FRA, 1928)
   WEDDING MARCH, THE (FRA/ITA, 1935)

WEDDING RINGS see DARK SWAN, THE

WEDNESDAY'S CHILD (RKO, 1934, based on the play by
   Leopold L. Atlas)
   CHILD OF DIVORCE (RKO, 1946)
   WEDNESDAY'S CHILD (NBC–TV, 1958)

WEDNESDAY'S CHILD see also IN TWO HANDS

WEEKEND AT THE WALDORF see GRAND HOTEL

WEIB IM DSCHUNGEL see LETTER, THE

WEIBSTEUFEL, DER see THY NAME IS WOMAN

WEIN TAŇZT   see   WALTZES FROM VIENNA

WEIRD WOMAN   (UN, 1944, based on the book by Fritz
  Leiber Jr.)
  BURN, WITCH, BURN   (AI, 1962)

WEISSE SPINNE, DIE   (GER, 1927, based on the book by
  Louis Weinert–Wilton)
  WEISSE SPINNE, DIE   (GER, 1963)

WEISSE TEUFEL, DER   (GER, 1930, based on the book,
  "Khadji Mourat," by Leo Tolstoy)
  KHADJI MOURAT, THE WHITE DEVIL   (ITA/YUG,
  1958)

WEISSEN ROSEN VON RAVENSBURG, DIE   (GER, 1919,
  based on the book by Adlersfeld--Ballestrem)
  WEISSEN ROSEN VON RAVENSBURG, DIE   (GER,
  1929)

WELCOME HOME   (PAR, 1925, based on the play by Edna
  Ferber and George S. Kaufman)
  EXPERT, THE   (WB, 1932)
  NO PLACE TO GO   (WB, 1939)

WELCOME STRANGER   (PAR, 1947, based on a story by
  Frank Butler)
  WELCOME STRANGER   (NBC–TV, 1954)

WELLS FARGO   (PAR, 1937, the second film consists of
  large sections of stock footage from the former)
  REDHEAD AND THE COWBOY, THE   (PAR, 1950)

WENN AM SONNTAGEBAND DIE DORFMUSIK SPIELT
  (GER, 1933, source unlisted)
  WENN AM SONNTEAGEBEND DIE DORFMUSIK SPIELT
  (GER, 1953)

WENN DU NOCH EINE MUTTER HAST   (GER, 1924, source
  unlisted)
  WENN DU NOCH EINE MUTTER HAST   (GER, 1956)

WENN WIR ALLE ENGEL WAREN   (GER, 1936, based on
  the book by Heinrich Spoerl)
  WENN WIR ALLE ENGEL WAREN   (GER, 1956)

WER WIRFT DEN ERSTEN STEIN?   (GER, 1922, source
  unlisted)
  WER WIRFT DEN ERSTEN STEIN?   (GER, 1927)

WE'RE NO ANGELS   (PAR, 1955, based on the play, "My
  Three Angels," by Albert Husson)
  MY THREE ANGELS   (NBC–TV, 1959)

WE'RE NOT DRESSING   see   BACK TO NATURE

WE'RE ON THE JURY   see   LADIES OF THE JURY

WERTHER   (FRA, 1910, based on the book, "Die Leiden
  des Jungen Werther" by Goethe)
  WERTHER   (FRA, 1938)
  BEGEGNUNG MIT WERTHER   (GER, 1949)

WEST OF SHANGHAI   see   BAD MAN, THE

WEST OF THE PECOS   (RKO, 1935, based on the book
  by Zane Grey)
  WEST OF THE PECOS   (RKO, 1945)

WEST OF ZANZIBAR   (MGM, 1929, based on a play by
  Chester Vonde and Kilbourn Gordon)
  KONGO   (MGM, 1932)

WEST SIDE STORY   see   ROMEO AND JULIET

WESTERNER, THE   see   TROUBLE AT TRES CRUCES

WESTMINSTER PASSION PLAY   see   PASSION PLAY, THE

WET PAINT   see   MUCH ADO ABOUT NOTHING

WHAT A CARVE UP   see   GHOUL, THE

WHAT A MAN   (WW, 1930, based on the book, "The Dark
  Chapter," author unlisted)
  ASI ES LA VIDA   (MEX, 1930)
  MERRILY WE LIVE   (MGM, 1938)

WHAT EVERY WOMAN KNOWS   (BRI, 1917, based on the
  play by Sir James Barrie)
  WHAT EVERY WOMAN KNOWS   (PAR, 1921)
  WHAT EVERY WOMAN KNOWS   (MGM, 1934)
  WHAT EVERY WOMAN KNOWS   (CBS--TV, 1959)

WHAT HAPPENED TO FATHER   (VIT, 1915, based on a
  story by Mary Roberts Rinehart)
  WHAT HAPPENED TO FATHER   (WB, 1927)

WHAT HAPPENED TO JONES   (WOR, 1915, based on the
  play by Georges Broadhurst)
  WHAT HAPPENED TO JONES   (PAR, 1920)
  WHAT HAPPENED TO JONES   (UN, 1925)

WHAT MAKES SAMMY RUN?   (NBC--TV, 1949, based on the
  book by Budd Schulberg)
  WHAT MAKES SAMMY RUN?   (NBC--TV, 1959)

WHAT PRICE GLORY?   (FOX, 1926, based on the play by
  Laurence Stallings and Maxwell Anderson)
  WHAT PRICE GLORY?   (FOX, 1952)

WHAT PRICE HOLLYWOOD?   (PAR, 1932, based on a story
  by Adela Rogers St. Johns)
  STAR IS BORN, A   (UA, 1937)
  STAR IS BORN, A   (NBC–TV, 1951)
  STAR IS BORN, A   (WB, 1954)
  STAR IS BORN, A   (BRA, 1975)
  STAR IS BORN, A   (WB, 1976)

WHATEVER HAPPENED TO DOBIE GILLIS?   see   AFFAIRS
  OF DOBIE GILLIS, THE

WHAT'S UP, TIGER LILY?   see   KIZINO KIZI

WHEELS OF FATE, THE   (SEL, 1913, based on a story by
  James Oliver Curwood)
  CODE OF THE MOUNTED   (AMB, 1935)
  DAWN ON THE GREAT DIVIDE   (MON, 1943)

WHEELS OF FATE   see   ROUE, LA

WHEN A MAN LOVES   see   MANON LESCAUT

WHEN A MAN SEES RED   (FOX, 1917, based on the story,
  "Painted Lady, The," by Larry Evans)
  PAINTED LADY, THE   (FOX, 1924)
  ONLY A WOMAN   (SPA, 1934)

PURSUED   (FOX, 1934)

WHEN A MAN'S A MAN   (FN, 1924, based on the book by
   Harold Bell Wright)
WHEN A MAN'S A MAN   (FOX, 1935)

WHEN KNIGHTHOOD WAS IN FLOWER   (PAR, 1922,
   based on the book by Charles Major)
SWORD AND THE ROSE, THE   (DIS, 1953)

WHEN KNIGHTS WERE BOLD   (BRI, 1916, based on the
   play by Charles Marlow)
WHEN KNIGHTS WERE BOLD   (IND, 1922)
WHEN KNIGHTS WERE BOLD   (BRI, 1929)
WHEN KNIGHTS WERE BOLD   (BRI, 1936)
WHEN KNIGHTS WERE BOLD   (IND, 1942)

WHEN LADIES MEET   (MGM, 1932, based on the play by
   Rachel Crothers)
WHEN LADIES MEET   (MGM, 1940)   (TV title:
   STRANGE SKIRTS)
WHEN LADIES MEET   (ABC--TV, 1952)

WHEN MY BABY SMILES AT ME   see   DANCE OF LIFE,
   THE

WHEN ROMANCE RIDES   (MGM, 1922, based on the book,
   "Wildfire," by Zane Grey)
RED CANYON   (UN, 1949)

WHEN THE DALTONS RODE   (UN, 1940, based on the lives
   of the gang of outlaws)
DALTONS RIDE AGAIN, THE   (UN, 1945)
DALTON GANG, THE   (SG, 1949)
DALTON GIRLS, THE   (UA, 1957)
END OF THE DALTON GANG, THE   (short)   (CBS--TV,
   1957)
DALTONS MUST DIE, THE   (NBC--TV, 1961)
LAST DAY, THE   (NBC--TV, 1975)

WHEN THINGS WERE ROTTEN   see   ROBIN HOOD AND
   HIS MERRY MEN

WHEN TOMORROW COMES   (UN, 1939, based on a story by
   James M. Cain)
INTERLUDE   (UN, 1957)

WHEN WE WERE 21   (PAT, 1920, based on a story by Henry
   V. Esmond)
TRUTH ABOUT YOUTH, THE   (FN, 1930)

WHEN WOMEN PLAYED DING--DONG   see   WARRIOR'S
   HUSBAND, THE

WHEN YOU'RE YOUNG   see   SMILIN' THROUGH

WHERE LOVE IS, GOD IS   (RUS, n.d., based on the story by
   Leo Tolstoy)
GUEST, THE   (short)   (FOX, 1951)
MICHAEL HAS COMPANY FOR COFFEE   (TV, 1951)
MARTIN, THE COBBLER   (short)   (IND, 1976)

WHERE SINNERS MEET   see   LITTLE ADVENTURESS,
   THE

WHERE THE BOYS MEET THE GIRLS   see   GIRL CRAZY

WHERE'S CHARLEY?   see   CHARLEY'S AUNT

WHICH WAY IS UP?   see   SEDUCTION OF MIMI, THE

WHICH WILL YOU HAVE?   see   BARABBAS

WHILE NEW YORK SLEEPS   (FOX, 1920, based on a story
   by C.J. Rubin)
WHILE NEW YORK SLEEPS   (FOX, 1939)

WHILE SATAN SLEEPS   see   PARSON OF PANAMINT, THE

WHIP, THE   (IND, 1917, based on the play by Cecil Raleigh
   and Henry Hamilton)
WHIP, THE   (FN, 1928)

WHISPERING CHORUS, THE   see   WAY OF ALL FLESH,
   THE

WHISPERING SMITH   (IND, 1916, based on the book by Frank
   H. Spearman)
WHISPERING SMITH RIDES   (serial)   (PDC, 1926)
LIGHTNING EXPRESS   (serial)   (UN, 1930)
WHISPERING SMITH SPEAKS   (FOX, 1936)
WHISPERING SMITH   (PAR, 1948)
WHISPERING SMITH VS. SCOTLAND YARD   (BRI, 1952)

WHISPERING SMITH RIDES   see   WHISPERING SMITH

WHISPERING SMITH SPEAKS   see   WHISPERING SMITH

WHISPERING SMITH VS. SCOTLAND YARD   see
   WHISPERING SMITH

WHISTLIN' DAN   see   BORDER LAW

WHISTLING IN THE DARK   (MGM, 1933, based on the play
   by Laurence Gross and Edward Childs Carpenter)
WHISTLING IN THE DARK   (MGM, 1941)

WHITE AND YELLOW   see   JACK LONDON'S TALES OF
   THE FISH PATROL

WHITE ANGEL   see   FLORENCE NIGHTINGALE

WHITE CARGO   (BRI, 1929, based on the play by Leon
   Gordon)
WHITE CARGO   (MGM, 1942)

WHITE CAT, THE   see   TWO SOUL WOMAN

WHITE CLIFFS OF DOVER, THE   (MGM, 1944, based on the
   poem by Alice Duer Miller)
WHITE CLIFFS OF DOVER, THE   (CBS--TV, 1946)

WHITE DOLLARS   see   IDLE RICH

WHITE DEVIL   (GER, 1930, based on a story by Leo Tolstoy)
WHITE WARRIOR, THE   (WB, 1961)

WHITE EAGLE, THE   see   SQUAW MAN, THE

WHITE FANG   (FBO, 1925, based on the book by Jack
   London)
WHITE FANG   (FOX, 1936)
WHITE FANG   (RUS, 1946)
WHITE FANG   (ITA/SPA, 1973)

WHITE--HAIRED GIRL, THE   (CHN, 1950, based on a
   Chinese play)
WHITE--HAIRED GIRL, THE   (CHN, 1972)
WHITE--HAIRED GIRL, THE   (PBS--TV, 1974)

WHITE HEAT (WB, 1949, based on a story by Virginia
    Kellogg)
  LAW VS. GANGSTERS, THE (WB--TV, 1959)

WHITE HELL see FOHN

WHITE HELL OF PITZ PALU, THE see FOHN

WHITE HOPE (BRI, 1915, based on the book by W.H.
    Trobridge)
  WHITE HOPE (BRI, 1922)

WHITE ICE see FOHN

WHITE NIGHTS (RUS, 1934, based on a book by Feyodor
    Dostoyevsky)
  WHITE NIGHTS (FRA/ITA, 1957)
  WHITE NIGHTS (RUS, 1959)
  FOUR NIGHTS OF A DREAMER (FRA, 1971)

WHITE NIGHTS see FEDORA

WHITE PONGO see PERILS OF THE JUNGLE

WHITE SHEIK, THE (ITA, 1952, based on a screenplay by
    Federico Fellini)
  WORLD'S GREATEST LOVER, THE (FOX, 1977)

WHITE SISTER, THE (ESS, 1915, based on the book by
    F. Marion Crawford)
  WHITE SISTER, THE (MGM, 1923)
  WHITE SISTER, THE (MGM, 1933)
  WHITE SISTER, THE (MEX, 1961)

WHITE THREADS OF THE CASCADES (JAP, 1933, source
    unlisted)
  WHITE THREADS OF THE CASCADES (JAP, 1952)

WHITE WARRIOR, THE see WHITE DEVIL

WHITE WOMAN (PAR, 1933, based on the play by Norman
    Reilly Raine and Frank Butler)
  ISLAND OF LOST MEN (PAR, 1939)

WHITE ZOMBIE (IND, 1932, based on a screenplay by
    Garnett Weston)
  CONDEMNED MEN (IND, 1940)

WHO ARE YOU? see TWO SOULS

WHO CARES? (IND, 1918, based on a story by Cosmo
    Hamilton)
  WHO CARES? (COL, 1925)

WHO HOLDS TOMORROW? see CASABLANCA

WHO KILLED ANNE FRANK? see DIARY OF ANNE
    FRANK, THE

WHO SLEW AUNTIE ROO? see HANSEL AND GRETEL

WHOLE TOWN'S TALKING, THE (UN, 1926, based on the
    play by John Emerson and Anita Loos)
  EX--BAD BOY (UN, 1931)
  WHOLE TOWN'S TALKING, THE (COL, 1935)

WHOLE WORLD IS WATCHING, THE (NBC--TV, 1969,
    based on a teleplay)
  LAWYERS, THE (series) (NBC--TV, 1971)

WHOM THE GODS LOVE (BRI, 1936, based on the life of
    the noted composer)
  MOZART (GER, 1940)
  MOZART AND HIS MUSIC (short) (COR, 1954)
  MOZART – REICH MIR DIE HAND, MEIN LEBEN
    (AUS, 1955)
  LIFE OF MOZART, THE (AUS/GER, 1967)
  MOZART (series) (ITA--TV, 1975)
  MOZART: A CHILDHOOD CHRONICLE (GER, 1976)

WHOM THE GODS WISH TO DESTROY see SIEGFRIED

WHOOPEE see NERVOUS WRECK, THE

WHO'S EARNEST? see IMPORTANCE OF BEING
    EARNEST, THE

WHO'S YOUR LADY FRIEND? see HERR OHNE WOH-
    NUNG, DER

WHY LEAVE HOME? see CRADLE SNATCHERS

WIDE OPEN see NARROW STREET, THE

. . . WIE EINST, LILI MARLEEN see TRUE STORY OF
    LILI MARLENE, THE

WIE ENST IM MAR (GER, 1926, source unlisted)
  WIE ENST IM MAR (GER, 1937)

WIENER HERZEN (GER, 1925, source unlisted)
  WIENER HERZEN (GER, 1930)

WIFE, HUSBAND AND FRIEND (FOX, 1939, based on a
    book by James M. Cain)
  EVERYBODY DOES IT (FOX, 1949)

WIFE OF MONTE CRISTO, THE see COUNT OF MONTE
    CRISTO, THE

WIFE TRAP, THE (PAR, 1922, based on the play, "Confession,
    The," by Ernst Vajda)
  WOMAN ON TRIAL (PAR, 1927)

WILD ASS'S SKIN, THE see PEAU D'ANE

WILD BILL HICKOCK (PAR, 1923, based on historical
    characters and the life of the western hero)
  GREAT ADVENTURES OF WILD BILL HICKOCK
    (serial) (COL, 1938)
  PLAINSMAN, THE (PAR, 1937)
  YOUNG BILL HICKOCK, THE (REP, 1940)
  BADLANDS OF DAKOTA (UN, 1941)
  WILD BILL HICKOCK RIDES (WB, 1941)
  WILD BILL HICKOCK (series) (ABC--TV, 1951)
  CALAMITY JANE (WB, 1953)
  WILD BILL HICKOCK -- LEGEND AND MAN (CBS--TV,
    1964)
  HEROES AND VILLAINS (sequence) (NET--TV, 1965)
  PLAINSMAN, THE (UN, 1966)
  WILD BUFFALO (UA, 1977)

WILD BILL HICKOCK -- LEGEND AND MAN see WILD
    BILL HICKOCK

WILD BILL HICKOCK RIDES see WILD BILL
    HICKOCK

WILD BOYS OF THE ROAD see ROAD OF LIFE

WILD BRIAN KENT (RKO, 1926, based on the book,
    "Recreation of Brian Kent, The," by Harold Bell Wright)
  WILD BRIAN KENT (RKO, 1936)

WILD BUFFALO see WILD BILL HICKOCK

WILD CHILD, THE (FRA, 1970, based on the book by Jean
    Itard)
  STALK THE WILD CHILD (NBC--TV, 1976)

WILD DUCK, THE (IND, 1915, based on the play by Hein--
    rich Ibsen)
  HAUS DER LUGE (GER, 1925)
  WILD DUCK, THE (GER--TV, 1977)

WILD GIRL see SALOMY JANE

WILD GRASS see DAME AUX CAMELIAS, LA and
    SEVENTH HEAVEN

WILD HORSE MESA (PAR, 1925, based on the novel by
    Zane Grey)
  WILD HORSE MESA (PAR, 1932)
  WILD HORSE MESA (RKO, 1947)

WILDFIRE see WHEN ROMANCE RIDES

WILDERNESS MAIL (SEL, 1914, based on a story by
    James Oliver Curwood)
  WILDERNESS MAIL (AMB, 1935)

WILHELM MEISTER see MIGNON

WILHELM TELL see GUILLAUME TELL ET LE CLOWN

WILL PENNY see LINE CAMP, THE

WILL ROGERS see STORY OF WILL ROGERS, THE

WILLIAM TELL see GUILLAUME TELL ET LE CLOWN

WILLIAM WILSON see STUDENT OF PRAGUE, A

WILSON (FOX, 1944, based on the life and times of the U.S.
    president)
  WOODROW WILSON: SPOKESMAN FOR TOMORROW
    (short) (MHF, 1956)
  WOODROW WILSON: THE FIGHT FOR PEACE (short)
    (CBS--TV, 1961)
  WOODROW WILSON (short) (MHF, 1963)
  WOODROW WILSON (NBC--TV, 1965)
  ORDEAL OF WOODROW WILSON, THE (short)
    (FNC, 1966)

WINCHESTER 73 (UN, 1950, based on a story by Stuart N.
    Lake)
  WINCHESTER 73 (UN, 1967)

WINDOW, THE (RKO, 1949, based on a story by Cornell
    Woolrich)
  BOY CRIED MURDER, THE (BRI, 1966)
  SUDDEN TERROR (NGP, 1971)
  BOY WHO CRIED WEREWOLF, THE (BRI, 1973)

WINDSTOSS, EIN see COUP DE VENT

WINE OF MORNING see BARABBAS

WINE, WOMEN AND HORSES see DARK HAZARD

WINGS OF THE SERF see IVAN THE TERRIBLE

WINGS OF VICTORY see GIRL FROM LENINGRAD, THE

WINSLOW BOY, THE (BRI, 1950, based on the play by
    Terence Rattigan)
  WINSLOW BOY, THE (CBS--TV, 1958)

WINTER'S TALE, A (ED, 1909, based on the play by
    William Shakespeare)
  TRAGEDIA ALLA CORTE DI SICILIA, UNA (ITA, 1913)
  WINTER'S TALE, A (GER, 1914)
  WINTER'S TALE, A (short) (BRI, 1953)
  WINTER'S TALE, A (BRI--TV, 1962)
  WINTER'S TALE, A (BRI, 1966)

WINTERSET (RKO, 1936, based on historical events and the
    play by Maxwell Anderson)
  WINTERSET (ABC--TV, 1951)
  THIS AGONY, THIS TRIUMPH (CBS-TV, 1958)
  WINTERSET (NBC--TV, 1959)
  SACCO AND VANZETTI STORY, THE (NBC-TV, 1960)
  SACCO AND VANZETTI (INTOLERANCE) (ITA, 1970)

WIR SCHALTEN UM AUF HOLLYWOOD see HOLLYWOOD
    REVUE OF 1929

WIRTSHAUS IM SPESSART, DAS (GER, 1923, based on the
    story by Wilhelm Hauff)
  WIRTSHAUS IM SPESSART, DAS (GER, 1957)

WIRTSHAUS VON DARTMOOR, DAS see COTTAGE ON
    DARTMOOR

WISDOM OF FATHER BROWN, THE see FATHER BROWN,
    DETECTIVE

WISH ON THE MOON (CBS--TV, 1953, based on a teleplay)
  WISH ON THE MOON (CBS--TV, 1959)

WITCHES' CURSE, THE see DANTE'S INFERNO

WITCHES OF SALEM see CRUCIBLE, THE

WITCHING HOUR, THE (FRO, 1916, based on the play by
    Augustus Thomas)
  WITCHING HOUR, THE (PAR, 1921)
  WITCHING HOUR, THE (PAR, 1934)

WITCH'S MILK see PETE 'N' TILLIE

WITH CAPTAIN SCOTT, R.N., TO THE SOUTH POLE see
    SCOTT ANTARCTIC EXPEDITION

WITH LAWRENCE IN ARABIA (IND, 1918, based on the
    book, "Lawrence of Arabia," by Thomas Edward
    Lawrence)
  LAWRENCE OF ARABIA (BRI, 1935)
  LAWRENCE OF ARABIA (COL, 1962)
  ROSS (BRI--TV, 1971)

WITHIN THE LAW (AUT, 1916, based on the play by Bayard
    Veiller)
  WITHIN THE LAW (VIT, 1917)
  WITHIN THE LAW (FN, 1923)
  PAID (MGM, 1930)
  WITHIN THE LAW (MGM, 1939)

WITHOUT REGRET see INTERFERENCE

WITNESS FOR THE PROSECUTION (CBS–TV, 1953, based
on the play by Agatha Christie)
WITNESS FOR THE PROSECUTION (UA, 1957)

WIVES OF HENRY VIII, THE see HENRY VIII

WIVES UNDER SUSPICION see KISS BEFORE THE
MIRROR, A

WIZ, THE see DOROTHY AND THE SCARECROW OF OZ

WIZARD, THE see BALAOO

WIZARD OF OZ, THE see DOROTHY AND THE SCARE--
CROW OF OZ

WIZARD'S APPRENTICE, THE (n.d., 1930, based on the
musical piece by Paul Dukas)
SORCERER'S APPRENTICE, THE (short) (IND, 1933)
FANTASIA (sequence) (DIS, 1940)
SORCERER'S APPRENTICE (short) (FOX, 1955)
SORCERER'S APPRENTICE, THE (RUM, c1960)

WO DIE LERCHE SINGT (GER, 1936, source unlisted)
WO DIE LERCHE SINGT (GER, 1956)

WOLF HUNTERS (IND, 1926, based on the book by James
Oliver Curwood)
TRAIL BEYOND, THE (MON, 1934)
WOLF HUNTERS (MON, 1949)

WOLF LARSEN see SEA WOLVES, THE

WOLFE AND MONTCALM see CHRONICLES OF
AMERICA: WOLFE AND MONTCALM

WOMAN, THE see TELEPHONE GIRL

WOMAN AND THE PUPPET, THE (GOL, 1920, based on the
book, "La Femme et le Pantin," by Pierre Louys)
FEMME ET LE PANTIN, LA (FRA, 1929)
DEVIL IS A WOMAN, THE (PAR, 1935)
DEVIL IS A WOMAN, THE (MEX, 1950)
FEMME ET LE PANTIN, LA (A WOMAN LIKE SATAN)
(FRA/ITA, 1959)
THAT OBSCURE OBJECT OF DESIRE (FRA/SPA, 1977)

WOMAN AND WIFE see JANE EYRE

WOMAN AT THE FAIR (RUS, 1928, based on the play
"Desire Under the Elms," by Eugene O'Neill)
DESIRE UNDER THE ELMS (PAR, 1958)

WOMAN BETWEEN, THE (UA, 1931, based on a screenplay
by Howard Estabrook)
FILS DE L'AUTRE, LE (FRA, 1931)

WOMAN DISPUTED, A (UA, 1928, based on the story,
"Boule de Suif," by Guy de Maupassant)
BOULE DE SUIF (RUS, 1934)
VIRGIN, THE (JAP, 1935)
MLLE. FIFI (RKO, 1944)
ANGEL AND SINNER (BOULE DE SUIF) (FRA, 1944)
MLLE. FIFI (TV, 1950)

WOMAN FROM MONTE CARLO, THE see VEILLE
D'ARMES

WOMAN FROM MOSCOW, THE see FEDORA

WOMAN FROM THE SEA see SEA GULL, THE

WOMAN GOD CHANGED, THE (PAR, 1921, based on the
short story, "Changeling," by Donn Byrne)
HIS CAPTIVE WOMAN (FN, 1929)

WOMAN HUNGRY see GREAT DIVIDE, THE

WOMAN I LOVE, THE see EQUIPAGE, L'

WOMAN I STOLE, THE see TAMPICO

WOMAN IN BLACK, THE (GER, 1928, based on the book,
"Die Dame in Schwarz," by Garai--Arvay)
WOMAN IN BLACK, THE (GER, 1951)

WOMAN IN RED, THE see MY NAME IS JULIA ROSS

WOMAN IN ROOM 13 (MGM, 1920, based on the play by
Samuel Shipman, Max Marcin and Percival Wilde)
WOMAN IN ROOM 13 (WW, 1929)
WOMAN IN ROOM 13 (FOX, 1932)
WOMAN IN ROOM 13 (WB, 1948)

WOMAN IN THE WINDOW, THE (RKO, 1944, based on a
book by J.H. Wallis)
WOMAN IN THE WINDOW, THE (NBC–TV, 1955)

WOMAN IN WHITE, THE (UN, 1912, based on the book by
Wilkie Collins)
DREAM WOMAN (IND, 1914)
TANGLED LIVES (FOX, 1917)
TWIN PAWNS (PAT, 1920)
WOMAN IN WHITE, THE (BRI, 1929)
CRIMES AT THE DARK HOUSE (BRI, 1940)
WOMAN IN WHITE, THE (WB, 1948)
WOMAN IN WHITE, THE (NBC–TV, 1960)

WOMAN LIKE SATAN, A see WOMAN AND THE PUPPET,
THE

WOMAN OF AFFAIRS, A (MGM, 1929, based on the book,
"The Green Hat," by Michael Arlen)
OUTCAST LADY (MGM, 1934)

WOMAN OF NO IMPORTANCE, A (BRI, 1921, based on the
play by Oscar Wilde)
WOMAN OF NO IMPORTANCE, A (GER, 1936)
WOMAN OF NO IMPORTANCE, A (FRA, 1937)
WOMAN OF NO IMPORTANCE, A (ARG, 1945)

WOMAN OF OSAKA (JAP, 1940, source unlisted)
WOMAN OF OSAKA (JAP, 1958)

WOMAN OF THE YEAR (MGM, 1942, based on a screenplay
by Ring Lardner Jr. and Michael Kanin)
DESIGNING WOMAN (MGM, 1957)
WOMAN OF THE YEAR (CBS–TV, 1976)

WOMAN ON TRIAL see WIFE TRAP, THE

WOMAN POWER (FOX, 1925, based on the book by Harold
McGrath)
RIGHT TO THE HEART (FOX, 1942)

WOMAN THE GERMANS SHOT, THE see NURSE CAVELL

WOMAN TO WOMAN (BRI, 1923, based on the play by

Michael Morton)
WOMAN TO WOMAN   (BRI, 1929)
WOMAN TO WOMAN   (BRI, 1946)

WOMAN WHO TOUCHED THE LEGS, THE   (JAP, 1952,
   source unlisted)
WOMAN WHO TOUCHED THE LEGS, THE   (JAP, 1960)

WOMAN'S FACE, A   (SWE, 1938, based on a play by Francis
   de Croisset)
WOMAN'S FACE, A   (MGM, 1941)

WOMAN'S LIFE, A   see   ONE LIFE

WOMAN'S RESURRECTION, A   see   RESURRECTION

WOMAN'S VENGEANCE, A   (UN, 1947, based on the play,
   "The Giaconda Smile," by Aldous Huxley)
GIOCONDA SMILE, THE   (CBS--TV, 1954)

WOMEN, THE   (MGM, 1939, based on the play by Claire
   Boothe Luce)
WOMEN, THE   (CBS--TV, 1955)
OPPOSITE SEX, THE   (MGM, 1956)

WOMEN IN GREEN HATS   see   DAMS AUX CHAPEAUX
   VERTS, CES

WOMEN LOVE ONCE   see   DADDY'S GONE A'HUNTING

WOMEN OF GLAMOUR   see   LADIES OF LEISURE

WOMEN PREFER THE MAMBO   see   TO HAVE AND HAVE
   NOT

WOMEN WITHOUT NAMES   see   LADIES OF THE BIG
   HOUSE

WONDER KID, THE   see   ENTFUEHRUNG INS GLUECK

WONDERFUL ADVENTURES OF NILS   (RUS, 1956, source
   unlisted)
WONDERFUL ADVENTURES OF NILS   (SWE, 1962)

WONDERFUL LAND OF OZ, THE   see   DOROTHY AND
   THE SCARECROW OF OZ

WONDERFUL LIE OF NINA PETROVNA, THE   (GER,
   1929, based on the book by Hans Szekely)
WONDERFUL LIE OF NINA PETROVNA, THE   (FRA,
   1937)

WONDERFUL STORY, THE   (BRI, 1922, based on a story
   by I.A.R. Wylie)
WONDERFUL STORY, THE   (BRI, 1932)

WONDERFUL TOWN   see   MY SISTER EILEEN

WONDERFUL WORLD OF THE BROTHERS GRIMM, THE
   (MGM, 1962, based on the lives and works of the
   children's story authors)
ONCE UPON A BROTHERS GRIMM   (CBS--TV, 1977)

WONDERFUL WORLD OF THE BROTHERS GRIMM, THE
   see   SHOEMAKER AND THE ELVES, THE

WONDERS OF ALADDIN   see   ALADDIN

WOODROW WILSON   see   WILSON

WOOING OF MILES STANDISH, THE   (IND, 1907, based on
   the poem, "The Courtship of Miles Standish," by Henry
   Wadsworth Longfellow)
COURTSHIP OF MILES STANDISH, THE   (BOS, 1910)
COURTSHIP OF MILES STANDISH, THE   (AE, 1923)

WORKING GIRLS   (FOX, 1931, based on the play, "Blind
   Mice," by Vera Caspary and Winifred Lenihan; the 1953
   remake also used as a source the play, "Loco," by Dale
   Eunson and Katherine Albert)
THREE BLIND MICE   (FOX, 1938)
MOON OVER MIAMI   (FOX, 1941)
THREE LITTLE GIRLS IN BLUE   (FOX, 1946)
HOW TO MARRY A MILLIONAIRE   (FOX, 1953)
HOW TO MARRY A MILLIONAIRE   (series)   (TV, 1958)

WORKING MAN, THE   (WB, 1933, based on a story by Edgar
   Franklin)
EVERYBODY'S OLD MAN   (FOX, 1936)

WORKS OF CHARLES DICKENS, THE   see   DICKENS
   WALKED HERE

WORKS OF WINSLOW HOMER AND JOHN MARIN   see
   YANKEE PAINTER – THE WORK OF WINSLOW
   HOMER

WORLD OF BEATRIX POTTER, THE   (TV, n.d., based on
   stories by Beatrix Potter)
(PETER RABBIT AND THE) TALES OF BEATRIX
   POTTER   (BRI, 1971)

WORLD OF HANS CHRISTIAN ANDERSEN, THE   see   HANS
   CHRISTIAN ANDERSEN

WORLD OF HORROR   see   CANTERVILLE GHOST, THE
   and   LORD ARTHUR SAVILLE'S CRIME

WORLD OF MARTIN LUTHER, THE   see   MARTIN
   LUTHER, THE NIGHTINGALE OF WITTENBERG

WORLD OF NICK ADAMS, THE   (CBS--TV, 1957, based on
   the book, "Adventures of a Young Man," by Ernest
   Hemingway)
HEMINGWAY'S ADVENTURES OF A YOUNG MAN
   (FOX, 1962)

WORLD OF SHALOM OF SAFED, THE   see   SHALOM OF
   SAFED

WORLD OF WONDERFUL REALITY, THE   see   CITY OF
   BEAUTIFUL NONSENSE, THE

WORLD, THE FLESH AND THE DEVIL, THE   (BRI, 1913,
   based on the play by Laurence Cowan)
WORLD, THE FLESH AND THE DEVIL, THE   (BRI, 1932)

WORLD'S GREATEST LOVER, THE   see   WHITE SHEIK,
   THE

WOULD--BE GENTLEMAN, THE   (NBC--TV, 1951, based on
   the play by Moliere)
WOULD--BE GENTLEMAN, THE   (NBC--TV, 1955)
WOULD--BE GENTELMAN, THE   (FRA, 1958)

WOZZECK   (GER, 1948, based on the opera by Alban Berg)
POSTMAN, THE   (ITA, 1972)

WRECK OF THE HESPERUS, THE   (short)   (BRI, 1926,

based on the poem by Henry Wadsworth Longfellow)
WRECK OF THE HESPERUS, THE   (PAR, 1927)
WRECK OF THE HESPERUS, THE   (COL, 1948)

WRECKER, THE   (TIF, 1929, based on the play by Arnold
    Ridley and Bernard Merivale)
SEVEN SINNERS   (BRI, 1936)

WRONG KIND OF WOMAN, THE   see   BUS STOP

WRONG MISS WRIGHT, THE   see   CRAZY LIKE A FOX

WRONG ROAD, THE   (REP, 1937, based on a story by Gordon
    Rigby)
OUT OF THE STORM   (REP, 1948)

WU–LI–CHANG   see   MR. WU

WUNSCHKONZERT   (GER, 1940, source unlisted)
WUNSCHKONZERT   (GER, 1955)

WUTHERING HEIGHTS   (BRI, 1920, based on the book by
    Emily Bronte: also the basis for the opera by Bernard
    Herrmann)
WUTHERING HEIGHTS   (UA, 1939)
WUTHERING HEIGHTS   (CBS–TV, 1950)
WUTHERING HEIGHTS   (TV, 1953)
ABISMOS DE PASION   (MEX, 1953)
WUTHERING HEIGHTS   (NBC--TV, 1956)
WUTHERING HEIGHTS   (CAN--TV, 1957)
WUTHERING HEIGHTS   (CBS–TV, 1958)
POKPOONGEA UHUNDUCK   (KOR, 1960)
WUTHERING HEIGHTS   (NET–TV, 1965)
WUTHERING HEIGHTS   (AI, 1971)

YANG KWEI FEI   see   EMPRESS YANG KWEI FEI

YANKEE DOODLE DANDY   (WB, 1942, based on the life of
     entertainer George M. Cohan)
   GEORGE M!   (CBS--TV, 1976)

YANKEE PAINTER -- THE WORK OF WINSLOW HOMER
     (short)   (MHF, 1964, based on the works of the noted
     painter)
   WORKS OF WINSLOW HOMER AND JOHN MARIN
     (sequence)   (EBE, 1965)

YEAR 1863   (POL, 1922, based on the book, "Le Fleuve
     Fidele," by Stefan Zeromski)
   FLEUVE FIDELE, LE   (POL, 1936)

YEAR OF THE CANNIBALS, THE   see   AMORE DE AMORE
     E ANTIGONE

YEARNING   (JAP, 1935, source unlisted)
   YEARNING   (JAP, 1955)

YEARS AGO   see   ACTRESS, THE

YEATS COUNTRY   see   W. B. YEATS -- A TRIBUTE

YELLOW JACK   (MGM, 1938, based on the play by Sidney
     Howard)
   YELLOW JACK   (ABC--TV, 1952)
   YELLOW JACK   (NBC--TV, 1955)

YELLOW SKY   (FOX, 1948, based on a story by W. R. Burnett)
   JACKALS, THE   (CBS--TV, 1956)

YELLOW TICKET   (PAT, 1918, based on the play by Michael
     Morton)
   YELLOW TICKET (ZLUTA KNIZKA)   (RUS, 1927)
   YELLOW TICKET   (FOX, 1931)

YES MADAM   (BRI, 1933, based on the book by K. R. G.
     Browne)
   YES MADAM   (BRI, 1938)

YIDDLE AND HIS FIDDLE   (BRI, 1912, based on a sketch
     by Harold Brett)
   YIDDLE AND HIS FIDDLE   (POL, 1938)

YOJIMBO   (JAP, 1961, based on a screenplay by Akira
     Kurosawa and others; remake is uncredited)
   FISTFUL OF DOLLARS, A   (ITA, 1966)

YOTSUYA KAIDAN   (JAP, 1949, source unlisted)
   YOTSUYA KAIDAN   (JAP, 1956)
   YOTSUYA KAIDAN   (JAP, 1959)

YOU ARE LIKE A WILD CHRYSANTHEMUM   (JAP, 1955,
     source unlisted)
   YOU ARE LIKE A WILD CHRYSANTHEMUM   (JAP, 1966)

YOU BELONG TO ME   (COL, 1941, based on a story by
     Dalton Trumbo)
   EMERGENCY WEDDING   (COL, 1950)

YOU CAN'T ALWAYS TELL   see   WOMAN POWER

YOU CAN'T CROSS THE BRIDGE   see   DEATH OF A
     SALESMAN

YOU CAN'T ESCAPE FOREVER   see   HI, NELLIE!

YOU CAN'T RUN AWAY FROM IT   see   IT HAPPENED
     ONE NIGHT

YOU CAN'T TAKE IT WITH YOU   (COL, 1938, based on the
     play by George S. Kaufman and Moss Hart)
   YOU CAN'T TAKE IT WITH YOU   (ABC--TV, 1950)
   FABULOUS SYCAMORES, THE   (NBC--TV, 1955)

YOUNG AMERICA   (ESS, 1922, based on a play by Fred
     Ballard and the "Mrs. Doray" stories by Pearl Franklin)
   YOUNG AMERICA   (FOX, 1932)
   YOUNG AMERICA   (FOX, 1942)

YOUNG AND GAY   see   OUR HEARTS WERE YOUNG AND
     GAY

YOUNG AND WILLING   (UA, 1943, based on the play, "Out
     of the Frying Pan," by Francis Swann)
   OUT OF THE FRYING PAN   (NBC--TV, 1957)

YOUNG ANDY JACKSON   see   OLD HICKORY

YOUNG AS YOU FEEL   see   HANDY ANDY

YOUNG AT HEART   see   FOUR DAUGHTERS

YOUNG BILL HICKOCK   see   WILD BILL HICKOCK

YOUNG DANIEL BOONE   see   DANIEL BOONE THRU THE
     WILDERNESS

YOUNG DANIEL BOONE   see   CHRONICLES OF AMERICA:
     DANIEL BOONE

YOUNG DONOVAN'S KID   see   BIG BROTHER

YOUNG EROTIC FANNY HILL, THE   see   FANNY HILL

YOUNG GIRLS IN PERU   see   MAEDCHEN IN UNIFORM

YOUNG IN HEART, THE   (UA, 1938, based on the book,
     "The Gay Banditti," by I.A.R. Wylie)
   YOUNG IN HEART, THE   (NBC--TV, 1951)

YOUNG LADY CHATTERLEY   see   LADY CHATTERLEY'S
     LOVER

YOUNG LAWYER IN NEW SALEM   see   ABRAHAM
     LINCOLN

YOUNG MAN FROM BOSTON, THE   see   MAKING OF THE
     PRESIDENT -- 1960, THE

YOUNG MAN FROM KENTUCKY   see   YOUNG MR.
     LINCOLN

YOUNG MISS   (JAP, 1930, source unlisted)
   YOUNG MISS   (JAP, 1937)

YOUNG MR. LINCOLN   (FOX, 1939, based on a screenplay
     by Lamar Trotti)
   YOUNG MAN FROM KENTUCKY   (CBS--TV, 1957)

YOUNG NOWHERES   (FN, 1929, based on the book by
     I. A. R. Wylie)
   THAT MAN'S HERE AGAIN   (WB, 1937)

YOUNG ONES, THE   (series)   (JAP--TV, 1966, based on a
     teleplay)

YOUNG ONES, THE   (JAP, 1967)

YOUNG STRANGER, THE   see   DEAL A BLOW

YOUNG TOM EDISON   (MGM, 1940, based on the life of the
   noted inventor)
  EDISON THE MAN   (MGM, 1940)
  EDISON THE MAN   (CBS--TV, 1954)
  THOMAS A. EDISON -- THE WIZARD OF MENLO PARK
   (MGM--TV, 1963)
  BOYHOOD OF THOMAS EDISON, THE   (short) (COR,
   1964)
  MAN CALLED EDISON, THE   (short) (STE, 1972)

YOUNG WINSTON   see   CHURCHILL -- MAN OF THE
   CENTURY

YOUNG WOODLEY   (BRI, 1929, based on the play by John
   van Druten)
  YOUNG WOODLEY   (BRI, 1930)

YOU'RE A SWEETHEART   (UN, 1937, based on a story by
   Warren Wilson, Maxwell Shane and William Thomas)
  COWBOY IN MANHATTAN   (UN, 1943)

YOU'RE NEVER TOO YOUNG   see   MAJOR AND THE
   MINOR, THE

YOU'RE TELLING ME   see   SO'S YOUR OLD MAN

YOUTHFUL TARO   see   SEISHUN TARO

YUKON GOLD   see   TRAIL OF THE YUKON

YVETTE   (RUS, 1917, based on a story by Guy de Maupassant)
  YVETTE   (BRI, 1929)
  YVETTE   (FRA, 1929)
  YVETTE   (GER, 1929)
  YVETTE   (GER, 1938)

ZAREWITSCH, DER (GER, 1928, based on the book by
    Gabriela Zapolska and the operetta by Franz Lehar)
  ZAREWITSCH, DER (GER, 1933)
  TSAREVITCH, LE (FRA/GER, 1954)

ZAZA (ITA, 1909, based on a book by Pierre Berton and
    Charles Simon)
  ZAZA (PAR, 1915)
  ZAZA (PAR, 1923)
  ZAZA (PAR, 1939)
  ZAZA (ITA, 1943)
  ZAZA (FRA, 1955)

ZEBRA, THE see GLAD EYE, THE

ZERO HOUR see FLIGHT INTO DANGER

ZIEGFELD: A MAN AND HIS WOMEN see GREAT
    ZIEGFELD, THE

ZIGEUNERBARON, DER (GER, 1927, based on the story,
    "Der Zigeunerbaron," by Maurus Jokai and the operetta
    by Johann Strauss)
  ZIGEUNERBARON, DER (GER, 1933)
  BARON TSIGANE, LE (FRA, 1935)
  BARON TSIGANE, LE (FRA/GER, 1954)
  GYPSY BARON, THE (RIN, 1959)
  PRINCESSE TSIGANE, LA (FRA/GER, 1962)

ZINKER, DER see SQUEAKER, THE

ZIVOT JE PES (A DOG'S LIFE) (CZE, 1933, based on a
    screenplay by Martin Frick and Hugo Haas)
  DOPPELBRAUTIGAM, DIE (GER, 1934)

ZLUTA KNIZKA see YELLOW TICKET

ZOBELPELZ, DER see GROSSTADTNACHT

ZOLA see LIFE OF EMILE ZOLA, THE

ZOMBIES OF THE STRATOSPHERE (serial) (REP, 1958,
    based on a screenplay by various authors; the remake is
    a condensation of the serial)

SATAN'S SATELLITES (REP, 1966)

ZONTAR, THE THING FROM VENUS see IT CONQUERED
    THE WORLD

ZORRO see MARK OF ZORRO, THE

ZORRO AND THE THREE MUSKETEERS see THREE
    MUSKETEERS, THE

ZUM GOLDENEN ANKER see MARIUS

ZUM PARADIES DER DAMEN (GER, 1922, based on the
    book, "Au Bonheur des dames," by Emile Zola)
  BONHEUR DES DAMES, AU (FRA, 1930)
  BONHEUR DES DAMES, AU (FRA, 1943)

ZWEI FRAUEN (GER, 1911, source unlisted)
  ZWEI FRAUEN (GER, 1938)

ZWEI HERZEN UND EIN SCHLAG (GER, 1932, source
    unlisted)
  FILLE ET LE GARCON, LA (FRA, 1932)

  ZWEI IM EINEM AUTO (GER, 1951)

ZWEI MENSCHEN (GER, 1930, based on the book by
    Richard Voss)
  ZWEI MENSCHEN (GER, 1952)

ZWEI WELTEN (GER, 1930, based on the book by Knud
    Hjorto)
  ZWEI WELTEN (GER, 1940)

ZWEIERLEI MASS see MEASURE FOR MEASURE

ZWEITE SCHUSS, DER (GER, 1923, source unlisted)
  ZWEITE SCHUSS, DER (GER, 1943)

ZWISCHEN HIMMEL UND ERDE see LEBEN UND TOD

ZWISCHEN NACHT UND MORGEN see DIRNENTRAGODIE

SEQUELS

ABSENT–MINDED PROFESSOR, THE (DIS, 1961)
SON OF FLUBBER (DIS, 1963)
    (based on a story by Samuel W. Taylor; these are the
    only two features Disney ever made in black–and–white)

ADVENTURES OF A ROOKIE (RKO, 1943)
ROOKIES IN BURMA (RKO, 1943)
    (based on a story by William Bowers and M. Coates
    Webster)

ADVENTURES OF THE WILDERNESS FAMILY, THE
    (IND, 1976)
FURTHER ADVENTURES OF THE WILDERNESS FAMILY,
    THE (IND, 1978)
    (based on a screenplay by Arthur R. Dubs)

ADVENTURES OF BARRY MCKENZIE, THE (AUT, 1972)
BARRY MCKENZIE HOLDS HIS OWN (AUT, 1974)
    (based on the comic strip, "The Wonderful World of
    Barry McKenzie," by Barry Humphries)

ADVENTURES OF P.C. 49 -- THE CASE OF THE GUARDIAN
    ANGEL, THE (BRI, 1949)
CASE FOR P.C. 49, A (BRI, 1951)
    (based on a radio series by Alan Stranks)

AFFAIRS OF ANABEL, THE (RKO, 1938)
ANABEL TAKES A TOUR (RKO, 1938)
    (based on a story by Charles Hoffman)

AGENT 3S3 – PASSPORT TO HELL (FRA/ITA/SPA, 1967)
3S3 – SPECIAL AGENT (FRA/ITA/SPA, 1967)
    (source unknown)

ALFIE (BRI, 1966)
OH, ALFIE (ALFIE, DARLING) (BRI, 1976)
    (based on the book by Bill Naughton)

ALL QUIET ON THE WESTERN FRONT (UN, 1930)
ROAD BACK, THE (UN, 1937)
    (based on books by Erich Maria Remarque)

AMAZING COLOSSAL MAN, THE (AI, 1957)
REVENGE OF THE COLOSSAL MAN, THE (WAR OF THE
    COLOSSAL BEAST) (AI, 1958)
    (based on a screenplay by Mark Hanna, Bert I. Gordon)

ANGELS WITH DIRTY FACES (WB, 1938)
ANGELS WASH THEIR FACES (WB, 1939)
    (based on a screenplay by John Wexley)

ANNE OF GREEN GABLES (RKO, 1934)
ANNE OF WINDY POPLARS (RKO, 1940)
    (based on the books of L.M. Montgomery)

APPLE DUMPLING GANG, THE (DIS, 1975)
RETURN OF THE APPLE DUMPLING GANG (DIS, 1978)
    (based on the book by Jack M. Bickham)

ARMATA BRANCALEONE, L' (ITA, 1966)
BRANCALEONE AND THE CRUSADES (ITA, 1970)
    (source unknown)

AVENGERS, THE (series) (BRI–TV, 1966)
NEW AVENGERS, THE (BRI–TV, 1976)
    (based on a teleplay)

AWFUL DR. ORLOFF, THE (FRA/SPA, 1961)
ORGIES OF DR. ORLOFF (FRA/SPA, 1966)
    (based on the book by David Kuhne)

BEAU GESTE (PAR, 1926)
BEAU SABREUR (PAR, 1928)
    (based on the book by Sir Percival Wren)

BEDTIME FOR BONZO (UN, 1951)
BONZO GOES TO COLLEGE (UN, 1952)
    (based on a story by Raphel David Blau and Ted Berkman)

BIGFOOT (IND, 1971)
CURSE OF BIGFOOT (IND, 1972)
    (source unknown)

BLACK CAESAR (AI, 1972)
HELL UP IN HARLEM (AI, 1973)
    (based on a screenplay by Larry Cohen)

BLACK CRUISE (FRA, 1926)
YELLOW CRUISE (FRA, 1934)
    (based on documentary footage)

BLACULA (AI, 1972)
SCREAM, BLACULA, SCREAM (AI, 1973)
    (suggested by the book, "Dracula," by Bram Stoker)

BLOB, THE (PAR, 1958)
SON OF BLOB (BEWARE THE BLOB) (IND, 1972)
    (based on an idea by Irvine H. Millgate)

BORSALINO (FRA, 1970)
BORSALINO AND CO. (FRA, 1974)
    (based on the book, "The Bandits of Marseilles," by
    Eugene Saccomano)

BOY NAMED CHARLIE BROWN, A (NGP, 1969)
SNOOPY COME HOME (NGP, 1971)
    (based on the comic strip, "Peanuts," by Charles Schulz)

BOY'S TOWN (MGM, 1938)
MEN OF BOY'S TOWN (MGM, 1941)
    (based on a story by Dore Schary and Eleanore Griffin)

BOZKURTS ARE COMING, THE (TUR, 1967)
VENGEANCE OF THE BOZKURTS, THE (TUR, 1967)
    (based on a screenplay by Cavit Yorukly and Vecdi
    Uygun)

BROTHER RAT (WB, 1938)
BROTHER RAT AND A BABY (WB, 1940)
    (based on the play by John Monks Jr. and Fred F.
    Finklehoffe)

BUCK PRIVATES (UN, 1941)
BUCK PRIVATES COME HOME (UN, 1947)
    (based on a screenplay by Arthur T. Horman)

CAPTIVE WILD WOMAN   (UN, 1943)
JUNGLE WOMAN   (UN, 1944)
   (based on a story by Ted Fithian and Neil P. Varnick)

CARPETBAGGERS, THE   (PAR, 1964)
NEVADA SMITH   (PAR, 1966)
   (based on the book by Harold Robbins)

CARTER CASE, THE   (serial)   (n.d., 1919)
CLUTCHING HAND, THE   (serial)   (SAS, 1936)
   (source unknown)

CAT PEOPLE, THE   (RKO, 1942)
CURSE OF THE CAT PEOPLE, THE   (RKO, 1944)
   (based on a screenplay by DeWitt Bodeen)

CHEAPER BY THE DOZEN   (FOX, 1950)
BELLES ON THEIR TOES   (FOX, 1952)
   (based on the book by Frank B. Gilbreth Jr. and
   Ernestine Gilbreth)

CHIMMIE FADDEN   (PAR, 1915)
CHIMMIE FADDEN OUT WEST   (PAR, 1915)
   (based on stories by Edward W. Townsend)

CIPHER BUREAU   (GN, 1938)
PANAMA PATROL   (GN, 1939)
   (based on a story by Arthur Hoerl and Monroe Shaff)

CLAUDIA   (FOX, 1943)
CLAUDIA AND DAVID   (FOX, 1946)
   (based on the play by Rose Franken)

CLEOPATRA JONES   (WB, 1973)
CLEOPATRA JONES MEETS THE DRAGON PRINCESS
  (WB, 1975)
   (based on a story by Max Julien)

CLEOPATRA WONG   (PHI, 1977)
VENGEANCE OF CLEOPATRA WONG, THE   (PHI, 1978)
   (source unlisted)

COTTON COMES TO HARLEM   (UA, 1970)
COME BACK, CHARLESTON BLUE   (WB, 1972)
   (based on the book by Chester Hines)

COUNT YORGA, VAMPIRE   (AI, 1970)
RETURN OF COUNT YORGA, THE   (AI, 1971)
   (based on a screenplay by Bob Kelljan)

CROWD, THE   (MGM, 1928)
OUR DAILY BREAD   (UA, 1933)
   (based on characters (John and Mary Simms) created by
   King Vidor)

CURSE OF NOSTRADAMUS   (MEX, 1960)
GENII OF DARKNESS   (MEX, 1962)
   (based on a screenplay by Charles Taboada and Alfred
   Ruanova)

DAUGHTERS OF JOSHUA McCABE, THE   (ABC–TV, 1972)
DAUGHTERS OF JOSHUA McCABE RETURN , THE
  (ABC–TV, 1976)
   (based on a teleplay)

DEEP THROAT   (IND, 1972)
DEEP THROAT II   (IND, 1974)
   (based on a screenplay by Gerry Gerard)

DESORDRE   (FRA, 1949)
DESORDRE IS 20 YEARS OLD   (FRA, 1967)
   (based on an idea by Jacques Baratier)

DETECTIVE FINN   (BRI, 1914)   (American title: SOCIETY
  DETECTIVE)
DETECTIVE FINN AND THE FOREIGN SPIES   (BRI, 1914)
   (based on a story by Charles Weston)

DEVIL BAT   (PRC, 1940)
DEVIL BAT'S DAUGHTER   (PRC, 1946)
   (based on a story by George Bricker)

DEVIL WITH HITLER, THE   (UA, 1942)
THAT NAZTY NUISANCE   (UA, 1943)
   (based on a screenplay by Al Martin)

DIAMOND FROM THE SKY, THE   (serial)   (IND, 1915)
SEQUEL TO DIAMOND FROM THE SKY   (serial)   (MUT,
  1916)
   (based on a story by Roy L. McCardell)

DIARY OF A SEX COUNSELLOR, THE   (JAP, 1968)
MASKED DOCTOR, THE   (JAP, 1968)
   (based on a screenplay by Fumi Takahashi)

DIRTY SEVEN, THE   (JAP, 1967)
RETURN OF THE DIRTY SEVEN, THE   JAP, 1967)
   (based on a story by Iwao Yamazaki)

DR. GOLDFOOT AND THE BIKINI MACHINE   (AI, 1965)
DR. GOLDFOOT AND THE GIRL BOMBS   (AI, 1966)
   (based on a story by James Hartford)

DR. SATAN   (MEX, 1966)
DR. SATAN AND THE BLACK MAGIC   (MEX, 1967)
   (based on a story by S. Tomas Be)

DON WINSLOW OF THE NAVY   (serial)   (UN, 1942)
DON WINSLOW OF THE COAST GUARD   (serial)   (UN,
  1943)
   (based on the comic strip by Frank V. Martinek)

DRACULA   (UN, 1931)
DRACULA'S DAUGHTER   (UA, 1936)
   (based on the book by Bram Stoker)

EIGHTEEN YEARS' IMPRISONMENT   (JAP, 1967)
EIGHTEEN YEARS' IMPRISONMENT – PAROLE   (JAP,
  1967)
   (based on a screenplay by Kazuo Kasahara and Shin
   Morita)

ELUSIVE AVENGERS, THE   (RUS, 1968)
FURTHER ADVENTURES OF THE ELUSIVE AVENGERS,
  THE   (RUS, 1969)
   (source unknown)

EMIGRANTS, THE   (SWE, 1971)
NEW LAND, THE   (SWE, 1973)
   (based on four books by Vilhelm Moberg)

EMMANUELLE   (COL, 1975)
EMMANUELLE 2   (PAR, 1976)
   (based on the book by Emmanuelle Arsan)

ENTER THE DRAGON   (WB, 1973)
WAY OF THE DRAGON   (WB, 1974)

(based on a screenplay by Michael Allin)

ESCAPE TO WITCH MOUNTAIN   (DIS, 1975)
RETURN FROM WITCH MOUNTAIN   (DIS, 1978)
   (based on characters created by Alexander Key)

EXORCIST, THE   (WB, 1974)
HERETIC, THE   (EXORCIST 2)   (WB, 1976)
   (based on the book by William Peter Blatty)

EYES IN THE NIGHT   (MGM, 1942)
HIDDEN EYE, THE   (MGM, 1945)
   (based on a book by Beynard Kendrick)

FX–18 SECRET AGENT – USA   (FRA, 1964)
FX–18 SUPER SPY   (FRA, 1965)
   (based on a screenplay by various authors)

FACES   (CON, 1968)
MINNIE AND MOSCOWITZ   (UN, 1971)
   (based on script and improvisations by John Cassavetes)

FANTASM   (AUT, 1977)
FANTASM COMES AGAIN   (AUT, 1978)
   (based on a screenplay by Ross Dimsey)

FEAR NO EVIL   (NBC–TV, 1969)
RITUAL OF EVIL   (NBC–TV, 1970)
   (based on a teleplay)

FIVE MEN AND ROSA   (DEN, 1964)
HANDSOME ARNE AND ROSA   (DEN, 1967)
   (based on a screenplay by Sven Methling)

FORBIDDEN PLANET, THE   (MGM, 1956)
INVISIBLE BOY, THE   (MGM, 1957)
   (based on a story by Irving Block and Allen Adler and the
   play, "The Tempest," by William Shakespeare)

FRANKENSTEIN'S BLOODY TERROR   (FRA/SPA, 1968)
NIGHTS OF THE WEREWOLF   (FRA/SPA, 1968)
   (based on a screenplay by Jacinto Molina)

FRENCH CONNECTION, THE   (FOX, 1971)
FRENCH CONNECTION II, THE   (FOX, 1975)
   (based on the book by Robin Moore)

FRESHMAN, THE   (PAT, 1925)
MAD WEDNESDAY   (THE SIN OF HAROLD DIDDLEBOCK)
   (UA, 1947)
   (based on a screenplay by various authors)

FRIENDS   (PAR, 1971)
PAUL AND MICHELLE   (PAR, 1974)
   (based on a screenplay by Jack Russell and Vernon
   Harris)

FRITZ THE CAT   (IND, 1972)
NINE LIVES OF FRITZ THE CAT, THE   (AI, 1974)
   (based on a screenplay by Ralph Bakshi)

FROSTY, THE SNOWMAN   (CBS–TV, 1969)
FROSTY'S WINTER WONDERLAND   (ABC–TV, 1976)
   (based on the song by Steve Nelson and Jack Rollins)

FUNNY GIRL   (COL, 1968)
FUNNY LADY   (COL, 1975)
   (based on the musical play with songs by Jule Styne and
   Bob Merrill)

GALLERY OF MADAME LIU TSONG   (series)   (TV, 1951)
MADAME LIU TSONG   (series)   (TV, 1952)
   (based on a teleplay)

GAMBLER'S WORLD, THE   (JAP, 1967)
GAMBLER'S WORLD II, THE   (JAP, 1967)
   (based on a screenplay by Goro Tanada and Yukio Iimura)

GENDARME OF ST. TROPEZ, THE   (FRA, 1965)
GENDARME IN NEW YORK, THE   (FRA, 1965)
   (source unknown)

GERT AND DAISY'S WEEKEND   (BRI, 1941)
GERT AND DAISY CLEAN UP   (BRI, 1942)
   (based on a screenplay by various authors)

GOAL FOR THE YOUNG   (JAP, 1967)
BURNING SUN   (JAP, 1967)
   (based on a screenplay by Katsuya Suzaki)

GODFATHER, THE   (PAR, 1972)
GODFATHER II, THE   (PAR, 1974)
   (based on the book by Mario Puzo)

GOING MY WAY   (PAR, 1944)
BELLS OF ST. MARY'S   (RKO, 1945)
   (based on a story by Leo McCarey)

GOLDENE SEE, DIE   (GER, 1919)
BRILLANTENSCHIFF, DAS   (GER, 1920)
   (source unknown)

GOODBYE, STORK, GOODBYE   (SPA, 1972)
CHILD IS OURS, THE   (SPA, 1973)
   (source unknown)

GREEN HORNET, THE   (serial)   (UN, 1940)
GREEN HORNET STRIKES AGAIN   (serial)   (UN, 1941)
   (based on the radio series by Fran Striker)

GUNFIGHT AT THE O.K. CORRAL   (PAR, 1957)
HOUR OF THE GUN   (UA, 1967)
   (based on the Wyatt Earp–Doc Holliday shootout)

HAPPY HOOKER, THE   (IND, 1975)
HAPPY HOOKER GOES TO WASHINGTON, THE   (IND,
   1977)
   (based on a book by Xaviera Hollander)

HARPER   (WB, 1966)
DROWNING POOL, THE   (WB, 1975)
   (based on the book, "The Moving Target," by Ross
   McDonald)

HARRAD EXPERIMENT, THE   (CIN, 1973)
HARRAD SUMMER, THE   (CIN, 1974)
   (based on the book by Robert H. Rimmer)

HAVING BABIES   (ABC–TV, 1976)
HAVING BABIES II   (ABC–TV, 1977)
   (based on a teleplay)

HAWAII   (UA, 1966)
HAWAIIANS, THE   (UA, 1970)
   (based on the book by James Michener)

HERE COMES MR. JORDAN   (COL, 1941)
DOWN TO EARTH   (COL, 1947)
   (based on the play, "Heaven Can Wait," by Harry Segall)

GREETINGS (IND, 1968)
HI, MOM (IND, 1969)
    (based on scripts by Brian de Palma)

HIS LORDSHIP REGRETS (BRI, 1938)
HIS LORDSHIP GOES TO PRESS (BRI, 1938)
    (based on the play, "Bees and Honey," by H.F. Maltby)

HONEYPOT, THE (BRI, 1920)
LOVE MAGGIE (BRI, 1921)
    (based on a book by Countess Barcynska)

HOOFS AND GOOFS (short) (COL, 1957)
HORSING AROUND (short) (COL, 1957)
    (based on a screenplay)

HORRIBLE DR. HICHCOCK, THE (ITA, 1962)
GHOST, THE (ITA, 1963)
    (based on a screenplay by Julyan Perry)

HOTEL FOR WOMEN (FOX, 1939)
FREE, BLONDE AND 21 (FOX, 1940)
    (based on a story by Elsa Maxwell and Kathryn Scola)

HOUSE OF DARK SHADOWS (MGM, 1970)
NIGHT OF DARK SHADOWS (MGM, 1971)
    (based on television series, "Dark Shadows," and a
    screenplay by Sam Hall and Gordon Russell)

IF . . . (BRI, 1968)
O LUCKY MAN! (BRI, 1973)
    (based on a story by David Sherwin and John Howlett)

ILSE, SHE--WOLF OF THE S.S. (IND, 1975)
ILSE, HAREMKEEPER OF THE OIL SHEIKS (IND, 1976)
    (source unknown)

IN SEARCH OF TREASURE (BRA, 1967)
JERRY THE BIG BOASTER (BRA, 1967)
    (based on the character of Jerry Adriani)

INGA (SWE, 1968)
SEDUCTION OF INGA, THE (SWE, 1972)
    (based on a screenplay by Joseph R. Sarno)

INNOCENTS, THE (FOX, 1961)
NIGHTCOMERS, THE (BRI, 1971)
    (based on the book, "Turn of the Screw," by Henry James)

INTERNS, THE (COL, 1962)
NEW INTERNS, THE (COL, 1964)
    (based on the book by Richard Frede)

INVASION OF THE SAUCER MEN (AI, 1957)
EYE CREATURES, THE (AI, 1965)
    (based on a story by Paul Fairman)

IT'S ALIVE! (WB, 1974)
IT LIVES AGAIN (WB, 1978)
    (based on a screenplay by Larry Cohen)

IVORY HUNTER, THE (WHERE NO VULTURES FLY)
  (BRI, 1951)
WEST OF ZANZIBAR (BRI, 1953)
    (based on a screenplay by Ralph Smart, W.P. Lipscomb
    and Leslie Norman)

IZUKOE (JAP, 1966)
TOO MANY MOONS (JAP, 1967)

    (based on the book by Yojiro Ishizaka)

JACK SLADE (AA, 1953)
RETURN OF JACK SLADE (AA, 1955)
    (based on a screenplay by Warren Douglas)

JAMES TONT, OPERATION U.N.O. (ITA, 1965)
JAMES TONT, OPERATION D.U.E. (FRA/ITA, 1966)
    (based on a screenplay by Bruno Corbucci and Gianni
    Grimaldi)

JANIE (WB, 1944)
JANIE GETS MARRIED (WB, 1946)
    (based on the play by Josephine Bentham and Herschel V.
    Williams Jr.)

JAWS (UN, 1976)
JAWS II (UN, 1978)
    (based on the book by Peter Benchley)

JESSE JAMES (FOX, 1939)
RETURN OF FRANK JAMES (FOX, 1940)
    (based on a screenplay by Nunnally Johnson)

JETTCHEN GEBERTS GESCHICHTE (GER, 1918)
HENRIETTE JACOBY (GER, 1918)
    (source unknown)

JOLSON STORY, THE (COL, 1946)
JOLSON SINGS AGAIN (COL, 1949)
    (based on the life of the noted entertainer)

JOSHUA IN A BOX (short) (IND, 1970)
JOSHUA AND THE BLOB (short) (IND, 1972)
    (based on animations by John C. Lange)

JUNGLE GIRL (serial) (REP, 1941)
PERILS OF NYOKA, THE (serial) (REP, 1942)
    (based on the book by Edgar Rice Burroughs)

JUNKET 89 (BRI, 1970)
TROUBLE WITH 2B, THE (BRI, 1972)
    (based on a story by David Ash)

KAMAKIRI (JAP, 1967)
STRONGER SEX, THE (JAP, 1967)
    (based on a screenplay by Ichiri Ikeda and Umeji Inoue)

KAMALI ZEYBEK VS. CAKIRCALI (TUR, 1967)
REVENGE OF KAMALI ZEYBEK (TUR, 1967)
    (based on a screenplay by Nuri Akinci)

KEEPING COMPANY (MGM, 1940)
THIS TIME FOR KEEPS (MGM, 1942)
    (based on a story by Herman J. Mankiewicz)

KEMAL, THE ENGLISHMAN (TUR, 1968)
SON OF KEMAL THE ENGLISHMAN, THE (TUR, 1968)
    (based on a screenplay by Burhan Bolan)

KIBA OKAMINOSUKE (JAP, 1966)
KIBA OKAMINOSUKE'S SWORD OF HELL (JAP, 1967)
    (based on a story by Hideo Gosha)

KING KONG (RKO, 1933)
SON OF KONG (RKO, 1934)
    (based on an idea by Edgar Wallace and Merian C. Cooper)

KON--TIKI (LES, 1951)

AKU–AKU (LES, 1964)
(based on films taken during the sea expeditions of Thor Heyerdahl)

LADY FOR A DAY (COL, 1933)
LADY BY CHOICE (COL, 1934)
(based on a story by Damon Runyon)

LAND THAT TIME FORGOT, THE (AI, 1975)
PEOPLE THAT TIME FORGOT, THE (AI, 1977)
(based on a story by Edgar Rice Burroughs)

LASSIE COME HOME (MGM, 1943)
SON OF LASSIE (MGM, 1945)
(based on the book by Eric Knight)

LEGEND OF BOGGY CREEK, THE (IND, 1973)
RETURN TO BOGGY CREEK, THE (IND, 1977)
(based on a story by Earl E. Smith)

LEGEND OF NIGGER CHARLEY (PAR, 1972)
SOUL OF NIGGER CHARLEY (PAR, 1973)
(based on a screenplay by Larry G. Spangler and Martin Goldman)

LIANA, JUNGLE GODDESS (GER, 1956)
LIANA, WHITE SLAVE (GER, 1957)
(source unknown)

LIFE AND TIMES OF GRIZZLY ADAMS, THE (IND, 1975)
LIFE AND TIMES OF GRIZZLY ADAMS, THE (series) (NBC--TV, 1977)
(based on a screenplay by Larry Dobkin)

LIFE WITH THE LYONS (BRI, 1953) (American title: FAMILY AFFAIR
LYONS IN PARIS, THE (BRI, 1954)
(based on a radio series by various authors)

LITTLE DRUMMER BOY, THE (short) (NBC--TV, 1974)
LITTLE DRUMMER BOY II, THE (short) (NBC--TV, 1976)
(based on a story by Ezra Jack Keats)

LITTLE FOXES, THE (RKO, 1941)
ANOTHER PART OF THE FOREST (UN, 1948)
(based on plays by Lillian Hellman)

LONGEST DAY, THE (FOX, 1962)
UP FROM THE BEACH (FOX, 1965)
(based on the book by Cornelius Ryan)

LOVE BOAT, THE (ABC--TV, 1976)
LOVE BOAT II, THE (ABC--TV, 1977)
(based on a teleplay)

MACON COUNTY LINE (AI, 1974)
RETURN TO MACON COUNTY (AI, 1975)
(based on a story by Max Baer)

MAD DOCTOR OF BLOOD ISLAND (PHI, 1969)
BEAST OF BLOOD (PHI, 1970)
(based on a screenplay by Reuben Conway)

MAGIC WORLD OF TOPO GIGIO (ITA, 1964)
TOPO GIGIO AND THE WAR MISSILE (ITA, 1967)
(based on a screenplay by various authors)

MALTESE FALCON, THE (WB, 1941)
BLACK BIRD (COL, 1975)

(based on the book by Dashiell Hammett)

MAN CALLED HORSE, A (UA, 1970)
RETURN OF A MAN CALLED HORSE, THE (UA, 1976)
(based on a story by Dorothy M. Johnson)

MAN FROM U.N.C.L.E., THE (series) (NBC--TV, 1964)
GIRL FROM U.N.C.L.E., THE (series) (NBC--TV, 1966)
(based on a teleplay)

MANDINGO (PAR, 1975)
DRUM (UA, 1976)
(based on books by Kyle Onstott)

MARK OF ZORRO, THE (UA, 1920)
DON Q. SON OF ZORRO (UA, 1925)
(based on the book, "The Curse of Capistrano," by Johnston McCulley)

ME AND MY KID BROTHER (DEN, 1967)
ME AND MY KID BROTHER AND THE SMUGGLERS (DEN, 1968)
(based on the book, "Brodrene Oastermanns Huskors," by Oscar Wennersten)

MEET THE GIRLS (FOX, 1938)
PARDON OUR NERVE (FOX, 1938)
(based on a screenplay by Marguerite Roberts)

MILLION EYES OF SUMURU, THE (GER/SPA, 1967)
RIO 70 (GER/SPA, 1970)
(based on characters created by Sax Rohmer)

MIRANDA (BRI, 1948)
MAD ABOUT MEN (BRI, 1954)
(based on the play by Peter Blackmore)

MISADVENTURES OF MERLIN JONES, THE (DIS, 1963)
MONKEY'S UNCLE, THE (DIS, 1966)
(based on a story by Bill Walsh)

MR. REEDER IN ROOM 13 (BRI, 1938) (American title: MYSTERY IN ROOM 13)
MIND OF MR. REEDER, THE (BRI, 1939) (American title: MYSTERIOUS MR. REEDER, THE)
(based on the book, "Room 13," by Edgar Wallace)

MR. ROBERTS (WB, 1955)
ENSIGN PULVER (WB, 1964)
(based on the book by Thomas Heggen and the play by Thomas Heggen and Joshua Logan)

MR. TUTT BAITS A HOOK (NBC--TV, 1956)
MR. TUTT GOES WEST (NBC--TV, 1956)
(based on a teleplay)

MR. VALIANT (JAP, 1954)
MR. VALIANT RIDES AGAIN (JAP, 1954)
(source unknown)

MRS. MINIVER (MGM, 1942)
MINIVER STORY, THE (MGM, 1950)
(based on the book by Jan Struther)

MONDO CANE (ITA, 1963)
MONDO PAZZO (MONO CANE NO. 2) (ITA, 1965)
(based on documentary footage taken all over the world)

MONSTERS, THE (ITA, 1962)

NEW MONSTERS, THE   (ITA, 1977)
    (anthology films with scripts by various authors)

MOUSE THAT ROARED, THE   (BRI, 1959)
MOUSE ON THE MOON   (BRI, 1963)
    (based on the book, "The Wrath of the Grapes," by
    Leonard Wibberley)

MUNCHHAUSEN   (GER, 1943)
MUNCHHAUSEN IN AFRICA   (GER, 1958)
    (based on a character created by R.E. Raspe)

MURDER GOES TO COLLEGE   (PAR, 1937)
PARTNERS IN CRIME   (PAR, 1937)
    (based on a book by Kurt Steel)

MY FRIEND FLICKA   (FOX, 1943)
THUNDERHEAD, SON OF FLICKA   (FOX, 1945)
    (based on the book by Mary O'Hara)

MY FRIEND IRMA   (PAR, 1949)
MY FRIEND IRMA GOES WEST   (PAR, 1950)
    (based on the radio series by Cy Howard)

NATHALIE   (FRA/ITA, 1957)
NATHALIE, SECRET AGENT   (FRA, 1959)
    (based on the book by Franck Marchal)

NATIONAL VELVET   (MGM, 1944)
INTERNATIONAL VELVET   (MGM, 1978)
    (based on the book by Enid Bagnold)

NIGHT CLUB LADY   (COL, 1932)
CIRCUS QUEEN MURDER, THE   (COL, 1933)
    (based on a story by Anthony Abbott)

NIGHT STALKER   (ABC–TV, 1971)
NIGHT STRANGLER   (ABC–TV, 1972)
    (based on a teleplay)

NO. 1 OF THE SECRET SERVICE   (BRI, 1977)
ORCHID FOR NO. 1, AN   (BRI, 1978)
    (based on a screenplay by Howard Craig)

OFFICE CHRISTMAS PARTY, THE   (DEN, 1977)
FACTORY OUTING, THE   (DEN, 1978)
    (based on a story by John Hilbard)

OMEN, THE   (FOX, 1976)
DAMIEN: THE OMEN (PART II)   (FOX, 1978)
    (based on a screenplay by David Seltzer)

ON MOONLIGHT BAY   (WB, 1951)
BY THE LIGHT OF THE SILVERY MOON   (WB, 1953)
    (based on the "Penrod" stories by Booth Tarkington)

ORGANIZED VIOLENCE   (JAP, 1967)
ORGANIZED VIOLENCE II   (JAP, 1967)
    (based on a screenplay by Kan Saji and Michio Suzuki)

OTHER SIDE OF THE MOUNTAIN, THE   (UN, 1975)
OTHER SIDE OF THE MOUNTAIN, THE -- PART 2   (UN,
    1978)
    (based on the book, "A Long Way Up," by E.G. Valens)

OUR YOUNG PRESIDENT   (JAP, 1967)
OPERATION RAINBOW   (JAP, 1967)
    (based on a screenplay by Ichiro Ikeda, Takeshi Yoshida
    and Kyuzo Kobayashi)

OVER THE HILL GANG, THE   (ABC–TV, 1969)
OVER THE HILL GANG RIDES AGAIN, THE   (ABC–TV,
    1970)
    (based on a teleplay)

PALEFACE, THE   (PAR, 1948)
SON OF PALEFACE   (PAR, 1952)
    (based on an original screenplay by Edmund Hartmann and
    Frank Tashlin)

PANDA AND THE MAGIC SERPENT   (JAP, 1968)
MADAME WHITE SNAKE   (CHN, 1975)
    (based on Oriental legend)

PARDON MON AFFAIRE   (FRA, 1977)
WE WILL ALL MEET IN PARADISE   (FRA, 1978)
    (based on a story by Jean–Loup Dabadie and Yves Robert)

PEYTON PLACE   (FOX, 1957)
RETURN TO PEYTON PLACE   (FOX, 1961)
    (based on the book by Grace Metalious)

PISTOL FOR RINGO, A   (ITA, 1964)
$100,000 FOR RINGO   (ITA, 1965)
    (based on a screenplay by Duccio Tessari)

PLOT THICKENS, THE   (RKO, 1936)
40 NAUGHTY GIRLS   (RKO, 1937)
    (based on a story by Stuart Palmer)

POM PON GIRLS, THE   (IND, 1976)
POM PON GIRLS II, THE   (IND, 1977)
    (based on a story by Joseph Ruben and Robert Rosenthal)

PREACHERMAN   (IND, 1973)
PREACHERMAN MEETS WIDDERWOMAN   (IND, 1974)
    (based on a screenplay by Harvey Flaxman and Albert
    T. Viola)

PRIVATE IZZY MURPHY   (WB, 1926)
SAILOR IZZY MURPHY   (WB, 1927)
    (based on a story by Edward Clark and Raymond L.
    Schrock)

PRIVATE SNUFFY SMITH   (MON, 1942)
HILLBILLY BLITZKREIG   (MON, 1942)
    (based on the comic strip, "Barney Google and Snuffy
    Smith," by Billy De Beck)

PROFESSOR ZAZUL   (POL, 1962)
PRZYJACIEL   (POL, 1963)
    (source unknown)

THE RASCALS OF THE FRONT BENCH: TO HELL WITH
    TEACHERS   (GER, 1968)
THE RASCALS OF THE FRONT BENCH: TO THE DEVIL
    WITH SCHOOL   (GER, 1968)
    (based on the book, "Zur Holle mit den Paukern," by
    Alexander Wolf)

REAL WEST, THE   (NBC–TV, 1961)
END OF THE TRAIL   (NBC–TV, 1965)
    (based on documentary footage of the American West)

RED STALLION   (EL, 1947)
RED STALLION IN THE ROCKIES   (EL, 1949)
    (based on a screenplay by Robert E. Kent and Crane Wilbur)

ROAD TO "SATURN," THE   (RUS, 1968)

END OF "SATURN," THE (RUS, 1968)
(based on the book, "Saturn is Barely Visible," by Vasili Ardamatski)

ROARING ROAD, THE (PAR, 1919)
EXCUSE MY DUST (PAR, 1920)
(based on a book by Byron Morgan)

ROBE, THE (FOX, 1953)
DEMITRIUS AND THE GLADIATORS (FOX, 1954)
(based on the book by Lloyd C. Douglas)

ROBOT (short) (YUG, 1960)
VENUS (short) (YUG, 1961)
(source unknown)

ROCK PRETTY BABY (UN, 1956)
SUMMER LOVE (UN, 1958)
(based on a screenplay by Herbert Margolis and William Raynor)

ROSEMARY'S BABY (PAR, 1968)
LOOK WHAT'S HAPPENED TO ROSEMARY'S BABY (ABC–TV, 1976)
(based on the book by Ira Levin)

RUDOLPH, THE RED–NOSED REINDEER (NBC–TV, 1967)
RUDOLPH'S SHINY NEW YEAR (ABC–TV, 1976)
(based on the story by Robert L. May)

SABATA (UA, 1970)
ADIOS, SABATA (UA, 1971)
(based on a screenplay by Renato Izzo and Gianfranco Parolini)

SALT AND PEPPER (UA, 1969)
ONE MORE TIME (UA, 1970)
(based on a screenplay by Michael Pertwee)

SALUTE THE TOFF (BRI, 1951)
HAMMER THE TOFF (BRI, 1952)
(based on books by John Creasy)

SCARLET PIMPERNEL, THE (BRI, 1935)
RETURN OF THE SCARLET PIMPERNEL, THE (BRI, 1938)
(based on the book by Baroness Orczy)

SECOND BEST SECRET AGENT IN THE WHOLE WIDE WORLD, THE (British title: LICENSED TO KILL) (BRI, 1966)
WHERE THE BULLETS FLY (BRI, 1967)
(based on a story by Lindsay Shonteff and Howard Griffiths)

SECRET AGENT X--9 (serial) (UN, 1937)
SECRET AGENT X--9 (serial) (UN, 1945)
(based on a story by Joseph O'Donnell and Harold C. Wire)

SECRET LOVE OF SANDRA BLAIN, THE (short) (IND, 1974)
NEW LIFE OF SANDRA BLAIN, THE (short) (IND, 1976)
(documentaries on the recovery of an alcoholic)

SEE HERE, PRIVATE HARGROVE (MGM, 1944)
WHAT NEXT, CORPORAL HARGROVE? (MGM, 1945)
(based on the book by Marion Hargrove)

SEVEN GOLDEN MEN (ITA, 1966)

GREAT BLOW OF THE SEVEN GOLDEN MEN, THE (ITA, 1968)
(based on a screenplay by Marco Vicario and Mariano Ozores)

SEVEN GUNS FOR THE MacGREGORS (ITA/SPA, 1965)
UP THE MacGREGORS (ITA/SPA, 1966)
(based on a story by David Moreno)

SHAGGY DOG, THE (DIS, 1959)
SHAGGY D.A., THE (DIS, 1976)
(based on the book, "The Hound of Florence," by Felix Salten)

SHARPSHOOTERS (FOX, 1938)
CHASING DANGER (FOX, 1939)
(based on a story by Maurice Rapf and Lester Ziffren)

SHE (MGM, 1965)
VENGEANCE OF SHE (FOX, 1968)
(based on the book by H. Rider Haggard)

SHEIK, THE (PAR, 1921)
SON OF THE SHEIK, THE (UA, 1926)
(based on books by Edith Maude Hull)

SHOGUN AND HIS MISTRESS, THE (JAP, 1967)
WOMEN AROUND THE SHOGUN, THE (JAP, 1967)
(based on a screenplay by various authors)

SIEGFRIED (GER, 1923)
KRIEMHELD'S REVENGE (GER, 1924)
(based on the Germanic legend, "Der Niebelungen")

SIX MILLION DOLLAR MAN, THE (series) (ABC--TV, 1975)
BIONIC WOMAN, THE (series) (ABC--TV, 1976)
(based on a teleplay)

SLAUGHTER (AI, 1972)
SLAUGHTER'S BIG RIP--OFF (AI, 1973)
(based on a screenplay by Mark Hanna and Don Williams)

SMILEY (BRI, 1958)
SMILEY GETS A GUN (BRI, 1959)
(based on the book by Moore Raymond)

SOUNDER (FOX, 1972)
PART 2, SOUNDER (GAM, 1976)
(based on the book by William H. Armstrong)

SPIDER'S WEB, THE (serial) (COL, 1938)
SPIDER RETURNS, THE (serial) (COL, 1941)
(based on the Spider stories)

SPINNING EARTH I (JAP, 1928)
SPINNING EARTH II (JAP, 1928)
(source unknown)

STRANGER IN TOWN, A (MGM, 1968)
STRANGER RETURNS, THE (MGM, 1968)
(based on a screenplay by Warren Garfield and Giuseppe Mangione)

STREETFIGHTER, THE (JAP, 1974)
RETURN OF THE STREETFIGHTER, THE (JAP, 1975)
(source unknown)

SUMMER OF '42 (WB, 1971)
CLASS OF '44 (WB, 1973)

(based on a screenplay by Herman Raucher)

SUPER FLY (WB, 1972)
SUPER FLY TNT (PAR, 1973)
(based on a screenplay by Philip Fenty)

SUPPORT YOUR LOCAL SHERIFF (UA, 1969)
SUPPORT YOUR LOCAL GUNFIGHTER (UA, 1971)
(based on a screenplay by William Bowers)

SWEENEY (BRI, 1976)
SWEENEY 2 (BRI, 1978)
(based on a teleplay)

TALL BLOND MAN WITH ONE BLACK SHOE, THE
(FRA, 1973)
RETURN OF THE BIG BLOND, THE (FRA, 1974)
(based on a screenplay by Robert Francis Veber)

TATOOED TEMPTRESS (JAP, 1968)
DEVIL IN MY FLESH (JAP, 1968)
(based on the book, "Hagoromo no Onna," by Akimitsu
Takagi)

TEACHER, TEACHER (NBC–TV, 1969)
EMILY, EMILY (NBC–TV, 1977)
(based on a teleplay)

THAT'LL BE THE DAY (BRI, 1973)
STARDUST (BRI, 1974)
(based on a story by Ray Connolly)

THEM THAR HILLS (short) (MGM, 1935)
TIT FOR TAT (short) (MGM, 1935)
(source unknown)

THERE'S ALWAYS A WOMAN (COL, 1938)
THERE'S THAT WOMAN AGAIN (COL, 1939)
(based on a story by Wilson Collinson)

THEY CALL HER CLEOPATRA WONG (HK, 1977)
VENGEANCE OF CLEOPATRA WONG, THE (HK, 1977)
(based on a screenplay)

THEY CALL ME TRINITY (ITA, 1970)
TRINITY IS STILL MY NAME (ITA, 1971)
(based on a screenplay by E.B. Clucher)

THIS MAN IS NEWS (BRI, 1938)
THIS MAN IN PARIS (BRI, 1939)
(based on a screenplay by various authors)

THREE MUSKETEERS, THE (FOX, 1973)
FOUR MUSKETEERS, THE (FOX, 1974)
(based on the book by Alexandre Dumas)

TIGHT LITTLE ISLAND (BRI, 1949) (British title:
WHISKEY GALORE)
MAD LITTLE ISLAND (BRI, 1958)
(based on the book, "Whiskey Galore," by Compton
Mackenzie)

TIL DEATH US DO PART (BRI, 1968) (American title:
ALF 'N' FAMILY)
GARNETT SAGA, THE (BRI, 1971)
(based on the British television series which was later
adapted into "All in the Family" by Johnny Speight)

TIME FOR BURNING, A (IND, 1966)

TIME FOR BUILDING, A (IND, 1967)
(based on incidents in the Lutheran Church in the United
States)

TONY ROME (FOX, 1967)
LADY IN CEMENT (FOX, 1968)
(based on the book, "Miami Mayhem," by Marvin H.
Albert)

TROUBLE WITH ANGELS, THE (COL, 1966)
WHERE ANGELS GO, TROUBLE FOLLOWS (COL, 1968)
(based on the book by Jane Trahey)

TWO HEROES (CHN, n.d.)
MEN FROM THE MONASTERY (CHN, 1974)
(source unknown)

TWO OF US, THE (FRA, 1968)
FIRST TIME, THE (FRA, 1976)
(based on a screenplay by Claude Berri)

UP FRONT (UN, 1951)
(WILLIE AND JOE) BACK AT THE FRONT (UN, 1952)
(based on the book by Bill Mauldin)

UP THE CREEK (BRI, 1958)
FURTHER UP THE CREEK (BRI, 1958)
(based on a story by various authors)

VAMPIRE, THE (MEX, 1957)
VAMPIRE'S COFFIN, THE (MEX, 1959)
(based on a story by Ramon Obon)

VILLAGE OF THE DAMNED (BRI, 1960)
CHILDREN OF THE DAMNED (BRI, 1963)
(based on the book, "The Midwitch Cuckoos," by John
Wyndham)

VIRGIN SOLDIERS, THE (BRI, 1969)
STAND UP, VIRGIN SOLDIERS (BRI, 1977)
(based on a book by Leslie Thomas)

WAI OLAWON (THAI, 1976)
RAK OTAROOT (THAI, 1977)
(based on a story by Boonrak Nilwong)

WALPURGIS NIGHT (SPA, 1970)
RETURN TO WALPURGIS (SPA, 1973)
(source unlisted)

WHEN THE DALTONS RODE (UN, 1940)
DALTONS RIDE AGAIN, THE (UN, 1945)
(based on the book by Emmett Dalton and Jack
Jungmeyer Jr.)

WHEN WOMEN HAD TAILS (ITA, 1970)
WHEN WOMEN LOST THEIR TAILS (ITA, 1971)
(based on a screenplay by Lina Wertmuller and others)

WHERE ARE YOUR CHILDREN? (MON, 1943)
ARE THESE OUR PARENTS? (MON, 1944)
(based on a story by Hilary Lynn)

WHITE LIGHTNING (UA, 1973)
GATOR (UA, 1976)
(based on a screenplay by William Norton)

WHO'S THAT KNOCKING AT MY DOOR? (IND, 1968)
MEAN STREETS (WB, 1973)

(based on a screenplay by Martin Scorsese)

WILLARD   (CIN, 1970)
BEN   (CIN, 1971)
    (based on the book, "Ratman's Notebooks," by Stephen
    Gilbert)

WOMEN'S PRISON   (JAP, 1968)
WOMEN'S ALL   (JAP, 1968)
    (based on a screenplay by Shozaburo Asai)

YOUNG PIONEERS, THE   (ABC–TV, 1975)

YOUNG PIONEERS CHRISTMAS   (ABC–TV, 1976)
    (based on a teleplay)

YOUNG TOM EDISON   (MGM, 1940)
EDISON THE MAN   (MGM, 1940)
    (based on the life of the noted inventor)

ZAMBO   (IN, 1937)
SON OF ZAMBO   (IN, 1938)
    (based on a story by S.B. Nayampally)

SERIES

ADDIE MILLS (based on stories by Gail Rock)
  THANKSGIVING TREASURE, A (CBS--TV, 1972)
  HOUSE WITHOUT A CHRISTMAS TREE, A (CBS--TV, 1973)
  EASTER PROMISE, AN (CBS--TV, 1975)
  ADDIE AND THE KING OF HEARTS (CBS--TV, 1976)

ADEMAI (source unlisted)
  ADEMAI JOSEPH (FRA, 1933)
  ADEMAI AVIATEUR (FRA, 1934)
  ADEMAI A L'O.N.M. (FRA, 1934)
  ADEMAI ET LA NATION ARMEE (FRA, 1934)
  ADEMAI AU MOYENAGE (FRA, 1935)
  ADEMAI BANDIT D'HONNEUR (FRA, 1942)

AGENT 69 (based on a story by Romy Galang)
  DOLLS FOR HIRE (PHI, 1967)
  EDEN BOYS (PHI, 1967)

AGENT X--44 (based on a story by Eliseo S. Corcuerro)
  ASSASSIN, THE (PHI, 1967)
  CRACK DOWN (PHI, 1967)
  FRAME--UP (PHI, 1967)
  MODUS OPERANDI (PHI, 1967)

AIRPORT (based on the book by Arthur Hailey and original screenplays)
  AIRPORT (UN, 1970)
  AIRPORT 1975 (UN, 1974)
  AIRPORT 1977 (UN, 1977)

ALL CREATURES -- (based on books by James Harriott)
  ALL CREATURES GREAT AND SMALL (BRI, 1975)
  IT SHOULDN'T HAPPEN TO A VET (BRI, 1976)
  ALL THINGS WISE AND WONDERFUL (BRI, 1977)
  ALL THINGS BRIGHT AND BEAUTIFUL (BRI, 1978)

ANGELIQUE (based on a book by Sergeanne Golon)
  RED ROSE FOR ANGELIQUE, A (ITA, 1966)
  ANGELIQUE AT THE OTTOMAN COURT (TUR, 1967)
  INDOMINATIBLE ANGELIQUE (FRA/GER/ITA, 1967)
  ANGELIQUE AND THE SULTAN (FRA/GER/ITA, 1968)
  ANGELIQUE -- THE ROAD TO VERSAILLES (FRA, 1968)

ALVIN PURPLE (based on the play by Alan Hopgood)
  ALVIN PURPLE (AUT, 1973)
  ALVIN RIDES AGAIN (AUT, 1974)
  ALVIN PURPLE (series) (AUT--TV, 1976)

ANTOINE DOINEL (based on screenplays by Francois Truffaut)
  400 BLOWS, THE (FRA, 1959)
  LOVE AT 20 (sequence) (FRA, 1963)
  STOLEN KISSES (FRA, 1969)
  BED AND BOARD (FRA, 1971)
  LOVE ON THE RUN (FRA, 1978)

ARLEN/DEVINE (based on original stories by Ben Pivar and others)
  MUTINY ON THE BLACKHAWK (UN, 1939)
  LEGION OF LOST FLYERS (UN, 1939)
  DANGER ON WHEELS (UN, 1940)

HOT STEEL (UN, 1940)
DEVIL'S PIPELINE, THE (UN, 1940)
LEATHER PUSHERS (UN, 1940)
LUCKY DEVILS (UN, 1940)
BLACK DIAMONDS (UN, 1940)
MAN FROM MONTREAL, THE (UN, 1940)
MUTINY IN THE ARCTIC (UN, 1940)
DANGEROUS GAME, A (UN, 1940)
MAN OF THE TIMBERLAND (UN, 1941)

ARSENE LUPIN (based on characters created by Maurice le Blanc)
  ARSENE LUPIN (BRI, 1916)
  ARSENE LUPIN (VIT, 1917)
  ARSENE LUPIN UTOLSO KALANDJA (HUN, 1921)
  813 (JAP, 1923)
  ARSENE LUPIN (MGM, 1932)
  ARSENE LUPIN, DETECTIVE (FRA, 1937)
  ARSENE LUPIN RETURNS (MGM, 1938)
  ENTER ARSENE LUPIN (UN, 1944)
  ADVENTURES OF ARSENE LUPIN (FRA, 1956)
  SIGNE ARSENE LUPIN (FRA, 1959)
  ARSENE LUPIN AGAINST ARSENE LUIPN (FRA, 1962)
  ARSENE LUPIN (series) (FRA--TV, 1971)
  ARRESTATION D'ARSENE LUPIN, L' (FRA, 1971)
  ARSENE LUPIN CONTRE "SHERLOCK HOLMES" (FRA 1971)

ASTERIX (based on a comic strip by Rene Goscinny and Albert Uderzo)
  ASTERIX THE GAUL (FRA, 1967)
  ASTERIX AND CLEOPATRA (BEL/FRA, 1968)
  12 LABORS OF ASTERIX, THE (FRA, 1976)

ATLAS (based on a legend)
  ATLAS (ITA, 1960)
  ATLAS AGAINST THE CYCLOPS (ITA, 1961)
  ATLAS AGAINST THE CZAR (ITA, 1964)

AZTEC MUMMY (based on an original screenplay)
  AZTEC MUMMY, THE (MEX, 1957)
  ROBOT VS. THE AZTEC MUMMY (MEX, 1959)
  CURSE OF THE AZTEC MUMMY (MEX, 1959)
  WRESTLING WOMEN VS. THE AZTEC MUMMY (MEX, 1964)

BAB (based on stories by Mary Roberts Rinehart)
  BAB'S BURGLAR (PAR, 1917)
  BAB'S DIARY (PAR, 1917)
  BAB'S MATINEE IDOL (PAR, 1917)
  BAB'S CANDIDATE (VIT, 1920)

BABY SANDY (based on a screenplay by Leonard Spigelgass and Charles Grayson)
  UNEXPECTED FATHER (UN, 1939)
  LITTLE ACCIDENT (UN, 1939)
  SANDY IS A LADY (UN, 1940)
  SANDY GETS HER MAN (UN, 1940)

BAD NEWS BEARS (based on characters created by Bill Lancaster)
  BAD NEWS BEARS, THE (PAR, 1975)
  BAD NEWS BEARS IN BREAKING TRAINING, THE

(PAR, 1977)
BAD NEWS BEARS GO TO JAPAN, THE (PAR, 1978)

BATMAN (based on the comic strip by Bob Kane)
  BATMAN (serial) (COL, 1943)
  BATMAN AND ROBIN (serial) (COL, 1949)
  BATMAN (series) (ABC--TV, 1965)
  BATMAN (FOX, 1966)
  BATMAN FIGHTS DRACULA (PHI, 1967)
  FANTOMA -- APOINTMENT IN ISTANBUL (TUR, 1967)
  SUPER FRIENDS (series) (ABC--TV, 1973)
  NEW ADVENTURES OF BATMAN, THE (series) (CBS--
    TV, 1977)

BEDSIDE (based on screenplays by Eric Soya)
  BEDSIDE MAZURKA (DEN, 1970)
  BEDSIDE DENTIST (DEN, 1971)
  MAZURKA AND THE HEADMASTER (DEN, 1972)
  BEDSIDE HEAD (DEN, 1972)
  BEDSIDE HIGHWAY (DEN, 1972)
  BEDSIDE RECTOR (DEN, 1972)
  BEDSIDE ROMANCE (DEN, 1973)
  JUMPIN' AT THE BEDSIDE (DEN, 1976)
  BEDSIDE SAILORS (DEN, 1976)

BEERY/ROGERS (based on a story by Donald Hough)
  DUDES ARE PRETTY PEOPLE (UA, 1942)
  CALABOOSE (UA, 1943)
  SLICK CHICK (UA, 1943)

BELLES OF ST. TRINIAN'S (based on cartoons by Ronald
    Searle; also the basis of the 1977 musical, "The Utter
    Glory of Morissey Hall")
  BELLES OF ST. TRINIAN'S, THE (BRI, 1955)
  BLUE MURDER AT ST. TRINIAN'S (BRI, 1958)
  PURE HELL AT ST. TRINIAN'S (BRI, 1961)
  GREAT ST. TRINIAN'S TRAIN ROBBERY, THE (BRI,
    1966)

BENDIX/SAWYER (based on a screenplay by Earle Snell and
    Clarence Marks)
  BROOKLYN ORCHID (UA, 1942)
  Mc GUERINS FROM BROOKLYN, THE (UA, 1943)
  TAXI, MISTER? (UA, 1943)

BENJI (based on a story by Joe Camp)
  BENJI (IND, 1974)
  FOR THE LOVE OF BENJI (IND, 1977)
  PHENOMENON OF BENJI, THE (ABC--TV, 1978)

BERRI TRILOGY (based on semi--autobiographical material
    by Claude Berri (Langmann))
  TWO OF US, THE (FRA, 1968)
  MARRY ME, MARRY ME! (FRA, 1969)
  FIRST TIME, THE (FRA, 1978)

BIG BROADCAST, THE (based on the play, "Wild Waves,"
    by William Ford Manley)
  BIG BROADCAST, THE (PAR, 1932)
  BIG BROADCAST OF 1936, THE (PAR, 1935)
  BIG BROADCAST OF 1937, THE (PAR, 1936)
  BIG BROADCAST OF 1938, THE (PAR, 1938)

BIG TOWN (based on a radio series by various authors)
  BIG TOWN (GUILTY ASSIGNMENT) (PAR, 1947)
  BIG TOWN AFTER DARK (UNDERWORLD AFTER DARK)
    (PAR, 1947)
  I COVER THE BIG TOWN (PAR, 1947)
  BIG TOWN SCANDAL (PAR, 1948)

BIG TOWN (series) (NBC--TV, 1950)

BILL CRANE (based on stories by Jonathan Latimer)
  WESTLAND CASE, THE (UN, 1937)
  LADY IN THE MORGUE (UN, 1938)
  LAST WARNING, THE (UN, 1938)

BILLY JACK
  BORN LOSERS (AI, 1967)
  BILLY JACK (WB, 1971)
  TRIAL OF BILLY JACK, THE (AI, 1974)
  BILLY JACK GOES TO WASHINGTON (IND, 1977)

BILLY THE KID (based on the life of outlaw William Bonner)
  BILLY THE KID (MGM, 1930)
  BILLY THE KID RETURNS (REP, 1938)
  BILLY THE KID'S GUN JUSTICE (PRC, 1940)
  BILLY THE KID IN TEXAS (PRC, 1940)
  BILLY THE KID OUTLAWED (PRC, 1940)
  BILLY THE KID IN SANTA FE (PRC, 1941)
  BILLY THE KID WANTED (PRC, 1941)
  BILLY THE KID (MGM, 1941)
  BILLY THE KID'S FIGHTING PALS (PRC, 1941)
  BILLY THE KID'S RANGE WAR (PRC, 1941)
  BILLY THE KID'S ROUNDUP (PRC, 1941)
  BILLY THE KID'S SMOKING GUNS (PRC, 1942)
  BILLY THE KID TRAPPED (PRC, 1942)
  LAW AND ORDER (PRC, 1942)
  FUGITIVE OF THE PLAINS (PRC, 1943)
  OUTLAW, THE (RKO, 1943)
  KID FROM TEXAS, THE (UN, 1950)
  BOY FROM OKLAHOMA (WB, 1954)
  LAW VS. BILLY THE KID, THE (COL, 1954)
  PARSON AND THE OUTLAW, THE (COL, 1957)
  LEFT--HANDED GUN, THE (WB, 1958)
  BILLY THE KID (SPA, 1962)
  MAN WHO KILLED BILLY THE KID (ITA/SPA, 1967)
  CHISUM (WB, 1970)
  ADVENTURES OF BILLY THE KID (FRA, 1971)
  DIRTY LITTLE BILLY (COL, 1972)

BLONDIE (based on the comic strip by Chick Young; also
    appeared as a radio series)
  BLONDIE (COL, 1938)
  BLONDIE BRINGS UP BABY (COL, 1939)
  BLONDIE MEETS THE BOSS (COL, 1939)
  BLONDIE TAKES A VACATION (COL, 1939)
  BLONDIE HAS SERVANT TROUBLE (COL, 1940)
  BLONDIE ON A BUDGET (COL, 1940)
  BLONDIE PLAYS CUPID (COL, 1940)
  BLONDIE GOES LATIN (COL, 1941)
  BLONDIE IN SOCIETY (COL, 1941)
  BLONDIE FOR VICTORY (COL, 1942)
  BLONDIE GOES TO COLLEGE (COL, 1942)
  BLONDIE'S BLESSED EVENT (COL, 1942)
  FOOTLIGHT GLAMOUR (COL, 1943)
  IT'S A GREAT LIFE (COL, 1943)
  LEAVE IT TO BLONDIE (COL, 1945)
  BLONDIE KNOWS BEST (COL, 1946)
  LIFE WITH BLONDIE (COL, 1946)
  BLONDIE'S LUCKY DAY (COL, 1946)
  BLONDIE IN THE DOUGH (COL, 1947)
  BLONDIE'S ANNIVERSARY (COL, 1947)
  BLONDIE'S BIG MOMENT (COL, 1947)
  BLONDIE'S HOLIDAY (COL, 1947)
  BLONDIE'S REWARD (COL, 1948)
  BLONDIE'S SECRET (COL, 1948)
  BLONDIE HITS THE JACKPOT (COL, 1949)
  BLONDIE'S BIG DEAL (COL, 1949)

BLONDIE'S HERO   (COL, 1950)
BEWARE OF BLONDIE   (COL, 1950)
BLONDIE   (series)   (NBC--TV, 1954)
BLONDIE   (series)   (CBS--TV, 1969)

BLUE DEMON   (source unlisted)
  BLUE DEMON VS. THE SATANICAL POWER   (MEX, 1964)
  BLUE DEMON VS. THE INFERNAL BRAINS   (MEX, 1967)
  BLUE DEMON AGAINST THE DIABOLICAL WOMEN (MEX, 1968)
  BLUE DEMON VS. THE SEDUCTRESS   (MEX, 1968)
  BLUE DEMON, SPY DESTROYER   (MEX, 1968)
  BLUE DEMON IN PASSPORT TO DEATH   (MEX, 1968)

BOM   (source unlisted)
  BOM THE SOLDIER   (SWE, 1948)
  FATHER BOM   (SWE, 1949)
  BOM, THE CUSTOMS AGENT   (SWE, 1951)
  BOM, THE AVIATOR   (SWE, 1952)
  BUM--BOM   (SWE, 1954)

BOMBA   (based on the "Bomba" books by Roy Lockwood)
  BOMBA, THE JUNGLE BOY   (MON, 1949)
  BOMBA AND THE HIDDEN CITY   (MON, 1950)
  BOMBA ON PANTHER ISLAND   (MON, 1950)
  BOMBA AND THE ELEPHANT STAMPEDE   (MON, 1951)
  LION HUNTERS   (MON, 1951)
  BOMBA AND THE JUNGLE GIRL   (MON, 1952)
  SAFARI DRUMS   (AA, 1953)
  GOLDEN IDOL, THE   (AA, 1954)
  KILLER LEOPARD   (AA, 1954)
  LORD OF THE JUNGLE   (AA, 1955)

BORDER G--MEN (SHAMROCK AND LUCKY)   (based on characters created by Ron Ormond)
  CROOKED RIVER   (LIP, 1950)
  COLORADO RANGER   (LIP, 1950)
  FAST ON THE DRAW   (LIP, 1950)
  HOSTILE COUNTRY   (LIP, 1950)
  MARSHAL OF HELLDORADO   (LIP, 1950)
  RANGELAND EMPIRE   (LIP, 1950)
  OUTLAW FURY   (LIP, 1950)
  SUDDEN DEATH   (LIP, 1950)
  WEST OF THE BRAZOS   (LIP, 1950)
  TEXANS NEVER CRY   (LIP, 1951)
  GHOST TOWN   (LIP, 1951)
  VALLEY OF FLAME   (LIP, 1951)

BORN FREE   (based on the book by Joy Adamson)
  BORN FREE   (BRI, 1966)
  LIONS ARE FREE   (BRI--TV, 1969)
  LIVING FREE   (BRI, 1972)
  FOREVER FREE   (BRI, 1974)
  CHRISTIAN THE LION   (BRI, 1977)

BOSTON BLACKIE   (based on stories by Jack Boyle; also appeared as a radio series)
  BOSTON BLACKIE'S LITTLE PAL   (MGM, 1918)
  BLACKIE'S REDEMPTION   (MGM, 1919)
  FACE IN THE FOG, A   (PAR, 1922)
  BOSTON BLACKIE   (FOX, 1923)
  RETURN OF BOSTON BLACKIE   (FD, 1927)
  MEET BOSTON BLACKIE   (COL, 1941)
  CONFESSIONS OF BOSTON BLACKIE   (COL, 1942)
  ALIAS BOSTON BLACKIE   (COL, 1942)
  BOSTON BLACKIE GOES TO WASHINGTON   (COL, 1942)
  BOSTON BLACKIE GOES HOLLYWOOD   (COL, 1942)

AFTER MIDNIGHT WITH BOSTON BLACKIE   (COL, 1943)
  CHANCE OF A LIFETIME   (COL, 1943)
  ONE MYSTERIOUS NIGHT   (COL, 1944)
  BOSTON BLACKIE BOOKED ON SUSPICION   (COL, 1945)
  BOSTON BLACKIE'S RENDEZVOUS   (COL, 1945)
  BOSTON BLACKIE AND THE LAW   (COL, 1946)
  PHANTOM THIEF, THE   (COL, 1946)
  CLOSE CALL FOR BOSTON BLACKIE, A   (COL, 1946)
  TRAPPED BY BOSTON BLACKIE   (COL, 1948)
  BOSTON BLACKIE'S CHINESE VENTURE   (COL, 1949)
  BOSTON BLACKIE   (series)   (NBC--TV, 1951)

BOWERY BOYS, THE   see   DEAD END KIDS

BRINGING UP FATHER   (based on the comic strip by George McManus)
  FATHER GETS INTO THE MOVIES   (short)   (IND, 1916)
  GREAT HANSOM CAB MYSTERY   (short)   (IND, 1917)
  HE TRIES HIS HAND AT HYPNOTISM   (short)   (IND, 1917)
  HOT TIME IN THE GYM   (short)   (IND, 1917)
  JUST LIKE A WOMAN   (short)   (IND, 1917)
  MUSIC HATH CHARMS   (short)   (IND, 1917)
  FATHER'S CLOSE SHAVE   (short)   (PAT, 1920)
  JIGGS AND THE SOCIAL LION   (short)   (PAT, 1920)
  JIGGS IN SOCIETY   (short)   (PAT, 1920)
  BRINGING UP FATHER   (MGM, 1928)
  BRINGING UP FATHER   (MON, 1946)
  JIGGS AND MAGGIE IN COURT   (MON, 1948)
  JIGGS AND MAGGIE IN SOCIETY   (MON, 1948)
  JACKPOT JITTERS   (MON, 1949)
  JIGGS AND MAGGIE OUT WEST   (MON, 1950)

BROADWAY MELODY   (based on original screenplays)
  BROADWAY MELODY   (MGM, 1929)
  BROADWAY MELODY OF 1936   (MGM, 1935)
  BROADWAY MELODY OF 1938   (MGM, 1937)
  BROADWAY MELODY OF 1940   (MGM, 1940)
  BROADWAY RHYTHM   (MGM, 1944)

BROWN/CARNEY   (based on a story by William Bowers and M. Coates Webster)
  ADVENTURES OF A ROOKIE   (RKO, 1943)
  ROOKIES IN BURMA   (RKO, 1943)
  SEVEN DAYS ASHORE   (RKO, 1944)
  ZOMBIES ON BROADWAY   (RKO, 1945)
  GENIUS AT WORK   (RKO, 1946)

BULLDOG DRUMMOND   (based on the books and plays of Herman Cyril McNeile [Sapper])
  BULLDOG DRUMMOND   (HOD, 1922)
  BULLDOG DRUMMOND   (BRI, 1923)
  THIRD ROUND, THE   (BRI, 1925)
  POPPIES OF FLANDERS   (BRI, 1928)
  BULLDOG DRUMMOND   (UA, 1929)
  BULLDOG DRUMMOND STRIKES BACK   (BRI, 1934)
  RETURN OF BULLDOG DRUMMOND   (BRI, 1935)
  ALIAS BULLDOG DRUMMOND   (BRI, 1935)
  BULLDOG DRUMMOND AT BAY   (BRI, 1937)
  BULLDOG DRUMMOND COMES BACK   (PAR, 1937)
  BULLDOG DRUMMOND ESCAPES   (PAR, 1937)
  BULLDOG DRUMMOND'S REVENGE   (PAR, 1937)
  BULLDOG DRUMMOND IN AFRICA   (PAR, 1938)
  BULLDOG DRUMMOND'S PERIL   (PAR, 1938)
  BULLDOG DRUMMOND'S BRIDE   (PAR, 1939)
  BULLDOG DRUMMOND'S SECRET POLICE   (PAR, 1939)
  ARREST BULLDOG DRUMMOND   (PAR, 1939)
  MR. AND MRS. BULLDOG DRUMMOND   (PAR, 1939)

BULLDOG DRUMMOND AT BAY (COL, 1947)
BULLDOG DRUMMOND STRIKES BACK (COL, 1947)
CHALLENGE, THE (FOX, 1948)
13 LEAD SOLDIERS (FOX, 1948)
CALLING BULLDOG DRUMMOND (MGM, 1951)
DEADLIER THAN THE MALE (BRI, 1967)
SOME GIRLS DO (BRI, 1968)

CAPPY RICKS (based on the books by Peter B. Kyne)
CAPPY RICKS (PAR, 1921)
MORE PAY, LESS WORK (FOX, 1926)
CAPPY RICKS RETURNS (REP, 1935)
AFFAIRS OF CAPPY RICKS, THE (REP, 1937)
GO--GETTER, THE (WB, 1937)

CAPTAIN BARNACLE (JOHN BUNNY) (based on original
    screenplays
CAPTAIN BARNACLE'S COURTSHIP (VIT, 1911)
CAPTAIN BARNACLE'S BABY (VIT, 1911)
CAPTAIN BARNACLE'S MESSMATE (VIT, 1912)

CAROLINE CHERIE (based on books by Cecil Saint--Laurent)
CAROLINE CHERIE (FRA, 1950)
CAPRICE OF CAROLINE CHERIE, THE (FRA, 1953)
SON OF CAROLINE CHERIE (FRA, 1954)
CAROLINE CHERIE (FRA/GER/ITA, 1967)

CARRY ON (based on original screenplays by various authors)
CARRY ON, SERGEANT (BRI, 1958)
CARRY ON, ADMIRAL (THE SHIP WAS LOADED) (BRI,
    1958)
CARRY ON, NURSE (BRI, 1959)
CARRY ON, TEACHER (BRI, 1959)
CARRY ON, CONSTABLE (BRI, 1960)
CARRY ON REGARDLESS (BRI, 1961)
CARRY ON CRUISING (BRI, 1962)
CARRY ON, CABBY (BRI, 1963)
CARRY ON, JACK (BRI, 1963)
CARRY ON TV (GET ON WITH IT) (BRI, 1963)
CARRY ON SPYING (BRI, 1964)
CARRY ON, CLEO (BRI, 1964)
CARRY ON, COWBOY (BRI, 1965)
DON'T LOSE YOUR HEAD (BRI, 1966)
CARRY ON, VENUS (BRI, 1966)
CARRY ON SCREAMING (BRI, 1966)
FOLLOW THAT CAMEL (BRI, 1967)
CARRY ON UP THE KHYBER (BRI, 1968)
CARRY ON, DOCTOR (BRI, 1969)
CARRY ON AGAIN, DOCTOR (BRI, 1969)
CARRY ON LOVING (BRI, 1970)
CARRY ON, JUNGLE BOY (CARRY ON UP THE JUNGLE)
    (BRI, 1970)
CARRY ON, COMRADE (BRI, 1971)
CARRY ON CAMPING (LET SLEEPING BAGS LIE) (BRI,
    1971)
CARRY ON, HENRY (BRI, 1971)
CARRY ON, MATRON (BRI, 1972)
CARRY ON ABROAD (BRI, 1973)
CARRY ON, GIRLS (BRI, 1973)
CARRY ON LAUGHING (series) (BRI--TV, 1974)
CARRY ON BEHIND (BRI, 1975)
CARRY ON ENGLAND (BRI, 1976)
CARRY ON, EMMANUELLE (BRI, 1978)

CHANDU THE MAGICIAN (based on the radio series by
    Harry A. Earnshaw, Vera M. Oldham and R. R. Morgan)
CHANDU THE MAGICIAN (FOX, 1932)
RETURN OF CHANDU, THE (serial) (PRI, 1934)
CHANDU ON THE MAGIC ISLAND (serial) (PRI, 1935)

CHARLIE CHAN (based on the books of Earl Derr Biggers
    and the character of Charlie Chan; some of the later
    Monogram films were remakes of the MR. WONG scripts)
HOUSE WITHOUT A KEY, THE (serial) (PAT, 1926)
CHINESE PARROT, THE (UN, 1927)
BEHIND THAT CURTAIN (FOX, 1929)
BLACK CAMEL, THE (FOX, 1931)
CHARLIE CHAN CARRIES ON (FOX, 1931)
CHARLIE CHAN'S CHANCE (FOX, 1932)
CHARLIE CHAN'S GREATEST CASE (FOX, 1933)
CHARLIE CHAN'S COURAGE (FOX, 1934)
CHARLIE CHAN IN LONDON (FOX, 1934)
CHARLIE CHAN IN EGYPT (FOX, 1935)
CHARLIE CHAN IN PARIS (FOX, 1935)
CHARLIE CHAN IN SHANGHAI (FOX, 1935)
CHARLIE CHAN AT THE CIRCUS (FOX, 1936)
CHARLIE CHAN AT THE OPERA (FOX, 1936)
CHARLIE CHAN AT THE RACE TRACK (FOX, 1936)
CHARLIE CHAN'S SECRET (FOX, 1936)
CHARLIE CHAN AT MONTE CARLO (FOX, 1937)
CHARLIE CHAN AT THE OLYMPICS (FOX, 1937)
CHARLIE CHAN ON BROADWAY (FOX, 1937)
CHARLIE CHAN IN HONOLULU (FOX, 1938)
CHARLIE CHAN AT TREASURE ISLAND (FOX, 1939)
CITY OF DARKNESS (FOX, 1939)
CHARLIE CHAN IN RENO (FOX, 1939)
CHARLIE CHAN'S MURDER CRUISE (FOX, 1940)
CHARLIE CHAN AT THE WAX MUSEUM (FOX, 1940)
CHARLIE CHAN IN PANAMA (FOX, 1940)
MURDER OVER NEW YORK (FOX, 1940)
CHARLIE CHAN IN RIO (FOX, 1941)
DEAD MEN TELL (FOX, 1941)
CASTLE IN THE DESERT (FOX, 1942)
JADE MASK, THE (MON, 1944)
CHINESE CAT, THE (MON, 1944)
BLACK MAGIC (MON, 1944)
CHARLIE CHAN IN THE SECRET SERVICE (MON, 1945)
SCARLET CLUE, THE (MON, 1945)
SHANGHAI COBRA, THE (MON, 1945)
RED DRAGON, THE (MON, 1945)
SHADOWS OVER CHINATOWN (MON, 1946)
TRAP, THE (MON, 1946)
DARK ALIBI (MON, 1946)
DANGEROUS MONEY (MON, 1946)
CHINESE RING, THE (MON, 1947)
SHANGHAI CHEST, THE (MON, 1948)
DOCKS OF NEW ORLEANS (MON, 1948)
GOLDEN EYE, THE (MON, 1948)
SKY DRAGON (MON, 1949)
FEATHERED SERPENT, THE (MON, 1949)
NEW ADVENTURES OF CHARLIE CHAN, THE (series)
    (TV, 1957)
HAPPINESS IS A WARM CLUE (CAN, 1970)
CHARLIE CHAN (NBC--TV, 1972)
AMAZING CHAN AND THE CHAN CLAN, THE (series)
    (CBS--TV, 1972)

CISCO KID, THE (based on a story by O. Henry and the
    character of the Cisco Kid)
CABALLERO'S WAY (FRA, 1914)
BORDER TERROR, THE (UN, 1919)
IN OLD ARIZONA (FOX, 1929)
ARIZONA KID, THE (FOX, 1930)
CISCO KID, THE (FOX, 1931)
RETURN OF THE CISCO KID, THE (FOX, 1939)
CISCO KID AND THE LADY, THE (FOX, 1940)
GAY CABALLERO, THE (FOX, 1940)
LUCKY CISCO KID (FOX, 1940)
VIVA CISCO KID (FOX, 1940)

ROMANCE OF THE RIO GRANDE   (FOX, 1941)
RIDE ON, VAQUERO   (FOX, 1941)
IN OLD NEW MEXICO   (MON, 1945)
SOUTH OF THE RIO GRANDE   (MON, 1945)
CISCO KID RETURNS, THE   (MON, 1945)
SOUTH OF MONTEREY   (MON, 1946)
BEAUTY AND THE BANDIT   (MON, 1946)
GAY CAVALIER, THE   (MON, 1946)
KING OF THE BANDITS   (MON, 1947)
ROBIN HOOD OF MONTEREY   (MON, 1947)
RIDING THE CALIFORNIA TRAIL   (MON, 1947)
DON AMIGO   (MON, 1948)   (unrealeased)
DARING CABALLERO, THE   (UA, 1949)
GAY AMIGO, THE   (UA, 1949)
SATAN'S CRADLE   (UA, 1949)
VALIANT HOMBRE   (UA, 1949)
GIRL FROM SAN LORENZO, THE   (UA, 1950)
CISCO KID, THE   (series)   (TV, 1951)

COCHISE   (based on the book, "Blood Brother," by Elliott
    Arnold)
BROKEN ARROW   (FOX, 1950)
BATTLE AT APACHE PASS, THE   (UN, 1952)
TAZA, SON OF COCHISE   (UN, 1954)

COHENS AND KELLYS   (based on the play, "Two Blocks
    Away," by Aaron Hoffman)
COHENS AND THE KELLYS, THE   (UN, 1926)
COHENS AND THE KELLYS IN ATLANTIC CITY, THE
    (UN, 1929)
COHENS AND THE KELLYS IN AFRICA, THE   (UN, 1930)
COHENS AND THE KELLYS IN PARIS, THE   (UN, 1930)
COHENS AND THE KELLYS IN SCOTLAND, THE   (UN,
    1930)
COHENS AND THE KELLYS IN HOLLYWOOD, THE
    (UN, 1932)
COHENS AND THE KELLYS IN TROUBLE, THE   (UN,
    1933)
NEVER MIND THE QUALITY – FEEL THE WIDTH   (BRI,
    1973)

COLOSSUS   (source unlisted)
COLOSSUS AND THE AMAZON QUEEN   (ITA, 1960)
COLOSSUS AND THE HEADHUNTERS   (ITA, 1960)
COLOSSUS AND THE HUNS   (ITA, 1960)
COLOSSUS OF THE ARENA   (ITA, 1960)

COMPUTER   see   MIDVILLE COLLEGE

CONFESSIONS   (based on a book by Timothy Lea)
CONFESSIONS OF A WINDOW CLEANER   (BRI, 1974)
CONFESSIONS OF A POP PERFORMER   (BRI, 1975)
CONFESSIONS OF A DRIVING INSTRUCTOR   (BRI,
    1976)
CONFESSIONS FROM A HOLIDAY CAMP   (BRI, 1977)

CORLISS ARCHER   (based on characters created by F. Hugh
    Herbert and the play, "Kiss and Tell")
KISS AND TELL   (COL, 1945)
KISS FOR CORLISS, A   (UA, 1949)
MEET CORLISS ARCHER   (series)   (TV, 1954)

CRAZY GANG, THE   (based on vaudeville acts by the Crazy
    Gang)
OKAY FOR SOUND   (BRI, 1937)
ALF'S BUTTON AFLOAT   (BRI, 1938)

FROZEN LIMITS, THE   (BRI, 1939)
GASBAGS   (BRI, 1940)
LIFE IS A CIRCUS   (BRI, 1954)

CREATURE, THE   (based on a story by Maurice Zimm)
CREATURE FROM THE BLACK LAGOON, THE   (UN,
    1954)
REVENGE OF THE CREATURE   (UN, 1955)
CREATURE WALKS AMONG US, THE   (UN, 1956)

CRICKET   (based on an idea and characters by Chuck Jones)
CRICKET IN TIMES SQUARE, A   (ABC--TV, 1972)
VERY MERRY CRICKET, A   (ABC--TV, 1973)
YANKEE DOODLE CRICKET, A   (ABC--TV, 1975)

CRIME CLUB   (based on various books which were "Crime
    Club" selections)
WESTLAND CASE, THE   (UN, 1937)
BLACK DOLL, THE   (UN, 1938)
LADY IN THE MORGUE, THE   (UN, 1938)
DANGER ON THE AIR   (UN, 1938)
LAST WARNING, THE   (UN, 1938)
LAST EXPRESS, THE   (UN, 1938)
WITNESS VANISHES, THE   (UN, 1939)

CRIME DOCTOR, THE   (based on the radio series by Max
    Marcin)
CRIME DOCTOR   (COL, 1943)
CRIME DOCTOR'S STRANGEST CASE   (COL, 1943)
SHADOWS IN THE NIGHT   (COL, 1944)
CRIME DOCTOR'S COURAGE   (COL, 1945)
CRIME DOCTOR'S WARNING   (COL, 1945)
CRIME DOCTOR'S MANHUNT   (COL, 1946)
JUST BEFORE DAWN   (COL, 1946)
CRIME DOCTOR'S GAMBLE   (COL, 1947)
MILLERSON CASE, THE   (COL, 1947)
GENTLEMAN FROM NOWHERE, THE   (COL, 1948)
CRIME DOCTOR'S DIARY   (COL, 1949)
DEVIL'S HENCHMAN, THE   (COL, 1949)

CRYING WOMAN, THE   (based on a Mexican legend)
CRYING WOMAN, THE   (MEX, 1933)
HERITAGE OF THE CRYING WOMAN   (MEX, 1946)
CRYING WOMAN, THE   (MEX, 1959)
CURSE OF THE CRYING WOMAN, THE   (MEX, 1961)

DARK SHADOWS   (based on a teleplay)
DARK SHADOWS   (serial)   (NBC--TV, 1966)
HOUSE OF DARK SHADOWS   (MGM, 1970)
NIGHT OF DARK SHADOWS   (MGM, 1971)

DAVY CROCKETT   (based on historical incidents and the life
    of the American frontiersman)
DAVY CROCKETT IN HEARTS DIVIDED   (n.d., 1908)
DAVY CROCKETT   (PAR, 1916)
DAVY CROCKETT AT THE FALL OF THE ALAMO
    (SUN, 1926)
REMEMBER THE ALAMO   (TCF, n.d.)
DAVY CROCKETT, INDIAN SCOUT   (UA, 1950)
DAVY CROCKETT, INDIAN FIGHTER   (ABC-TV, 1954)
DAVY CROCKETT, KING OF THE WILD FRONTIER
    (DIS, 1955)
DAVY CROCKETT GOES TO CONGRESS   (ABC-TV,
    1955)
DAVY CROCKETT AT THE ALAMO   (ABC--TV, 1955)
DAVY CROCKETT AND THE KEELBOAT RACE   (ABC-
    TV, 1955)
DAVY CROCKETT AND THE RIVER PIRATES   (DIS,
    1956)

DEAD END KIDS/LITTLE TOUGH GUYS/EAST SIDE KIDS/
    THE BOWERY BOYS (based on characters in the play,
    "Dead End," by Sidney Kingsley. The four original Dead
    End Kids moved on to Warners, then Universal, then
    Monogram where they evolved from the Dead End Kids to
    the Little Tough Guys and on to the East Side Kids and
    finally the Bowery Boys, which became the longest--
    running series in film history)
    DEAD END (UA, 1937)
    ANGELS WITH DIRTY FACES (WB, 1938)
    CRIME SCHOOL (WB, 1938)
    LITTLE TOUGH GUYS (UN, 1938)
    THEY MADE ME A CRIMINAL (WB, 1939)
    LITTLE TOUGH GUYS IN SOCIETY (UN, 1938)
    ANGELS WASH THEIR FACES (WB, 1939)
    HELL'S KITCHEN (WB, 1939)
    ON DRESS PARADE (WB, 1939)
    NEWSBOY'S HOME (UN, 1939)
    CALL A MESSENGER (UN, 1939)
    CODE OF THE STREETS (UN, 1939)
    GIVE US WINGS (UN, 1940)
    EAST SIDE KIDS (MON, 1940)
    YOU'RE NOT SO TOUGH (UN, 1940)
    BOYS OF THE CITY (THE GHOST CREEPS) (MON, 1940)
    THAT GANG OF MINE (MON, 1940)
    HIT THE ROAD (UN, 1941)
    BOWERY BLITZKRIEG (MON, 1941)
    PRIDE OF THE BOWERY (MON, 1941)
    MOB TOWN (UN, 1941)
    FLYING WILD (MON, 1941)
    SPOOKS RUN WILD (MON, 1941)
    SEA RAIDERS (serial) (UN, 1942)
    MUG TOWN (UN, 1942)
    TOUGH AS THEY COME (UN, 1942)
    JUNIOR G--MEN OF THE AIR (serial) (UN, 1942)
    LET'S GET TOUGH (MON, 1942)
    SMART ALECS (MON, 1942)
    MR. WISE GUY (MON, 1942)
    'NEATH BROOKLYN BRIDGE (MON, 1942)
    KEEP 'EM SLUGGING (UN, 1943)
    KID DYNAMITE (MON, 1943)
    MR. MUGGS STEPS OUT (MON, 1943)
    CLANCY STREET BOYS, THE (MON, 1943)
    GHOSTS ON THE LOOSE (MON, 1943)
    FOLLOW THE LEADER (MON, 1944)
    MILLION DOLLAR KID (MON, 1944)
    BLOCK BUSTERS (MON, 1944)
    CRAZY KNIGHTS (MON, 1944)
    BOWERY CHAMPS (MON, 1944)
    TROUBLE CHASERS (MON, 1945)
    COME OUT FIGHTING (MON, 1945)
    DOCKS OF NEW YORK (MON, 1945)
    MR. MUGGS RIDES AGAIN (MON, 1945)
    IN FAST COMPANY (MON, 1946)
    LIVE WIRES (MON, 1946)
    SPOOK BUSTERS (MON, 1946)
    MR. HEX (MON, 1946)
    SMUGGLER'S COVE (MON, 1946)
    BOWERY BOMBSHELL (MON, 1946)
    BOWERY BUCKAROOS (MON, 1947)
    HARD BOILED MAHONEY (MON, 1947)
    NEWS HOUNDS (MON, 1947)
    TROUBLE MAKERS (MON, 1948)
    JINX MONEY (MON, 1948)
    ANGEL'S ALLEY (MON, 1948)
    SMART POLITICS (MON, 1948)
    SMUGGLER'S COVE (MON, 1948)
    MASTER MINDS (MON, 1949)
    FIGHTING FOOLS (MON, 1949)

    ANGELS IN DISGUISE (MON, 1949)
    HOLD THAT BABY (MON, 1949)
    BLONDE DYNAMITE (MON, 1950)
    TRIPLE TROUBLE (MON, 1950)
    LUCKY LOSERS (MON, 1950)
    BLUES BUSTERS (MON, 1951)
    GHOST CATCHERS (MON, 1951)
    CRAZY OVER HORSES (MON, 1951)
    LET'S GO NAVY (MON, 1951)
    BOWERY BATALLION (MON, 1951)
    NO HOLDS BARRED (MON, 1952)
    FEUDIN' FOOLS (MON, 1952)
    HERE COME THE MARINES (MON, 1952)
    HOLD THAT LINE (MON, 1952)
    PRIVATE EYES (AA, 1953)
    LOOSE IN LONDON (AA, 1953)
    CLIPPED WINGS (AA, 1953)
    JALOPY (AA, 1953)
    HOT NEWS (AA, 1953)
    PARIS PLAYBOYS (AA, 1954)
    JUNGLE GENTS (AA, 1954)
    BOWERY BOYS MEET THE MONSTERS (AA, 1954)
    BOWERY TO BAGDAD (AA, 1954)
    SPY CHASERS (AA, 1955)
    JAIL BUSTERS (AA, 1955)
    HIGH SOCIETY (AA, 1955)
    HOT SHOTS (AA, 1956)
    FIGHTING TROUBLE (AA, 1956)
    DIG THAT URANIUM (AA, 1956)
    CRASHING LAS VEGAS (AA, 1956)
    SPOOK CHASERS (AA, 1957)
    HOLD THAT HYPNOTIST (AA, 1957)
    LOOKING FOR DANGER (AA, 1957)
    UP IN SMOKE (AA, 1957)
    IN THE MONEY (AA, 1958)

DEAR RUTH (based on the play by Norman Krasna)
    DEAR RUTH (PAR, 1947)
    DEAR WIFE (PAR, 1949)
    DEAR BRAT (PAR, 1951)

DEREK FLINT (based on characters created by Hal Fimberg)
    OUR MAN FLINT (FOX, 1966)
    IN LIKE FLINT (FOX, 1967)
    OUR MAN FLINT: DEAD ON TARGET (TV, 1976)

DEUXIEME BUREAU (source unlisted)
    ALERT THE DEUXIEME BUREAU (FRA, 1956)
    DEUXIEME BUREAU AGAINST THE UNKNOWN (FRA,
    1957)
    RAPT AU DEUXIEME BUREAU (FRA, 1958)
    DEUXIEME BUREAU AGAINST THE TERRORISTS
    (FRA, 1961)

DICK BARTON (based on the radio serial by Edward J. Mason)
    DICK BARTON, DETECTIVE (BRI, 1948)
    DICK BARTON, SPECIAL AGENT (BRI, 1948)
    DICK BARTON STRIKES BACK (BRI, 1949)
    DICK BARTON AT BAY (BRI, 1950)

DICK TRACY (based on the comic strip by Chester Gould;
    also appeared as a radio series)
    DICK TRACY (serial) (REP, 1937)
    DICK TRACY RETURNS (serial) (REP, 1938)
    DICK TRACY'S G--MEN (serial) (REP, 1939)
    DICK TRACY VS. CRIME INC. (serial) (REP, 1941)
    DICK TRACY (RKO, 1943)
    DICK TRACY VS. CUEBALL (RKO, 1946)
    DICK TRACY MEETS GRUESOME (RKO, 1947)

DICK TRACY'S DILEMMA (RKO, 1947)
DICK TRACY (series) (ABC--TV, 1950)
DICK TRACY VS. THE PHANTOM EMPIRE (serial)
  (REP, 1952)
DICK TRACY SHOW, THE (series) (UPA, 1960)
DICK TRACY (MR. MAGOO) (UPA, 1964)

DIONNE QUINTUPLETS (based on screenplays with the
  quintuplets playing themselves and not appearing in
  dramatic roles in any of the films)
COUNTRY DOCTOR, THE (FOX, 1936)
REUNION (FOX, 1936)
FIVE OF A KIND (FOX, 1938)

DIRTY HARRY (based on a story by Harry Julian Fink and
  R. M. Fink)
DIRTY HARRY (WB, 1971)
MAGNUM FORCE (WB, 1973)
ENFORCER, THE (WB, 1976)

DJANGO (source unlisted)
PROSCRITO DEL RIO COLORADO, EL (SPA, 1965)
DJANGO (SPA, 1966)
DOS MIL DOLARES POR COYOTE (SPA, 1966)
MESTIZO (SPA, 1966)
DJANGO SHOOTS FIRST (SPA, 1966)
DON'T WAIT FOR DJANGO, SHOOT! (GER/ITA, 1967)
DOLLAR A HEAD, A (ITA, 1967)
GOOD, THE BAD AND THE UGLY, THE (UA, 1968)
DJANGO -- EIN SARG VOLL BLUT (GER/ITA, 1967)
POKER D'AS POUR DJANGO (FRA/ITA, 1968)
DJANGO -- DIE GEIER STEHEN SCHLANGE (GER/ITA,
  1969)
STRANGER, THE (ITA, 1973)
STRANGER'S GUNDOWN, THE (ITA, 1974)

DOBERMANS (source unlisted)
DOBERMAN GANG, THE (IND, 1972)
DARING DOBERMANS, THE (IND, 1973)
AMAZING DOBERMANS, THE (IND, 1976)

DR. CHRISTIAN (based on the radio series)
MEET DR. CHRISTIAN (RKO, 1939)
COURAGEOUS DR. CHRISTIAN (RKO, 1940)
DR. CHRISTIAN MEETS THE WOMEN (RKO, 1940)
REMEDY FOR RICHES (RKO, 1940)
MELODY FOR THREE (RKO, 1941)
THEY MEET AGAIN (RKO, 1941)
DR. CHRISTIAN (series) (ABC--TV, 1956)

DR. KILDARE (based on the stories by Max Brand (Frederick
  Faust); also appeared as a radio series)
INTERNES CAN'T TAKE MONEY (PAR, 1937)
YOUNG DR. KILDARE (MGM, 1938)
CALLING DR. KILDARE (MGM, 1939)
SECRET OF DR. KILDARE, THE (MGM, 1939)
DR. KILDARE GOES HOME (MGM, 1940)
DR. KILDARE'S CRISIS (MGM, 1940)
DR. KILDARE'S STRANGEST CASE (MGM, 1940)
DR. KILDARE'S VICTORY (MGM, 1941)
DR. KILDARE'S WEDDING DAY (MGM, 1941)
PEOPLE VS. DR. KILDARE, THE (MGM, 1941)
CALLING DR. GILLESPIE (MGM, 1942)
DR. GILLESPIE'S NEW ASSISTANT (MGM, 1942)
DR. GILLESPIE'S CRIMINAL CASE (MGM, 1943)
THREE MEN IN WHITE (MGM, 1944)
BETWEEN TWO WOMEN (MGM, 1944)
DARK DELUSION (MGM, 1947)
DR. KILDARE (series) (NBC--TV, 1961)

DR. KILDARE (series) (NBC--TV, 1965)
YOUNG DR. KILDARE (series) (TV, 1972)

DR. MABUSE (based on original screenplays)
DR. MABUSE, DER SPIELER (GER, 1922)
INFERNO (GER, 1922)
TESTAMENT OF DR. MABUSE, THE (FRA, 1932)
TESTAMENT OF DR. MABUSE, THE (GER, 1932)
1,000 EYES OF DR. MABUSE, THE (GER, 1960)
INVISIBLE DR. MABUSE, THE (GER, 1960)
TESTAMENT OF DR. MABUSE, THE (GER, 1960)
RETURN OF DR. MABUSE, THE (GER, 1961)
DEATH RAY OF DR. MABUSE, THE (GER, 1962)
LAST WILL OF DR. MABUSE, THE (GER, 1962)
SECRET OF DR. MABUSE, THE (FRA/GER/ITA, 1962)
SCOTLAND YARD VS. DR. MABUSE (GER, 1963)
TERROR OF DR. MABUSE, THE (GER, 1964)
SECRET OF DR. MABUSE, THE (GER, 1964)
DR. MABUSE (GER/SPA, 1971)

DR. ORLOF (source unlisted)
AWFUL DR. ORLOF, THE (FRA/SPA, 1961)
DR. ORLOF'S MONSTER (FRA/SPA, 1964)
DIABOLICAL DR. Z, THE (FRA/SPA, 1965)
SOLO UN ATAUD (FRA/SPA, 1966)
DR. ORLOFF'S SECRET (SPA, 1967)
ORLOF AND THE INVISIBLE MAN (FRA/SPA, 1970)

DR. SIMON SPARROW (based on the book by Richard
  Gordon)
DOCTOR IN THE HOUSE (BRI, 1955)
DOCTOR AT SEA (BRI, 1956)
DOCTOR AT LARGE (BRI, 1957)
DOCTOR IN LOVE (BRI, 1962)
DOCTOR IN DISTRESS (BRI, 1964)
DOCTOR IN CLOVER (BRI, 1966)
CARNABY M. D. (BRI, 1968)
DOCTOR IN TROUBLE (BRI, 1970)
DOCTOR IN THE HOUSE (series) (BRI--TV, 1970)
DOCTOR AT SEA (series) (BRI--TV, 1974)

DR. WHO (based on the teleplay by Terry Nation)
DR. WHO AND THE DALEKS (BRI, 1965)
DALEKS -- INVASION EARTH 2150 A. D. (BRI, 1966)
DR. WHO (series) (BRI--TV, 1970)
DR. WHO (series) (BRI--TV, 1977)

DON CAMILLO (based on the books by Giovanni Guareschi)
LITTLE WORLD OF DON CAMILLO, THE (ITA, 1953)
DON CAMILLO'S LAST ROUND (ITA, 1955)
RETURN OF DON CAMILLO, THE (ITA, 1956)
COMPANION OF DON CAMILLO, THE (ITA, n.d.)
DON CAMILLO, A MAN WHO IS STILL NOT TOO MUCH
  (ITA, n.d.)
DON CAMILLO AND THE HONORABLE PEPPONE (ITA,
  n.d.)
DON CAMILLO IN RUSSIA (ITA, 1968)
DON CAMILLO, PEPPONE AND THE NEW GENERATION
  (ITA, 1970)

DRACULA (based on the book by Bram Stoker and the
  character of Count Dracula)
DRACULA (HUN, 1921)
NOSFERATU (GER, 1922)
DRACULA (UN, 1931)
DRACULA'S DAUGHTER (UN, 1936)
HOUSE OF DRACULA (UN, 1945)
DRACULA IN ISTANBUL (TUR, 1953)
DRACULA (NBC--TV, 1957)

HORROR OF DRACULA (UN, 1958)
BRIDES OF DRACULA (UN, 1960)
KISS OF THE VAMPIRE (UN, 1963)
SECRETS OF DRACULA (PHI, 1964)
DRACULA, PRINCE OF DARKNESS (FOX, 1966)
TASTE OF BLOOD, A (IND, 1967)
BATMAN FIGHTS DRACULA (PHI, 1967)
BLOOD OF DRACULA'S CASTLE (IND, 1967)
EMPIRE OF DRACULA, THE (MEX, 1967)
DRACULA HAS RISEN FROM THE GRAVE (BRI, 1968)
VAMPIRES, THE (MEX, 1968)
GUESS WHAT HAPPENED TO COUNT DRACULA (IND, 1969)
DRACULA (BRI--TV, 1969)
DRACULA'S VAMPIRE LUST (SWI, 1970)
DRACULA HUNTS FRANKENSTEIN (GER/ITA/SPA, 1970)
COUNT DRACULA (BRI/GER/ITA/SPA, 1970)
HERITAGE OF DRACULA, THE (GER, 1970)
COUNTESS DRACULA (BRI, 1970)
SCARS OF DRACULA (BRI, 1970)
LAKE OF DRACULA (JAP, 1971)
THEY'VE CHANGED FACES (ITA, 1971)
DRACULA VS. DR. FRANKENSTEIN (FRA/SPA, 1971)
BLACULA (AI, 1972)
DRACULA IM SCHLOSS DES SCHRECKENS (FRA/GER/ITA, 1972)
DRACULA A.D. 1972 (DRACULA TODAY) (BRI, 1972)
DRACULA'S GREAT LOVE (SPA, 1972)
DRACULA VS. FRANKENSTEIN (SPA, 1972)
SAGA OF DRACULA (SPA, 1972)
VAMPIRA (BRI, 1973)
DRACULA (CAN--TV, 1973)
DRACULA (CBS--TV, 1973)
DRACULA (IND, 1973)
SATANIC RITES OF DRACULA, THE (WB, 1973)
ANDY WARHOL'S DRACULA (WAR, 1973)
BLOOD (IND, 1974)
OLD DRACULA (BRI, 1974)
EVIL OF DRACULA (JAP, 1975)
DRACULA (short) (IND, 1976)
DRACULA, FATHER AND SON (FRA, 1976)
COUNT DRACULA (BRI--TV, 1977)
DRACULA'S DOG (CRO, 1978)

DRAGNET (based on an idea by Jack Webb)
DRAGNET (series) (NBC–TV, 1952)
DRAGNET (WB, 1954)
DRAGNET (series) (NBC–TV, 1967)

DURANGO KID, THE (based on original screenplays)
LAW OF THE PLAINS (COL, 1938)
CALL OF THE ROCKIES (COL, 1938)
CATTLE RAIDERS (COL)
WEST OF CHEYENNE (COL, 1938)
COLORADO TRAIL (COL, 1938)
SOUTH OF ARIZONA (COL, 1938)
OUTLAWS OF THE PRAIRIE (COL, 1938)
WEST OF SANTA FE (COL, 1939)
SPOILERS OF THE RANGE (COL, 1939)
WESTERN CARAVANS (COL, 1939)
MAN FROM SUNDOWN, THE (COL, 1939)
RIDERS OF BLACK RIVER (COL, 1939)
OUTPOST OF THE MOUNTIES (COL, 1939)
STRANGER FROM TEXAS (COL, 1939)
BULLETS FOR RUSTLERS (COL, 1940)
BLAZING SIX--SHOOTERS (COL, 1940)
TWO--FISTED RANGERS (COL, 1940)
TEXAS STAGECOACH (COL, 1940)

WEST OF ABILENE (COL, 1940)
DURANGO KID, THE (COL, 1940)
THUNDERING FRONTIER (COL, 1940)
OUTLAWS OF THE PANHANDLE (COL, 1941)
PINTO KID, THE (COL, 1941)
MEDICO OF PAINTED SPRINGS, THE (COL, 1941)
THUNDER OVER THE PRAIRIE (COL, 1941)
PRAIRIE STRANGER (COL, 1941)
WEST OF TOMBSTONE (COL, 1942)
LAWLESS PLAINSMEN (COL, 1942)
DOWN RIO GRANDE WAY (COL, 1942)
RIDERS OF THE NORTHLAND (COL, 1942)
BAD MEN OF THE HILLS (COL, 1942)
OVERLAND TO DEADWOOD (COL, 1942)
RIDING THROUGH NEVADA (COL, 1943)
FIGHTING BUCKAROO (COL, 1943)
HEROES OF THE SAGEBRUSH (COL, 1943)
TEXAS RIFLES (COL, 1943)
COWBOY IN THE CLOUDS (COL, 1943)
PARDON MY GUN (COL, 1943)
LAW OF THE NORTHWEST (COL, 1943)
ROBIN HOOD OF THE RANGE (COL, 1943)
HAIL TO THE RANGERS! (COL, 1943)
SUNDOWN VALLEY (COL, 1944)
COWBOY CANTEEN (COL, 1944)
RIDING WEST (COL, 1944)
SAGEBRUSH HEROES (COL, 1944)
CYCLONE PRAIRIE RANGERS (COL, 1944)
COWBOY FROM LONESOME RIVER (COL, 1944)
SADDLE LEATHER LAW (COL, 1944)
BLAZING THE WESTERN TRAIL (COL, 1945)
BOTH BARRELS BLAZING (COL, 1945)
LAWLESS EMPIRE (COL, 1945)
OUTLAWS OF THE ROCKIES (COL, 1945)
RETURN OF THE DURANGO KID (COL, 1945)
ROUGH RIDIN' JUSTICE (COL, 1945)
RUSTLERS OF THE BADLANDS (COL, 1945)
DESERT HORSEMAN, THE (COL, 1946)
FIGHTING FRONTIERSMAN (COL, 1946)
FRONTIER GUN LAW (COL, 1946)
GALLOPING THUNDER (COL, 1946)
GUNNING FOR VENGEANCE (COL, 1946)
LAND RUSH (COL, 1946)
ROARING RANGERS (COL, 1946)
TWO--FISTED STRANGER (COL, 1946)
HEADING WEST (COL, 1946)
TEXAS PANHANDLE (COL, 1946)
LONE HAND TEXAN (COL, 1947)
TERROR TRAIL (COL, 1947)
WEST OF DODGE CITY (COL, 1947)
LAW OF THE CANYON (COL, 1947)
PRAIRIE RAIDERS (COL, 1947)
SOUTH OF THE CHISHOLM TRAIL (COL, 1947)
RIDERS OF THE LONE STAR (COL, 1947)
STRANGER FROM PONCA CITY, THE (COL, 1947)
BUCKAROOS FROM POWDER RIVER (COL, 1948)
LAST DAYS OF BOOT HILL (COL, 1948)
PHANTOM VALLEY (COL, 1948)
SIX--GUN LAW (COL, 1948)
WEST OF SONORA (COL, 1948)
WHIRLWIND RAIDERS (COL, 1948)
TRAIL TO LAREDO (COL, 1948)
BLAZING ACROSS THE PECOS (COL, 1948)
BLAZING TRAIL (COL, 1949)
CHALLENGE OF THE RANGE (COL, 1949)
DESERT VIGILANTE (COL, 1949)
EL DORADO PASS (COL, 1949)
HORSEMEN OF THE SIERRAS (COL, 1949)
LARAMIE (COL, 1949)

SOUTH OF DEATH VALLEY (COL, 1949)
OUTCAST OF BLACK MESA (COL, 1950)
TEXAS DYNAMO (COL, 1950)
TRAIL OF THE RUSTLER (COL, 1950)
STREETS OF GHOST TOWN (COL, 1950)
ACROSS THE BADLANDS (COL, 1950)
RAIDERS OF TOMAHAWK (COL, 1950)
LIGHTNING GUNS (COL, 1950)
RIDING THE OUTLAW TRAIL (COL, 1951)
PRAIRIE ROUNDUP (COL, 1951)
SNAKE RIVER DESPERADOES (COL, 1951)
FORT SAVAGE RAIDERS (COL, 1951)
BONANZA TOWN (COL, 1951)
CYCLONE FURY (COL, 1951)
KID FROM AMARILLO, THE (COL, 1951)
PECOS RIVER (COL, 1951)
SMOKY CANYON (COL, 1952)
HAWK OF WILD RIVER, THE (COL, 1952)
KID FROM BROKEN GUN, THE (COL, 1952)
ROUGH TOUGH WEST, THE (COL, 1952)
JUNCTION CITY (COL, 1952)
LARAMIE MOUNTAINS (COL, 1952)

EDGAR (based on stories by an unknown author)
EDGAR AND THE TEACHER'S PET (short) (IND, 1920)
EDGAR'S HAMLET (short) (IND, 1920)
EDGAR'S LITTLE SAW (short) (IND, 1920)
EDGAR CAMPS OUT (short) (IND, 1921)
GET RICH QUICK EDGAR (short) (IND, 1921)

ELLERY QUEEN (based on stories and books by Ellery
    Queen; also appeared as a radio series)
SPANISH CAPE MYSTERY, THE (REP, 1935)
MANDARIN MYSTERY, THE (REP, 1936)
CRIME NOBODY SAW, THE (PAR, 1937)
ELLERY QUEEN, MASTER DETECTIVE (COL, 1940)
ELLERY QUEEN'S PENTHOUSE MYSTERY (COL, 1941)
ELLERY QUEEN AND THE PERFECT CRIME (COL,
    1941)
ELLERY QUEEN AND THE MURDER RING (COL, 1941)
CLOSE CALL FOR ELLERY QUEEN, A (COL, 1942)
DESPERATE CHANCE FOR ELLERY QUEEN, A (COL,
    1942)
ENEMY AGENTS MEET ELLERY QUEEN (COL, 1942)
MYSTERY IS MY BUSINESS (ADVENTURES OF ELLERY
    QUEEN) (series) (TV, 1954)
FURTHER ADVENTURES OF ELLERY QUEEN, THE
    (series) (NBC--TV, 1958)
10 DAYS' WONDER (FRA, 1971)
ELLERY QUEEN: DON'T LOOK BEHIND YOU (NBC--
    TV, 1971)
ELLERY QUEEN (series) (NBC--TV, 1975)

EMMANUELLE (based on the book by Emmanuelle Arsan)
EMMANUELLE, THE JOYS OF A WOMAN (FRA, 1976)
EMMANUELLE II (FRA, 1977)
GOODBYE EMMANUELLE (FRA, 1978)

ERZABETH BATHORY (based on the legend of Countess
    Erzabeth Bathory, a "female Dracula")
VAMPIRES, THE (ITA, 1956)
COUNTESS DRACULA (BRI, 1970)
NECROPOLIS (sequence) (ITA, 1970)
WALPURGIS NIGHT (GER/SPA, 1970)
FEMALE BUTCHER (ITA/SPA, 1972)
BLOOD CEREMONY (IND, 1973)
BLOODY COUNTESS, THE (GER, 1973)
DEVIL'S WEDDING, THE (BRI, 1973)
RETURN TO WALPURGIS, THE (SPA, 1973)

IMMORTAL TALES (FRA, 1974)

F.P.L. (based on the book by Kurt Siodmak)
F. P. L ANTWORTET NICHT (GER, 1932)
SECRETS OF F. P. L (BRI, 1933)
I. F. 1 NE REPOND PLUS (FRA, 1933)

FALCON, THE (based on characters and stories created by
    Michael Arlen)
GAY FALCON, THE (RKO, 1941)
DATE WITH THE FALCON, A (RKO, 1941)
FALCON TAKES OVER, THE (RKO, 1942)
FALCON'S BROTHER, THE (RKO, 1942)
FALCON STRIKES BACK, THE (RKO, 1943)
FALCON AND THE COEDS, THE (RKO, 1943)
FALCON IN DANGER, THE (RKO, 1943)
FALCON IN HOLLYWOOD, THE (RKO, 1944)
FALCON IN MEXICO, THE (RKO, 1944)
FALCON OUT WEST, THE (RKO, 1944)
NIGHT OF ADVENTURE, A (RKO, 1944)
FALCON IN SAN FRANCISCO, THE (RKO, 1945)
TWO O'CLOCK COURAGE (RKO, 1945)
FALCON'S ADVENTURE, THE (RKO, 1946)
FALCON'S ALIBI, THE (RKO, 1946)
DEVIL'S CARGO (FC, 1948)
APPOINTMENT WITH MURDER (FC, 1948)
SEARCH FOR DANGER (FC, 1949)
ADVENTURES OF THE FALCON (series) (TV, 1954)

FATHER OF THE BRIDE (based on the book by Edward
    Streeter)
FATHER OF THE BRIDE (MGM, 1950)
FATHER'S LITTLE DIVIDEND (MGM, 1951)
FATHER OF THE BRIDE (series) (CBS--TV, 1961)

FEDERAL AGENT (based on original screenplays)
YELLOW CARGO (GN, 1936)
NAVY SPY (GN, 1937)
GOLD RACKET (GN, 1937)
BANK ALARM (GN, 1937)

FIBBER Mc GEE AND MOLLY (based on the radio series by
    Don Quinn)
THIS WAY PLEASE (PAR, 1938)
LOOK WHO'S LAUGHING (RKO, 1941)
HERE WE GO AGAIN (RKO, 1942)
HEAVENLY DAYS (RKO, 1944)
FIBBER Mc GEE AND MOLLY (series) (NBC--TV, 1959)

FIVE GENTS (source unlisted)
FIVE GENTS' TRICK BOOK (JAP, 1965)
FIVE GENTS AT SUNRISE (JAP, 1966)
FIVE GENTS ON THE SPIT (JAP, 1966)
FIVE GENTS PREFER GEISHA (JAP, 1967)
FIVE GENTS AND A CHINESE MERCHANT (JAP, 1968)
FIVE GENTS AND KARATE GRANDPA (JAP, 1968)

FIVE LITTLE PEPPERS (based on the book by Margaret
    Sidney)
FIVE LITTLE PEPPERS AND HOW THEY GREW (COL,
    1939)
OUT WEST WITH THE PEPPERS (COL, 1940)
FIVE LITTLE PEPPERS AT HOME (COL, 1940)
FIVE LITTLE PEPPERS IN TROUBLE (COL, 1940)

FLAGG AND QUIRT (based on the play by Laurence Stallings
    and Maxwell Anderson; also appeared as a radio series)
WHAT PRICE GLORY? (FOX, 1926)
COCKEYED WORLD (FOX, 1929)

WOMEN OF ALL NATIONS   (FOX, 1931)
HOT PEPPER   (FOX, 1933)
WHAT PRICE GLORY?   (FOX, 1952)

FLASH GORDON   (based on the comic strip by Alex Raymond)
FLASH GORDON   (serial)   (UN, 1936)
FLASH GORDON'S TRIP TO MARS   (serial)   (UN, 1938)
FLASH GORDON CONQUERS THE UNIVERSE   (serial)
   (UN, 1940)
FLASH GORDON   (series)   (TV, 1951)
FLASH GORDON'S BATTLE IN SPACE   (TUR, 1967)

FLICKA   (based on the book by Mary O'Hara)
MY FRIEND FLICKA   (FOX, 1943)
THUNDERHEAD, SON OF FLICKA   (FOX, 1945)
MY FRIEND FLICKA   (series)   (CBS--TV, 1956)

FLY, THE   (based on the story by George Langelaan)
FLY, THE   (FOX, 1958)
RETURN OF THE FLY   (FOX, 1959)
CURSE OF THE FLY, THE   (FOX, 1965)

FLINTSTONES, THE   (developed by the Hanna--Barbera
   creative staff)
FLINTSTONES, THE   (series)   (TV, 1960)
MAN CALLED FLINTSTONE, A   (COL, 1966)
PEBBLES AND BAM BAM   (series)   (TV, 1971)
FLINTSTONES COMEDY SHOW, THE   (series)   (TV, 1972)

FLIPPER   (based on a story by Ricou Browning and Jack
   Cowden)
FLIPPER   (MGM, 1963)
FLIPPER   (series)   (NBC--TV, 1964)
FLIPPER'S NEW ADVENTURE   (MGM, 1964)

FORAN/CARILLO   (based on original screenplays)
HORROR ISLAND   (UN, 1941)
KID FROM KANSAS, THE   (UN, 1941)
ROAD AGENT   (UN, 1941)
UNSEEN ENEMY   (UN, 1942)

FOUR ARTILLERYMEN   (source unlisted)
FOUR ARTILLERYMEN AND A DOG I   (POL, 1968)
FOUR ARTILLERYMEN AND A DOG II   (POL, 1968)
FOUR ARTILLERYMEN AND A DOG III   (POL, 1968)
FOUR ARTILLERYMEN AND A DOG IV   (POL, 1968)

FOUR DAUGHTERS   (based on a story by Fannie Hurst)
FOUR DAUGHTERS   (WB, 1938)
DAUGHTERS COURAGEOUS   (WB, 1939)
FOUR WIVES   (WB, 1939)
FOUR MOTHERS   (WB, 1941)

FRANCIS, THE TALKING MULE   (based on the novel by
   David Stern)
FRANCIS   (UN, 1949)
FRANCIS GOES TO THE RACES   (UN, 1951)
FRANCIS GOES TO WEST POINT   (UN, 1952)
FRANCIS COVERS THE BIG TOWN   (UN, 1953)
FRANCIS JOINS THE WACS   (UN, 1954)
FRANCIS IN THE NAVY   (UN, 1955)
FRANCIS IN THE HAUNTED HOUSE   (UN, 1956)

FRANKENSTEIN   (based on the novel by Mary Shelley and
   the character of the Frankenstein monster)
LIFE WITHOUT SOUL   (IND, 1915)
MONSTER OF FRANKENSTEIN   (ITA, 1920)
FRANKENSTEIN   (UN, 1931)
BRIDE OF FRANKENSTEIN   (UN, 1935)

SON OF FRANKENSTEIN   (UN, 1939)
GHOST OF FRANKENSTEIN   (UN, 1942)
FRANKENSTEIN MEETS THE WOLF MAN   (UN, 1943)
HOUSE OF FRANKENSTEIN   (UN, 1944)
ABBOTT & COSTELLO MEET FRANKENSTEIN   (UN,
   1947)
I WAS A TEENAGE FRANKENSTEIN   (AI, 1957)
CURSE OF FRANKENSTEIN   (BRI, 1957)
REVENGE OF FRANKENSTEIN   (BRI, 1958)
FRANKENSTEIN 1970   (AA, 1958)
FRANKENSTEIN'S DAUGHTER   (IND, 1958)
FRANKENSTEIN, THE VAMPIRE & CO.   (MEX, 1961)
TESTAMENT OF FRANKENSTEIN, THE   (FRA/SPA,
   1964)
EVIL OF FRANKENSTEIN, THE   (BRI, 1964)
FRANKENSTEIN MEETS THE SPACE MONSTER   (AA,
   1966)
FRANKENSTEIN CONQUERS THE WORLD   (JAP, 1966)
FRANKENSTEIN CREATED WOMAN   (BRI, 1968)
FRANKENSTEIN MUST BE DESTROYED   (BRI, 1969)
HORROR OF FRANKENSTEIN, THE   (BRI, 1970)
DRACULA HUNTS FRANKENSTEIN   (GER/ITA/SPA,
   1970)
DRACULA VS. FRANKENSTEIN   (GER/ITA/SPA, 1971)
PASTEL DE SANGRE   (SPA, 1971)
FRANKENSTEIN'S BLOODY TERROR   (SPA, 1972)
FRANKENSTEIN AND THE MONSTER FROM HELL
   (BRI, 1972)
YOUNG FRANKENSTEIN   (FOX, 1974)
FRANKENSTEIN -- ITALIAN STYLE   (ITA, 1977)

THE FRED CHRONICLES   (based on screenplays by Curtis
   Imrie)
YOUNG AMERICAN DREAM   (IND, n.d.)
JACKASSES ON THE RUN   (IND, n.d.)
OUTLAW IN THE CHURCH   (IND, n.d.)
ONE ON ONE   (IND, n.d.)
U.S. 50   (IND, n.d.)

FU MANCHU   (based on the books and characters by Sax
   Rohmer)
CRY OF THE NIGHT HAWK   (BRI, 1923)
FIERY HAND, THE   (BRI, 1923)
MAN WITH THE LAMP, THE   (BRI, 1923)
CALL OF SIVA   (BRI, 1923)
FUNGI CELLARS, THE   (BRI, 1923)
MYSTERY OF DR. FU MANCHU, THE   (serial)   (BRI,
   1923)
MIRACLE, THE   (BRI, 1923)
QUEEN OF HEARTS   (BRI, 1923)
SACRED ORDER, THE   (BRI, 1923)
SCENTED ENVELOPE, THE   (BRI, 1923)
SHRINE OF THE SEVEN LAMPS, THE   (BRI, 1923)
SILVER BUDDHA   (BRI, 1923)
COUGHING HORROR   (BRI, 1924)
MIDNIGHT SUMMONS   (BRI, 1924)
GREEN MIST, THE   (BRI, 1924)
CAFE L'EGYPTE, THE   (BRI, 1924)
KARAMANEH   (BRI, 1924)
GREYWATER PARK   (BRI, 1924)
FURTHER MYSTERIES OF DR. FU MANCHU   (serial)
   (BRI, 1924)
CRAGMIRE TOWER   (BRI, 1924)
GOLDEN POMEGRANATES, THE   (BRI, 1924)
MYSTERIOUS DR. FU MANCHU (INSIDIOUS DR. FU
   MANCHU, THE)   (PAR, 1929)
PARAMOUNT ON PARADE   (sequence)   (PAR, 1930)
RETURN O FU MANCHU   (PAR, 1931)
DAUGHTER OF THE DRAGON   (PAR, 1931)
MASK OF FU MANCHU, THE   (MGM, 1931)

DRUMS OF FU MANCHU (serial) (REP, 1940)
ADVENTURES OF FU MANCHU, THE (series) (TV, 1956)
FACE OF FU MANCHU, THE (BRI, 1965)
BRIDES OF FU MANCHU, THE (BRI, 1966)
VENGEANCE OF FU MANCHU, THE (BRI, 1967)
CASTLE OF FU MANCHU (BRI, 1968)
KISS AND KILL (FU MANCHU AND THE KISS OF DEATH) (BRI, 1968)
AGAINST ALL ODDS (BRI, 1970)

GALLEGHER (based on the book by Richard Harding Davis)
GALLEGHER (DIS, 1965)
FURTHER ADVENTURES OF GALLEGHER (DIS, 1965)
GALLEGHER GOES WEST (DIS, 1966)

GAMBINI FAMILY (based on original screenplays)
SPEED TO BURN (FOX, 1938)
ROAD DEMON (FOX, 1938)
WINNER TAKE ALL (FOX, 1939)

GAS HOUSE KIDS (based on an original screenplay)
GAS HOUSE KIDS, THE (PRC, 1946)
GAS HOUSE KIDS GO WEST, THE (PRC, 1947)
GAS HOUSE KIDS IN HOLLYWOOD, THE (EL, 1947)

GENE AUTRY (based on original screenplays)
IN OLD SANTA FE (MAS, 1934)
MYSTERY MOUNTAIN (MAS, 1934)
PHANTOM EMPIRE, THE (MAS, 1935)
TUMBLING TUMBLEWEEDS (REP, 1935)
SAGEBRUSH TROUBADOR (REP, 1935)
MELODY TRAIL (REP, 1935)
SINGING VAGABOND (REP, 1936)
RED RIVER VALLEY (REP, 1936) (TV title: MAN OF THE FRONTIER)
COMIN' 'ROUND THE MOUNTAIN (REP, 1936)
SINGING COWBOY, THE (REP, 1936)
GUNS AND GUITARS (REP, 1936)
OH, SUSANNAH! (REP, 1936)
RIDE, RANGER, RIDE (REP, 1936)
BIG SHOW, THE (REP, 1936)
OLD CORRAL, THE (REP, 1936)
ROUND–UP TIME IN TEXAS (REP, 1937)
GIT ALONG, LITTLE DOGIES (REP, 1937)
ROOTIN' TOOTIN' RHYTHM (REP, 1937)
YODELIN' KID FROM PINE RIDGE (REP, 1937)
PUBLIC COWBOY NUMBER 1 (REP, 1937)
BOOTS AND SADDLES (REP, 1937)
MANHATTAN MERRY–GO–ROUND (REP, 1937)
SPRINGTIME IN THE ROCKIES (REP, 1937)
OLD BARN DANCE, THE (REP, 1938)
GOLD MINE IN THE SKY (REP, 1938)
MAN FROM MUSIC MOUNTAIN (REP, 1938)
PRAIRIE MOON (REP, 1938)
RHYTHM OF THE SADDLE (REP, 1938)
WESTERN JAMBOREE (REP, 1938)
HOME ON THE PRAIRIE (REP, 1939)
MEXICALI ROSE (REP, 1939)
BLUE MONTANA SKIES (REP, 1939)
MOUNTAIN RHYTHM (REP, 1939)
COLORADO SUNSET (REP, 1939)
IN OLD MONTEREY (REP, 1939)
ROVIN' TUMBLEWEEDS (REP, 1939)
SOUTH OF THE BORDER (REP, 1939)
RANCHO GRANDE (REP, 1940)
SHOOTING HIGH (FOX, 1940)
GAUCHO SERENADE (REP, 1940)
CAROLINA MOON (REP, 1940)

RIDE, TENDERFOOT, RIDE (REP, 1940)
MELODY RANCH (REP, 1940)
RIDIN' ON A RAINBOW (REP, 1941)
BACK IN THE SADDLE (REP, 1941)
SINGING HILLS, THE (REP, 1941)
SUNSET IN WYOMING (REP, 1941)
UNDER FIESTA STARS (REP, 1941)
DOWN MEXICO WAY (REP, 1941)
SIERRA SUE (REP, 1941)
COWBOY SERENADE (REP, 1942)
HEART OF THE RIO GRANDE (REP, 1942)
HOME IN WYOMIN' (REP, 1942)
STARDUST ON THE SAGE (REP, 1942)
CALL OF THE CANYON (REP, 1942)
BELLS OF CAPISTRANO (REP, 1942)
SIOUX CITY SUE (REP, 1946)
TRAIL TO SAN ANTONE (REP, 1947)
TWILIGHT ON THE RIO GRANDE (REP, 1947)
SADDLE PALS (REP, 1947)
ROBIN HOOD OF TEXAS (REP, 1947)
LAST ROUND--UP, THE (COL, 1947)
STRAWBERRY ROAN (COL, 1948)
LOADED PISTOLS (COL, 1949)
BIG SOMBRERO, THE (COL, 1949)
RIDERS OF THE WHISTLING PINES (COL, 1949)
RIM OF THE CANYON (COL, 1949)
COWBOY AND THE INDIANS, THE (COL, 1949)
RIDERS IN THE SKY (COL, 1949)
SONS OF NEW MEXICO (COL, 1950)
MULE TRAIN (COL, 1950)
COW TOWN (COL, 1950)
BEYOND THE PURPLE HILLS (COL, 1950)
INDIAN TERRITORY (COL, 1950)
BLAZING HILLS, THE (COL, 1950)
GENE AUTRY AND THE MOUNTIES (COL, 1951)
TEXANS NEVER CRY (COL, 1951)
WHIRLWIND, THE (COL, 1951)
SILVER CANYON (COL, 1951)
HILLS OF UTAH (COL, 1951)
GENE AUTRY SHOW, THE (series) (TV, 1951)
VALLEY OF FIRE (COL, 1951)
OLD WEST, THE (COL, 1952)
NIGHT STAGE TO GALVESTON (COL, 1952)
APACHE COUNTRY (COL, 1952)
BARBED WIRE (COL, 1952)
WAGON TEAM (COL, 1952)
BLUE CANADIAN ROCKIES (COL, 1952)
WINNING OF THE WEST (COL, 1953)
ON TOP OF OLD SMOKY (COL, 1953)
GOLDTOWN GHOST RIDERS (COL, 1953)
PACK TRAIN (COL, 1953)
SAGINAW TRAIL (COL, 1953)
LAST OF THE PONY RIDERS (COL, 1953)

GERALD McBOING BOING (shorts) (based on an idea by Stephen Bosustow)
GERALD McBOING BOING (COL, 1950)
GERALD McBOING BOING'S SYMPHONY (COL, 1952)
HOW NOW BOING BOING (COL, 1954)
GERALD McBOING BOING ON THE PLANET MOO (COL, 1955)

GIDGET (based on characters created by Frederick Kohner)
GIDGET (COL, 1959)
GIDGET GOES HAWAIIAN (COL, 1961)
GIDGET GOES TO ROME (COL, 1963)
GIDGET (series) (ABC--TV, 1965)
GIDGET GROWS UP (ABC--TV, 1969)
GIDGET GETS MARRIED (ABC--TV, 1972)

GILBERT/HOWARD/ROSENBLOOM (based on original
    screenplays)
  3 OF A KIND (MON, 1944)
  CRAZY KNIGHTS (MON, 1944)
  TROUBLE CHASERS (MON, 1945)

GINGER (based on original screenplays)
  GINGER (IND, 1971)
  ABDUCTORS, THE (IND, 1972)
  GIRLS ARE FOR LOVING (IND, 1973)

GODZILLA (based on original screenplays)
  GODZILLA (JAP, 1954)
  GODZILLA'S COUNTERATTACK (JAP, 1955)
  KING KONG VS. GODZILLA (JAP, 1962)
  SON OF GODZILLA (short) (BRI, 1963)
  GODZILLA VS. THE SEA MONSTER (JAP, 1966)
  EBIRAH, HORROR OF THE DEEP (JAP, 1966)
  SON OF GODZILLA (JAP, 1967)
  GODZILLA'S REVENGE (JAP, 1971)
  GODZILLA VS. THE SMOG MONSTER (GODZILLA VS.
    HEDORA) (JAP, 1972)
  GODZILLA VS. GIGAN (JAP, 1973)
  GODZILLA VS. MECHAGODZILLA (JAP, 1975)
  GODZILLA VS. MEGALON (JAP, 1976)
  GODZILLA ON MONSTER ISLAND (JAP, 1978)

GOLD DIGGERS (based on the play by Avery Hopwood)
  GOLD DIGGERS, THE (WB, 1923)
  GOLD DIGGERS OF BROADWAY (WB, 1929)
  GOLD DIGGERS OF 1933 (WB, 1933)
  GOLD DIGGERS OF 1935 (WB, 1935)
  GOLD DIGGERS OF 1937 (WB, 1936)
  GOLD DIGGERS IN PARIS (WB, 1938)

GOLIATH (based on original screenplays)
  GOLIATH AND THE BARBARIANS (ITA, 1960)
  GOLIATH AND THE DRAGON (ITA, 1960)
  GOLIATH AGAINST THE GIANTS (ITA, 1962)
  GOLIATH, THE REBEL SLAVE (ITA, 1963)
  GOLIATH AT THE CONQUEST OF DAMASCUS (ITA,
    1964)

GORILLA, THE (based on books by Antoine Dominque)
  GORILLE VOUS SALUE BIEN, LE (FRA, 1958)
  VALSE DU GORILLE, LA (FRA, 1959)
  GORILLE A MORDU L'ARCHEVEQUE, LE (FRA, 1962)

GORKY TRILOGY, THE (based on books by Maxim Gorky)
  YOUTH OF MAXIM (CHILDHOOD OF MAXIM GORKY,
    THE) (RUS, 1938)
  RETURN OF MAXIM, THE (OUT IN THE WORLD OR,
    MY APPRENTICESHIP) (RUS, 1939)
  MAXIM IN VYBORG (UNIVERSITY OF LIFE OR, MY
    UNIVERSITIES (RUS, 1940)

GREAT GILDERSLEEVE, THE (based on a radio series
    which was a spinoff from the "Fibber McGee and Molly"
    series)
  GREAT GILDERSLEEVE, THE (RKO, 1942)
  GILDERSLEEVE'S BAD DAY (RKO, 1943)
  GILDERSLEEVE ON BROADWAY (RKO, 1943)
  GILDERSLEEVE'S GHOST (RKO, 1944)
  GREAT GILDERSLEEVE, THE (series) (TV, 1955)

GREEN HORNET (based on a screenplay by various authors)
  GREEN HORNET, THE (serial) (UN, 1940)
  GREEN HORNET STRIKES AGAIN (serial) (UN, 1940)
  GREEN HORNET, THE (series) (ABC--TV, 1966)

HARDY FAMILY, THE (based on characters created by
    Aurania Rouverol from her play)
  FAMILY AFFAIR, A (MGM, 1937)
  YOU'RE ONLY YOUNG ONCE (MGM, 1938)
  OUT WEST WITH THE HARDYS (MGM, 1938)
  JUDGE HARDY'S CHILDREN (MGM, 1938)
  LOVE FINDS ANDY HARDY (MGM, 1938)
  HARDYS RIDE HIGH, THE (MGM, 1939)
  JUDGE HARDY AND SON (MGM, 1939)
  ANDY HARDY GETS SPRING FEVER (MGM, 1939)
  ANDY HARDY MEETS A DEBUTANTE (MGM, 1940)
  LIFE BEGINS FOR ANDY HARDY (MGM, 1941)
  ANDY HARDY'S PRIVATE SECRETARY (MGM, 1941)
  COURTSHIP OF ANDY HARDY, THE (MGM, 1942)
  ANDY HARDY'S DOUBLE LIFE (MGM, 1942)
  ANDY HARDY'S BLONDE TROUBLE (MGM, 1944)
  LOVE LAUGHS AT ANDY HARDY (MGM, 1946)
  ANDY HARDY COMES HOME (MGM, 1958)

HARRY PALMER (based on books by Len Deighton)
  IPCRESS FILE, THE (UN, 1965)
  FUNERAL IN BERLIN (PAR, 1966)
  BILLION DOLLAR BRAIN (UA, 1967)

HELGA (source unlisted)
  HELGA (GER, 1968)
  MICHAEL AND HELGA (GER, 1969)
  HELGA AND THE SEXUAL REVOLUTION (GER, 1969)

HENRY (based on a story by D.D. Beauchamp)
  HENRY THE RAINMAKER (MON, 1949)
  LEAVE IT TO HENRY (MON, 1949)
  FATHER MAKES GOOD (MON, 1950)
  FATHER'S WILD GAME (MON, 1951)
  FATHER TAKES THE AIR (MON, 1951)

HENRY ALDRICH (based on the play by Clifford Goldsmith;
    also appeared as a radio series after debuting on "The Kate
    Smith Show")
  WHAT A LIFE (PAR, 1939)
  LIFE WITH HENRY (PAR, 1941)
  HENRY ALDRICH FOR PRESIDENT (PAR, 1941)
  HENRY AND DIZZY (PAR, 1942)
  HENRY ALDRICH, EDITOR (PAR, 1942)
  ALDRICH FAMILY GETS IN THE SCRAP, THE (short)
    (PAR, 1943)
  HENRY ALDRICH GETS GLAMOUR (PAR, 1943)
  HENRY ALDRICH HAUNTS A HOUSE (PAR, 1943)
  HENRY ALDRICH SWINGS IT (PAR, 1943)
  HENRY ALDRICH, BOY SCOUT (PAR, 1944)
  HENRY ALDRICH PLAYS CUPID (PAR, 1944)
  HENRY ALDRICH'S LITTLE SECRET (PAR, 1944)

HERCULE POIROT (based on books by Agatha Christie; also
    appeared as a radio series)
  ALIBI (BRI, 1931)
  BLACK COFFEE (BRI, 1931)
  LORD EDGEWARE DIES (BRI, 1934)
  HERCULE POIROT (CBS--TV, 1962)
  ALPHABET MURDERS, THE (MGM, 1966)
  MURDER ON THE ORIENT EXPRESS (EMB, 1974)
  MURDER ON THE NILE (BRI, 1978)

HERCULES (based on the Hercules legend)
  HERCULES AND THE BIG STICK (FRA, 1910)
  HERCULES (ITA, 1959)
  HERCULES UNCHAINED (ITA, 1959)
  HERCULES AND THE TREASURE OF THE INCAS (ITA,
    1960)

HERCULES AND THE BLACK PIRATES (ITA, 1960)
HERCULES AGAINST THE MASKED RIDER (ITA, 1960)
HERCULES AGAINST THE MONGOLS (ITA, 1960)
HERCULES CONQUERS ATLANTIS (ITA, 1961)
HERCULES IN THE CENTER OF THE EARTH (ITA, 1961)
HERCULES IN THE HAUNTED WORLD (ITA, 1961)
HERCULES IN THE VALE OF WOE (ITA, 1962)
HERCULES VS. ULYSSES (ITA, 1962)
FURY OF HERCULES (ITA, 1962)
HERCULES THE INVINCIBLE (ITA, 1963)
HERCULES AGAINST THE SONS OF THE SUN (ITA, 1963)
HERO OF BABYLON (ITA, 1963)
CONQUEST OF MYCENE (ITA, 1963)
HERCULES AGAINST ROME (ITA, 1964)
HERCULES, PRISONER OF EVIL (ITA, 1964)
HERCULES AGAINST THE BARBARIANS (ITA, 1964)
HERCULES IN THE DESERT (ITA, 1964)
HERCULES AND THE TEN AVENGERS (ITA, 1964)
HERCULES AND THE TYRANTS OF BABYLON (ITA, 1964)
LOVES OF HERCULES, THE (ITA, 1964)
TRIUMPH OF HERCULES (ITA, 1964)
HERCULES AGAINST THE MOON MEN (ITA, 1964)
HERCULES, SAMSON AND ULYSSES (ITA, 1965)
HERCULES IN NEW YORK (ITA, 1965)
HERCULES AND THE PRINCESS OF TROY (ABC–TV, 1965)

HERCULES, SONS OF (based on the legend)
ULYSSES AGAINST THE SON OF HERCULES (ITA, 1961)
SON OF HERCULES IN THE LAND OF FIRE (ITA, 1962)
TRIUMPH OF THE SONS OF HERCULES (ITA, 1963)
MOLE MEN AGAINST THE SONS OF HERCULES (ITA, 1963)
TERROR OF ROME AGAINST THE SONS OF HERCULES (ITA, 1963)
TYRANT OF LYDIA AGAINST THE SONS OF HERCULES (ITA, 1963)
MESALINA AGAINST THE SONS OF HERCULES (ITA, 1963)
SON OF HERCULES IN THE LAND OF DARKNESS (ITA, 1963)
MEDUSA AGAINST THE SON OF HERCULES (ITA, 1963)
DEVIL OF THE DESERT AGAINST THE SONS OF HERCULES (ITA, 1964)

HIGGINS FAMILY, THE (based on a story by Richard English)
HIGGINS FAMILY, THE (REP, 1938)
SHOULD HUSBANDS WORK? (REP, 1939)
EARL OF PUDDLESTONE (REP, 1940)
MEET THE MISSUS (REP, 1940)
GRANDPA GOES TO TOWN (REP, 1940)
PETTICOAT POLITICS (REP, 1941)

HIGH–SCHOOLERS, THE (based on a screenplay by Arthur Dreifuss and Hal Collins)
HIGH SCHOOL HERO (MON, 1946)
JUNIOR PROM (MON, 1946)
SARGE GOES TO COLLEGE (MON, 1947)
VACATION DAYS (MON, 1947)
CAMPUS SLEUTHS (MON, 1948)
SMART POLITICS (MON, 1948)

HILDEGARDE WITHERS (based on stories by Stuart Palmer)
PENGUIN POOL MURDER, THE (RKO, 1932)

MURDER ON THE BLACKBOARD (RKO, 1933)
MURDER ON A HONEYMOON (RKO, 1935)
MURDER ON A BRIDLE PATH (RKO, 1936)
PLOT THICKENS, THE (RKO, 1936)
FORTY NAUGHTY GIRLS (RKO, 1937)
WE'RE ON THE JURY (RKO, 1937)
VERY MISSING PERSON, A (TV, 1972)

HIT PARADE, THE (based on original screenplays and suggested by the radio program)
HIT PARADE, THE (REP, 1937) (TV title: I'LL REACH FOR A STAR)
HIT PARADE OF 1941, THE (REP, 1940)
HIT PARADE OF 1943, THE (REP, 1943)
HIT PARADE OF 1947, THE (REP, 1947) (TV title: HIGH AND HAPPY)
HIT PARADE OF 1951, THE (REP, 1950) (TV title: SONG PARADE, THE)

HOMER PRICE (based on stories by Robert McCloskey)
DOUGHNUTS (WW, 1964)
CASE OF THE COSMIC COMIC, THE (WW, 1976)
HOMER AND THE WACKY DOUGHNUT MACHINE (CBS–TV, 1977)

HOODLUM SOLDIER (source unlisted)
HOODLUM SOLDIER (JAP, 1965)
HOODLUM SOLDIER DESERTS AGAIN (JAP, 1966)
HOODLUM SOLDIER, FLAG BEARER (JAP, 1967)
HOODLUM SOLDIER AND $100,000 (JAP, 1968)

HOPALONG CASSIDY (based on books and characters created by Clarence E. Mulford)
BOSS OF BAR 20 (UN, 1924)
HOPALONG CASSIDY ENTERS (PAR, 1935)
BAR 20 RIDES AGAIN (PAR, 1935)
EAGLE'S BROOD, THE (PAR, 1935)
CALL OF THE PRAIRIE (PAR, 1936)
HOPALONG CASSIDY RETURNS (PAR, 1936)
HEART OF THE WEST (PAR, 1936)
THREE ON THE TRAIL (PAR, 1936)
TRAIL DUST (PAR, 1936)
BORDERLAND (PAR, 1937)
HILLS OF OLD WYOMING (PAR, 1937)
HOPALONG RIDES AGAIN (PAR, 1937)
NORTH OF THE RIO GRANDE (PAR, 1937)
RUSTLER'S VALLEY (PAR, 1937)
TEXAS TRAIL (PAR, 1937)
BAR 20 JUSTICE (PAR, 1938)
CASSIDY OF THE BAR 20 (PAR, 1938)
FRONTIERSMAN, THE (PAR, 1938)
PRIDE OF THE WEST (PAR, 1938)
HEART OF ARIZONA (PAR, 1938)
SUNSET TRAIL, THE (PAR, 1938)
IN OLD MEXICO (PAR, 1938)
PARTNERS OF THE PLAINS (PAR, 1938)
LAW OF THE PAMPAS (PAR, 1939)
RANGE WAR (PAR, 1939)
RENEGADE TRAIL (PAR, 1939)
SILVER ON THE SAGE (PAR, 1939)
HIDDEN GOLD (PAR, 1940)
SANTA FE MARSHAL (PAR, 1940)
SHOWDOWN (PAR, 1940)
STAGECOACH WAR (PAR, 1940)
THREE MEN FROM TEXAS (PAR, 1940)
BORDER VIGILANTES (PAR, 1941)
DOOMED CARAVAN (PAR, 1941)
OUTLAWS OF THE DESERT (PAR, 1941)
IN OLD COLORADO (PAR, 1941)

PIRATES ON HORSEBACK (PAR, 1941)
RIDERS OF THE TIMBERLINE (PAR, 1941)
TWILIGHT ON THE TRAIL (PAR, 1941)
SECRET OF THE WASTELANDS (PAR, 1941)
WIDE OPEN TOWN (PAR, 1941)
STICK TO YOUR GUNS (PAR, 1941)
HOPPY SERVES A WRIT (UA, 1942)
LOST CANYON (UA, 1942)
UNDERCOVER MAN (UA, 1942)
BAR 20 (UA, 1943)
BORDER PATROL (UA, 1943)
COLT COMRADES (UA, 1943)
FALSE COLORS (UA, 1943)
LEATHER BURNERS (UA, 1943)
TEXAS MASQUERADE (UA, 1943)
RIDERS OF THE DEADLINE (UA, 1943)
FORTY THIEVES (UA, 1944)
LUMBERJACK (UA, 1944)
MYSTERY MAN, THE (UA, 1944)
DEVIL'S PLAYGROUND, THE (UA, 1946)
DANGEROUS VENTURE (UA, 1947)
FOOL'S GOLD (UA, 1947)
HOPPY'S HOLIDAY (UA, 1947)
MARAUDERS, THE (UA, 1947)
UNEXPECTED GUEST (UA, 1947)
BORROWED TROUBLE (UA, 1948)
DEAD DON'T DREAM, THE (UA, 1948)
FALSE PARADISE (UA, 1948)
SILENT CONFLICT (UA, 1948)
SINISTER JOURNEY (UA, 1948)
STRANGE GAMBLE (UA, 1948)
HOPALONG CASSIDY (series) (TV, 1951)

HOSTESS, THE (source unlisted)
HOSTESS OF THE LAHN, THE (GER, 1967)
HOSTESS ALSO HAS A COUNT, THE (GER, 1968)
HOSTESS ALSO HAS A NIECE, THE (GER, 1969)
HOSTESS ALSO LIKES TO BLOW THE HORN, THE
   (GER, 1970)
HOSTESS EXCEEDS ALL BOUNDS, THE (GER, 1970)

HOTEL FOR WOMEN (based on a story by Elsa Maxwell)
ELSA MAXWELL'S HOTEL FOR WOMEN (FOX, 1939)
FREE, BLONDE AND 21 (FOX, 1940)
GIRLS IN 313, THE (FOX, 1940)

HUGGETTS, THE (based on characters created by Godfrey
   Winn)
HERE COME THE HUGGETTS (BRI, 1948)
VOTE FOR HUGGETT (BRI, 1948)
HUGGETTS ABROAD, THE (BRI, 1948)

I, A WOMAN (based on the book by Siv Holm)
I, A WOMAN (DEN, 1965)
I, A WOMAN PART 2 (DEN, 1969)
DAUGHTER, THE (I, A WOMAN PART 3) (DEN, 1970)

I LOVE A MYSTERY (based on the radio serial by Carleton
   E. Morse)
I LOVE A MYSTERY (COL, 1945)
DEVIL'S MASK, THE (COL, 1946)
UNKNOWN, THE (COL, 1946)
I LOVE A MYSTERY (NBC--TV, 1973)

INNER SANCTUM (based on the radio series created by
   Himan Brown)
CALLING DR. DEATH (UN, 1943)
DEAD MAN'S EYES (UN, 1944)
WEIRD WOMAN (UN, 1944)

FROZEN GHOST, THE (UN, 1945)
STRANGE CONFESSION (UN, 1945)
PILLOW OF DEATH (UN, 1945)

INSPECTOR CLOUSEAU (based on an idea by Blake Edwards
   and the play, "A Shot in the Dark," by Harry Kurnitz;
   also the basis for two cartoon series, "The Inspector" and
   "The Pink Panther" plus a TV series)
PINK PANTHER, THE (UA, 1964)
SHOT IN THE DARK, A (UA, 1964)
INSPECTOR CLOUSEAU (UA, 1968)
RETURN OF THE PINK PANTHER, THE (UA, 1975)
REVENGE OF THE PINK PANTHER (UA, 1978)

INSPECTOR DUGGAN (based on stories by James Eastwood)
INSIDE INFORMATION (short) (BRI, 1957)
MAIL VAN MURDER, THE (short) (BRI, 1957)
WHITE CLIFFS MYSTERY, THE (short) (BRI, 1957)
NIGHT CROSSING (short) (BRI, 1957)

INSPECTOR HANAUD (based on the book, "At the Villa
   Rose," by A.E.W. Mason)
AT THE VILLA ROSE (BRI, 1920)
HOUSE OF THE ARROW (BRI, 1930)
AT THE VILLA ROSE (BRI, 1930)
MYSTERY AT THE VILLA ROSE (FRA, 1930)
AT THE VILLA ROSE (HOUSE OF MYSTERY) (BRI,
   1939)
HOUSE OF THE ARROW (BRI, 1940)
HOUSE OF THE ARROW (BRI, 1952)

INSPECTOR HORNLEIGH (based on the radio series by Hans
   Wolfgang Priwin)
INSPECTOR HORNLEIGH (BRI, 1939)
THIS MAN IN PARIS (BRI, 1939)
INSPECTOR HORNLEIGH ON HOLIDAY (BRI, 1939)
INSPECTOR HORNLEIGH GOES TO IT (BRI, 1941)
INSPECTOR HORNLEIGH INVESTIGATES (BRI, 1941)
MAIL TRAIN (BRI, 1941)

INSPECTOR MAIGRET (based on the books by George
   Simenon)
TETE D'UN HOMME, LA (FRA, 1933)
MAN ON THE EIFFEL TOWER, THE (RKO, 1950)
TEMOIGNAGE D'UN ENFANT DE CHOEUR, LE (FRA,
   1952)
MAIGRET DIRIGE L'ENGUETE (FRA--TV, 1955)
INSPECTOR MAIGRET (WOMAN BAIT) (FRA, 1958)
MAIGRET TEND UN PIEGE (FRA, 1958)
MAIGRET AND THE SAINT--FIACRE AFFAIR (FRA/
   ITA, 1959)
MAIGRET SEES RED (FRA/ITA, 1962)
MAIGRET UND SEIN GROSSTER FALL (AUS/FRA/GER,
   1966)
MAIGRET A PIGALLE (FRA/ITA, 1966)
ENTER INSPECTOR MAIGRET (FRA, 1967)
MIRROR OF MAIGRET, THE (FRA--TV, 1971)

INVISIBLE MAN, THE (based on the book and character by
   H.G. Wells)
INVISIBLE MAN, THE (UN, 1933)
INVISIBLE MAN RETURNS, THE (UN, 1940)
INVISIBLE WOMAN, THE (UN, 1941)
INVISIBLE AGENT, THE (UN, 1942)
INVISIBLE MAN'S REVENGE, THE (UN, 1944)
ABBOTT & COSTELLO MEET THE INVISIBLE MAN
   (UN, 1951)
INVISIBLE MAN IN ISTANBUL, THE (TUR, 1956)
NEW INVISIBLE MAN, THE (MEX, 1957)
INVISIBLE MAN, THE (series) (TV, 1958)

INVISIBLE MAN ATTACKS, THE (ARG, 1967)
INVISIBLE MAN, THE (series) (NBC--TV, 1975)
GEMINI MAN, THE (series) (TV, 1976)

IZZY (source unlisted)
IZZY AND HIS RIVAL (MUT, 1914)
IZZY AND THE DIAMOND (MUT, 1914)
IZZY'S NIGHT OUT (MUT, 1914)
IZZY THE DETECTIVE (MUT, 1914)

JAMES BOND (based on the books by Ian Fleming)
DR. NO (UA, 1963)
FROM RUSSIA WITH LOVE (UA, 1964)
GOLDFINGER (UA, 1965)
THUNDERBALL (UA, 1966)
CASINO ROYALE (COL, 1967)
YOU ONLY LIVE TWICE (UA, 1967)
ON HER MAJESTY'S SECRET SERVICE (UA, 1969)
DIAMONDS ARE FOREVER (UA, 1971)
LIVE AND LET DIE (UA, 1973)
SPY WHO LOVED ME, THE (UA, 1977)

JEFF GORDON, SPECIAL AGENT (source unlisted)
JEFF GORDON, SPECIAL AGENT (FRA, 1963)
JEFF GORDON STRIKES AGAIN (FRA, 1963)
JEFF GORDON AND THE COUNTERFEITERS (FRA, 1963)
FRISSONS PARTOUT, FIDA, DES (FRA, 1964)
LAISSEZ TIERER LES TIEREURS, FIDA (FRA, 1964)
CES DAMES S'EN MELENT, FIDA (FRA, 1965)

JERRY COTTON (source unlisted)
SHOTS FROM A VIOLIN CASE (VIOLIN CASE MURDER) (GER, 1965)
MILLION EYES OF SU--MURU (GER, 1967)
HOUSE OF A THOUSAND DOLLS, THE (GER, 1967)
DEATH IN A RED JAGUAR (GER, 1968)
MURDER CLUB FROM BROOKLYN (GER, 1968)
DYNAMITE IN GREEN SILK (GER, 1968)
OPERATION HURRICANE (GER, 1968)
DEADLY SHOTS FROM MANHATTAN (DEADLY SHOTS ON BROADWAY) (GER, 1969)

JERUSALEM (based on books by Selma Lagerhof)
JERUSALEM I--II (SWE, 1919)
JERUSALEM III (SWE, 1920)
JERUSALEM IV--V (GER/SWE, 1926)

JOE PALOOKA (based on the comic strip by Ham Fisher)
PALOOKA (UA, 1934)
CALLING ALL KIDS (short) (WB, 1937)
JOE PALOOKA, CHAMP (MON, 1946)
GENTLEMAN JOE PALOOKA (MON, 1946)
KNOCKOUT, THE (MON, 1947)
WINNER TAKE ALL (MON, 1948)
COUNTERPUNCH, THE (MON, 1949)
BIG FIGHT, THE (MON, 1949)
JOE PALOOKA MEETS HUMPHREY (MON, 1950)
HUMPHREY TAKES A CHANCE (MON, 1950)
TRIPLE CROSS (MON, 1951)
SQUARED CIRCLE, THE (MON, 1951)
JOE PALOOKA STORY, THE (series) (TV, 1954)

JONES FAMILY, THE (based on characters created by Katherine Kavanaugh)
EDUCATING FATHER (FOX, 1935)
EVERY SATURDAY NIGHT (FOX, 1936)
BIG BUSINESS (FOX, 1937)
OFF TO THE RACES (FOX, 1937)

HOT WATER (FOX,1937)
BORROWING TROUBLE (FOX, 1937)
TRIP TO PARIS, A (FOX, 1938)
SAFETY IN NUMBERS (FOX, 1938)
DOWN ON THE FARM (FOX, 1938)
LOVE ON A BUDGET (FOX, 1938)
JONES FAMILY IN HOLLYWOOD, THE (FOX, 1939)
TOO BUSY TO WORK (FOX, 1939)
QUICK MILLIONS (FOX, 1939)
EVERYBODY'S BABY (FOX, 1939)
ON THEIR OWN (FOX, 1940)
YOUNG AS YOU FEEL (FOX, 1940)

JOSSER (based on the play by Ernest Lotinga and Norman Lee)
DR. JOSSER, K.C. (BRI, 1931)
P.C. JOSSER (BRI, 1931)
JOSSER JOINS THE NAVY (BRI, 1932)
JOSSER ON THE RIVER (BRI, 1932)
JOSSER IN THE ARMY (BRI, 1932)
JOSSER ON THE FARM (BRI, 1934)

JUNGLE JIM (based on the comic strip by Alex Raymond)
JUNGLE JIM (serial) (UN, 1937)
JUNGLE JIM (COL, 1949)
LOST TRIBE, THE (COL, 1949)
MARK OF THE GORILLA (COL, 1950)
CAPTIVE GIRL (COL, 1950)
PYGMY ISLAND (COL, 1950)
FURY OF THE CONGO (COL, 1951)
JUNGLE MANHUNT (COL, 1951)
VOODOO TIGER (COL, 1952)
FORBIDDEN ISLAND (COL, 1952)
SAVAGE MUTINY (COL, 1953)
KILLER APE (COL, 1953)
CANNIBAL ATTACK (COL, 1954)
JUNGLE JIM (series) (TV, 1955)
JUNGLE MOON MEN (COL, 1955)

KING KONG (based on an idea by Edgar Wallace and Merian C. Cooper)
KING KONG (RKO, 1933)
SON OF KONG (RKO, 1934)
KING KONG VS. GODZILLA (UN, 1963)
KING KONG SHOW (series) (ABC--TV, 1966)
KING KONG ESCAPES (UN, 1968)
KING KONG (PAR, 1976)

KITTY O'DAY (based on a story by Victor Hammond)
DETECTIVE KITTY O'DAY (MON, 1944)
ADVENTURES OF KITTY O'DAY (MON, 1944)
FASHION MODEL (MON, 1945)

LASSIE
LASSIE COME HOME (MGM, 1943)
SON OF LASSIE (MGM, 1945)
COURAGE OF LASSIE (MGM, 1946)
HILLS OF HOME, THE (MGM, 1948)
SUN COMES UP, THE (MGM, 1949)
CHALLENGE TO LASSIE (MGM, 1949)
PAINTED HILLS, THE (MGM, 1951)
LASSIE (series) (CBS–TV, 1954) (TV title: JEFF'S COLLIE)

LEMMY CAUTION   (source unlisted)
  POISON IVY   (FRA, 1953)
  THIS MAN IS DANGEROUS   (FRA, 1953)
  FEMMES S'EN BALANCENT, LES   (FRA, 1954)
  VOUZ PIGEZ?   (FRA, 1956)
  DIAMOND MACHINE, THE   (FRA, 1956)
  COMMENT QU'ELLE EST!   (FRA, 1960)
  LEMMY AND THE GIRLS   (FRA, 1962)
  CARDS ON THE TABLE   (FRA, 1962)
  BIG BITE, THE   (FRA, 1962)
  LADIES MAN   (FRA, 1962)
  LADIES FIRST   (FRA, 1962)
  BIG BLUFF, THE   (FRA, 1963)
  YOUR TURN, DARLING   (FRA, 1963)
  ALPHAVILLE   (FRA, 1965)

LIEUTENANT DARING   (based on screenplays)
  LIEUTENANT DARING AND THE MYSTERY OF ROOM
    41   (BRI, 1913)
  DETECTIVE DARING AND THE THAMES CORNERS
    (BRI, 1913)
  LIEUTENANT DARING, AERIAL SCOUT   (BRI, 1913)
  LIEUTENANT DARING AND THE WATER RATS   (BRI,
    1922)
  LIEUTENANT DARING, R.N.   (BRI, 1935)

LONE RANGER, THE   (based on the comic strip and radio
    series by Fran Striker)
  LONE RANGER, THE   (serial)   (REP, 1938)
  LONE RANGER RIDES AGAIN, THE   (serial)   (REP,
    1939)
  HI--YO SILVER   (REP, 1940)
  LONE RANGER, THE   (series)   (TV, 1952)
  LONE RANGER, THE   (WB, 1956)
  LONE RANGER AND THE LOST CITY OF GOLD, THE
    (UA, 1958)
  LONE RANGER, THE   (series)   (CBS--TV, 1966)
  FIVE MASKED MEN   (TUR, 1968)
  RETURN OF THE FIVE MASKED MEN   (TUR, 1968)
  LANDLESS WOLVES, THE   (TUR, 1968)

LONE RIDER, THE   (based on a screenplay)
  LONE RIDER RIDES ON, THE   (PRC, 1941)
  LONE RIDER CROSSES THE RIO   (PRC, 1941)
  LONE RIDER IN GHOST TOWN, THE   (PRC, 1941)
  LONE RIDER IN FRONTIER FURY, THE   (PRC, 1941)
  LONE RIDER AMBUSHED, THE   (PRC, 1941)
  LONE RIDER FIGHTS BACK, THE   (PRC, 1941)
  LONE RIDER AND THE BANDIT, THE   (PRC, 1942)
  LONE RIDER IN CHEYENNE, THE   (PRC, 1942)
  TEXAS JUSTICE   (PRC, 1942)
  LONE RIDER'S BORDER ROUNDUP, THE   (PRC, 1942)
  OUTLAW OF BOULDER PASS   (PRC, 1942)
  OVERLAND STAGECOACH   (PRC, 1942)
  WILD HORSE RUSTLERS   (PRC, 1943)
  DEATH RIDES THE PLAINS   (PRC, 1943)
  WOLVES OF THE RANGE   (PRC, 1944)
  LAW OF THE SADDLE   (PRC, 1944)
  RAIDERS OF RED GAP   (PRC, 1944)

LONE WOLF, THE   (based on a book by Louis Joseph Vance)
  LONE WOLF, THE   (SEZ, 1917)
  FALSE FACES   (INC, 1918)
  LONE WOLF'S DAUGHTER, THE   (HOD, 1919)
  LONE WOLF'S LAST ADVENTURE, THE   (COL, 1924)
  LONE WOLF RETURNS, THE   (COL, 1926)
  ALIAS THE LONE WOLF   (COL, 1927)
  LONE WOLF'S DAUGHTER, THE   (COL, 1929)
  LAST OF THE LONE WOLF, THE   (COL, 1930)

CHEATERS AT PLAY   (FOX, 1932)
LONE WOLF RETURNS, THE   (COL, 1936)
LONE WOLF IN PARIS, THE   (COL, 1938)
LONE WOLF SPY HUNT, THE   (COL, 1939)
LONE WOLF MEETS A LADY, THE   (COL, 1940)
LONE WOLF STRIKES, THE   (COL, 1940)
LONE WOLF KEEPS A DATE, THE   (COL, 1941)
SECRETS OF THE LONE WOLF   (COL, 1941)
LONE WOLF TAKES A CHANCE, THE   (COL, 1941)
COUNTER ESPIONAGE   (COL, 1942)
ONE DANGEROUS NIGHT   (COL, 1943)
PASSPORT TO SUEZ   (COL, 1943)
NOTORIOUS LONE WOLF, THE   (COL, 1946)
LONE WOLF IN LONDON, THE   (COL, 1947)
LONE WOLF IN MEXICO, THE   (COL, 1947)
LONE WOLF AND HIS LADY, THE   (COL, 1949)
STREETS OF DANGER   (series)   (TV, 1954)

LORD PETER WHIMSEY   (based on a character created by
    Dorothy L. Sayers)
  SILENT PASSENGER, THE   (BRI, 1935)
  HAUNTED HONEYMOON   (BUSMAN'S HONEYMOON)
    (MGM, 1940)
  LORD PETER WHIMSEY   (PBS--TV, 1973)
  FIVE RED HERRINGS   (series)   (PBS--TV, 1976)

LOVE BUG   (based on a story, "Car--Boy--Girl," by Gordon
    Buford)
  LOVE BUG, THE   (DIS, 1968)
  HERBIE RIDES AGAIN   (DIS, 1974)
  HERBIE GOES TO MONTE CARLO   (DIS, 1977)

LUM 'N' ABNER   (based on the radio series)
  DREAMING OUT LOUD   (RKO, 1940)
  BASHFUL BACHELOR, THE   (RKO, 1942)
  SO THIS IS WASHINGTON   (RKO, 1943)
  TWO WEEKS TO LIVE   (RKO, 1943)
  GOIN' TO TOWN   (RKO, 1944)
  PARTNERS IN TIME   (RKO, 1946)
  LUM 'N' ABNER   (series)   (CBS--TV, 1949)
  LUM 'N' ABNER ABROAD   (HOW, 1955)

MA AND PA KETTLE   (based on the book by Betty McDonald)
  EGG AND I, THE   (UN, 1947)
  MA AND PA KETTLE   (UN, 1949)
  MA AND PA KETTLE GO TO TOWN   (UN, 1950)
  MA AND PA KETTLE BACK ON THE FARM   (UN, 1951)
  MA AND PA KETTLE AT THE FAIR   (UN, 1952)
  MA AND PA KETTLE ON VACATION   (UN, 1953)
  MA AND PA KETTLE AT WAIKIKI   (UN, 1955)
  KETTLES IN THE OZARKS, THE   (UN, 1956)
  KETTLES ON OLD MACDONALD'S FARM, THE   (UN,
    1957)

MacGREGORS, THE   (based on a screenplay)
  UP THE MacGREGORS   (ITA/SPA, 1968)
  7 GUNS FOR THE MacGREGORS   (ITA/SPA, 1968)
  SEVEN WIVES FOR THE MacGREGORS   (ITA/SPA,
    1968)
  MORE DOLLARS FOR THE MacGREGORS   (ITA/SPA,
    1971)

MACISTE   (based on the Italian legend)
  MACISTE   (ITA, 1915)
  MACISTE ALPINO   (ITA, 1916)
  MACISTE BERSAGLIERE   (ITA, 1916)
  MACISTE AGAINST MACISTE   (ITA, 1917)
  MACISTE – STRONG MAN   (ITA, 1918)
  MACISTE IN THE LIBERATOR   (ITA, 1919)

MACISTE VS. DEATH (ITA, 1919)
MACISTE IN LOVE (ITA, 1920)
MACISTE – SUPER MAN (ITA, 1920)
MACISTE IN THE LION'S DEN (ITA, 1926)
MACISTE IN HELL (ITA, 1926)
MACISTE THE MIGHTY (ITA, 1960)
SAMSON AND THE 7 MIRACLES (ITA, 1961)
GOLIATH AND THE VAMPIRES (ITA, 1961)
STRONGEST MAN IN THE WORLD, THE (ITA, 1971)
CYCLOPS, THE (ITA, 1961)
MACISTE IN HELL (ITA, 1962)
COLOSSUS AND THE HEAD HUNTERS (ITA, 1962)
COLOSSUS OF THE STONE AGE (ITA, 1962)
MACISTE AGAINST THE SHEIK (ITA, 1962)
DEATH IN THE ARENA (ITA, 1962)
SAMSON IN KING SOLOMON'S MINES (ITA, 1963)
GOLIATH AND THE SINS OF BABYLON (ITA, 1963)
MACISTE AND THE 100 GLADIATORS (ITA, 1964)
HERCULES AGAINST THE BARBARIANS (ITA, 1964)
MACISTE AGAINST THE MONGOLS (ITA, 1964)
MACISTE AND THE LOST TOMB (ITA, 1964)
MACISTE AGAINST THE CZAR (ITA, 1964)

MADELINE (based on stories by Ludwig Bemelmans)
MADELINE (short) (COL, 1952)
MADELINE AND THE BAD HAT (short) (FRA, 1966)
MADELINE AND THE GYPSIES (short) (FRA, 1966)

MAGGIE AND JIGGS (see BRINGING UP FATHER)

MAGNIFICENT SEVEN, THE (based on the Japanese film,
    "The Magnificent Seven")
MAGNIFICENT SEVEN, THE (UA, 1960)
RETURN OF THE SEVEN (UA, 1966)
GUNS OF THE MAGNIFICENT SEVEN (UA, 1969)
MAGNIFICENT SEVEN RIDE, THE (UA, 1972)

MAIGRET (see INSPECTOR MAIGRET)

MAISIE (based on a book by Wilson Collinson; also appeared
    as a radio series)
MAISIE (MGM, 1939)
MAISIE WAS A LADY (MGM, 1940)
CONGO MAISIE (MGM, 1940)
RINGSIDE MAISIE (MGM, 1941)
MAISIE GETS HER MAN (MGM, 1942)
SWING SHIFT MAISIE (MGM, 1943)
MAISIE GOES TO RENO (MGM, 1944)
UP GOES MAISIE (MGM, 1946)
UNDERCOVER MAISIE (MGM, 1947)

MAJIN (based on a screenplay by Tetsuo Yoshida)
MAJIN, THE TERROR MONSTER (JAP, 1966)
MAJIN STRIKES BACK (JAP, 1966)
MAJIN, THE HIDEOUS IDOL (JAP, 1968)
RETURN OF MAJIN, THE (JAP, 1969)

MAN FROM U.N.C.L.E., THE (based on a teleplay)
SPY WITH MY FACE, THE (MGM, 1965)
ONE OF OUR SPIES IS MISSING (MGM, 1966)
ONE SPY TOO MANY (MGM, 1966)
SPY IN THE GREEN HAT, THE (MGM, 1966)
HELICOPTER SPIES, THE (MGM, 1967)
KARATE KILLERS, THE (MGM, 1967)
HOW TO STEAL THE WORLD (MGM, 1968)

MAN WITHOUT A NAME, THE (based on a story by Tonio
    Alombi)
FISTFUL OF DOLLARS, A (ITA, 1966)

FOR A FEW DOLLARS MORE (ITA, 1967)
STRANGER RETURNS, THE (ITA, 1968)

MASTER CRIMINAL "KILLING" (based on screenplays by
    various authors)
"KILLING" -- KING OF CRIMINALS (TUR, 1967)
"KILLING" VS. FRANKENSTEIN (TUR, 1967)
"KILLING" IN ISTANBUL (TUR, 1967)
"KILLING" CORPSES DO NOT TALK (TUR, 1967)
MANDRAKE VS. "KILLING" (TUR, 1967)
STUNNED DETECTIVE VS. "KILLING," THE (TUR,
    1967)
FLYING–MAN VS. "KILLING" (TUR, 1967)

MASTER DETECTIVE (source unlisted)
BLOOMKVIST, THE MASTER DETECTIVE (SWE, 1947)
MASTER DETECTIVE AND RASMUS (SWE, 1953)
MASTER DETECTIVE LEADS A DANGEROUS LIFE
    (SWE, 1957)

MATT HELM (based on books by Donald Hamilton)
SILENCERS, THE (COL, 1966)
MURDERER'S ROW (COL, 1967)
AMBUSHERS, THE (COL, 1967)
WRECKING CREW, THE (COL, 1968)
MATT HELM (ABC--TV, 1975)
MATT HELM (series) (ABC–TV, 1975)

MEXICAN SPITFIRE (based on a story by Lionel Houser)
GIRL FROM MEXICO, THE (RKO, 1939)
MEXICAN SPITFIRE (RKO, 1939)
MEXICAN SPITFIRE OUT WEST (RKO, 1940)
MEXICAN SPITFIRE'S BABY (RKO, 1941)
MEXICAN SPITFIRE AT SEA (RKO, 1942)
MEXICAN SPITFIRE SEES A GHOST (RKO, 1942)
MEXICAN SPITFIRE'S ELEPHANT (RKO, 1942)
MEXICAN SPITFIRE'S BLESSED EVENT (RKO, 1943)

MICHAEL SHAYNE (based on books by Brett Halliday)
MICHAEL SHAYNE, PRIVATE DETECTIVE (FOX, 1940)
SLEEPERS WEST (FOX, 1941)
DRESSED TO KILL (FOX, 1941)
BLUE, WHITE AND PERFECT (FOX, 1941)
MAN WHO WOULDN'T DIE, THE (FOX, 1942)
TIME TO KILL (FOX, 1942)
JUST OFF BROADWAY (FOX, 1942)
BLONDE FOR A DAY (PRC, 1946)
LARCENY IN HER HEART (PRC, 1946)
MURDER IS MY BUSINESS (PRC, 1946)
THREE ON A TICKET (PRC, 1947)
TOO MANY WINNERS (PRC, 1947)
MICHAEL SHAYNE (series) (NBC--TV, 1960)

MIDVILLE (MEDFIELD) COLLEGE (based on screenplays by
    Joseph L. McEveety)
COMPUTER WORE TENNIS SHOES, THE (DIS, 1969)
NOW YOU SEE HIM, NOW YOU DON'T (DIS, 1972)
STRONGEST MAN IN THE WORLD, THE (DIS, 1975)

MIKE AND JAKE (source unlisted)
MIKE AND JAKE AS HEROES (UN, 1913)
MIKE AND JAKE AS PUGILISTS (UN, 1913)
MIKE AND JAKE IN MEXICO (UN, 1913)
MIKE AND JAKE IN SOCIETY (UN, 1913)
MIKE AND JAKE IN THE WILD WEST (UN, 1913)

MIKE HAMMER (based on books by Mickey Spillane)
I, THE JURY (UA, 1953)
LONG WAIT, THE (UA, 1954)

KISS ME DEADLY (UA, 1955)
MY GUN IS QUICK (UA, 1957)
MICKEY SPILLANE'S MIKE HAMMER (series) (TV, 1957)
GIRL HUNTERS, THE (UA, 1965)
DELTA FACTOR, THE (CON, 1970)

MISS HILDEGARDE WITHERS see HILDEGARDE WITHERS

MISS JANE MARPLE (based on books by Agatha Christie)
MURDER SHE SAID (BRI, 1962)
MURDER AT THE GALLOP (BRI, 1963)
MURDER AHOY (BRI, 1964)
MURDER MOST FOUL (BRI, 1964)

MR. ANATOL (source unlisted)
MR. ANATOL'S HAT (POL, 1958)
MR. ANATOL SEEKS A MILLION (POL, 1961)
MR. ANATOL'S INSPECTION (POL, 1961)

MR. BELVEDERE (based on a book by Gwen Davenport)
SITTING PRETTY (FOX, 1948)
MR. BELVEDERE GOES TO COLLEGE (FOX, 1949)
MR. BELVEDERE RINGS THE BELL (FOX, 1951)

MR. DISTRICT ATTORNEY (based on a radio series)
MR. DISTRICT ATTORNEY (REP, 1941)
MR. DISTRICT ATTORNEY AND THE CARTER CASE (REP, 1941)
SECRETS OF THE UNDERGROUND (REP, 1943)
MR. DISTRICT ATTORNEY (series) (TV, 1954)

M. HULOT (based on an original character created by Jacques Tati)
JOUR DE FETE (THE BIG DAY) (FRA, 1952)
MR. HULOT'S HOLIDAY (FRA, 1954)
MY UNCLE (FRA, 1958)
PLAYTIME (FRA, 1969)
TRAFFIC (FRA, 1971)

MR. MOTO (based on books by John P. Marquand)
THINK FAST, MR. MOTO (FOX, 1937)
THANK YOU, MR. MOTO (FOX, 1937)
MR. MOTO'S GAMBLE (FOX, 1938)
MYSTERIOUS MR. MOTO (FOX, 1938)
MR. MOTO TAKES A CHANCE (FOX, 1938)
MR. MOTO TAKES A VACATION (FOX, 1939)
DANGER ISLAND (FOX, 1939)
MR. MOTO'S LAST WARNING (FOX, 1939)
RETURN OF MR. MOTO, THE (ABC–TV, 1952)
RETURN OF MR. MOTO, THE (FOX, 1965)

MR. TIBBS (based on a book by John Ball)
IN THE HEAT OF THE NIGHT (UA, 1967)
THEY CALL ME MISTER TIBBS (UA, 1970)
ORGANIZATION, THE (UA, 1971)

MR. WONG (based on stories by Hugh Wiley)
MR. WONG, DETECTIVE (MON, 1938)
MYSTERY OF MR. WONG (MON, 1939)
MR. WONG IN CHINATOWN (MON, 1939)
FATAL HOUR, THE (MON, 1940)
DOOMED TO DIE (MON, 1940)
PHANTOM OF CHINATOWN, THE (MON, 1940)

MONOCLE (source unlisted)
BLACK MONOCLE, THE (FRA, 1961)
EYE OF THE MONOCLE, THE (FRA, 1962)
MONOCLE GIVES A SICKLY SMILE, THE (FRA, 1963)

MUMMY, THE (based on a story by Nina Wilcox Putnam and Richard Schayer)
MUMMY, THE (UN, 1932)
MUMMY'S HAND, THE (UN, 1940)
MUMMY'S TOMB, THE (UN, 1942)
MUMMY'S GHOST, THE (UN, 1943)
MUMMY'S CURSE, THE (UN, 1945)
ABBOTT & COSTELLO MEET THE MUMMY (UN, 1955)
MUMMY, THE (BRI, 1958)
CURSE OF THE MUMMY'S TOMB, THE (BRI, 1964)
MUMMY'S SHROUD, THE (BRI, 1967)
BLOOD FROM THE MUMMY'S TOMB (BRI, 1972)

MUSASHI MIYAMOTO (source unlisted)
MUSASHI MIYAMOTO (JAP, 1940)
MUSASHI MIYAMOTO (JAP, 1944)
SAMURAI (JAP, 1954)
UNTAMED FURY (JAP, 1961)
DUEL WITHOUT END (JAP, 1962)
WORTHLESS DUEL (JAP, 1963)
DUEL AT ICHIJOJI (JAP, 1964)
LAST DUEL, THE (JAP, 1965)

MY FRIEND IRMA (based on the radio series by Cy Howard)
MY FRIEND IRMA (PAR, 1949)
MY FRIEND IRMA GOES WEST (PAR, 1950)
MY FRIEND IRMA (series) (TV, n.d.)

NANCY DREW (based on books by Carolyn Keen)
NANCY DREW, DETECTIVE (WB, 1938)
NANCY DREW, TROUBLESHOOTER (WB, 1939)
NANCY DREW, REPORTER (WB, 1939)
NANCY DREW AND THE HIDDEN STAIRCASE (WB, 1939)
NANCY DREW AND THE HARDY BOYS (series) (ABC–TV, 1977)

NEUTRON (source unlisted)
NEUTRON AND THE BLACK MASK (MEX, 1961)
NEUTRON AGAINST THE DEATH ROBOTS (MEX, 1961)
NEUTRON BATTLES THE KARATE ASSASSINS (MEX, 1961)
NEUTRON VS. THE MANIAC (MEX, 1962)
NEUTRON VS. THE AMAZING DR. CARONTE (MEX, 1963)
NEUTRON TRAPS THE INVISIBLE KILLERS (MEX, 1964)

NICK CARTER (based on stories by the Rev. Sam Spalding)
NICK CARTER (serial) (FRA, 1908)
MYSTERE DU LIT BLANC, LE (FRA, 1911)
ZIGOMAR AGAINST NICK CARTER (FRA, 1911)
NICK CARTER, MASTER DETECTIVE (MGM, 1939)
SKY MURDER (MGM, 1940)
PHANTOM RAIDERS (MGM, 1940)
LICENSE TO KILL (FRA, 1964)
BOMBS UNDER THE TABLE (FRA/ITA, 1965)
NICK CARTER ET LE TREFLE ROUGE (FRA, 1965)
ADVENTURE OF NICK CARTER, THE (ABC–TV, 1972)

NOSTRADAMUS (based on the writings of the noted visionary)

NOSTRADAMUS (MEX, 1937)
NOSTRADAMUS (short) (MGM, 1938)
MORE ABOUT NOSTRADAMUS (short) (MGM, 1940)
CURSE OF NOSTRADAMUS (MEX, 1960)
MONSTER DEMOLISHER (MEX, 1960)
GENII OF DARKNESS (MEX, 1960)
BLOOD OF NOSTRADAMUS (MEX, 1960)
PROPHECIES OF NOSTRADAMUS (JAP, 1975)

08/15 (source unlisted)
  08/15 I (GER, 1954)
  08/15 II (GER, 1955)
  08/15 IN DER HEIMAT (GER, 1955)

OSS 117 (based on books by Jean and Josette Bruce)
  OSS 117 IS NOT DEAD (FRA, 1956)
  OSS 117 SE DECHAINE (FRA/ITA, 1963)
  JACKPOT IN BANGKOK FOR OSS 117 (SHADOW OF
    EVIL) (FRA/ITA, 1964)
  FURY IN BAHIA FOR OSS 117 (FRA/ITA, 1965)
  OSS 117 – MISSION FOR A KILLER (FRA/ITA, 1966)
  HEART TRUMP IN TOKYO FOR OSS 117 (TERROR IN
    TOKYO) (FRA/ITA, 1966)
  NO ROSES FOR OSS 117 (FRA/ITA, 1968)
  OSS 117 TAKES A HOLIDAY (FRA/ITA, 1969)

OILY MAN, THE (source unlisted)
  PONTIANAK MEETS THE OILY MAN (HK, 1957)
  OILY MAN, THE (HK, 1958)
  OILY MAN STRIKES AGAIN, THE (HK, 1958)
  CURSE OF THE OILY MAN, THE (HK, 1958)

OLD MOTHER RILEY (based on a screenplay)
  OLD MOTHER RILEY (BRI, 1937)
  OLD MOTHER RILEY IN PARIS (BRI, 1938)
  OLD MOTHER RILEY M.P. (BRI, 1939)
  OLD MOTHER RILEY OVERSEAS (BRI, 1944)
  OLD MOTHER RILEY JOINS UP (BRI, 1945)
  OLD MOTHER RILEY'S CIRCUS (BRI, 1945)
  OLD MOTHER RILEY AT HOME (BRI, 1946)
  MY SON, THE VAMPIRE (BRI, 1946)
  OLD MOTHER RILEY IN BUSINESS (BRI, 1946)
  OLD MOTHER RILEY, DETECTIVE (BRI, 1947)
  OLD MOTHER RILEY IN SOCIETY (BRI, 1947)
  OLD MOTHER RILEY'S GHOSTS (BRI, 1948)
  OLD MOTHER RILEY'S NEW VENTURE (BRI, 1949)
  OLD MOTHER RILEY, HEADMISTRESS (BRI, 1950)
  OLD MOTHER RILEY'S JUNGLE TREASURE (BRI,
    1951)
  OLD MOTHER RILEY MEETS THE VAMPIRE (BRI,
    1952)

OLSEN GANG, THE (source unlisted)
  OLSEN GANG, THE (DEN, 1968)
  OLSEN GANG IN A FIX, THE (DEN, 1969)
  OLSEN GANG IN JUTLAND (DEN, 1971)
  OLSEN GANG'S BIG SCORE, THE (DEN, 1972)
  OLSEN GANG RUNS AMOK, THE (DEN, 1973)
  OLSEN GANG SEES RED, THE (DEN, 1976)
  OLSEN GANG OUTTA SIGHT, THE (DEN, 1977)

ONE–ARMED SWORDSMAN (source unlisted)
  ONE–ARMED SWORDSMAN, THE (CHN, 1968)
  RETURN OF THE ONE–ARMED SWORDSMAN, THE
    (CHN, 1969)
  ZATOICHI AND THE ONE–ARMED SWORDSMAN (CHN,
    1970)
  NEW ONE–ARMED SWORDSMAN, THE (CHN,
    1970)

ONESIME HORLOGER (source unlisted)
  ONESIME HORLOGER (FRA, 1912)
  ONESIME IN HELL (FRA, 1912)
  ONESIME AND THE HAUNTED HOUSE (FRA, 1913)
  ONESIME AND THE CLUBMAN (FRA, 1914)

ON THE BUSES (based on a television series)
  ON THE BUSES (BRI, 1971)
  UP THE BUSES (BRI, 1972)
  MUTINY ON THE BUSES (BRI, 1972)
  HOLIDAY ON THE BUSES (BRI, 1973)

OWNY O'REILLY (based on a teleplay)
  SALVATION OF OWNY O'REILLY, THE (ABC--TV, 1960)
  RETURN OF OWNY O'REILLY, THE (ABC–TV, 1960)
  OWNY O'REILLY, ESQ. (ABC--TV, 1961)

PAUL SLEUTH (based on a screenplay, author unknown)
  PAUL SLEUTH, CRIME INVESTIGATOR: THE BURG--
    LARY SYNDICATE (BRI, 1912)
  PAUL SLEUTH – THE MYSTERY OF THE ASTORIAN
    CROWN PRINCE (BRI, 1912)
  PAUL SLEUTH AND THE MYSTIC SEVEN (BRI, 1914)

PAUL TEMPLE (based on a radio serial by Francis Durbridge)
  SEND FOR PAUL TEMPLE (BRI, 1946)
  CALLING PAUL TEMPLE (BRI, 1948)
  PAUL TEMPLE'S TRIUMPH (BRI, 1950)
  PAUL TEMPLE RETURNS (BRI, 1952)
  PAUL TEMPLE (BRI--TV, n.d.)

PAULA, THE APE WOMAN (based on a story by Ted Fithian
    and Neil P. Varnick)
  CAPTIVE WILD WOMAN (UN, 1943)
  JUNGLE WOMAN (UN, 1944)
  JUNGLE CAPTIVE (UN, 1945)

PEANUTS (based on the comic strip, "Peanuts," by Charles
    Shulz)
  YOU'RE IN LOVE, CHARLIE BROWN (CBS--TV, 1965)
  CHARLIE BROWN CHRISTMAS, A (CBS--TV, 1965)
  CHARLIE BROWN THANKSGIVING, A (CBS--TV, 1965)
  CHARLIE BROWN'S ALL-STARS (CBS--TV, 1965)
  HE'S YOUR DOG, CHARLIE BROWN (CBS--TV, 1965)
  IT'S A MYSTERY, CHARLIE BROWN (CBS--TV, 1965)
  IT'S THE GREAT PUMPKIN, CHARLIE BROWN (CBS--
    TV, 1965)
  IT WAS A SHORT SUMMER, CHARLIE BROWN (CBS--
    TV, 1965)
  PLAY IT AGAIN, CHARLIE BROWN (CBS--TV, 1965)
  THERE'S NO TIME FOR LOVE, CHARLIE BROWN
    (CBS--TV, 1965)
  YOU'RE ELECTED, CHARLIE BROWN (CBS--TV, 1965)
  BOY NAMED CHARLIE BROWN, A (NGP, 1970)
  SNOOPY COME HOME (NGP, 1972)
  RACE FOR YOUR LIFE, CHARLIE BROWN (PAR, 1977)

PERRY MASON (based on books by Erle Stanley Gardner)
  CASE OF THE HOWLING DOG, THE (WB, 1934)
  CASE OF THE CURIOUS BRIDE, THE (WB, 1935)
  CASE OF THE LUCKY LEGS, THE (WB, 1936)
  CASE OF THE BLACK CAT, THE (WB, 1936)
  SPECIAL INVESTIGATOR (WB, 1936)
  CASE OF THE STUTTERING BISHOP, THE (WB, 1937)
  CASE OF THE BLACK PARROT, THE (WB, 1941)
  PERRY MASON (series) (CBS--TV, 1958)
  NEW PERRY MASON, THE (series) (NBC--TV, 1973)

PERSONS IN HIDING (based on a book by J. Edgar Hoover)

PERSONS IN HIDING (PAR, 1939)
UNDERCOVER DOCTOR (PAR, 1939)
PAROLE FIXER (PAR, 1940)
QUEEN OF THE MOB (PAR, 1940)

PHILIP MARLOWE (based on books by Raymond Chandler)
MURDER MY SWEET (RKO, 1944)
LADY IN THE LAKE (MGM, 1946)
BIG SLEEP, THE (WB, 1946)
BRASHER DOUBLOON, THE (FOX, 1947)
LITTLE SISTER (TV, n.d.)
LONG GOODBYE, THE (CBS–TV, 1954)
PHILIP MARLOWE (series) (ABC--TV, 1959)
MARLOWE (MGM, 1969)
LONG GOODBYE, THE (UA, 1973)
FAREWELL MY LOVELY (EMB, 1975)
BIG SLEEP, THE (UA, 1978)

PHILO VANCE (based on books and stories by S.S. van Dyne;
    also appeared as a radio series)
CANARY MURDER CASE, THE (PAR, 1929)
GREENE MURDER CASE, THE (PAR, 1929)
BISHOP MURDER CASE, THE (PAR, 1929)
BENSON MURDER CASE, THE (PAR, 1930)
CORPUS DELECTI, THE (ARG, 1930)
CLYDE MYSTERY, THE (short) (WB, 1931)
WALL STREET MYSTERY, THE (short) (WB, 1931)
WEEKEND MYSTERY, THE (short) (WB, 1931)
SYMPHONY MURDER MYSTERY, THE (short) (WB,
    1931)
STUDIO MURDER MYSTERY, THE (short) (WB, 1932)
SKULL MURDER MYSTERY, THE (short) (WB, 1932)
COLE CASE, THE (short) (WB, 1932)
MURDER IN THE PULLMAN (short) (WB, 1932)
SIDE SHOW MYSTERY, THE (short) (WB, 1932)
CAMPUS MYSTERY, THE (short) (WB, 1932)
CRANE POISON CASE, THE (short) (WB, 1932)
TRANSATLANTIC MYSTERY, THE (short) (WB, 1932)
GIRL MISSING (WB, 1933)
KENNEL MURDER CASE, THE (WB, 1933)
DRAGON MURDER CASE, THE (WB, 1934)
CASINO MURDER CASE, THE (MGM, 1935)
GARDEN MURDER CASE, THE (MGM, 1936)
PRESIDENT'S MYSTERY, THE (REP, 1936)
SCARAB MURDER CASE, THE (BRI, 1937)
NIGHT OF MYSTERY (PAR, 1937)
GRACIE ALLEN MURDER CASE, THE (PAR, 1939)
CALLING PHILO VANCE (WB, 1940)
PHILO VANCE RETURNS (PRC, 1947)
PHILO VANCE'S GAMBLE (PRC, 1947)
PHILO VANCE'S SECRET MISSION (PRC, 1947)

PIPPI LONGSTOCKING (based on the "Fifi Brindacier" books
    by Astrid Lindgren)
PIPPI LONGSTOCKING (GER/SWE, 1969)
PIPPI IN THE SOUTH SEAS (GER/SWE, 1970)
PIPPI GOES ON BOARD (GER/SWE, 1971)
PIPPI ON THE RUN (GER/SWE, 1972)

PLANET OF THE APES (based on the book by Pierre Boulle)
PLANET OF THE APES (FOX, 1968)
BENEATH THE PLANET OF THE APES (FOX, 1970)
ESCAPE FROM THE PLANET OF THE APES (FOX,
    1971)
CONQUEST OF THE PLANET OF THE APES (FOX,
    1972)
BATTLE FOR THE PLANET OF THE APES (FOX, 1973)
PLANET OF THE APES (series) (CBS--TV, 1974)
RETURN TO THE PLANET OF THE APES (series)

(NBC–TV, 1975)

PONTIANAK (source unlisted)
PONTIANAK (HK, 1957)
PONTIANAK MEETS THE OILY MAN (HK, 1957)
PONTIANAK STRIKES AGAIN (HK, 1957)
BLOOD OF PONTIANAK (HK, 1958)
TERROR OF PONTIANAK (HK, 1958)
ANAK PONTIANAK (HK, 1958)
SUMPAH PONTIANAK (HK, 1958)
PONTIANAK KEMBALI (HK, 1963)
PONTIANAK GUA MUSANG (HK, 1964)

POTASH AND PERLMUTTER (based on a play by Montague
    Glass and Charles Klein)
POTASH AND PERLMUTTER (FN, 1923)
IN HOLLYWOOD WITH POTASH AND PERLMUTTER
    (FN, 1924)
PARTNERS AGAIN (UA, 1926)

PUSHKIN (based on the life of the noted writer, Alexander
    Pushkin)
PUSHKIN (RUS, 1949)
PUSHKIN AND MIKHAILOVSKY (RUS, 1950)
PUSHKIN AT ST. PETERSBURG (RUS, 1950)

PUSSY CAT (source unlisted)
PUSSY CAT (PHI, 1969)
PUSSY CAT STRIKES AGAIN (PHI, 1969)
WILD, WILD PUSSY CAT (PHI, 1970)

QUATERMASS (based on a British television series)
QUATERMASS (series) (BRI–TV, 1953)
CREEPING UNKNOWN, THE (BRI, 1956)
ENEMY FROM SPACE (BRI, 1957)
FIVE MILLION YEARS TO EARTH (BRI, 1967)

QUILLER (based on books by Adam Hall)
QUILLER MEMORANDUM, THE (FOX, 1967)
QUILLER: PRICE OF VIOLENCE (BRI–TV, 1975)
QUILLER: NIGHT OF THE FATHER (BRI--TV, 1975)

RAMAR (adapted from the television series)
RAMAR AND THE BURNING BARRIERS (TV, 1964)
RAMAR AND THE DEADLY FEMALES (TV, 1964)
RAMAR AND THE JUNGLE SECRETS (TV, 1964)
RAMAR AND THE SAVAGE CHALLENGES (TV, 1964)
RAMAR AND THE UNKNOWN TERROR (TV, 1964)
RAMAR'S MISSION TO INDIA (TV, 1964)

RANGE BUSTERS, THE (based on an original screenplay)
RANGE BUSTERS, THE (MON, 1940)
FUGITIVE VALLEY (MON, 1941)
KID'S LAST RIDE, THE (MON, 1941)
SADDLE MOUNTAIN ROUNDUP (MON, 1941)
TONTO BASIN OUTLAWS (MON, 1941)
TRAIL OF THE SILVER SPURS (MON, 1941)
TUMBLEDOWN RANCH IN ARIZONA (MON, 1941)
UNDERGROUND RUSTLERS (MON, 1941)
WRANGLER'S ROOST (MON, 1941)
BOOT HILL BANDITS (MON, 1942)
ROCK RIVER RENEGADES (MON, 1942)
TEXAS TO BATAAN (MON, 1942)
THUNDER RIVER FEUD (MON, 1942)
TRAIL RIDERS (MON, 1942)
TWO–FISTED JUSTICE (MON, 1942)
WAR DOGS (MON, 1942)
BLACK MARKET RUSTLERS (MON, 1943)
BULLETS AND SADDLES (MON, 1943)

COWBOY COMMANDOS (MON, 1943)
HAUNTED RANCH (MON, 1943)
LAND OF HUNTED MEN (MON, 1943)

RAY TRILOGY (based on an original screenplay)
PATHER PANCHALI (IN, 1958)
APARAJITO (IN, 1959)
WORLD OF APU, THE (IN, 1960)

RED RYDER (based on the comic strip by Fred Harman;
    also appeared as a radio series)
ADVENTURES OF RED RYDER (serial) (REP, 1940)
VIGILANTES OF DODGE CITY (REP, 1944)
TUCSON RAIDERS (REP, 1944)
CHEYENNE WILDCAT (REP, 1944)
MARSHAL OF RENO (REP, 1944)
SAN ANTONIO KID, THE (REP, 1944)
SHERIFF OF LAS VEGAS (REP, 1944)
MARSHAL OF LOREDO (REP, 1945)
LONE TEXAS RANGER (REP, 1945)
GREAT STAGECOACH ROBBERY, THE (REP, 1945)
PHANTOM OF THE PLAINS (REP, 1945)
COLORADO PIONEERS (REP, 1945)
WAGON WHEELS WESTWARD (REP, 1945)
SUN VALLEY CYCLONE (REP, 1946)
SANTA FE UPRISING (REP, 1946)
SHERIFF OF REDWOOD VALLEY (REP, 1946)
STAGECOACH TO DENVER (REP, 1946)
CALIFORNIA GOLD RUSH (REP, 1946)
CONQUEST OF CHEYENNE (REP, 1946)
HOMESTEADERS OF PARADISE VALLEY (REP, 1947)
RUSTLERS OF DEVIL'S CANYON (REP, 1947)
VIGILANTES OF BOOMTOWN (REP, 1947)
MARSHAL OF CRIPPLE CREEK (REP, 1947)
OREGON TRAIL SCOUTS (REP, 1947)
FIGHTING REDHEAD, THE (EL, 1949)
COWBOY AND THE PRIZE FIGHTER, THE (EL, 1949)
ROLL, THUNDER, ROLL (EL, 1949)
RED RYDER (series) (TV, 1956)

RENFREW OF THE ROYAL MOUNTED (based on stories
    by Laurie York Erskine; also appeared as a radio series)
RENFREW OF THE ROYAL MOUNTED (GN, 1937)
CRASHING THRU (MON, 1939)
FIGHTING MAD (MON, 1939)
DANGER AHEAD (MON, 1940)
YUKON FLIGHT (MON, 1940)
MURDER ON THE YUKON (MON, 1940)
SKY BANDITS (MON, 1940)
RENFREW OF THE ROYAL MOUNTED (series) (CBS–
    TV, 1953)

RIFIFI (based on the book by Auguste le Breton)
RIFIFI (FRA, 1955)
RIFIFI AND THE GIRLS (FRA, 1959)
RIFIFI IN TOKYO (FRA/ITA, 1963)
RIFIFI IN PANAMA (FRA/GER/ITA, 1966)

"ROAD" SERIES (based on an original screenplay)
ROAD TO SINGAPORE (PAR, 1940)
ROAD TO ZANZIBAR (PAR, 1941)
ROAD TO MOROCCO (PAR, 1942)
ROAD TO UTOPIA (PAR, 1945)
ROAD TO RIO (PAR, 1947)
ROAD TO BALI (PAR, 1952)
ROAD TO HONG KONG (UA, 1962)

ROOM AT THE TOP (based on the book by John Braine)
ROOM AT THE TOP (BRI, 1959)

LIFE AT THE TOP (BRI, 1965)
MAN AT THE TOP (BRI, 1973)

ROULETABILLE (based on books by Gaston Leroux)
MYSTERE DE LA CHAMBRE JAUNE, LA (FRA, 1913)
PARFUM DE LA DAME EN NOIR, LE (FRA, 1914)
MYSTERY OF THE YELLOW ROOM, THE (REA, 1919)
ROULETABILLE CHEZ LES BOHEMIENS (FRA, 1922)
MYSTERE DE LA CHAMBRE JAUNE, LA (FRA, 1931)
PARFUM DE LA DAME EN NOIR, LE (FRA, 1931)
ROULETABILLE AVIATEUR (FRA, 1932)
ROULETABILLE JOU ET GAGNE (FRA, 1947)
ROULETABILLE CONTRE LA DAME DE PIQUE (FRA,
    1948)
MYSTERE DE LA CHAMBRE JAUNE, LE (FRA, 1949)
PARFUM DE LA DAME EN NOIR, LE (FRA, 1949)

ROVING REPORTERS (based on an original screenplay)
TIME OUT FOR MURDER (FOX, 1938)
WHILE NEW YORK SLEEPS (FOX, 1938)
INSIDE STORY (FOX, 1938)

RUSTY (based on a story by Al Martin)
ADVENTURES OF RUSTY, THE (COL, 1945)
RETURN OF RUSTY, THE (COL, 1946)
SON OF RUSTY (COL, 1947)
FOR THE LOVE OF RUSTY (COL, 1947)
RUSTY LEADS THE WAY (COL, 1948)
MY DOG RUSTY (COL, 1948)
RUSTY SAVES A LIFE (COL, 1949)
RUSTY'S BIRTHDAY (COL, 1950)

SAINT, THE (based on books by Leslie Charteris; also appeared
    as a radio series)
SAINT IN NEW YORK, THE (RKO, 1938)
SAINT STRIKES BACK, THE (RKO, 1939)
SAINT IN LONDON, THE (RKO, 1939)
SAINT TAKES OVER, THE (RKO, 1940)
SAINT'S DOUBLE TROUBLE, THE (RKO, 1940)
SAINT IN PALM SPRINGS, THE (RKO, 1941)
SAINT'S VACATION, THE (RKO, 1941)
SAINT MEETS THE TIGER, THE (BRI, 1941)
SAINT'S GIRL FRIDAY, THE (RKO, 1943)
SAINT PRENT L'AFFIRT, LE (FRA, 1966)
SAINT, THE (series) (NBC–TV, 1967)

SAMMIE JOHNSIN (based on a screenplay by Pat Sullivan)
SAMMIE JOHNSIN (UN, 1916)
SAMMIE JOHNSIN AND HIS WONDERFUL LAMP (UN,
    1916)
SAMMIE JOHNSIN, MAGICIAN (UN, 1916)
SAMMIE JOHNSIN, STRONG MAN (UN, 1916)
SAMMIE JOHNSIN IN MEXICO (UN, 1916)
SAMMIE JOHNSIN GETS A JOB (UN, 1916)
SAMMIE JOHNSIN AT THE SEASIDE (UN, 1916)
SAMMIE JOHNSIN, HUNTER (UN, 1916)
SAMMIE MINDS THE BABY (UN, 1916)
SAMMIE JOHNSIN'S LOVE AFFAIR (UN, 1916)
SAMMIE JOHNSIN SLUMBERS NOT (UN, 1916)

SAMSON (based on screenplays from the legend of Samson
    in the Bible)
SAMSON (ITA, 1960)
SAMSON AGAINST THE SHEIK (ITA, 1960)
SON OF SAMSON (ITA, 1961)
SAMSON AND THE SEVEN MIRACLES OF THE WORLD
    (ITA, 1961)
SAMSON VS. THE GIANT KING (ITA, 1962)
SAMSON AND THE SEA BEASTS (ITA, 1963)

SAMSON AND THE SLAVE QUEEN   (ITA, 1963)
SAMSON AND THE MIGHTY CHALLENGE   (ITA, 1964)
SAMSON AND THE SEVEN CHALLENGES   (ITA, 1964)
SAMSON IN KING SOLOMON'S MINES   (ITA, 1964)
HERCULES, SAMSON AND ULYSSES   (ITA, 1965)

SANDOKAN   (based on the character created by Emilio
    Salgari)
  SANDOKAN, THE TIGER OF MOMPRACEM   (FRA/ITA/
    SPA, 1963)
  SANDOKAN AGAINST THE LEOPARD OF SARAWAK
    (ITA, 1964)
  SANDOKAN FIGHTS BACK   (ITA, 1964)
  SANDOKAN THE GREAT   (ITA, 1965)
  SANDOKAN   (serial)   (ITA--TV, 1976)

SANTO   (based on a screenplay)
  SANTO VS. THE ZOMBIES   (MEX, 1962)
  SANTO EN EL HOTEL DE LA MUERTE   (MEX, 1962)
  SANTO IN THE WAX MUSEUM   (MEX, 1963)
  SANTO CONTRA EL REY DEL CRIMEN   (MEX, 1963)
  SANTO VS. LOS MUJERES VAMPIROS   (MEX, 1963)
  SANTO ATTACKS THE WITCHES   (MEX, 1964)
  SANTO CONTRA EL CEREBRO DIABOLICO   (MEX,
    1964)
  SANTO CONTRA EL ESTRANGULADOR   (MEX, 1964)
  ESPECTRO VS. BARON DRAKOLA   (MEX, 1965)
  SANTO CONTRA EL ESPECTRO   (MEX, 1965)
  FROGANADORES DE TUMBRAS   (MEX, 1966)
  SANTO VS. INVASION DE LOS MARCIANOS   (MEX,
    1967)
  SANTO VS. LOS VILLANOS DEL RING   (MEX, 1967)
  SANTO VS. THE BLUE DEMON IN ATLANTIS   (MEX,
    1968)
  SANTO AND THE REVENGE OF THE VAMPIRE WOMEN
    (MEX, 1968)
  SANTO VS. DRACULA'S TREASURE   (MEX, 1968)
  SANTO AND THE BLUE DEMON VS. THE MONSTERS
    (MEX, 1968)
  VAMPIRO Y EL SEXO, EL   (MEX, 1968)
  WORLD OF THE DEAD   (MEX, 1969)
  SANTO VS. THE HEAD HUNTERS   (MEX, 1969)
  SANTO VS. THE MAFIA MURDERS   (MEX, 1970)
  ASSASSINS OF OTHER WORLDS   (MEX, 1971)
  SANTO AND THE VENGEANCE OF THE MUMMY   (MEX,
    1971)
  SANTO VS. CAPULINA   (MEX, 1971)
  SANTO VS. THE DAUGHTER OF FRANKENSTEIN
    (MEX, 1971)
  SANTO VS. THE ROYAL EAGLE   (MEX, 1971)
  SUICIDE MISSION   (MEX, 1971)
  SANTO IN FRONT OF DEATH   (MEX, 1972)
  SANTO VS. BLACK MAGIC   (MEX, 1972)
  SANTO AND THE BLUE DEMON VS. DRACULA AND
    THE WOLF MAN   (MEX, 1972)

SCATTERGOOD BAINES   (based on the radio series)
  SCATTERGOOD BAINES   (RKO, 1941)
  SCATTERGOOD MEETS BROADWAY   (RKO, 1941)
  SCATTERGOOD PULLS THE STRINGS   (RKO, 1941)
  SCATTERGOOD RIDES HIGH   (RKO, 1942)
  SCATTERGOOD SURVIVES A MURDER   (RKO, 1942)

SECRET SERVICE   (based on material compiled by W.H.
    Moran)
  SECRET SERVICE OF THE AIR   (WB, 1939)
  CODE OF THE SECRET SERVICE   (WB, 1939)
  SMASHING THE MONEY RING   (WB, 1939)
  MURDER IN THE AIR   (WB, 1940)

SEXTON BLAKE   (based on characters by Harry Blyth)
  SEXTON BLAKE   (BRI, 1909)
  JEWEL THIEVES TURN TO EARTH BY SEXTON
    BLAKE   (BRI, 1910)
  SEXTON BLAKE VS. BARON KETTLER   (BRI, 1912)
  MYSTERY OF THE DIAMOND BELT   (BRI, 1914)
  KAISER'S SPIES, THE   (BRI, 1914)
  THORNTON JEWEL MYSTERY, THE   (BRI, 1915)
  COUNTERFEITERS, THE   (BRI, 1915)
  FURTHER EXPLOITS OF SEXTON BLAKE, THE   (BRI,
    1919)
  MYSTERY OF THE SILENT DEATH   (short)   (BRI, 1928)
  CLUE OF THE SECOND GOBLET, THE   (short)   (BRI,
    1928)
  BLAKE THE LAWBREAKER   (short)   (BRI, 1928)
  SEXTON BLAKE, GAMBLER   (short)   (BRI, 1928)
  SILKEN THREADS   (short)   (BRI, 1928)
  GREAT OFFICE MYSTERY, THE   (short)   (BRI, 1928)
  SEXTON BLAKE AND THE BEARDED DOCTOR   (BRI,
    1935)
  SEXTON BLAKE AND THE MADEMOISELLE   (BRI, 1935)
  SEXTON BLAKE AND THE HOODED TERROR   (BRI,
    1938)
  MEET SEXTON BLAKE   (BRI, 1944)
  ECHO MURDERS, THE   (BRI, 1945)
  MURDER AT SITE THREE   (BRI, 1959)
  SEXTON BLAKE   (series)   (BRI--TV, n.d.)

SEXY SUSAN   (source unlisted)
  SWEET SINS OF SEXY SUSAN   (ITA, 1968)
  SEXY SUSAN SINS AGAIN   (ITA, 1969)
  SEXY SUSAN AND NAPOLEON   (ITA, 1970)

SHADOW, THE   (based on a character in the radio series)
  BURGLAR TO THE RESCUE, A   (short)   (UN, 1931)
  HOUSE OF MYSTERY   (short)   (UN, 1931)
  SEALED LIPS   (short)   (UN, 1931)
  TRAPPED   (short)   (UN, 1931)
  CIRCUS SHOW--UP   (short)   (UN, 1932)
  RED SHADOWS, THE   (short)   (UN, 1932)
  SHADOW STRIKES, THE   (GN, 1937)
  INTERNATIONAL CRIME   (GN, 1938)
  SHADOW, THE   (serial)   (COL, 1940)
  SHADOW RETURNS, THE   (MON, 1946)
  BEHIND THE MASK   (MON, 1946)
  MISSING LADY, THE   (MON, 1946)
  INVISIBLE AVENGER, THE   (BOURBON STREET
    SHADOWS)   (REP, 1958)

SHAFT   (based on the book by Ernest Tidyman)
  SHAFT   (MGM, 1971)
  SHAFT'S BIG SCORE   (MGM, 1972)
  SHAFT IN AFRICA   (MGM, 1973)
  SHAFT   (series)   (CBS--TV, 1973)

SHERLOCK HOLMES   (based on the books, stories and
    characters of Sir Arthur Conan Doyle; also appeared as a
    radio series. The 1912 French films and the 1921--23
    British films were 2--reel shorts)
  SHERLOCK HOLMES BAFFLED   (BIO, 1903)
  ADVENTURES OF SHERLOCK HOLMES, THE   (BRI,
    1905)
  ADVENTURES OF SHERLOCK HOLMES, THE   (BIO,
    1908)
  RIVAL SHERLOCK HOLMES, A   (ITA, 1908)
  SHERLOCK HOLMES IN THE GREAT MURDER MYSTERY
    (IND, 1908)
  SHERLOCK HOLMES   (DEN, 1908)
  SHERLOCK HOLMES IN THE GAS CHAMBER   (DEN,

1908)
GREY DANE, THE   (DEN. 1909)
MURDER IN BAKER STREET, THE   (DEN, 1910)
BERYL CORONET, THE   (FRA, 1912)
REYGATE SQUIRES   (FRA, 1912)
SPECKLED BAND, THE   (FRA, 1912)
COPPER BEECHES   (FRA, 1912)
MYSTERY OF BASCOMBE VALE   (FRA, 1912)
SILVER BLAZE, THE   (FRA, 1912)
STOLEN PAPERS   (FRA, 1912)
MUSGRAVE RITUAL, THE   (FRA, 1912)
SHERLOCK HOLMES SOLVES THE SIGN OF THE FOUR
   (THA, 1913)
STUDY IN SCARLET, A   (FRA, 1914)
HOUND OF THE BASKERVILLES, THE   (FRA, 1915)
ISOLATED HOUSE, THE   (IND, 1915)
VALLEY OF FEAR   (BRI, 1916)
SHERLOCK HOLMES   (ESS, 1916)
HOUND OF THE BASKERVILLES, THE   (GER, 1917)
BERYL CORONET, THE   (BRI, 1921)
CASE OF IDENTITY, A   (BRI, 1921)
COPPER BEECHES, THE   (BRI, 1921)
DEVIL'S FOOT, THE   (BRI, 1921)
DYING DETECTIVE, THE   (BRI, 1921)
EMPTY HOUSE, THE   (BRI, 1921)
HOUND OF THE BASKERVILLES, THE   (BRI, 1921)
MAN WITH THE TWISTED LIP, THE   (BRI, 1921)
NOBLE BACHELOR, THE   (BRI, 1921)
PRIORY SCHOOL, THE   (BRI, 1921)
REDHEADED LEAGUE, THE   (BRI, 1921)
RESIDENT PATIENT, THE   (BRI, 1921)
SCANDAL IN BOHEMIA, A   (BRI, 1921)
SOLITARY CYCLIST, THE   (BRI, 1921)
TIGER OF SAN PEDRO   (BRI, 1921)
YELLOW FACE, THE   (BRI, 1921)
ABBEY GRANDE   (BRI, 1921)
ADVENTURES OF SHERLOCK HOLMES, THE   (BRI,
   1922)
HOUND OF THE BASKERVILLES, THE   (FBO, 1922)
BLACK PETER   (BRI, 1922)
BOSCOMBE VALLEY MYSTERY, THE   (BRI, 1922)
BRUCE PARTINGTON PLANS, THE   (BRI, 1922)
CHARLES AUGUSTUS MILVERTON   (BRI, 1922)
GOLDEN PINCE--NEZ, THE   (BRI, 1922)
GREEK INTERPRETER, THE   (BRI, 1922)
MUSGRAVE RITUAL, THE   (BRI, 1922)
NAVAL TREATY, THE   (BRI, 1922)
NORWOOD BUILDER, THE   (BRI, 1922)
RED CIRCLE, THE   (BRI, 1922)
REYGATE SQUIRES, THE   (BRI, 1922)
SHERLOCK HOLMES   (MGM, 1922)
SECOND STAIN, THE   (BRI, 1922)
SIX NAPOLEONS, THE   (BRI, 1922)
STOCKBROKER'S CLERK, THE   (BRI, 1922)
BLUE CARBUNCLE, THE   (BRI, 1923)
CARDBOARD BOX, THE   (BRI, 1923)
CROOKED MAN, THE   (BRI, 1923)
DANCING MEN, THE   (BRI, 1923)
DISAPPEARANCE OF LADY FRANCIS CARFAX, THE
   (BRI, 1923)
ENGINEER'S THUMB, THE   (BRI, 1923)
FINAL PROBLEM, THE   (BRI, 1923)
GLORIA SCOTT, THE   (BRI, 1923)
HIS LAST BOW   (BRI, 1923)
MAZARIN STONE, THE   (BRI, 1923)
MISSING THREE--QUARTER, THE   (BRI, 1923)
MYSTERY OF THOR BRIDGE, THE   (BRI, 1923)
SIGN OF FOUR, THE   (BRI, 1923)
SILVER BLAZE, THE   (BRI, 1923)

SPECKLED BAND, THE   (BRI, 1923)
THREE STUDENTS, THE   (BRI, 1923)
BLACK SHERLOCK HOLMES, A   (IND, 1927)
HOUND OF THE BASKERVILLES, THE   (GER, 1929)
RETURN OF SHERLOCK HOLMES, THE   (PAR, 1929)
SHERLOCK HOLMES' FATAL HOUR   (BRI, 1931)
   (British title: SLEEPING CARDINAL, THE)
SPECKLED BAND, THE   (short)   (BRI, 1931)
ADVENTURE OF THE MISSING REMBRANDT, THE
   (BRI, 1932)
SHERLOCK HOLMES   (FOX, 1932)
SIGN OF FOUR, THE   (BRI, 1932)
HOUND OF THE BASKERVILLES, THE   (BRI, 1932)
STUDY IN SCARLET, A   (WW, 1933)
HOUND OF THE BASKERVILLES, THE   (BRI, 1934)
TRIUMPH OF SHERLOCK HOLMES, THE   (BRI, 1935)
HOUND OF THE BASKERVILLES, THE   (GER, 1936)
SHERLOCK HOLMES AND THE SILVER BLAZE   (BRI,
   1936)
GRAUE DAME, DIE   (GER, 1937)
MAN WHO WAS SHERLOCK HOLMES, THE   (GER, 1937)
ADVENTURES OF SHERLOCK HOLMES, THE   (FOX,
   1939)
HOUND OF THE BASKERVILLES, THE   (FOX, 1939)
SHERLOCK HOLMES AND THE SECRET WEAPON
   (UN, 1942)
SHERLOCK HOLMES AND THE VOICE OF TERROR
   (UN, 1942)
SHERLOCK HOLMES FACES DEATH   (UN, 1943)
SHERLOCK HOLMES IN WASHINGTON   (UN, 1943)
SCARLET CLAW, THE   (UN, 1944)
SPIDER WOMAN, THE   (UN, 1944)
HOUSE OF FEAR, THE   (UN, 1944)
PEARL OF DEATH, THE   (UN, 1944)
WOMAN IN GREEN, THE   (UN, 1945)
PURSUIT TO ALGIERS   (UN, 1945)
DRESSED TO KILL   (UN, 1946)
TERROR BY NIGHT   (UN, 1946)
MAN WITH THE TWISTED LIP, THE   (short)   (BRI, 1951)
ADVENTURES OF SHERLOCK HOLMES, THE   (series)
   (NBC--TV, 1954)
HOUND OF THE BASKERVILLES, THE   (BRI, 1959)
SHERLOCK HOLMES AND THE DEADLY NECKLACE
   (GER, 1962)
VALLEY OF FEAR   (GER, 1964)
MR. MAGOO -- MAN OF MYSTERY   (UPA, 1964)
FOG   (BRI, 1965)
STUDY IN TERROR, A   (BRI, 1966)
PRIVATE LIFE OF SHERLOCK HOLMES, THE   (UA,
   1970)
LONGING OF SHERLOCK HOLMES, THE   (CZE, 1971)
HOUND OF THE BASKERVILLES, THE   (ABC--TV, 1972)
RETURN OF THE WORLD'S GREATEST DETECTIVE,
   THE   (NBC--TV, 1976)
SHERLOCK HOLMES IN NEW YORK   (NBC--TV, 1976)
SILVER BLAZE, THE   (short)   (LCA, 1976)
SEVEN PER CENT SOLUTION   (UN, 1976)
MR. SHERLOCK HOLMES OF LONDON   (short)
   (CAL, 1976)

SINBAD   (based on the legend and the "Arabian Nights"
   stories)
   MAGIC VOYAGE OF SINBAD, THE   (COL, 1962)
   GOLDEN VOYAGE OF SINBAD, THE   (COL, 1974)
   SINBAD AND THE EYE OF THE TIGER   (COL, 1977)

SISSI   (source unlisted)
   SISSI   (GER, 1956)
   SISSI DIE JUNGE KAISERIN   (GER, 1957)

SISSI SCHICKSALSJAHRE EINER KAISERIN (GER, 1958)

SIX MORAL TALES (based on screenplays by Eric Rohmer)
    BOULANGERE DE MONCEAU, LA (FRA, 1962)
    CARRIERE DE SUZANNE, LA (FRA, 1963)
    COLLECTIONIEUSE, LA (FRA, 1970)
    MY NIGHT AT MAUD'S (FRA, 1970)
    CLAIRE'S KNEE (FRA, 1971)
    CHLOE IN THE AFTERNOON (FRA, 1972)

SLOANES, THE (based on a book by Harry Kurnitz)
    FAST COMPANY (MGM, 1938) (TV title: KING OF SPORTS)
    FAST AND LOOSE (MGM, 1939)
    FAST AND FURIOUS (MGM, 1939)

SNUFFY SMITH (based on the comic strip by Billy De Beck)
    PRIVATE SNUFFY SMITH (MON, 1941)
    HILLBILLY BLITZKREIG (MON, 1942)
    SNUFFY SMITH, YARDBIRD (MON, 1942)
    BARNEY GOOGLE AND SNUFFY SMITH (series) (TV, 1963)

SOPHIE LANG (based on stories by Frederick Irving Anderson)
    NOTORIOUS SOPHIE LANG (PAR, 1934)
    RETURN OF SOPHIE LANG (PAR, 1936)
    SOPHIE LANG GOES WEST (PAR, 1937)

SPLINTERS (based on a screenplay by W.P. Lipscome)
    SPLINTERS (BRI, 1929)
    SPLINTERS IN THE NAVY (BRI, 1931)
    SPLINTERS IN THE AIR (BRI, 1937)

SQUIBS (based on the play by Clifford Seyler and George Pearson)
    SQUIBS (BRI, 1921)
    SQUIBS WINS THE CALCUTTA SWEEP (BRI, 1922)
    SQUIB'S HONEYMOON (BRI, 1923)
    SQUIBS, M.P. (BRI, 1923)
    SQUIBS (BRI, 1935)

SUPER GIANT (source unlisted)
    SUPER GIANT 1 (JAP, 1956)
    SUPER GIANT 2 (JAP, 1956)
    SUPER GIANT 3 (JAP, 1957)
    SUPER GIANT 4 (JAP, 1957)
    SUPER GIANT 5 (JAP, 1957)
    SUPER GIANT 6 (JAP, 1958)
    SUPER GIANT 7 (JAP, 1958)
    SUPER GIANT 8 (JAP, 1959)
    SUPER GIANT 9 (JAP, 1959)

SUPERARGO (based on a story by Julio Buchs)
    NEW YORK CHIAMA SUPERARGO (FRA/ITA, 1966)
    SUPERARGO VS. DIABOLICUS (FRA/ITA, 1966)
    SUPERARGO AND THE FACELESS GIANTS (ITA/SPA, 1967)
    CRIMINAL KING, THE (ITA/SPA, 1967)

SUPERMAN (based on the comic strip by Jerry Siegel and Joe Shuster)
    SUPERMAN (PAR, 1941)
    SUPERMAN IN THE MECHANICAL MONSTERS (PAR, 1941)
    SUPERMAN IN BILLION DOLLAR LIMITED (PAR, 1942)
    SUPERMAN IN DESTRUCTION INC. (PAR, 1942)

SUPERMAN IN ELECTRIC EARTHQUAKE (PAR, 1942)
SUPERMAN IN SHOWDOWN (PAR, 1942)
SUPERMAN IN TERROR ON THE MIDWAY (PAR, 1942)
SUPERMAN IN THE ARCTIC GIANT (PAR, 1942)
SUPERMAN IN THE BULLETEERS (PAR, 1942)
SUPERMAN IN THE ELEVENTH HOUR (PAR, 1942)
SUPERMAN IN THE JAPOTEURS (PAR, 1942)
SUPERMAN IN THE MAGNETIC TELESCOPE (PAR, 1942)
SUPERMAN IN VOLCANO (PAR, 1942)
SUPERMAN IN JUNGLE DRUMS (PAR, 1943)
SUPERMAN IN SECRET AGENT (PAR, 1943)
SUPERMAN IN THE MUMMY STRIKES (PAR, 1943)
SUPERMAN IN THE UNDERGROUND WORLD (PAR, 1943)
SUPERMAN (serial) (COL, 1948)
ATOM MAN VS. SUPERMAN (serial) (COL, 1950)
SUPERMAN AND THE MOLE MEN (TV, 1951)
SUPERMAN (series) (TV, 1952)
SUPERMAN AND THE JUNGLE DEVIL (TV, 1953)
SUPERMAN FLIES AGAIN (TV, 1954)
SUPERMAN VS. THE GORILLA GANG (IND, 1965)
NEW ADVENTURES OF SUPERMAN, THE (series) (CBS-TV, 1966)
SUPERMAN–AQUAMAN HOUR OF ADVENTURE (series) (CBS--TV, 1967)
SUPER FRIENDS (series) (ABC--TV, 1973)
IT'S A BIRD, IT'S A PLANE, IT'S SUPERMAN (ABC--TV, 1975)

SYBERBERG TRILOGY (based on original screenplays)
    LUDWIG II: REQUIEM FOR A VIRGIN KING (GER, 1971)
    HANS MAY (GER, 1974)
    HITLER, A FILM FROM GERMANY (GER, 1977)

TAILSPIN TOMMY (based on the comic strip by Hal Forrest; also appeared as a radio series)
    TAILSPIN TOMMY (serial) (UN, 1934)
    TAILSPIN TOMMY IN THE GREAT AIR MYSTERY (serial) (UN, 1935)
    MYSTERY PLANE (MON, 1939)
    STUNT PILOT (MON, 1939)

TAMMY (based on the book, "Tammy Out of Time" by Cid Ricketts Sumner)
    TAMMY AND THE BACHELOR (UN, 1957)
    TAMMY AND THE DOCTOR (UN, 1963)
    TAMMY (series) (ABC--TV, 1965)
    TAMMY AND THE MILLIONAIRE (UN, 1967)

TARZAN (based on the books by Edgar Rice Burroughs)
    TARZAN OF THE APES (FN, 1918)
    ROMANCE OF TARZAN (FN, 1918)
    RETURN OF TARZAN (MGM, 1920)
    REVENGE OF TARZAN (IND, 1920)
    SON OF TARZAN (serial) (IND, 1920)
    ADVENTURES OF TARZAN (serial) (IND, 1921)
    JUNGLE TRAIL OF THE SON OF TARZAN (NAT, 1923)
    TARZAN AND THE GOLDEN LION (FBO, 1927)
    TARZAN THE MIGHTY (serial) (UN, 1928)
    ADVENTURES OF TARZAN (serial) (IND, 1928)
    TARZAN THE TIGER (serial) (UN, 1929)
    TARZAN THE APE MAN (MGM, 1932)
    TARZAN THE FEARLESS (serial) (IND, 1933)
    TARZAN AND HIS MATE (MGM, 1934)
    NEW ADVENTURES OF TARZAN, THE (serial) (IND, 1935)
    TARZAN ESCAPES (MGM, 1936)

TYPHOON (IN, 1937)
TARZAN'S REVENGE (FOX, 1938)
TARZAN AND THE GREEN GODDESS (IND, 1938)
TARZAN FINDS A SON (MGM, 1939)
ADVENTURES OF A CHINESE TARZAN (CHN, 1940)
TARZAN'S SECRET TREASURE (MGM, 1941)
TARZAN'S NEW YORK ADVENTURE (MGM, 1942)
TARZAN TRIUMPHS (RKO, 1943)
TARZAN'S DESERT MYSTERY (RKO, 1943)
TARZAN AND THE AMAZONS (RKO, 1945)
TARZAN AND THE LEOPARD WOMAN (RKO, 1946)
TARZAN AND THE HUNTRESS (RKO, 1947)
TARZAN AND THE MERMAIDS (RKO, 1948)
TARZAN'S MAGIC FOUNTAIN (RKO, 1949)
TARZAN AND THE SLAVE GIRL (RKO, 1950)
TARZAN'S PERIL (RKO, 1951)
TARZAN'S SAVAGE FURY (RKO, 1952)
TARZAN IN ISTANBUL (TUR, 1952)
TARZAN AND THE SHE--DEVILS (RKO, 1953)
TARZAN'S HIDDEN JUNGLE (RKO, 1955)
TARZAN AND THE LOST SAFARI (MGM, 1957)
TARZAN'S FIGHT FOR LIFE (MGM, 1958)
TARZAN AND THE TRAPPERS (NBC--TV, 1958)
TARZAN'S GREATEST ADVENTURE (PAR, 1959)
TARZAN THE MAGNIFICENT (PAR, 1960)
TARZAN THE APE MAN (MGM, 1960)
TYPHOON TARZAN (IN, 1962)
TARZAN GOES TO INDIA (MGM, 1962)
ROCKET TARZAN (IN, 1963)
TARZAN'S THREE CHALLENGES (MGM, 1963)
TARZAN AND KING KONG (IN, 1963)
TARZAN COMES TO DELHI (IN, c1964)
TARZAN AND THE GORILLA (IN, 1964)
TARZAN AND CLEOPATRA (IN, 1964)
TARZAN'S BELOVED (IN, c1964)
TARZAN AND THE MAGICIAN (IN, c1964)
TARZAN AND CAPTAIN KISHORE (IN, 1965)
TARZAN AND THE CIRCUS (IN, 1965)
TARZAN AND THE VALLEY OF GOLD (AI, 1966)
TARZAN (series) (NBC--TV, 1966)
TARZAN AND THE GREAT RIVER (PAR, 1968)
TARZAN AND THE JUNGLE BOY (PAR, 1968)
TARZAN AND THE GROTTO OF GOLD (ITA/SPA, 1969)
TARZAN'S JUNGLE REBELLION (NGP, 1970)
TARZAN'S DEADLY SILENCE (NGP, 1970)
TARZAN AND THE RAINBOW (ITA/SPA, 1972)
TARZAN, LORD OF THE JUNGLE (series) (CBS--TV, 1976)

TEMPEST CODY (based on stories by Jacques Jaccard and Dorothy Rockfort)
TEMPEST CODY HITS THE TRAIL (UN, 1919)
TEMPEST CODY FLIRTS WITH DEATH (UN, 1919)
TEMPEST CODY RUNS WILD (UN, 1919)
TEMPEST CODY'S MANHUNT (UN, 1919)
TEMPEST CODY PLAYS DETECTIVE (UN, 1919)
TEMPEST CODY GETS HER MAN (UN, 1919)
TEMPEST CODY TURNS THE TABLES (UN, 1919)
TEMPEST CODY BUCKS THE TRUST (UN, 1919)
TEMPEST CODY, KIDNAPPER (UN, 1919)

TENAMONYA (based on a story by Toshio Kagawa)
TENAMONYA (series) (JAP--TV, 1966)
TENAMONYA: CONFUSION IN THE LAST DAYS OF THE TOKUGAWA REGIME (JAP, 1967)
GHOST JOURNEY (JAP, 1967)

TEXAS RANGERS, THE (based on a screenplay by Elmer Clifton)

RANGERS TAKE OVER, THE (PRC, 1943)
BAD MEN OF THUNDER GAP (PRC, 1943)
BORDER BUCKAROOS (PRC, 1943)
WEST OF TEXAS (PRC, 1943)
BOSS OF RAWHIDE (PRC, 1944)
SPOOK TOWN (PRC, 1944)
GUNS OF THE LAW (PRC, 1944)
THUNDERGAP OUTLAWS (PRC, 1944)
OUTLAW ROUNDUP (PRC, 1944)
PINTO BANDIT, THE (PRC, 1944)
TRAIL OF TERROR (PRC, 1944)
RETURN OF THE RANGERS (PRC, 1944)
GANGSTERS OF THE FRONTIER (PRC, 1944)
WHISPERING SKULL, THE (PRC, 1944)
DEAD OR ALIVE (PRC, 1944)
ENEMY OF THE LAW (PRC, 1945)
FLAMING BULLETS (PRC, 1945)
THREE IN THE SADDLE (PRC, 1945)
MARKED FOR MURDER (PRC, 1945)
FRONTIER FUGITIVES (PRC, 1946)

THATCHER COLT (based on stories by Anthony Abbot [Fulton Oursler] ; also appeared as a radio series)
NIGHT CLUB LADY (COL, 1932)
CIRCUS QUEEN MURDER, THE (COL, 1933)
PANTHER'S CLAW, THE (PRC, 1942)

THIN MAN, THE (based on books by Dashiell Hammett)
THIN MAN, THE (MGM, 1934)
AFTER THE THIN MAN (MGM, 1936)
ANOTHER THIN MAN (MGM, 1939)
SHADOW OF THE THIN MAN (MGM, 1941)
THIN MAN GOES HOME, THE (MGM, 1944)
SONG OF THE THIN MAN (MGM, 1947)
THIN MAN, THE (series) (NBC--TV, 1957)
NICK AND NORA (series) (ABC--TV, 1975)

THREE MESQUITEERS, THE (based on books by William Colt MacDonald)
POWDERSMOKE RANGE (RKO, 1935)
THREE MESQUITEERS, THE (REP, 1936)
LAST OUTLAW, THE (PAR, 1936)
GHOST TOWN GOLD (REP, 1936)
ROARIN' LEAD (REP, 1936)
TRIGGER TRIO (REP, 1937)
RIDERS OF THE WHISTLING SKULL (REP, 1937)
HIT THE SADDLE (REP, 1937)
GUNSMOKE RANCH (REP, 1937)
COME ON COWBOYS (REP, 1937)
RANGE DEFENDERS (REP, 1937)
HEART OF THE ROCKIES (REP, 1937)
WILD HORSE RODEO (REP, 1937)
LAW WEST OF TOMBSTONE (RKO, 1938)
RED RIVER RANGE (REP, 1938)
CALL THE MESQUITEERS (REP, 1938)
RIDERS OF THE BLACK HILLS (REP, 1938)
PALS OF THE SADDLE (REP, 1938)
PURPLE VIGILANTES (REP, 1938)
OVERLAND STAGE RAIDERS (REP, 1938)
OUTLAWS OF SONORA (REP, 1938)
SANTA FE STAMPEDE (REP, 1938)
HEROES OF THE HILLS (REP, 1938)
COWBOYS FROM TEXAS (REP, 1939)
NEW FRONTIER, THE (REP, 1939)
NIGHT RIDERS (REP, 1939)
KANSAS TERRORS, THE (REP, 1939)
THREE TEXAS STEERS (REP, 1939)
WYOMING OUTLAWS (REP, 1939)
ROCKY MOUNTAIN RANGERS (REP, 1940)

TRAIL BLAZERS (REP, 1940)
OKLAHOMA RENEGADES (REP, 1940)
PIONEERS OF THE WEST (REP, 1940)
COVERED WAGON DAYS (REP, 1940)
ROCKY MOUNTAIN RANGERS (REP, 1940)
HEROES OF THE SADDLE (REP, 1940)
LONE STAR RAIDERS (REP, 1940)
UNDER TEXAS SKIES (REP, 1940)
GAUCHOS OF EL DORADO (REP, 1941)
GANGS OF SONORA (REP, 1941)
PALS OF THE PECOS (REP, 1941)
PRAIRIE PIONEERS (REP, 1941)
WEST OF CIMARRON (REP, 1941)
SADDLEMATES (REP, 1941)
CODE OF THE OUTLAW (REP, 1942)
OUTLAWS OF THE CHEROKEE TRAIL (REP, 1941)
PHANTOM PLAINSMAN, THE (REP, 1942)
RAIDERS OF THE RANGE (REP, 1942)
SHADOWS ON THE SAGE (REP, 1942)
VALLEY OF HUNTED MEN (REP, 1942)
WESTWARD HO! (REP, 1942)
BLOCKED TRAIL, THE (REP, 1943)
RAIDERS OF THE RIO GRANDE (REP, 1943)
SHADOWS ON THE SAGE (REP, 1943)
SANTA FE SCOUTS (REP, 1943)
THUNDERING TRAILS (REP, 1943)

THREE SMART GIRLS (based on a story by Adele
    Comandini)
    THREE SMART GIRLS (UN, 1936)
    THREE SMART GIRLS GROW UP (UN, 1939)
    HERS TO HOLD (UN, 1943)

TINTIN (based on the comic strip by George Remi)
    CRABE AUX PINCES D'OR, LA (BEL, 1947)
    TINTIN AND THE MYSTERY OF THE GOLDEN FLEECE
        (BEL, 1961)
    TINTIN (series) (FRA--TV, 1961)
    OBJECTIVE MOON (BEL, 1962)
    MYSTERY OF THE BLUE ORANGES (BEL, 1965)
    TINTIN AND THE TEMPLE OF THE SUN (BEL, 1969)
    TINTIN AND THE LAKE OF SHARKS (BEL, 1972)
    I, TINTIN (BEL, 1976)

TOLSTOY TRILOGY (based on books by Leo Tolstoy)
    SISTERS, THE (RUS, 1957)
    1918 (RUS, 1958)
    BLEAK MORNING (RUS, 1959)

TOONERVILLE TROLLEY (based on the comic strip,
    "Toonerville Folks," by Fontaine Fox)
    TOONERVILLE TROLLEY (series) (IND, 1921)
    MICKEY MCGUIRE (series) (IND, 1927)
    TOONERVILLE TROLLEY (short) (IND, 1936)
    TOONERVILLE PICNIC (short) (IND, 1936)

TOPO GIGIO (based on Italian puppet characters)
    TRIP TO THE MOON, A (ITA, 1963)
    MAGIC WORLD OF TOPO GIGIO, THE (ITA/JAP, 1965)
    TOPO GIGIO AND THE MISSILE WAR (ITA/JAP, 1967)

TOPPER (based on the book by Thorne Smith)
    TOPPER (MGM, 1937)
    TOPPER TAKES A TRIP (UA, 1939)
    TOPPER RETURNS (UA, 1941)
    TOPPER (series) (NBC--TV, 1953)

TORCHY BLANE (based on characters created by Frederick
    Nebel)

SMART BLONDE (WB, 1936)
ADVENTUROUS BLONDE (WB, 1937)
FLY AWAY BABY (WB, 1937)
TORCHY BLANE IN PANAMA (WB, 1938)
BLONDES AT WORK (WB, 1938)
TORCHY GETS HER MAN (WB, 1938)
TORCHY BLANE IN CHINATOWN (WB, 1939)
TORCHY RUNS FOR MAYOR (WB, 1939)
TORCHY PLAYS WITH DYNAMITE (WB, 1939)

TOTO (source unlisted)
    TOTO THE SHEIK (ITA, 1950)
    TOTO A COLORI (ITA, 1952)
    TOTO IN HELL (ITA, 1955)
    TOTO CERCA PACE (ITA, 1957)
    TOTO E I RE DI ROMA (ITA, 1958)
    TOTO ON THE MOON (ITA, 1958)
    TOTO, PEPPINO E I FUORILEGGE (ITA, 1959)
    TOTO VS. MACISTE (ITA, 1961)
    TOTO E PEPPINO DIVISI A BERLINO (ITA, 1963)
    TOTO CONTRO I 4 (ITA, 1965)
    TOTO DIABOLICO (ITA, 1966)

TOUGH GUY (source unlisted)
    TOUGH GUY I (JAP, 1960)
    TOUGH GUY II (JAP, 1961)
    TOUGH GUY III (JAP, 1963)

TRACY/SAWYER (based on a screenplay by various authors)
    TANKS A MILLION (UA, 1941)
    HAY FOOT (UA, 1941)
    ABOUT FACE (UA, 1942)
    FALL IN (UA, 1943)
    YANKS AHOY (UA, 1943)

TUGBOAT ANNIE (based on stories by Norman Reilly Raine)
    TUGBOAT ANNIE (MGM, 1933)
    TUGBOAT ANNIE SAILS AGAIN (WB, 1940)
    CAPTAIN TUGBOAT ANNIE (REP, 1945)
    ADVENTURES OF TUGBOAT ANNIE, THE (series)
        (TV, 1956)

ULTUS (based on a screenplay by George Pearson)
    ULTUS: MAN FROM THE DEAD (BRI, 1916)
    ULTUS AND THE GREY LADY (BRI, 1916)
    ULTUS AND THE SECRET OF THE NIGHT (BRI, 1917)
    ULTUS AND THE THREE BUTTON MYSTERY (BRI,
        1917)

VIRGIL TIBBS (see MR. TIBBS)

WAJDA TRILOGY (based on a script by Bohdan Czeszko)
    GENERATION, A (POL, 1954)
    KANAL (POL, 1956)
    ASHES AND DIAMONDS (POL, 1958)

WALKING TALL (based on a screenplay by Mort Briskin and
    the life of Sheriff Buford Pusser)
    WALKING TALL (CIN, 1973)
    WALKING TALL II (CIN, 1975)
    FINAL CHAPTER WALKING TALL (AI, 1977)

THE WEAVER BROTHERS AND ELVIRY (based on original
    screenplays by various authors)
    DOWN IN "ARKANSAW" (REP, 1938)
    JEEPERS CREEPERS (REP, 1939)
    IN OLD MISSOURI (REP, 1940)
    FRIENDLY NEIGHBORS (REP, 1940)
    ARKANSAS JUDGE, THE (REP, 1941)

MOUNTAIN MOONLIGHT   (REP, 1941)
SHEPHERD OF THE OZARKS   (REP, 1942)
OLD HOMESTEAD, THE   (REP, 1942)
MOUNTAIN RHYTHM   (REP, 1943)
TUXEDO JUNCTION   (REP, 1943)

WHEELER & WOOLSEY   (based on a screenplay)
CUCKOOS, THE   (RKO, 1930)
HALF SHOT AT SUNRISE   (RKO, 1930)
HOOK, LINE AND SINKER   (RKO, 1930)
CRACKED NUTS   (RKO, 1931)
CAUGHT PLASTERED   (RKO, 1931)
PEACH O'RENO   (RKO, 1931)
GIRL CRAZY   (RKO, 1932)
HOLD 'EM JAIL   (RKO, 1932)
SO THIS IS AFRICA   (COL, 1933)
DIPLOMANIACS   (RKO, 1933)
HIPS, HIPS, HOORAY   (RKO, 1934)
COCKEYED CAVALIERS   (RKO, 1934)
KENTUCKY KERNELS   (RKO, 1934)
NITWITS, THE   (RKO, 1935)
RAINMAKERS, THE   (RKO, 1935)
SILLY BILLIES   (RKO, 1936)
MUMMY'S BOYS   (RKO, 1936)
ON AGAIN, OFF AGAIN   (RKO, 1937)
HIGH FLYERS   (RKO, 1937)

WHISTLER, THE   (based on the CBS radio series)
WHISTLER, THE   (COL, 1944)
MARK OF THE WHISTLER   (COL, 1944)
POWER OF THE WHISTLER   (COL, 1944)
VOICE OF THE WHISTLER, THE   (COL, 1945)
MYSTERIOUS INTRUDER, THE   (COL, 1946)
SECRET OF THE WHISTLER, THE   (COL, 1946)
THIRTEENTH HOUR, THE   (COL, 1947)
RETURN OF THE WHISTLER, THE   (COL, 1948)
WHISTLER, THE   (series)   (TV, 1954)

WHISTLING   (THE FOX)   (based on the play by Laurence
     Gross and Edward Childs Carpenter)
WHISTLING IN THE DARK   (MGM, 1941)
WHISTLING IN DIXIE   (MGM, 1942)
WHISTLING IN BROOKLYN   (MGM, 1943)

WINNETOU   (based on stories by Dr. Karl May)
WINNETOU UNS DAS HALBBLUT APANATSCHI   (GER,
     1966)
WINNETOU UND SEIM FREUND OLD FIREHAND
     (GER, 1966)
WINNETOU UND SHATTERHAND IM TAL DER TOTEN
     (GER, 1968)

WINNIE THE POOH   (based on the books by A.A. Milne)
WINNIE THE POOH AND THE HONEY TREE   (DIS,
     1965)
WINNIE THE POOH AND THE BLUSTERY DAY   (DIS,
     1968)
WINNIE THE POOH AND TIGGER TOO   (DIS, 1974)

WOLF MAN   (based on a screenplay by Curt Siodmak)
WOLF MAN, THE   (UN, 1941)
FRANKENSTEIN MEETS THE WOLF MAN   (UN, 1943)
HOUSE OF FRANKENSTEIN   (UN, 1944)
HOUSE OF DRACULA   (UN, 1945)

BLOOD   (IND, 1974)

WRESTLING WOMEN   (source unlisted)
DOCTOR OF DOOM   (MEX, 1962)
WRESTLING WOMEN VS. THE AZTEC MUMMY, THE
     (MEX, 1964)
WRESTLING WOMEN   (MEX, 1966)
WRESTLING WOMEN VS. THE MURDERING ROBOT
     (MEX, 1969)

YOSHIDA TRILOGY   (based on screenplays by Toshiro
     Ishido)
JOEN   (JAP, 1967)
HONOO TO ONNA   (JAP, 1967)
FLICKER OF THE SILVER THAW   (JAP, 1968)

THE YOUNG GUY
LET'S GO, YOUNG GUY!   (JAP, 1967)
JUDO CHAMPION   (JAP, 1967)
SKIING ON THE SUMMIT   (JAP, 1967)
YOUNG GUY GOES TO RIO   (JAP, 1968)
YOUNG GUY GRADUATES   (JAP, 1969)
YOUNG GUY ON MT. COOK   (JAP, 1969)

ZATOICHI   (THE BLIND SWORDSMAN)   (based on a book
     by Kan Shimozawa)
ZATOICHI   (JAP, 1966)
SHOWDOWN FOR ZATOICHI   (JAP, 1967)
BLIND SWORDSMAN'S CANE SWORD, THE   (JAP, 1967)
BLIND SWORDSMAN'S RESCUE, THE   (JAP, 1967)
ZATOICHI CHALLENGED   (JAP, 1968)
BLIND SWORDSMAN AND THE FUGITIVE, THE   (JAP,
     1968)
BLIND SWORDSMAN SAMARITAN, THE   (JAP, 1968)
ZATOICHI MEETS HIS EQUAL   (JAP, 1971)
ZATOICHI TO YOJIMBO   (JAP, 1971)
ZATOICHI AT LARGE   (JAP, 1972)
ZATOICHI, CONSPIRACY IN ANCESTRAL LAND   (JAP,
     1973)

ZIGOMAR   (based on the book by Leon Sazie)
ZIGOMAR   (FRA, 1911)
ZIGOMAR VS. NICK CARTER   (FRA, 1912)
ZIGOMAR PEAU D'ANGUILLE   (FRA, 1912)

ZORRO   (based on the book, "Curse of Capistrano," by
     Johnston McCulley)
MARK OF ZORRO, THE   (UA, 1920)
DON Q, SON OF ZORRO   (UA, 1925)
BOLD CABALLERO, THE   (REP, 1936)
ZORRO RIDES AGAIN   (serial)   (REP, 1937)
ZORRO'S FIGHTING LEGION   (serial)   (REP, 1939)
MARK OF ZORRO, THE   (FOX, 1940)
ZORRO'S BLACK WHIP   (serial)   (REP, 1944)
SIGN OF ZORRO, THE   (ITA, 1951)
SIGN OF ZORRO, THE   (DIS, 1960)
ZORRO'S SHADOW   (SPA, 1962)
ZORRO, THE AVENGER   (ITA/SPA, 1963)
BEHIND THE MASK OF ZORRO   (ITA, 1964)
THREE SWORDS OF ZORRO   (ITA, 1964)
ZORRO THE REBEL   (ITA, 1966)
MASK OF ZORRO, THE   (ABC--TV, 1974)
ZORRO   (FRA/ITA, 1975)